P9-AQH-376

BOOKS BY ERNEST GRUENING

These United States (editor), 1923
Mexico and Its Heritage, 1928
The Public Pays, 1931
The State of Alaska, 1954
An Alaskan Reader (editor), 1967
The Battle for Alaska Statehood, 1967
Vietnam Folly (with Herbert Beaser), 1968

MANY BATTLES

MANY BATTLES

The Autobiography of
Ernest Gruening

329
G886m

LIVERIGHT NEW YORK

Copyright © 1973 by Ernest Gruening.
All rights reserved. No part of this book
may be reproduced in any form without
permission in writing from the publisher.

1.987654321

International Standard Book Number: 0-87140-565-2
Library of Congress Catalog Card Number: 72-97492

Designed by Mary Ahern
Manufactured in the United States of America

For *Dorothy, my beloved wife, devoted comrade through the years; our dear son Huntington; our lovely daughter-in-law Oline; and our grandchildren, Clark, Winthrop, Bradford, Kimberly, Peter and Tiffany.*

And to the cherished memory of Ernest, Jr., and Peter Brown Gruening.

51439

N. C. WESLEYAN COLLEGE LIBRARY
ROCKY MOUNT, N. C. 27801

CONTENTS

FOREWORD

It can scarcely be gainsaid that, born in 1887, I have lived during the period of greatest change in all human history, and by that token the most provocative and exciting era in the experience of mankind. The great scientific discoveries and technological inventions of the twentieth century have altered the ways of earth's inhabitants almost beyond imagination; no future generation will witness such a profound transformation. My father, a physician in New York City, had one of the first telephones. It seemed miraculous that one could talk over a wire to someone several "blocks" away; that was the way we measured distance in the 1880s. Wireless communication—globe-wide and instantaneous—and television were undreamed of. Ford's "horseless carriage," still a joke in the 1890s, and the airplane would revolutionize man's sedentary and static existence still further.

Indeed, the shrinkage of our planet perhaps best summarizes the principal effect of the twentieth century metamorphosis, although there has been much else—especially in the *mores* of people who deem themselves civilized. The full implications of these changes remain to be grasped. For the ever-increasing acceleration of change makes it difficult to visualize the world of tomorrow with any certainty. As I began this autobiography in 1969, my lifelong optimism was assailed by doubts about our country's—and indeed mankind's—future, an apprehension intensified by the events of the 1960s.

This mood may change. But, as of now, it would seem that man has developed no concomitant moral equivalent to his technological gains; his greater knowledge has not brought greater wisdom; despite greater general education the gap between the informed and the ignorant widens; violence throughout the world has increasingly replaced reason; and the nineteenth-century American dream of inevitable progress has been negated by the evidences of regression, mounting crime, and man-made deterioration of the environment.

But while the foreseeable future is less clear, it affords an increasing challenge to man's inventiveness and posits the need for reappraising and coordinating the great values of the past with the potentialities of the future. However great the changes, the Golden Rule would seem to be, and is, fortunately, immutable and unimpaired as a guide for man's conduct.

MANY BATTLES

1

CHILDHOOD

I find that the chance for appreciation is much increased by being the son of an appreciator.

—RALPH WALDO EMERSON

My earliest dream was of a big waterwheel on a stream in a beautiful glen with a waterfall in the middle distance. There was a friendly donkey in the foreground, and beyond, the glen stretched entrancingly into high mountains. I referred to this idyllic picture then and thereafter as my Esel-Muehlbach Traum, evidence that my first language was German. I also remember, at the age of four, standing at the door of my father's bedroom on April 1st, and after knocking loudly to awaken him, I called out, *"Ein Löwe steht vor deiner Tür!"* ("A lion is standing in front of your door!") Soon, English predominated in our family conversation, but as small children we were all bilingual and used both languages interchangeably.

My father, as I will always remember him, had a full white beard, a high forehead, very blue eyes and a pleasant smile. He was a handsome man. He was forty-five when I was born in New York City on February 6, 1887. He had left his native town, Inowraclaw, in East Prussia's Province of Posen, in 1861 at the age of nineteen. He would shortly have been drafted into the King of Prussia's army, but fighting in wars against Prussia's neighbors for the greater glory of king and fatherland did not appeal to young Emil. Posen had been a battleground for centuries between Poles, Teutons, Tartars, Muscovites, Cossacks, and Swedes. He wanted no part of it, but the war across the sea in the land of freedom for the preservation of the Union held a powerful appeal. It resulted in his enlisting in the Seventh New Jersey Volunteer Infantry. In his early days in America he lived in Hoboken where this regiment was in part recruited. Prussia's subsequent wars in that decade—against Denmark, Austria-Hungary and France—confirmed the wisdom of his decision. Inowraclaw had been included in the territory ceded to Prussia in the first partition of Poland in 1772. The Germans later renamed the town Hohensalza, but the Treaty of Versailles restored it once again to Poland. In the 1930s and 1940s the Nazis exterminated a third of its population and, after World War II it suffered the oppression of Kremlin-directed communism. My father, who died on Memorial Day, 1914, did not live to know the agonies suffered by his birthplace successively under two forms of totalitarianism. He had had the vision to seek a new world.

As a Union soldier, Father fought in the Battle of Five Forks and was among the cheering boys in blue at the surrender of General Lee at Appomattox. I still treasure the brass numeral 7 which adorned his cap. I received it a few weeks after his death in a letter from Alameda, California, which read in part:

> My dear Ernest: I am sending you to-day the treasured token which has been in my keeping for nearly fifty years. This will best speak for the value in which I held it, and will give you some idea of my feelings as I pass it on to the son of the old friend of my girlhood days. Your dear father gave it to me just after his return from the war. The cloth to which the number was fastened has long since crumbled away. Time was successful with its destruction, but with nothing else. He and his ally, Distance, made as little impression on our friendship and affection as was made on the metal.
>
> *Hedwig Falkenau*

My father had three sisters, Cecilia, Eugenie and Frances. Cecilia, the eldest, also came to America, settled in California and was happily married there. Eugenie stayed with her parents. Frances, after visiting California, came East and lived with us at various times during our childhood. She adored her elder brother Emil and carried that love to his children. She had been a beautiful girl and had several eager suitors, but she never married. "I was waiting for the prince to come," Aunt "Frank" once told me sadly in her later years.

After mustering out, Father resumed his studies at the Columbia University Medical School—the College of Physicians and Surgeons. He worked his way through by tutoring in German, Latin, Greek and mathematics. His training in the *Gymnasium Hochschule* in Inowraclaw had been thorough. And his savings financed a return to Europe for postgraduate work in Paris, London and Berlin. There he studied optics and acoustics under Helmholtz, the inventor of the ophthalmoscope, and Albrecht von Graefe, the founder of modern ophthalmology. Returning to New York, he served as assistant in the office of Dr. Herman Knapp, one of the pioneer ophthalmologists, and hung out his own shingle in 1870.

In the next forty-four years, thanks to a rugged constitution, he did not miss a single day from his office on account of illness. Once, while he was strolling through Central Park, a carriage driven by two horses staged a runaway. Father leaped to the bridle—it was an instinctive reaction, he explained—and was dragged some fifty feet before the frightened horses were brought to a halt. I watched him rubbing linament on his bruises that night. But he was back in his office the next morning.

Although in his later years he became one of the last of his profession in New York to treat both eye and ear (for those specialties had for some time been separated in our larger cities), he was eminent in both. In 1903 he was elected president of the American Otological Society and in 1910 of the American Ophthalmological Society. On more than one occasion he told me that practice in each of these specialties was helpful in the other, but, he once remarked humorously, "That doesn't prevent some of my colleagues from saying that I am great in the other specialty. 'Gruening's a great eye man,' say the ear men, and the eye men say, 'He's a great ear man.' "

In 1875 my father was invited to go to San Francisco to perform an operation on Major-General John Franklin Miller. Miller had been collector of the Port of San Francisco but had declined President Andrew Johnson's offer of reappointment to become president of the Alaska Commercial Company which had received from the U.S. Treasury Department a twenty-year lease on the fur-seal fisheries of the Pribilof Islands. General Miller had been wounded in battle during his service in the Union Army. A Confederate bullet had struck him above the eye, had worked its way down behind the eye-ball and had become painful. My father removed the bullet. Later Miller was elected to the U.S. Senate from California. In my father's papers I found the following message written in longhand on a sheet of Alaska Commercial Company stationery from its address at 310 Sansome Street, San Francisco:

Friend Gruening. I am directed by Genl. Miller to pay your bill for the operation performed on his eye, if you will be kind enough to have it presented to the above office. I'll see it is settled. Truly yours,
Emanuel Neumann.
(Neumann was the treasurer of the company.)

I still wonder why a relatively young practitioner was invited to cross the country—a long and difficult trip in those days—to perform this

operation on one of California's leading citizens. Were there no competent oculists in San Francisco, or was my father's reputation already known from coast to coast? Unfortunately, all the records and papers pertaining to the operation were destroyed in the fire that followed the 1906 San Francisco earthquake, but I have always been intrigued by the fact that my father, too, had—at least indirectly—a niche in Alaska's history.

In New York, Father developed a large and busy practice. Twenty-third Street, where we lived and Father had his office, was wholly residential when he began. But soon thereafter an optician, Meyrowitz, established himself across the street to fill Dr. Gruening's prescriptions for eyeglasses and later developed a chain of stores of international reputation. A druggist, Kalisch, moved to the southeast corner of Fourth Avenue and Twenty-third Street to fill Dr. Gruening's other prescriptions,

*Our childhood home on Twenty-third
Street, in New York City
Ernest, aged two*

and in appreciation for this business he would decline to charge the
Gruening children for ice-cream sodas, a happy arrangement which continued until I unwisely boasted of it to Father. He notified Kalisch that
his children would thereafter pay for their sodas.

My father's career was long and distinguished. He was a pioneer in the
diagnosis of mastoiditis and the development of its cure through the mas-
toid operation. He was the first to operate successfully on a brain abscess
of aural origin, and he was able to advance the knowledge and treatment
of cerebral complications following suppurative diseases of the middle ear.
He was also the first to call attention to the danger of wood alcohol as a
cause of blindness. He introduced the use of platinum instruments in
ophthalmic surgery and his name was identified with a number of surgical
instruments.

In addition to his practice, he was for many years Professor of
Ophthalmology at the New York Polyclinic and belonged to numerous
medical societies. He was president of the Society for the Relief of Widows and Orphans of Medical Men, and he gave generously of his services
to the indigents in the three hospitals with which he was associated
throughout his career, Mount Sinai, the German Hospital (renamed
Lenox Hill Hospital as a result of the World War I hysteria) and the
New York Eye and Ear Infirmary. He once told me that the only unpleasant concomitant of the practice of medicine was that one had to
charge for one's services. So he frequently found it easy to dispense with
doing it. Ministers, teachers, artists, widows, anyone for whom his services might prove to be a financial hardship, would be told "There is no
charge."

Many subsequently eminent eye and ear specialists received their train-

ing in his office, including Dr. William Holland Wilmer who founded
the world-renowned Wilmer Ophthalmic Institute of Johns Hopkins
University. Dr. Wilmer wrote me after Father's death that his friendship
meant more to him than that of any man except his own father. And
through the years in widely scattered places I have encountered people
who recall being treated by my father. Several have mentioned that he
treated four or five generations of their family. Even as late as October
1968, one New Yorker reminded me that my father had prescribed glasses
for him at the age of eleven.

In his obituary in the *Archives of Ophthalmology*, Dr. Wilmer, after
listing Father's professional achievements, also wrote:

> In his profession, as in all other relations, Dr. Gruening held to the
> highest ideals. With him everything was subordinated to principle.
> He knew no clique. Material considerations, expediency, favoritism,
> were no part of his mental make-up. Character and ability alone
> counted with him and his adherence to his principles was unwaver-
> ing. He demanded the truth no matter what the cost. Though a hard
> task master to himself, he was most tolerant of the failings of others.
> He never sought honors having a profound belief that one's work
> must speak for itself.

In fact, Father carried out that belief to a quixotic degree; he invariably
threw the blanks he received from *Who's Who in America* into the
wastebasket.

Dr. Wilmer also called attention to another nonmedical aspect in the
life of his former teacher:

> It was characteristic that he never associated himself with a pa-
> triotic or military organization. He had answered the call of his
> newly adopted country, but, the war over, he turned quietly to the
> conquests of peace, finding his reward not in past glories, but in the
> satisfaction of work well done and of humanity benefited.

In 1874 my father married Rose Fridenberg, the eldest of a family of
ten children. Their parents, Henry and Bertha, had emigrated from Inowraclaw some years before Father. Rose, aged twenty-one, died of ty-
phoid fever in 1876 at the same time as she was giving birth to a daughter, also named Rose. It was a tragic event in Father's life. Four years
later he married her sister, Phebe, my mother, the eldest of the other
daughters.

Mother was a cheerful soul with a keen sense of humor, a ready wit
and a fine gift of mimicry. We adored each other.

Eventually there were five Gruening children—Rose, Clara, Marie
—who was two years older than I and who later chose to be called
May—and Martha, who was two years younger than I. Growing up,
we lived on the north side of Twenty-third Street between Fourth and
Lexington Avenues. Our parents owned three small brownstone houses of
three stories each—numbers 109, 111, and 113—set back from the
street behind an earthen plot adorned by a maple, which through the
years never seemed to grow. There was also a huge mallow bush with
large white blossoms and a wisteria vine with profuse pendant lilac clus-
ters which climbed all the way to the roof. Father's offices were in number 109, we lived in number 111 and rented number 113, but as the family grew and needed more space we occupied that house, too. On both
the ground and top floors, passageways had been broken through between the houses, and my sisters and I used to play a great joke, or so we
thought, on the salesmen and peddlers who came to call. When a peddler
pulled the bell at 109, May, Martha and I would open the door and say,
"No thank you." Then we would rush through to 111 and greet him
again with the same giggled refusal. But imagine the peddler's surprise
and consternation—and our joy—when the same trio met him at the
door of 113.

There was a big yard in back of 109 and 111 surrounded by a high
white fence. The yard was paved with concrete, but around its edges was
a flower bed from which ivy climbed up the fence and where Mother
raised lilies of the valley, her favorite flower. When we moved into 113
we cut through the fence and added to our private playground. Right in
the middle of the yard's concrete was a little grating into which we could
look down some twenty feet and see clear running water. It was part of
Gramercy Creek, which must have been a beautiful stream in the early
days of Manhattan, but was now completely buried. The fence, which
continued beyond our homes down the block and separated the yards of
other houses facing on Twenty-third and Twenty-fourth Streets, was an
invitation to exploration. I could reach its ten-foot height by shinnying
up a conveniently placed ailanthus tree, a species which flourished in
New York backyards where other trees would not. As the fence was only
about three inches wide, walking along it was risky. But sitting astride
and working myself forward was easy, I thought, although my mother
informed me it was hard on my trousers. From the top of the fence, I
could look into the back of the Ashland House, a long-departed hostelry
on Fourth Avenue just around the corner, and into the backyard of our
grocer, Plumb and Evers. As I grew older, I gave up that kind of acro-
batic act, but part of the western fence was of white brick, and later,
when I began playing tennis, that wall and the paved yard proved to be
an ideal practice court.

Ernest's mother, Phebe, and her sisters Clara, May and Martha in a Rockport cornfield, 1915

Twenty-third Street was a fascinating neighborhood in those days. The next block to the north was lined with livery stables and used to exercise racehorses. The clanking of sledge and anvil as horseshoes were hammered out, the clatter of hoofs as the horses got a workout, the warm stable odors, all left a pleasant impress on our senses. Gramercy Park, only a block east and two blocks south, was a charming oasis of trees, grass and flowerbeds surrounded by a high iron fence. It was open only to those who lived in the surrounding homes, but occasionally, we would slip, with a sense of triumph, through one of the gates when a legitimate user obligingly unlocked it with his key. Madison Square Park was even closer and not quite so exclusive. It afforded roller-skating which the flagstone pavements on the sidewalks—at that time not laid too evenly—did not.

Another sidewalk game developed by accident when walking along Twenty-Third Street with Aunt Frank. She dropped a glove and it was immediately picked up: "You dropped this madam." This suggested to us that we see how often it would happen. It always did. We could not "lose" anything. Those were the days when one (if male) got up in a crowded street car to give his seat to a lady. Some years later when subways had been built, reminiscing about these vanished gallant days with Franklin Pierce Adams, the conductor of the humorous "Conning Tower" column in the New York *Tribune*, I observed that now to have

Rose Gruening   *Dr. Emil Gruening*

a seat yielded to her a woman would have to be visibly pregnant, on crutches, or a nun. "Probably all three," remarked F. P. A.

Farther west on the north side of Twenty-third Street was the then-famous institution known as the Eden Musée, a waxworks museum. In the corner of the lobby next to the admissions booth was a huge policeman in the blue uniform and domelike helmet of that day's force. Most people did not realize until they got close to him that he was a wax figure and this suggested a game to us. We would stand near him, just inside the door, motionless and in deliberately awkward positions. When the visitors approached the ticket booth and looked at us, their comment would be, "Don't they look natural?" Then we would come to life with peals of laughter.

The principal exhibits—world celebrities and scenes from history— filled the main floor: Washington crossing the Delaware, Pickett's charge at Gettysburg, Barbara Fritchie hanging out her flag, the last moments of John Brown, Custer's last stand. Those were patriotic times. In the basement was the chamber of horrors. We children had been strictly forbidden by our parents to go there; but somehow we always managed to escape the mademoiselle, fraülein or nurse in charge and visited it breathlessly. There were exhibits showing the execution of a criminal in India by having an elephant step on his head, and the burning alive of a beautiful Indian maiden in the practice of suttee. Many of the figures were animated, and the breast of the Indian maiden heaved as she emitted audible sighs. It was very moving. But most entrancing was a huge gorilla who had invaded an African village and seized another fair maiden who, strangely enough, was white. He was carrying her away in his hairy arms and at intervals would turn his head, bare his fangs and emit a hideous roar.

Another fascinating exhibit was the cinematograph, an early form of motion picture without a plot. It showed people diving from a springboard into a pool and then the film was reversed so that the divers flew backward through the air and landed on the springboard. Pretty heady stuff. The Musée also exhibited "Ajeeb, the Chess Automaton," a robed oriental figure whose hands moved the pieces on a chessboard. To show there was no human being inside, an attendant would open panels about a foot square in his chest and back to reveal a network of rods through which one could see daylight beyond. The identity of the player was not revealed, nor from where he operated the robot. He was reputed to be invincible, a myth which in my later school years when I had learned to play chess, I was able to dissipate. My father had taught me to play. Ajeeb would nod his head once for "check" and twice for "checkmate." When he was beaten, he would sweep the chessmen off the board. There was no reward for winning, just satisfaction.

Another of the remembered joys of my childhood was known as "tasting around at Huyler's," the famous candy store on the west side of Broadway near Eighteenth Street. Alluring trays of chocolates and bonbons were spread out on the counters and the practice was to sample them, preparatory, presumably, to making a purchase. How could you tell what you wanted until you had tasted? But alas, one day, probably noting that the practice of tasting had been abused, the management shielded the trays behind glass partitions, and like the free sodas at Kalisch's drugstore, another good thing came to an end.

The great event in our young lives was our first trip to Europe. Father felt his children should learn French, and in June of 1894, Mother, my sisters, Clara, May, Martha and I embarked on the Hamburg-American liner *Normannia*. The cabins had bunks, not beds, and we all clamored for the privilege of sleeping in an upper. We landed in England, crossed the Channel to Le Havre in a ferry, and took a train to Paris where we stayed for a few days at a hostel opposite the Gare Saint Lazare. Soon we had established ourselves in a suburb called Chatou. Our home was set in a beautiful garden with a Japanese kiosk, a sort of summer house, where we could eat out of doors. In the rear of the garden was a miniature grotto with a little statue of a saint. There was also a *potager*—a kitchen garden—with vegetables and herbs growing in neat rows. Apple, pear and plum trees had been trained to spread close to the ground so that the fruit could be reached easily. And there was a henhouse with chickens we delighted in feeding.

A month later Father and my sister Rose, who had just completed her junior year at Vassar, arrived. Under Father's guidance sightseeing began and we visited the Louvre, the Luxembourg, the Musée Cluny, and the palaces at Saint Germain, Saint Cloud and Versailles. And of course we ascended the Eiffel Tower, which at that time was the tallest structure in the world.

Father and Rose returned to America in September, but the rest of the family stayed on in Paris. I was sent to the Petit Lycée Condorcet on the Rue D'Amsterdam, Clara and May went to a semi-boarding school run by a Mademoiselle des Essarts on the Rue du Bac, and Martha went to a small private school in the Trocadero section to which we had moved. My most memorable experience at the Lycée occurred when a boy sitting in back of me jabbed my behind with a pen which he had contrived to fasten into his shoelaces. While he sat innocently in his seat, his leg would commit his acts of aggression. As I was not able to expose him and convey my indignation in words, I turned around after the third or fourth jab and pulled his ear so hard that it bled. He screamed. The teacher rushed over. The pen had disappeared and I was unable to explain the provocation. I was rushed downstairs to the office of *le proviseur*, the principal, who wrote a note to my mother saying that I was being sent home in disgrace *"pour avoir tiré l'oreille d'un autre élève."* The principal blotted the letter with blue sand. But all was set to rights the next day when my mother sent me back with an explanation of what had happened. The pen-wielding culprit was called down and we were both told not to do it again.

I went to school five days a week from half past eight until half past five. Our day off was Thursday, not Saturday, and we were allowed to play in the beautiful Parc Monceau or in the Tuileries. We brought our lunch to school, but every day at four o'clock we were given a *goûter*—a bar of chocolate one day, jam and crackers the next. I still have a steel napkin ring with my initials and the number 186 engraved on it.

Later in the year I transferred to a small private school conducted by a Madame Marie at 40 Rue de Londres, and on Thursday and Sunday mornings I had a piano lesson. My teacher was a very young girl— perhaps no older than nineteen or twenty—and very lovely. I asked her to write in my autograph book, and she penned these appropriate lines on February 17, 1895:

> *Comme le flot que le vent chasse et qui a*
> *nos pieds vient mourir, ainsi dans la vie tout passe*
> *Excepté. . . . le souvenir!*
>
> *Emma Blanc*

Rose and Father were with us again in July of 1895, Rose having graduated from Vassar, and that summer we traveled in western Germany, taking the boat trip down the Rhine, past its picturesque hilltop castles, and visiting Wiesbaden, Mainz and Frankfurt, which was getting ready to celebrate the 25th anniversary of the Battle of Sedan. Then we went to Bern and to Geneva where we enjoyed many boat rides on the lake. Once we went as far as Territet and from there took a train to the Castle of Chillon, set against the snow-covered Dents du Midi, where we heard tales of the cruelties to prisoners in times past and saw the chains with which they were fastened to the stone walls. We also ascended the Petit Salève and the Grand Salève, rocky hills at the far side of a plain extending south from Geneva, and from the top gazed on the splendor of Mont Blanc. Toward the end of September we returned to Paris and after a few days there started home from Le Havre on the *Champagne* of the Compagnie Générale Transatlantique. We came back speaking French fluently and filled with happy recollections. But it was wonderful to be home again.

My memory of the summer of 1897, spent on the charming estate of Charles Loring Brace at Dobbs Ferry, is aided because Father required each of us to keep a diary, and he read our daily output critically. For this I have ever been grateful. Along with this literary exercise, we all early acquired the reading habit. In our youngest days we read German juvenile classics, such as *Strubbelpeter*, an illustrated account of a boy whose hair was long and unkempt, *Münchener Bilderbogen*, a profusely illustrated miscellany, and an annual volume, *Deutscher Jugendfreund*, with the subtitle *"für Unterhaltung und Veredelung der Jugend"* (for the entertainment and ennobling of youth). We also read Grimm's and Hoffman's fairy tales in German and became familiar with Greek mythology, the *Iliad* and the *Odyssey*. Hector, Patroclus, Achilles, Odysseus, Diomede, Idomeneus and the two Ajaxes were my heroes and I read of their exploits again and again. To these were added adventure stories, *Robert der Schiffsjunge*, *Kreuz und Quer durch Indien* and *Robinson Crusoe*. Nor were we allowed to forget our newly acquired French. We subscribed to an illustrated weekly, *Mon Journal* and our reading included the fascinating science fiction of Jules Verne, whose fantastic prophecies of flights to the moon and navigation under the sea would be fulfilled in my lifetime.

But soon English predominated. *St. Nicholas Magazine* arrived regularly and each installment of *The Lakerim Athletic Club* by Rupert Hughes was eagerly awaited. There were the adventure stories of Kirk Munroe, *The Flamingo Feather* and *With Crockett and Bowie*, and the Brace's library contained the works of Frederick Marryat, the British naval officer turned novelist. I also read *Midshipman Easy* and *Osceola, the Seminole* by Mayne Reid, but my favorite author was G. A. Henty, a British writer of historical novels for youngsters. I asked for them for Christmas and birthday presents and read at least thirty. My favorite was *Under Drake's Flag*. Except in accounts of ancient times, the hero was almost always a British lad who had all the manly virtues. Two Hentys, however, I did not like: *True to the Old Flag*, a tale of the American War for Independence, whose hero does not support America's cause and goes back to England, and *With Lee in Virginia* which espoused the Confederate cause. Thomas Bailey Aldrich's *The Story of a Bad Boy* was more to my liking, as were Cooper's *Leatherstocking Tales*, Scott's *Ivanhoe* and *Quentin Durward*, and Bulwer-Lytton's *The Last of the Barons* and *The Last Days of Pompeii*.

That fall I entered the Drisler School at 9 East Forty-ninth Street. It was conducted by two brothers whose father was a professor at Columbia University, then located a block away at Forty-ninth Street and Madison Avenue. An entry in my diary reported on the city election of that year:

We had a holiday and in the evening Papa, Mama, Uncle Albert, Rose, May, Martha and I went to see the returns on Twenty-third street opposite the headquarters of the Citizens Union. The returns were shown on a house by a magic lantern. There was only one district which had a majority of votes for Low. Van Wyck was victorious in every district except one.

Low was Seth Low, president of Columbia University and a candidate of the reform element against Tammany Hall, then led by its boss Richard Croker. Father said he had voted for Low, who lost but ran again and was elected Mayor four years later. Father was nominally a Republican. It was the "respectable" party at that time and place. But in 1884 he told me he had been a "mugwump"; he had voted for Grover Cleveland, and did so again in 1892.

My diary also recorded my attendance at a Sunday school whose principal was a tall, kindly, attractive man named John Lovejoy Elliott. The school was conducted by the Society for Ethical Culture which had been founded in New York City by Dr. Felix Adler with an emphasis on ethical conduct in all the relations of life. That was as near as we came to an organized religion in my family. Father was a freethinker and we children followed in that course until later in life when we came to our own conclusions in the realm of faith.

The family played a very important part in our young lives and it was dominated by Father in patriarchal fashion. He followed my studies closely and helped me with my homework, particularly Latin. He also took a keen interest in national and world affairs and discussed them in the evening at the dinner table. He subscribed to the New York *Tribune*, the *Neu-Yorker Staats-Zeitung* and the *Evening Post* whose editorials he would sometimes read aloud and comment upon. He seemed to be informed on every subject, but while his appreciation of European cultures was keen, he had no doubt that American institutions and ideals made for a better life. After dinner the whole family gathered around the piano to sing German songs and the familiar tunes of the day. Rose, an accomplished pianist, played the accompaniments. We also went as a family to the Metropolitan Opera House to hear Wagner, and to productions of Gilbert and Sullivan's *The Mikado, H.M.S. Pinafore* and *The Pirates of Penzance*. At the Irving Place Theater a competent cast played the German classics, Lessing's *Nathan der Weise* and Schiller's *Don Carlos, Ipigenie in Aulis* and *Wilhelm Tell*. I still remember the tension when the tyrant Gessler orders Tell on pain of death to shoot an apple off the head of his son, the agony while Tell begs vainly for mercy, the suspense before the successful shot, Tell's imprisonment when Gessler concludes that

Tell's second arrow was intended for him, and finally Tell's lying in wait for Gessler and shooting him with his crossbow.

In the summer of 1898, I went to Europe with my father for the second time, a trip that was both pleasant and of enduring educational value. We visited the museums, monuments, palaces and other "sights" of Berlin, Amsterdam, The Hague, Antwerp, Brussels and London, and under Father's informed guidance I learned lessons in history as well as art.

My second year at the Drisler School was much like the first, except that I was now "an old boy" and able to appraise the newcomers condescendingly. I was too young and too small to play on the school football or hockey teams. Our chief rival was the Cutler School just a block away on Fiftieth Street and it generally won. My extracurricular sport was shinny, a game played on the asphalted crosstown streets with hockey sticks and a hard rubber ball by any number of players above two on a side. The great hazard was losing the ball down the sewer. It was here that we first encountered gang warfare. Each block of each street had a gang and in our neighborhood warfare was rather gentlemanly. We never went much further than pulling caps off each others' heads, and the battle would end quickly when someone's mother appeared at the top of the "stoop" of her house. But occasionally a gang from the other side of Third Avenue would invade our block. They took caps, hockey sticks and whatever else they could for keeps, and picked fights with no holds barred. We generally beat a strategic retreat after the first skirmish.

As I had been the specially favored child the previous summer with a trip to Europe, it was decided that the whole family would go the next time. Father's plan was to spend most of our vacation in a region known as Saxon Switzerland, the hilly country on both sides of the Elbe. Its most striking features were sandstone rock pillars, grottoes and arches eroded by the action of the elements, and picturesque glens and hills which provided inviting climbs and hikes, but these outdoor physical excursions were supplemented by the rich cultural offerings of Dresden. It was a rigorous summer and we were happy to return once again to Paris. May and I strolled along the boulevards and through the Tuileries. We rode on the top of the horsedrawn buses with delightful names indicating their points of departure and destination: "Madeleine-Bastille," "Les Halles-Vaugirard." We visited the churches and crossed the Seine to *flâner* among the *bouquinistes* along the river's bank. And we sat at the tables of the sidewalk cafes, feeling very grown up and very much at home. Paris became our favorite city. And we liked the French people, in part, no doubt, because we could converse with them.

In the fall of 1898 I transferred from the Drisler School to Sachs's Collegiate Institute at 38 West Fifty-ninth Street. Father, after some checking, had concluded that the teaching there would furnish a better preparation for college. I was sorry to leave Drisler, but there was no question about the high quality of my new school's instruction. Its headmaster, Dr. Julius Sachs, had degrees in pedagogy from both American and German universities; he had been a Professor of Secondary Education at Columbia and had assembled a galaxy of excellent teachers. We expected to study hard, and we did. There were school football, hockey and baseball teams, but it was made clear that athletics were secondary. Debating, however, was an important extracurricular study in which we all took part. We were encouraged to write for the school paper, *The Red and Blue*, and I contributed articles on visits to Governor's Island and to the Statue of Liberty. We also had a chess team of which I was a member.

Another change in our lives came with the move from our childhood home. Manhattan was gradually spreading uptown. Residential areas were being taken over by businesses, and more and more stores were filling up our block. Father's patients were moving to the forties, fifties and even beyond. We children hated to leave Twenty-third Street, but we found ourselves at the turn of the century in a new home at 36 East Fifty-seventh Street, just east of Madison Avenue.

The house was less commodious for the younger children. Our parents, Rose and Clara occupied large rooms, but May, Martha and I had hall bedrooms, mine on the top floor. There were five stories, counting the basement, where we had our dining room, as one. It had been remodeled with oak paneling capped by a narrow shelf for holding suitable objects against a frieze of Pompeian red, and there was a big fireplace of light mottled bricks. Father's waiting room and offices occupied the entire floor above, the third floor contained the sitting room and the top two floors our bedrooms. Aunt Frank did not come with us; she had a desire for independence. For a while she occupied one of the Twenty-third Street houses and took in boarders, including some promising literary lights of that period, and later, when the three houses were sold, she continued this occupation in the neighborhood of Columbia University.

We children were growing up. Rose was interesting herself in social work. Clara, after preparation at Miss Gerrish's boarding school in Englewood, New Jersey, had entered Barnard College and would graduate four years later with the Class of '03. She achieved the distinction of being Barnard's sole representative on the editorial board of *The Morningside*, Columbia College's undergraduate publication, to which she contributed verse and prose.

We spent the summer of 1900 at Far Rockaway where we rented a cottage with substantial acreage on which we built a tennis court. Tennis was increasingly my favorite sport. It was still considered a bit highbrow, however, and if one walked along the village street with a tennis racket, the boys lounging in front of the drugstore were apt to say something unflattering like "Ah there, Algernon!"

Of course we bathed, swam and sunned on the then not-too-crowded beaches. The girls' enjoyment was diminished by the necessity of wearing bathing costumes encumbered by skirts and stockings. Clara, then aged eighteen, objected and declared she would bathe without them. "No, my child, that would not be proper," Father told her, and his dictum prevailed. Clara was always ahead of her time. Men and boys were—as always—more privileged but an "upper" was strictly required. Trunks alone would not have been countenanced.

The automobile, still referred to as "the horseless carriage" was not yet universal, but the "bike" was becoming popular with young and old alike. We all had one, with names like "Crawford," "Rambler" and "Columbia," but again the girls with their voluminous skirts were at a disadvantage. The murmurings that presaged change were beginning to be heard, but bloomers and their equivalents were still not quite respectable, and there were other feminine prohibitions. Serious damage could be done to a lady's reputation if it were whispered that "she paints." Needless to say, none of the girls in my family did.

That fall one aspect of my education took a pleasant and fortuitous turn. Although I had no talent for music—much as I enjoyed singing —Father wanted me to take lessons on both the piano and the violin. The violin lessons were short-lived; the teacher quickly concluded that his time and Father's money could be better spent. My piano teacher was a delightful gentleman named Ulysse Buehler, and while he taught me to play and sing a few pieces that I liked, I really did not make much progress. However, I am greatly indebted to him for introducing me to astronomy. He would take me out of doors at night—on his own time. —and teach me to identify the constellations and the planets. Manhattan's atmosphere was not smog-laden in those days, and while buildings limited the horizon, skyscrapers were in their infancy. The recently constructed Flat-iron Building on Twenty-third Street was still one of the wonders of the day. The East River waterfront gave us the unlimited vision of the heavens we needed.

The night skies opened up a new world for me. The procession of the seasons was signaled by the three great first-magnitude stars—gold Arcturus, harbinger of spring; steel-blue Vega, summer's emblem; and white Capella, heralding autumn. Mr. Buehler started his instruction with the easily recognizable stars, but I soon learned the constellations and their Latin names, although it was difficult to picture the mythical creatures they were supposed to represent. I took particular delight in following the planets as they circulated through the Zodiac; Venus the most brilliant, visible in the morning or evening sky; Jupiter, the next largest starlike object; red Mars and yellow Saturn. We watched them move from night to night between the fixed stars. We were never sure that we saw Mercury, but one night in February 1901, when I was confident I knew the constellations and their principal stars, I was startled and puzzled by a very bright star just below Cassiopeia's five-star W. It was as bright as Jupiter, but I knew that planets did not wander off course. I reported it to Mr. Buehler who said I must be mistaken. I wanted to show it to him, but the next two nights were clouded. Then the newspapers told of a Nova in the constellation Perseus, a star that through collision with another star or from some other cause bursts into unequalled brightness. Had I known enough and been sure of myself I might have reported that discovery. We watched it gradually fade, and in a few weeks it was no longer visible to the naked eye.

2

YOUTH

You send your boys to the schoolmaster,
but it is the schoolboys who educate him.
—RALPH WALDO EMERSON

As graduation from the Sachs's Collegiate Institute with the Class of '02 was in prospect, with the likelihood that I would pass a sufficient number of entrance examinations to be admitted to Harvard, Father nevertheless considered it advisable that I take another year at a good preparatory school. The average entrance age for Harvard College at that time was eighteen. If I had entered in the fall of 1902, I would have been fifteen and one-half and I was small for my age. Father thought I needed a little more maturity and physical development before entering college. He was quite right. The Hotchkiss School was selected.

Hotchkiss, in Lakeville, Connecticut, was much younger and smaller than its better-known counterparts such as Andover, Exeter or Lawrenceville. It was only ten years old. The school was pleasantly situated on high ground overlooking a lake in the foothills of the Berkshires. It had only two principal buildings: Main, which included a dormitory, dining hall and classrooms, with one-story enclosed corridors connecting with the chapel and gymnasium; and Bissell Hall, a dormitory. The school was undergoing an administrative change at that time. Edward G. Coy, known familiarly as "Nibsy" Coy, a Yale graduate in the class of 1869, was the headmaster who had directed Hotchkiss from its beginning and given it its character and repute, but he was retiring because of failing health. Tall and handsome with white hair, a white mustache and "burnsides," he was a popular man and his impending retirement was deemed a serious loss by the trustees, faculty and students. One of his sons, Sher-

man, had been, and another son, Edward, would become famous Yale
football stars. "Ted," the younger, was at that time in the lower middle
class. He was as close a replica of a Greek god as anyone I have ever
known.

In retrospect, it seems that extracurricular activities, especially athletics,
were given heavy emphasis at Hotchkiss, in part because of the popularity and ability of the physical training master, Otto M. Monahan, who
was referred to affectionately as "Mogie." The school had football, baseball, track and hockey teams and all did well in their contests with other
schools. But the competitive spirit was vigorously instilled in every student. In one practice game between two teams of the football squad, an
upper middler named Starr Donaldson, attempting an end run, was forced
back as he tried to evade the onrushing tacklers and was downed for a
several-yard loss. Coach Monahan halted the play, called the luckless half-
back to the sidelines and gave him a dressing down before all the players
and spectators. "Donaldson," he said, "you're the first Hotchkiss man ever
to run backward. No Hotchkiss man ever ran backward before." It was a
rebuke not easily forgotten by any of us.

This strong competitive urge "on the playing field" was in accord with
the spirit of the times, and I was all for it. Like everyone else, I cheered
myself hoarse at our teams' touchdowns, runs or goals. It was perhaps also
in keeping with the spirit of the times that the members of the Latin class
groaned when I translated a passage from Cicero without difficulty. It
was no feat; I was going over familiar ground, having passed my Latin
entrance exams for Harvard. The teacher, John Edmund Barss, by way of
mild rebuke to the groaners, expressed the hope that I would not be intimidated by this evidence of disapproval and would continue to recite as
well on subsequent occasions. But I regret to admit that I had already
made up my mind to stumble through future recitations.

Nicknames were the custom, and being the smallest in the class, I became known as "Mouse." Another custom consisted of invading other
boys' bedrooms after they had retired, turning their mattresses over on
top of them and then vanishing before you could be identified. This was
easy to do as the doors of the little cubicles that were our rooms were not
locked, and the lights were out. I took part in one of these raids. Bolder
spirits proposed that we "turn" one of the masters, Alfred Bates Hall—
teacher of history and English—known as "Peanut Hall," who was
unmarried and whose room was, like mine, on the second floor of Main.
To add to the excitement I attached a cord to the clapper of the bell
which was in the hall not far from my room and slipped the cord
through my door, so I could sound an alarm while presumably sleeping
peacefully. We "turned" Peanut Hall and escaped without immediate de-

tection, but the string attached to the bell's clapper was, not surprisingly, traced to my room by the irate Mr. Hall.

The penalty? I was banished from Main and forced to take up residence in a cottage some distance from the school known as "the Pesthouse," since students with ailments were hospitalized there. But as it was the month of May, this did not seem too severe a punishment. Besides I had the pleasant company of several other culprits.

My first days at Harvard the following fall filled me with a sense of exaltation. Walking through the "Yard," I did not doubt that I had the good fortune to be in the greatest institution of higher learning in America. A most attractive member of the senior class, the president of the *Crimson*, had welcomed the freshmen at Phillips Brooks House, the university's social-religious center. His name was Franklin Delano Roosevelt. His warmth and charm made us feel—as he bade us feel—at home, as he told of Harvard's great past, its present objectives and its promise for the future. He made clear that we had every right to be proud to be Harvard men, and suggested our responsibility to cherish and maintain Harvard's high standards and traditions.

There were 734 of us and at first I knew very few of my classmates. Two had come with me from Hotchkiss, Howard Earl Kramer and Paul Theodore Christie. A third, who had left Hotchkiss in his last year and now sought me out, was John Dolbeare White, a most attractive young man who became our junior class president and first marshall at Commencement. But soon other acquaintances developed into friendship—two in particular, Richard John Walsh and Earl Derr Biggers. Both had literary talent and were to be on the editorial boards of the *Advocate* and the *Lampoon*. Eating at Memorial Hall—at tables of ten—rapidly enlarged acquaintance. The food, of course, was subject to the usual undergraduate grousing. To describe the bean soup, one of my table companions drew on Omar Khayyam: "I came like water and like wind I go." Occasionally we would vary our diet by breakfasting at one of the several places on Harvard Square. It is hard to believe now, but a hearty "combination" breakfast of fruit, cereal and cream, eggs and bacon, rolls and coffee cost twenty-five cents. A favorite spot for late-night snacks was "Rammy's Rathskeller," a tiny one-room joint a few feet below sidewalk level on Holyoke Street, whose walls were adorned with some amusing and mildly risqué prints. "Rammy"—I never knew his full name— was popular and on occasion would treat the boys he knew to a bottle of champagne when he met them dining in a Boston restaurant. Other memorable figures of that day were John the Orangeman, whose donkey pulling a cart emblazoned with a crimson H was a feature at every football or baseball game; Max Keezer, the secondhand clothes dealer, and white-bearded "Billy the Postman." There was also a freshman proctor, living in Hollis Hall, Charles Minor Stearns, who was irreverently dubbed Charles Minus Sperms.

On "Bloody Monday," the first Monday after college opening, it was traditional for the sophomore class to rush the freshmen, engage them in physical combat and haze them in their rooms thereafter. We were on the receiving end our freshman year and on the giving end our sophomore year, but that was its last occurrence. Our class had the good sense to abolish the custom.

My room faced the Yard from the fourth floor of Weld Hall. It was a fair-sized room with a bay-window and a fireplace equipped with gas logs, but, unfortunately, there was no running water and the toilets were in the basement, five floors below. The water pitcher would be filled each day by the "goodie," as we called the aged maid in current Harvardese. I lived in 48 Weld my first three years. The fourth year I was on the top floor of Stoughton, Number 32, once occupied by Ralph Waldo Emerson. The effort to get as many seniors as possible to move into the three venerable dormitories, Holworthy, Hollis and Stoughton, also originated with our class. This was first opposed by the Corporation—the ruling body of the University—but it yielded when our class raised the funds to make some needed repairs.

Harvard College at that time had the "elective system" for undergraduates—a reform ascribed to President Charles William Eliot, a revered aristocrat to whom the adjective "Olympian" was not inappropriate. With the exception of a freshman course in English composition, we were free to choose whatever courses we wanted. In English A my instructor was Henry Milner Rideout, a refutation of the later wheeze that "those who can, do; those who can't, teach," and particularly that if they couldn't "do" or "teach" anything else, they became teachers of English. Rideout's credentials were the publication of his short stories in *The Saturday Evening Post*, then and for a long time thereafter in the heyday of its popularity.

While I never took a course with him, I came to know Charles Townsend Copeland, '82—"Copey" as he was known to us all—and attended some of his "readings" in his room in Hollis. "Copey" was an inspiration to generations of Harvard men who wanted to write, but during his earlier years on the faculty, he was not particularly appreciated by the administration, presumably because he had not "published." "Copey" continued in President Eliot's régime as a mere "instructor," but his gifts as a teacher and inspirer of good writing brought such support from alumni who had benefited from them that he became successively an assistant professor, an associate professor and finally Boylston Professor of

Rhetoric and Oratory. Like so many other notable men, "Copey" was not without some affectation and some eccentric mannerisms, but almost everyone loved them and him.

In retrospect, I have to confess that I failed to take advantage of the great opportunities that Harvard offered. I know now, and knew not long after graduation, that I was still very immature and that the unlimited freedom we enjoyed had not been utilized—by me—as it should have been. My scholastic achievements were mediocre, and my extracurricular activities, other than contributing two satirical pieces to the *Advocate*, and playing on the Harvard chess team, were negligible. But my four years at Harvard were unqualifiedly happy. My intramural diversions were tennis, poker and bridge—before the coming of auction and contract bridge. There was an annual class dinner at some hotel in town, and occasional class "beer nights" in the Harvard Union, a new institution which furnished both a fine library and other recreational opportunities. It brought some good lecturers, including ex-President Theodore Roosevelt, William Jennings Bryan, Dr. Wilfred Grenfell, Major Henry Lee Higginson and Jacob Riis. One of our long-since-vanished joys was to attend the "ten, twenty, thirties" at an "Opera House" in Boston, where such thrillers as *Why Women Sin, The Evil Men Do* and *Nellie, the Cloakmodel* were performed to audiences that took them seriously, hissing the villain and cheering the hero.

Our social life was also enlivened by dances sponsored by the All Souls Church Lend-a-Hand Club in Roxbury, then a reasonably respectable outlying part of Boston. Our groups were not included in the bluest of blue Boston circles, which were reserved largely for the graduates of Groton, Saint Mark's and Saint Paul's, but in our junior year our class produced for the first time a junior dance, open to everyone in the class. It was planned as an effort to establish a greater measure of social democracy, for there was a certain amount of snobbery at Harvard. Perhaps one-seventh of the class—the ten tens who would "make" the Institute of 1770, D. K. E., the Hasty Pudding, Porcellian, A. D. and Fly, and the few more who aspired to these clubs and were disappointed—set themselves apart from the rest of their classmates, living in private dormitories on Mount Auburn Street—Claverly, Westmorely and Randolph— and avoiding the Yard in their early college years until their social aspirations were achieved or not. There were some rumblings of revolt in our senior year initiated in the freshman class, the class of 1910, against "the Street"—meaning Mount Auburn Street—but it was not until a generation later, in the thirties, that this undergraduate schism would largely disappear with the coming of the House system.

Again, retrospectively, I am not at all proud of my performance at

LIBRARY
N. C. WESLEYAN COLLEGE
ROCKY MOUNT, N. C. 27801

51439

Harvard. The opportunities were there, but I failed to take advantage of them. I spent much time in the library of the Union and perhaps got more education out of my browsing there than in the lecture halls or classrooms. In seeking later to analyze my want of enterprise and my scholastic mediocrity, I was astonished to discover a plaint of a really distinguished Harvard alumnus which in a way parallels my experience. Charles Francis Adams of the Class of 1856, son of another Charles Francis Adams, a grandson of President John Quincy Adams, and for twenty-four years a member of the Board of Overseers of the university, wrote of his college days:

> As it was, I was tumbled into the common hopper to emerge therefrom as God willed. No instructor produced or undertook to produce, the slightest impression on me, no spark of enthusiasm was sought to be infused into me. . . . And it was exactly the same as with my father before me. From the recitation room I got as nearly as I can now see almost nothing at all; from the college atmosphere and the close contact with a generation of generous young fellows containing then, as the result showed, infinite possibilities, I got much of all that I have ever had of quickening and good. So after all I owe a great debt to Harvard.

It was from my classmates and my contemporaries in the classes just senior or junior to 1907 that I, too, received what I owe Harvard. Many years later in considering to what college it would be best to counsel my youngest son Peter to go, I sought advice from my knowledgeable friend, Felix Frankfurter. "The faculty at Harvard," he said, "is good, but I doubt whether it is better than Columbia's or Chicago's. But what *is* better is the student body. Harvard's is the fastest, the most brilliant of any of the colleges' student bodies."

My contemporaries certainly lived up to that description. Behind me in the class of 1910 were Heywood Broun, Walter Lippmann, and T. S. Eliot who distinguished themselves in the field of literature; Harlow Shapley, the astronomer; Robert Edmund Jones, the stage designer; and Dr. Carl Binger, the psychiatrist, among so many others.

Our '07 class, in literature and publishing, had Maxwell Perkins, who at Scribner's would edit the works of Thomas Wolfe and Scott Fitzgerald; Richard Walsh who established his own publishing house, and brought out Pearl Buck; Earl Derr Biggers, playwright and novelist, who created one of the enduring characters in detective fiction, Charlie Chan; John Gould Fletcher, Norreys Jephson O'Connor and Hermann Hagedorn, all poets. In the field of art, Waldo Pierce, painter; in archeology, Sylvanus

Griswold Morley, a decipherer of Maya hieroglyphics and the foremost American authority on the ancient Maya. To medicine our class contributed James Howard Means, for more than a quarter century Jackson Professor of Clinical Medicine at Harvard Medical School. To the Foreign Service went John Campbell White, Leland Harrison, Orme Wilson and Franklin Mott Gunther, all of whom served as Chiefs of Mission. In law, while 1907 produced no judges, it adorned the profession with Harrison Tweed and Walter Heilprin Pollak. And in business and finance, with accompanying philanthropy and public service, there were Ward Murphey Canaday, Harper Sibley, Winthrop W. Aldrich, George Whitney, Daniel W. Streeter and Edgar Bloom Stern. Perhaps Harvard's greatest benefaction to me stemmed from the atmosphere of independent thought and intellectual leadership that influenced such men as these.

It had always been taken for granted that I would be a physician: "You're going to follow in Father's footsteps." My father never urged it upon me, but at the end of my junior year when he learned that I could have graduated in June and gone to medical school that fall, he expressed some disappointment. He was then sixty-four years old and had undoubtedly reckoned that with four years of medical school, two years of general internship, and possibly a further internship for eye and ear, he would be seventy, or older, before I could join him in practice. I am sure I should have been more understanding and given up the pleasure of an easy senior year in college. Even so, he raised the question of whether I might not prefer to study law, lapsing into German: "*Wenn du umsatteln willst*," which means literally "if you wish to change your saddle; that is, your steed." I did not take his suggestion seriously; I intended to proceed with medicine as planned, yet I knew the decision had to be my own. My father's remark had revealed his feeling that *a* profession was the proper choice of an educated man, but that profession need not necessarily be medicine.

I entered Harvard Medical School in the fall of 1907. The school had just moved into five impressive new buildings, joined in a harmonious whole on three sides of a rectangle in the Longwood district of Brookline. The faculty, too, was impressive; it included pioneers and leaders in the many specialties of the medical profession. At the end of this century's first decade, the services which may be grouped together as "the healing arts," while no longer in their infancy, were still in their adolescence. Insulin, the sulfa drugs, antibiotics, penicillin—as yet undiscovered— had not worked their revolutionary remedial powers, and there was even a professorship of syphilis, which later pharmaceutical discoveries would render obsolete. We were horrified when bandage removal revealed wounds swarming with maggots which we promptly eliminated. World

War I would shortly demonstrate the bactericidal value of these larvae. Preventive medicine was just beginning to come into its own, and the lecture on alcoholism began with: "There are three classes of drinkers, the moderate drinker, the heavy drinker and the man who drinks before breakfast, and for this last there is no hope." Great breakthroughs still lay ahead in this and every other medical field, particularly in the field of birth control.

I received my first awareness of this problem in the second half of my third year when we went, in pairs, on obstetrical service in the slums of South Boston. There, the children came as fast as nature permitted. Often they were sickly, undernourished, rickety, deformed, and the health of the mother impaired by excessive childbearing. They lived in cramped quarters, sometimes with six or seven to a room. Contraception, impeded by restrictive legislation, was undreamed of, and even if it were legal would have been rejected on religious grounds by these Irish Catholic parents. Contraceptive techniques were not taught at Harvard Medical School.

It was during my obstetrical service that a minor incident started a train of thought that altered my life. One early morning hour as we tumbled into bed in the Lying-in-Hospital after twenty-six hours of duty, I said to my team-mate, Edwin Lee Miller, "I wonder whether we'll have any time for reading after we get into practice."

"Well," he replied, "I'll tell you what my future father-in-law does." He was engaged to the daughter of a nationally known surgeon, Dr. John Fairbairn Binnie of Kansas City. "He sets his alarm clock at five every morning and reads until seven when he gets up."

The idea that this busy surgeon would consider his reading so important intrigued me. "What does he read?" I asked.

"Well, he starts with the *Journal of the American Medical Association*, then he reads the *Journal of Gynecology and Obstetrics*, then the London *Lancet*," and he named several other surgical and medical publications.

I was about to say, "I don't mean that kind of reading." I was thinking of contemporary fiction, current history, social and economic comment which was burgeoning at that time of the "muck-rakers;" even those delightful commentaries on the manners and customs of the period, George Ade's *Fables* and Finley Peter Dunne's *Mr. Dooley*. But I refrained. I felt that my team-mate would wonder what kind of queer duck I was, preparing for a career in medicine and interested in so many other things.

But I was interested. I had found medicine absorbing, but not to the exclusion of everything else. In fact, I was already dabbling in journalism. My best friend, Earl Biggers, had become the dramatic critic of the Boston *Traveler*. When several plays opened at the same time, he had given me the chance to review those he could not attend, including a performance by Sarah Bernhardt. I enjoyed doing it, and my reviews were highly praised by Marlen Pew, the paper's managing editor. But all this had nothing to do with medicine. I was also following national and international events. Would I be able to take care of my professional responsibilities and still keep abreast of what was happening in the world? The question troubled me. Nor was I sure, as I gave the dilemma more thought, that I could be absolutely devoted to treating bodily ailments, which I believed should be a doctor's overriding concern. At the same time, the careers of my closest friends in journalism had an increasing appeal. Dick Walsh was a reporter on the Boston *Herald*, Lucian Price was writing editorials for the *Globe*, Fred Spayde was day city editor on the Boston *American*.

As my perplexity grew, I thought of a way to find out what I should do. In the fourth year of medical school, internships were open competitively. At that time there were three principal hospitals in Boston—the Massachusetts General, the Boston City and the newly established Peter Bent Brigham—which offered both medical and surgical internships. The successful applicant would leave medical school at the end of the first semester, January 31, and his internship would not begin until March 1. If I were successful, I would have a month to experiment. I resolved to try and received an appointment to the First Surgical Service of the Boston City Hospital. I had a guilty feeling when the head of that service, Dr. John Bapst Blake, one of our instructors in surgery, congratulated me; my classmates' congratulations made me feel even more foolish. About thirty of our ninety-one members had come from Harvard '07, and there were a few from '08 who had completed college in three years, among them Paul Dudley White who would become a world-famous cardiologist. Still, I resolved to see where my interest in journalism would carry me.

I had discussed my problem with my newspaper friends and their advice was "Start with Hearst. You won't want to stay there, but you'll get a type of experience that you won't get anywhere else." They were right. The Hearst newspapers featured what was known as "yellow journalism," stories designed to build circulation but not always too concerned with accuracy. Yet it was a much livelier press than the general run of staid, stodgy dailies. The Hearst papers had better comics and cartoons, they attracted a galaxy of star reporters, and they often turned the spotlight on corruption and malfeasance in public office, digging below the surface for scandals other papers would not touch. They were papers for the masses, and for better or worse, represented a new and different kind of journalism.

Hearst owned the Boston *American*. When I called at the office, I saw

the city editor, Jim Reardon, and explained my problem and how I hoped
to solve it. He listened sympathetically. His interest was aroused by the
freakishness of it all. "We can probably give you a job as a cub reporter,"
he said, "but don't do it, my boy. Anyone who would give up medicine
for this must be crazy. Even if you get to be managing editor of *The
New York Times*, you'd make a mistake to give up that fine practice
your father has." Charles O. Power, the Sunday Editor, gave me similar
advice.

I told them that I had not yet burned my bridges, but that I would like
to try newspaper work. Reardon told me to keep on applying. I did, and
after several days of repeated calls, I was hired at fifteen dollars a week.

3

NEWSPAPER MAN

*If, as it has been so wittily said, Boston is
the abandoned farm of American literature,
journalistically it is the country's poor farm.*
—OSWALD GARRISON VILLARD

On my first day as a newspaper man, city editor Jim Reardon handed me
a small clipping concerning a speech made by Judge Charles A. DeCourcy
of the Massachusetts Supreme Court to the senior class at Boston University Law School. The judge deprecated the law's delays, the frequency of
second trials and recommended some reforms—including the repeal of
the Third and Fourth Amendments of the Constitution. He was to be at
Harvard's Stillman Infirmary that morning and I was to catch him there,
interview him and get enough to make a full-page story for the Sunday
edition.

"You've got to be very accurate," Reardon said, "and report his words
exactly. We really ought to send a stenographer, but you've got to do the
best you can. Of course," he added, "the ideal thing would be to get the
notes from which he spoke, but I suppose that's out of the question."

I went to Cambridge and the Stillman Infirmary. Looking over the list
of sick students, I discovered J. DeCourcy '14, and went to his private
room. He was a nice young freshman who told me that he had been expecting his father, the judge, for the last hour and could not understand
why he had not shown up or where he was. I telephoned the court house
but got no satisfaction there. Then young DeCourcy gave me his father's
private number, and when I called I was informed that the judge had
been taken ill suddenly and had gone to his home in Lawrence. So I decided to go to Lawrence, an hour's train ride. I telephoned the judge's

home. His wife answered and when I explained my purpose she told me that the judge had had a heart attack and was under doctor's orders to see no one. My first assignment and I felt I was stuck for fair.

Then, thinking it over, I reasoned that other newspapers might have a more detailed story. The somewhat lowbrow *Post* would not be interested in such matters as constitutional amendments, but maybe the other newspapers would have a longer account from which I could patch together a fuller story. So I went to Amee Brothers on Harvard Square and bought all the morning papers. The accounts in the *Herald* and the *Globe* were useless but the *Journal* had a two-column write-up filled with long quotations. My first conclusion was that it had been taken down by a stenographer, but the *Journal*, which had been acquired by Frank A. Munsey, a chain-store grocery man, had a reputation for being tight-fisted and this did not seem likely. Then in rereading the article I noted that between the long well-phrased passages in quotations there were shorter passages less skillfully worded, which suggested that the *Journal* reporter had gotten the judge's notes and had summarized what was not directly quoted. I wondered if by any chance the notes were still at the *Journal* office.

I called and asked for the city editor. "What do you want?" said a voice. Assuming an imperious tone, I asked why the manuscript of Judge DeCourcy's speech had not been returned. Presently another voice replied, "That manuscript is just about to be mailed to Judge DeCourcy's home in Lawrence." I was so overjoyed that I stuttered but finally managed to say, "Never mind, I'll come in for it right away. Hold it for me."

They did just that and when I picked it up, I saw that it was not merely notes but the entire speech, long enough for several Sunday stories. It filled a full page. A city editor's praise was supposed to be hard to come by, but when Reardon found out how I got the speech, he said, "Good work, my boy, I think you'll do." I was not so sure. I still had a lot to learn.

The Boston afternoon papers, of which the *American* was one, published half-a-dozen editions, the first going to press about 9:00 A.M. for street and out-of-town circulation. Competition with the *Traveler*, *Evening Herald* and *Evening Globe* was keen, and when these papers were brought in, the staff clustered around the day city editor's desk to see what stories they had. If they had something we had missed, orders were barked out to rewrite their story and reporters were sent out to develop some new angle which was telephoned in to make the next edition. Among the rewrite men was young Ben Ames Williams who would later make a name for himself as a novelist. And in the sports department another young man, Ring Lardner, was sharpening his literary talents. The pace was fairly hectic and the city room was noisy. Loud calls of "Boy!" from the city editor or one of the rewrite men kept us on our toes. My hours were 6:00 A.M. to 3:30 P.M., but I soon learned that you worked around the clock, if necessary, to "get that story."

There were frequent changes of executives. Someone from headquarters in New York or San Francisco, reputed to be a "big shot" in the organization, would come in and bawl out some orders to indicate that things were going to be different. These men, we were informed, were high up in Hearst's confidence. The new managing editor, Arthur Clarke, we were told, had done a terrific job building up the Hearst paper in Chicago. I ventured to differ from him only once.

In a laboratory at the Harvard Medical School, some research on nutrition was being conducted by Dr. Francis G. Benedict and the *American* had assigned a reporter named Fred McIsaac to find out about it. The doctor obviously wanted no publicity—especially not in the *American* —and refused to admit McIsaac. But the reporter had put his foot in the door so that it could not be shut, whereupon Dr. Benedict pushed him out bodily. McIsaac's stories thereafter told of the mysterious disappearance of children's pets and of the various horrors that befell them in Dr. Benedict's laboratory. It was a Hearst policy to oppose animal experimentation and vivisection, but McIsaac's stories were so obviously malicious fabrications that I went to the managing editor's desk and registered a protest. I was not prepared for the consequences.

In a thunderous voice that echoed and re-echoed through the city room Clarke roared out, "Do you know what that man did? He laid hands on one of my reporters. Out in Chicago, when I was managing editor of the *American*, a man laid hands on one of my reporters, and I didn't stop until I landed him behind bars in Joliet. And I won't stop until I get this doc behind bars!"

I was properly rebuked, but needless to say nothing more serious happened to Dr. Benedict than a continuing misrepresentation of what was going on in his laboratory.

One morning, Sunday editor Charlie Power called me to his desk and said, "The Chilton Club has applied for a liquor license. It looks like a good story. See what you can find out." I found that some of Boston's blue-blooded ladies had decided to have a club of their own; it was called The Chilton and it would rival Boston's exclusive men's clubs. Their clubhouse in the Back Bay was nearing completion, and the "good story" consisted of the fact that, in blue-stocking Boston, the ladies were planning to serve liquor.

I sought out Mrs. Robert Lovett, vice president of the club. She was reticent and clearly did not relish publicity, but since it was known that the club had applied for a liquor license, she explained that the governing board felt that they could not properly entertain their male guests without serving them drinks. "We can't just serve them ginger ale." But she hastened to emphasize that there would be no bar and that the drinks would be brought into the dining room on a tray, which, she felt, would lessen any criticism that might be offered. In further evidence of the club's conservatism she added that no smoking would be allowed in the dining room, but would be limited to the roof-garden where members and their guests gathered before and after meals. Would the ladies smoke there? I asked. "Yes, but only there" was her answer. Moreover, while the men could smoke anything they brought along, the club would furnish only cigarettes.

It is difficult to conceive, over half a century later, that the story of these twin evils, liquor and tobacco, being served in a woman's club would constitute a sensation. But it did. It blossomed with a three-line, four-column headline on the Sunday *American's* front page: COCKTAILS AND CIGARETTES! WHERE? IN EXCLUSIVE BOSTON WOMAN'S CLUB! Of course, Boston's temperance faction picked up the hue and cry. In his next Sunday's sermon, the Reverend Cortland Myers, pastor of Tremont Temple, the city's leading Baptist church, denounced the Chilton Club as "the vestibule of Hell," and other clergymen followed suit. Since it was an "exclusive" *American* story, the other Boston newspapers gave the affair slight mention or ignored it completely, but the *American*, in the best tradition of Hearst journalism, kept it alive for weeks.

That it was a different age with different *mores* was reconfirmed not much later when Mrs. Emmeline Pankhurst, the noted British feminist, who had come to America with her daughter Sylvia to assist in the women's suffrage struggle, was asked to leave the Hotel Thorndike, one of Boston's leading hostelries, because she had lighted a cigarette in the dining room. She declined to comment on the incident when I sought to interview her, but she was obviously more amused than annoyed by it.

Another of my assignments was to write full-page Sunday stories about Massachusetts towns. They were intended as circulation builders and were illustrated with photos of local notables and buildings. I was instructed to stress only the favorable features of every town. Local authorities and Chamber of Commerce officials were tremendously pleased by this kind of publicity. They wrote approving letters to the paper and after half-a-dozen articles I was given a "by-line." What they did not know was that the story appeared only in the copies of the paper that went to their town. I protested to Reardon that this was a fraud, but he replied, "They are free to buy as many extra copies as they want and send them out."

In the manufacturing city of Chicopee I ran across what I thought was a new angle. I interviewed M. A. Rawlinsen, the general manager of the Chicopee Manufacturing Company which produced a variety of textiles and was the city's oldest industry and largest employer with 1300 operatives.

"Perhaps you'd like to hear about our pension system," he said. I was certainly interested in such an unprecedented example of social welfare.

"Yes," said the manager, "after an employee has been with us for a period of years, we retire him at half-pay for life."

"That's wonderful," I said. "How long do they have to work?"

"Fifty years."

"How many do you have now drawing the pension?"

"Just one so far, but several others are close."

"How much does he get?"

"It's a she. She was being paid $6 a week. She is now getting $3 a week for life."

"How old is she?"

"Sixty-two. She began working when she was twelve."

I reported that conversation, but I was chagrined to find that only the fifty-years' service period was mentioned. The fact that only one employee was pensioned and at what amount had been deleted.

A retirement system was rare in both private industry and government in those days. I wrote up the plight of the employees of the Life Saving Service, a branch of the Revenue Cutter Service, later known as the U.S. Coast Guard. These men were paid $65 a month and $9 for rations, but when they were disabled in the line of duty or retired because of age, they did not receive another penny from the government. My story urged the necessary legislation which, I am happy to say, was eventually passed.

Making ends meet was a problem then as now, but more so then, and I reported another hardship story from quite a different quarter. Insisting that they had posed long enough for much too little, several artists' models were interested in forming a models' union, the first of its kind, in Boston. Margaret Johnson, whom I interviewed, was not only beautiful, but witty. "Our demands may not be palatable to the painters but they'll find that a canvas of the models will show we're together for better pay," she said. "The sculptors needn't think they can give us the marble heart or chisel down our rates. It's the hardest kind of toil, and only one who has carefully trained herself for the various positions and poses for many months can be a successful model. If you think posing for periods of twenty-five minutes, with only five minutes in between isn't hard work, try it."

Maude Brooks, another model, talked of the model's high living expenses: "The strain of continuous posing is great and its effects have to be
compensated for by Turkish baths, massages and similar treatments that
are considered luxuries, but are necessities in this calling." Their calling
paid them as little as 25 cents an hour and the models felt that 75 cents an
hour would be a fair rate.

But the biggest story that broke while I was on the *American* was the
death of a choir singer named Avis Linnell. She had been seduced by the
pastor of her church, the Reverend Clarence V. T. Richeson, who had
promised to marry her. She became pregnant and the pastor sent her some
medicine which he told her would take care of her problem. It was potas-
sium cyanide. The first newspaper stories described Miss Linnell's death
as a suicide, but Dr. Timothy Leary, the astute Boston Medical Examiner,
came to another conclusion. Richeson was tried, convicted and sentenced
to death. His lawyers pleaded insanity as a defense. I was assigned to report the examination performed by the doctors which found him sane.
He was electrocuted.

As the year rolled on, I decided to return to medical school, take the
fourth year's second semester and get my degree. My father was pleased;
he no doubt hoped that, once back in school, I would stick to medicine.
But while I had decided to leave Hearst, I wanted to stay in journalism.
The *American* had treated me well. I had covered fires, court cases,
elopements, accidents, public meetings, visiting celebrities and various
oddities. My pay had been raised twice—three dollars each time—
without my asking. From my point of view at least, my experiment had
been successful. I had sampled the power of the press not merely to report events but to lead public opinion. That, I decided, would be my
profession.

An event that would make my life much more pleasant, and bring the
members of my family together again, was Father's decision to build a
summer home in Rockport, Massachusetts. In recent years the family had
spent its summer vacations in several different resorts; we all agreed that it
would be better to settle down in one place. A summer in Gloucester had
acquainted us with the charm of Cape Ann and Clara and I now explored
it in a horsedrawn buggy. Our eyes lighted on a beautiful meadow sloping to the sea with a "for sale" sign on it. Offshore to the left was Straitsmouth Island with its small lighthouse; to the right, Thacher's Island with
its tall twin lighthouses. The land was on a winding country road that
came to a dead end about a mile to the south where there was an inn, the
Turk's Head, and a fine sandy beach; its ocean frontage was part stony
beach and part granite rock. The water was deep off these rocks and we
could dive safely from them into the cool, clear salt water. The meadow,

abundant with tall grass, red clover and daisies, was treeless except for a few willows which grew alongside a brook that trickled seaward. It was a beautiful spot.

Father agreed to buy the twelve-acre meadow and engaged Robert Coit, a well-known Boston architect, to build a house. As the plans proceeded in the spring of 1911, I was more or less in charge simply because I was in Boston, and what I lacked in judgment I made up for in enthusiasm. Under my direction, a third floor was added to the original plan, and when Mother and my sister May came up in the late summer, they were horrified at the house's size. Father expressed doubt that we would be able to keep it after he had gone. Nevertheless, we all loved the house and got a full measure of enjoyment from it for many years.

Our weekend houseparties in Rockport are among my pleasantest memories, and were a welcome relief from the hustle and bustle of Boston. I lived in Cambridge, and one of my friends there, W. Cleveland Cogswell '06, a lawyer, whom I got to know through our mutual interest in chess, had a summer home in North Scituate on the South Shore to which he invited me each of several summers. In July of 1908, he and his younger brother John and I had paddled the length of Lakes Champlain and George. Then, in the summer of 1909, after playing tennis at North Scituate's Hatherly Club, I met a Vassar graduate of that year who had been watching us. Her name was Dorothy Elizabeth Smith. Her parents had a cottage on the beach at Minot and their home was in Norwood where her father was a partner in the Norwood Press which printed books for the Macmillan Company. Her mother, Laura Huntington Smith, was also a graduate of Vassar, Class of '78, when it took considerable gumption for a girl to go to college. The next day I proposed a swim to Minot Light, about a mile from the shore. Cleveland Cogswell agreed to row alongside. Dorothy was a good swimmer and could have made it, but the water was icy and halfway out she climbed back in the boat. I kept on to the light, no doubt to impress Dorothy, but I was glad to get warm by rowing back. Dorothy was among the girls who made our Rockport houseparties so enjoyable. She soon became the only girl in my life. I fell in love with her, courted her during the following years when she was secretary of the Salem Young Women's Association, proposed in 1913 and we were married at her parents' home in Norwood on November 19, 1914.

I held fast to my decision to stay with journalism. After graduating from medical school in June 1912, I had a wide choice of newspapers in Boston. Besides the *American* and the Hearst morning paper—the *Advertiser*—there were the Boston *Post*—the morning paper with the largest circulation—the *Journal*, the *Traveler* and the *Record* which were evening papers, and the *Herald* and the *Globe* which published both morning and

LEFT: *Dorothy at the time of our engagement*

BELOW: *Dorothy Gruening with Ernest Jr., Huntington, and Peter*

OPPOSITE TOP: *Our summer home in Rockport, Maine, 1911–1931*

OPPOSITE BELOW: *Musical trio—Ernest Jr., Huntington, and Peter in Portland, 1930*

evening editions. There were also two rather special newspapers, the *Transcript*, a highbrow afternoon paper of limited circulation, read by "the best families," and the *Christian Science Monitor* which was national and international in its coverage, and at that time followed closely Mary Baker Eddy's religious precepts by omitting crime and disaster stories. When the *Titanic*, on her maiden voyage in 1912, sank after colliding with an iceberg, the *Monitor* omitted the names of those who perished and printed only the roster of those who had been saved. I applied for work on the *Evening Herald* and was hired at $25 a week. Three weeks later the *Traveler* and the *Evening Herald* were amalgamated, a consolidation similar to those that would in the next half century drastically reduce the number of metropolitan dailies and profoundly alter the character of the "newspaper game." Invariably when this happened, a lot of newspaper men (and women) found themselves jobless and became, under the whimsical current definition, "journalists"—*i.e.* "newspaper men out of work." I was not one of the victims, but I was shifted to the morning *Herald*, which meant entirely different working hours. And once again I plunged into the busy life of a reporter.

That summer there was an International Congress of Otologists at the Harvard Medical School and I was, not surprisingly, assigned to cover it. My father was there and was pleased by my incidental welding of medicine and journalism. The most newsworthy feature of the meeting was the presentation, for the first time at such a gathering, of deaf-mutes who had been taught to speak, among them Helen Keller who, besides being deaf since infancy, was also blind. Miss Keller's voice was high-pitched with a peculiar metallic ring, but her speech was remarkably clear. She had never before been interviewed for publication, so I communicated with her teacher-companion, Anne Sullivan Macy, and on securing assent went to their home in Wrentham.

Miss Keller came out on the porch to greet me and, asking me to sit beside her, told me to put the fore and middle fingers of her right hand on my lips. By that means she could understand everything I said.

She spoke with enthusiasm of her aspirations to help others who were deaf and blind, and revealed that she was a socialist, repeatedly referring to socialism as the cure for the nation's economic ills. The special development of her other senses also came to light in the course of our interview.

"When you speak to an audience, do you know that there are many people in the room?" I asked. "For instance, when you were speaking at the Harvard Medical School did you know there was a crowd there?"

"I should say I did," Miss Keller replied. "I could feel them and smell them."

"How did you feel them?"

"By any number of vibrations through the air, and through the floor, from the moving of feet or the scraping of chairs, and by the warmth when there are people around."

"How could you tell by your sense of smell?"

"There was the doctors' odor."

"Do you mean to say that doctors have a special odor which you can recognize?"

"A very decided odor," Miss Keller said. "It's partly the smell of ether and partly the smell that lingers from the sick rooms in which they have been. But I can tell many professions from their odor."

"Which ones?" I asked.

"Doctors, painters, sculptors, masons, carpenters, druggists, and cooks."

"What does the carpenter smell like, and the druggist?"

"The carpenter is always accompanied by the odor of wood. The druggist is saturated with various drugs. There is a painter who comes here often and I can always tell the minute he comes anywhere near me."

"Could you tell my work in that way?" I asked. "Do you smell any ink?"

"No, a typewriter, I think," Miss Keller answered quickly, laughing.

"Could you really tell that?"

Miss Keller's rippling laugh continued. "I'm afraid that was a guess," she admitted.

"Do you receive many sensations by means of vibrations?" I asked. "Can you distinguish between noise and music?"

"Oh yes, there is the rhythm," Miss Keller replied.

"Aside from the rhythm if someone were to beat rhythmically with a hammer, could you tell?"

"There is an entirely different feeling between music, which is pleasant, and noise, which is harsh."

"Can you understand German as well as English?"

"Not nearly so well," Miss Keller said. "I can understand it as well to read, but I haven't had the practice in reading lips in German."

"*Können sie mich jetzt verstehen?*" I asked without any intimation of the sudden change.

Miss Keller hesitated for just a moment longer than usual. "*Jawohl, Ich verstehe ja ganz gut,*" she answered with perfect fluency.

I visited the house and saw her library printed in Braille, including her own works, *The Story of My Life* and *The World I Live In.*

She gave me a photograph of herself, a lovely profile, and sat down at a typewriter to type under it a verse from a poem which she said had been her inspiration. It was the first verse of William Ernest Henley's "Invictus."

Out of the night that covers me
Black as the pit from pole to pole
I thank whatever gods may be
For my unconquerable soul.

And she printed her name underneath in longhand.

The interview was published in full in the *Herald* along with Miss Keller's photograph. As it was her first interview and revealed much that had not been known about her sensory faculties, the story was sent out by the Associated Press and called attention to the potential for other deaf-mutes. But I feared that for those without Helen Keller's character, determination and patience, coupled with those same qualities in her devoted teacher, Anne Sullivan, her achievement would not be easily duplicated.

I took part in another first when I was assigned to cover the air show at the Squantum field on Boston's southern outskirts. While this was not the first show of its kind, the airplane was a great novelty, and flying, considered daring and hazardous—as indeed it still was—attracted crowds. Because two women were taking part in the show—referred to in the headlines of the day as "bird-women,"—a woman reporter, Gertrude Stevenson, was given the assignment to be a passenger on one of the planes flown either by Harriet Quimby or Blanche Scott. This would be a "first"—a woman flown in a plane piloted by a woman.

Miss Quimby was a jolly, good-looking girl, tanned by sun and wind. She told me she had flown the English Channel in April in her Bleriot open-cockpit monoplane—the plane she was now using—and had reached an altitude of 6,000 feet, which she said was a world record for an aviatrix. Miss Stevenson got into the two-seated plane beside her. At this point the manager of the air show, William Willard, joined us at the plane to remind Miss Quimby that she had agreed he would be her first passenger, but that he would be glad to yield to the lady reporter. Miss Stevenson, however, obligingly climbed out. The crowd watched the plane take off, circle several times to attain altitude and then head northward across the waters of Dorchester Bay. When it returned some minutes later, there was applause from the grandstand. It circled at about 1,000 feet and began to descend. Suddenly, it went into a headspin and the crowd was horrified to see two figures tumble out of the plane, their bodies turning over and over in the air as they fell. Willard's teenage son was in the crowd which rushed to the water's edge. It was an unnerving experience, particularly for Miss Stevenson. The bodies were quickly recovered from the shallow water. Both had died instantly. The tragedy made all the front pages the next day, but it was not the "lead" story.

That came from Baltimore where the Democratic National Convention was about to nominate Woodrow Wilson and Thomas Riley Marshall, whose most memorable contribution to history during his vice-presidency was his statement that "What this country needs is a good five-cent cigar."

Politically it was a lively summer and fall with the unprecedented participation of three major parties—Republican, Democratic and Progressive, which was generally called "Bull Moose." I was one of half a dozen reporters sent to cover "Teddy" when he came to Boston. At that time political campaigners did not send advance copies of their speeches to the newspapers; they had to rely on reporters to take down what was said in longhand. Addressing a large cheering crowd in the Boston Common, Roosevelt urged that the Golden Rule be applied to politics which, he said, he would continue to do; and he let all know that both the old parties were hopelessly corrupt and incompetent. To a voice in the crowd that called, "Tell us about Taft," he responded, "I don't discuss dead issues."

Roosevelt mingled a lot of platitudes with his remarks but did it with such hearty gusto that he carried his audience with him. In fact, the crowds did not care too much what he said; they were for him no matter what.

That was not quite true of those who came to hear President William Howard Taft. When he spoke at Faneuil Hall, the postal employees were given time off to go. He addressed them as "my fellow servants in the government," and explained that he had vetoed a bill giving them a seven-year tenure because he wanted to give them a longer one. Their enthusiasm was restrained.

Woodrow Wilson at a noon rally at Tremont Temple urged tariff reductions to curb monopoly and the "trusts." It was a scholarly, professional presentation, but it evoked only moderate applause.

Throughout 1912 industrial strife on a major scale had broken out in the textile mills of Lawrence. In that city of 90,000 people, the wages of women and workers under sixteen had been cut thirty cents a day, the price of three loaves of bread. The cut resulted indirectly from enactment by the state legislature of a law reducing the work week from fifty-eight hours or longer, to not more than fifty-four hours. When, without previous notification, the workers found $1.80 less in their pay envelopes, and the industry refused to arbitrate, they struck. The strike leaders were Joseph Ettor and Arturo Giovanitti, aided by Carlo Tresca, William Haywood and Elizabeth Gurley Flynn, who were seeking to organize the workers in the Industrial Workers of the World. Violence broke out; the strikers tried to block access to the mills and the police used their clubs freely. When a woman striker was shot and killed, the police arrested Ettor, Giovanitti and Joseph Caruso, charging them with murder.

The miserable conditions in the crowded, foul, mill-owned tenements and the mills themselves made me sympathetic to the strikers' cause—it was my first contact with some of the realities of the industry-labor struggle—but the general public's thought was that these foreign-born anarchist leaders were not to be tolerated and the editorial position of the newspapers reflected that view. The *Herald*'s attitude was slightly modified after a policeman's well-directed kick smashed the camera of *Herald* photographer, Arthur Waldron, who had taken some pictures of police clubbing, an incident I witnessed at close range and reported.

The workers' walkout continued in protest against the imprisonment of Ettor and Giovanitti. A huge Sunday rally was held on the Boston Common at which some 15,000 workers, who had come from Lawrence, Lynn, Haverhill and other industrial towns, were addressed by Elizabeth Gurley Flynn, a dynamic orator. After congratulating them for choosing "rather to starve on the picket line than starve in the mill," she urged all to abstain from violence, but said that those who went back to work while their leaders were jailed would be looked upon with shame by all the world.

A startling development occurred when William M. Wood, President of the American Woolen Company, and three other men were indicted by a grand jury for "conspiracy to place explosives—to wit dynamite —in certain buildings and premises in the City of Lawrence with intent to use unlawfully to injure certain mill owners." Apparently it was their intention to blame the strikers for the damage.

The indictment came as a bombshell. Wood was president of various woolen mills in cities other than Lawrence, a bank director and a multimillionaire. All four men pleaded not guilty, but while the lesser figures in the conspiracy were sentenced, Wood's participation was not proved to the jury's satisfaction.

The strikers' paycuts were ultimately restored and Ettor, Giovanitti and Caruso were found not guilty. The IWW distintegrated with the subsequent conviction of its leaders on various other charges after the entry of the United States into the first World War, when their activities were equated with disloyalty. But their activity in Lawrence and in other Bay State cities undoubtedly won important gains for the workers. Ninety-four new AFL unions came into being in Massachusetts in 1912, and organized labor was beginning to become a force.

One unusual, but little-noticed episode in the spring of 1913, which I enjoyed, involved my friend "Bob" Benchley who had graduated from Harvard the previous June and had acquired some local fame as an after-dinner wit and impersonator. A dinner was scheduled at the Copley-Plaza hotel by the officers of the First Naval District to greet President Wilson's appointee as Secretary of the Navy on his first visit to New England after assuming his new duties.

He was Josephus Daniels, North Carolina newspaper editor and publisher. One of his first acts as Secretary had been to ban the use of liquor aboard Naval vessels, a custom prevalent since John Paul Jones. This action was highly unpopular with the officers at that time. Daniels was viewed with disapprobation and apprehension by most of the Navy "brass." Clearly the new chief was no "He-man."

As the diners assembled, it was announced that while, unfortunately, due to the press of official duties, Secretary Daniels had been obliged to cancel his visit, he had sent his personal secretary, Jeremiah Beasley, to represent him and impart to the assembled Navy officers some of his ideas, purposes and plans. Beasley was Benchley, but only the perpetrator of this impish spoof and I—assigned to report Secretary Daniels's visit—were aware of it.

When Bob rose to speak to the assembled admirals, captains, commanders and lesser officers, he was aware of the frostiness of the atmosphere. He saw no smiling countenances, but he sailed on gaily.

After expressing the regrets of his chief, the Secretary of the Navy, at his inability to be there in person, and conveying his greetings to the officers who served on the nation's first line of defense, he said that his chief was sure that they would like to hear of some of his ideas, plans, and some of the reforms that he looked forward to making. At the mention of reforms the already chilly atmosphere became icy.

"Yes," said Daniels's personal secretary, "my chief feels that the Navy has not been sufficiently democratic—with a small "d" of course, heh, heh, heh—and to rectify that, a matter to which he has given special attention, he's going to have tea served every afternoon on the quarter deck. Both officers and men will be invited." At this, Bob told me later, he could see some of the old salts turning purple.

"Yes," he continued engagingly, "my chief hopes this will break down some of the class barriers between officers and enlisted men, and create a new *esprit de corps*, if I may use that expression."

At that point a four-striper jumped up, and with grimly bitter emphasis asked:

"Will niggers be invited to those teas?"

"Well, it did not come up when he was briefing me, but I'll be glad to carry the idea back to him, and I'm sure he'll be happy to see it done."

The scowling faces, the blood mounting in them to apoplectic levels, made Bob fearful of a general walkout, perhaps open denunciation, or even physical violence; so he felt he'd better broaden his spiel, so that they'd catch on.

"Moreover," he continued cheerfully, "my chief feels that the Navy also has a function as an educational institution. While training for naval duties, we must not forget our role as citizens. To emphasize that, he's planning to have a little red schoolhouse painted on every funnel."

At this point, some in the audience caught on and one of the admirals roared with laughter and began applauding. But defrosting was not easy. Even after Bob had concluded and was mingling with the diners he could see and feel a chilly lingering resentment.

Perhaps the officers felt it had been too near a possibility to be funny.

I wanted to broaden my newspaper experience and I sought the chance to work on the copy desk and do "rewrite"—take the stories telephoned in and prepare them for publication. So after a year, except for some Sunday feature stories, my reporting ceased. One story that I did cover, however, involved two members of my family. My sisters Clara and Martha were active suffragists. Martha, while at Smith College, was Secretary of the National College Equal Suffrage League. A meeting on behalf of the cause was held at the Straitsmouth Inn at Rockport. Clara presided and the speakers were State Senator Roger Sherman Hoar, and Martha. Her speech was persuasive: "Antisuffragists say that woman's place is in the home and that therefore she is not entitled to vote. Man's place is in the office, but that is never given as a reason that men should not vote." And, of course, she was right.

I also started to submit editorials. The first three were rejected with kindly criticism, but finally one, and thereafter, several were accepted. One evening I received a note from the editor, Robert Lincoln O'Brien, telling me to go into his office and write enough editorials to complete the three columns allotted to them in the next morning's paper. His assistant editorial writer was going on vacation. Later that night O'Brien dropped in and told me that I was to write editorials for a while. The assignment would be temporary, however; an experienced editorial writer was coming from the West to take over the job. But after several weeks O'Brien told me that the editorial writer from the West was a fiction, designed to spare my feelings if I had not made good. I got the job and the title of assistant editor.

My pay was $25 a week, as it had been since I had joined the *Traveler* a year and a half earlier. I knew that my predecessor had been getting $60 a week and I went home in a glow of euphoria. I was planning to get married to Dorothy and $60 a week would put us on Easy Street. But when I opened my next pay envelope, I found my salary had been raised to $27.

I was struck by the humor of it, and when O'Brien came in I said, "There seems to be a slight typographical error in my pay check." He was mildly embarrassed and said, "We'll correct it next week." My next check was for $50 and I was content to let the matter rest.

I cannot say that in the next two years I produced any editorial gems. I was largely confined to subjects that were not too controversial. O'Brien wrote the editorials on national matters which reflected the *Herald*'s Republican position and became increasingly critical of Woodrow Wilson's "New Freedom" and his social and economic policies. But in one field I was able to be useful, writing on medical subjects about which the press generally was ill-informed. Various fake cures for cancer, tuberculosis and other ailments were being swallowed whole by a gullible public. I was able to give the facts, and these editorials were reprinted in medical journals and commented upon favorably. My contributions in this field helped reconcile my father to my having given up medicine.

My father died on May 30, 1914. I rushed to New York after my sister Clara telephoned that he had had a stroke and that the end was near. Unable to speak when I came to his bedside and bent over to kiss him, he could still give me his wonderful smile. Dear Father! He had exemplified "the American dream" and left his children a priceless legacy of integrity and love for the values he embodied and cherished.

With the outbreak of the war in Europe at the end of July 1914, my background of travel seemed to fit me for a special position on the *Herald*, namely handling the war-news. I became a part managing editor. I was violently pro-Ally but my bias was held in check by O'Brien. I was outraged by the German invasion of Belgium in violation of solemn treaty commitments which German Chancellor Von Bethmann-Hollweg brushed off as a mere "scrap of paper," and by the subsequent German atrocities in Belgium. My father and I, when we were together, had followed the course of Prussian "junkerism," highlighted by the Zabern affair, in which a German officer had sabered a lame shoemaker in Alsace and instead of being punished for it, was lionized. I suggested various cartoons to the *Herald*'s cartoonist, Hayden Jones, some of which O'Brien deemed too strong. One, showing the Kaiser's hands dripping with the blood of his Belgian victims and seeking peace in the face of advancing bayonets, O'Brien deleted after the *Herald*'s first edition. I saved it for my scrapbook.

In October of that year I got another promotion. I became managing editor of the *Traveler* which was the *Herald*'s afternoon paper. It had been losing circulation, and it was hoped I would reverse the trend.

4

MANAGING EDITOR

Who would not be an editor
To write the magic we, of such enormous might;
To be so great beyond the common span
It takes the plural to express the man.

— I. G. SAXE

Boston journalism in the century's second decade was in varying degrees subject to the pressures of special interests. Advertisers could and did influence its news columns, keeping out stories they deemed distasteful, and securing insertion of material that was not newsworthy but was of financial benefit to them. Labor troubles in department stores were never mentioned. Except in the *Transcript*, dramatic and literary "criticism" consisted of fulsome puffs for plays and books. In addition, there were "keep-outs," "must-nots" and "sacred cows" affecting many individuals and institutions.

My friend and Harvard classmate, Earl Biggers, had been dramatic critic of the Boston *Traveler* and had married one of its most talented reporters and feature writers, Eleanor Ladd. When he heard of my appointment as managing editor, he wrote:

> I hope you may do wonders with the Traveler—but somehow, in the eyes of both Eleanor and myself, each new move like that ties you more firmly to Boston and the rotten game there, rouses new doubts as to whether you are doing the wisest thing to stay on. Not always blest is the tie that binds, particularly when it binds to what has so long seemed a hopeless proposition to us—the Boston Traveler. . . . I know you will win *if they let you*—and I hope when

you have won, the next step will be onward and upward, out of the graveyard of ideals.

I knew what Earl meant and had resolved to draw my battle-lines accordingly. Indeed, I had witnessed a most amusing example of the stupidity of the *Herald*'s "sacred cow" practices.

One night in 1913 while I was in the outer sanctum writing editorials, a tall gentleman walked in asking to see Mr. O'Brien, who emerged from his inner room and introduced the visitor as Mr. Billings. I gathered from O'Brien's manner that Billings was a man of some importance. "Mr. O'Brien, there is something coming up about me shortly," Mr. Billings said, "and I hope the *Herald* will treat me kindly."

"You may count upon it, Mr. Billings," said O'Brien.

Billings left, and opening the door to the city room O'Brien called out, "There'll be something about Edmund Billings coming out shortly. The *Herald* must not print a line of it, not a line of it," which was duly noted by the night editor and copy desk. O'Brien assumed that the "something" would be unfavorable to Mr. Billings.

O'Brien was out of reach in the Maine woods when several days later the Associated Press flashed the news that President Wilson had appointed Edmund Billings Collector of the Port of Boston. It was a front-page story, with pictures and laudatory editorials, in every paper but the *Herald*. O'Brien was quite upset when he returned, but his staff had simply obeyed the boss's orders.

The *Traveler* staff made no secret of welcoming my arrival. Its morale was low; the man I replaced had been a sports editor and interested in little else. We had a good staff and I hoped that with encouragement and leadership we could produce a fine daily. The city editor, Moses Williams, was an extremely able newspaperman.

On my first day, as I looked out from my office on the third floor into the city room, an old lady shuffled by with a cane. She was Margaret Maginnis, referred to by all as Madam Maginnis, the oldest journalist in Boston both in age and years of service. She was eighty-seven and had worked on the *Traveler* for forty-three years. Her greatest journalistic exploit had been covering the Jesse Pomeroy case. Pomeroy, a sexual pervert, as a teenager some forty years before had murdered several children. On account of his youth he was spared the death penalty and sentenced to solitary imprisonment for life. Through the years, Madam Maginnis had covered every kind of story, but now she wrote a daily column of church notes preceded with a selection of her choosing from the Scriptures. For that she was paid ten dollars a week, which had been her wage through the years. Of course, she should have retired long before, but there was no pension plan on the *Herald* or the *Traveler*.

I went out into the city room and said, "Madam, you shouldn't be coming into the office on a day like this." It was raining.

She looked at me in surprise. "But my copy? I have to bring in my copy."

"Send it in by messenger," I said. That was unheard of. Messenger service cost fifty cents.

I was afraid that Madam Maginnis would become ill, and three weeks later my fears were realized. She was rushed to the hospital and when she came to some hours later, her first words were "What about my copy?" I went to see her and told her not to worry about her copy; someone else would do her column until she got back.

Two weeks later, I was called into O'Brien's office.

"I see you've continued Madam Maginnis on the payroll," he said.

"Yes, I have."

"How long do you purpose to do that?"

"Until she gets well."

"The Boston *Herald* is not an eleemosynary institution," said O'Brien, enunciating his words with cutting emphasis. "If you wish to do charity, do it out of your own pocket."

"It never occurred to me," I said, "that there was any element of charity in it. Don't you think that a person who has worked for the paper for forty-three years is entitled to it?"

"Dammit, Gruening, didn't she get paid all the time she was working?"

"Yes, the munificent sum of $10 a week."

"Well," said O'Brien, "take her off the payroll at the end of the week."

"I will not," I said.

There was a succession of "I won'ts, you wills," at the end of which O'Brien said:

"She goes off the payroll next Saturday."

"I can't prevent you from taking her off the payroll," I said, "but if you do, I'll have one of the office boys pass the hat and he'll come to solicit you, too."

"I don't want you to humiliate the *Herald* in this manner," O'Brien said with a show of anger.

"Then it mustn't put itself in a position where it's got to be humiliated." And I went out, slamming the door. Our loud tones had carried into the city room, and several of the staff were shaking their clasped hands.

There was no change in that week's payroll. But the next week I was called to the office of James H. Higgins, the general manager. Higgins, who also owned the daily papers in Gloucester and Newburyport, had been brought up in the school of hard knocks in which a nickel was a nickel, as he had told me on a previous occasion. O'Brien was there and I knew something was up.

"Gruening," Higgins began, "I'm sorry to touch on a matter that has been greatly troubling Mr. O'Brien and me. It's a painful subject. It's one we'd like to avoid. I refer to the sad case of Madam Maginnis. Of course, if we were to follow the inclination of our hearts, there's no question what we would do; we'd keep her on the payroll. But we have no right to do that. We are, after all, trustees for the owners. We have a duty to our stockholders, and we must be faithful to that duty."

I found it difficult to keep a straight face. I felt as if we were in some play by Galsworthy or Bernard Shaw. While Higgins paused, I collected my thoughts. "Mr. Higgins," I said, "you've put this matter to me in an entirely new light. I can see now that we have an obligation to the stockholders. But you have shown the way out. Let us follow, as you suggest, the inclination of our hearts, and we three make up Madam Maginnis's salary."

O'Brien was out of his chair in protest. "That would be setting a bad precedent," he said. "We can't do that." Higgins agreed.

"Well, it's one or the other," I said.

"But she might be sick for years," O'Brien said, and then he came up with a new idea. "You know there are these institutions where they put old people and you pay a certain amount down, and they gamble—so to speak—that the person won't live too long."

"Would you like to put your mother in such a place?" I asked.

"Leave my mother out of it," said O'Brien.

"All right," I said, "I've given you an alternative. I'm willing to do my part to relieve the stockholders. If you don't want to do that, she'll stay on the payroll. The day she comes off, I'll be off too." And I got up and left.

Margaret Maginnis continued on the payroll. She returned to the paper three months later in as good health as her age permitted.

One of my first directives to the staff, tacked on the city-room bulletin board, read as follows:

TO THE MEMBERS OF THE *Traveler* DESK

In editing stories which involve Negroes please handle as follows:

Ask yourselves how the story would read if the word Jew, Irishman, or Swede was substituted for the word Negro.

Refer to the color of the individual only when it is of particular and special interest and when the story is manifestly incomplete and inaccurate if the color of the person involved is concealed. This would appy to lynchings, interracial marriages and when a colored person gains unusual and exceptional prominence, such as the ranking of a colored girl at the head of a class of white children.

In crime cases where the description of a principal is of importance, the color should be brought into the story but as a *part of the description* such as, for instance, in describing an unidentified assailant you would say that he was of medium height, wore a black cap, had a moustache and looked like an Italian, so similarly, you may state that the man was colored, but never say that five Negroes were arrested in a raid, etc. or that a Negro burglar entered the house of ———, or that Martha Jones, thirty-five, colored, while crossing Northampton Street, was run over by a street car.

In other words, I would like the colored people treated with approximately the same fairness that we accord other racial groups in the community.

This proposed practice, which seemed to me a matter of elementary fairness, had not been followed by any Boston newspaper, nor, as far as I could ascertain, by dailies anywhere else. In supplementing my written instructions in a discussion with Jim Towne, the head of the copy desk, I asked him what he supposed would happen if the story of a disorder in which three men named O'Brien, Dooley and Finnegan were arrested were headlined "Three Irishmen Arrested in Raid." Jim roared with laughter and said, "We'd have Irish confetti breaking every window in the place."

I was also determined to have honest dramatic criticism as a regular department of the *Traveler*. There were a number of legitimate theaters in Boston, most of which presented week-long or longer runs of Broadway productions. On the *Traveler* the practice had been to make every review a rave, and to permit theatrical press agents to load the paper with ridiculous stories and pictures in exchange for increased advertising space. I did not like it and called a meeting of the local theater managers, some of whom came accompanied by visiting press agents from their New York offices. I told them the *Traveler* would have legitimate criticism henceforth and that shows would be rated as the critic felt they should be. Further, we would gladly accept news and feature stories about the plays and the actors in them, but we would not accept the kind of self-servicing rubbish that press agents usually supplied.

The managers' reaction to my proposals were unfavorable, of course. They said that since they were paying good money for advertising they did not relish reviews that might keep people away.

The issue was shortly to be tested. William Hodge was starring in *The Man from Home*, a splendid comedy by Booth Tarkington. Solita Solano, our critic and later the author of several novels, reviewed it glowingly. So far all was well. Then I was called to the office of the advertising manager, Dr. William R. Ellis. O'Brien was also present.

"We've arranged for a half-page ad from the Hodge show for next Sunday's *Herald*," O'Brien announced. Theatrical advertising sold at a high rate and a half-page was quite a plum. "What they want you to do," O'Brien continued, "is to have a daily cartoon by Hodge on your editorial page for the next two weeks entitled 'As William Hodge Sees It.'"

"Can Hodge draw?" I asked.

"No," said Dr. Ellis, "it would have to be done by someone else, but Hodge would sign it."

"I can't do it," I said. "That would be phoney." And I told of my hopes for legitimate stage stories. In this case it would be easy. In the cast was Ida Vernon, a distinguished actress who, in her youth, had played with Edwin Booth. I said we would be glad to interview her at length, have her give her recollections of Booth and tell the story of her many years on the stage. Then I agreed that Hodge could also be interviewed on the type of homespun, small-town Midwest American he was portraying in *The Man from Home*. Either or both of these would be far more valuable publicity for the play and would also have reader interest.

"That's not what they want," said Ellis. "We've got to give them what they want."

"What they want is no good, either for them or for the *Traveler*," I insisted.

"Of course," said Ellis sarcastically, addressing O'Brien. "We can break our necks to get advertising. We haven't had a half-page theater ad since God knows when. It's worth $320. And these young squirts in the news end want to throw all that out of the window. They have no right to undo all our hard work to promote their fancy ideas."

"Why not put my proposal to Mr. Hodge?" I suggested.

"Don't be obstinate," O'Brien said, and the meeting broke up.

That night I received a typewritten note from him saying, "You were not hired to let your ideas jeopardize the *Herald*'s revenues." That was too much. I wrote out a check to the *Herald* for $320 and sent it back to O'Brien along with his note. The check was not cashed, but apparently it was a matter of high-level discussion, for Mr. Higgins telephoned me the next day to say that while he disagreed with my position, the *Herald* would not accept the check. It was returned to me with "Payable only on April 1" written across it.

The next day, Friday, November 19, Dorothy and I were married at the Smiths' Norwood home. Earl Biggers was my best man and it was a happy occasion. The next morning all of us went to New Haven to see the Harvard-Yale game, the first event in the great new Yale bowl. Harvard christened it by winning 36-0. After the game Dorothy and I continued our honeymoon by driving to Stockbridge in the Berkshires. Our cup was running over. When the Sunday Boston *Herald* arrived, there was the half-page ad from *The Man from Home*. It had been secured without any of the free publicity requested or offered. I had won my point, and the attitude of the *Herald*'s business office changed. I would now have its support in the battle for legitimate criticism.

But the battle was not yet over. Three weeks later, Eugene Walter's *Just a Woman* opened at the Wilbur Theater and was unfavorably reviewed. The next day the advertising for all three Shubert theaters— the Majestic and the Shubert as well as the Wilbur—was withdrawn from the *Traveler* and no tickets were sent for next Monday's opening at the Shubert. We purchased them and reviewed the play anyway, but the boycott continued and would do so, we were told, as long as Miss Solano was the reviewer. In reply I asked advertising manager Ellis to tell the Shuberts that if they persisted, their ads would be thrown out of the *Herald*, too. O'Brien and Ellis were fearful that it would mean an additional loss of revenue, but I offered to bet them that the Shuberts would cave in. They could not, I felt sure, do without both papers. And so it proved. Honest dramatic criticism in the *Traveler* was off to a good start.

A similar fight against the Shuberts was being waged in other cities where they had physically excluded offending reviewers even when they bought their own tickets, among them such nationally known critics as Alexander Woollcott, Channing Pollock and Percy Hammond. The counter-offensive was headed by Samuel Hopkins Adams in the *New York Tribune*, who was also leading a one-man crusade against medical advertising of worthless and even harmful nostrums. Having established a kinship in the field of dramatic criticism, I urged Adams to come to Boston to open up on medical advertising and induced the Boston Chamber of Commerce to invite him to speak. He came and distributed a fair share of knocks and boosts. The *Herald* and *Traveler* carried less medical advertising than the *American, Post* and *Globe;* not that our management would have refused it, but the purveyors of this quackery considered them inferior to other dailies as sales media. Adams's visit was beneficial and influenced the gradual elimination of the most flagrant medical frauds from the Boston papers. One which ran in the *Post*, and had always amused me, was an ad extolling the virtues of "Old Doctor Jones, Specialist, All Diseases."

Because of the intense competition among the afternoon papers where headlines produced street sales, it was desirable to get a new and challenging "lead" wherever possible, and to change it from edition to edition. We depended on the Associated Press for national and international news, but all too often AP-wire stories merely rehashed news that had already appeared in the morning papers. I noticed that the headlines in the Scripps-Howard papers in other cities were based on United Press stories which often had more punch than the AP. I wanted very much to take on the UP which no Boston paper had, but I had a tough time selling it to publisher Higgins who saw no reason why he should add to his operating costs. Finally I persuaded him to let me take it on a trial basis and within days we beat the other papers on a steamboat disaster on the Great Lakes; the UP-wire story was not only minutes ahead of the AP but was also more accurate as to the number of casualties. It happened again with another story, probably because the UP was a young organization, staffed by youngsters full of pep and initiative, while the AP had slipped into a kind of easygoing torpor. When AP officials came to town at Higgins's request to "unsell" me, I was able to show them several examples favorable to the UP. We kept the UP.

From Atlanta, Georgia, came a story that would stay in both the morning and afternoon headlines for some time. A young man named Leo Frank, a graduate of Cornell and a newcomer to the state, had been tried, convicted and sentenced to death for the rape-murder of a fourteen-year-old girl named Mary Phagan who worked in the pencil factory of which he was manager. The girl's body was found in its basement. The trial had been conducted in an atmosphere of hysteria and hate fanned by the demagogic incitement of a widely read weekly edited by Thomas E. Watson, who had served years earlier as a Congressman elected on the Populist ticket. Antisemitism was a dominant element in his propaganda and he aroused such feelings in Atlanta against Jews that there was widespread fear of violent reprisals against them if Frank were not convicted and executed. Georgia militiamen had guarded the courtroom during the trial.

Throughout the nation many men, including members of the bench and bar, were convinced of Frank's innocence and said so. I shared that view. Pertinent were the doubts of Judge L. S. Roan, who had presided at Frank's trial and sentenced him, doubts which he expressed in a letter to Frank's attorneys, saying that he would ask the Georgia Board of Pardons to recommend commutation to life imprisonment so that if the jury had erred, the error could be rectified. The United States Supreme Court declined to reverse, but the dissenting opinions of Justices Charles Evans Hughes and Oliver Wendell Holmes questioned Frank's guilt and the unfairness of his trial. "Mob law does not become due process of law by securing the assent of a terrorized jury," wrote Justice Holmes.

The *Traveler* covered the Frank case and editorialized about it. We printed letters of protest against the verdict and urged the signing of petitions asking for commutation. The campaign for commutation culminated in a mass-meeting in Faneuil Hall, presided over by Samuel J. Elder, president of the Massachusetts Bar Association. Three thousand people crowded into the hall and hundreds more could not gain admittance. Among the dozen speakers were former Massachusetts Governor Eugene N. Foss. The meeting adopted without dissent a resolution asking Georgia's Governor John Marshall Slaton to commute Frank's sentence to life imprisonment and approved sending a delegation representing New England to present some 50,000 names petitioning for such action. Nominated and appointed as members of the delegation were former Governor Foss; John W. Coughlin, Democratic National Committeeman and former Mayor of Fall River; Alexander Brin, former *Herald-Traveler* newsboy and writer for the weekly *Jewish Advocate* of which he would later become editor; and myself. Although the pro-Frank movement was admittedly a *Traveler* crusade, all the other Boston papers covered it fully. The story had assumed an importance that no one could ignore.

We traveled to Atlanta, my first journey south of the Mason-Dixon line, visited Leo Frank in prison and spoke to him through the bars. He was clearly an intelligent, civilized young man, and we were convinced of his innocence even more than ever. Then we spoke to the three members of the Board of Pardons and presented our petition to Governor Slaton.

"Petitions do not necessarily carry weight with me," he told us. "If I find that Frank is guilty, he shall hang. No appeal or power on earth could stay that sentence. If there is a doubt, a possibility of error in his conviction, I shall exercise clemency and commute his sentence. If I believe that he has been unjustly convicted and that he is not the man, I shall give him back his liberty. Of that you may rest assured."

We were hopeful after seeing the Governor, but the anti-Frank sentiment in and around Atlanta was virulent. I had never seen such hard, cruel faces as those crowded before the Board of Pardons when it met. "If Frank doesn't hang there'll be more lynchings in Georgia than ever before," said President N. M. Sessions of the Sessions Loan Company in opening a mass meeting in the Marietta Court House while the hearings were underway in Atlanta. There were roars of approval from the hundreds gathered to protest against commutation. "Let him hang!" roared John Tucker Dorsey, a cousin of Glen Dorsey who had been the prosecutor, and the crowd roared again. "She was only a poor factory girl," shouted State Representative Fred Morris. "What chance would she have against Jew money?"

The feeling throughout Georgia was not wholly of that kind. Leaders of the Savannah, Macon, Columbus and Rome bars had that day voiced their doubt of Frank's guilt before the Board of Pardons to the jeers of most of those present. It took courage to lift one's voice against the mob, but finally Governor Slaton commuted Frank's sentence to life imprisonment.

Shortly thereafter while sleeping in his cell Frank was slashed in the throat by a convict. He recovered, but a few weeks later some twenty-five men entered the prison, overpowered the warden, carried Frank to a remote spot near Marietta, where Mary Phagan had lived, and lynched him. No adequate precautions to prevent the lynching had been taken. Photographs were made of Frank's hanging corpse and widely sold as picture postcards.

In commuting Frank's sentence Governor Slaton had signed his political death warrant and he resigned soon after. Had he set Frank free, it might have proved a physical death sentence as well.

There was no question in my mind that Thomas E. Watson's weekly fulminations after Frank's commutation had incited the lynching. He attacked the Governor with equal vehemence and ironically, he was elected to the United States Senate in 1920 largely on the basis of his anti-Frank and anti-Slaton crusade.

In the following months, I found myself handling a number of other political "hot potatoes." With Europe at war and with the increasing likelihood of American involvement, "preparedness" became an issue. We had urged it editorially in the *Traveler* and I was asked to defend our position in a speech and in a debate under the auspices of the New England Fabian Society. Women's suffrage was another issue I was asked to promote, and did.

The *Traveler* was gaining circulation. In October 1914, when I became managing editor, it was 84,618. The following October it was 96,854, not a great gain, but a reversal of the previous downward trend. By the following March it had risen to 109,344. The management was delighted and inclined to be more tolerant of what O'Brien called my "quirks," among them my refusal to let the advertising department slip some favorable mention of products it advertised—or wanted to advertise—into our household column which I tried to make a trustworthy consumer's service. But this tolerance, I soon discovered, had its limits.

Following a court case which prosecuted the distribution of birth-control literature, I wrote an editorial criticizing the Massachusetts statute which made it a criminal offense for physicians to impart birth-control information to a patient even when a mother's life was imperiled. When O'Brien saw it in the *Traveler*'s first edition, he ordered the presses stopped and the editorial removed. He said he agreed with my view but that its publication could be disastrous from a circulation and advertising standpoint.

O'Brien had come to the *Herald* from the *Transcript*. In his younger days he had been personal secretary to President Grover Cleveland during his second term, largely because he knew shorthand, relatively rare in those days. With his White House background he was a valuable Washington correspondent on the *Transcript* for the next eleven years and then moved to Boston as its editorial-page editor. When his views were deemed to be sufficiently "sound," he was invited to become the editor of the *Herald*, reorganized after bankruptcy. A brilliant conversationalist and a witty after-dinner speaker, O'Brien brought to the paper a vast knowledge of national affairs, and his editorials were fine examples of literary craftsmanship, but his acquisitiveness on behalf of the paper often submerged what should have been his ethical standards. When the Barnstable fair held a Governor's Day in honor of Governor Samuel W. McCall, the *Herald*'s headline "McCall and Moxie at Barnstable Fair" was an undignified and cheap bit of commercialism; the *Herald* was trying to get Moxie advertising. O'Brien approved the headline over my and others' protests.

When the Sunday *Herald* started a rotogravure section—then a new and improved medium of display—a plan was conceived to print half-page pictures of the summer residences of prominent citizens, who liked the idea until they found they were expected to pay $400. When they declined, they were told that the goodwill of so influential a paper was something they could not wisely disregard. It was a form of blackmail. Nevertheless the practice continued with varying success until Mr. Morton Plant, a large *Herald* stockholder, was approached. When he declined and was given the spiel about the desirability of keeping the *Herald*'s goodwill, the solicitors were shown the door and O'Brien got a call on the telephone. The project was canceled abruptly.

My association with O'Brien and the *Traveler* was destined to come to an end in a way that I did not anticipate. I had long thought that America's treatment of its Negro citizens was the worst blot on a nation that in every other way I admired. Not only were they the victims of segregation and discrimination, but every year several score were lynched— murdered without trial—often for a trifling offense, or innocent of any offense; some were even tortured and burned alive. I was an early member of the National Association for the Advancement of Colored People and became acquainted with the members of the Boston branch, particularly a charming elderly couple, the Butler Wilsons. I also came to know another Negro leader, William Monroe Trotter, who was the moving spirit of the Boston branch of the National Independent Equal Rights

League, an organization like, but somewhat to the left of, the NAACP, but without its prestige and white support. It published a weekly called *The Guardian* of which Trotter was the editor.

I wrote editorials in the *Traveler* about the unfair treatment of Negroes and even tried to translate my words into deeds. A good friend, who was the top executive of a large new Boston department store, was an enlightened man, totally without racial prejudice. I asked him why his store, Filene's, would not employ Negro salesgirls. He said that he would like to do it, that it ought to be done, but that the employees had a social organization which gave dances and so on, and would object to having black girls participate. I pointed out that this prejudice would be obliged to yield if the store firmly adopted a policy of disregarding color, but the store's policy did not change. Several decades had to pass before that happened.

On my trip to Georgia in the effort to save Leo Frank, I had had a first-hand view of one very special aspect of racial discrimination in the South. A friend and Harvard classmate, Arthur Andrews, had given me a letter to an uncle and aunt of his, a Mr. and Mrs. Oscar Elsas. Mr. Elsas was president of the Fulton Bag and Cotton Mills. They were Jewish, concerned about the Frank case and in almost every way kind and civilized people. Yet one day when we boarded a bus, they explained and accepted the Southern view of the Negro's odor to justify the segregation which placed us in the forward section while blacks had to take the rear seats. We were sitting in about the fourth row and I noticed a large black woman in the very first row. When I pointed her out, Mr. Elsas jumped up in alarm and surprise. Then he smiled as he sat down. "You didn't see it, but she has an infant on her lap," he said. So I learned that if a Negro passenger was a nurse carrying a white baby, that deodorized and desegregated her.

The motion picture *The Birth of a Nation* had opened at Boston's Tremont Theater. It was a dramatization of the novel *The Klansman* by Thomas Dixon, a Baptist minister, author and playwright, and glorified the Ku Klux Klan in its heyday after the Civil War, portraying its members as gallant knights while Negroes were pictured as subhuman brutes. Produced by David Wark Griffith, it was technically a masterpiece, far ahead of the other films of that time, but was clearly an incitement to race hatred. I attacked the picture in the *Traveler*'s editorial columns, bringing upon the paper not only the threat of cancellation of advertising if I persisted, but actual cancellation because I did persist. This time I did not have the management's support. O'Brien told me to desist and I told him I would resign first. He wrote me a memorandum chiding me for the loss of revenue.

The *Traveler* was not alone in its opposition. Although there was none from the other Boston newspapers, several prominent citizens had raised their voices in protest and I felt justified in appealing to Mayor James Michael Curley, who held the office of municipal censor, either to stop the picture or at least delete some of the most violence-inciting passages. He told me that he was wholly in sympathy with my view but that he had no power under the existing law. He would need legislation giving him authority to act when a show incited to violence or was otherwise contrary to the public interest, and he urged me to try to get the necessary legislation.

I had such an amendment introduced in the Massachusetts legislature. The bill, enacted into law, created a Board of Three Censors that included, besides the Mayor, the Chief Judge of the Municipal Court and Boston's Chief of Police. I began to doubt that seeking such legislation was wise, although the provocation was great. Before long I came to the conclusion that all censorship is undesirable and has no place in a free society. I was convinced of it when Curley reneged on his promise, ignored the other two board members and began arbitrarily censoring other productions to satisfy his own predilections.

He stopped the performance of a play by Eugene Brieux, the noted French dramatist, *Damaged Goods*, renamed *Maternity* in the English translation, which had played at the Odeon in Paris and in several eastern cities without objection. He stopped David Belasco's *Marie Odile* which likewise had played in many other American cities, and closed down a play by Hall Caine because one of the characters, a Catholic bishop, while not portrayed objectionably, was not made out to be a saint. When the workers for equal suffrage staged a Greek pageant to raise funds, the chorus wore sandals on bare feet. Curley ordered them to wear shoes and stockings. He imposed the same restrictions on Anna Pavlova—probably the world's foremost ballerina—who generally performed barefoot, and on Isadora Duncan. "Bare feet are indecent," declared Mayor Curley.

Then a picture called *Where Are My Children?* came to Boston. Abortion was its theme, and it was presented in a way that was nothing short of indecent and vile. It was luridly advertised, with challenges to Curley to stop the film, yet he let it run. I was naturally suspicious of this sudden censorial insensitivity and voiced that suspicion in an editorial. Then I got a tip that Curley had gone to Washington to see Senator Boies Penrose, the Republican boss of Pennsylvania, to ask him to use his influence to have the State Board of Censors, which had barred the picture from the Keystone State as "too indecent to be shown," reverse their verdict.

I sent John W. English, our star reporter, to Washington. Senator Penrose confirmed the tip and added that Curley told him that he had an interest in the film. The *Traveler* printed the whole story with banner headlines. It was too important for the other Boston papers to ignore. They all "played" it with credit to the *Traveler*.

When he was interviewed, Curley admitted the truth of the story but said he had "done it for a friend." Taking this disculpation at its face value, which few did, it scarcely diminished the gravity of the Mayor's offense nor the devastating character of the revelation. It was recalled that years before, when he had been sent to jail for impersonating someone else in taking a Civil Service examination, he had also "done it for a friend." Apparently he thought better of his confession; the next day he brought a civil suit for $25,000 against the *Traveler* and one for criminal libel against me as managing editor and against O'Brien. He retained Daniel Coakley, a shrewd Boston lawyer, as his attorney.

The *Herald*'s attorney was not alarmed. "Cuttlefish tactics," he said. "He's caught with the goods. Nothing to be worried about." Even the cautious O'Brien expressed his delight. "That finishes Curley," he said gleefully. But he was not gleeful for long.

To understand what was about to happen requires a retrospective glance at the *Herald*'s history. It had been a great newspaper but had declined in quality and appeal, and had gone into bankruptcy. Two principal supporters were found to save it; one was the United Shoe Machinery Company, headed by Sidney Winslow, and the other was Morton Plant, a wealthy steamship operator. Their investments netted each a forty-four percent stock ownership. The United Shoe Machinery Company was facing antitrust prosecution from the federal government, was active in politics and wanted to use the paper to serve its own ends. Morton Plant, on the other hand, simply hoped to profit from his investment. Two lesser subscribers, one aligned with United Shoe and the other with Plant, each held an additional four percent. The remaining four percent—which, because of the equal division of stock, would control the company— came into the hands of Winthrop Murray Crane, head of the paper firm of Eaton, Crane and Pike, former Governor of Massachusetts, United States Senator and at that time also Chairman of the Republican National Committee. In the reorganization O'Brien represented the Morton Plant interests. James H. Higgins represented those of the United Shoe Machinery Company.

After O'Brien expressed his satisfaction over Curley's forthcoming political demise, he said, "I think I'll go down and twit Louis Coolidge." Coolidge was the treasurer of United Shoe which was close to Curley politically. But O'Brien returned from this visit with a worried look. Coolidge had said to him, "This *Traveler* story will not be pleasing to a certain gentleman in the western part of the state." The gentleman in question was Winthrop Murray Crane, whose residence was in Dalton in western Massachusetts.

O'Brien decided to go to Dalton and see Crane. Crane was evasive at first, but when O'Brien said, "Mr. Crane, I came up here solely to get your views on the Curley matter," Crane closed his eyes, paused for some moments and then said slowly, "I think, if I were you, I would do what I thought was right."

That answer did not satisfy O'Brien. He was still worried and later he asked me, "Do you know who William Morgan Butler is?"

I had heard the name but had little other information.

"William Morgan Butler," continued O'Brien, "is a man of importance. He is a lawyer, he is the president of the Boston and Worcester Railway, he is the owner of textile mills in Fall River and New Bedford, and," lowering his voice, "he is Mr. Dalton's representative in Boston."

O'Brien seldom mentioned Crane by name but referred to him as "Mr. Dalton" or as "the gentleman in the western part of the state."

"Mr. Butler," said O'Brien, "is disturbed about the Curley story and thinks we should not go on with it."

"We're not going on with it," I said. "We've published the story and Curley has admitted its truth. He is the one who is going on with it. Mr. Butler ought to speak to Curley, not to us."

"I agree," said O'Brien, "but he thinks we ought to publish a retraction."

"A retraction!" I almost yelled. "What the devil is there to retract?"

"That's what I told him," said O'Brien. "But, Gruening, I think this is the real message from Crane. You know he never acts directly."

Then, struck by a new idea, he said, "You go down and see Butler and explain our point of view to him."

I agreed reluctantly, but when O'Brien got Butler on the phone, it was clear that he was very much displeased that I had been allowed to learn of his interest in the matter. O'Brien had some difficulty in persuading him to see me, but finally it was arranged and I went to his office bearing a letter of identification which Butler had insisted O'Brien give me.

I had to get by several secretaries before I was ushered into what appeared to be a Board of Directors' room. At the head of the long table sat a small man with graying hair and a drooping gray mustache.

I was feeling rather jaunty, confident that I would have no difficulty in convincing Mr. Butler of the justice of the *Traveler*'s position. But Butler eyed me coldly. "Sit down," he said crisply. I sat down and waited.

After a pause Butler began shaking his head slowly from side to side. "Well, this is a nasty mess you're in. You've printed this story. You've offended the Mayor, who considers the story very damaging, which it is. He has engaged the ablest and undoubtedly the crookedest lawyer in Boston, and they've gone together to get the support of the crookedest district attorney in the United States. They won't have the slightest trouble getting a grand jury to indict you and a petit jury to convict you. And that," he said with sudden grimness, pointing his finger at me, "means jail."

I had a feeling that Butler was putting on an act, as indeed he was. "With all respect to you, Mr. Butler," I said, "you're a lawyer and an older and wiser man than I am, but that just isn't going to happen. The *Traveler* printed only facts, the truth of which Curley has admitted."

Mr. Butler made a gesture of brushing aside my contention. "But you certainly don't want to be dragged through all the mess and troubles of a suit and trial," he said. "Why, these fellows wouldn't hesitate to frame up a woman story on you."

"That wouldn't worry me in the slightest," I said. "My life is an open book. I am happily married. Every night after I finish at the office I go home."

Mr. Butler did not allow me to develop further the impregnability of my private life. "Avoiding trouble is always good policy," he said, then paused and leaned forward to convey a new thought. "It can be done very easily by printing a small retraction, saying simply that upon mature reflection the paper realizes that it has been hasty and . . ."

"But that wouldn't be true," I interrupted.

"And in justice to all concerned," Butler continued unperturbed, "it desires to retract its statement and apologize for any harm done."

"Don't you think, Mr. Butler," I said when he had finished and was apparently waiting to note the effect of his proposal, "that a newspaper owes some duty to the public?"

"An uncontrolled newspaper is—what shall I say—" he stroked his chin searching for a definition, "a Utopian myth. And this is a practical world, young man. What difference do a few printed words make?"

I told him that "a few printed words" made a big difference to me, that I would rather go to jail than knowingly print a palpable and cowardly falsehood.

"Perhaps," Mr. Butler said sarcastically, "you will not be given the opportunity of going to jail." He rose and the interview was ended.

I reported the exchange to O'Brien. He was obviously nervous but agreed that printing a retraction was out of the question.

"What," I asked him, "can be the connection between a man like Winthrop Murray Crane and a crooked municipal politician like Curley?"

"I'd like to know myself," O'Brien answered with evident sincerity. "I've wondered about that. It may be Otis elevators. You know Crane controls Otis, and Curley is having Otis elevators installed in various municipal buildings. Or it may be something else. There may be a working arrangement between them to have Curley line up some Democratic votes in the city on behalf of certain matters that Mr. Crane is interested in."

Our discussion ended with O'Brien still supporting my side of the dispute, but several hours later he returned to my office. "It's all settled," he said briskly. "I have just come from Mr. Butler's office and have conferred with Mr. Coakley. Here is the retraction we will print in the *Traveler* on Monday."

I was stunned by his sudden about-face. I wondered what had made him change his mind. Had Butler threatened him, too? I never found out, but I had no intention of changing mine.

"What do you mean by *we?*" I asked. "I'll have nothing to do with it. I won't be here."

Only once in the next few days did O'Brien waver. I urged him to check again with Crane to make sure Butler was not acting on his own behalf, and finally, he decided to do so. He reached Crane by phone at the Hotel Biltmore in New York. "Mr. Crane, I hate to bother you again on the Curley matter," he said. "I just want to make sure that Mr. Butler represents your wishes in the matter." Crane's reply was "Mr. Butler is my personal representative in Boston."

"Thank you, that's all I wanted to know," said O'Brien, and thus the matter was settled.

Both O'Brien and Higgins asked me to reconsider my resignation.

"You'd be very foolish to leave," said O'Brien. "Where can you get as good a job as this?" My salary had been raised to $100 a week when the *Traveler*'s circulation passed the 100,000 mark.

"I thought it was a good job," I said, "but if this retraction goes through, I'll find that I've been working in a cesspool and I want to get out and get disinfected."

The retraction was set in type and Monday morning I went to the composing room and took my name off the masthead. Then I went to the city room, and told the staff what had happened. They cheered me and urged me to reconsider, but I could not. My resignation caused many repercussions in Boston and in the newspaper world and I received a flood of congratulatory condolences. My friend Earl Biggers wrote:

> When Hell finally gets O'Brien he will be compelled to walk for all eternity with a "for sale" sign hung around his neck. And no one will make him an offer; that would be Hell for him.

Margaret Maginnis, now eighty-nine years old, had been failing in the past few months. Before my successor as managing editor, Walter Emerson, could find out what it was all about, she was fired. When she died two months later, she got a two-column cut on the front page and a fine editorial praising her long and devoted service.

5

THE BOSTON
JOURNAL

*Freedom of the press from governmental
interference is guaranteed by the Bill of
Rights. Yet the press is not free if it accepts
dictation from other sources and submits to
the pressures of private interests.*
—GILSON GARDNER

As soon as it became known that I had left the *Traveler*, I received two
newspaper offers, and one to become the executive secretary of the
NAACP in New York. The latter invitation came from Mary White
Ovington, one of its founders, then acting chairman. My sister Martha,
who was deeply interested in the Negro cause, urged me to accept, but
naturally I preferred to stay in journalism which I not only enjoyed, but
in which I felt I could be more helpful to this cause and perhaps others.
One newspaper offer came from the *American* to be its city editor, the
other was from the Boston *Journal.*

The *Journal* had a long history under various managements. Under its
previous owner, Frank A. Munsey, the paper had declined in circulation
and revenue and he was prepared to shut it down. But in 1913 a group of
young Harvard graduates, "Bull Moosers" dedicated to the promotion of
the Progressive Party, had acquired it at a nominal cost though with the
obligation to pay its debts. They were Matthew Hale, Walton Atwater
Green, Charles Eliot Ware and Alexander Kendall. Green became the editor and publisher, Ware the president and general manager, and Alexander Kendall the treasurer. They were idealists and had established—

from my standpoint—the *Journal*'s credentials as an honest and independent daily. Charles Ware telephoned me that the *Journal*'s managing editor, Edgar Davenport Shaw, was leaving to take a position with the *Washington Times* and that I could succeed him, functioning in the meantime as city editor. He explained, however, that the *Journal*'s future was anything but bright; it was incurring a substantial deficit each week and he was doubtful whether he could continue to raise the funds to keep going.

I accepted the offer and quickly discovered he had spoken the truth; there was a question each Thursday whether the Saturday payroll would be forthcoming. One week, having no other prospect, Ware played the stock market and was rewarded with a lucky rise that enabled him to meet the weekend payroll. The established position of the other Boston newspapers as advertising media rendered the *Journal*'s outlook gloomy. Against such heavy competition it got only the crumbs. But it was a pleasure to work again briefly under Edgar Shaw. I had done so three years earlier when he was managing editor of the *Traveler* and I was a reporter. He was one of the most considerate bosses I had ever encountered.

We had a reasonably good collection of features. Anthony Arnoux wrote a daily interpretation of the war news, and in another column answered questions about the war. On the sports pages we carried Rube Goldberg's inimitable cartoons, with Franklin Collier, a local cartoonist, for the events at home. Bob Dunbar's sporting chat, a syndicated column, and a group of volunteer reporters marshaled by the enthusiasm of Francis Eaton, the sports editor, enabled us to proclaim immodestly "the best sports pages in New England." Our other columnists, Franklin P. Adams whose "Conning Tower" was syndicated by the New York *Tribune*, and John D. Barry, whose daily "Ways of the World" gently philosophized on almost any subject, had a devoted following. Barry had one idiosyncrasy. He maintained that writing should closely resemble—indeed scarcely differ from—spoken words and his style consisted of relatively short and uncomplicated sentences. I argued that speech was modified and amplified by inflection, emphasis, expression, pauses, gestures, which were unavailable to the writer, and that written language required a different technique. We never fully agreed.

Solita Solano had come over from the *Traveler* and was writing excellent dramatic reviews. On the feature page we had Dr. W. A. Evans's "How to Keep Well," Zoe Beckley's "Diary of a War Wife," "My Funniest Story" collected from *Journal* readers, and the required household, dressmaking, recipe, and social columns. Our financial editor, Donald R. Hanson, did himself proud by exposing Emerson Motors, whose stock-promotion campaign, carried in large advertisements in other Boston papers but refused by the *Journal* on Hanson's advice, had defrauded large numbers of New England buyers. When the bubble burst and the promoters were arrested, the *Journal* was able to claim the lion's share of the credit.

But the feature that attracted the most attention was the *Journal* "Mail Bag." Other Boston papers were reluctant to print letters differing sharply from their editorial policy or espousing generally unaccepted views. The *Journal* threw its columns wide open, cheerfully printing letters denouncing our editorials, although occasionally replying. We closed the doors to no letters except those clearly libelous.

Because of the financial straits the *Journal* confronted, I took it upon myself to write editorials. Walton Green had gone to the Plattsburg Officers Training Camp and thence overseas, and I was left in full charge. The year was 1917. The war in Europe was going badly for the Allies. The toll of their shipping taken by Germany's U-boat campaign was mounting disastrously. United States involvement on a major scale was becoming more certain. We supported America's increasing participation in the war effort fervently, and when war was declared, we accepted unquestioningly Woodrow Wilson's dictum that "the world must be made safe for democracy." But we were outspoken against the violations of democratic practices at home and opposed Wilson's efforts to impose censorship on the press and the activities of his Postmaster General Omar Burleson in suppressing newspapers and magazines. We also supported the draft but criticized its administration and the defects in its application. We objected to the drafting of married men with children, to the inclusion of aliens—who were exempt from the draft—in the count on which the quotas from each district were based, and to the requirement that the registrants' race and color be stated in the draft forms. We enlisted the support of the Massachusetts Congressional delegation against drafting married men and on August 18 announced the decision in Washington that married men would not be drafted until all single registrants had been taken. The *Journal* had won that part of its battle, but "Jim Crow" registration continued.

There were other battles. We backed Herbert Hoover's efforts to prevent profiteering in food and fuel and received a letter of appreciation from him for our support. We applauded the appointment of Dr. H. A. Garfield, president of Williams College, as "fuel dictator," and James J. Storrow as his representative for Massachusetts. Then in an editorial entitled "The Indictment is Read: Now We Want Action," we declared that coal consumers were sick and tired of being told by the Federal Trade Commission that they had been bilked, and that while not all coal dealers were guilty of profiteering, we wanted the names of those who were and would publish them. That threat proved effective and Boston retail coal prices were uniformly made to conform to prices established by Garfield.

Adequate taxation of war profits was another *Journal* crusade. Munitions makers' profits had soared in the last few years but the House had enacted a revenue bill providing only moderate tax increases. The bill was fought in the Senate with Massachusetts Senator Henry Cabot Lodge leading the opposition; the *Journal* printed the names of the senators supporting and opposing the higher taxes. The *Journal* also protested against violent and arbitrary actions against peaceful dissenters and against the proscription of all things German. The war had bred fanatical patriotism in some quarters. Sauerkraut had become "liberty cabbage," and on July 1, in Boston, a Socialist parade was broken up by men in the uniforms of the Army, Navy and National Guard. The paraders were beaten up, the party's headquarters wrecked, and its literature burned. Two days later, a mob of whites in East Saint Louis set fire to the houses in a Negro neighborhood and shot the residents as they fled from their burning homes; some 250 were reported killed while police and soldiers let the rioters run loose. The *Journal*'s Fourth of July editorial suggested that the Germans were not the only threat to the goals and ideals of democracy.

The aphorism that in wartime "truth is the first casualty" was illustrated by widely current reports that the Germans in Belgium had cut off the hands of Belgian children. When the story was again propagated by a contributor to the *Journal*'s "Mail Bag," I felt compelled to reply:

> There are not and never have been Belgian children maimed by the Germans. The best proof thereof lies in the negative evidence that there never have been any photographs of such children. Had any mutilated children existed their pictures would have been Exhibit A in the case against Germany. . . . No intelligent people credit those stories any more. Even the official British propaganda has given up trying to make use of them, relying on the horrors which can be substantiated.

The possible origin of this macabre allegation may have been from quite another source. When the Congo was a Belgian colony under King Leopold I, the hands and feet of Congolese children were cut off as penalties for not bringing in a sufficient supply of rubber. This horror was exposed and documented with photographs by Sir Arthur Conan Doyle in his book *The Crime of the Congo*. I myself saw the book in the library of the Harvard Club of New York, but it mysteriously disappeared from the shelves during the war.

While war abroad and at home captured most of the headlines and

filled most of the news columns, occasionally a local story proved of surpassing interest. One of these was the charge against a Boston broker,
Frederick Lincoln Small, of murdering his wife. I happened to know
Small. He was a member, as I was, of the Boston Chess Club, which had
barnlike quarters on the second floor of a building on Tremont Street.
He was an unpleasant fellow and unpopular among the other members,
but I recall no effort to expel him. Small had a cottage on Lake Ossipee,
New Hampshire, and one morning he called for a horse and buggy to
drive him to the railroad station where he would take the train to Boston.
When the driver appeared, he was surprised to find Small in hat and
overcoat waiting on the porch. There was no sign of Mrs. Small, but he
called through the closed door, "Goodbye, darling."

In Boston that night he learned that his cottage had been totally consumed by fire. As the news of the fire was reported by wire, members of
the press went to interview him. The *Journal*'s reporter, Gertrude Steven-
sen, was intrigued by Small's doleful comment "I've lost my pet." She
wondered how he knew that his wife had perished in the flames. One unforeseen circumstance proved Small's undoing. When the cottage's floor
was destroyed by flames, the body of Mrs. Small fell into the cellar beneath it and her head and shoulders landed in a pool of water which preserved them from incineration. A rope was tightly wound around her
throat.

Small was arrested and evidence was produced to show the fire had
been set deliberately. Of course Small protested his innocence and suggested that some passing tramp or enemy in Ossipee could have murdered
his wife and set the fire. His motive was a $20,000 insurance policy on his
wife's life. He was found guilty, and hanged.

The news and editorial policies on the *Journal* were as different from
the *Traveler*'s as night from day. There were no "sacred cows" and we
did not cater to even the few advertisers we were able to attract. One, the
president of a chain grocery store, asked that we kill the story of a
holdup in one of his stores. I refused and when I met him later he said, "I
want to congratulate you. You are the only Boston newspaper editor
with any guts." When the graduating class of the Quincy High School
suffered ptomaine poisoning at a school banquet, we were again asked,
by the restaurant chain that had supplied the food, to kill the story. We
were told that all the other papers had agreed to do so.

"Have you," I asked the manager, "ever said you can't believe what
you read in the newspapers, or heard someone else say it?"

He admitted he had.

"We're trying to make the *Journal* a paper of which no one can say
that." We were the only Boston paper to print the story.

We also made a conscientious effort to publish all the news. When Representative William E. Mason of Illinois made a speech in the House attacking the policy of sending draftees and National Guardsmen abroad and announced that he was sponsoring a constitutional amendment to forbid it, a correspondent to our "Mail Bag" sent us a summary of the speech and charged that the failure of Boston papers, including the *Journal,* to print it was evidence that the press was subsidized, prostituted and otherwise controlled by sinister forces. We agreed, but the sinister force in this case was the Associated Press which was supposed to transmit all the news of national interest from the Capitol. I wrote to Melville E. Stone, the general manager of the AP, and asked why it had not carried Mason's speech. He replied that he did not consider it news, and that while the International News Service had carried it, he did not believe the AP should lend itself to attacks of the kind that Congressman Mason had delivered. We expressed our dissent from Stone's judgment and printed our contributor's extract from Mason's speech.

The battle for equal suffrage was coming to a head and the *Journal* supported it enthusiastically. The struggle was thrust upon the public's consciousness once again by a determined group of women who picketed the White House to remind President Wilson of his campaign pledge and to recommend to Congress the so-called Susan B. Anthony Amendment which would extend the vote to women. The members of the National Woman's Party who took part in the demonstrations were shamefully treated by the Washington authorities. They were roughed up by government employees while the police stood aside; they were arrested and sentenced to jail for "disturbing the peace" or "obstructing traffic." The *Journal* expressed its outrage and Alice Paul, the chairman of the National Woman's Party, wrote to thank us for our support. Three years later the Nineteenth Amendment would be passed into law, but fifty years later, the remarkable Alice Paul would still be battling in Washington for equal rights and fuller participation for women in our society.

Unlike my experience on the *Traveler,* I was free to editorialize about birth control. A young man, Van Kleeck Allison, had been given a heavy sentence for distributing birth-control literature. We pointed out that the severity of the sentence was not surprising, the prosecution having been personally handled by District Attorney Joseph A. Pelletier—a rare event. We recommended appeal to a higher court and cited the precedent recently established by federal authorities in dropping a similar case against Margaret Sanger. The whole subject was taboo—not surprisingly at that time and place—and there was an organized effort to prevent its discussion. A factual article on the birth-control movement, its status in other countries where contraception was permitted, and a discussion of the laws in our country forbidding it, which we published on the *Journal*'s woman's page, led to cancellation of several advertisements.

And then there was the question of academic freedom. In New York, two professors had been expelled by Columbia University President Nicholas Murray Butler. Their offenses? James McKeen Cattell, a professor of psychology for over a quarter of a century, had written to certain members of Congress urging them to support a measure against sending conscipts to fight in Europe against their will. Professor Henry Wadsworth Longfellow Dana was a member of the People's Council, a group often critical of President Wilson's policies. A third professor, Charles A. Beard, the distinguished historian, had resigned from the Columbia faculty in protest. I wrote an editorial in the *Journal* criticizing this flagrant violation of academic freedom, and then wrote to Harvard's president, A. Lawrence Lowell, suggesting that he invite these three scholars to join the Harvard faculty. I thought surely they would receive better treatment there. I was wrong. Neatly sidestepping the real issue, President Lowell wrote back labeling Cattell a "mischief-maker" and chastising Dana because of "a tendency in his brothers to love eccentricity." Then, after extolling academic freedom at Harvard, he dismissed my suggestion by concluding ". . . whatever their qualifications, under present conditions, and facing—as this University will—an enormous deficit, we could not think of appointing additional professors."

The blow that Charles Eliot Ware had feared, had warned me of when he asked me to come to the *Journal*, and had worked indefatigably to avert, was imminent. Our circulation had soared, but the deficits had continued. On October 6, the announcement that would sadden a body of loyal and devoted readers appeared at the top of our front page. No one was sadder than I, for the *Journal* had been acquired by my old employer, the *Herald*. The announcement was drafted by Ware who, as part of the arrangement with the *Herald*, was obliged to paint an optimistic but scarcely realistic picture of a Boston *Journal* living on after its forced extinction.

We went down with colors flying. Our leading editorial on that last day, "A Blot On America's Escutcheon," condemned Postmaster General Burleson's suppression of the *Milwaukee Leader* not for particular articles, editorials or cartoons but because of its general tendency. This and similar suspensions, including that of *The Masses*, a brilliant publication under the editorship of Max Eastman, tainted the Wilson administration's conduct of the war. Under Burleson's ruling, a single editorial, article or cartoon which his censorship found objectionable, deprived the publication of subsequent use of the mails.

I also wrote the *Journal*'s "obituary," expressing hope for its future which, being familiar with the *Herald*, I knew was unwarranted. But the sale—sought by the *Herald* because it wanted to acquire the *Journal's* circulation—helped Ware and others out of their financial hole and recognition of their problems, as well as good sportsmanship, required me to do no less.

My friend Stuart Chase wrote:

> So liberty gets another wallop in these glorious days of democracy—but, then, she is used to 'em! It must have been a discouraging experience for you—for once in my life I longed to be a capitalist, so that I might plunk down a cool, staggering check on your desk and bid the Powers of Newspaper Darkness Come On!

> For you did a wonderful job, old man. You gave us a taste of what a real newspaper ought to be and these thousands of us who have drunk of that cup will neither forget it nor be permanently satisfied until we have more of it. Your day is dawning, but it will probably be some years before the sun will shine as brightly as it ought. But I think you have driven a wedge into journalism that will widen and widen . . .

My years in Boston were coming to an end, although I did not know it then. They had been happy years. Dorothy and I lived in Cambridge and often spent weekends with my family in Rockport. Our first child, Ernest Junior, was born on October 20, 1915, and our second son, Huntington Sanders, on September 11, 1916. I was a member of the Union Boat Club, where I was more interested in squash and handball than in rowing or sculling, and shortly after the *Traveler* blow-up, I had been invited to join the Saint Botolph Club whose members included a distinguished list of writers, artists, musicians, publishers, professors and other professional men. But with the demise of the *Journal* I was out of a job, so when Frank Munsey telephoned and said, "If you're not doing anything else, I'd like to have you come to New York and tell me what's wrong with the *Sun*," I thought to myself: Why not? Maybe I can do some good.

In buying, selling and amalgamating newspapers, Munsey had acquired the New York *Sun*, the daily made famous under the editorship of Charles A. Dana. I had heard tales of Munsey's eccentricities when he owned the *Journal*. One night he announced that he would write an editorial for the next morning's paper. "Very good," said the editor, "the deadline is midnight; that's when our first edition goes to press." As midnight neared, the editor entered Munsey's office to remind him of the approaching deadline. "You have fifteen minutes, Mr. Munsey." He was back ten minutes later. "We've really got to have your copy in the next five minutes." Munsey waved him aside. At midnight the editor was back. "If you want to make the first edition, we have to have your copy now."

"Cancel the first edition," ordered Munsey.

"You can't do that," said the editor in surprise and alarm.

"You heard me," said Munsey.

Munsey was known for his incredible and costly abuses of power, and I went to New York to see him with some apprehension.

"I have given orders that you are to have free access to the news and composing rooms," he told me. "Browse around. Take your time and let me know what's wrong with the *Sun*." Those were his only instructions.

I found the *Sun* to be a well-run newspaper under the experienced hand of Keats Speed, the managing editor. But one night when I was sitting beside him at his desk, after the first edition had gone to press, his phone rang. It was Munsey calling.

"Who wrote that goddam story on page eight, column six?" he bellowed. Before Speed could answer, Munsey said, "I didn't like it. Kill it."

Speed did not try to find out what Munsey disliked about the story. He said "OK" and ordered the presses stopped, the plates containing the story removed, and another plate cut with a new story put in its place. The press run was suspended meantime.

"Does Munsey do that often?" I asked.

"Yes, and that's not the worst of it. The other night he walked in here and took a look at the boys working around the copy desk. One of them was decidedly overweight. 'Fire him,' said Munsey, 'he's too fat.' He was a good man, too," Speed added.

It did not take me long to conclude that the only thing wrong with the *Sun* was its owner; without his capricious and arbitrary interference, it would have been a smooth-running, professional operation. I could do nothing other than tell Mr. Munsey so. "If you could keep your hands off entirely, you'd have a fine shop," I said.

Naturally our arrangement was ended. It had lasted three weeks, and I returned to Boston to look for another job.

While I was on the *Journal*, I had been requested to make a report to the Federal Trade Commission on the supply and consumption of newsprint, its concern being the utilization for other purposes of raw materials which were in short supply. The request came from William Julius Harris, acting chairman, later United States Senator from Georgia. I had also had some correspondence on the subject with Joseph E. Davies, another member of the commission. Now I received a letter from Chairman Harris telling me that the War Trade Board was about to establish a Bureau of Imports, and asking whether I would like to help organize it. I wrote him that my ignorance of imports was virtually total, but he urged me, nonetheless, to come to Washington.

I accepted his offer and took on my first government assignment. The bureau's job was to stop imports from enemy countries. I learned then, as thereafter, that it does not take long to learn the routine of any new job if you are interested.

Dorothy, the children and I moved to Washington and rented a house in adjacent Chevy Chase, sharing it with some friends, David Bradlee Childs and his wife, Emily. David had been Harvard '10 and we had gotten to know each other on the chess team. As my salary on the War Trade Board was $2,400 a year, we decided to take in boarders, and found two who were delighted to be part of our menage, a delight we shared. One was John D. Barry whose daily column for the *San Francisco Bulletin* we had carried in the Boston *Journal*. He introduced us to a young man named Irving Caesar whom he had come to know when both were passengers on Henry Ford's peace ship, which Ford had chartered and taken to Europe in 1915 in an effort to persuade the belligerents to stop the war. Caesar played the piano incessantly, improvising tunes and songs. He would later become famous as the composer of "Tea for Two." Both he and Barry had excellent voices and entertained us after dinner with old English ballads and popular songs. Next door to us were Robert and Gertrude Benchley with their three-year-old son Nathaniel. Bob was doing publicity for the Aircraft Board. The Gruenings, Benchleys and Childs planted a kitchen garden together and Bob's humor enlivened all our domestic activities—including such chores as tending the furnace—no mean task in the cold winter of 1918. He later used some of our experiences together as material for his amusing essays and skits.

During these months I commuted to New York each weekend to see my mother who was seriously ill. And I had decided to go into the army as soon as the Bureau of Imports was well organized. I was offered a commission in the Sanitary Corps for which my medical training was a good preparation, but I preferred combat and made application for a newly organized Field Artillery Officers Training Camp located near Louisville, Kentucky.

My plans were interrupted, however, by a call from Garet Garrett, the executive editor of the *New York Tribune* who said he was on his way to Washington. He came and offered me the managing editorship of the *Tribune*. I told him I was planning to go into military service, but in any case I did not like the *Tribune*'s undisguised hostility toward President Wilson. Garrett urged me to keep my mind open while he discussed the matter with the *Tribune*'s management. A week later I was visited by G.

Vernor Rogers, business manager and vice-president of the *Tribune* and a brother of Helen Rogers Reid, wife of Ogden Mills Reid, the *Tribune*'s owner. He told me that my criticism of the *Tribune* policies had been discussed with the Reids and they particularly wanted me *because* of my views. He also argued persuasively that in directing a great newspaper I could do far more for the war effort than by enlisting in the Field Artillery. It was a tempting offer—my first opportunity to run a daily in the nation's biggest city. I accepted, but stipulated that our contract be for one year only—to see how we got along.

So Dorothy and I moved once again. My mother and two of my sisters had occupied an apartment at the corner of Riverside Drive and 103rd Street. Sadly, my mother died just a few weeks before our return, but my sisters invited us to occupy the apartment and welcomed us back to New York.

6

NEW YORK TRIBUNE

*In wartime failure to lie is negligence, the
doubting of a lie is a misdemeanor, the
declaration of the truth, a crime.*
—ARTHUR PONSONBY, M.P.

Garet Garrett was in charge at the *Tribune*, with control of the editorial
page and—implicitly—of news management. Ogden Reid, who had
the title of Editor and Publisher on the *Tribune*'s masthead, rarely appeared, and during my months there he never wrote an editorial. Mrs.
Reid, who seemed to be the brains of the family, was seen more frequently and was liked by everyone. Garrett, despite his birth and lifetime
residence in the United States, spoke with something resembling a British
accent and was a practised and persuasive editorial writer. Heywood
Broun, who was running the dramatic department and whom I had
known well since our Harvard days, referred to him as a "Svengali." Garrett had pretty well inculcated the idea in the staff that the conduct of the
war was being bungled by President Wilson, and that somehow it was
the *Tribune*'s function to correct this. I had presumed that the *Tribune*'s
dislike of the President would not be unfairly reflected in the news and
editorial columns, but Garrett's antipathy was pervasive, occasionally
over my objections. The President was generally referred to by Garrett
and others as "that son of a bitch Wilson," and his secretary of War,
Newton D. Baker, as "that bastard Baker." Garrett told me he was suspicious of Baker because—Garrett alleged—he had been a pacifist before the war, and his middle name, Diehl, was German. However, the
Tribune's chief crusade, which had begun before my arrival, was against
William Randolph Hearst, a campaign which appeared in full pages every

Sunday, in items of varying size during the week and was captioned: COILED IN THE FLAG — HEAR—S—S—S—T. The letters of the caption were entwined by a snake, with its head above the letter H and the tail extended above the letter T.

Early in June 1918 the *Tribune* reported the action of the Department of Justice in depriving of his citizenship a naturalized citizen who had shown support for Germany's cause. It was an unprecedented step, but two days later Neal Jones, the city editor, came to me with a story listing a number of other naturalized citizens against whom similar action was shortly expected. The list included Morris Hillquit and Abraham Cahan, neither of whom I had ever met though I knew both by reputation. Hillquit, who was born in Riga and had emigrated to America with his parents in 1886 at the age of seventeen, had been the Socialist Party's candidate for mayor of New York in 1917. Cahan, born in Vilna, Russia, had come to America in 1882 at the age of twenty-two. He was the editor and publisher of the Jewish daily *Forward*, the author of short stories in Yiddish and English and had written a best-selling novel *The Rise of Abraham Levitsky*. Both were respected men, although their socialist views were in general disfavor.

"Has the Department of Justice announced definitely that it is going to act?" I asked Jones.

"No, but I am sure it will" was his answer.

"When it does take such action, we'll print the story," I said. "Can't you see that otherwise it would be libelous as well as unfair?"

Jones disagreed. "Let's get the sons of bitches," he said.

I stopped the story and Jones complained to Garrett.

"How come you killed Jones's story?" he asked me.

I gave him my reasons.

"Well, it's a pretty safe conjecture they'll act," he answered, "and the story might give them a little encouragement." But from then on, I think there was no doubt that Garrett suspected my "loyalty," too. Of course no such action by the Department of Justice followed.

Another man Garrett and Jones wanted to "get" was Hermann Hagedorn. No one could have been more enthusiastically loyal to America's cause than he, although his German-born parents were not. He was an idolator of Theodore Roosevelt. Indeed, along with Julian Street, Charles Hanson Towne and Porter E. Browne, he had founded the "Vigilantes," a writers' organization to present America's case in the war. Again, I vetoed the proposed story. Hagedorn, years later in an inscription to me in his book, *The Hyphenated Family*, wrote "in grateful remembrance of his defense of me on a certain day in June 1918, when I desperately needed defending."

The *Tribune* featured a new twelve-page Sunday picture section called the "Graphic," and I asked Bob Benchley, who had previously worked for the paper, to be its editor. His job in Washington for the Aircraft Board had petered out since military aircraft production—or rather, the lack of it—had become a scandal. So Bob came back to the *Tribune* and began to edit the "Graphic" section with great success, even eliciting a word of praise from *Tribune* vice president G. Vernor Rogers. Then Sunday, June 7, he scheduled a half-page picture of a contingent of Negroes of Colonel Hayward's 169th Infantry which had distinguished itself in recent engagements in France, and two of whom—their pictures were shown separately—had been decorated with the *Croix de Guerre* for bravery in action. As the page was being made up, Bob received a photograph of the lynching of a Negro man in Georgia being witnessed by a large crowd. Bob thought that running these pictures together might prove useful as a plea for racial tolerance and I agreed. What followed is described in Nathaniel Benchley's biography of his father: *

The page went to press . . . and the first copy hadn't been upstairs more than three minutes when there was a dropping of pencils, a ringing of bells, and then a great clanking sigh as the presses ground to an emergency stop. Robert was summoned down to the office of Garet Garrett and there he found Garrett, Rogers and Ogden Reid, the Editor in Chief standing in a semi-circle and looking with frozen horror at the lynching picture. He was told it was pro-German, that it was a terrible thing to run "at this time" and that he would damned well get another picture to replace it because the Alco Company had already been notified to make a new press cylinder. Robert hunted up an innocuous picture of some horses that would fit the space and then went to see Gruening. He and Ernest were sure they had been right in trying to run the page, so they didn't feel too badly, but Robert said he knew from the way Rogers and Garrett looked at him, that they were out to get him.

This was apparently confirmed when Garrett began to criticize Robert's choice of pictures with remarkable vigor. . . . He and Gruening had a long argument about a picture of the Kaiser that Robert had run, Garrett maintaining that to show the Kaiser as a normal human being, walking down the street, tended to weaken the public's hate for him. The policy was that any picture that showed a German not cutting off a child's hand was a bad picture. Gruening

* Nathaniel Benchley, *Robert Benchley: A Biography* (New York: McGraw-Hill Book Co., 1955).

disagreed and told Garrett exactly what he thought of such a policy, but it had no effect. Three days later Garrett pounced on a picture Robert had scheduled . . . showing a U-boat crew picking up survivors of a ship they had torpedoed. This, it seemed, was as good as a pro-German picture, because they weren't machine gunning the survivors; so in the interest of what little harmony was left, Robert killed it. . . .

Our days on the *Tribune* were clearly numbered and they finally came to an end through a bizarre combination of circumstances. On July 9, a story "broke" that furnished page-one headlines for all the newspapers. Dr. Edward H. Rumely, the publisher of the *Evening Mail*, was arrested in connection with the purchase of that paper. It was alleged that he bought the paper from its previous owner—Henry L. Stoddard—with money furnished by the German government and he was charged with perjury in a report to the Alien Property Custodian. The assumption was that he was running a pro-German paper, although as Henry Stoddard, the former owner, said in an interview: "It would seem that Rumely misrepresented the situation, but I cannot for the life of me see where Germany got one cent's worth of value for each dollar expended. It is conceded by the government that the paper since we went to war has been one hundred percent American." But this apparent contradiction between German ownership and a hundred-percent pro-American policy was explained away by the conjecture that the *Mail* would work for favorable peace terms for Germany after the war.

The Rumelys lived in the Clearfield on the corner of 103rd Street and Riverside Drive, the same apartment house where Dorothy and I and our two children had been living since my mother's death. Our apartments were side by side, but we had never set eyes on each other, no doubt because my morning-paper hours did not coincide with those of an afternoon-paper executive. But the proximity of the two apartments proved to be explosive fuel in the prevailing atmosphere of suspicion and distrust.

That fuel was ignited by another curious coincidence. As a public relations stunt, William Randolph Hearst had invited the entire Congress to come to New York at his expense for the July Fourth celebration, to review the parade with him and be his guests at the "Follies" that evening. Only forty-nine accepted his invitation, an item which the *Tribune* exultingly featured, as for it, Hearst himself was always fair game. On the day of the parade, city editor Neal Jones assigned a reporter, Robert H. Rohde, to cover it from the Fifth Avenue grandstand where Hearst, his Congressional guests and other notables were assembled. Rohde reported that when the American flag passed, Hearst remained seated and kept his hat on. I had suspected that Jones could not be relied upon to provide an unbiased account of anything having to do with Hearst or others on the *Tribune*'s suspect list. So I had assigned another man who reported the story that we did publish, namely that when the American flag went by Hearst stood up and bared his head as did all others.

I later discovered that Rohde had been nowhere near Hearst at the time of the parade; he was in a bar at some distance from the scene. When I confronted him with this information, he at first denied, then admitted it and I suspended him without pay for a week. I should have fired him. He went directly to the office of the Hearst *American-Journal* and was subsequently assigned to cover the story of the suspicious proximity of the Rumely and Gruening apartments. He did a first-rate job of it. He reported that the switchboard operator at the Clearfield had told him that Gruening and Rumely were constantly in each other's apartments, that when you called one of them and could not get him in his own apartment, he could be found in his neighbor's. In fact, there was no switchboard in the Clearfield. It, and the report of its nonexistent operator, were Rohde inventions. But Hearst's *Journal* leaped at this anti-*Tribune* scoop with understandable relish; "*Tribune* Editor Rumely Pal" was its headline.

The *Tribune* reacted immediately. When I got to my office on Friday afternoon, July 12, I was met by Garrett who told me that my further presence was highly embarrassing to the paper and requested me to leave. I called my attorney, my 1907 classmate, Walter Heilprin Pollak, who advised me to hold fast until he got there. Pollak met with Garrett and Rogers; incredibly enough, both insisted that whatever the facts in the case, my continuing presence on the *Tribune* was out of the question.

Obviously, they had panicked. For the first time I became conscious that my Germanic surname was also a factor in their decision. I told Pollak that under the circumstances I had no desire to stay but I did wish to prevent the *Tribune* from voiding my contract. Garrett clearly intended to do just that, and when the matter later came to court, he testified that I had voluntarily resigned, thus nullifying the *Tribune*'s contractual obligation. The *Tribune* lost the case and paid me the balance of my year's salary.

My departure from the *Tribune* caused a flurry of rumors; from all appearances, I was in league with Rumely and the *Tribune* made no effort to deny it. The Hearst papers even instructed their staff that I was fleeing to Canada and I should be overtaken and interviewed. In fact, I was in Bayshore on Long Island, where Dorothy and I had rented a cottage for the summer, and the members of the press discovered me at home by telephone.

Finally, on Sunday July 19, the *Tribune* clarified the situation with the following story:

Dr. Ernest H. Gruening, who until Friday evening was managing editor of the *Tribune* appeared yesterday in the office of Assistant United States Attorney Harper in answer to the rumor that he had been friendly with Dr. Edward A. Rumely. Afterward Mr. Harper made the following statement:

"This office has no evidence whatever that Dr. Gruening was connected in any way with Dr. Rumely in the transaction of the purchase of the *Evening Mail* by Von Bernsdorff and the Imperial German Government. Dr. Gruening's name had been given me as a person who might possess some information upon a particular matter connected with the investigation of the *Mail*. Dr. Gruening himself had not been under investigation by this office. I have questioned him and he states that he has not the information that I thought he might have. That is his whole connection as far as is known to this office."

Captain Lloyd, of the Military Intelligence Service who was in Mr. Harper's office at the time, said in reply to a question: "We have nothing against Dr. Gruening."

Bob Benchley rose to my support, convinced that his letter of resignation from the *Tribune* preceded a letter from it, firing him. He wrote:

Mr. Ogden Reid, Mr. Rogers, Mr. Garrett:

Gentlemen:
Without any rational proof that Dr. Gruening was guilty of the burlesque charge made against him (except the heinous one of living at 324 West 103rd Street) you took steps, which on the slightest examination could have been proved unwarranted, to smirch the character and newspaper career of the first man in three years who has been able to make the *Tribune* look like a newspaper.
I haven't the slightest idea who is boss on this sheet, so I am sending this resignation to three whom I suspect.

With the *Tribune* behind me, I renewed my application to the Field Artillery Officers Training School at Camp Zachary Taylor, six miles south of Louisville, Kentucky. I was accepted a few weeks later by the

Forty-fifth Training Battery and after mastering the rudiments of drill, my equestrian proficiency was tried out on wooden horses, since at that time the field artillery and caissons were still horsedrawn.

One amusing incident gave me some unexpected attention. When my eyesight was being tested, I was confronted with the charts I had grown up with in my father's office. Naturally I knew them by heart. If you were able to read the seventh line from the top, your vision was 20-20. I rattled off the much tinier ninth line without a pause. The medical officer felt he had encountered a unique phenomenon in ocularity.

Neither my horsemanship nor my eyemanship proved to be of any use. Scarcely a month after my training began, the armistice was declared and the war was over. It took us all by surprise, and I believe that almost without exception there was widespread disappointment—at least at first—which I shared. We were told that if we completed our training and qualified, we would be commissioned in the Field Artillery Reserve. But my interest in doing that was slight. On December 1, I left Louisville and headed north for home. I had no idea what New York held in store for me, but one minor camp incident would help guide my future interest. Picking up a newspaper one day, I read that the US Marines were bombing Haitian villages and killing quite a few of the natives. This struck me as so inconsistent with President Wilson's pronouncements that I vowed, if the opportunity offered, to find out how such a thing could happen.

I would get that opportunity before long. Meanwhile, again on the lookout for a job in New York, I met a friend, Paul Hollister, who told me about an interesting acquaintance of his. He was José Aymar Camprubí, a graduate of both Harvard and Hotchkiss, a naturalized citizen from Spain and a successful businessman. Camprubí was eager to promote better relations between the United States and the Spanish-speaking countries and wanted to acquire a Spanish language newspaper in New York. There was such a newspaper, a weekly, *La Prensa*, and Camprubí asked me to study the situation.

La Prensa was published in two second-floor lofts on Canal Street by an Italian firm, the Nicoletti Brothers. Its editor was a Chilean, Alfredo von der Heyde Collao. I spent a month there and elsewhere around New York trying to decide which of several alternatives would enable Camprubí to carry out his purpose. Should he buy *La Prensa* and publish it in the existing plant? Should he try to acquire another plant somewhere else in the city? Or should he start a new newspaper? Finally I recommended purchasing the Canal Street plant and transforming *La Prensa* into a daily.

I thought that was the end of it, but Camprubí then asked me to stay with the paper and put my recommendations into effect. This meant

going somewhat beyond my previous newspaper experience, which had
been wholly in the news and editorial departments, but in my month's
survey I had learned a good deal about the mechanical problems of production and distribution, and I was enthusiastic about the potential of a
newspaper that would not only cater to the Spanish-speaking residents of
New York but might also help promote understanding between the Spanish and American cultures. I found Camprubí to be a charming, intelligent and cultured man with whom I was glad to be associated.

I had to start virtually from scratch; distribution, advertising, news
coverage and the mechanics of production were all gravely deficient.
With the proposed expansion, we desperately needed more space which
we finally acquired in the same building, and because news coverage had
consisted of rewriting and translating items from other papers, we applied
for and acquired an Associated Press franchise and tapped new sources
for local news. But our most pressing problem came from another source.
The production staff consisted, strangely enough, of operators who knew
no Spanish, and as a result some glaring typographical errors appeared.
The men were not organized; it was an "open" shop. I found that if we
organized the composing room, we could get some Spanish-speaking or
even bilingual compositors and linotypists. It would mean, however, a
substantial increase in cost; the union scale was over twice what the Italian management had been paying. Money was tight, but Camprubí said
we could afford it. The shop was unionized and there was an immediate
improvement. But I soon discovered that there was a related unsolved
problem.

When Camprubí purchased the plant and newspaper, its circulation
was only about 6,000. Some 5,500 went to newsstands and the remaining
several hundred were wrapped and mailed out to individual subscribers
by a single mailer, who came to work at nine o'clock six nights a week, and
with a hand-wrapping machine, did his job in an hour, for which he was
paid 18 dollars a week. His salary was the equivalent of three dollars an
hour, a good wage at that time, and he had not requested a raise. A week
after we had unionized the composing room I was visited by two representatives of the Mailers' Union.

"We see you've organized the composin' room," said the spokesman.
"You've got to organize the mailin' room." He spoke with a strong Irish
brogue.

"What will it cost me?" I asked. Obviously the union scale would be
higher.

"The union wage is thirty-foive dollars a week."

"So you want me to pay thirty-five dollars for what I am now getting for
eighteen?"

"It'll cost you more than that," he said.

"How's that?" I asked.

"For the number of papers you're printin' you requires two mailers."

"Don't be ridiculous," I retorted; "You have an eight-hour day. Our mailer gets done in an hour."

"Them's the union rules," he came back.

"So you want me to pay $70 for what I'm now getting for $18?"

"It'll cost you more than that," he asserted.

"How's that?" I asked for the second time.

"When there's two mailers, one of them is a foreman and the foreman's wage is $37.50 a week."

"So you want me to pay $72.50 for what I am now getting for $18?"

"It'll cost you more than that."

"What more can you think of?" I inquired.

"The union day ends at foive, and the union night begins at eleven. Anything in between is toime-and-a-half."

"So you want me to pay$108.75 for what I'm now getting for $18? It's been nice knowing you," I said, and got up.

"You better had; you'll be sorry if you don't," he said.

"Are you threatening me?" I asked.

"You'll see," he said.

The next night, sabotage of our newsstand deliveries began. Our papers were thrown off the delivery trucks and from the newsstands.

Camprubí was outraged. "To Hell with those Union bastards," he said. "I won't be blackmailed. We'll deunionize the composing room. I don't care how many typographical errors we make. I won't submit to such outrageous extortion." And it was done. The union linotypers were dropped.

Shortly after, the unions started a Spanish-language daily to compete with *La Prensa*. It was short-lived.

This was an experience I have never forgotten. I recalled that in Boston, when the mechanical departments were unionized, the typographical union had imposed the practice known as "setting bogus." This consisted of compelling the resetting, making up, proof reading and correcting of every advertisement sent in by an advertiser or advertising agency even if submitted in plate form—a general practice to secure uniformity in appearance of the copy. The reset copy was then thrown away. This type of featherbedding persists today.

This and other similar union practices have been largely responsible for the consolidation, elimination and extinction of many newspapers—a tragic blow to the democratic process which is nourished by the diversity of opinion in editorial treatment and news coverage that only several newspapers under different managements can offer. The decline in the number of newspapers, to the point where in most American cities there is but one daily, or perhaps a morning and evening paper under the same management—and the trend has not yet run its course—has been ascribed to the advent of radio and television. No doubt these do compete with newspapers, both in news coverage and for advertising revenue. But radio and television were insignificant half a century ago when the elimination of dailies was already well underway. The strikes initiated by the well-paid mechanical-department workers on newspapers have had serious consequences far beyond the diminution of sales in department stores and lesser mercantile establishments. When newspapers are forced to suspend publication even temporarily, plays are not reviewed and their runs are shortlived to the injury of the playwright, producer, actors and others —not to mention the unionized stagehands; books are not reviewed, with the same damage to authors and publishers. A newspaper strike differs in its effects from one in a brick plant or steel mill where the interruption of production results in little permanent damage and the costs, if the strike's objectives are secured, are merely passed on to the public.

But when a newspaper "folds," which is too often the result of a prolonged strike, a whole category of professional and semiprofessional workers are thrown out of employment, not temporarily but often permanently. Editorial writers, reporters, special feature writers, columnists, cartoonists and photographers are left stranded with no place to go. And the mechanical-department employees may suffer equally. While printers can usually find work in book-printing, the pressmen cannot. Finally, despite the great benefits of radio and television, there is in many respects no substitute for the printed word. A newspaper story can be read and reread, clipped, filed and stored for future reference. An ephemeral radio or television broadcast cannot.

In the case of *La Prensa*, I might have been willing, for no very good reason, had Camprubí agreed, to try to work out a compromise with the union demands. I was strongly sympathetic with the organized-labor movement, having noted the ruthless exploitation of the textile workers in Lawrence and other New England cities, and the general plight of most wage-earners in the early decades of this century. It was clear that the organized-labor movement had done much to lessen economic injustices, to raise the standard of living and improve working conditions, and thereby benefit our whole society. But the rapacity of the Mailers' Union demands on that occasion, and their violent tactics, made yielding obviously impossible.

The news staff of *La Prensa* included some excellent journalists and interesting personalities. At times, they were political or economic exiles from their country, and welcomed the chance for even a very modest livelihood and self-expression. They included Dr. Luis Lara Pardo, physician, sociologist, journalist, former member of the Mexican Chamber of Deputies, whose scholarly *La Prostitucion en Mexico* had been published both in Mexico City and in Paris; Ernesto Montenegro, a distinguished Chilean journalist; Tulio Cestero, a Dominican, author of *Estados Unidos y las Antillas,* a history of the interventional policies of the United States in the Caribbean, and later in his country's diplomatic service.

Interesting visitors from various countries would call and be entertained by Camprubí. One of them was Blasco Ibañez whose *Four Horsemen of the Apocalypse* had been a best seller in English. He asked me to accompany him to the Grand Central Depot where he was starting on a tour of the country. While there, we saw a girl scout troop. Its leader was an enormously fat woman. She was wearing shorts, which emphasized her obesity. Blasco Ibanez called my attention to her:

"You are a wonderful people, you Americans. You can accomplish anything. You have no sense of the ridiculous."

In spite of our problems, we made headway on *La Prensa* and the paper became a going concern. It was an education for me; I learned the mechanics of putting out a newspaper and I became acquainted with the ideas and concerns of our Spanish-speaking citizens and our Latin American neighbors, which would prove an invaluable background in my later career. Still, I preferred the writing and editorial end of journalism, and in May 1920, when Oswald Garrison Villard, owner and editor of *The Nation,* asked me to become its managing editor, I accepted his offer.

7

ON *THE NATION*

Who so would be a man must be a non-
conformist. . . . Nothing is at last sacred
but the integrity of our mind.
—RALPH WALDO EMERSON

My name first appeared as managing editor on *The Nation*'s masthead, May 15, 1921. A weekly journal devoted to "politics, literature, science, drama, music, art and finance," *The Nation* had been founded in 1865 and over the years had established a reputation for independence and integrity that attracted an impressive list of contributors and a loyal audience. The interests of the magazine had varied under different editors since the forceful leadership of its first editor, Edwin Laurence Godkin. Its articles had always been marked by high literary quality, but now under Oswald Garrison Villard's direction it would increasingly be the voice of dissent, and inevitably seek and publish material on issues ignored by the daily press. That, all of us on *The Nation*'s staff agreed, was our principal mission.

We were a congenial group. Weekly staff meetings on Tuesdays, after the previous issue had been "put to bed" and we were planning the next week's, were spiced with hilarity and wit. Lewis Stiles Gannett, a Harvard '13 graduate, who had joined the staff at the same time as I, would prove to be a perceptive and versatile journalist with great personal charm. Ludwig Lewisohn, who wrote brilliant dramatic criticism and book reviews, would shortly replace Arthur Gleason, specializing on labor subjects, as an associate editor. The Van Dorens, Carl, his wife Irita, his brother Mark and Dorothy Graffe, who would shortly marry Mark, were a scintillating quartette. To me it was more than a pleasant group; it was intellectually the "fastest company" of my experience.

A glance through the issues of that year reveals the range and depth of their interests, and the caliber of the men and women who wrote about them. Each issue contained editorial "shorts" and a longer editorial or two on some topic of current importance, the dramatic and book review sections, and the international relations section, devoted to the vast new field of foreign affairs and ably edited by Freda Kirchwey. Special articles made up the bulk of each issue and they almost invariably shed some new light on a wide variety of national and international concerns. Mexico, which had just passed through a decade of violent revolution, took a large part of one issue with contributions by my *La Prensa* associate, Luis Lara Pardo, Mary Austin, Professor Arthur Livingston and L. J. de Bekker. The same issue carried an article by Mary Heaton Vorse about the Amalgamated Clothing Workers and an exposé by Arthur Gleason, "West Virginia—Private Ownership of Public Offices," which revealed how the coal-mining interests controlled the state's officialdom. And on the international scene, an article by Henry W. Nevinson urged the course of action which a few years later would establish Ireland's new political status. This was one of many instances when *The Nation* promoted an unpopular policy that would be subsequently adopted.

The misconduct of our relations with Latin American countries received special attention in *The Nation's* pages. In Haiti, as well as in other Caribbean and Central American republics, powerful financial interests backed up by American military might sought to exploit the economies of these small and helpless nations. It was "gunboat diplomacy" at its worst, a policy initiated in the century's first decade and amplified and intensified by armed intervention under the Wilson Administration. The ruthless marine invasions of Haiti, the Dominican Republic and Nicaragua—all in violation of existing treaties and international law— had been concealed by strict naval censorship and the facts kept from the American people. *The Nation* was the first publication to "break" the story and begin a ten-year crusade against such flagrant abuses of power.

The Nation also made a continuing effort to establish understanding with the new regime in Soviet Russia. A brilliant, two-part article by Bertrand Russell, based upon his own firsthand experience, was as fine and balanced a guide to the truth about Russia as could be found in any American publication, at a time when misrepresentation and distortion prevailed.

Another of *The Nation's* concerns was the treatment—or rather mistreatment—of minorities. A long editorial condemned the campaign in California to deprive Japanese residents of land ownership; and we published in full the report of the Sir Stuart Samuel Commission about the pogroms in Poland which had been largely suppressed in the daily newspapers by the Associated Press. On the treatment of Negroes, an editorial paragraph epitomized its horror and one gratifying reaction to it by a Southern governor, Thomas Walter Bickett of North Carolina. A Negro charged with assaulting a white girl had been taken from jail and lynched; the next day his white employer revealed that the victim was innocent. When, a week later, three Negroes charged with assault were jailed, Bickett ordered the National Guard out to protect them "at all hazards," with instructions to shoot members of the mob which had formed, if necessary—an unprecedented action.

Another issue that concerned *The Nation* was industrial espionage and it published the report of the Commission of the Inter-Church on these practices in the steel industry. The objective was to impede unionization, which was being strenuously fought by Judge Elbert Gary, the steel industry's mogul. We also published an early warning against efforts on the part of power interests to invade Yellowstone National Park. And, of course, we hailed the passage of the Susan B. Anthony Amendment— the Nineteenth Amendment to the Constitution—and expressed the hope that the newly enfranchised women, would, unlike the men, see to it that the same right was extended to their black sisters in the South.

As the year progressed, we added other contributing editors to an already distinguished list. Henry L. Mencken, whose lusty iconoclasm spared neither the left nor the right; Robert Herrick, whose novels had raised provocative social issues; John A. Hobson, the British economist; and Anatole France, then his country's foremost man of letters who began to write regularly for *The Nation* on current and other affairs, beginning with his "Message to Frenchmen" which urged them to outgrow their hostility to the Germans. Another new feature was the cartoons of Art Young, a pink-faced, rolypoly cherub with a delicious and irreverent sense of humor. Along with Max Eastman and other editors of *The Masses*, he had been a target of Postmaster General Burleson and was tried for dissent from America's participation in the war. In one memorable cartoon, he depicted himself gently snoring in the courtroom with the title, "Art Young on trial for his life."

Editors and contributors like these were not easily intimidated, nor were they afraid to speak out on unpopular issues and personalities in the news. Sir Roger Casement, while in the British consular service, had exposed the atrocities perpetrated on the laborers in the rubber plantations in the Congo and in the Putumayo district bordering Colombia and Peru. For these services he had been knighted, but his persistent struggle for Irish freedom led him to the error of seeking to enlist German aid for this cause in wartime and he was tried for treason, convicted and hanged. *The Nation* published his diaries. Cherishing our own freedom, we kept a vigilant watch at home and abroad for violations of the freedom of others. We covered the seething events in India's struggle for independence led by the towering figure of Gandhi. We printed discussions of antisemitism and in particular focused on President A. Laurence Lowell's effort to establish at Harvard a quota for the admission of Jews. *The Nation*'s airing of this otherwise unpublicized Lowellian design proved effective in preventing it.

We also published a number of valuable series. Carl Van Doren wrote incursive criticism of contemporary American novelists who were widely read in that and the previous decade. In another series Villard took on American newspapers and wrote penetrating dissections which revealed their omissions, distortions and suppressions as well as their valuable contributions. I conceived another series on the States of the Union. It was designed to bring out the individual character of each state and its inhabitants and to reveal their own particular and special flavor. William Allen White began the series with "Kansas, a Puritan Survival," and I was able to enlist a galaxy of other writers: Henry Mencken on Maryland, Sinclair Lewis on Minnesota, Dorothy Canfield on Vermont, Zona Gale on Wisconsin, Robert Herrick on Maine, Willa Cather on Nebraska, Sherwood Anderson on Ohio, Theodore Dreiser on Indiana, Douglas Southall Freeman on Virginia, W. E. B. DuBois on Georgia and Edmund Wilson on New Jersey.*

Nineteen-twenty was a happy and eventful year for me. The mood of America at the beginning of the century's third decade seemed to me, and to most of my friends in journalism, to be one of boundless and justified optimism. Our country had performed the incredible feat of sending more than a million men under arms overseas, and had brought to a successful conclusion what we saw as a great crusade for democracy. America, we felt, had rescued our hard-pressed, gallant European allies from defeat at the hands of Prussian militarism. True, we had serious reservations about other aspects of our foreign policy, particularly in Latin America, and we deplored the repression of the rights of minorities and dissenters at home, best exemplified by the sentencing and imprisonment of Eugene Debs for voicing his pacifist convictions. But these regrettable mistakes could and would be rectified, we felt, now that we were at peace and with the prospect of new political leadership.

Nineteen-twenty was an election year and, of course, *The Nation* was right in the thick of it, publishing perceptive articles on Hiram Johnson, Henry T. Allen, Calvin Coolidge, Warren G. Harding and other presi-

---

* These were published in two volumes in 1923 by Boni and Liveright. After being out of print for some years, they were republished in 1971 by Books for Libraries Press.

dential possibilities. But, to me, one man—never considered a political figure—seemed to stand apart from the others, to be "above the battle." He had effectively managed our essential food and fuel supply during the war; his energies and talents had then been applied to feeding its starving victims. His public expressions were generous and liberal and seemed not inconsistent with reformist aspirations. His name was Herbert Hoover.

The enthusiasm Hoover was beginning to generate seemed to come from every quarter and cross the usual party lines. A few "literary people" gathered in our apartment on 103rd Street to promote the cause, but we soon required larger meeting places. We got an impressive list of endorsements and circulated Hoover literature. Many of us felt that the man was more important than the party and were prepared to support Hoover as either a Republican or a Democrat. He finally cast his lot with the Republicans in a telegram to the Republican Club of his state—California —published in the morning newspapers of March 31, 1920. He said that he would not seek the Republican nomination, but if "it is demanded of me, I cannot refuse service."

The movement to nominate Hoover had little effective organization and no backing from the party regulars who were openly hostile. At a gathering of Republicans in New York's Fifteenth Assembly District, his name was greeted with hoots and jeers. Our group, meeting at the New York Harvard Club, voted to send a representative to the convention anyway, to do whatever might be done by an amateur, politically inexperienced organization. Dorothy and I were elected for that mission. In Chicago we circulated among the state delegations, leaving Hoover pamphlets and talking to any and everyone who wore a delegate's badge. Our advances were pleasantly received, obviously because our candidate did not stand a chance. But more than once we were told, prophetically, "You're eight years ahead of your time."

Successive balloting eliminated the three most prominent candidates, Governor Frank O. Lowden of Illinois, Senator Hiram Johnson of California, and Major-General Leonard Wood. It was then, during a recess, that Senator Warren G. Harding of Ohio emerged from the proverbial "smoke-filled room" with Calvin Coolidge as his running mate.

We felt considerably deflated. The mood of our group in New York alternated between rebelliousness and depression. We could not know then, of course, that Harding's would be one of the most corrupt administrations in American history. Nor were we inspired by the results of the Democratic Convention which nominated Governor James M. Cox of Ohio as the presidential candidate and Franklin Delano Roosevelt as Vice President. None of us had an inkling that years later we would develop great enthusiasm for Roosevelt.

My colleagues on *The Nation* had not shared my opinion of Hoover, and because neither of the major party candidates appealed to me, I thought of casting my vote for one of the minor party leaders—either Eugene Debs on the Socialist ticket, who was still in prison, or Parley P. Christensen on the Farmer-Labor ticket. *The Nation*'s staff lunched with Christensen that summer and I found him a genial and intelligent man with a keen sense of humor. I voted for him in November.

Later events modified some of my views about our 1920 "man of the hour." But I never had reason to doubt that Hoover's nomination and inevitable election that year would have obviated the degradation of the Harding Administration and relieved some of the political bleakness of the ensuing twenties. And fate would doubtless have been kinder to Herbert Hoover in the early 1920s than it was a decade later.

8

GUNNING AGAINST

"GUNBOAT DIPLOMACY"

*Extending the blessings of civilization to
our Brother who sits in darkness has been a
good trade and paid well, on the whole, and
there is money in it yet, if carefully worked.*
—SAMUEL L. CLEMENS

Our campaign on *The Nation* to restore civil self-government to Haiti
and the Dominican Republic and terminate an American policy which
we considered damaging not only to those small Caribbean nations, but to
America's honor, required some extra-journalistic effort. In Haiti a group
of intellectuals and other leading citizens had organized the *Union Patriotique Haitienne* to break through the military censorship and lay Haiti's
case before world—and particularly American—opinion. Its chairman was Georges Sylvain, former Haitian minister to France and to the
Vatican, and an officer of the French Legion of Honor, some of whose
works had been cited by the French Academy. The general secretary was
Perceval Thoby, a former Chargé d'Affaires of the Haitian legation in
Washington, and a former Inspector-General of the Consular Service.
This organization, which was now sending a delegation to the United
States, consisting of: Sylvain, Thoby, and a former Haitian Secretary of
State, H. Pauléus Sannon, had drafted a "Memoir on the Political, Economic
and Financial Conditions Relating to the Republic of Haiti under the
American Occupation." It was some 30,000 words in length and was
printed in full in the May 25, 1921, issue of *The Nation*. The story it told
was not a pretty one.

The forerunner of American military intervention in Haiti was the purchase by the National City Bank of New York of some of the capital stock in the National Bank of Haiti. This bank, founded in 1881 with French capital, had been entrusted with the administration of the treasury of the Haitian government. A railroad from Port-au-Prince to Cape Haitien was also under construction financed with funds loaned by the National City Bank, but work had been suspended and the contract thereby unfulfilled after three separate sections had been built. Other American interests were eyeing Haiti with its rich soil, tropical climate and abundant cheap labor for extensive cotton and sugar development. Difficulties between the bank's new American management and the Haitian government were followed by the State Department's effort to arrange a treaty with Haiti for the control of its finances. The Haitian Congress rejected it in the belief that it would lead to the status of an American protectorate, and that reports that the government of President Vilbrun Guillaume Sam was negotiating with the United States were a factor in a revolution which broke out against him. Then a squad of United States Marines landed from the gunboat *Machias*, removed $500,000 in gold from the bank and shipped it to New York, where it was deposited in the vaults of the National City Bank. The Haitian Secretary of State protested and twice asked for an explanation which was not forthcoming. On July 27, 1915, revolutionaries attacked the President's palace. He fled, taking refuge in the French legation from which he was dragged and killed following the execution of some of the revolutionaries who had been imprisoned in the palace.

The next day marines and bluejackets from the cruiser *George Washington* landed in Port-au-Prince, seized the customs houses, the chief sources of revenue, and Admiral W. B. Caperton, United States Navy, took charge. Meanwhile, the two houses of the Haitian Congress had met and elected Sudre Dartiguenave as president. He was told that the military occupation would remain until the conditions the Haitians had previously rejected were approved, including the right of foreigners to acquire land in Haiti, which every Haitian government from the nation's birth had opposed. Until the United States got what it wanted, funds for salaries and wages of government employees were withheld by the occupation. Not long after, the Haitian Congress was dissolved by orders of the military and a new constitution ratified in an election in which only the "yes" ballots were available. It was thenceforth a rule of force, with consistent violations by the military, of the treaty which they had imposed. As a result of forced road labor, revolts broke out during which over 3,000 Haitians were killed.

The facts were at last laid before the American public in the Memoir published in *The Nation*, and the Haitian spokesmen demanded immediate abolition of martial law and the withdrawal of occupation forces, abrogation of the Treaty of 1915 and the convocation of a constituent assembly with all the guarantees of electoral liberty, demands which they felt were not inconsistent with continuing friendship and cooperation between the Haitian and American governments. They presented these demands to the State Department, which did not accord them an interview, and to the Foreign Relations Committee of the Senate.

Meanwhile, we at *The Nation* had organized a "Haiti-Santo Domingo Independence Society" with Moorfield Storey—former president of the American Bar Association—as chairman, James Weldon Johnson as vice-chairman, Helena Hill Weed, a daughter of Representative Ebenezer J. Hill of Connecticut, as secretary, and Robert Herrick as treasurer. There was also an advisory council of prominent men and women interested in the cause. One of the society's functions was to secure speaking engagements for the Haitian visitors. There was a mass-meeting for them in Tremont Temple, Boston, at which H. Pauléus Sannon, James Weldon Johnson and I spoke, and there were other meetings in Philadelphia, Chicago and New York. The fate of both Haiti and Santo Domingo became an issue in the 1920 presidential campaign, and our cause received an unexpected boost when Franklin Delano Roosevelt, who was campaigning for the Vice Presidency on the Democratic ticket, emitted a notable "blooper." As Assistant Secretary of the Navy, he admitted proudly, "You know I had something to do with running a couple of little republics. The facts are that I wrote Haiti's constitution myself and if I do say it, I think it is a pretty good constitution."

Warren G. Harding, campaigning from his front porch at Marion, Ohio, picked up the Roosevelt boner and ran with it. "If I am elected President of this just and honorable republic," he said, "I shall not empower an Assistant Secretary of the Navy to draft a constitution for helpless neighbors in the West Indies and jam it down their throats at the point of bayonets borne by United States Marines." And Medill McCormick, a newspaper man of the *Chicago Tribune* family, elected to the United States Senate from Illinois in 1918, joined the chorus. I asked him to present his views in *The Nation*, which he did right after the presidential election. But while he was ready to blast the Democrats' malfeasance, his purpose was none other than to continue it, expressing his belief that the occupation should remain for twenty years. *The Nation* took issue with that belief in a long footnote.

Nevertheless, McCormick was willing to sponsor the Senate investigation which we had urged. He introduced a resolution on July 27, 1921, providing for a "Select Committee" of five senators "to inquire into the occupation and administration of the territories of the Republic of Haiti and the Dominican Republic by the forces of the United States." The resolution was adopted and McCormick, as its sponsor, became chairman. The other members of the committee were Philander Chase Knox of Pennsylvania and Tasker L. Oddie of Nevada, Republicans; and Atlee Pomerene of Ohio and Andrieus Aristieus Jones of New Mexico, Democrats. Knox, however, was taken ill shortly thereafter and did not sit.

The Senate hearings revealed an even grimmer picture of unwarranted military intervention, rigged elections, censorship, forced labor and political assassination than the Memoir printed in *The Nation*. The committee then decided to visit Haiti and the Dominican Republic and continue the hearings there. Senator McCormick invited me to go along, but a week before the scheduled departure he informed me that the committee would not have much time in Haiti—a maximum of three days—and requested that I go on ahead and sort out the witnesses, so that an effective presentation could be made in the limited time available. I was disappointed that the committee would attempt to investigate six years of military occupation in three days, and said so, but that was the decision. Nevertheless, I was pleased to have at least a semiofficial status with the committee. I boarded the Panama Line Steamer *Colon* and arrived at Port-au-Prince on November 9, 1921.

It was my first visit to the tropics. It was night when we docked and overhead was the brilliant star, Canopus, the second brightest star in the firmament, which I had never seen before because it was not visible in northern latitudes. I was cordially welcomed, taken to the Hotel Bellevue, and awakened too soon the next morning by the citywide crowing of cocks. After breakfast I was escorted to an office that had been made ready for my exclusive use by the Haitians. There I was interviewed by the representatives of half-a-dozen newspapers, and then conducted to a gathering in the square in front of the beautiful Gothic cathedral where I was expected to speak. It was my first public address in French and I found I was not quite as fluent as I had thought I was. Paraphrasing Napoleon's words to his troops in Egypt, I pointed to the surrounding mountains and said that from their heights one hundred and seventeen years of liberty "are contemplating you." I spoke of our efforts and hopes, and when I finished, I was voted a *citoyen honoraire de Port-au-Prince* and the mayor fastened a decoration in my buttonhole. Everyone seemed happy. They considered my coming in advance of the committee a good omen.

However, I was startled to learn that the members of the senatorial delegation were to be the house guests of the United States Marine Corps, then headed by Colonel John H. Russell. This struck me as shocking. How could an investigation be objective while the senators were house guests of the people they were to investigate? I found that I could reserve ample space for the entire delegation at the Hotel Montagne, which was then the leading hotel, but how to communicate that to the senators? Martial law prevailed, strict censorship was in effect and I feared that any message I tried to send might not be transmitted.

It happened that before leaving *The Nation* offices, I had picked up Lewis Gannett's copy of Burt's English-French and French-English dictionary in red cover. So using page and word numbers I devised a code and sent the following message to Gannett:

Marine occupation plans to have Senatorial delegation as its house guests. I consider this highly improper. It will destroy any confidence Haitians may have in objectiveness of Committee. I have reserved ample accommodations at Hotel Montagne. Please communicate to chairman.

I preceded the telegram with the phrase "Your missing red volume," and hoped that Lewis would figure out the numbers, but unfortunately, he had not missed the book, and wired back that he did not know what I was talking about. I had to find a way to enlighten him without revealing the contents of my message to the occupation. We had a friend, Burt Morgan Dennis, who had worked on the Boston *Traveler* and later became well-known as an illustrator of the advertisements for Black and White whiskey. He had married a girl named Helen Bishop whom Dorothy and I knew well. So I wired Gannett: "Ask Dorothy for the first name of Helen Bishop's husband and you will know to which volume I refer." This was done. Lewis deciphered the message and took it up with Senator McCormick.

Two days later a marine officer came to see me at the Hotel Bellevue and said, somewhat sourly, "We understand that you have made reservations for the senatorial committee and they want to take up these reservations." I was delighted and moved into the Hotel Montagne myself to await the delegation which, with my wife and the wives of several of the senators, was sailing for Port-au-Prince on an army transport, the *Argonne.*

Knowing Senator McCormick to be a man of the world, I suspected he would be far more interested in being entertained by the Haitians than by the military; and I also knew that social contacts with the Haitians would be just as important as the hearings themselves for the exchange of information. So I went to Georges Léger, one of the Haitians active in the *Union Patriotique* and the son of Jacques N. Léger, who had been Haiti's Ambassador to the United States, and asked him to entertain the delegation. Léger demurred; he told me that when the occupation first came to Haiti, even though Haitians resented it, its officers and men were most hospitably received and invited to the Haitians' homes, but some months later when the American wives arrived, all social intercourse ceased. In fact, during my visit an American newspaper representative was requested by the management of the Hotel Montagne not to receive Haitians except on the back porch; complaints had been made by American officers who were guests in the hotel. The Haitians, Léger told me, did not care to expose themselves to additional social insults. Despite my urging that it would be different with the senatorial party, my efforts seemed destined to fail, leaving the field wholly to the occupation hosts.

I received some unexpected support in a telegram from Senator McCormick asking what entertainment the Haitians planned. So I returned to Léger, and renewed my request. He replied that under these circumstances he would be happy to entertain the delegation and would consult the occupation forces to find out what arrangements had been made for the three nights of the senators' visit.

"That is very considerate of you," I said, "but let me remind you that this is your country, and I suggest you make whatever arrangements you think desirable, invite the senatorial party, and then notify the occupation."

Léger, however, felt that he should first consult the occupation authorities, and when he did so, he found—as might have been expected— that every night had been preempted. But after he spoke to Colonel Russell, it was agreed that the second night would be the Haitians', and they planned a reception, dinner and dance at the Cercle Bellevue, their leading social club.

When Léger told me of this arrangement, I asked him whether he had forwarded his invitation to the senatorial party aboard the *Argonne*. He said he had left the transmission of the message to the occupation. Something told me I had better notify the senatorial party myself and make sure the message had been sent. Besides, McCormick's inquiry had been addressed to me and warranted a personal reply. I went to the occupation headquarters and said I wanted to send a message to Senator McCormick. I was met with a scowl by the lieutenant at the desk and the brusque reply, "Well, I'll see whether you can." He left to find out, and there, right in front of me on his desk, were the flimsies of other radio messages that had been sent. The top one was addressed to Senator McCormick and read: "Haitians planning no entertainment whatever. You are therefore free to accept previous invitations for all three nights. (Signed) Jordan, United States Attaché"

I could hardly believe my eyes. The United States attaché, unless he had been misinformed, was deliberately double-crossing the Haitians. How high up this connivance went, I never found, although I resolved to tell Senator McCormick about it and let him make his own inquiries. My message was transmitted and the social insult that Léger feared was narrowly averted. Later, Dorothy told me that there was considerable disappointment on board ship when Jordan's wire arrived, but everyone was greatly cheered by my subsequent message.

When the *Argonne* finally docked, the senatorial delegation was greeted by a tremendous and enthusiastic crowd, but clearly visible were placards which read "The United States Has Been Betrayed in Haiti," "Three Thousand Slain Haitians Ask for Justice," "End Martial Law," "Shall Haiti Be Your Belgium?" Under the circumstances, these sentiments were certainly justified and were based, naively perhaps, on the belief that America stood by the principles enunciated in the Declaration of Independence, and in the utterances of our great statesmen, Washington, Jefferson and Lincoln.

Unfortunately, the hearings got off to a poor start. Senator McCormick, who spoke French, was not present; he was touring the island with Marine Corps officers. So the presiding was left to Senator Atlee Pomerene, a Babbitt (or Claghorn, to use a more recent caricature). The opening presentation was made by Georges Sylvain who thanked the senators for coming, and said that the Haitian people were convinced that once they learned all the facts, they would promptly move to remedy the situation. He then went on to express his regret that in anticipation of the hearings the senators had not seen fit to have martial law lifted. Because of that, he said, Haitians had been imprisoned for criticizing the occupation, and many therefore felt intimidated and would not testify.

A marine officer with a limited knowledge of French was translating Sylvain's remarks, and at this point Senator Pomerene called out, "Let the witness give the names and addresses of any who have been intimidated."

"*Ne m'attendant pas à cette demande,*" replied Sylvain. "*Je n'ai pas actuellement les noms,*" which correctly translated would be: "Not expecting this request, I do not have the names with me at this time." But the interpreter translated, "I do not actually have the names." Whereupon Pomerene bellowed, "The United States Senate will not entertain vague and slanderous charges of this nature. If the witness has facts, let him produce them, or remain silent."

Then followed a period of heckling by Senator Pomerene which widened the breach. He wanted to know all about "this here Union *Patrique.*" Reassured that it did represent the sentiments of the country and was not hostile to the United States, Senator Pomerene started a new line of questions. Who, he wanted to know with some grimness, had been responsible for the inscriptions on the placards at the welcoming demonstrations, in particular the one that read "Shall Haiti Be Your Belgium?" The *Union Patriotique*, of course, was the answer. What was the purpose of these devices? Pomerene wanted to know. Did they seek to arouse and inflame the populace? Did they think thereby to intimidate the United States Senators? The answer was that they represented the Haitians' feelings.

The Senator was clearly displeased and there followed hours of questions about Haitian history and education, all designed to bring out the backwardness of the country. It was difficult to avoid the impression that the committee was hostile, and that the Haitians' high hopes would again be dashed.

Ernest Angell and his wife Katrina, Helena Weed, Dorothy and I tried to reassure the Haitians, and the party at the Cercle Bellevue the next night would, we hoped, help repair these unfortunate first impressions. It did. Senator McCormick's charm and gaiety, and his gracious words of appreciation in faultless French soothed a lot of ruffled feelings.

The hearings the following day were congeries of unrelieved horror stories. One Haitian after another, men and women, told of arrests, imprisonment, beatings and other tortures. A French priest, Father Le Sidaner, described the burning of Haitian homes. A man named Polydor Saint Pierre exhibited a back and legs seared with the scars of a red-hot iron deliberately applied in the prison at Saint Marc by Captain Fitzgerald Brown of the Marine Corps. A witness put forward by the occupation denied it, but it was established beyond contradiction that the torture had been inflicted in the prison, where the victim was subsequently treated for five months for his burns, and that the prison was in charge of Captain Brown.

J. Jolibois, one of the editors of the *Currier Haitien* whom I had visited in prison, testified on the reasons for his imprisonment. When the order instituting martial law was issued, his paper was already on the press. His equipment was primitive. He had no linotypes. Composition was by hand. An article criticizing the occupation was already in type. In order not to scrap the entire issue, Jolibois extracted from the type all sentences that he considered could possibly be objectionable, leaving the spaces blank. But the court-martial decided that inflammatory sentiments could be read into the blanks.

The hearings concluded in Port-au-Prince on schedule; the senators went overland to Santo Domingo and held hearings at the interim points on the way. The rest of us went to Santo Domingo on the *Argonne*. The situation in the Dominican Republic resembled and yet differed from that

*Welcoming United States Senatorial commission at Port-au-Prince, Haiti,
1923*

in Haiti. Here, too, unable to secure assent from the Dominican authorities to a treaty drafted by the State Department, military forces abolished the legally constituted government. Captain Harry Shepard Knapp, United States Navy, proclaimed martial law and declared himself to be "the supreme executive, the supreme legislator and the supreme judge." Unlike Haiti, however, the occupation had been unable to find a compliant Dominican who would do its bidding and give its actions the semblance of legality and consent. Dr. Francisco Henriques Y Carvajal, the constitutionally elected president, refused to sign anything that he considered disadvantageous to his country. Furthermore, while the French Catholic hierarchy in Haiti did not oppose the occupation, in Santo Domingo it found a resolute and outspoken opponent in Archbishop Adolfo Nouel. My interview with him, which *The Nation* printed under the title "Santo Domingo's Cardinal Mercier," was widely reprinted throughout Latin America. But the abuses by the occupation in both countries were alike: censorship, imprisonment, killing and torture.

An interesting revelation of the nature of military justice in a conquered country was furnished me by William H. Jackson, who for eight years was United States District Judge in Panama and later presiding judge of the Land Court established by the occupation. When Fabio Fiallo, the Dominican poet and journalist, was placed on trial, the Judge Advocate in charge of the prosecution asked Judge Jackson to appear before the court to testify as an expert in Spanish as to the incendiary character of an article by Fiallo in his own newspaper, *La Bandera Libre*. Judge Jackson read the article and informed the Judge Advocate that in his opinion the article was not incendiary and not actionable. "In that case," said the Judge Advocate, "we shall not call you." Judge Jackson was not called, and the court-martial found Fiallo guilty and sentenced him to three years imprisonment and a $5,000 fine. The sentence had such wide repercussions throughout Latin America that Washington was later obliged to reverse the verdict, but it did more to bring the Dominican cause before the world than any other of the military's ruthless and tyrannical acts.

The hearings in Santo Domingo got off to a better start than in Haiti. The Dominicans were represented by a retired American diplomat, Horace G. Knowles, previously United States Minister to Nicaragua, and the first witness was an attorney, Francisco J. Peynado, whose favorable reception by the committee was due in part to his ability to speak in English, his assertion that he was not a politician and had no political connections, and the fact that—to all appearances—he was white. He said that he had offered to serve his country as treasurer, but without a salary, and added that since all the public revenues had been seized by the occupation, he would be the nation's first treasurer without a treasury as well. The story that he and other witnesses told paralleled the tragedy in Haiti. Clearly, the only reason for the occupation was to bail out American investors.

The senatorial delegation returned to Washington and the hearings continued there. I was called to testify, but by far the most effective Haitian witness was an attorney, Pierre Hudicourt, who had never held an elective office and was not a member of the *Union Patriotique*. He was a professor at the National Law School, President of the Port-au-Prince Bar Association and a member of the commission appointed by the Haitian government in connection with its negotiations with the National City Bank. He came to Washington at his own expense and testified for two days, revealing how the National City Bank and its affiliates had used the State Department and the Armed Forces of the United States to get what they wanted.

The hearings were widely publicized and public opinion was beginning to mobilize. A joint committee representing the Federal Council of the Churches of Christ in America, the Home Missions Council, and the Committee on Cooperation with Latin America presented a brief to the Senate committee urging that United States' relations with Haiti be based on free consent. Another brief resulted in part from a visit I made to Louis Marshall, an eminent member of the New York Bar and a man of great public spirit. He was a Republican and I suggested that he take up the matter with Secretary of State Charles Evans Hughes. He did just that, but Hughes rebuffed him as a meddler and Marshall was furious. Returning to New York together on the train, I gave Marshall some additional pages from the hearing record which he had not seen. As he read on, he exploded, "This is the worst thing in our history!" Then he decided to voice his protest in another form. He and his associates drafted a brief which analyzed the Haitian occupation at length and took the United States government to task for its violation of the principles of democracy and international law. The brief was sponsored by the Foreign Policy Association of New York and by the National Popular Government League of Washington, and it was signed by twenty-four influential members of the bar.

There were other protests and mass-meetings, and finally on July 20, 1922, The Nation printed a full-page editorial entitled "The Retreat from Santo Domingo." We had won the battle for the Dominican Republic. The occupation was ended in response to the pressure of public opinion at home and abroad, and the unflinching passive resistance of the Dominicans. Haiti, however, was another story. Harding's campaign pledge was honored in the breach. Not only was the status quo of military and financial control maintained, but Brigadier General John H. Russell was made High Commissioner—nothing short of a dictator. But our fight would continue in the years ahead. The 1924 elections swept both Medill McCormick and Atlee Pomerene out of office, which I did not deplore, but I was deeply grieved when I learned of McCormick's death by suicide. This proud and sensitive man could not take his defeat.

The Nation had its finger in a great many pies in the tumultuous years of the early 1920s. It was not "ivory tower" journalism, by any means; we often found ourselves involved in person with the causes we supported in print. I had met and corresponded with Margaret Sanger even before coming back to New York in 1918 and greatly admired her pioneering struggle to make contraceptive information available to those who wanted it in spite of the federal and state laws against it and the militant opposition of the Catholic Church. Mrs. Sanger had gone to jail repeatedly for her efforts on behalf of "birth control"—a term she originated—but she continued her crusade in public speeches and pamphlets, and through her publications. The Woman Rebel and The Birth Control Review, which she published and edited from 1917 to 1928 included contributions from men like Havelock Ellis, H. G. Wells, Julian Huxley and Sigmund Freud.

Now she had organized "The First American Birth Control Confer-

ence" in the fall of 1921, in an effort "to show that the conclusions attained by scientists and social authorities indicate birth control is the first
and fundamental step toward national and racial health, the abolition of
poverty, disarmament and world peace." She asked Dorothy and me to be
members of the Conference Committee and we accepted with enthusiasm.
Two full days at the Hotel Plaza were devoted to discussions of health
and social problems, overpopulation as a causative factor of war, and the
legal obstacles to birth control in the United States. A private session for
members of the medical profession, by invitation only, was devoted to
contraceptive methods. We had arranged a mass-meeting at Town Hall
for the third day, Sunday, November 13, where Margaret Sanger and Harold Cox, editor of the *Edinburgh Review* and a former member of Parliament, were to discuss "Birth Control, Is It Moral?"

I attended some of the meetings at the Plaza on Friday and Saturday,
and on Sunday night I went to Town Hall early to get a good seat. I expected it would be filled to capacity, and it nearly was, when a police
sergeant stepped out on the stage, announced that the meeting would not
be held and told the audience to leave. At that point Margaret Sanger and
Harold Cox came into the hall. Mrs. Sanger walked to the platform and
began to speak, but she was interrupted by a policeman who took her by
the arm and told her that if she continued to speak she would be arrested.
She tried, and was arrested.

There were cries of indignation from the audience which now started
singing, "My country, 'tis of thee, sweet land of liberty." Then Captain
Thomas Donahue stepped forward and announced he was taking Margaret Sanger and her associate Mary Winsor to the police station. People
began to shout in protest; someone offered to take them to the police station by car. "They'll go in the patrol wagon," Captain Donahue said.
"No, we'll walk," said Margaret Sanger.

Much of the audience was crowding around her; it looked for a few
moments as if there might be violence. Captain Donahue backed down
and I was part of the great crowd that followed Margaret Sanger in a
march up Seventh Avenue to the Forty-seventh Street police station.

Mrs. Sanger and Mary Winsor were arraigned in night court and released on bail by Magistrate Francis X. McQuade. In court the next
morning, she was charged with "disorderly conduct" but discharged
by Magistrate Joseph L. Corrigan on the grounds of insufficient
evidence.

It was front-page news Monday morning, and according to *The New
York Times* the police raid had been ordered by the Most Reverend Patrick Hayes, Archbishop of New York. The story quoted Monsignor Dineen, the Archbishop's secretary:

I was present from the start. The Archbishop had received an invitation from Mrs. Sanger to attend the meeting and I went there as his representative. The Archbishop is delighted at the action of the police, as I am. . . . I am confident that in this great city of ours the majority of the women are too pure, clearminded and self-respecting to want to attend or hear a discussion of such a revolting subject.

While all the newspapers reported the episode fully, I noted that they did not comment editorially. I had seen Mrs. Ogden Reid at Town Hall and heard her express her indignation at the police action. Still there was no editorial reflection of that view in the New York *Tribune* of which her husband was owner and editor. The *Tribune* did print various letters of protest under the heading "Police Prussianism," but that evaded the essential point that the police action had originated with the head of the Catholic hierarchy. *The Nation*, however, pointed to the obvious truth:

. . . the Archbishop has furnished the birth control movement with advertising worth thousands of dollars. He has given all anti-clericals definite and specific evidence of clerical interference in government and hostility to the fundamental American rights of free speech which will be used in those anti-Catholic campaigns which *The Nation* has deplored.

Archbishop Hayes continued, unwittingly, to aid the birth-control movement. He denounced it in unsparing terms, promoted Monsignor Dineen to be Chancellor of the Archdiocese, and published his view that practitioners of birth control were worse than murderers. In his Christmas pastoral he said:

Children troop down from Heaven because God wills it. He alone has the right to stay their coming; while he blesses some homes with many, others with few, or with none at all. They come in the way ordained by his wisdom. Woe to them who degrade, pervert or do violence to that law of nature as fixed by the eternal decree of God himself. Even though some little angels in the flesh, through the moral, mental or physical deformity of parents may appear to human eyes misshapen, a blot on civilized society, we must not lose sight of this Christian thought that under and with such visible malformation there lives the immortal soul to be saved and glorified for all eternity among the blessed in Heaven.

I thought it advisable to balance the fulminations of Archbishop Hayes—shortly to be made Cardinal—with the views of another prominent interpreter of the divine purpose. At my request, Walter R. Inge, Dean of Saint Paul's Cathedral in London, wrote an article for *The Nation* which began:

The control of parenthood is perhaps the most important movement in our time. It is not only universal in the civilized world, but the degree to which it is practiced is a very fair gauge of the position of that country in the scale of civilization.

I continued my own activities in behalf of the birth-control movement which for the next third of a century continued to be opposed by the same forces against which Margaret Sanger had battled so indomitably. But a breakthrough was coming.

9

GETTING ACQUAINTED
WITH MEXICO

*It should be clear that if we wish to
establish friendly relations with the Latin-
American nations, we must begin with our
adjacent neighbor, Mexico. Both of these
sister republics have everything to gain by a
policy of friendship, cooperation and goodwill. Each has much to give and to learn
from the other.*

—SAMUEL GUY INMAN

Mexico in the 1920s emerged from a decade of bloody and devastating
revolution, and its new president, Alvaro Obregon, was trying to put the
country back on its feet. Yet the Harding Administration, under the pre-
ceptorial direction of Secretary of State Charles Evans Hughes, denied it
recognition. This in itself was a formidable obstacle to Mexico's recovery,
for it brought similar action from Great Britain and France, and was interpreted as an open invitation to hostile forces, both internal and external, to upset the government in office. Such a force was personified by
Albert B. Fall, former United States Senator from New Mexico and now
Secretary of the Interior in the Harding Cabinet. As a member of the
Senate Foreign Relations Committee, he had sponsored hearings on the
"outrages" suffered by American citizens, and the "destruction, confiscation and larceny" of American property that had occurred during the
revolution, and then wrote a highly prejudicial report recommending that
none of the provisions of the Mexican Constitution of 1917 be held appli-

cable to United States citizens. These recommendations were, in effect, the Harding Administration's Mexican policy, and it was obvious that it was designed to compel the Mexicans to give up the premises and objectives of their revolution. Nonrecognition and concomitant agitation for armed intervention were expected to achieve that goal.

The Nation kept fully abreast of Mexican developments. Early in 1921 we sent Paul Hanna, an able reporter, fluent in Spanish, to Mexico, and published five articles by him in successive issues. We also published an article by John Kenneth Turner, "Why the Obregon Government has Not Been Recognized," which disclosed the activities of American oil companies in blocking recognition and fomenting intervention. Fall's close association with these oil companies would shortly be exposed when he was tried, convicted and sent to prison for accepting a $100,000 bribe from Edward L. Doheny, president of two oil companies in Mexico. Yet this man was the chief architect of our Mexican policy which, through the State Department, demanded that Mexico promise *in writing* not to apply the terms of its constitution to American citizens and companies.

With few exceptions, news stories about Mexico were both inaccurate and inflammatory; the Hearst papers in particular proclaimed regularly that Mexico was overrun by "reds" and bandits. I felt that more firsthand information about the country should be made available and I spoke to my Harvard classmate, Richard John Walsh, at that time the editor of *Collier's Weekly*. He agreed with me and said he would publish my reports if I went to Mexico. *Collier's* was a magazine of wide circulation and influence. It would reach a readership many times that of *The Nation.* So I decided to go.

In mid-December, Dorothy, our two sons, then aged seven and six, and I sailed from New York on a Ward Line steamer in the middle of a snowstorm. The ship collided with a freighter almost immediately and the damage was sufficient to send it back to port. After passing an impatient week at a midtown hotel, we finally reembarked on the Ward Liner *Morro Castle.* The service was so bad that we were not surprised when, some years later, that ill-fated ship burned at sea. Fortunately, the voyage to Vera Cruz took only four days. Our stay there was brief; the Mexico City train timed its departure to the ship's arrival and we began the slow climb from the coast to the capital. En route, barefoot Indian women in colorful native dress offered us tamales, fruit, homemade confections and flowers. We circled the base of Mount Orizaba, its shining cone rising over 18,000 feet into eternal snow, and we noted the changing vegetation, palm to pine, as we gradually climbed from tropical sea-level to the mile-and-a-half-high plateau. By coincidence, the first Secretary of the United States Embassy, Lanier Winslow, was also on board. I listened eagerly to his account of Mexico until he said, quite seriously, that it would be a great country if it could be dipped in the sea for half an hour and all the Mexicans drowned.

I had written President Obregon and when we reached Mexico City and registered at the Hotel Genève, we received an invitation from him to a dance at the Salon Briones. There we were formally introduced by Roberto Pesqueira, a charming young Sonoran who had instructions to look out for us. While the President did not dance, he enjoyed promenading with the señoras and señoritas, and from time to time, between dances, groups of men gathered around him for lively and informal discussions. Obviously he was very democratic, and a very popular man. I was invited to dine with the President the following Monday, and as was the custom, we dined out in a nearby Chapultepec restaurant. Again Obregon was greeted warmly and informally. Evidently he was a familiar figure there; his food was brought in already cut up. He had lost his right arm in the Battle of Trinidad fighting Pancho Villa's men and he explained to me, with subtle humor, that no doubt he had been favored in the election because the people knew he had only one hand to reach into the treasury.

We talked about the expropriation of lands, and he said that under Porfirio Diaz vast areas had been turned over to large landowners, many of them foreign, and the natives had been reduced to virtual peonage. He remarked that he could have created immediate prosperity by mortgaging the land and resources of his country, but that he knew it was his duty not to do so. His hope was to create an understanding between the people of the United States and Mexico, but there would be no yielding in Mexico's present policy to carry out the principles of the revolution as set forth in the Constitution of 1917. I came away feeling that I had been talking to a great man, a statesman, a view strengthened by repeated visits and interviews in the coming months.

Telling him of my mission, I asked for a letter of introduction that would help me get the information I needed and he sent me one which opened every door. I was plunged into a new world, framed in an unforgettable first impression of the luminous Valley of Mexico with its backdrop of white-crested Ixtacihuatl and the snowy cone of Popocatepetl soaring into the clear azure sky. It was, in 1922, a world of contrasts and paradoxes, of exquisite beauty and unbelievable squalor, where past and present mingled. Along with men and women in modern dress on the streets of the captial, there were white-pyjama-clad peasants, barefoot or shod with *huaraches*, a bright serape flung over the shoulders of the men, women shawled in the blue *rebozo;* working-class men and women carried huge loads on their backs, horsemen of a middle class in *charro* garb rode by on prancing steeds, and the rich rolled by in limousines.

There was color everywhere on the storefronts, painted with intriguing figures and legends. Flowers were in abundance: bloodred poinsettia, crimson hibiscus, orange *flamboyan*, roses, tulips, lillies, and draped over age-tinted walls, bougainvillea with magenta, red, pink, orange and yellow blossoms. The air was filled with their fragrance and with such earthy odors as frying cornmeal. The sounds were equally fascinating: the pat-a-pat as the *tortillera* shaped the cornmeal into the Mexican staple, the *tamale*, both food and eating utensil; and floating even from the humblest hut, the songs and music of the people.

Everywhere there was the rising hum of revolutionary fervor, of a people reborn, of hopes rekindled. It was symbolized by the robust and jovial Diego Rivera on a scaffold in the Escuela Preparatoria, laying on vivid colors in broad strokes depicting life in Mexico and the events of the revolution. He was one of several painters whom José Vasconcelos, Obregon's Secretary of Education, had enlisted to record Mexico's past and present on the walls of public buildings. Diego Rivera was a national institution and an ardent spokesman for Mexico, frankly combining great art with propaganda. *A mestizo*, he declared himself proudest of his Amerind blood. "The only civilization that is really worthwhile in Mexico," he told me, "is the Indian. It is different from what we know as civilization in Europe, but it is civilization nonetheless. The only places where you can really see it, in all its loveliness and fullness, is in remote spots far from the contact of the invading Spaniard. Where the civilizations have clashed and mingled, as in, or close to, our great cities, the Indian's has been destroyed. Here he has lost his knowledge of how to live from the land and has degenerated."

Rivera said his contract paid him eight pesos a square meter, and a similar arrangement was made with other artists such as José Clemente Orozco, whose frescoes starkly depicted the savagery and cruelty of Mexico's struggles. Others, such as Francisco Goitia and David Alfaro Siqueiros, were commissioned to produce smaller paintings which were then purchased and hung on the walls of government offices. Many of these men, thus starting their careers, went on to achieve lasting fame.

While art was an important product of the revolution, battling against sheer ignorance took precedence. "Eighty-five percent of Mexicans are illiterate," Secretary of Education Vasconcelos told me. "We have never had popular education. We have had a compulsory education law for fifty years, but like many others of our laws it existed on paper only. During the thirty-four years of Porfirio Diaz the federal budget for education never exceeded eight million pesos. In many areas there were no schools at all. The school population which should be twenty percent of the total was slightly over six. Even in Mexico City—the show place of our Republic in the old days—there were schools for but half the children. Now the administration has enacted a new educational law which has created a ministry of public education. Last year we succeeded in getting an appropriation of forty-five million pesos, but considering the magnitude of the task this is far from sufficient. For our masses have almost everything to learn."

It was also found that most children were undernourished and that school breakfasts of hot milk and rolls were a necessity. This need was being met in a program conducted by Elena Torres, a remarkable young woman who was president of the newly formed Feminist League of Mexico. Education was given a further impetus by the Sub-Secretary of Education, Moises Saenz, a *mestizo* who developed a rural school system designed for the Indian *campesino* population. *Misioneros* from the capital visited remote villages where there had never been a school, got the people interested, obligating them to build a schoolhouse and to accept teacher training for the best qualified villager.

One of the foremost figures in the new cultural revival was the archeologist and ethnologist, Manuel Gamio. I soon found that these two professions were inseparable in Mexico. Gamio had been chiefly instrumental in uncovering, restoring and interpreting the great pyramids of San Juan Teotihuacan not far from the capital. His book *Forjando Patria* ("Forging the Fatherland"), written in 1916, was an enlightened expression of the new Mexican aspirations and a guide to their fulfillment. He briefed me on the vast archeological treasures of Mexico, the great pre-Columbian temples and cities, only a few of which had been excavated and studied. The profound differences between the histories of the United States and Mexico began to dawn on me. Ours began with the successive landings of the Old World colonists who systematically displaced and virtually destroyed the native Indian population and its culture. But Mexico's history reached back far beyond Montezuma's empire which Cortez overthrew, and the heritages of these earlier civilizations, however suppressed, had persisted. The basic differences then in the history of the two nations was that North America was settled, Mexico (and Latin America generally) conquered; and in Mexico the conquerors and their white descendants enslaved much of the indigenous population, creating a caste and class society. Furthermore, the newcomers to what would become the United States brought their own women; the *Conquistadores* did not, and mated with the indigenous population, hence the *mestizaje*, the miscegenation which is largely characteristic of the Mexican people. Mexico's preconquest heritage, much of which survives visibly, racially and culturally, was beginning to reemerge and found a new appreciation in a revolution not merely against Porfirio Diaz, but against four centuries of absentee and alien control. No statue to Cortez existed anywhere in Mexico, but those he conquered were honored in stone and bronze on the capital's principal thoroughfares.

In my first weeks in Mexico I sought information from any and all who would give it. I talked with government officials, businessmen, journalists, artists, labor leaders, long-time American residents, vendors in the markets. I visited the slums—the *casas de vecindad*—where human beings shared their quarters with chickens and pigs. Dorothy and I also made friends with a small group of Americans in the capital who found Mexico an agreeable place to live. They included Frances Toor who edited a monthly magazine, *Mexican Folkways,* and published a "Guide to Mexico"; Jerome Hess, an attorney with offices both in New York and Mexico City; Frank McLaughlin, a Californian interested in developing various business projects; Anita Brenner, a lifelong resident, born in Mexico of American parents, who was starting a notable journalistic career; Robert Hammond Murray, formerly the Mexican correspondent of the *New York World,* now retired; William Spratling, master craftsman, artist, author, who revived the silver-craft industry at Taxco, using all kinds of Mexican materials—metals, stone and wood—to create wholly new and distinctive artifacts; and from time to time Carleton Beals, then at work on the first of his many books on Mexico. All of these men and women were sympathetic with Mexico's postrevolutionary efforts, in contrast to the American business community which longed for a return to "the good old days of Porfirio Diaz," expressed contempt for Mexicans and echoed the views of First Secretary of the United States Embassy, Lanier Winslow, and other members of the embassy staff. I could not but feel that these "eyes and ears" of our State Department were singularly defective.

With the exception of John Kenneth Turner's exposé of the tyranny and oppressions of the Diaz regime published in 1910, nothing, save some violently hostile tracts, had been published in the English language about the revolution; in fact, relatively little had been published in Spanish in Mexico. Since virtually all the Mexican officialdom had been participants and eyewitnesses to the events of the revolutionary decade, I sought to elicit as many firsthand accounts as I could. Thus Isidro Fabela, who had been the *Oficial Mayor* in the Secretariat of Foreign Relations, gave me a full account—from the Mexican standpoint—of the United States naval bombardment and occupation of Vera Cruz in 1914. Although President Wilson's action was designed to oust Victoriano Huerta who had deposed, imprisoned and murdered President Francisco Madero, even Huerta's bitterest enemies in the revolutionary camp were resentful of Wilson's interference and the deaths his military intervention caused.

Similarly, they resented General Pershing's expedition into Sonora to capture Pancho Villa, however atrocious the acts for which he was being pursued.

I also sought firsthand information on current conditions in Mexico, and after a few weeks in Mexico City and the surrounding federal district, I began to travel to other states to interview their governors. They all responded courteously to my questions—Obregon's letter insured that—but generally they gave me only a favorable picture of conditions that other informants disputed. Most of these men seemed to me to be *politicos* of little principle or scruple who used their office to enrich themselves. But a governor of another type was Rafael Nieto of San Luis Potosi, a former diplomat and an enlightened man who filled in many gaps in my information of the previous decade. Another governor who impressed me most favorably was José Parres of Morelos, whom I interviewed in the state's capital, Cuernavaca. He was an active agrarian reformer, which was not surprising in a region dominated by Emiliano Zapata until his death, who more than any other Mexican revolutionary embodied the people's demand for land, the most basic of the revolution's aspirations.

At Governor Parres's home I met other leading agrarian reformers, Antonio Diaz Soto y Gama, Felipe Santibañez and Rodrigo Gomez, all of whom drew a graphic picture of the land problem throughout Mexico before the revolution. Beginning with the conquest in the early sixteenth century, there had been a continued struggle between the Spaniards and the Indians for the possession of land. The Indians had always held and farmed large areas of land in and around their villages. Some of it was lost in succeeding centuries, but they still managed to retain a substantial portion when Mexico achieved independence. Then under Diaz, by force and fraud, the Indians were gradually deprived of their lands and converted into landless peons, in effect serfs. All the land in Morelos was owned by twenty-seven *hacendados* who lived in splendor in the capital or abroad. Their haciendas were run by an *amo* (boss) who treated the peons worse than the cattle. It was the contrast between the care of horses at some haciendas' luxurious stables and the care of men, Parres told me, that first aroused Zapata to launch his fiery declaration for "*Tierra y Libertad.*" In the closing years of the Diaz regime, the workers received a few centavos a day as wages, and a measure of corn, and were kept in perpetual debt by the cost of their few store-bought requirements. The revolution provided for the break-up of the big estates and the return of the village lands to the villagers. My informants were not hesitant to admit the obstacles to a successful implementation of this program: inexperience, inefficiency, corruption, failure to supplement the land grants with adequate tools, seeds and fertilizer. There was hostility among some *jefes de operaciones*, and the old *hacendados* still wielded considerable influence. But they all expressed the conviction that these obstacles would in time be overcome.

Before 1911, the city workers were little better off than the rural peons. Labor unions were forbidden and strikes were bloodily suppressed. A recalcitrant worker could be shipped into the chattel slavery of the Valle Nacional from which none returned. The factory working day was twelve hours. If a worker lost an arm in an unprotected machine, he was turned out to beg. If he lost his life in an accident, his family was turned out of the company-owned hovel. The revolution sought to redress these evils, too, and the Constitution of 1917 established an eight-hour day, a seven-hour night, one day's rest in seven, equal pay for equal work regardless of sex and abolished labor for children under twelve.

The major labor organization was the *Confederacion Regional Obrera Mexicana*, headed by Luis Morones. The CROM had established close relations with the American Federation of Labor but was more radical in its ideology. It waved a red and black flag—*la bandera roji-negra*—and in 1922 proclaimed its belief in class warfare. Labor conditions varied widely throughout the country. Like the land program, labor reforms could not be accomplished overnight.

Mexico was a vast country. I could not see it all, but when we discussed an itinerary, President Obregon said that Yucatan was a "must." Its governor, Felipe Carrillo Puerto, was a dynamic and enlightened reformer. My friend, Charles W. Ervin, decided to come along with me. Born in Philadelphia in 1867 of Scotch-Irish descent, the son of a rock-ribbed Republican manufacturer, Charles had early become interested in the reform movements that fought municipal corruption. Then, disgusted with both the Republican and Democratic parties, he joined the Socialist Party and was its candidate for representative-at-large to Congress from Pennsylvania. For six years he ran the *New York Call*, a Socialist daily, and in 1922 he took on a public relations job for the Amalgamated Clothing Workers. While he called himself a socialist, he was a democrat in the best sense of the word. The promise of the Mexican Revolution had attracted his interest and he had taken leave from his job to see it for himself. I could not have had a more perceptive and stimulating traveling companion.

We took the train to Vera Cruz, then a disheveled and filthy port in the hands of labor extremists who abused their newfound power. From there we traveled by ship to Yucatan's port, Progreso, and took the train to the capital, Mérida, where we were met by Governor Felipe Carillo Puerto. Although he claimed descent from Natchikokom, a chieftain in the pre-Cortez days of Maya glory, he looked like the captain of a varsity crew might, twenty years after. We drove through clean, paved streets lined with houses in pastel shades of blue and orange. Then we stopped at the Governor's unpretentious stucco house where we dined simply with a half-dozen state officials.

In the next few days, we discovered that Carillo's reputation as a reformer was completely justified. He had been elected governor in what even the *hacendados* admitted was the first honest election ever held in Yucatan. When he took office, the sisal industry, virtually Yucatan's sole crop which was used to make twine, was in serious trouble. The state government took over the industry, regulated production and prices, and by 1922 the industry was back on its feet. Agrarian reforms were also handled intelligently.

"We have not taken over a single hacienda although we have reduced them slightly in size to provide garden plots for the workers so they may raise their own vegetables," Carillo told me. "The same *hacendado* is still the owner, but we fix the price of his hemp and the conditions of the employment of his labor. Then, in return, we guarantee him his labor supply, his profit and his market. Meanwhile we get his services as a plantation manager. It was absolutely essential to act as we did. The state depends largely on the taxes from the sisal industry for its revenues. By taking control of it we saved the state, the planters and the workers."

I wanted to get "the other side" of the story and located a young man from one of the former great landowning families, who was running a hat store in Mérida. "The old days are gone," he told me, "but I have no kick coming. I used to spend most of my time in New York or Paris squandering the lavish allowance that was sent me. Two of my brothers are now living on their haciendas and managing them, instead of living in Mérida or abroad. We shall all probably have to continue to work, but none of us will starve. Some of the old guard don't like him, but Carillo is honest and is doing what he believes to be right."

Other Carillo reforms included the first birth-control clinic to be legally established in the western hemisphere. It was opened in Mérida with the assistance of Anne Kennedy, secretary of the American Birth Control League. He also established a school in every village and made them co-educational, something new for Mexico. The villagers built the school and the state supplied the teachers. The filthy Yucatecan penitentiary had become a penological model under his leadership. Stripes and numbers were abolished, mail was no longer censored, visitors were admitted daily, and a man's wife or sweetheart was allowed to spend one day a week with him. Education was carried on within prison walls and each inmate became an expert in a craft of his own choosing.

Another Carillo accomplishment was highway construction. One not yet completed was headed for the ancient Mayan city of Chichen Itza which we visited on horseback. There, impressive monuments to a great civilization were crumbling, and around some of the buildings the jungle had wrapped its coils. Carillo intended to restore these ruins and make them accessible, not only because of their historic and esthetic value but to revive the Mayan pride. Two American archeologists working there, Edward H. Thompson and Sylvanus Griswald Morley, a former Harvard classmate of mine, told me that Carillo had done more for archeology than all the governors in the last four centuries.

Charlie Ervin and I parted company in Mérida; he returned to the United States and I went back to Vera Cruz. I wanted to see the infamous Valle Nacional, the hell-hole where *enganchados*, the enslaved workers, were sent to work and die on tobacco plantations in the days before the revolution. I wondered what it would be like fifteen years later, and wanted to compare and contrast life there before and after the Revolution. We entered the port shortly before noon, but instead of docking, the ship anchored offshore. I asked the captain the cause of the delay, and when we would land.

"The longshoremen are having their siesta," he said, "and we will not dock till three."

"But my train leaves Vera Cruz at two-thirty," I said, "and there won't be another for three days. Can't I be put ashore?"

"Impossible," he said. "The crew would not move the boat and the longshoremen would not warp her to the dock."

I produced Obregon's letter. The captain read it, shouted some orders, went back to the bridge. The anchor was weighed, the engines throbbed, the ship moved. As we neared the dock, the captain shouted some orders to the dock-workers through a megaphone. Lines were thrown, the ship was made fast, and I debarked.

I would need a horse to travel up the Valle Nacional, and so I went to the local army headquarters, the *Jefatura de operaciones*, to ask whether the general would help me out. I was met by a tousle-headed colonel whose unbuttoned uniform indicated I had disturbed his siesta, and to whom I explained my problem. Only the general—Gudalupe Sanchez—could authorize my getting a horse, but he was having his siesta and could not be awakened for two hours. I produced Obregon's letter. The general was awakened. He was a tall, dark, handsome Indian with a hairline mustache. After reading the letter, he ordered a telegram sent to El Hule, to provide not only a horse but a mounted escort for me. I had not asked for that, but the general explained it would be desirable for so long a ride.

So I caught my train from Vera Cruz to the sizzling banana center of El

Hule, and from there boarded a launch for a four-hour trip up the muddy
Papaloapam, the limit of navigation. I was met by a young lieutenant and
lodged for the night in a small barracks. The next morning we traveled for
fifty miles on horseback into the Oaxaca Sierra, recrossing the river five
times in dugouts while the horses swam. The trail led through a jungle
paradise humming with insect life. Giant blue butterflies fluttered by;
indigo and scarlet birds gleamed from the green tangle, heavy with tropical
scent. Wherever the dense foliage wall opened, forested mountains filled
the sky in receding tiers of olive, green and blue.

In clearings where the river bent into greater width, neatly thatched,
even-rowed houses revealed a village culture holding its own, far from
the modern civilization that had once made a slave-labor camp of this
peaceful jungle. In the villages along the way, the Indians spoke of the
horrors endured by the *enganchados,* and when I finally reached my destination, Albino Vega, the *Presidente Municipal* of Valle Nacional, a fine
old Mixtec, showed me a slender rod, heavier for its size than any wood I
had ever hefted and flexible as rubber. "This is *bejuco* of the region," he
said. "With it they scourged the slaves of the Valle Nacional."

Cantering through the long valley in the morning coolness, I tried to
imagine it as it had been fifteen years before. The slaves were forced to
work for long hours to make every inch of ground productive; very few
were able to survive such inhuman treatment. Now much of the land was
idle. Here and there white-pyjama-clad Indians were gardening for their
own use. Young boys splashed in the river, and below them, kneeling on
the rocks, women patiently scrubbed bright red, white and blue garments
in the stream. The Revolution had again brought peace to the valley.

I returned to Mexico City where Dorothy and I had rented a house on
Calle Colima and began to write the articles that were the purpose of
our trip. Then in March an event of great importance to Mexico occurred. The Southern Pacific Railroad—which had suspended construction of a line down the west coast of Mexico in 1914 because of revolutionary turmoil—decided to resume work on the project. Here was
recognition by American business interests of the stability of Mexico's
postrevolutionary regime and an indirect rebuke to the Harding Administration. It was a great feather in Obregon's cap and the presidential train
was readied to travel to the Pacific coast for an official celebration. Dorothy and I were invited to go along, and as we left the capital in the late
afternoon, I found myself in the rear club car with Obregon, his cabinet,
generals, newspaper reporters and other guests. *Copitas* of *tequila* were
being passed around; it was an occasion for rejoicing. Obregon greeted
me warmly and asked me how I liked Mexico. Across the valley the
snowy cone of Popocatepetl was crimson in the evening sky.

"It's magnificent," I said, "but there's one thing I miss."

"What is it? We'll endeavor to supply it," said Obregon.

"Where are the bandits that I expected to see in the countryside?"

"When I left the country and came to the capital," Obregon replied, "I brought the bandits in with me. I have them in my cabinet." There was a roar of laughter in which those who had heard the exchange joined.

On another occasion he said to me with deadpan seriousness, "Dr. Gruening, you are studying the history of my country. You should also be acquainted with our legends. Do you know the legend of the miracle of San Antonio?"

I told him I did not.

"Well, this is the story of San Antonio—not San Antonio, Texas, formerly of Mexico, but of the saint, Antonio, who was a very pious man. One time when he was bathing, nude, in the Rio Bravo, the devil sent two beautiful nymphs to tempt him. But San Antonio, not wishing to be tempted, rushed to the river's shore, took up his *sombrero* and held it in front of himself. The devil, furious at being foiled, sent two wasps to sting San Antonio and defeat his modesty. The wasps stung him, one on each ear, and San Antonio's hands flew to his ears, letting go of his hat. And then is when the miracle took place. The hat did not fall!"

At Tepic where work on the railway was to be resumed, there were suitable ceremonies and celebrations, including bullfights in which several of the government officials in our party played matador in their city clothes. At a banquet that evening, both Mexico and the United States were toasted in a glow of warm feeling. It was only the beginning of better relations between the two countries, but I felt it was a good beginning.

Collier's and *The Nation* had been publishing my articles, but now the time had come for Dorothy, the boys and me to return home. I wrote to the President thanking him for his help and notifying him of our departure. An hour before we were to leave for the station, the doorbell in our courtyard rang and our *galopina* rushed in breathlessly. "El Presidente!"

President Obregon came to say goodbye and brought with him an autographed copy of his book *Ocho Mil Kilometros en Campana*, a thick volume bound in red cloth which told the story of his military campaigns.

"Like Julius Caesar's *Commentaries*," I said, as I thanked him.

He nodded, then put his hand on my shoulder. "You will return soon, I hope," he said. "You have conquered far more terrain in Mexico than General Pershing."

Back in New York, I wanted others to see Mexico as I had seen it. I decided to write a book—*the* book, I hoped—describing the roots of

President Alvaro Obregon

the Revolution deep in the past, its present accomplishments and its prospects for the future. But when I visited several New York publishing houses, I found little enthusiasm for my idea. Then Glenn Frank, editor of the *Century* magazine, to whom I had sold a couple of articles on Mexico, interceded with the book-publishing end of his company. "It won't sell," I was told, "but maybe we can break even." With those encouraging words, I went to our Rockport summer home, where Dorothy and the boys were waiting for me, and started writing. Producing a book—one's first book—is always a formidable undertaking. But I was fortunate in having a sympathetic editor, Lyman B. Sturgis, and I remembered Heywood Broun's advice: "Get down the first sentence; that's always the hardest. After that it comes easy."

It was an eventful summer even in peaceful and secluded Rockport. On July twenty-eighth, our third son was born and named Peter Brown. Then in the middle of all that excitement a friend sent me a copy of the Chicago *Tribune*. Printed under a front-page headline—U.S. WAR DODGER STEERS MEXICO TO BOLSHEVISM—was a fantastic tale of a small group of disreputable American expatriates, draft evaders and wife deserters who were bolshevising Mexico and, having succeeded there, were planning to turn over the whole American continent to Moscow. The kingpin in this conspiracy, according to the article, was Roberto Haberman. The story was so ridiculous that I was chuckling until, turning to page three, I read this final paragraph:

> Although living in the United States, Dr. Ernest Gruening, Editor of *The Nation*, is considered an important part of the Haberman machine. He has spent considerable time in Mexico.

My amusement turned to anger and I wrote my attorney, Walter Pollak, asking him—if he agreed that the story was libelous—to take the appropriate action. He wrote Colonel Robert R. McCormick, the *Tribune*'s owner, publisher and editor, requesting a retraction. McCormick replied that the *Tribune* would listen to my side of the story but would not turn over its columns to me in any particular. He left us no alternative but to initiate a court action.

Suing the powerful Chicago *Tribune* was not an easy undertaking. Trying our case in Chicago would be costly, but because the *Tribune* owned property in New York, we were able to bring the action there. Preliminary hearings were held to test the likelihood of an out-of-court settlement, but the *Tribune* showed no sign of relenting. By a curious coincidence, Colonel McCormick had just given an address before the Pulitzer School of Journalism at Columbia University on "The New Racket, Suing Newspapers for Libel." The gist of his remarks was that every respectable newspaper would cheerfully print a retraction and apology for a story that had libeled anyone, if the errors were called to its attention. We had done just that, without any luck, so we subpoenaed the Colonel himself. He was a huge and haughty man, and during the course of his examination in the United States District Court, he acted as if he could not recall the circumstances of the suit. Then it came to him. "Oh yes, Gruening," he said. "Why, he was born in Germany and was a German spy during the war."

We won our action. The *Tribune* settled for $15,000 and printed the retraction drafted by my attorneys.

I was making some progress on my book, in spite of interruptions, and I followed closely the proceedings of the United States-Mexican Commission which had been established to seek compromise solutions to the problems that existed between the two countries. I had talked to both the Mexican commissioners—Ramon Ross and Fernando Gonzalez Roa— and to the United States commissioners—Charles Beecher Warren and John Barton Payne—and had given the latter two my impressions of the laudable purposes of the Obregon government. I concluded hopefully from them that the Harding Administration might modify its rigid stand on nonrecognition. And so it did when Mexico agreed that the Constitution's provisions concerning subsoil ownership would not be enforced retroactively, consented to return the railways to their former foreign owners and assented to a reduced debt settlement with a committee of international bankers headed by Thomas Lamont. The hearings finally concluded and in August of 1923, the Harding Administration recognized Obregon. Things appeared to be looking up for Mexico.

Then, scarcely four months later, Mexico was again wracked by revolution. Five Mexican states rose up in open rebellion against President Obregon. I was shocked and dismayed, and I immediately wrote friends in Mexico for "inside" information. The man behind the rebellion was Adolfo de la Huerta who had been one of the Sonora triumvirate with Obregon and Plutarco Ellias Calles, the provisional president in the six months preceding Obregon's inauguration, and Secretary of the Treasury in Obregon's cabinet. He wished to succeed Obregon in the presidency, and chose duplicity and armed force to satisfy his ambition. I had met de la Huerta who, in our conversations, had given lip-service to the goals of the revolution, but now I realized that he and his supporters were primarily concerned with personal power and self-enrichment. I had also met the three principal rebel army leaders, General Guadalupe Sanchez at Vera Cruz, General Enrique Estrada in command at Guadalajara, and Fortunato Maycotte, the *Jefe* in Oaxaca. All three were *divisionarios*, the highest rank in the army. They announced that there would be a military dictatorship and that the constitutional procedures would be suspended until 1928. It was therefore unlikely that de la Huerta, a civilian, could ever have achieved the presidency; nevertheless he had plunged into bloodshed and physical destruction that would undo much that had been accomplished under Obregon.

My friend Felipe Carillo Puerto was one of the first victims of this tragic uprising. The Mérida garrison, under the command of Colonel Juan Ricardez Broca, and bribed by the *hacendados*, revolted and then restored by decree the pre-Carillo ownership of the sisal plantations. Carillo, wishing to avoid needless slaughter, discouraged his *campesinos* from pitting their machetes against the military's rifles and slipped quietly out of Mérida. He had a boat waiting for him at a small northern port from which he planned to escape to the United States and there arrange for the purchase of arms. A tremendous *Norte* wrecked the vessel and an armed column took him and his three brothers back to prison in Mérida. Informed of their capture, de la Huerta wired Broca, congratulating him and urging him to "proceed with all energy," a cryptic command that

was well understood. Carillo, his brothers and eight others, after a per-
functory court-martial, were shot in cold blood.

Calvin Coolidge had become President with the sudden death of Harding. His administration, having recognized Obregon, was persuaded to
sell it arms, and in a few months the rebellion was crushed, de la Huerta
escaping into exile in the United States. But in my opinion, Mexico's future was far from secure. How serious were the wounds the rebellion had
inflicted? Would the Obregon policies be continued? Would the Calles
presidency, which now seemed assured, signify important changes? I had
to have the answers to these questions to continue my book; the voluminous information I had gathered in my six months in Mexico was not
enough. I could have produced a journalistic "quickie," but not the book
I wanted to write. So I laid aside the chapters I had completed in the
hope of returning to Mexico at some future time and resuming my research.

10

SUING HEARST

It is impossible to estimate the damage done to our Mexican relations by the publication in 1928 by the Hearst newspapers purporting to reveal that certain United States Senators were bribed by the Mexican government.

—PETER ODEGARD

My life took a new turn in 1924. I continued to write freelance magazine articles—one in *Harper's* on "The Conquest of Scarlet Fever" and another in *The Century* entitled "Can Journalism Be a Profession?"—but my interest in the impending Presidential race drew me back into politics. I was enthusiastic about New York's governor, Alfred E. Smith. I hoped the Democrats would nominate him and I attended their convention as one of his rooters. But the prolonged balloting between William G. Mac-Adoo and John W. Davis, who was ultimately chosen on the 103rd ballot, with its overtones of anti-Smith, anti-Catholic prejudice ruined the Democrats' chances. The Republicans offered Calvin Coolidge, and with Coolidge and Davis as tweedledum and tweedledee alternatives of stand-patism and reaction, there was clearly room for a third party. The Progressive Party reemerged to fill the gap, and at the party's convention in Cleveland, which Walter Pollak and I attended, it nominated, amid great enthusiasm, Senator Robert Marion La Follette of Wisconsin for President and Senator Burton Kendall Wheeler of Montana for Vice President.

The records of both men were outstanding. As Governor of Wisconsin, La Follette had made the Badger State a pioneer in political, economic and social legislation, then deemed radical but later widely adopted. It was there that the direct primary first replaced the boss-ridden convention system; that workmen's compensation, employers' liability and safety appliance legislation was enacted; that railroad rate regulation with abolition of secret rebates was adopted. In Congress, La Follette successfully sponsored parcel post, the Seamen's Act and a federal Department of Labor. "Burt" Wheeler had successfully bucked the powerful influence of the Anaconda Copper Company while he was in the Montana legislature, had been a fearless United States District Attorney and in the Senate had led the battle to expose the corruption of Harding's Attorney General, Harry M. Daugherty (retained in office by Coolidge) and the rest of the "Ohio gang."

I made no secret of my enthusiasm for both men and the platform on which they stood; so I was pleased when La Follette sent word through Charlie Ervin that he wanted me to be Director of Publicity for his campaign. I moved to Washington and conferred with the Senator and his twenty-nine-year-old son Bob, who had served as his father's secretary in the Senate. The party had little in the way of support with the exception of organized labor, and we had consultations with Samuel Gompers of the AFL, William H. Johnston of the Machinists' Union, and Sidney Hillman and Jacob Potofsky of the Amalgamated Clothing Workers. Our limited funds came from these organizations and from the individual contributions of thousands of so-called little people. Needless to say, no one in our devoted little organization, staffed with volunteers, had any expectation of winning. But we all felt strongly that the basic issues which the Progressive ticket represented should be aired. We were spurred on by "Fighting Bob," who on his occasional visits to our office between speaking trips, would say, "There's a ground swell, there's no telling," and we would dream a bit about what "might just happen."

Both the Republicans and the Democrats took us sufficiently seriously to denounce us. Half-page advertisements blossomed all over the country digging up La Follette's opposition to United States entry into World War I, and condemning his reform measures as "socialistic." Our office countered with a barrage of news releases sent to every variety of publication. Of course much that we issued was never printed. Almost all the dailies were in the old parties' camp and even our advertisements were censored. But every setback seemed to inspire new efforts.

We worked tirelessly all through the fall. Then shortly before election day, Bob Jr. said to me quietly, "I think we've done everything possible with the means at our disposal. We'll get a substantial popular vote, but we'll carry only Wisconsin." He was right. The Progressive ticket polled five million votes, but had a majority only in Bob's home state.

Just a few days before the election, the newspapers reported that Mexico's President-elect Plutarco Elias Calles, who had left his country right after his victory in July for a three-month trip to Europe (presumably to escape the importunities of office-seekers), would return via the United States. He was banqueted in New York by American business interests and accorded appropriate courtesies by the municipal authorities. I was informed by Manuel Tellez, the Chargé d'Affaires of the Mexican Embassy, that Calles would stop in Washington to pay a courtesy call on President Coolidge. I went to Washington's Union Station to greet the President-elect. A red carpet had been laid out; the State Department was there in full force in cutaways and striped trousers. I waited until they had greeted General Calles, and when it was my turn, he gave me, not a formal handshake, but a warm *abrazo*.

"You are coming to my inauguration as my guest," he said.

Manuel Tellez had told me that I would ride to the embassy with him and Calles. There General Calles elaborated on his invitation; a Standard Fruit Company boat was leaving New Orleans the following Tuesday and a cabin had been reserved for me. It was a tempting invitation, but Tuesday was Election Day, and I did not want to leave my duties with the La Follette campaign until the returns were in. I spoke to young Bob who assured me there was nothing of significance that I could accomplish in the last twenty-four hours and urged me to accept Calles's invitation. So I took a train for New Orleans on Monday and spent the night aboard the Standard's *Atlantic*. We sailed shortly after noon the next day.

General Calles was thought to be a strong, impassive man. But as we sat together on the deck of the ship, he impressed me with his friendliness and his simple, unaffected speech. In response to my inquiries about his past, he said that he had been born in poverty and became a schoolteacher. "That was my profession and I am still a schoolteacher at heart." He told me that I was his only personal guest at his inauguration; that President Obregon and he had appreciated my articles about Mexico in *The Nation* and elsewhere, not only because they were understanding of the revolution, but also because they leveled criticism where criticism was deserved. He inquired about my book. I told him that it was in a state of suspension because of the unexpected upheaval of the de la Huerta rebellion, but that I now looked forward to returning to it with renewed enthusiasm.

When we discussed the current state of affairs in Mexico, Calles said that *dépuración*—housecleaning of government officialdom—was the first essential. The principles and objectives of the revolution were sound, but they had been repeatedly betrayed by faithless public servants who stole the public's money. His first concern would be to stop that. He also told me that he was making Manuel Tellez Ambassador to the United

States. He pointed out that it was not usual in the foreign service to promote a lesser official to be Chief of Mission in the same embassy, but Tellez, who had served during the difficult years of nonrecognition, deserved it, and he was glad to hear that I approved. I expressed my view that the greatest current obstacle to Mexico's progress was the army, with its corrupt generals whose loyalty was less to their country than to their own fortunes. Calles agreed, but pointed out that it was part of Mexico's unhappy heritage; there had never been a national army, only bands loyal to local chieftains: a Zapata army, a Villa army, a Pablo Gonzalez army.

When we reached Tampico, the welcome was tumultuous; crowds filled every inch of the dock-space and adjacent plaza. A brass band played the Mexican national anthem. Hundreds of red, white and green Mexican flags were waved. There was a reception, a bullfight and a banquet before the presidential train left for Mexico City at midnight.

We reached the first stop, Cardenas, by daylight. Calles spoke from the rear platform, then mingled with the crowd. People had assembled at every station along the way. At one stop, a local speaker had finished his words of welcome and Calles had responded, but the train started to move just as another speaker began his greeting. The crowd laughed, but Calles ordered the train stopped and backed up. "We want you to finish your speech," said the president-elect. His own speeches were restrained and dignified; he spoke of the goals of the revolution and said their attainment depended on the determination of the Mexican people.

President Obregon headed the welcoming party in Mexico City, and there, too, the crowds were immense and enthusiastic. The ceremonies over, an official car drove me to the Hotel Princesa, where a sitting room, bedroom and bath had been reserved for me.

"I don't need a sitting room," I told the manager. "I expect to be here sometime and my funds are limited."

"You are the guest of the President," he answered.

"I have enjoyed the President's hospitality on the boat and train," I told him, "now I want to pay for my lodgings."

"Impossible. The President's orders."

I tried to make clear that while I was a guest of the President for the inauguration, I intended to stay on and pursue my studies of Mexico, and felt that I could not indefinitely accept the President's hospitality.

The manager smiled. "The President's orders are that you are his guest as long as you stay."

Finally, I delivered an ultimatum. "Unless you move me into a bedroom and bill me for it, I will move to another hotel."

He said he would have to take the matter up with the *Presidencia.*

He reported later that Calles said, "Nothing like this ever happened before." But I had my way. I wanted to feel free of any further financial obligation to the administration about which I would be writing.

The inauguration in the Chamber of Deputies was a serious and impressive affair. Calles's theme was the need to extend to Mexico's people—nearly all of whom were workers—equal benefits in education, health and economic opportunity of which so many had long been deprived. He spoke firmly but with moderation and it made me feel that despite the setbacks of the de la Huerta revolt, the government had once again achieved stability and that relations with the United States would enter a new era of friendliness and cooperation.

This last illusion was shortly to be shattered. I discovered that James R. Sheffield, who had been appointed United States Ambassador to succeed Charles Beecher Warren, had adopted the hostile view of the resident American colony toward Mexico's postrevolutionary regimes. I had paid a courtesy call on Mr. Sheffield and hoped for a friendly exchange of views, but I found him deliberately icy. I suspected, and soon confirmed that I was *persona non grata* at the embassy. Through Bob Murray, who kept in touch with the American newspaper correspondents although he himself had retired, I learned that the Ambassador had condemned me by saying, "Gruening's playing around with all those Mexicans." Unfortunately, the principal American correspondents shared Ambassador Sheffield's views of the government. "I would never have imagined that a group of correspondents in a foreign capital could be so hostile to the country and the people to which they are assigned," Bob Murray remarked to me. "It doesn't make for objective reporting." My own observations confirmed this. It was true of Joseph T. DeCourcy of the New York *Times*, John Page of the Hearst newspapers and John F. Wright of the Chicago *Tribune*.

Then out of an already clouded sky a bombshell was dropped by Frank B. Kellogg, who had succeeded Charles Evans Hughes as Secretary of State. Kellogg stated that he had gone over Mexican affairs "at great length with Ambassador Sheffield," and that they were not satisfied with the rate of indemnification for American properties. Further, he said that he had "seen statements published in the press that another revolutionary movement may be impending in Mexico" and concluded that "the Government of Mexico is now on trial before the world."

The message took the people of both countries by surprise because commissions had been working diligently to settle American claims. The needless reference to "another revolutionary movement" was viewed in both countries as an incitement to such a movement.

As soon as the story blazed across the front pages of Mexico City's newspapers I sought an appointment with President Calles at his retreat, the "Quinta del Lago," a cottage on a small lake at the capital's outskirts. "This is the voice of Wall Street," he said and then read me his reply. It was a dignified refutation and rejection of Kellogg's allegations.

I was convinced of the sincerity of Calles's efforts to settle the mountainous American claims without betraying the promises of the revolution, and I decided to do what I could to clarify the issues between the two governments, as I saw them, and to prevent, if possible, worsening of relations. I spent the next four weeks in the United States working with Charlie Ervin, Samuel Guy Inman who represented various church groups, Hubert Herring and William English Walling, all of whom shared a similar goal. I also spoke to newspaper editors and to members of Congress, and except where the newspapers were implacably hostile— Hearst's and the Chicago *Tribune*, particularly—I had a fair hearing.

Hubert Herring had an idea, which I liked, that if a number of representative Americans could be brought each year to see firsthand what the Mexicans were trying to do, they would help form a useful body of public opinion. The first of these seminars was held in 1925, when relations between the two countries were tense. The group, which I had joined, met with President Calles in the Palacio Nacional and he explained why it had been necessary for the government to act drastically in breaking up the large estates, even if that reform appeared to violate foreign interests. At that point one of the group interrupted to ask, "Would you arbitrate that question, Mr. President?"

Calles hesitated and then said, "The right of a nation to legislate in its domestic affairs cannot be properly called in question. This is not an issue that we should be asked to arbitrate. Nevertheless, I would be glad to arbitrate. I believe in arbitration."

His statement made headlines in America. Telegrams requesting arbitration poured in on members of Congress. Only a few weeks earlier President Coolidge had flatly rejected a request that he consider arbitration: "You cannot arbitrate the confiscation of American property." But the tenor of the telegrams to Congress was that if the President of Mexico was willing to arbitrate, why should not the President of the United States? Within three weeks a resolution—introduced by Senator Joseph T. Robinson of Arkansas—calling on the President to arbitrate was voted unanimously by the United States Senate. The tension was broken. The initial seminar had played a part in writing history. Thereafter the seminars became an annual affair sponsored by The Committee on Cultural Relations with Latin America, a group of a hundred distinguished men and women from half the states of the Union.

I traveled back and forth frequently between Mexico and the U.S., doing what I could to promote better understanding, and the balance of my time was spent between my research and writing and a job as consultant for various enterprises that my friend Frank McLaughlin sought to promote in Mexico. They were all projects which would develop resources, give employment and aid the national economy. Frank was an enlightened businessman who had discovered that seeing the other fellow's point of view was often the best way to achieve your own objectives. Unfortunately, I was too often separated from my family, but I hoped to make up for that in the summer of 1926 on a trip to Europe, much like the trips I had made as a boy. Dorothy and our three sons left for Paris early in the year, the boys were put in school, hopefully to acquire French as my sisters and I had, and I joined them at the end of the school term. We spent many happy hours in Paris, visiting the scenes of my childhood experiences thirty years earlier. Then we traveled to Chartres, Rouen and Mont-Saint-Michel, turned south along the French Atlantic coast, and visited Toulouse, Carcassonne and Perpignan en route to Spain. I was, of course, particularly interested in Mexico's Spanish heritage, and after visiting Barcelona, Tarragona, Zaragoza, Valencia and Toledo, I spent many profitable hours in the Royal Library in Madrid.

July found us on Lake Annecy, a jewel in the French Alps. At Talloires with ample frontage on the lake's east shore, Donald MacJannet, a graduate of Tufts and an Air Corps lieutenant in World War I, had that year established a boys' and girls' camp. We enrolled the two older boys, and Dorothy, Peter and I lodged in the nearby Hotel de l'Abbaye, a thirteenth-century monastery that had been modernized yet retained all its ancient charm. We often joined the boys and their counselors on mountain-climbing expeditions, and in the peaceful gardens of the hotel I continued my writing on Mexico, making use of books on the French intervention that I had acquired in Paris.

When the camp closed at the end of August, we went to Zermatt, my favorite spot in the Alps, and then returned to Paris to put the boys in the École Alsacienne. Paris of that day was a mecca for American artists and writers, and among the journalists whom I met there, the conversation frequently turned to Mexico. I met Lincoln Steffens who had had extensive experience in Mexico and I was glad to compare notes with him. He was pessimistic about staving off American intervention. "There are too many riches in Mexico and powerful interests in the United States that want them," he said.

Paris had not lost any of its old fascination, but I felt I must return to my task. With the boys in day-school and Dorothy safely housed in an apartment on the Rue de Quatrefages near the old Roman arena, the "Arènes de Lutèce," I went back to New York. There I once again teamed up with Charlie Ervin, and we planned a quiet campaign to enlist labor, church and anti-imperialist groups against the interventionist forces. Little progress had been made in settling American claims and anti-Mexican sentiment was growing stronger. Then our cause received another setback by a flare-up of the old religious conflict between the Catholic hierarchy and the government. It had been brewing even before the adoption of the Constitution of 1917, an echo and recurrence of the mid-nineteenth-century struggles between the clergy and Benito Juarez. But it came to a head in January 1926, with the Mexican Episcopate's unanimous repudiation of the Constitution of 1917.

The Catholic hierarchy had legitimate grievances. Restrictions on the clergy were unduly severe. But a year later the church destroyed its case by turning to armed rebellion. On April 20, 1927, four hundred men shouting the battle-cry "Long Live Christ the King" attacked the Guadalajara-Mexico City train. The attack, the government charged, was led by three priests. The Episcopate replied that the priests were there as chaplains, but various survivors testified that the priests were actively directing the assault. The entire train-guard and fifty-four passengers—including women and twenty children—were killed. A number of the wounded were burned alive when the attackers poured kerosene on the cars and set fire to them. One man traveling with his mother, wife and three children lost them all—and his reason. When dawn broke, he was found wandering amid the charred wreckage, with a burnt baby's corpse in his arms.

Two days later the Mexican government ordered the expulsion of the archbishops and bishops remaining in the country. Although the Episcopate denied responsibility for the Guadalajara incident, the Archbishop of Durango, José Maria Gonzalez y Valencia, issued a pastoral letter from Rome in which he quoted Pope Pius XI as approving all the acts of the *Cristeros*, as these rebels were called. Predictably enough, American Catholic sentiment rose up against the troubled Calles government.

The appointment that September by President Coolidge of his Amherst '95 college classmate, Dwight Morrow, to be Ambassador to Mexico, replacing the inept Sheffield, provided a small ray of hope for Mexican-American relations. Morrow's enlightened performance and his successful effort to understand Mexico's problems would prove invaluable. He had been a member of the firm of J. P. Morgan and Company, and another member of that same firm, Thomas Lamont, headed the group of bankers who were trying to recover as much as possible of Mexico's unpaid debt. But that association never caused the slightest divergence in Morrow's ambassadorial service in behalf of better understanding between the two countries.

The old interventionist forces were far from dead, however. Dorothy and the boys had returned from Europe and we all spent the summer of 1927 in Rockport, where I was able to devote more time to my book. In September we moved to Portland, Maine, and I embarked on a new journalistic venture, but Mexico was never far from my thoughts. Then, in mid-November Charlie Ervin telephoned me from New York to say that the first of a series of startling exposés, alleging that Mexico was plotting against the United States, would appear in all the Hearst newspapers and that I was to be exhibit number one on the front page of the *New York American*. It claimed to have a document revealing that I had received $10,000 from President Calles to go to England and work with the striking coal-miners there.

I was just finishing my book. The charge that I had received money from the Mexican government could be damaging in more ways than one. I told Charlie to let the Hearst management know in no uncertain terms that the document on which they based their accusation was a forgery and asked him to send me a copy. But before it arrived I obtained a copy of the *Boston American*, and there on page one was a photostatic reproduction of a letter allegedly written and signed by President Calles, on his official stationery, dated February 2, 1924, to his Secretary of the Treasury.

You will please direct the Treasurer General of the Nation to order the issuance of a pay warrant for the sum of $10,000 (Ten Thousand Dollars) in favor of Dr. Don Ernesto H. Gruening, for expenses on a voyage for the discharge of a mission confided to him by the Executive, the purpose of which is to study the situation of the striking coal miners in London.

You will please charge this pay warrant to secret expenditures of the Executive and excuse the interested person from the necessity of submitting an account of his expenditures.

The Hearst papers elaborated this alleged mission into the assumption that I was being sent to England to ascertain if the British coal-miners were sufficiently interested in the cause of world revolution to justify the Calles government's making a contribution to them.

I immediately wired Hearst requesting publication in all his papers that the document was a forgery. I demanded an apology and a retraction, and then issued my own statement to the Associated and United Presses. I said that the Hearst allegation was an absolute and outrageous lie. I had never discussed the British coal strike with President Calles, directly or indirectly; I was never authorized by President Calles to go on this, or any other mission; I never received a cent of money from President Calles; and I was not in England in 1926. What is more, I was not even in Mexico on the date that the order was supposedly written. I concluded my statement by saying that it would have been a simple matter for the Hearst papers to have checked up on the facts, but I had never even been approached by any Hearst representative. Then I repeated that the material published was utterly and maliciously false, and that I was taking the necessary legal steps to secure redress.

I knew who the forger was. He was a Mexican-American named Miguel Avila who a year earlier had offered to sell me some sensational documents allegedly disclosing malfeasance by United States and Mexican officials. I recognized him as a faker and told him I was not interested. Later that year Bob Murray informed me that he had heard that documents purporting to prove that I had received money from the Mexican government had been shown to various newspaper men in the American Embassy. I wrote Ambassador Sheffield in protest but received only an acknowledgement from the embassy's second secretary. It had taken a while, but apparently the documents finally found their way to Hearst.

Not content with merely smearing me, the Hearst series continued with even more fantastic allegations. According to John Page, the author of the series, President Calles had spent millions of dollars to "champion the cause of unrest in England as elsewhere in the world," including $100,000 to the striking British coalminers, $250,000 to Russia, and similar amounts to China and Central America for "the furtherance of the general Bolshevik scheme." It was even claimed that Mexico had signed a secret treaty with Japan, inviting colonization by Japanese immigrants and their possible use in warlike operations. Newspaper syndicates and American periodicals had also been paid for favorable propaganda, and four United States senators, who were not named, had been bribed $25,000 each to work in favor of Mexico. Naturally, the Hearst papers alleged they had the documents to prove all this.

My attorneys filed a $500,000 libel suit against the *New York American* and announced that similar action would follow against all twenty-six Hearst newspapers. Whether as a result or not, the identity of the alleged American recipients of Calles's bounty was thereafter deleted from the stories, thus eliminating the likelihood of successful libel action. That in itself strengthened my case, but the four senators were finally named and that was an even greater break. The Senate promptly created a special committee to investigate the allegation, consisting of David A. Reed of Pennsylvania as Chairman; Wesley L. Jones of Washington and Hiram W. Johnson of California, Republicans; Joseph T. Robinson of Arkansas and William Cabell Bruce of Maryland, Democrats.

The hearings opened in Washington on December 15, continued until January 7, 1928, and filled 294 printed pages. The senators accused of receiving money from the Mexican government were William E. Borah of Idaho, George W. Norris of Nebraska, Robert M. La Follette, of Wisconsin and Thomas J. Heflin of Alabama. All promptly filed their denials and William Randolph Hearst was the first witness. He admitted that little or no investigation had been made to determine the authenticity of the documents, but he stated that they had been "submitted to Ambassador Sheffield and to the Counsellor of the Embassy, Arthur Schoenfeldt, who had been unable to find any indication of lack of genuineness."

The hearings revealed that Avila was the procurer as well as the forger of the "documents" and that John Page was aware of their spuriousness. It was also revealed that a year earlier, Page—then working for the Philadelphia *Public Ledger*—had sought to print a letter allegedly written by Senator La Follette to Calles in which he promised his support and that of Senators Johnson, Swanson, Borah and Wheeler in any difficulties with the United States. But Robert Barry, the *Ledger's* Washington correspondent, recognized it as an obvious forgery and the *Ledger* declined to print it. La Follette, properly indignant, asked Secretary Kellogg, who had received a copy of the letter from Ambassador Sheffield, to make a thorough investigation and if possible bring the perpetrators of this hoax to justice. Kellogg had declined to act.

The Senate committee, in its final report on January 7, labeled the documents "crude forgeries" and added that they were "so clearly trumped up and fraudulent as not to have required an explanation or denial by the Senators named therein." But it had not one word of criticism or condemnation for the whole shabby fraud, treating Hearst and his confederates with undue consideration. No mention was made of them in the report. But addressing the Senate subsequently, Chairman Reed stated that both Avila and Page had testified falsely, and as both had been under oath it is difficult to understand why no prosecution was considered.

Senator Norris alone spoke forthrightly, labeling the Hearst papers as "the sewer system of American journalism" and inserting in the *Congressional Record* a long editorial from the Los Angeles *Times*, also reprinted in the Washington *News*, from which this paragraph, he told me, expressed his own view of Hearst's performance as it did mine:

It is a black record, the blackest in American journalism, the most gross abuse of the right of a free press in this or any other country's history. To call his proven fakes inflammatory is to understate their tenor. They accused a neighbor country of repeated acts of war; accused Japan of plotting against the peace of the United States; they accused the United States Senators of Treason; they accused dozens of high and reputed officials and prominent citizens of the blackest of crimes against patriotism; all without investigation, equivalent or mitigation.

I assumed that after the committee's verdict—conceded by Hearst —that all the documents were forgeries, there would be a prompt settlement of my libel suit. But Hearst had not given up on me yet. He sent two investigators to Mexico to "follow Gruening's trail." The trail led nowhere and a year later he settled for $75,000 and a retraction. My New York attorneys received one-third of this sum, and the lawyers in each of the other cities where Hearst published divided another third.

There would be, however, one more tragic incident in Mexico's postrevolutionary history, and a series of events that would completely vindicate President Calles. His term of office expired in 1928, and through a special amendment to the Constitution of 1917, Obregon was reelected to replace him on July 1, for a term that would begin on December 1. Then on July 17, Obregon was assassinated by a young religious fanatic. By a cruel irony, Obregon was planning to seek modification of some of the restrictions on the clergy, and had an appointment with Ambassador Morrow to discuss the matter on the day he was shot. His murder hit Mexico with the impact of a major earthquake; confusion, anger, apprehension reigned. Who would replace him; who could steer the ship of state when Calles's term ended on December 1?

Almost immediately a movement developed to urge Calles to stay in office by amending the Constitution even further. The pressure was great, but Calles refused all entreaties; too many Mexican "strong men" had perpetuated themselves in office in the same way, to the country's detriment. Calles suppressed a military revolt by a number of generals, designed to place one of them in the presidency; then he persuaded the Congress to provide for the election of a provisional president who, in turn, would arrange for the election of a constitutional president by popular vote. Thus it was largely through his wisdom and leadership that Mexico survived its tumultuous postrevolution decade.

11

STARTING A NEWSPAPER

*It is my feeling that the only pressure to
which editors as a whole yield, is the pressure of the* mores *of the time, the pressure
of the generally accepted stereotyped con-
ceptions in all fields of thought.*
—WILLIAM ALLEN WHITE

While writing away at Rockport, in the late summer of 1927, I learned
from my friend and newspaper associate, C. Harry Tobey, that there was
a move to start a daily newspaper in Portland, Maine. Tobey had been
advertising manager of the Boston *Herald* and *Traveler* during the latter
part of my editorship there, and had gone in the same capacity to the
Boston *American*. Then he had been asked by Philip F. Chapman, a Portland lawyer and banker, to assume the business management of a daily
that Chapman wanted to start. They needed an editor and Tobey had
recommended me. It was an attractive prospect and I went to Portland to
see Chapman, to whom I took an immediate liking. In his early forties, he
was president of a bank that bore his name and a member of the law firm
of Chapman, Brewster and Smith, Brewster being Ralph Owen Brewster
who in 1925 had been elected governor of Maine on the Republican
ticket.

Chapman explained that there was need of an independent daily in the
state's metropolis, that at present all the newspapers there—the morning
Press-Herald, the evening *Express* and the Sunday *Telegram*—were
owned by one man, Guy P. Gannett, and all of them supported Samuel
Insull, the Chicago utility tycoon, who had acquired Maine's power resources and wanted to export hydroelectric current. This had been for-

bidden by state law—the Fernald Act—in the belief that keeping power within the state would attract industry to Maine. Insull, who had acquired the hydroelectric resources of neighboring New Hampshire and Vermont and was exporting their power, wanted to do the same in Maine. Chapman represented citizens who felt that reversing the established state policy would be unwise. Moreover, there were other aspects of Insullism—corruption and political control—that Chapman and his friends viewed with alarm. A newspaper was needed that would support what they considered Maine's best interests.

I was familiar with the high-pressure tactics and shady practices that had made Insull notorious. Among them was his policy of making war on publicly owned municipal utilities, not by argument and reason, but by "pinning the Bolshevist tag" on anyone who favored them. Here was a challenging assignment, but would I have a free hand? I presented my ideas of what an independent newspaper should be and proposed that I be the one to determine its editorial and news policy. It was a presumptuous proposal. I argued that Chapman and I should discuss any divergence of views and that we could, no doubt, arrive at a meeting of minds, but that the final determination would be mine. As I look back on it, I am amazed that Chapman was willing to agree and to stick to it. It was almost unprecedented in American journalism. We also agreed on my salary, but one minor obstacle remained. I still had some weeks' work to complete my book on Mexico, and I could scarcely visualize launching a daily in a strange town and continuing my writing. But Chapman insisted that we get to work at once; he said I could do my writing at night.

I went to Portland about mid-September, hired a staff, engaged features, purchased equipment and the first issue of the *Portland Evening News* rolled off the press in the basement of our building on Monument Square on October 3. We were almost immediately confronted by an issue of fundamental importance—free speech. The Portland Federation of Churches had invited Lucia Ames Mead to address it on October 10, "International Friendship Day." Mrs. Mead and her husband, Edwin Doak Mead, who were both in their seventies, had been lifelong workers in the peace movement, highly respected not only in New England but nationally. Yet the local posts of the American Legion and Veterans of Foreign Wars had initiated a campaign to prevent her appearance, denouncing not only her but the Protestant clergymen who sponsored her. The local clergy, some of whom had received abusive letters and telephone threats, were fearful and came to see me. I promised them our support and gave it in the following editorial:

It seems almost incredible that individuals representing or purporting to represent patriotic and military organizations would seriously contemplate any attempt to prevent a woman—invited as a speaker by the Federation of Church Societies on International Friendship Day—from addressing that organization on the ground that she is a pacifist. Such an attempt would be a negation of the very designations "patriotic" and "military." Nothing could be less patriotic than to assault the American principle of freedom of speech. Nothing could be less military, nothing less worthy of officers and gentlemen, than to attempt to inflame sentiment against a woman; nothing less soldierly than to be fearful of the consequences that might follow from her spoken words.

The Portland *Evening News* prefers to believe no such misguided, ungallant, and unintelligent attempt will be made. It could only reflect discredit on its proponents. And it would tend to discredit and make ridiculous the community in which the attempt was made.

The opposition to Mrs. Mead collapsed. Her speech turned out to be a mild plea to have the United States join the World Court, but the incident helped to establish firm and friendly relations with the clergymen of various denominations and the *News* got a running start as a paper with ideas and ideals that it was not afraid to voice. Of course, we also incurred a reputation for being "pink," a designation that would be assiduously cultivated by our rivals.

Defeated in their attempt to stifle Mrs. Mead, the local "patriots" invited a speaker who would set things right. He was the Reverend Herbert Spencer Johnson of Boston, a Baptist who had held several pastorates in Massachusetts. His speech was needlessly jingoistic and in denouncing pacifism he remarked, "I am so good a pacifist that I left my pulpit during the World War and went overseas. And I hold a commission as a major in the Reserve Infantry." I wondered why he had not gone overseas as a chaplain, and I decided to do a little checking with the War Department. As a result I was able to expose him when, two years later at an Armistice Day service in Boston, he violently denounced President Hoover for his alleged pacifism. I had discovered that Johnson had not gone overseas during the war at all. He had joined the American Red Cross and had gone to Czechoslovakia in April 1919, five months after the war's end; and it was not until six years later, in 1925, that he was commissioned as a major in the infantry reserve. As he had made his denunciatory speech of the Commander in Chief in uniform, the *News* called attention to his violation of the Articles of War. A group of contrite legionnaires called on me to say that they would spread the word in their organization and Johnson would not again be invited as a "patriotic" speaker.

I soon understood Phil Chapman's desire to get the *News* started in a hurry. A move to abolish the state primary and substitute a convention system had been launched. It had attracted little attention and seemed likely to be adopted. The *News* editorialized against it, calling it a backward step, a return to "boss" rule, and a diminution of the people's participation in government. The convention-system proposal was defeated. Municipal changes where also in the wind. Portland, like almost all American cities, had long had the mayor-and-council form of municipal government. The idea of having a city manager was proposed, but it was a new idea and not many people were familiar with it. I knew how the system worked and was aware of its advantages because Norwood, Massachusetts, where Dorothy's parents lived, had a city manager. I was therefore able through the *News*'s editorial columns to present the arguments, widely accepted decades later, that the affairs of a city required the professional direction of a man knowledgeable in water supply and sewage disposal, paving, lighting, fire and police protection. Portland was a conservative community, but this reasoning proved persuasive and the city-manager form of government was adopted.

The *News* even had a hand in solving a murder case after the Cumberland County authorities declared the victim's death to be accidental. The crime took place in Yarmouth, a few miles east of Portland. A young man named Kenneth Williams reported that he had left his wife in their home shortly after seven o'clock in the evening to go to a nearby drugstore to buy cigarettes. Before he left they had agreed to meet at the home of a next-door neighbor to play cards. Returning from the drugstore, Williams explained, he passed through the neighbor's barn, a short cut which he and his wife invariably used to go next door. There, at the foot of some steep, rickety steps, he found his wife lying face up, dead. There were several deep gashes in her head. Questioned by County Attorney Ralph M. Ingalls, Williams explained that his wife was pregnant and subject to fainting fits. This was confirmed by neighbors and Ingalls accepted the explanation that she had fallen accidentally and struck her head on the steps.

When I heard that there were several gashes on Mrs. Williams's head, I was immediately skeptical. The wooden steps were only six feet high, and if she had fallen, one gash would probably have been the limit and even that unlikely. Nor was it likely that gashes sufficiently deep to cause death would have resulted from a fall. Moreover, the position of her body, face up and stretched out at full length with the head away from the stairs, seemed to indicate that she had not fallen at all. Without further checking, I wrote an editorial denouncing the county attorney's verdict as nonsensical and called for the case to be reopened. Ingalls declined to act and issued a statement rebuking the *News*. But I challenged the verdict again and requested that Dr. George Burgess McGrath, the medical examiner of Suffolk County, Massachusetts, and a medicolegal expert, be called. McGrath had been one of my teachers at Harvard Medical School. Ingalls yielded; McGrath was summoned and quickly came to the conclusion that the woman had received heavy blows from a blunt instrument and had bled to death.

Ingalls questioned the husband again and allowed me to be present. The grilling lasted for some time, but Williams stuck to his story. Ingalls motioned me to step outside and said, "Well, I can't shake him." I had noticed that before answering, Williams always repeated the county attorney's question. I suggested that he ask Williams a lot of different questions, or put the same questions in a different way, and insist that he not repeat the question, but answer immediately. Ingalls did just that and before long Williams broke down and confessed that he had tired of his wife and had murdered her with a rolling-pin. He was sentenced to life imprisonment.

The Williams case attracted wide attention and accounts of it were published in various magazines dealing with crime and crime detection.

Nineteen hundred and twenty-eight was an election year and President Coolidge surprised the country and his party by declaring that he did not "choose to run." The Republican leadership in Maine, after vainly trying to persuade Coolidge to reconsider, decided to support Vice President Charles G. Dawes for the presidential nomination. The *News* favored Secretary of Commerce Herbert Hoover and ran a series of editorials urging his nomination and the Maine GOP finally yielded. I received half-a-dozen letters from Hoover expressing his appreciation for our support. But in spite of my earlier enthusiasm, Hoover's campaign was disappointing. His opponent was the much more colorful Alfred E. Smith, governor of New York. I deplored the thinly disguised opposition to him because he was a Catholic, and felt that bigotry should not be the deciding factor. So we tapered off our support of Hoover, and while printing the arguments set forth on behalf of each candidate and trying to keep the scales even, we finally endorsed neither one.

I ran into the religious issue in another disconcerting way. In 1928 Governor Brewster had decided to challenge Senator Frederick Hale for the Senate seat in the Republican primary. Maine was so overwhelmingly Republican that the nominee was certain of election. Fred Hale was the heir to a senatorial dynasty. His father, Eugene Hale, a powerful conservative, had sat ten years in the House of Representatives and was elected for five consecutive terms to the United States Senate, serving from 1881 to 1911—at that time a record for senatorial longevity. He could doubtless have been elected to a sixth term and would have lived beyond it, but he had passed the crown to his son, who through his mother was also the grandson of Zachariah Chandler, the influential senator from Michigan and one of the founders of the Republican Party. This heritage was almost unbeatable, although the family's political potency seemed to have petered out in "Freddie," who was generally considered pretty much of a lightweight and was dubbed a "pipsqueak" by some of his intimates.

Governor Brewster had incurred the enmity of the Insull interests and the Gannett papers by vetoing a bill enacted by the previous legislature permitting the export of power, an issue of major importance. He had been an active and energetic governor. He had supported the primary against the convention system, and as Chapman's law partner he was, so to speak, "in the family." But even if he had not been, there were valid reasons for opposing Fred Hale. In the preceding winter the case of Colonel Frank Leslie Smith, elected to the United States Senate from Illinois, came into public view. It was revealed that Smith had accepted contributions improperly when he was a member of the Illinois Commerce Commission, and the *News* alone among Maine's newspapers had urged editorially that he not be confirmed. Smith was rejected, but Hale voted not only with the Senate minority but with a minority of his own party. A further examination of Hale's record showed that he had supported Denby and Fall in the Teapot Dome episode. As a member of the Naval Affairs Committee he should have been especially vigilant. So the *News* supported Brewster.

The primary election was on Monday, June 18. The day before, Sunday, a pastoral letter by Bishop John Gregory Murray was read in every Catholic Church in Maine. It called on the faithful to contribute to the rebuilding of a chapel—on the reservation of the Passamaquoddy Indians—which had been destroyed by fire. The pastoral charged that Governor Brewster had blocked an appropriation for that purpose. Actually, the chapel had been insured for $10,000 which was made available, and Brewster could see no justification for additional state funds to rebuild a religious edifice. But there was no time for rebuttal, and an outpouring of Catholic voters for Hale followed, although he would probably have been nominated without the Bishop's pastoral.

I was outraged and—no doubt, naively—expressed my views to Bishop Murray. I told him that I had always battled religious bigotry and had defended the Catholic Church against its detractors, but that his action was a blow to my confidence in the positions I had taken. Bishop Murray blandly denied any political motive. I asked him how he happened to pick the day before the primary for his pastoral. He said it was a coincidence; the information on the increased cost of rebuilding the chapel had just been compiled and he wanted to raise the funds promptly so that the construction could proceed during the summer season. I was not convinced. Not long after, Bishop Murray was made Archbishop of Saint Paul, Minnesota.

Dorothy and I had rented a comfortable house at 27 Storer Street and we discovered that in Maine people were slow to take up with strangers, at least at first. Also, the *News* was considered "anti-establishment," and that may have made those who were part of the establishment a trifle wary. But all this changed after people got to know us. Our social life was interesting and varied, although during this era of Prohibition, we had to surmount the difficulty of satisfying both the "wets" and the "drys" by serving tomato juice which was "spiked" for the wets and not for the drys at our dinner parties. Dorothy was asked to be program chairman of the Portland Woman's Club. A speaker was scheduled once a week and we had the privilege of entertaining a galaxy of brilliant people. I remember one in particular, Tsuruke Tsurumi, the Japanese writer, who sounded a warning which unfortunately went unheeded, that Japan's military was likely to plunge his country into war. He was later imprisoned for his efforts to avert that disaster.

The *News* carried a good literary page once a week, an innovation in Portland. Book reviews were contributed by members of the faculties of Maine's four institutions of higher learning, Bowdoin, Bates, Colby and the University of Maine, all of which I made a point of visiting. I discovered that Colby was wedged between the tracks of the Maine Central Railroad at Waterville, and I pointed out in a *News* editorial that its growth would always be stunted there and recommended that it move to another location. I also wrote its president, urging the move.

Seventeen years later, Franklin Johnson, president of Colby College, wrote me, "Your letter contained the first suggestion for the moving of Colby College. At the time it seemed visionary. . . . It was not long, however, before I realized the wisdom of your suggestion and we undertook the project." More years later, in 1967, I had the pleasure of visiting the beautiful new Colby campus on Mayflower Hill.

The *News* sought in every way to stimulate Portland's civic pride. It spearheaded a drive for a municipal golf course and urged the improvement of the city's shoreline by converting the smelly tidal flats into a park. It also took a hand in selecting the site for a new post office, or rather urged the citizens of Portland to take a hand. Senator Hale was seeking to repay a political favor to the owner of the city's only theater, the Jefferson. With the decline of legitimate drama, it had become a white elephant, and Hale had arranged to have the federal government buy it for a post office. It was not a good site; it was in the heart of the business district and a post office there would have increased the already

considerable traffic. And it obviously would be very costly to purchase
the theater and then tear it down. The *News* concluded that the people
of Portland should have a voice in deciding where the post office should
be located, so we ran a daily poll of five possible sites. One of the sites
was owned by Philip Chapman and as the polling got underway, he told
me that while he would like to sell it, the *News* must do nothing to favor
it. We did not. The Jefferson site fared badly in the poll. The site facing
a park, Deering Oaks, was overwhelmingly approved, and there the post
office was built. Chapman's site came in second.

The *News* was an "open shop." In the mechanical departments, we
paid a dollar a day more for an eight-hour day than the union scale, and
gave every employee a two-week vacation with pay, which the union did
not. No attempt was made to unionize us, and it was obvious that an
open shop gave us a flexibility which a union shop would have denied.
The same man could operate a linotype, make up the forms and pull
proofs, thereby avoiding the wasteful limitation of separate work categories which the typographical union imposed. Remembering my experience at *La Prensa*, I was glad the issue was never raised. We had a happy
shop.

We were also gaining steadily in circulation. Six months after our
founding, our readership had climbed to twenty thousand, but while circulation was growing, the paper was still far from breaking even. It was
being boycotted by Portland's four department stores which were advertising extensively in the Gannett papers. We would discover just how
powerful all these vested interests were when we finally tangled with the
Insull utility empire.

An interlocking directorate between Portland's largest bank, the Fidelity Trust Company, the Gannett newspapers and the Insull interests was
extending its influence all over the state. The Insull interests had acquired
all but one of Maine's power companies and were buying banks in one
community after another, as well as other industries, and mayors, legislators, county officials and others were "retained" to support Insull policies.

Meanwhile, a bill giving the power companies the right of unlimited
eminent domain to string their lines anywhere was introduced in the
Maine legislature, an unprecedented act which rendered everybody's farm
open to invasion without the owner's consent. When the bill came up in
the House of Representatives, there was a tie vote. It was broken in favor
of the bill by the Speaker, Robert Hale, a cousin of Senator Hale, in private life an attorney and a member of the Portland firm of Verrill, Hale,
Booth and Ives, which represented the Insull interests. The next day the
News's leading editorial asked the question, "Can a Man Serve Two
Masters?" It retired Hale from public life for a decade. It was not until

1942, when the memory of his conflict-of-interest vote had faded, that he was elected to Congress.

A bill to export power from Maine had been enacted by the 1926 legislature but had been vetoed by Governor Brewster. However, a similar bill had been enacted by a subsequent legislature and signed by Brewster's successor, Governor William Tudor Gardiner. But the vote was sufficiently close, so a referendum clause was attached to the act. The decision whether to export or retain Maine's hydroelectric power would be made by the electorate.

Under the power structure which Insull had been building in Maine, the rates for electricity were excessive. They were supporting an increasingly top-heavy structure of holding companies whose sole income was derived from the generating company at the bottom. If rates were reduced to something approximating the cost of generation and distribution plus a reasonable profit, the superimposed financial structure would collapse, destroying the equity of the investors in the holding companies. Little of this was generally understood, yet it was of vital concern to consumers as well as to investors. This was illustrated in the twin cities of Lewiston and Auburn where power was supplied by the generating company, the Lewiston and Auburn Electric Light Company. Its stock was owned by the Androscoggin Electric Light Company which was owned by the Central Maine Power Company, which owned several other power companies throughout Maine, including the Cumberland Light and Power Company serving Cumberland County in which Portland was situated. These Maine companies, together with Insull-owned power companies in New Hampshire and Vermont, were in turn held by the New England Public Service Company. Its common stock, together with that of still more widely scattered holding companies, was held by Middle West Utilities with headquarters at the seat of the Insull empire, Chicago. On top of this pyramid were two more layers, Insull Securities, Inc., and Insull Son & Co.

We explained to our readers both the cause of high electric rates, and the danger to investors, and—of course—were penalized. When the *News* advertising manager sought an advertisement from the Cumberland Light and Power Company similar to those running daily in the Gannett papers, he was told, "I'm extremely sorry, but my orders are not to give the *Portland Evening News* a line of advertising. I got those orders from Mr. Gordon, Mr. Gordon got his orders from Mr. Wyman. Mr. Wyman gets his orders from Mr. Insull. Go to Chicago." Walter Wyman was president of the Central Maine Power Company, but he was also president of the Fidelity Trust Company and Guy P. Gannett was its vice president. Newspapers, banks and Insull-owned power companies were inextricably entwined through office holders and common-stock ownership, and when the *News* revealed all these facts, they tried to muzzle us. Companies which had loans at the Fidelity Trust Company were warned that if they did not cease advertising in the *News*, their loans would be called. The paper could not be sold at the Augusta House, the state capital's leading hotel; it was owned by Walter Wyman. But our newsboys stood in front of the hotel and called out, "Buy your *Portland Evening News* here; you can't buy it inside."

The battle was on and it began to attract national attention on two counts, first as a flagrant attempt to kill a newspaper enterprise, and second as an equally flagrant attempt to manipulate the country's power resources. The issues were debated in the United States Senate, and as a result, the Senate enacted a resolution sponsored by Senator Thomas J. Walsh, Montana Democrat, to investigate the propaganda activities of the privately owned utilities. The resolution was referred to the Federal Trade Commission whose investigators would shortly come to Maine.

Meanwhile, the power interests were spending a fortune to promote the cause of power export. Ours was the only paper in the state to oppose it, and our case received a last-moment boost when the Maine Grange asked Walter Wyman and me to debate. The meeting, ten days before the referendum, was held in a Grange hall in Richmond, a small community south of Augusta. Farmers had come from miles around in their "flivvers." The hall was packed, but the front rows were occupied by legislators, lawyers, magistrates and power-company officials to provide a good "claque" for their man Wyman. The president of the Maine State Grange made a few introductory remarks and then called on me. We were to debate the question "Shall Power Be Exported From Maine?" and the speaker on the affirmative side, Mr. Wyman, should have been called on first. I rose and without going to the platform said, "The question which my adversary, Mr. Wyman, and I have been asked to debate is 'Shall Power Be Exported From Maine?' As Mr. Wyman is taking the affirmative side and I the negative, it is proper, and it was understood, that he speak first." And I sat down.

There was a pause and some whispered consultation in the front rows. Then Wyman rose and went to the platform. I had seen him on various occasions, but now I was startled by his appearance. Usually faultlessly dressed, he wore a brown shirt, a baggy coat and trousers and his opening remarks made clear why. "I don't think it matters who speaks first to my fellow farmers," he said. "I've always been a farmer and I feel at home among them." It was true; he did own a large farm, in addition to his other interests. Then he went on to say that he favored the export of power because it would lower the rates to the farmers. But he forgot himself and began telling how wonderful the power business was and how it had "doubled and doubled and doubled again."

When it was my turn, I pointed out how high the cost of electricity was and then asked why, if the power business was so profitable, the promised reductions had not taken place. I also wondered who was paying for the high-priced referendum campaign—full and double pages in the newspapers, posters everywhere, five different kinds of pamphlets mailed to every voter. Having asked the question, I answered it myself. "The Maine light and power consumer," I said, "and he'll pay the costs whether the referendum wins or loses."

"That's a damn lie," Mr. Wyman called out angrily. "The Maine consumer won't pay a cent of it."

I then read Wyman's own testimony at a hearing before a committee of the legislature the previous March. The committee was trying to determine the basis for power rates, and Wyman had admitted that lobbying expenses were included in the costs of operation and hence were passed on to the consumer. At this point Wyman jumped to his feet and said that the cost of lobbying in the legislature had nothing to do with the present campaign.

"Who, then," I asked, "does pay the costs of this expensive campaign?"

"That comes out of some money we made in a deal in Texas," Wyman answered.

"Texas?" I echoed incredulously.

It was a fatal admission on Wyman's part. He had suddenly revealed the nationwide nature of the Insull utility empire and disclosed that a vast sum was being transferred from elsewhere to capture a Maine election.

"Well, if Texas is paying for it," I said, "won't Maine people have to pay for a deal with Texas?"

It was not a wholly logical question, but the thrust went home and Wyman lost his temper. Shaking his fist at me he yelled, "I don't know who's paid you to do this! Tell us who's paying you!" He waited for my reply.

"No one pays me, except as editor of the Portland Evening News," I said. "But it's a natural question for my opponent to ask. He is so accustomed to buying people—senators, representatives, mayors, newspaper men—buying their bodies and their souls, that he just can't understand that a man can be for something just because he believes in it."

It was a bit demagogic, I admit, but the audience knew that some of the bodies Wyman had bought were sitting in the hall and it responded with a roar of approval.

The meeting was over. The crowds poured out. The news spread rapidly. I was hopeful that we had turned the corner. We had. The referendum was held September 9, 1929, and when the ballots were counted, power export had been defeated by 8,000 votes.

Gannett's *Evening Express* was not a good loser. It said the people of Maine had been deceived by "a paid communist" who had not been in Maine long enough to know what was good for the state. I was obviously the "paid communist," but as the writer did not identify me as such, there were no grounds for a libel suit. The *News* was content to let bygones be bygones if the existing abuses could be rectified, even though I was getting tired of having a "bolshevist tag" pinned on me, and indeed on anyone who opposed obsolescent, manifestly stupid or even corrupt policies and practices. Our stand was completely vindicated, a short time later, by the collapse of the top-heavy Insull empire. The Middle West Utilities Company went into receivership and Insull's Maine banks were closed. The losses to depositors and stockholders were estimated at 2.5 billion dollars.

When the Federal Trade Commission investigated the power industry, its report on Maine listed the recipients of Insull bounty and the amounts they had received. Needless to say, there were many red faces in the Pine Tree State. The Trade Commission reports, which ultimately filled eighty-four volumes, attracted much attention at first, for they exposed the power trust's activities in every state, including the machinations of the "high and mighty," their addiction to "frenzied finance," their corruption of public officials, their milking of consumers, their perversion of the sources of information, press and radio, even their prostitution of university faculty members. It seemed to me that all this should be brought home to the victims and the public generally to prevent repetition of these abuses, and I chose the subject for a speech at a joint meeting of the American Political Science and American Economic Association in Chicago. The assembled schoolmen listened with keen interest and I was urged to expand my material into a book.

The point was made that the Trade Commission reports were inaccessible to the general public, so I decided to summarize the millions of words of testimony and exhibits in a volume that was published in 1932 by the Vanguard Press entitled *The Public Pays*. The book was updated and enlarged in 1964 to include the more recent propaganda efforts of the private utilities. It was appropriately retitled *The Public Pays . . . And Still Pays*.

My investigations into the shaky Insull empire should have made me wary of the perils of "high finance," but, unfortunately, they did not. In 1928 and early 1929 I engaged in a common folly. I got into the stock market. It began when Guy F. Dunton, vice president of the Chapman bank, told me of a pool he and a few others were organizing. Stocks were rising and there was an opportunity to make a little profit. Every subscriber would invest at least $5,000 which would then be used to buy stocks on margin. I explained to Dunton that my father had never bought stocks. He considered them risky and uncertain gambles and had invested his earnings in gilt-edge bonds, which seemed to me a sound and sensible policy.

"It's a very sound policy," Dunton agreed condescendingly, "but you'll never build up an estate that way."

Everyone was doing it, and I followed the crowd. I had inherited $50,000 in bonds carrying five percent interest from my father's estate. My broker, Hayden Stone, one of the most reputable brokerage houses, suggested some very attractive stocks that were sure to go up. And for a while they did.

Every week there seemed to be a new story of the enormous profits someone had made, usually a "friend of a friend," and every day the office buzzed with a new "tip." One such tip came from a no less reliable source than a vice president of Crosley Radio who was passing through Portland and advised a local car salesman to buy Crosley. The salesman, Tim Donahue, repeated the tip to me. Affecting new-found wisdom, I said, "That's the kind of talk one should be careful of. I'm going to check with my broker." So I asked Hayden Stone to give me a report on Crosley. The report was very favorable; Crosley stock was due for a big move. It was then selling at 103 and I bought ten shares. There was a big move all right. A few months later it had dropped to 3. Other similar gullibilities wiped out my patrimony. I was not alone, of course. The stock-market crash wiped out thousands of others, rich and poor alike. It was a tragic climax to the heedless exuberance and optimism of the postwar decade, and a blow from which it would take the country another decade to recover.

The year 1931 brought a deep, personal tragedy into our lives. "Happy is the family where the parents are young and the children small," wrote William Allen White in his autobiography. The Gruenings were that family when we came to Portland in 1927. Our boys were healthy and happy; they enjoyed each other thoroughly and had no trouble making friends. Dorothy and I had always encouraged them to do their own thinking and to arrive at their own decisions. Ernest, Jr., whom we called Sonny, was twelve; Huntington, who was nicknamed Hunny, was eleven; and Peter was four. The older boys attended Portland Country Day School and little Peter fitted happily into the youngest class at Waynfleete. They all did well in their studies. Sonny was an honor-roll student and both he and Hunny were active Boy Scouts.

Our first summer, 1928, we rented a cottage on Long Lake, some twenty miles northwest of Portland from which I could commute to work. Sonny and Hunny were very much at home in the water, and we all joined in teaching Peter to swim. The summer before he had fallen into the water accidentally and Sonny dove in and promptly rescued him.

The next summer, 1929, we rented a cottage on Little Diamond Island in Casco Bay, that beautiful protected body of water, dotted with islands, which extends twenty miles northeasterly from the Portland waterfront. The owner of the cottage, the father of a Harvard classmate, Cyrus Woodman, included a motorboat with the exotic name of *Huitzilihuitl* —the Aztec word for butterfly—in the lease. We used the boat on weekends to travel the length of Casco Bay and picnic on some of its small uninhabited islands. Sonny and Hunny, who had a mechanical knack their father lacked, were both able to operate it.

One early morning when a passing motorboat developed engine trouble in front of Little Diamond and attracted our attention through a megaphone, Sonny and Hunny, shouting "to the rescue!" shed their pyjamas and in a matter of seconds were running toward our float. Peter came pattering after them calling out, "Wait for me!" trying to shed his wrapper on the way. They launched the *Huitzilihuitl* and a hundred feet from shore gave the crippled motorboat a tow to land. I remember wondering, as we sat down to breakfast that morning, how I could be the father of three such wonderful sons.

Our third summer, 1930, we rented a cottage on the shore at "Wildwood" a development at Falmouth Foreside, a few miles east of town, owned by Philip Chapman. That August we went on a tour, exploring the clear sandy beaches, rocky cliffs and pine- and spruce-covered offshore islands of the Maine coast. We visited Wiscasset, Camden and other well-kept towns. Skirting the west coast of Penobscot Bay and moving northward, we came to a region of lakes and forests from which rose five-thousand-foot Mount Katahdin, Maine's loftiest peak. We climbed the mountain, sleeping on its summit on blankets laid on the ground and awakening to the sunrise.

That fall Sonny entered Milton Academy near Boston and Hunny went to Deering High in Portland. Sonny would expect to graduate from Milton in 1933. If all went well, that would make him a member of Harvard's class of '37, and we reckoned that some of his and my '07 reunions would coincide. He liked Milton, and from the reports we got, Milton liked him. He was on the school's wrestling team, 135-pound class, Captain of Team A (one of six teams) in the senior baseball league, and played the trumpet in the school orchestra.

Late May of 1931 Sonny came home for a weekend and with some friends went for a midnight swim in a nearby lake. He returned to school

and a few days later William L. W. Field, Milton's headmaster, telephoned to say that Sonny had a temperature and an earache and was in
the Milton infirmary. I went there immediately, and learned that he had a
middle-ear infection. I took him to Dr. Philip Hammond, a well-known
Boston otologist, who performed a paracentesis of the ear drum and inserted the appropriate drainage. Then we took him to Portland in an ambulance and placed him in the Maine General Hospital under the care of
Dr. Fisher, a Portland otologist.

He continued to run a temperature and soon it was clear that the mas-
toid bone was involved. An operation was performed but the temperature
continued. After two weeks Dr. Fisher spoke the ominous words, "Ernest
is septic." A culture showed that the infecting microbe was the deadly
streptococcus hemoliticus.

A few years later with the discovery of the bactericidal properties of
penicillin and the sulfa drugs, an injection would have disposed of the
infection, but the remedies known at that time were ineffective. Early in
July the doctors decided that another operation to clean out the infection
was necessary. I was alarmed and doubtful. We called another well-
known otologist from Boston whom I had known in medical school,
Harry Cahill. He concurred.

We hated to break the news to Sonny that another operation was necessary. As he lay on the operating table prior to being anesthetized for the
operation which presented the last hope of saving his life, he saw the tears
running from Dorothy's eyes as she bent over to kiss him.

"Don't cry, Mother, it'll be all right," he said. He extracted his hand
from the sheet which wrapped him, reached up and patted her cheek.

He came through the operation, but the streptococcus septicemia swept
through his body. I suggested to Dr. Richard Small, who was our devoted family doctor in Portland, that a blood transfusion might help. He
agreed, and as my blood flowed into Sonny's veins, I hoped against hope
that it might somehow stimulate the needed resistance. But it did not. We
stayed at his bedside those desperate hours praying that some miracle
would save him. He breathed his last early on July 5.

It is difficult as I write this, even now so many years later, to keep back
the tears when I think of Sonny. Friends who had known him shared our
grief and our stunned bewilderment that a boy so fitted to live was no
more. We received letters from near and far, many from Sonny's teachers
who scarcely knew Dorothy and me, but whose lives had been touched
by our son. In the dreary weeks that followed, we tried to buoy up the
spirits of Hunny and Peter and keep our own grief as far away from them
as we could. We knew Hunny had been hit hard. He and Sonny—with
only ten and a half months difference in their ages—had been inseparable

playmates and companions. In replying to the letters Dorothy and I had received, I said that we were trying to fix our minds not on what we had lost, but on what we had had, and what we would always have in remembering our son. He had given us and all who knew him the gift of happiness.

There was a memorial service for Ernest at Milton Academy the following October 20, which would have been his sixteenth birthday. A tablet to his memory was placed in the school chapel inscribed with these words:

> Faithful to Duty
> Eager for Knowledge
> Thoughtful of Others
> Gallant and Joyous—Always

I was grateful, in the following months, for the continuing pressures and demands of my work on the *News*. As 1932 approached, we sought to promote a gubernatorial candidacy that would eliminate the incumbent, William Tudor Gardiner. Gardiner of Gardiner, Maine, lawyer, Groton and Harvard graduate, was an aristrocrat and a dull and reactionary executive. He had all the prejudices of his class and had supported the Insull shenanigans. But he had tradition and wealth behind him, and was considered certain for renomination and hence reelection. A possible opponent was John Wilson, Mayor of Bangor. He was also a blue-blood and his brother was in the foreign service, a guarantee of family respectability. But his views were not wholly those of his class. His published statements revealed his desire for improvements in the state's governmental structure, and for greater consideration of the needs of the state's farmers and workers whose interests had been ignored by Gardiner. Wilson entered the race, the *News* supported him, and what had seemed like a forlorn political hope began to look possible. The Gardiner forces were worried, and Augustus Merrill, our astute political editor, never given to unwarranted fancy, became convinced that Wilson could be, and in the closing days of the campaign, *would* be nominated.

The concluding pre-election event in Maine in those days was a gathering of the candidates on the top floor of the Eastland Hotel for a final statement over Station WCSH. Everyone in the state would be listening. I was at home and heard Gardiner, who spoke first, review his own past term as an argument for renomination. Then the radio announced that the next speaker would be John Wilson.

There was a pause. A minute, then two minutes, went by. I began to be apprehensive. Then the announcer declared that Mayor Wilson had been taken ill and his speech would be read for him. I suspected what had happened. John Wilson had reportedly been an alcoholic, but as far as we knew, he had overcome his weakness. He had not touched liquor in months.

The phone rang and my apprehensions were confirmed. It was Lloyd Jordan, Sheriff of Cumberland County, a strong Gardiner supporter. "Gruening, you ought to come up here and take a look at your candidate," he said. "You know what I mean, don't you?" he added mockingly.

The phone rang again. It was Wallace H. White, Jr., who had been a member of Congress and would soon be elected United States Senator. We were on friendly terms politically and personally. "Ernest," he said, "you'd better come up here and take care of John. He's in bad shape."

I rushed to the Eastland and there I found John Wilson, alone and bleary-eyed, barely able to stand. "Let's go to your room," I said. He fumbled for and produced his key. I was obliged to steady him. "Do you know what you've done?" I asked bitterly, as I set him on the bed. He was too drunk to make a coherent reply.

Most of the thousands who had been listening to the radio knew what had happened. The rest of the electorate were, not surprisingly, informed by the Gardiner forces. Yet Wilson lost the nomination by only 5,000 votes. I never found out how it was done. But those of us who had hoped for his election felt sure that someone in the opposite camp, knowing Wilson's weakness, had tempted him, successfully.

Toward the end of 1932 I heard from Freda Kirchwey, who had succeeded me as managing editor of *The Nation*. Several of the editors were seeking to acquire it from Oswald Villard and their plan was to have four of us old-time editors, imbued with *Nation* traditions, to run it. Besides Freda they would be Joseph Wood Krutch, Henry Hazlitt, and me, if I agreed.

I did agree. Franklin Delano Roosevelt had been elected and had pledged a "New Deal." Tremendous problems faced the country, but it would be headed by a man likely to solve them. I enjoyed life in Portland and my work there; I could not have had a better "boss" than Phil Chapman who never reneged on his agreement to give me a free hand. Yet Portland was, I felt, a bit remote from what would now be the center of activity. I wanted to be closer to the coming domestic struggle in whose objectives I believed. The *Portland Evening News* was a going concern. The advertisers' boycott had ended with the collapse of the Insull empire; some of the boycotters had gone out of business. My only concern was that under a different editorship the *News* might not continue the policies which had made it an influential force. That is exactly what happened. After I left, the business office took over and pursued a policy of offending no one. The qualities that had distinguished the *News* petered out. The paper continued for four years and then folded. Its demise evoked the following comment in a column in the *Bangor News* entitled "Cause and Effect," which said in part:

The decline of the *Evening News* began on the day that Ernest Gruening left it. He was the heart and soul of it. They never got another Gruening. So now they have a corpse. Thus again, for the thousandth time, is demonstrated the fact that a stream can rise no higher than its source, and that, by the same token, no newspaper can be better than the men who make it.

12

THE TWILIT TWENTIES AND
THE GREAT REBOUND

*The great achievement in the past seven
years in the United States has not been the
saving of the nation from economic chaos,
not the great series of laws to avert destitution and improve our social standards, but
it has been the awakening of many millions
of American men and women to an understanding of the processes of their own governments, local, state and federal. . . . In
every community, large and small, people
are taking a greater interest in decent government, in forward-looking government,
than ever before.*
—FRANKLIN DELANO ROOSEVELT
February 10, 1940

The 1930s were years of national introspection, reform and hard work as
the country struggled to recover from the debauchery of the previous decade. The reformist impulse was a direct reaction to the blatant 1920s, a
renewal of the social exploration initiated in the century's first decade by
the Muckrakers, but side-tracked by the First World War and the ex-
cesses of the boom-and-bust postwar years. The country had run head-
long into a wall, and now, dazed and disenchanted, it had no alternative
but to search for new solutions for old problems.

The reform movement at last had come into its own, and my sisters,

Clara, May and Martha, were, in different ways, active in the current ferment. They all worked for liberal causes and wrote for liberal publications. Clara's outstanding contribution was a scholarly and readable biography, *Samuel Butler, A Mid-Victorian Modern.* Butler, whose life spanned the last two-thirds of the nineteenth century, was one of the most versatile of philosophers and writers in that era of great British creativity. Perhaps he is best remembered for *Erewhon*, a novel about a mythical country where the foibles and rigidities of contemporary British society were delicately satirized; but no less important was his novel, *The Way of All Flesh*, which portrayed a revolt against existing orthodoxies, dissected generally assumed values and pictured in an Anglican family what— three-quarters of a century later—would come to be known as "the generation gap."

My sister Rose devoted a full lifetime of service to a field that had its beginnings in the nineteenth century and its apogee in the first third of the twentieth—social work. She and many others were motivated by a compassionate desire to help the poverty-stricken improve their lot. Jane Addams's Hull House in Chicago and Lillian Wald's Henry Street Settlement in New York were outstanding examples of their achievements. Rose was a volunteer social worker in Madison House, the Ethical Culture Society's settlement on New York's Lower East Side. In 1907, convinced of the need for country vacations for the settlement's ghetto dwellers, she persuaded the trustees to acquire land along a creek, the Moodna River, at Mountainville, New York, not far from Newburgh. But housing and its costs seemed to present an unsurmountable obstacle until Rose read in the newspapers that the city's transit lines were converting to trolley and cable cars and that the old horsedrawn cars were to be sold at whatever price they might bring. She promptly preempted twenty of them and was able to persuade the company to defray part of the cost of transporting them to Mountainville. Refurbished by enthusiastic prospective occupants, they became the camp's dormitories and their uniqueness attracted wide attention and support.

Camp Moodna was filled to overflowing for many summers; occasionally mothers, as well as their children, enjoyed relief there from crowded tenement life in the hot city. In time the streetcars, having served their purpose, were replaced by cabins. Rose had a cottage adjacent to the camp; we visited her on several occasions and our boys played happily with the children from the slums.

In 1916, noting that Madison House was strained beyond its capacity, Rose founded a new settlement on Division Street, which she named Arnold Toynbee House after the British social worker who had established the first settlement house in London. Soon, even larger quarters were needed, and a successful drive for funds permitted removal to a four-story building on East Broadway. In 1925 its name was changed to the Grand Street Settlement.

Rose took a personal interest in every one of her charges. When young boys and girls seemed ambitious for higher education, she always found ways to help them, either by lending her own funds or by soliciting them from others. She worked without compensation all her life and found her happiness in helping others. After many years of devoted service, she became known as "The Angel of Grand Street," although she disliked the apellation.

Rose died in 1934 and something of her legacy was illuminated in a letter my sister Clara wrote me two years later.

> I'm sending you under another cover the program of the 20th anniversary of the Rose Gruening Mothers Club I attended last night. . . . I can't convey to you the atmosphere of this gathering. The spirit of Rose seemed to be there and all spoke of it. . . . One of the mothers said: "She taught us to think of something besides our wash tubs. Now we are raising scholarships for our young people and sending them to Albany to talk to the legislators." . . . Martha and I were conducted around to all the tables and introduced to the mothers who clapped and many a one pulled me by the hand to pour into my ears all that Rose had done for her. . . . I can only tell you it was thrilling. I spoke a few words and was glad to be able to represent the family.

Rose's death in 1934, Jane Addams's the year following, and Lillian Wald's in 1940 coincided with the decline and eventual disappearance of the social work concept as it had been conceived and brought into being during their lifetimes. Social security, work relief and other measures adopted by the Roosevelt Administration in the 1930s transformed the care of the indigent and the underpriviledged from a voluntary and private concern to a public responsibility. The financial burden would thereafter be placed where it belonged, on all of society, and no longer on a few compassionate individuals. Some of their devotion was no doubt lost, but the change was overdue and imperative.

Change in other fields was necessary and inevitable after the great depression precipitated by the follies of the 1920s. For me it was a stimulating experience to work as a journalist in an atmosphere of new ideas and in what was really a peaceful revolution. That is what FDR's "New Deal" was, and no two-word phrase or slogan could have epitomized it better. Repeal of prohibition after a decade of it under three Republican administrations was a token of the impending and returning joyousness. On the domestic front the overriding problem was to liquidate the vast army of unemployed, to put people back to work, to restore their livelihood as well as their hope, self-respect, and confidence in America.

During my previous stint on *The Nation*, I had been an ardent admirer of Fiorello H. La Guardia. As a member of the House of Representatives from 1917 to 1919, and 1923 to 1933 he had taken an independent and fearless stand on every major social and economic issue. He voted for United States entry into World War I, and then took the unusual action of absenting himself from Congress in order to enlist, serving as a bomber pilot on the Italian front and rising to the rank of major. After retiring from Congress in 1919, he had been elected president of the New York City Board of Aldermen. In 1922, he was again elected to Congress for five successive terms, running first as a Republican, then as a Socialist when the Republicans denied him the nomination, and finally as a Republican-Progressive for his next three terms. But in 1932 he lost his seat to James D. Lanzetta in the Roosevelt landslide.

Back on *The Nation*, and again involved in New York City politics, I joined the chorus of voices urging this dynamic and mercurial man to run for mayor. Cleaning up the city's Augean stables of graft required a man of La Guardia's integrity and courage. But La Guardia, while interested in the challenge, doubted he could win. In 1929 he had lost the mayoralty to "Jimmie" Walker by half a million votes, and while the Tammany sachems had been pretty well discredited, the "cohesive force of public plunder" was still powerful. Besides there seemed every likelihood that even with a somewhat purged Tammany Hall, the national Democratic Party, directed by James A. Farley and New York's Bronx boss, Ed Flynn, would want to keep New York City in Democratic ranks, although the movement that was hoping to back and elect La Guardia would be labeled a "Fusion" ticket. That was what happened. Mayor Walker, having been forced out of office by scandals in his regime, the incumbent, Mayor John P. O'Brien, was challenged by Joseph V. McKee, a young and more attractive candidate who in an earlier mayoralty election had polled nearly a quarter of a million votes as an independent. This time he would run as a Democrat.

I pleaded with Fiorello to throw his hat—the broad-brimmed black hat that had become his trademark—into the ring, but he continued to have serious doubts that he could be elected. He was considered too radical by the Republican organization and with the Democrats committed to McKee, he did not see how he could make it. I enlisted a friend, Ira Hirschmann, who was then the executive vice president of Lord and Taylor's department store, and he added his persuasive voice, offering to put his public-relations know-how to work in the campaign.

At dinner in our apartment, Dorothy, who was active in the League of Women Voters and Chairman of its Manhattan Living Costs Committee, asked La Guardia if he would let League members serve as poll watchers if he should run. Of course he would, provided that they would commit themselves not to leave for even one minute. "If they tell you your house is on fire, and that your child has been run over by a truck, you must promise to disregard it," he said with the high squeak that occasionally came into his voice.

Having discussed it with my editorial colleagues, I was able to assure him of *The Nation*'s support. Finally, yielding to pressure from all sides, he consented to run. "La Guardia for Mayor of New York" on the cover of the July 19 issue of *The Nation* was our opening gun with an article by Arthur Garfield Hays, the eminent lawyer, author and active worker for civil liberties. Other articles followed, along with endorsements by a number of influential public figures, and campaigning as only he could, La Guardia began to gather a full head of steam.

Yet, as Election Day approached, McKee looked like the winner, although there was hope in the La Guardia camp that O'Brien and he would split the opposition vote. But there was a skeleton in McKee's closet. He was alleged to have written a viciously antisemitic article in the *Catholic World* some years previously, entitled "A Serious Problem." But no copy of the issue of May 1913 could be located. In every library where the bound volumes of this monthly magazine, published by the Paulist Fathers, were kept, either the volume was missing or the article —listed in the table of contents—had been excised. It was not to be found in the New York Public Library or in the libraries of Columbia, Fordham, Manhattan College, Harvard, Boston College, Yale or Princeton. Even at the office of the *Catholic World*, at 120 West Sixtieth Street, the Paulist Fathers deeply regretted that their volume had been missing for sometime. This obviously organized attempt to conceal the article whetted our desire to find it. Finally I was able to locate it in the library of the Presbyterian Seminary in Princeton. I had it photostatted and the pertinent passages were printed in *The Nation* in a two-and-a-half-page article by Paul Blanshard, "La Guardia versus McKee," on October 25. The issue sold like hot cakes. The quoted passages were devastating to the McKee candidacy.

When the votes were tallied, La Guardia received 858,000, McKee 504,000 and O'Brien 586,000 votes. For the next ten years New York City would have the best government in its history, an administration rigidly honest, imaginative, unceasingly active and dominated at all times by the warm, pervasive personality of that restive and versatile human dynamo. *The Nation*, quite correctly, was editorially critical of Farley for his "ill-judged adventure with McKee" and for "risking Roosevelt's prestige in a situation when it was not involved." But that was promptly overlooked by La Guardia, and for the next decade his and Roosevelt's administrations cooperated closely for their common objectives.

I saw Fiorello from time to time during those years and felt increasingly that he was one of our country's all-time great men, and a heartening example of what one individual can accomplish.

In the foreign field, wishing to discuss Latin-American policy, I sought an appointment with President Roosevelt. He would shortly enunciate the "good neighbor" policy, a statement in general terms I had urged him to make, which, if properly implemented, would go far to erase the resentment at our consistently imperialistic actions toward our Latin-American neighbors. These had included annexing a large part of Mexico following the war with that country, which, while history long past, had not been forgotten by Mexicans and was echoed in our time by other United States armed interventions. There was FDR's unfortunate boast in his 1920 vice-presidential campaign that he had, as Woodrow Wilson's Assistant Secretary of the Navy, written Haiti's constitution and that in League of Nations procedures he held Haiti's and the votes of half-a-dozen Caribbean and Central-American countries in his pocket. This was made a campaign issue by Candidate Warren G. Harding. Now as President, Roosevelt had apparently made another blunder in appointing North Carolina editor Josephus Daniels, Ambassador to Mexico, having forgotten that nearly two decades earlier, as Secretary of the Navy, Daniels had sent our fleet to bombard and take possession of Vera Cruz as part of President Wilson's purpose to oust the dictator Victoriano Huerta, who had imprisoned and murdered Mexico's duly elected President Francisco Madero and Vice President Pino Suarez. Some 200 Mexicans, mostly cadets in Mexico's naval academy, were killed. Although Huerta would no doubt have been overthrown by Mexicans whose revolution he had interrupted, they were virtually unanimous in opposing United States intervention.

At the Gridiron Club's dinner in the late spring of 1933, Roosevelt and Daniels appeared as of 1914.

Daniels: "I've ordered the fleet to take Vera Cruz."

Roosevelt: "The Mexicans will love you for that."

Daniels: "I'll march the marines to Mexico City and take Montezuma's palace."

Roosevelt: "I can hear them shouting 'Viva Daniels.' "

Daniels: "I'll drive Victoriano Huerta and the Mexican government out of their country."

Roosevelt suddenly bursts out laughing.

Daniels: "What are you laughing about?"

Roosevelt: "I was just thinking how funny it would be if I ever became President and appointed you Ambassador to Mexico."

Daniels: "I can't imagine anything as funny as that ever happening."

President Roosevelt asked me to present my views on Latin-American affairs to Secretary of State Cordell Hull, which I had already sought to do. I had previously discussed the Haitian mess with Felix Frankfurter, ever helpful and prolific with good counsel. He asked me whether I knew Colonel House. I did not. Edward Mandell House, a Texan, had been an intimate advisor of President Wilson. He was now retired, living on the "North Shore" of Massachusetts, but still interested in current affairs and in the Roosevelt Administration's success. He knew Secretary Hull well and if I could interest him, it would serve as a good entrée to the Secretary. So I went to Pride's Crossing, found House sympathetic and got a warm note of introduction to Hull.

I had never met Cordell Hull, but I found him a friendly, informal and courteous gentleman of the "old school." His qualifications had won him eleven elections to the House of Representatives and a senatorship, but he was comparatively new to the intricacies of our Latin-American affairs. He listened attentively as I related the whole story of our Haitian intervention and how President Hoover's efforts to extricate the United States had been frustrated by his own State Department. When I told him of its latest subterfuge to achieve by executive agreement what it had failed to achieve by treaty, he said, "I've been away at London. It wouldn't have happened if I had been here."

"Mr. Secretary," I said, "even if you had been here, you would have been told by the same State Department officials that the arrangement was in the best interests of the United States and Haiti."

Hull pressed a button for one of his aides. "Find out who negotiated the agreement with Haiti," he said.

His aide picked up a phone and called the Latin-American desk. "Who handled Haiti?" he asked. The answer came back: "Wilson and McGurk." It was an interesting revelation of how obscure individuals— "unseen men"—could make national policy. I was to find it happening again and again.

I saw Secretary Hull once more at his request. The Seventh Inter-American Conference was scheduled to be held in Montevideo, Uruguay, in December and I outlined what I thought the conference should try to achieve. We should cease all military interventions, make the Monroe Doctrine multilateral and scrap the Platt amendment. I told him that the United States had lost ground at the two previous Inter-American conferences. At Santiago, Chile, in 1923, efforts to modify United States domination of the Pan-American Union had been opposed by our delegation.

Mexico had not been represented at all because we had not yet recognized the Obregon government; and to make matters worse, the Haitian and Dominican delegations had joined forces to protest United States intervention in their countries, had distributed pamphlets to all the delegates and had aired their grievances in a receptive Chilean press, which spread their protests all over Latin America.

The 1928 conference at Havana, I told the Secretary further, had also been a disaster. Secretary of State and Delegation Chairman Charles Evans Hughes had firmly rebuffed every Latin-American effort to bring up the issue of American intervention and had indicated that it would continue to be practiced at the discretion of the United States. He had also let it be known in no uncertain terms that the Monroe Doctrine was unilateral and would remain so. Several delegates from various countries had resigned in protest and it was certain that these suppressed issues would come up with increased vehemence in Montevideo.

I felt that Hull was sympathetic to my point of view, and those feelings were confirmed in mid-October when I received a letter from him. He said that the President wished to appoint me as an advisor to the United States delegation to the Montevideo Conference. I was elated, but it would not be easy for me to get away. Henry Hazlitt was leaving *The Nation* to go with the *American Mercury*, and Freda Kirchwey and Joe Krutch would have to do the work that four of us had shared. And when I learned that the six-member delegation would include Alexander Weddell, our Ambassador to Argentina, J. Butler Wright, our Minister to Uruguay, and Spruille Braden of New York, I had serious reservations. Braden was of a family that owned vast copper deposits in Chile. He had wanted to be our Ambassador to Chile, but as he had married a Chilean, that was ruled out and he was given a seat on the delegation as a consolation prize.

I saw Secretary Hull and told him of my reservations. "The way this delegation is shaping up," I said, "you will get completely reactionary advice—no change from our present dollar diplomacy—and my views won't be considered at all."

"That is all the more reason I shall need you," Hull said sweetly, "and I assure you that you will be able to see me at any time and give me the benefit of your ideas."

Thus reassured, I said, "Why don't you name someone to the delegation who is not a career diplomat or a businessman with investments in Latin America—a woman, a poet, a professor, a college president?"

Hull said two places were to be filled, and one would have to go to a Republican. Under consideration were William S. Culbertson who had been our Ambassador to Chile, and Reuben Clark who had been Under-

Secretary of State. Hull asked me which I would recommend. I did not know Culbertson but I had come to know Clark in Mexico where he was Ambassador Morrow's right hand. I thought that some of Morrow might have rubbed off on Clark, and said so. He was appointed. For the sixth member, Hull named Sophonisba P. Breckenridge, Professor of Social Work at the University of Chicago. "She fills two of your requirements, a woman and a professor," he said to me with a smile.

A big crowd saw us off on November 11 at the Hudson River pier of the Munson Line steamer *American Legion*. On board, besides Secretary and Mrs. Hull, were Spruille and Maria Braden, Miss Breckenridge, Reuben Clark and a number of advisors and assistants. I was grateful that Hull himself was heading the delegation. It was an indication of the high priority Roosevelt put on his Good Neighbor Policy, and it precluded Sumner Welles being a delegate. To me, the stiff, unapproachable Under-Secretary symbolized the State Department's *status quo* policies.

Both the Cuban and Haitian delegations were aboard. The Cubans were Angel Alberto Giraudy, a gaunt windswept figure; Herminio Portell-Vilá, a youthful professor of history at the University of Havana; and Alfredo Nogueira. It would have been a good opportunity for Secretary Hull to get a firsthand account of Cuba's problems, but he took what seemed to me the regrettable position that since the United States had not recognized the administration of Grau San Martin, he could have no intercourse with its delegates. Nevertheless, he said to me, "You go mingle with those Cubans. Tell them Ah'm their fwiend." (Cordell Hull had a defect in his speech. He could not pronounce his *r*s. He also dropped his terminal *g*s. and had a Tennessee accent.) I did mingle with the Cubans. They were depressed about our Cuban policy and the continued nonrecognition of Grau San Martin. I also got to know the Haitian delegation and had no difficulty in arranging for them to see Hull in person.

To my surprise, the American delegation met for the first time on board. There had been no prior briefings or conferences. Secretary Hull explained that the President had decided we should not get involved in economic and financial questions which would be divisive. Our purpose was simply to make friends, and there was hope that our mutual treaty of nonaggression between the American States would be ratified. When it was pointed out that the Foreign Minister of Argentina, Carlos Saavedra Lamas, had a similar treaty and had been trying to line up support for it in various countries, Secretary Hull asked what we should do about it.

Reuben Clark said, "He is just stealing our stuff; we should have nothing to do with it."

I asked whether the Argentine proposal differed from ours. The answer was that they were virtually identical. "Then why not support it and win his friendship?" I suggested. Hull agreed.

I was disappointed by what seemed to me a wholly negligible agenda and felt I had better raise the issue I considered most important when alone with Hull, as I suspected that the career State Department men would oppose my ideas. I had plenty of opportunity as Hull and I sat together on deck.

"Mr. Secretary," I said, "the one issue that concerns every Latin-American country is intervention. We should come out strongly for a resolution abjuring it."

"Ah'm against intervention," Hull said, "but what am Ah goin' to do when chaos breaks out in one of those countries, and armed bands go woamin' awound, burnin', pillagin' and murdewin' Amewicans? How can I tell mah people that we cain't intervene?"

"Mr. Secretary, that usually happens *after* we have intervened."

"If Ah were to come out against intervention," Hull said, "the Hearst papers would attack me fwom coast to coast."

"Mr. Secretary," I responded, "if I could achieve that for you, I would feel that I had not come in vain."

Hull looked doubtful. "Wemember, Gwuening, Mr. Woosevelt and Ah have to be weelected. You don't have to wun."

"Coming out against intervention would help you get reelected." I insisted. I was able to speak so frankly because I was not a State Department employee. I doubted that any bureaucrat would feel free to argue so vigorously with his chief, and to disagree with him.

The other members of the delegation joined us when we landed in Montevideo and we were lodged at the Hotel Parque. The inaugural session at the Legislative Palace on December 3 was addressed by Dr. Gabriel Terra, President of Uruguay. The opening plenary session, which was scheduled for the next day, was to be addressed by a representative of the host country, Dr. Alberto Mañé, and the response—according to established practice—would be by the head of the delegation from the country which had held the previous conference, Cuba. But it was reported that the chief of the Cuban delegation was not to be permitted to speak because his address would contain an attack on the United States.

I blew up and asked Secretary Hull if the report I had heard was true. His reply was: "Ah had nothing to do with it."

I nearly exploded. "No one will believe that. Everyone knows that what the US says here goes. We have got to stand for freedom of speech."

"Whah," said Secretary Hull somewhat petulantly, "should we let them attack us? Ah fought in Cuba for the Cubans. Ah got fever down there."

"Mr. Secretary," I said, "if Cuba is prevented from speaking, we might as well pack up and go home. It doesn't make any difference what's in the speech. Even if it's a violent attack, it will probably get no more than a couple of inches in the New York *Times*. But if it is not given, it will be published in full all over the world as the speech the United States suppressed."

"Ah had nothing to do with it. That's up to the Uwuguayans," said Hull, and walked away.

I was greatly concerned and went to see Ambassador Wright. "Are you responsible for suppressing the Cubans' speech?" I asked accusingly.

"Well, we don't want to start off with disharmony," he said. "But it wasn't our decision. It was Uruguay's."

I went back to Hull. "Do you mind if I see the Cubans and get a look at that speech? Maybe it can be modified."

"Go ahead by all means," Hull said.

I had established friendly relations with the Cuban delegation on the journey, and when I asked them if their speech was to be suppressed, they said it was true.

"Do you mind if I read it?"

"Of course not."

I read the speech with mounting amazement. The United States was not even mentioned. It was a typically Latin-American oration, an ornate, fulsome, emotional elaboration of the Cubans' suffering and their thwarted aspirations for freedom. It did contain, however, one symbolic reference to the fears generated in the hearts of the people in small

United States Delegation to the Seventh Inter-American Conference, Montevideo, 1933

Latin-American countries when eagles appeared in the northern sky. And the final paragraph was an apostrophe to non-Cubans who had helped Cuba win its independence from Spain, whom the speech named individually, together with their country.

"There is absolutely no reason why you shouldn't make this speech," I said with all the emphasis I could muster. "But I have just one suggestion. Did you know that Cordell Hull fought for you in Cuba and contracted fever there? Can't you add his name to the list of the men who fought for your independence?"

"Of course. We didn't know that he had fought in Cuba, we'll be glad to add his name."

I went back to Hull. "There's not a word in that speech that is objectionable," I said. "If I had written it, I could have done a much better job denouncing our policy in Cuba."

Word got around that the Cubans would speak, and there was tense expectancy as to what their spokesman would say. I sat three seats away from where Ambassador Wright was translating the speech to Hull as it was being delivered. Hull looked apprehensive, but when the final sentences were delivered and the speaker said that it gave him "pleasure to record that the Honorable Cordell Hull, now United States Secretary of State, in 1898 was one of those brave Americans who fought side by side with us against Spain," Hull beamed. There was tremendous and prolonged applause. The day was saved.

But soon another issue loomed. The Argentine delegation headed by its Minister of Foreign Affairs, Carlos Saavedra Lamas, was very hostile. The Buenos Aires newspapers coming over daily by air reflected that hostility in editorials, news articles and cartoons.

When I walked into the Secretary's study where a delegation conference was scheduled, the gloom was unmistakable.

"What's wrong?" I asked.

"Haven't you heard?" I hadn't.

"Saavedra Lamas has introduced a resolution providing for an observer from the mother-country, Spain."

"What's so bad about that?" I asked.

"Can't you see, Gruening," said Clark. "It will be an observer at this Conference. At the next it will be a delegate from Spain. It will then no longer be an Inter-American Conference. It will be an Inter-Hispanic Conference. The Spanish-speaking countries outnumber us eighteen to three if you count Brazil and Haiti on our side. They'll run it right through. We haven't a chance to stop it."

It struck me as a wholly needless alarm. "There's nothing to that," I said airily.

"What do you suggest?" asked Clark.

"That's easy. We should support the resolution in principle. We should say that it will enrich our discussions. We should get the Brazilians to request an observer from their mother-country, Portugal. I think I can get my Haitian friends to request an observer from their mother-country, France, maybe one from Africa.

"We should explain that we're all for it, but that we're embarrassed, because if we ask for an observer from the mother-country, England, the Irish will get mad, and we'll have to yield because we can't afford to lose the Irish vote. But if Ireland is in, we'll also have to have an observer from Scotland and one from Wales."

By this time the gloom was lifting. The group was beginning to laugh.

"Wait a minute," I said. "I'm not through yet. If we have four from the British Isles, how about our Germans, Dutch, French, Italians, Scandinavians and all the rest that made America? We can explain that we'd be in a pack of trouble, if we leave them out. But how many mother-countries can we insist upon?"

The word spread. In a few hours the idea of mother-country observers was laughed out of existence.

Our days were not all work. It was very hot and an inviting beach lined the bay in front of our hotel. Hubert Herring, who had come down by plane, and I decided to go in swimming. But the water was very dirty—and smelly—although it was part of the sea. As we emerged from our first dip we saw hundreds of floating objects which at first we took to be jellyfish. They proved to be condoms. The city's sewers were emptying into the bay. We returned to the shore.

"There's the title for your magazine article," I said to Hubert: "Across South America; or from Condom to Condor."

Cordell Hull was doing a magnificent job in public relations. He called personally on each of the delegations' chairmen. In the past, I was informed, they were expected first to call on the head of the United States delegation. Hull was winning widespread sympathy. But Saavedra Lamas was still hostile. I had a firsthand account of how Hull met the problem.

He said to Saavedra that of all the great names whose fame had reached him for years, that of Carlos Saavedra Lamas ranked foremost. (Hull had never heard of him till we were on the boat.) Now there was an unfortunate war going on in the Chaco, the swampy area of the Bolivian lowlands bordering on Paraguay. Bolivians and Paraguayans were engaged in bloody combat. This was a tragic negation of all the wonderful peace efforts for which you, sir, have striven for years. It is a negation of our hopes for your peace treaty which we of the United States delegation are strongly supporting. Now if the great Argentine statesman whom I have the honor to be addressing could see his way clear to go up into the Chaco to mediate between the contending forces, bringing his great prestige to bear upon them, he could then become not only the great hemispheric figure that he already was, but a world figure, and if successful, he, Cordell Hull, would recommend him for the Nobel Peace Prize.

Saavedra Lamas accepted both the encomium and the assignment. He went to the Chaco. An armistice was arranged while the Montevideo Conference was still in session. Peace followed. (Subsequently Cordell Hull did recommend Saavedra Lamas for the Nobel Peace Prize and it was awarded him.)

Saavedra Lamas had become our friend!

Hull's task was not being made any easier by the State Department back in Washington. Despite Sumner Welles's forecast that the Grau San Martin regime could not last a week, it had lasted four months without United States recognition; yet it was clear that the State Department's determination to impose its choice would prevail.

Hull had assured the Haitian delegation in an oral statement that was then reduced to writing that he would oppose the maintenance of the fiscal Occupation for the life of the loan which had been imposed upon them and that he would seek to end the financial as well as the military control speedily. It was therefore a shock when the wires brought the news that President Roosevelt had written President Vincent of Haiti in response to a letter from him that the United States had "an unescapable obligation to the bond holders to carry out the Treaty of 1915 and the Protocol of 1917," and to remain in occupation until that was done.

It was hard for me to believe it could happen again. Cordell Hull was visibly upset, the Haitian delegates were flabbergasted, and the whole American image which Cordell Hull had built up so painstakingly was severely damaged. (The explanation which was soon forthcoming was that President Roosevelt had signed a letter drafted for him which represented the policy of Wilson and McGurk; although the draft had been submitted by the prestigious William Phillips, Acting Secretary.)

Moreover, Cordell was now about to face an issue in the Conference —the issue of intervention. I had not been able to persuade him that we should not wait till it was brought up in a plenary session when the recommendations of the Committee on the Rights and Duties of States would be presented. To me the success or failure of the Conference would hang on our taking a positive stand against intervention.

The day before as I came into his room Hull was smiling.

"Well, it's settled," he said. When the resolution against intervention is presented, Saavedra Lamas will take the floor to say that this is too complex a matter to be settled right here and now, and he will move to have it referred to a learned committee of jurists who will meet in Rio next year."

"That will never happen," I said. "No Latin-American delegate will do other than support the resolution against intervention."

"You're a bright young man," said the Secretary, "but you're quite mistaken this time. It's all arranged and Saavedra Lamas's motion will be seconded by Cruchaga Tocornal, the Chilean Foreign Minister."

"I can't believe it," I said, "and we shouldn't allow it to happen."

"You'll see," said Secretary Hull, "and I will say that I agree with the wise recommendations of the distinguished Argentine Foreign Minister."

I shook my head, sadly.

The plenary session was packed to the limit. Raimondo Rivas of Colombia, Chairman of the Committee on the Rights and Duties of States, made a vigorous attack on the practice of intervention. It violated all the principles of sovereignty and freedom. He made no direct reference to the United States but no one could mistake the target that was implicit in his remarks.

Then Saavedra Lamas took the floor. Far from proposing a referral of the resolution to a future committee he vigorously supported Rivas's presentation.

I was sitting five seats from where Butler Wright was translating to Hull. I could not resist sending him a note. "Your dear friend has let you down, now do your stuff."

Hull read it, pulled a manuscript from his pocket and began writing. In the meantime Cruchaga Tocornal also supported the resolution against intervention.

Then Hull rose to the occasion magnificently. He, personally, he said, had always opposed intervention. "May I," he said, continuing with the deep sincerity which he felt and the historic occasion required, "for a moment direct attention to the significance of this broad policy as my country is steadily carrying it into effect under the Roosevelt Administration, the extent and nature of which should be familiar to each of the nations here represented? My government is doing its utmost, with due regard to commitments made in the past, to end with all possible speed engagements which have been set up by previous circumstances. There are some engagements which can be removed more speedily than others. In some instances disentanglement from obligations of another era can only be brought about through the exercise of some patience. The United States is determined that its new policy of the New Deal—of enlightened liberalism—shall have full effect and shall be recognized in its fullest import by its neighbors. The people of my country strongly feel that the so-called right-of-conquest must forever be banished from this hemisphere and, most of all, they shun and reject that so-called right for themselves. The New Deal indeed would be an empty boast if it did not mean that."

When he concluded, the whole assembly broke out in thunderous applause and cheers.

The Seventh-Inter-American Conference was a success—so acclaimed throughout Latin America and at home. Every delegation had signed everyone else's peace treaty. A new high point in hemispheric solidarity and friendship had been achieved. Secretary Hull had demonstrated how much one individual imbued with high purpose can accomplish.

Even before we left South America came the gratifying news of President Roosevelt's ratification of our efforts. At the dinner of the Woodrow Wilson foundation on December 28 he said:

> The definite policy of the United States from now on is one opposed to armed intervention. The maintenance of constitutional government in other nations is not a sacred obligation devolving upon the United States alone. The maintenance of law and the orderly processes of government in this hemisphere is the concern of each individual nation within its borders first of all.
>
> It is only when the failure of orderly processes affects the nations of the continent, that it becomes their concern, and the point to stress is that in such event it becomes the joint concern of a whole continent in which we are all neighbors.

This made headlines in the newspapers of Buenos Aires where Hubert Herring and I spent four days. We then flew over the Andes in a tri-motored Ford plane to Santiago, awed by the stupendous scenery as we passed between Aconcagua, the Western Hemisphere's loftiest peak, and the great bulk of Tupungato only a few hundred feet lower. We dallied two days at Santiago and at Valparaiso, discovering as we swam at Viña del Mar, the coldness of the Humboldt current. We stopped at Lima and planned to visit Cuzco and Quito. But our program was upset by my coming down with amoebic dysentery. Whether it was contracted in the sewage-laden bay at Montevideo or from the screenless dining room of the Hotel Parque where the flies were legion, I shall never know. But the British-American Hospital knew just what to do and in two weeks I was on my way home.

Stopping off at Havana I was met by our new Ambassador Jefferson Caffery. Grau San Martin had retired three days before, having lasted four and a half months. He had been succeeded by Carlos Hevia, a fine young man, a graduate of the United States Naval Academy, who was acceptable to the followers of Grau San Martin but not to Caffery. I called on Hevia at the Gubernatorial palace and found him and his wife planning, as new householders do, the rearrangement of the furniture. Twenty-four hours later they were out, replaced by Colonel Carlos Mendieta whom Caffery had appointed as Cuba's new chief.

"Don't you think we should recognize him?" Caffery asked me.

I had to laugh. "Of course we should," I said. "But wouldn't it look pretty crude if we gave Mendieta instant approval when we had denied it to Grau San Martin for months? Shouldn't we wait at least a week and be apparently going through the motions of determining his qualifications?" (He was recognized after five days.)

I was feeling pretty cynical about our past performance in Cuba, but was hopeful that the forthcoming scrapping of the Platt amendment which Hull had promised he would work for, would phase out our ambassadorial determination of not only a Cuban president's incumbency, but that of the presidents in any Caribbean or Central-American country. For a quarter of a century their tenure in office had depended pretty much on the affirmative nod or the negative shake of the head of the State Department. Nicaragua—from which we had finally withdrawn the Marines but installed a dynasty agreeable to the State Department—was a case in point.

On my return I communicated with Secretary Hull in the effort to button up Caribbean matters. On February 7, 1934, he wrote me:

We are ready to open negotiations on all phases of the Platt amendment. It seems to be desirable first to get the financial and sugar phases somewhat in hand as the first and immediate step of the next few days. [The Platt amendment was abrogated in May.] I am having every attention given to overhauling the San Domingan, the Haitian and other conditions which give concern.

And so Hull reversed the Haitian policy established by the State Department career boys in his absence. A new treaty abrogating the forced commitments of 1915 and 1919 was drawn up and approved by the Haitian assembly and the Congress. The evacuation of both military and financial personnel did not wait until the expiration of the 1915 Treaty in 1936.

But there was more. I went to see James H. Perkins, the new president of the National City Bank in New York, who had replaced the discredited Charles E. Mitchell. I told him the whole Haitian story, including the piratical role of the bank under its previous managements. He agreed to sell its branch in Haiti to Haiti on reasonable terms and sever all other entanglements.

So the final chapter in our Occupation provided a generous and creditable *dénouement*. Haiti's future, for better or worse, was in its own hands. The sequel in the Dominican Republic where a bloody monster had seized power was a possible eventuality in Haiti, and in Cuba. But entry by *force majeure* of an alien power, even if well-intentioned, offered no solution. Each nation, each people, had to learn through trial and error to be the master of its fate. Its salvation, sooner or later, would have to depend upon itself.

I was able at long last to write "At Last We're Getting Out of Haiti" in the June 20 issue of *The Nation* where we had begun the fight fourteen years before, and to describe in detail the rise, wane and imminent ending of "dollar" or "gunboat" diplomacy in a two-and-a-half-page article in the New York *Times* Magazine, Sunday, June 19, 1934. It was headlined:

OUR ERA OF 'IMPERIALISM' NEARS ITS END

*"Manifest Destiny" Is Giving Way to the New Policy of
'Equal Dealing With All Nations' "*

13

IN METROPOLITAN
JOURNALISM—BRIEFLY

*The misfortune of the liberal is that he
must suffer the censure of both his friends
and his enemies. His friends are particularly
severe, for naturally enough, they hold him
to much higher standards of intellectual de-
portment than those with whom they disagree.*
—JOHN KENNETH GALBRAITH

In Santiago, on my way home from the Montevideo conference, I heard
from J. David Stern, the owner of *The Philadelphia Record* and *The
Camden Courier*, who had just purchased *The New York Evening Post*.
This ancient newspaper, founded by Alexander Hamilton, had had a distinguished history, but in recent years had passed through various less
competent managements, had steadily lost its prestige and was now at low
ebb. Stern telephoned to ask whether I would become its managing editor.

Stern was a liberal and was more or less familiar with my work on *The
Nation*, and my Boston and Portland daily newspaper experience had
been called to his attention by a friend, James Coveney, who was in the
newspaper advertising field and had founded an organization called
"Media Records" which supplied advertisers with data about newspaper
circulations. I was interested in Stern's offer, and when I returned to
New York, we discussed terms. I told him that I wanted to become not
merely the managing editor but the editor with responsibility for the

news, for features and for editorial-page policies. He agreed, but then I said there was one final condition. There must be no "sacred cows," no "keep outs," no "must nots." Stern said that was entirely in harmony with his own views and that one of his desires for the new editorial management was to get "the news behind the news." That suited me perfectly. I regretted leaving *The Nation*, but here was an opportunity to reach a much wider audience.

On my first day in the office, Monday, February 19, 1934, I made one amusing discovery. When I looked up my file in the *Post*'s "morgue," I found a brown envelope stamped in large letters: GRUENING, ERNEST— WATCH OUT FOR LIBEL. Enclosed were various clippings about me and a letter dated January 1928 to a former *Post* managing editor, Ralph E. Renaud, from a member of the then *Post*'s firm of attorneys. It cautioned him that the paper should be careful about printing anything derogatory about me unless certain of the facts, because I was in the habit of suing and that had proved costly to other newspapers. The file contained clippings of my Chicago *Tribune* and Hearst suits.

As one of my first acts as editor, I gave the staff the same instructions for handling stories dealing with Negroes that I had given on the Boston *Traveler* and Boston *Journal* more than a decade and a half earlier. Unfortunately, there had been no improvement in black-white relationships. A flagrant example of racial discrimination brought about an editorial on February 23 which condemned the ejection from the public restaurant on the House side of the nation's Capitol of a black welfare worker, Mabel Byrd, a Ph.D. who had been brought to Washington as a member of the National Recovery Act investigating staff.

A similar incident took place shortly thereafter in the public restaurant on the Senate side of the Capitol, and this time the incident involved an outstanding young white woman whom I had come to know well, Dorothy Detzer. As executive secretary of the Women's International League for Peace and Freedom, she was lobbying in Washington for the anti-lynching bill sponsored by Senator Edward P. Costigan of Colorado. Several black journalists had come to the Capitol for the same purpose.

Outraged by the incident in the House, a number of citizens, headed by Howard K. Beale, whom I had known as an assistant professor of history at Bowdoin, decided to put the situation to a test on the Senate side. The plan was to bring one Negro guest to the Senate restaurant every day, and on the first day Dorothy Detzer came accompanied by a young, black graduate of Bryn Mawr. They sat down at a counter and gave their orders which were served by Paul Johnson, the Negro headwaiter. At that moment the manager of the restaurant swooped down on the two young ladies with a loud bellow.

"Miss Detzer," he yelled, "you know you can't do this to me."

"Do what?" she asked.

"You know we don't allow niggers in this dining room."

"Please look around you," Miss Detzer said. "There are six Negroes here already. Only they are standing up and my friend is sitting down; that's the only difference." (She was referring to the waiters.)

This enraged the manager even further. He grabbed the girl's plate. "You can have your lunch, but that nigger can't."

"Are you game?" Miss Detzer asked her friend quietly, and pushing her plate between them, said, "We can share my lunch."

With that the manager rushed out and returned with a policeman, a well-known figure on Capitol Hill because of his enormous size. He laid his hand on Miss Detzer's shoulder. "I've got to arrest you for disturbing the peace." Then with his hand on the black girl's shoulder, he led them away.

"Where are you taking us?" Miss Detzer asked.

"We got a calaboose downstairs."

But in the corridor, the three encountered Senator Arthur Capper of Kansas.

"What's this all about?" he said.

"She's been obstructing the peace," replied the policeman.

"Oh no," said the Senator, "Miss Detzer would never do that," and putting an arm around each of the girls he steered them away from the policeman.

The incident received wide publicity and helped dramatize the shameful discrimination in a building built and maintained by all the American people, but this indecency was not rectified for some time to come. When I visited Washington some weeks later, I discovered that hotels and restaurants were all "Jim Crowed," and the only public place where one could lunch or dine with a Negro friend was in the Union Station.

In New York, Mayor La Guardia was trying to fulfill his campaign promises. He wanted a new charter for the city, and legislation that would improve living conditions in the metropolis—better transportation, lower light and power rates, adequate housing, better educational facilities. These objectives were supported by Governor Herbert Lehman, but they were repeatedly thwarted in the state legislature by a combination of upstate Republican conservatives and Tammany Hall Democrats from the city's five boroughs.

Public opinion supported the Mayor, but the legislators seemed indifferent to it. I suspected that few New Yorkers even knew who their legislators were, let alone how they voted on these important issues. So to test my suspicions and if possible to inform and arouse the voters, I proposed that the *Post* conduct a general poll. Our reporters were assigned to interview a hundred New Yorkers every day for a month and ask them if they knew who represented them on the City Council, in the Albany legislature and in Congress. We tabulated and reported the results daily, and they developed into a monumental exhibition of political illiteracy. On some days, not a single person interviewed was able to identify even one of his representatives. In our final tabulation of 3,000 interviews, we found that 1,367 people could not identify a single representative, and four out of five did not know the name of their assemblyman, state senator or congressman. Obviously, the legislators were aware of their constituents' ignorance and therefore felt free to disregard the public interest.

As a result of our polls and the revelation of the city's widespread political ignorance, an information service was established by the city's economic council to educate the voters. The *Post* printed maps showing the various assembly and senatorial districts in each of the five boroughs and put the name of each assemblyman and senator on the map in his district. Then we recorded how each voted on the important measures that came up in Albany. So for the first time it was possible for a reader to find out at a glance how his elected representatives in both houses of the state legislature had performed. In time the results of this exposure would have some effect.

So far in my work on the *Post*, Stern had given me a free hand as he had promised, and I made every effort to print "the news behind the news." But I was soon to discover that some of that news was about Stern himself. The *Post*'s Washington correspondent was Robert S. Allen, who also represented Stern's other newspapers and was the co-author with Drew Pearson of the widely syndicated column, "Washington Merry-go-Round." Allen told me he was on the track of a whale of a story. There was a crooked federal judge operating in Harrisburg, Pennsylvania's capital, who had violated the judicial code, had handed out "masterships" to relatives and in other ways had been guilty of acts that would justify his impeachment. The Attorney General of the United States was Homer Cummings of Connecticut, appointed by Roosevelt after the death of Thomas J. Walsh. Cummings had served in Connecticut as a district attorney and would be wholly familiar with criminal practice and procedure. I told Bob Allen to assemble all his facts, and then ask Cummings why he had not laid the case before the House of Representatives for impeachment proceedings.

Two days later Bob called and said he had just had the shock of his life. This is what he told me:

I went to see Cummings and asked him why he had not proceeded with impeachment proceedings against Judge Albert W. Johnson of the United States District Court in the Middle District of Pennsylvania. He was sitting behind his desk, smoking a big cigar, and said, "Bob, if I tell you, what will you do with the story?"

I told him it was a big story whether he acted or not. It would make the front pages of the *Post*, the Philadelphia *Record* and the Camden *Courier*, but that wasn't all. It would be carried by the AP and the UP all over the country.

"That's very interesting," Cummings said. "Now if I tell you just why I haven't as yet proceeded against Johnson, will you be sure and print exactly what I say?"

"Of course," I said. "That's what I'm here for."

"All right," Cummings said, "don't miss a word of what I am going to say. Get this. The only reason I have not yet proceeded against Johnson is that the publisher of the Philadelphia *Record*, the Camden *Courier* and the New York *Post*, Mr. J. David Stern, has been to see me several times and pleaded with me on bended knee not to proceed because of the many favors Judge Johnson has done for him."

I went to Stern and told him what Bob Allen had reported.

Stern replied airily, "Oh, you've got to allow me a few fat cats."

"I thought you promised me I wouldn't be working in a cat house," I told him.

We clashed again over another issue. Tenement fires seemed to be an almost daily occurrence in New York. These shabby, overcrowded buildings were scarcely fit for human habitation, and when they caught fire, whole families were burned to death in the blaze. In one disastrous fire, an entire family of five and the mother and two children of another had perished, when flames swept through their tenement. The *Post* featured the story and a few days later we published pictures of a march staged by five hundred children to protest these firetraps.

I discovered that many of these tenements were owned by Vincent Astor, heir to the great Astor fortune, much of it invested in New York real estate. So I wrote an editorial entitled "An Open Letter to Vincent Astor," which called attention to every landlord's responsibility to make his property habitable and fireproof. I scheduled the editorial for the front page. When it failed to appear, I found that Stern had ordered it killed.

"How did that happen?" I asked him.

"Well, if you must know," Stern answered, "I am trying to get Astor to lend me $200,000 for the *Post*."

There were other such incidents and I felt that despite Stern's reputation as a liberal, which he had demonstrated conspicuously in various ways, our views on the conduct of a newspaper were not compatible. He shared that view and we agreed to part company. Before I left, we pursued the firetrap issue vigorously and my chief regret in leaving the *Post* was that I could not stay to see this fight through. And retribution, although wholly inadequate, finally overtook Judge Johnson. A subcommittee of the House Judiciary Committee headed by Representative Estes Kefauver of Tennessee found that "For more than fifteen years Judge Johnson used, and permitted his court to be used, as a medium in the formation and operation of an inconceivable, a despicable, and a degrading conspiracy against the administration of justice. . . ." The committee recommended impeachment, but because Johnson resigned and waived all rights, including those of pension and retirement, it was felt that impeachment would serve no purpose. He got off far too easily. I never did find out what favors he had granted J. David Stern.

No sooner had I left the *Post* than I was asked to be a member of a commission to study Cuban affairs and to make recommendations for Cuba's economic and social rehabilitation. The study was sponsored by the Foreign Policy Association, of which I was a director, and financed by the Rockefeller Foundation. An invitation to make such a study had been extended by Cuba's president, Carlos Mendieta. Raymond Leslie Buell, a political scientist and president of the Foreign Policy Association, was chairman, and each of the other ten members of the commission were specialists in such fields as economics, social welfare, public health, education, agriculture and labor. We spent several weeks in Cuba, visiting every one of its six provinces and the Isle of Pines. We then assembled in Richmond, Massachusetts, for a week's interim work on the report. While each of us produced the chapters in our assigned specialty, we were all concerned with the overall conclusions and recommendations.

The report was a substantial volume of 522 pages, divided into twenty-one chapters with maps, charts and graphs, which was issued in both English and Spanish under the title *Problems of the New Cuba*. We had the benefit of the advice of many enlightened Cubans who offered valuable suggestions, read our manuscripts and submitted useful criticisms. While advocating measures for the maintenance of markets and the price of sugar, the report stressed the need for agricultural diversification to lessen the dependence of the island's economy, and especially of its labor, on one crop. We recommended that the workers cultivate other crops for their own sustenance and for export, which would involve redistribution of land to achieve family ownership of small tracts. We also recommended changes and improvements in the fields of finance, health, education and public utilities.

We were, of course, fully aware of Cuba's heritage of corruption and violence. In fact, several outbreaks took place while we were in Havana. Thus our report made clear that while it dealt primarily with economic and social problems, their solution would depend largely on whether Cuba had a government desirous of carrying out long-needed reforms, and the capacity to do so. We were frankly skeptical that the island's pressing political problems could be solved. Nor did we shrink from discussing the conflict posed by absentee capital control and the resulting difficulties in the relations of American-owned enterprises and Cuban labor. And we pointed out that "the fundamental obstacle to good relations between Cuba and the United States is the widespread belief in Cuba that the American State Department attempts to make and unmake governments, and that the present disturbed situation is an outgrowth of a plan for provisional government which Washington induced the Cubans to accept."

Unfortunately, despite the abrogation of the Platt amendment and the good intentions of President Roosevelt and Cordell Hull, there was no "New Deal" in Cuba. The United States had twice rejected a popular Cuban choice for the presidency that might well have led to the realization of the island's aspirations. Sumner Welles's pique had denied them Grau San Martin; Ambassador Caffery never gave Carlos Hevia a chance. His choice, Carlos Mendieta, was a pawn in the hands of Fulgencio Batista who, with the support of the State Department and American bankers and sugar barons, soon came to power and established a right-wing dictatorship so oppressive that it was in time replaced by a no-less-oppressive dictatorship of the left, that of Fidel Castro. The victims were the Cuban people, and the shortsightedness of successive United States administrations was in large measure responsible for what happened to them.

With the completion of the Cuban report, I accepted an invitation to join the faculty of another of Hubert Herring's seminars in Mexico. They had already played a part in informing the American public and mobilizing its sentiment for a friendlier government policy toward our southern neighbor. But now our relations with Mexico, which had been so greatly improved by Ambassador Morrow, were facing a new crisis. Newly elected President Lazaro Cardenas had announced his determination to expropriate all foreign oil holdings.

Josephus Daniels, North Carolina newspaper publisher, was our new Ambassador in Mexico City. He had been Secretary of the Navy in the Wilson Administration and Franklin Roosevelt had been his assistant secretary. When Roosevelt was elected President, he offered his former "chief" whatever post he desired and Daniels opted for the Ambassadorship to Mexico. Incredibly, as I related earlier, both had apparently forgotten that as Secretary of the Navy Daniels had, in 1914, following Woodrow Wilson's instructions, sent the following telegram to Admiral Frank Fletcher, the commander of United States Naval Forces off Vera Cruz:

Seize custom house. Do not permit war supplies to be delivered to Huerta government or to any other party.

In the ensuing bombardment and landing operations, 126 Mexicans had been killed and 195 wounded. Under these circumstances was the appointment a colossal blunder? Would the Mexicans accept Daniels, and if they did, would not the memory of Vera Cruz prevent his effective functioning?

The Mexicans, however, won over by Roosevelt's New Deal policies, in which they saw close resemblances to their own programs, and aware of Daniels's liberal record, did accept him. Daniels lost no time in expressing his sympathy for Mexico's aspirations and implementing Roosevelt's Good Neighbor Policy. The close personal relationship between the two men gave Daniels a freedom unprecedented in our diplomatic history. It enabled him to bypass the State Department which was under great pressure from American oil men and interventionists to block nationalization of Mexico's oil.

The issue finally resolved itself into what indemnification Mexico would offer for the oil. The oil companies asked for almost 400 million dollars, a figure based on the estimated value of the oil remaining in the ground. Mexico was, of course, unwilling to pay for the loss of future revenues, but it was willing to reimburse the oil companies for whatever sums they had invested. The situation continued tense.

Working directly with Roosevelt, Daniels secured an agreement that an expert from each country would determine the amount of compensation to be paid and that their determination would be binding on all parties. The United States was represented by Morris Llewellyn Cooke, a distinguished consulting engineer who had been the administrator of the Rural Electrification Administration, one of the New Deal's achievements. He met with his Mexican counterpart, Manuel J. Zevada, and they arrived at a figure of $23,995,991. The money was paid and the problem was solved.

I looked forward to meeting Daniels when I was in Mexico City with the seminar. Shortly after his appointment, he had written to compliment me on my book, *Mexico and Its Heritage*, which had been published in 1928, and as a result we had corresponded, but we had never met. On our first night in Mexico City, a few of the seminarians dined at the American Embassy and I found the Ambassador and his wife to be charming and gracious hosts. The Ambassador addressed the seminar a few days later, and in the course of his remarks, he praised Mexico's prevailing concern for universal education and quoted a sentence from one of Calles's last speeches, an endorsement of public-school education. His remarks were picked up by the *Catholic Review of Baltimore* and distorted as an attack on the Catholic Church because elsewhere in the same speech Calles had criticized the clergy for its opposition to public-school education.

The incident developed into a furor. Various members of Congress—Hamilton Fish and Martin J. Kennedy of New York, William Patrick Connery, Jr. of Massachusetts, and Clare Gerald Fenerty of Pennsylvania—called for Daniels's removal and the campaign was taken up by the Knights of Columbus headed by Martin H. Carmody. It created a worrisome problem both for Ambassador Daniels and President Roosevelt. Back in New York, I wrote the Ambassador that because I had been present on the occasion, I would be most happy to testify that nothing seemed more remote from the meaning and obvious purpose of his address than the intent with which he was charged. Ambassador Daniels replied that he had forwarded copies of my letter to President Roosevelt and Secretary Hull, and that it was helpful in allaying their fears that he might have committed an indiscretion.

14

NEW POLICIES FOR

PUERTO RICO

*The New Deal was a program of
dynamism and vitality, a period of promise,
hope and brand new concepts for tens of
millions of Americans. Through it we
learned by trial and error something of the
unlimited capacity of a free people to produce a prosperous and well-balanced society.*

—CHESTER BOWLES

In the summer of 1934, President Roosevelt, apparently pleased with my
work as an advisor at Montevideo, asked me to join his administration. In
May of that year, he had by executive order created a new agency in the
Department of the Interior, the Division of Territories and Island Possessions, which would supervise federal relations with our outlying and dependent areas and assist them in every way possible to compensate for
their lack of voting representation in the Congress. Alaska and Hawaii
were represented in the House by a delegate who could speak but was
not permitted to vote even on a matter affecting his territory. In Puerto
Rico and the Philippines, the corresponding official was titled Resident
Commissioner. The Virgin Islands lacked even that type of representation. Further, the responsibility for these areas had been scattered in various government departments. Hawaii and Alaska were in the Interior
Department's chief clerk's office, as were the Virgin Islands after President Hoover transferred them from the Navy Department. Puerto Rico
was transferred from the War Department's Insular Bureau to the new

agency. Now they had all been brought together in this new division and I was to be its director.

I was conscious of my inadequacy to head the division. I had never visited three of its four prospective wards, Alaska, Hawaii and the Virgin Islands; and I had spent only one day in Puerto Rico in the course of a 1931 seminar in the Caribbean. I did not advertise my lack of firsthand experience and, fortunately, none of the newspapermen who interviewed me raised the question. In fact, the editorial comments on my appointment were uniformly favorable.

Accompanied by Oscar L. Chapman, the Assistant Secretary of the Interior, I journeyed to Hyde Park to get my instructions from the President. When we arrived he was in a conference—to which we listened —with Harry Hopkins, the Federal Relief Administrator, and Rexford Guy Tugwell, the Under-Secretary of Agriculture. They were discussing a shelter belt of trees which would extend along the western edge of the Prairie States to help prevent further wind-erosion in the areas known as dust bowls.

When they had finished, the President turned to Chapman and me. "Now, about the territories," he said. He had just returned from a trip to the Pacific. "Hawaii is in good shape. There's too much concentration of land there in the big estates. Alaska needs more people and we ought to do something to promote agriculture. Next spring I would like you to move a thousand or fifteen hundred people from the drought-stricken areas of the Middle West and give them a chance to start life anew in Alaska. The Virgin Islands were called an effective poorhouse by my predecessor and we must do what we can to improve that situation. Let me know what plans you will develop. As for Puerto Rico, that place is hopeless, *hopeless*," and he raised his arms above his head to emphasize his feeling.

"This new division is really the equivalent of the British colonial office, isn't it, Mr. President?" I asked.

"I suppose it is," he replied.

"Well, a democracy shouldn't have any colonies," I ventured.

The President smiled, and then extending his arms forward, palms up, he said, "I think you're right. Let's see what you can develop."

No more was said, but I gathered that any steps I might take to diminish the territories' colonial status would have his approval.

The only specific assignment the President had given me related to Alaska. I soon found that the budgeted appropriations for the Interior Department did not include funds for transferring settlers to Alaska. But Harry Hopkins had heard the conversation at Hyde Park and, as Federal Relief Administrator, had ample funds to be used at his discretion. So I called on him and asked if he would supply the needed financing.

"Yes," he said, "provided I run it."

Word of the proposed resettlement had broken in the press. Recovery from the Depression had barely begun and to many thousands it sounded like an alluring project and a new chance in life. Letters poured into the White House, the Interior Department and the Relief Administration from every state in the Union. I felt that these letters should furnish the basis for the selection of the new settlers. The mere fact that they wanted to go was, I felt, a good indication of their need and their willingness to work. But Hopkins decided that the settlers should come from only three states—Michigan, Wisconsin and Minnesota—on the assumption that they were climatically similar to Alaska and the settlers would have an easier time adapting. I urged that applicants from the Dakotas, Montana, Wyoming, Idaho and eastern Washington should be equally acceptable, and even some applicants from more southerly states, if they appeared to have the qualifications. The larger number would offer a wider choice, but Hopkins refused. The thousands of applicants' letters were totally ignored.

Instead, selections in the three states designated by Hopkins were made from the relief rolls by social workers and county agents who, in some cases, actually went out and solicited settlers. Before long a substantial number of those selected to go felt they were doing Uncle Sam a favor, and this attitude was increased by the fanfare that accompanied their journey. One train bearing them went by way of Seattle, one by way of San Francisco. They were greeted with cheers along the route and feted in the ports of embarkation. Among them were some of the problem cases the social workers wanted to get rid of; a few were physically or temperamentally unfit and were soon on their way back to the States.

Their destination was the Matanuska Valley which had been selected by Otto Ohlson, the manager of the government-owned Alaska Railroad, and Don Irwin of the Department of Agriculture. It was an excellent choice, and the project served to publicize Alaska as a new frontier of opportunity and promise. It was another of the imaginative undertakings characteristic of the Roosevelt Administration. Despite inevitable mistakes, it would serve its purpose.

My first weeks in the Interior Department were devoted to organizing the new division. I brought my faithful secretary, Estella Draper, who had followed me to *The Nation* and the *Post*, and I was lucky to secure as counsel the services of Irwin Silverman, an able young lawyer, keenly interested in the wide diversity of problems we would try to solve. I was also fortunate in finding as assistant director Ruth Hampton, a hearty cheerful, level-headed and very able woman. And last but not least, I admired my "boss," Secretary of the Interior Harold L. Ickes. I had never met Ickes, but what I knew of him, or thought I knew of him, gave me assurance that I would be working for an intellectually and spiritually congenial man. He was known as a progressive who for years had been battling in the Middle West for liberal causes—unsuccessfully, most of the time, until the advent of the New Deal. His departmental appointments were also most reassuring. They included Harry Slattery, who as a newspaperman had uncovered "the little green house on K Street," where some of the crooked deals that were to tarnish the Harding Administration had been concocted; Oscar Chapman, a lawyer who had worked with Judge Ben Lindsey in Denver's juvenile court; Louis Glavis, who had been fired by the Taft Administration for exposing Secretary of the Interior Richard Achilles Ballinger's performance on behalf of the questionable Cunningham coal claims in Alaska; and John Collier, who had battled for a new approach to the problems of the American Indian. I felt that men with records like these would be a great asset to the New Deal. I was confident I would be happy in the Department and told my friends so. I was soon to be disillusioned.

The Secretary of the Virgin Islands, Boyd Brown, the second-ranking official with the additional title of Lieutenant-Governor of Saint Croix, was being transferred to the presidency of the newly formed Virgin Island Company, the government agency which was to develop the economy of the three islands, and lift them from the "poorhouse" status to which President Hoover had consigned them. The vacancy had to be filled, and as Director of the Division of Territories and Island Possessions, I considered it my duty to find a suitable successor. It seemed to me that Robert Herrick, the nationally known novelist who had just retired as Professor of English Literature at the University of Chicago, would make an ideal appointee. A highly urbane and knowledgeable man, he had also written a book on the Caribbean. I had known Herrick for years and his credentials were further called to my attention by Felix Frankfurter. I asked him if he would be interested in the job and Herrick said he would be delighted to accept.

Then I mentioned his name to Ebert K. Burlew, Ickes's administrative assistant. "Did you speak to Herrick about it? he asked. I said I had. "You had no business to do that. The Secretary wants to make the offers of employment."

"I didn't offer it to him; I merely asked him whether he'd be interested."

"You violated one of the Secretary's standing orders," said Burlew.

I went to see Ickes and explained that I had been unaware of his ruling, but in any event, Herrick would be glad to serve if appointed and I considered him a good choice.

"I won't have him," Ickes said curtly. "He's a snob."

I was so taken aback by this brusque rejection that for the moment I was speechless. Then I came to Herrick's defense, but Ickes again said, "I won't have him," and ended the interview.

The more I thought about it, the less I understood Ickes's objections. At a subsequent meeting I spoke again of Herrick's qualifications, but Ickes cut me short. "I told you I won't have him," he said in a tone that implied I should not have bothered him again. I had no alternative but to notify Herrick and tell him how much I regretted Ickes's decision.

Two weeks later I received a letter from Ickes addressed to me as Director of the Division of Territories and Island Possessions. It ran about as follows:

> If you insist that I hire Robert Herrick as Secretary of the Virgin Islands as a CAF-13 at a salary of $5,600, I cannot go along with you. I have to be vigilant in protecting the public purse. But if you are willing to have him put on as a CAF-12 at a salary of $4,600, I am prepared to give him the appointment.

My head swam. I had never insisted on any such thing; I did not even know at that time what the initials "CAF" (Clerical, Administrative, Fiscal) meant. In my bewilderment I took the letter to Assistant Secretary Oscar Chapman and asked him whether he could throw any light on the mystery.

Oscar grinned broadly. "Don't you know what this means?" he said. "It's called 'building the record.' You may not realize it, but since Herrick's rejection has become known, the Secretary has had protests from persons whose opinions he values. He's heard from Felix Frankfurter; he's heard from Jane Addams; he's heard from the president of the University of Chicago, he's heard from Robert Morss Lovett. Now the record will show that it was you and not he who blocked Herrick's appointment."

"You mean he *has* appointed Herrick?"

"That's right."

"Well, I'll be damned," I said. "Why doesn't he tell the truth and say he changed his mind?"

Still boiling, I sought out Burlew and—very unwisely—showed him Ickes's letter and gave him my opinion of the Secretary's underhanded tactics. He listened carefully and then took the letter. The more I thought about it, the more inexcusable Ickes's performance seemed, and several days later, to preserve a copy of his letter, I went to the file of our correspondence. The letter was not there. In its place, identically dated, was another letter, wholly innocuous, which merely said that he had decided to appoint Herrick. I wondered if that was how Ickes intended to conduct the Department of the Interior. If so, I knew it would be impossible to trust him.

I learned later from Robert Lovett that a rebuke Professor Herrick had given in class to a somewhat contentious pupil named Harold Ickes years before at the University of Chicago had probably rankled in Ickes's mind. But once the appointment was made and Herrick assumed his post, Ickes became enthusiastic about his services. Indeed, during his four years as Secretary and at times as Acting Governor of the Virgin Islands—until his sudden death in 1938—Herrick carried out his duties with distinction and dignity.

Herrick and I sailed to the Virgin Islands together. It was my first view of the white beaches and deep blue waters of Saint Thomas. Hillsides rose steeply all around the harbor, and the streets and pastel-tinted buildings of the town retained the flavor of the island's Danish heritage. A proposal had been made during the navy's rule, and was now being renewed, to rename some of the streets to conform to the new sovereignty, but it seemed desirable to me that the cultural vestiges of the civilized Danes be preserved. There was no good reason to rechristen Grooningens Gade, Main Street; and I found it easy to insist that the town itself should retain its name of Charlotte Amalie.

The islands were certainly among the most beautiful in the Carribean, and their Old World atmosphere and near-perfect climate were great assets for tourism. But as yet they were still "undiscovered"; only three tourist ships had visited Saint Thomas in 1933 and only eighteen in 1934. Almost our first project was to convert Bluebeard's Castle—the historic fort of an eighteenth-century pirate overlooking the harbor—into a modern hotel, and to construct adjacent accommodations. In time, other hotels would be built and the islands would become a tourist mecca, providing the islanders with their most important source of income. But that was still in the future; in 1934 it was clear that beauty and atmosphere alone were not enough to support the islands' economy.

No one was more aware of this fact than Governor Paul Pearson, a Hoover appointee. His first report had summarized conditions in the islands as "desperate," and although Hoover had declared that the islands' "people cannot be self-supporting either in living or government without discovery of new methods and new revenues," the necessary funds were not made available. As a result most of the islands' laborers were out of work and the Red Cross had been feeding twenty-five percent of the population. The death rate was about three times that of the United States, and in the face of endemic respiratory and intestinal diseases, epidemics of malaria, measles and whooping cough—further aggravated by widespread malnutrition—the federal appropriations for health had declined year after year in the previous decade from $16,904 to $5,960 in 1934.

In addition to providing better health services, it was our task to find the "new methods and revenues" which President Hoover had posited but had done nothing to secure. To supplement tourist revenue we established a craft cooperative on Saint Thomas to make baskets, hats and tablemats using indigenous reeds and fibers, pottery, tortoiseshell ornaments, mahogany bowls and tropical-fruit jams and jellies. The skills to produce some of these products did not exist and the trained craftsmen who would teach them had to be imported. We also tried to increase the production of bay oil and bay rum from the sparsely inhabited island of Saint John which also figured in our tourist plans.

Prohibition had obliterated the islands' chief industry and source of revenue, rum. The sugar factories and distilleries which had produced it on the island of Saint Croix had been abandoned and the acreage previously devoted to sugarcane was overgrown with weeds. It was impossible at that time, although we tried, to attract private capital. So the newly created government-owned Virgin Island Company purchased five thousand acres, cleared them, planted cane, and acquired and rehabilitated the old distilleries. After considerable discussion the name of the product approved by President Roosevelt was "Government House Rum." He also personally selected one of several attractive labels for it, but he rejected with a laugh my suggestion to call it Fine Distilled Rum.

We also started some needed housing and initiated a general public works program. And believing that greater political liberties should march hand in hand with economic improvement, and that an increase in local autonomy was due, we drafted a new Organic Act for the Virgin Islands. It replaced limited male suffrage based on property with universal suffrage, subject only to a literacy test. It abolished the gubernatorially appointed members of the colonial councils of Saint Thomas, Saint John and Saint Croix and made them elective. And it limited the Governor's veto power.

Our efforts were not wholly untroubled. In March of 1935 the cane planters struck, protesting the Virgin Island Company's wage of 45 cents a day. The strike was settled by raising it to 60 cents a day. But the chief trouble came from the frustrations and the pessimism of a tropically impoverished people. Their expectations had been raised by what the government and what the New Deal promised to do for them. But only with time and hard work by the people themselves would these promises become a reality.

Puerto Rico's problems were somewhat different, if no less severe. President Roosevelt's characterization of the island as "hopeless," was perhaps an exaggeration, but clearly it should and would be my division's major concern. In fact, Secretary Ickes told me to give it priority over the other three wards. When I learned of my forthcoming responsibilities, I went to Oyster Bay to visit the island's former governor, Theodore Roosevelt. His advice confirmed the gloomy view of his cousin Franklin.

Unlike the Virgin Islands, Puerto Rico could not blame the American government for all its problems. On the contrary, it had been generous. The Foraker Act of 1900 forbade corporations from owning more than five hundred acres of land, a provision reaffirmed in the Jones Act of 1917 which also conferred American citizenship on the Puerto Ricans, established a bicameral legislature and limited the number of presidential appointments. All federal taxes and customs receipts reverted not to the American treasury but to Puerto Rico's. Nevertheless, in violation of the five-hundred-acre provision, sugar companies had acquired some one hundred thousand acres of the best land, ending many small holdings. But the responsibility for that lay clearly with the Puerto Ricans, whose legislature, subservient to the absentee interests, never sought to enforce its provisions which they had the power to do. By the 1930s this illegal acquisition had become a well-established vested interest and Puerto Rico had fallen victim to economic rather than political imperialism. In consequence, the small tracts, previously locally owned, passed to the absentee corporations, compelling the former occupants to work as *colonos*, small capitalist sharecroppers, or as agricultural laborers at pitifully low wages. Sugar profits were exported and benefitted the absentee owners, but the workers had to pay for their imported food at high prices. And the Jones-Costigan Act had just reduced Puerto Rico's sugar quota, thereby adding several thousand workers to the ranks of the unemployed.

Puerto Rico's other important crop, coffee, occupied nearly two hundred thousand acres in the mountainous regions. Small, locally owned plantations employed both men and women, supplied a living for a third of the population and provided not only a livelihood but a place on the land. But in September 1928, the most devastating hurricane in Puerto Rico's history had swept the island. It left thousands homeless, destroyed growing crops and uprooted the coffee trees. But the Puerto Ricans went bravely back to work, assisted by the Red Cross and a five-million-dollar loan from Congress, and were breathing feebly again when a second hurricane almost as destructive as the first swept the island in 1932. This time it also uprooted the people, who took refuge in the already overcrowded cities, increasing the pressure for nonexistent jobs and adding to the relief rolls. It was estimated that the unemployed and their families numbered 350,000. The third agricultural crop, tobacco, had also become largely absentee-owned, but its value was impaired by the decline in the consumption of cigars in favor of cigarette smoking. Thus the distress of the Puerto Ricans, who were victims of distant economic forces beyond their reach or control, confronted them and us with problems of the utmost urgency.

A rehabilitation program for Puerto Rico was already in being, but only on paper. The previous March when the island was still under the jurisdiction of the War Department, Rexford Guy Tugwell, acting under instructions from the President, had gone there and formed a committee of local leaders which became known as the President's Policy Committee on Puerto Rico. Its report was accepted in principle by the President as a working basis for Puerto Rican rehabilitation. Our problem was to create an agency that could effectively carry out the committee's proposals and find the means of funding them. It was an experience in frustration. We felt we could not wait for action by the Congress. Various schemes were hatched in the Solicitor's Office of the Department of the Interior and after bureaucratic and maddening delays, rejected. At an interview with the President early in November, we wondered whether our programs could not be financed by an anticipation of processing taxes. He said it would have to be approved by Comptroller General J. C. McCarl, whose crustiness he deplored, and whose office, being a creation of Congress, could be as independent of the executive as its incumbent pleased. The President called in Steve Early to ask him what McCarl's first name was, and found that he was familiarly called by his initials "JC". So the President called him in my presence and, turning on all his charm, asked him to discuss the question of financing our programs with me. I met with McCarl's General Counsel, Rudolph L. Golze, the next day, accompanied by Colonel W. C. Rigby, the counsel for Puerto Rico, and Frederick Bernays Wiener, a member of the Department of the Interior's Solicitor's staff. We waited several weeks for the decision, which was "no."

Proposals to model the agency after the Virgin Island Company, the Inland Waterways Authority and other alternatives also met with implacable rejections from McCarl. The Puerto Ricans were, understandably, growing more and more restive, as the only action taken by the administration after two years in office was an inadequate supply of relief funds. But by April the Emergency Relief Appropriation Act provided a way out and the Solicitor's Office proposed a reconstruction board of seven to be appointed by the Secretary of the Interior, with himself as Chairman. The proposal was sent to the President so that he could issue an Executive Order, but this time the Bureau of the Budget objected, recommending a single administrator instead of a board. So the order was redrafted with the space for the administrator's name left blank. The President signed it on May 28, 1935, the Puerto Rican Reconstruction Administration (PRRA) came into being, and my name appeared as Administrator. The appointment was a complete surprise to me. My first information came from the press. I was rather overwhelmed at the prospect of trying to carry on the duties of two offices. Ickes was not pleased and questioned me sharply. Had I requested the President to appoint me? Had I asked an intermediary to do so? Had I discussed the appointment with the President? The answer was "no" to all of these questions.

There was a further delay on funding. Finally, the gratifying news came on August 1, in a letter from the President that $35 million had been segregated from the general funds appropriated by Public Resolution No. 11-74 in Congress, and that there would be additional funds which the President hoped would total $100 million. "The Administration's program," he wrote, "intends not merely relief but permanent reconstruction for the Island. To this end the projects in contemplation will seek to insure every person on the Island a position of reasonable independence and security. . . . I am anxious that the Government of the United States shall discharge fully its responsibilities to the Puerto Rican people and urge upon you that this work be carried forward with the greatest dispatch consistent with a sound and considered rehabilitation program."

My first task was to find a competent general counsel, and after several weeks of being unable to come up with a satisfactory candidate, I turned to Felix Frankfurter. He recommended Francis Michael Shea, a 1928 Harvard Law School graduate who had just resigned as chief of the opinion section of the legal division of the Agricultural Adjustment Administration under circumstances that appeared to me highly creditable to him. He proved a first-rate choice.

A further Executive Order issued on September 6, authorized the PRRA to make loans "for the purpose of financing, in whole or in part, the purchase by farmers, farm tenants, croppers, or farm laborers, of farm lands and of necessary equipment for the production, preparation and preservation of farm and rural community products for distribution and use, where such purchases are incidental and necessary to the effectuation of authorized projects of rural rehabilitation." This authority was necessary to carry out the objective of enforcing the five-hundred-acre limitation on corporate holdings and making the lands thus acquired available to small farmers.

It was a major step forward and the means that a few enlightened Puerto Ricans had sought to break up the large land holdings. Their leader was Luis Muñoz Marin, a highly intelligent and dedicated young man. His father, Luis Muñoz Rivera, had been Resident Commissioner of Puerto Rico, and Muñoz Marin had served as his secretary. Equally fluent in English and Spanish, he was now the editor of a daily newspaper in

San Juan founded by his father, *La Democracia*, the organ of the Liberal
Party, and had been elected Senator "at large." I had known Muñoz
Marin since the early 1920s when he had contributed articles on Puerto
Rico to *The Nation*. When I returned to *The Nation* in 1933, he had
written me a letter describing the "objectives" of Puerto Rico's three political parties. Two of them he said, the Republican and Socialist, with
very different ideologies, had formed a coalition for an obvious purpose
which transcended all ideologies: the spoils of political power. His letter
should have served me as a warning of the turmoil into which the PRRA
would be thrust, but of that I was as yet innocently unaware.

I had visited San Juan briefly in November of 1934 on my way to the
Virgin Islands. At that time plans for reconstruction were still uncertain,
but every newspaperman asked my views on Puerto Rico's future political status and my reply was invariably that it should be determined by
the Puerto Ricans. To the further question as to which status, statehood
or independence, I personally favored, I responded that I favored whatever the Puerto Ricans decided. My answer was at first generally approved, but soon I was charged with evasiveness. I meant it, nevertheless,
and emphasized the necessity for Puerto Rico's social and economic rehabilitation before we faced the issue of the island's political future.

In the frustrating ten months that elapsed before the authorizations for
our program permitted my return to Puerto Rico, the tension that had
been so evident during my earlier visits had markedly increased. But my
first job had to be the organization of the PRRA. I hoped to be able to
give Puerto Ricans as many positions and as much responsibility as possible. I was interested in their qualifications, not their political affiliations,
but I soon discovered that five of the six Puerto Rican executives I chose
were members of the Liberal Party. Their appointment aroused the bitter
opposition of the Republican-Socialist coalition, whose press soon began a
campaign of intemperate denunciation that far exceeded any mainland expressions in my experience. I should, of course, have realized that these
jobs did signify political control, and, although it was not my intention to
make the PRRA a vehicle for partisan employment, it became so to a
considerable extent. I have to take the blame for that. Nevertheless, it was
the Liberal Party that had in the preceding months devised the program
which formed the basis of our reconstruction plans, whereas it was reasonably plain that the Republican officials of the coalition, closely allied
with absentee interests, were opposed to the plan's principal features, especially the land purchase and redistribution, and the electrification programs.

In the long painful months spent in Washington waiting for the legislation and appropriations necessary to create the PRRA, I had received

almost daily letters and memoranda from Muñoz Marin apprising me of the activities of the coalition leaders, and of their efforts to get the governor to appoint their men to various offices. He often wrote of his frustrations at not having a "New Dealer" operating from La Fortaleza, the historic gubernatorial residence, and his complaints were justified. Puerto Rico had recently suffered a worse than inept governor, Robert Gore, appointed through Jim Farley's efforts as a reward for a campaign contribution and the unwavering six Puerto Rican votes for Roosevelt at the Chicago Democratic convention. Gore was forced to resign after six months, and Roosevelt wisely decided not to pay campaign debts with that office again. The Insular Bureau of the War Department, still in charge, secured the appointment, in February 1934, of Major-General Blanton Winship, just retired as Judge-Advocate General.

I had, after Gore's departure, forwarded to the President, Muñoz Marin's recommendation that a qualified Puerto Rican, Martin Travieso, be named governor. A Cornell graduate, he had been appointed by Woodrow Wilson as Secretary of the Territory and had acted in the governor's absence, the first time that responsibility was granted a Puerto Rican. It would have been a fine move at that time. But Roosevelt was imbued with a strong naval tradition; the Caribbean was an American lake. Winship was a decent, able man, but the obsolescence of appointing almost any non-Puerto Rican to that difficult and delicate post, and especially a military man who would convey a proconsular aura, had not yet dawned on the nation's executive consciousness.

Muñoz Marin's almost daily communications were supplemented by Ruby Black, the Washington correspondent of La Democracia. I had known her since my early days on The Nation and had made her the Washington correspondent for The Portland Evening News. She now carried in Puerto Rican Liberal Party circles the unofficial title of "advisor on continental psychology." An active New Dealer, she had established friendly relations with Eleanor Roosevelt, and as a conduit to her was a great asset to Muñoz Marin's objectives.

While I was no less concerned than Muñoz Marin with bringing the New Deal to Puerto Rico, and as Director of Territories and Island Possessions, had a vague and undefined authority over our territorial governors, I did not see how I could impose my choices of appointees on Winship. After all, Winship had to deal with a majority which controlled the Puerto Rican legislature, even if by coalition. In any event, President Roosevelt approved of Winship and it was my duty to work with him as best I could. He had been called to Washington so that we could brief him on our reconstruction program, and there was no evidence that he would not cooperate to the best of his ability.

In setting up the machinery for the PRRA, I discovered that Muñoz Marin's assessment of the island's political situation was depressingly accurate. But I had not counted on bureaucratic delays and indifference from Washington. I hoped for an enactment of legislation that would permit the revenues from PRRA enterprises, and particularly from the repayment of its loans, to go back into a revolving fund for agency use instead of reverting to the federal treasury. The idea had the President's warm support and I returned to Washington to fight for the necessary legislation. Introduced in the Senate on May 13, 1935, it came up on the consent calendar on July 20, but was objected to by Senator Wallace White of Maine, who stated that he had never heard of the proposed legislation until that morning when he was apprised that it permitted "the Federal Government to go into Puerto Rico and to engage in any sort of agricultural or industrial enterprise" it saw fit. Of course the bill did just that, but similar authorization had already been provided by the President's Executive Order creating the PRRA; it was the revolving fund provision that mattered. But Senator White thought it sounded "socialistic" and his objection, under the rules, prevented action. I had been friends with the Senator since the years I spent in Maine, so I sought him out and presented my side of the case. A few minor modifications in the wording of the measure were made, the Senator withdrew his objections and the bill passed the Senate on August 13. I learned later that the men who had sounded the socialist alarm were Senator Martinez Nadal, the president of Puerto Rico's Republican Party, and Mr. Louis Obergh, a lawyer representing Santiago Iglesias, Puerto Rico's resident commissioner. When the bill came up in the House, Iglesias's absence evidenced his lack of interest and the bill failed to get the necessary majority. I knew I could overcome this opposition. The bill was reintroduced and passed both houses the following February.

We could not wait for Washington to make up its mind, and our reconstruction plans began to get underway early in 1936. Our first notable victory came in mid-February when Secretary Ickes announced that proceedings to enforce the five-hundred-acre provisions of the land law would begin. The logical official to carry the cases to court was Puerto Rico's Attorney General, Benjamin Horton. But Horton, another Farley political appointee, was incompetent and there seemed to be no way to get rid of him. While this prickly situation was being studied, it was decided in the interests of speedy action to retain a competent Puerto Rican lawyer, and Miguel Guerra Mondragon carried the land cases to court. The sugar companies were resistant although their land was to be acquired at a fair negotiated price. In spite of this problem and the resistance of the coalition, land reform was proceeding.

We negotiated to acquire land everywhere. In the rich Plata Valley some 4,300 acres of the best tobacco land were owned by American Suppliers, an absentee corporation. This we were to divide into some five hundred units of from five to ten acres each. Several other large holdings in the coffee regions were similarly to be subdivided. In addition to growing the traditional revenue crops, sugar, tobacco and coffee, farmers were encouraged to raise subsistence crops, and vanilla, citron and perfume plants to provide additional income. Newly established service farms would supply seeds, fertilizer and know-how to the farmers. Poultry, hog and goat-raising were also to be encouraged, and pedigreed nannies were imported to improve the quality and quantity of the breed. And plans were made to teach home-canning to preserve food products for future use.

Other reconstruction projects also got underway. For generations soil erosion had depleted the richness of Puerto Rico's earth. After every heavy rain, the surrounding seawater would be streaked with the eroded soil. Contour plowing was being inculcated for the first time. The coconut bedrot was being eliminated to bring back the supply of that useful fruit. Electrification to provide power at a reasonable cost was to be sought by building two new dams with a total capacity of eight million kilowatt-hours. Transmission lines were being projected, and negotiations were begun to acquire the privately owned Mayaguez and the absentee-owned Ponce generating plants and to incorporate them into the insular grid system.

Schools were under construction to accommodate the half-million children not in school. Existing roads were being improved and new ones built. A new plant for the University of Puerto Rico at Rio Piedras was being designed. A design for an enlarged and rebuilt School of Tropical Medicine in San Juan was also on the drawing boards.

Plans were also being made to build homes on the little plots of land carved out of the large holdings. Wood previously used was subject to termites and hurricane destruction; concrete was essential for maintenance and safety. But cement imported from the United States was costly. So we were designing a thousand-barrel-a-day cement plant. However, I received a letter from President Roosevelt himself disapproving our plans for the plant. He was in Warm Springs, Georgia, and I flew there immediately, convinced that the project was both necessary and urgent, and equipped with figures to show how much money could be saved if we manufactured cement in Puerto Rico. He was persuaded, and the project proceeded.

Another PRRA project was the restoration of San Juan's historic fortifications—one of the finest architectural monuments of the Spanish Empire in the western hemisphere, surpassing even Havana's El Morro and the great fortifications of Cartagena, Colombia—they had been neglected by the United States military authorities; not only had they fallen into disrepair, but some wholly inappropriate wooden structures had been imposed upon them. I had called Secretary Ickes's attention to the project, and he had secured the introduction of a bill to Congress to make the massive crenelated battlements and jutting stone sentry-boxes a national monument. Included in the restoration would be the Casa Blanca, the house built by Ponce de Leon during his governorship from 1509 to 1512, and now the residence of the commanding army officer. It was the oldest house continuously occupied in the New World. Both the house and the fortifications had great historic value and were potential tourist attractions; indeed the jutting sentry-boxes would become a tourist trademark.

Secretary Ickes visited the island in January of 1936. His plane was delayed by head winds and he missed the governor's dinner in his honor, but the following day our tour of inspection included the fortifications. We were accompanied by the commanding officer, Colonel Otis R. Cole, who was known to be a heavy drinker. He was certainly "under the influence" that morning. A professor of history at the University of Puerto Rico, Rafael Ramirez de Arellano y Asenjo, was our guide, and just as he was pointing to an embrasure in the walls saying, "Here is where the Spanish repelled the Dutch," Colonel Cole, who was six feet four and weighed 250 pounds, seized him by both shoulders and flinging him aside roared, "We don't want to hear about the Spaniards. This is America!" This unpleasant incident, viewed by the entire entourage, was only the beginning of Cole's remarkable performance.

A stag luncheon in Ickes's honor had been planned at a picnic ground on the slopes of El Yunque, the highest peak in the western part of the island in the heart of Luquillo National Forest, the only tropical rain forest under the American flag. Our host was the regional forester, Evan Hadley, and the guests, about fifty in number, included the members of the Supreme Court and other federal and insular officials and legislators.

After the luncheon, Ickes spoke a few words to the company. He said he had been inspecting the fortifications and it was clear that the army did not appreciate their historic value. He proposed transferring them to the Interior Department's National Park Service and securing the services of Colonel Cole as superintendent of the national monument. As for the Luquillo National Forest, he felt that it, too, should be taken over by the National Park Service with Evan Hadley in charge. The speech was light and obviously in a humorous vein, but as Hadley rose to thank the guests for their presence, Colonel Cole staggered to his feet and in hoarse tones delivered himself as follows:

"Mishter Shecretary, I don't know a God-damn thing about the Department of the Interior, and you don't know a God-damn thing about the army, but I want to tell you that if you take away our base, we'll be back here with machine guns to put these people down!"

The astounded audience was further electrified when he keeled over backward and was caught by his second-in-command and a half-a-dozen GIs who carried him off on a stretcher, which had been prudently provided.

Ickes spent two days in Puerto Rico and two in the Virgin Islands, and then returned to the mainland, the Cole incident apparently forgotten. I could not forget it, and when I returned to Washington, I mentioned it to President Roosevelt.

"Get me Malin Craig," he told his aide, Major-General "Pop" Watson. Craig was Chief-of-Staff.

"Your commanding officer in Puerto Rico was beastly drunk when the Secretary of the Interior was on his first official visit to the island. What have you got to say?" said the President.

"Ample provocation," replied Craig.

"Well, you better take care of it," the President ordered.

Cole was retired shortly thereafter and I was able to secure as his successor a splendid officer, John Womack Wright, who did much to erase the blemish of Colonel Cole's misconduct.

Another project that I felt was of great importance to the Puerto Rican economy was the acquisition of at least one sugar "central"—that is, a sugar-processing plant—to operate as a yardstick and measure its performance under the optimum conditions of wages and hours against that of the other centrals. However, there was some question whether the PRRA could do this under the terms of the executive order. I decided to see what I could do with Comptroller General McCarl. He was not as unapproachable and impregnable as was generally assumed, provided one started with the assumption that he was God. I asked him to show me how we could translate the provision permitting the PRRA to supply agricultural implements into an authorization to acquire a sugar factory.

"If you use the right language," McCarl said, "you can do anything." And we did.

The "central" would be run as a cooperative and I insisted that its lands be equal to the best in the island, and that the mill be at least as well equipped as many of the other "centrals" against whose production the efficiency of our operation would be measured. We made an extensive survey of the mills to find one that would meet these conditions, and in a number of cases, prices skyrocketed the moment the PRRA expressed an interest. We finally decided on "Central" Lafayette owned by French interests. Working out the details of its management was a long and complex job, but soon the mill was a going operation.

So matters were progressing on the economic front, but there were unexpected clouds on the horizon. Our problem was one man, Pedro Albizu Campos, leader of the Nationalist Party. He was of mixed Spanish and Negro blood, the illegitimate son of a wealthy white Ponce businessman and one of his house-servants. His father sent him to Harvard. He was not Negroid in appearance, and as he was not considered a Negro but a Latin American, he encountered none of the prejudice that he would otherwise have experienced. Harvard in the century's second decade—as in my time—did not discriminate against Negroes, but they did suffer a kind of isolation and were forced to associate chiefly with other black students.* Albizu Campos escaped all that. Known as "Pete," he was a popular student and was elected president of the Cosmopolitan Club whose membership consisted of students from foreign countries. When the United States entered the war, he was filled with patriotic fervor and wanted to be among the first to go and fight the Kaiser. He returned to Puerto Rico and was assigned to a Negro regiment. It was a new experience for Albizu Campos; his regiment trained in the South and for the first time he learned what it was to be a Negro, not only in the army, but in America. All his love for America turned to hate.

When he returned to Puerto Rico, he voiced his hatred for all things American, announced that the transfer of Puerto Rico from Spain, having been achieved by force, was null and void, and that he would use force to drive out the Americans. He declared himself President of the Republic of Puerto Rico, assumed the trappings of power, referred to himself as "my person" and combined a fierce fanaticism with a paranoid megalomania. He organized his young followers into a "liberation army," uniformed in black shirts and equipped with rifles. His activities were tolerated and eventually led to bloodshed.

Unable to enlist the support of the student body at the University of Puerto Rico, Albizu Campos reviled the boys as homosexuals and the girls as prostitutes—perversions brought about, he declared, by American influence. Indignant, the students resolved to hold a protest meeting and declare him *persona non grata* to the university. Determined to prevent the meeting, he sent an automobile-load of heavily armed Nationalists to

---

* In the early 1920s, we on *The Nation* learned that Negroes were being excluded from Harvard's new freshman dormitories, a policy which had the support of President A. Lawrence Lowell. We started a round robin of protest among Harvard alumni. I wrote personal letters to members of my '07 class. Lewis Gannett, '13, asked his father, the Reverend William Channing Gannett, '60, to secure the signatures of the ten surviving members of that Civil War class. Like a similar campaign to protest Lowell's intention to establish a quota for Jews at Harvard, our tactics were effective. The Negro exclusion policy was dropped.

break it up. But informed of his intention, the police intercepted the car at the university gate and ordered its occupants to turn around and head for the police station. A policeman stationed himself on the running board. A shot from within the car felled him. The police returned the fire. In the fusillade four Nationalists and an innocent bystander were killed. At the Nationalists' funeral Albizu Campos declared them to be patriots and martyrs to independence, and pledged that for every life taken, the life of one "continental oppressor" would be forfeited. He named Francis Riggs, Chief of the Insular Police, as one who would be singled out for reprisal. A few days later, as he was leaving church, unarmed, Riggs was murdered by two young Nationalists. The assassins were caught, taken to the police station and killed by the police who alleged they were reaching for guns.

Riggs was not a typical police chief. A retired army colonel, he had served as a military attaché and in various diplomatic posts abroad. He was a kind, cultured man, fluent in Spanish and sincerely interested in Puerto Rico's needs and aspirations. Both Muñoz Marin and I deplored the death of Riggs and I asked Muñoz if he was going to make a statement.

"I am not," he said.

"I mean a statement regretting his death."

"I am not. I have taken on the coalition. I'm not going to take on the Nationalists, too."

"You *should* take them on and denounce their campaign of terrorism," I said, puzzled and indignant at his refusal.

"I'm not going to" was his emphatic reply.

I felt my indignation rising. "I'm afraid you're just another politician. I thought you were something different."

He laid his hand on my shoulder. "Ernest, you're excited. Many lives may have to be lost in the liberation of Puerto Rico. I take the long-range view in contemplating the destiny of my country."

"I'm afraid you are just contemplating the destiny of Muñoz Marin."

"The destiny of Muñoz Marin and the destiny of Puerto Rico are inseparable."

I recorded our conversation that evening because it shocked me profoundly. I confess I was greatly disillusioned. I had had implicit faith in Muñoz Marin, in his integrity, his vision, his statesmanship. Now by his silence he was condoning murder, and indeed the whole Nationalist campaign of violence. We had disagreed on other occasions; only a few days before he had berated me because I had appointed the Territorial Commissioner of Health, Dr. Garrido Morales, to an advisory board in connection with a medical problem. My offense was that Garrido Morales was a Republican. Muñoz Marin was an exacting man, it was true, but I had always supported his views. Now I began to feel that we were working at cross-purposes.

I was deeply troubled and after a sleepless night, I went to him and again pleaded that a simple statement of sorrow at Riggs's death was the minimum of decency. I could not budge him. Subsequent events would widen the breach between us.

Then a political bomb exploded. In April of 1936, Senator Millard Tydings of Maryland introduced a bill "to provide for a referendum in Puerto Rico on the question of independence." There had been no warning—not even a rumor—of any such legislation in Puerto Rico. I had heard about it myself only three weeks earlier in Washington when Senator Tydings had asked me to come see him at the Capitol. "I'm going to introduce a bill to provide a referendum in Puerto Rico on independence and to give it to them if they want it," he said. "I've always been opposed to the United States taking over countries with cultures and traditions alien to ours. That's why I introduced my bill for Philippine independence."

"Have you talked to the President about it?" I asked.

"I have. He said, 'Why not try it? It may be a good idea, but I don't want it considered an administration measure.'"

"Have you talked to Secretary Ickes about it?" I asked.

"I have. He's all in favor of it."

When I spoke to Secretary Ickes, he said he strongly favored giving the people of Puerto Rico a chance to decide whether they wanted independence or not. If they wanted it, they should have it, but if they rejected it, it should put an end to the unrest aroused by their uncertainty about their future.

The bill was drafted by one of the Department of the Interior's lawyers, Frederick Bernays Wiener, and was modeled after the Tydings-McDuffie Act for the Philippines. It provided that the referendum would take place on the first Monday in November 1937, and that if the people of Puerto Rico voted for it, the legislature would convene a constitutional convention to draft a constitution for the Commonwealth of Puerto Rico. Then if the constitution was ratified by popular vote, Puerto Rico would achieve its independence in four years.

In Puerto Rico the coalition leaders declaimed violently against the bill. Muñoz Marin was also extremely indignant; in a public statement he charged me with its authorship and by implication with an act of treachery. I was intrigued at his backing away from the independence he had always advocated, but he said it was a brutal act, and very unfair to Puerto Rico. In this he was partly right; the bill was not nearly as generous as it should have been. The provisions that particularly aroused him stipulated that after independence, Puerto Rico would receive no further federal appropriations; that the activities of our federal agencies would cease; and that the tariff on Puerto Rican goods would be established at twenty-five percent for four years and then put on a par with other countries' imports to the United States.

Replying to Muñoz Marin's heated objections, I said, "What do you expect? You can't have your cake and eat it too. If you want independence and get it, you can't expect to have all the benefits Puerto Rico now enjoys by being under our flag. Of course, we can improve the bill by adding some 'going away presents' and other more generous terms."

"You can't impale me on that 'have your cake and eat it too,'" he exploded. "That is just what I *do* want."

Here was born the germ of an idea that would eventuate in a status for Puerto Rico that would permit it to have its cake and eat it too, a solution which would in a few years be achieved by Muñoz Marin's leadership and the generosity of the American people.

But at that time there was only anger and I was one of the targets. I was in the doghouse with virtually all Puerto Rican elements, and some newspaper comments were indeed scurrilous. *La Linterna*, one of the organs of the Republican Party, wrote:

> Roosevelt, the crippled and mentally unbalanced White House dweller, through his drunken agents, Ickes, Gruening and Tydings, does not hide his black hatred for the majority party in Puerto Rico, the Coalition. . . . Men like Ickes (read, habitual drunkard); men like Gruening (read, people of the lowest sort); men like Tydings (read, scented thief) who are the ones in power . . . ought to be behind bars in some penitentiary, for the good and the honor of humanity.

I made no secret of my belief that the Tydings bill would be useful in making it clear that the government and the people of the United States had no desire to keep Puerto Rico if its people wanted independence, but I also expressed my personal view that independence would be a mistake for the Puerto Ricans. It was a difficult position to be in, and even more difficult to defend, but it was motivated in part by my desire to achieve what I felt would benefit Puerto Rico the most, and in part by my fear that the island was not yet ready for independence. That fear had been deepened by the Nationalist violence of recent months, the failure of the Liberal Party leaders to disavow it, and the lack of restraint of a substantial section of the press. I knew that after more than a century of independence, every Latin-American country—with the possible exception of Costa Rica—had been torn by chaos and revolution, and the electoral process overturned by a succession of military dictatorships. Whatever the shortcomings of United States rule, it was trying to correct the economic inequities from which Puerto Rico had suffered, and to establish a firm belief in the democratic process, both in principle and in practice. We were making headway on both fronts, but in my opinion the job was not yet over.

To further complicate my position, I fell out of favor with the Catholic Church over an issue that had claimed my support many times before— birth control. By August of 1936, eleven months after the PRRA had been organized, we had put 59,000 people to work. It was only a temporary inroad on the problem of unemployment, for Puerto Rico's rapidly growing population—now at 1,750,000 with a density of 541 to the square mile, and increasing at double the birth rate of the United States —would eventually wreck our program. Unless some steps were taken to slow down the population growth, our efforts would be nullified.

I called on the Bishop of San Juan, the Right Reverend Edwin V. Byrne with whom I had established friendly personal relations. Francis Shea and I had visited him several times and the bishop was obviously pleased that our general counsel was a Catholic. Shea shared my views on birth control, but when we had brought up the subject on a previous visit, the bishop had understandably expressed his opposition. Now I felt it essential to try again.

I presented my case, with all the facts and figures at my command about the unemployment, poverty and ill-health of the burgeoning Puerto Rican population, and then proposed birth-control clinics as an essential and practical approach to the solution to these problems. In conclusion I asked for his tacit support. "If we started a program of maternal health clinics where good Puerto Rican Catholic mothers, who had had eight, nine and ten children but did not want to have eleven, twelve and thirteen, could get the necessary advice and information, wouldn't you be willing to look the other way?"

Bishop Byrne thought for a while, then asked, "Would there be any publicity about these centers?"

"Not," I said, "if it would prevent your looking the other way."

"I will look the other way," said Bishop Byrne.

"Bishop, you're wonderful," I said.

I called in the health and welfare staffs. "We're going to open maternal health clinics," I told them, "one in every *municipio* (of which there were seventy-seven) and as many as possible in San Juan." But we were able to start only fourteen because of staff limitations and the scarcity of birth-control information and contraceptive devices. And I left happily for Washington to report to the Congress on the progress of our reconstruction programs, confident that the birth-control clinics were an important part of our overall objective.

A week later in the Interior Department, my secretary laid a newspaper on my desk—the *Catholic Review* of Baltimore. There on the front page was an attack on our maternal health clinics written by Reverend M. J. Conley, at the request, he said, of the Most Reverend Bishop Byrne of San Juan. It referred to the maternal health centers as an "insidious and sophisticated crime against God and humanity" and labeled them in the headlines as "attacks on the Church." While I was wondering what might have caused the Bishop to reverse his stand, the phone rang.

"New York is calling. Democratic National Committee Headquarters." It was Jim Farley.

"Gruening, what in hell is going on in Puerto Rico?"

"What *is* going on in Puerto Rico?" I said.

"Well, whatever it is, stop it. We've had three bishops in here this morning. Have you seen this week's *Tablet?*" (The organ of the Brooklyn Archdiocese.)

"Have you seen this week's issue of *America?*" (The Jesuit Weekly.)

"No, I haven't."

"Well, take a look at them. This is hurting us in the campaign. I'm going to Hyde Park tomorrow, and I want to be able to tell the boss that whatever we've been doing, we're not doing any more."

Who was I to jeopardize Roosevelt's campaign for reelection? That November he would carry only forty-six out of forty-eight states.

I returned to Puerto Rico and immediately called on Bishop Byrne. After an exchange of greetings, I said, "I saw your article in the *Catholic Review* of Baltimore. I thought you'd agreed to look the other way."

Bishop Byrne laid his hand on his heart and sighed, "I had no idea you'd do it on such a scale."

Of course, that was not the answer. I learned later that word of the maternal health clinics had reached Cardinal Hayes in New York and that he had called the Bishop.

The next day at the PRRA office, I told the social workers and medical staff what had happened. I expressed my deep regret—which they all shared—and said that no one on the PRRA payroll could take part in these clinics any longer. My instructions were carried out. Yet most of the clinics continued. They were so popular that doctors, nurses and others working as volunteers kept them going.

That was not the end of the story. When the Puerto Rican legislature met the following January, a bill was introduced to void the restrictions in the law forbidding the dissemination and use of contraceptive materials. It passed the House and when it was up before the Senate, Bishop

Byrne heard about it. I was again in Washington and Governor Winship phoned to tell me that the Bishop had come to him and had demanded that he veto the bill. The Catholic Church was opposed to it, he had said, and a Protestant governor had no right to impose his ideas on a Catholic country. He had been very angry and the governor was much perturbed.

"What do you think I should do?" he asked.

"I'll tell you what you should do," I said. "The bill is about to pass the Senate. When it does, leave Puerto Rico and appoint Rafael Menendez Ramos, the Commissioner of Agriculture, as acting governor. You've appointed him before. He's a devout Catholic, but he'll sign the bill. Then it will have been the work of a Catholic House, a Catholic Senate and a Catholic Puerto Rican governor."

"But I don't want to seem to be running away from this issue. I've talked to several people since I talked with the Bishop, and I'm convinced it's a desirable bill."

"You won't be running away from it. If you feel inclined, you can say you favor the bill before you leave. But by letting Menendez Ramos sign it into law, you'll refute the Bishop's contention that it's a Protestant imposition."

The governor came to Washington and Acting Governor Rafael Menendez Ramos signed the bill. The maternal health clinics continued and under Puerto Rican auspices. They were now sanctioned by law.

I was extremely proud of the work the PRRA had been able to accomplish in spite of the opposition we had encountered. Its employees, many of whom I had appointed, were able men and I was distressed to learn that they were being pressured for contributions to the Liberal Party. I asked our Director of Personnel, Luis Raul Esteves, to investigate. Colonel Esteves was the adjutant-general of the Puerto Rico National Guard. I had appointed him because of his integrity and because he was known to be apolitical, although his brother Guillermo, the assistant regional administrator, was a member of the Liberal Party. Colonel Esteves uncovered a widespread system of kickbacks. Employees were pressured to join in a "socioeconomic" society called *Renovacion*, a front that channeled their membership dues to the Liberal Party. Some of the money thus collected went to pay the salary and expenses of Ruby Black in Washington.

It was a deeply disturbing revelation to me. I had obviously been misguided in letting the PRRA become a political arm of the Liberal Party. Political contributions were illegal, in violation of the federal criminal code, and those participating could have been prosecuted. The Chief Counsel of the PRRA, Moses Huberman, who had succeeded Francis

Shea when he left to become Dean of the University of Buffalo Law School, advised me that I had no choice but to fire everyone who had contributed to *Renovacion*. It would have meant discharging most of our employees and that was obviously impossible. I requested the resignation of six division chiefs who had initiated the scheme and had been active in its conduct.

My action further widened the breach with Muñoz Marin. When he left for Washington soon after, the newspapers announced that one of his objectives was to have me removed as administrator of the PRRA and as Director of the Division of Territories and Island Possessions.

Government action against the Nationalists further separated us. Their assassinations and attempted assassinations had continued. Santiago Iglesias, Puerto Rico's resident commissioner, was fired on several times and wounded while delivering a speech in the public square at Mayaguez. One shot which struck the microphone would, but for its interception, have killed him. Shots were fired at Governor Winship while he was reviewing a parade. Albizu Campos and six Nationalist leaders had been arrested and charged with conspiracy to overthrow the government by force. This lesser charge—instead of prosecuting them for being accessories to murder—was the result of Nationalist intimidations. Prospective jurors got letters threatening them with death if they served, and there was some difficulty in impaneling a jury. But finally, Albizu and six of his associates were tried in the United States District Court at San Juan and sentenced to six- to ten-year prison terms in the federal penitentiary at Atlanta. On appeal their sentences were affirmed by the First Circuit Court in Boston.

Muñoz Marin took the position that these Nationalists were the victims of political persecution and sought to hold me responsible. In a letter to Secretary Ickes, he enclosed a clipping from *The New York Times* which reported a speech made at the Pan-American Peace Conference that was being held in Buenos Aires. The speaker was a member of Puerto Rico's Liberal Party and one of the attorneys in the PRRA's legal division who had taken leave without revealing his purpose. His speech was an attack on United States imperialism in Puerto Rico.

Muñoz Marin also wrote Ickes that my policy of prosecuting the Nationalists for political offenses was destroying goodwill toward America. It was part of his plan to discredit me, and I replied to Ickes at length, pointing out that I had nothing to do with the prosecution of the Nationalists. It was entirely in the hands of the Department of Justice and they had been tried not for "political offenses" but for their complicity in murder and terrorism which, apparently, Muñoz Marin condoned. I also pointed out that he was behind the anti-American attack in Buenos Aires and, as part of his policy to achieve Puerto Rican independence and become the first president of Puerto Rico, he was attempting to stir up as much antagonism as possible toward the United States, both in Puerto Rico and in other Latin-American countries.

The attack on the administration's policies in Puerto Rico did not go unanswered in Buenos Aires. Feeling that Roosevelt's Good Neighbor Policy and his efforts in Puerto Rico should be truthfully presented, I had written the President several weeks earlier recommending the appointment of Emilio del Toro, Chief Justice of Puerto Rico's Supreme Court, as a member of the United States delegation to the Buenos Aires Conference. He was appointed and accompanied President Roosevelt to Buenos Aires where he refuted the misrepresentation of United States policy in Puerto Rico. His appointment also served to initiate the practice of utilizing qualified Puerto Ricans in our Foreign Service in Spanish-speaking countries.

Clearly, my differences with Muñoz Marin—and through him with the Liberal Party—seemed now irreconcilable, a fact further demonstrated by the resignation of Carlos E. Chardon as the PRRA's regional administrator. He had been a member of the President's Policy Commission on Puerto Rico which had drawn up the recommendations that formed the basis of PRRA programs, and had proved to be one of its most able executives. The reason he gave for his resignation was that I had entrusted the legal work connected with the purchase of the "Central" Lafayette to American lawyers on the PRRA staff rather than Puerto Ricans, and that this indicated my lack of confidence in Puerto Rican talent and integrity.

I could not believe that this was the real reason for his resignation. I suspected that he was under pressure from the Liberal Party leadership. The employment of "continental" lawyers was not a new issue. It had been raised early in the organization of the PRRA by the Puerto Rico Bar Association, and the *importados* were a continuing subject of adverse newspaper criticism. Actually we had three times as many Puerto Rican lawyers on our staff as Americans; we had entrusted our most important legal task—that of bringing *quo warranto* proceedings against the sugar companies for violation of the five-hundred-acre law—to a Puerto Rican attorney, Guerra Mondragon. But the few American lawyers who successively headed our legal division, and the others whose services they engaged, were familiar with the intricacies of United States legal and budget procedures, and their employment was essential. Moreover they were earnest, young New Dealers who were deeply dedicated to our programs. I was grateful, and proud of them.

I tried by phone and proxy to persuade Chardon to reconsider but gave up when I became convinced that it was a political ploy. In his place, I appointed Miles Fairbanks who had extensive administrative experience in agriculture, both in Maryland and in Puerto Rico. He replaced the PRRA officials who had been let out as a result of the *Renovacion* investigation with men of ability regardless of their party affiliation. But *La Democracia* and *Imparcial*—which, under the editorship of Antonio Ayuso Valdivieso, was an indefatigable spewer of distortion and hate against Americans—charged me with turning over the PRRA to the coalition. Actually, I had left all the appointments to Fairbanks.

I would not have been surprised if Chardon's resignation had been followed by wholesale resignations of other PRRA officials. But except for his brother and one or two other personal associates, the Puerto Ricans who held positions of authority stayed on. The Esteves brothers, Antonio Luchetti, and Dr. Moralea Otero, the head of our health division, told me they had no intention of resigning and made clear that they did not sympathize with Chardon's action. Guillermo Esteves proved a tower of strength, efficiency and loyalty, and as Miles Fairbanks had, of necessity, to spend much of his time in the field with "Central" Lafayette and the other agricultural cooperatives, Esteves carried a large part of the PRRA administrative burdens on his own shoulders. Indeed the work went more smoothly than before. Even so, the press campaign continued with undiminished virulence.

Then on Palm Sunday March 27, 1937, a tragic incident took place in Ponce that further inflamed the animosity of the Liberal Party. There will probably always be two different versions of what quickly came to be called the "Ponce Massacre." A group of Nationalists had sought a permit to parade, which had been granted with the understanding that it would be a civil demonstration. But on learning that the marchers would wear the uniforms of the Liberation Army, the permit was withdrawn for fear the demonstration would lead to bloodshed, and every effort was made to persuade the Nationalists not to parade. They refused. The marchers assembled and the chief of the Ponce police, Captain Soldevila, faced the Nationalist columns, calling out in a loud voice that the parade was prohibited. At that moment, shots rang out and a policeman standing at Soldevila's side fell, killed by a bullet. A volley of shots then came from the nearby Nationalist headquarters and another policeman fell, mortally wounded. The police returned fire, and nineteen were killed and several wounded in the bloody fusillade.

The unresolved question was: Who fired first? The Nationalists and their Liberal Party supporters maintained that it was the police. Subsequently, Arthur Garfield Hays, of the American Civil Liberties Union, made a study of the affair and of the whole question of civil liberties in

Puerto Rico. He produced what seemed to me a biased report which evaded the reality that it was the Nationalists with their campaign of assassinations and terrorism who were the real foes of civil liberties.

I was in Washington when the "Ponce Massacre" took place. After considering all the accounts, reading the subsequent testimony at the inquest and studying the photographs taken on the scene, I concluded that the Nationalists had provoked the disaster and fired the first shots. Most of my liberal friends thought otherwise. When my views became known, I was the object of journalistic attacks in Puerto Rico and the United States. After consulting with Ruby Black, John Franklin Carter, Jr., writing in a syndicated column under the pen name of Jay Franklin, urged that Governor Winship and I resign, and that if we did not, President Roosevelt should fire us.

Another sore spot in our relations with Puerto Rico revolved around the issue of teaching English. Both the Liberal Party and the Nationalists opposed it. Muñoz Marin, whose bilingualism was a major factor in his influence and effectiveness, might have been expected to support it as an economic benefit to his fellow Puerto Ricans, but he was uninterested. The incident which brought the issue to a head was the refusal to renew the teaching contract of a very spirited young woman, Inez Mendoza de Pallacios, who had for ten years been a teacher in the Central High School. Her subject was Spanish, but she was charged with having fought against the use of English as the language of instruction in the lower grades. Señorita Mendoza was an *Independentista* and later married Muñoz Marin, and her position was probably pedagogically correct, but it became a part of the larger controversy over English instruction. The matter never came to my attention, but it was the subject of animated correspondence between Secretary Ickes and Arthur Garfield Hays, who had been asked to interest the American Civil Liberties Union in her cause. Inez Mendoza carried her protest to President and Mrs. Roosevelt, but Ickes sided with the insular educational authorities on the grounds that she had been needlessly insubordinate. The language controversy was resolved when Dr. José Gallardo was appointed the island's new commissioner of education. President Roosevelt accompanied his notification of the appointment with a letter which represented the views he had expressed to both Secretary Ickes and to me. It regretted that hundreds of thousands of Puerto Ricans had virtually no knowledge of English and that it was "an inescapable part of American policy that the coming generation of American citizens of Puerto Rico grow up with complete facility in the English language." The draft of the letter was mine. Ickes approved it and President Roosevelt signed it on April 8, 1937.

It seemed to me that I had won President Roosevelt's confidence and support as PRRA administrator, but my relationship with Secretary Ickes was clearly another matter. That spring, Walter Flavius McCaleb presented himself to me as a journalist who wanted to write a book on the new developments in Puerto Rico. He was given much of my time and that of PRRA officials who took him on tours of all our projects. He turned out to be a spy sent by Ickes. I encountered him in the Secretary's outer office in Washington several weeks later, and he was embarrassed when I asked him how his book was coming along and who would publish it.

In June, Ickes wired to ask Governor Winship and me to come to Washington. We were met at the airport by Ebert K. Burlew, who told us that the Secretary had been ill and was recuperating at his home in Maryland. On the way out, Burlew began to put on an act. Shaking his head, he told Governor Winship that he was in deep trouble; the Senate was considering investigating his administration in Puerto Rico. When I asked what senators were considering this, he was at a loss, and then came up with the name of La Follette. I suspected that this was false because I had kept in touch with "young Bob," and knew that if he had entertained questions about Puerto Rican affairs he would have communicated with me. Burlew's ploy was a prelude to a plan of the Secretary's.

Ickes received us in his bedroom. He followed Burlew's line by saying that there was discontent on the Hill with affairs in Puerto Rico and that he felt it his duty to send a commission to investigate the situation to forestall a Congressional inquiry. Specifically he requested that Winship ask for the investigation through me as Director of the Division of Territories and Island Possessions. Winship replied that he would be delighted to have a Congressional inquiry, but that he could not see his way clear to asking for a commission that Ickes would appoint. Ickes renewed his request. Winship said he would think it over.

I called Bob La Follette that afternoon and asked whether there was any truth in the report that he wanted to investigate affairs in Puerto Rico. "It's the first I've heard of it," he said.

I secured an appointment at the White House the next day and reported to the President on the PRRA, the aftermath of the "Ponce Massacre" and on conditions generally. Then the President said, "Secretary Ickes wants to have an investigation of Puerto Rican affairs. He thinks he can stall off a Congressional investigation. What do you think of it?"

"I think it would be a great mistake," I said. "I have found no evidence of any pending Congressional investigation. Just this morning's paper tells of a fusillade by Nationalists on Judge Cooper as he was riding in his car. (Robert A. Cooper was the United States District Court judge in Puerto Rico who had tried the Nationalists.) Fortunately he wasn't hurt. An investigation now would be taken as evidence of lack of confidence, would increase the ferment, and encourage violence at a time when your administration should show its support of Governor Winship."

"There will be no investigation by Secretary Ickes," said the President.

Several days later when Ickes returned to his office, he had words for me. "What do you mean by opposing my plan to have an investigation of Puerto Rico?" he said. "That was a distinct act of disloyalty on your part. I have a good mind to ask for your resignation immediately."

"Mr. Secretary," I said, "the President asked for my opinion and I gave it to him. I told him I thought it unwise. I didn't know that you wanted to be surrounded by 'yes men.' "

"I wouldn't know what to do with them," he said, "but once a policy has been decided upon, I expect conformity."

"Well, obviously the policy hadn't been decided upon since the President raised the question. And I shall always give my opinions on any matter the President asks me about."

Ickes had, in fact, already picked out his commission and he was boiling mad that he could not send it. He wanted to use it to get rid of Winship, but that in my view was hardly the time or the way to do it.

There were a number of pleasant developments in Puerto Rico when I returned in June. Colonel John Womack Wright had undertaken to improve the relationship between the American military and the Puerto Rican people, with happy results. I had come to know Wright in Portland where he was commanding officer. In addition to his army career —he was both a scholar and a military historian—he had served in Cuba, Mexico, and the Philippines, and spoke Spanish fluently. President Roosevelt had assigned him to succeed Colonel Cole on my recommendation.

Wright was enthusiastic about restoring the fortifications, but funds had been denied, and I could not let PRRA funds be used for the purpose, much as I favored the restoration. It was clearly the War Department's responsibility. Working on it together with an assist from President Roosevelt, we enlisted the active support of Major General Frank McCoy, who commanded the Second Corps which included Puerto Rico, and the money was found.

Wright also arranged for an historic pageant in which his soldiers, garbed in seventeenth-century uniforms, reenacted the attempted landing and the repulse of the Dutch fleet in 1625. He had erected an arch over one of the gateways to the Casa Blanca with the coat of arms of Ponce de Leon. The unveiling of the new arch took place amid great acclaim.

These and other activities brought a great appreciation for Wright and helped erase the memory of his predecessor's performance. The Puerto

Rican legislature adopted a concurrent resolution asking that the rank of the army's commanding officer in Puerto Rico be made a brigadier-generalcy and that Colonel Wright, on whom the resolution bestowed glowing praise, be promoted to it—an unprecedented legislative action. Unfortunately, a new army regulation prevented his promotion, so he retired as a colonel, having established a warm spot in the hearts of the Puerto Ricans by his conduct in a post that he had made as much diplomatic as military.

After only a year and a half, the PRRA was making great strides in its reconstruction programs. Land distribution was well underway and hundreds of hurricane- and termite-proof houses, constructed with cement from our own plant, were already tenanted. "Central" Lafayette was functioning as a cooperative. Our islandwide power program was achieving its objectives of increased hydroelectric output and reduced rates, and for the first time electricity was made available to many outlying rural areas. We had rehabilitated 8,672 coffee farmers, 366 fruit growers, 1900 tobacco growers and 163 cotton planters. We had produced food crops among the cash crops on 61,198 acres. We had planted 30,490,000 trees and our nurseries were producing some twenty million seedlings annually. We had built forty-five medical dispensaries, nineteen health units, two municipal hospitals, treated 96,800 patients and given dental care to 25,760. We had constructed eight new buildings for the university and some twenty-four other school buildings. We had rebuilt the School of Tropical Medicine.

There was much more to be done, of course, but I felt, with the PRRA functioning so well, that I should take care of my long-neglected responsibilities in other areas. I had made only one brief trip to Alaska and none to Hawaii. The Philippines were being added to the responsibilities of the Division of Territories and Island Possessions and I had never been there. So I wrote the President accordingly, submitting my resignation as administrator of the PRRA.

The President waited for over a month and then replied on July 13, 1937:

. . . I would hesitate to accede to this request at this time were it not that I know that through your directorship of the Division of Territories and Island Possessions you will continue to keep close watch on the conduct and progress of affairs in Puerto Rico.

15

ALASKA, HO!

There is one word of advice and caution to be given those intending to visit Alaska for pleasure, for sightseeing. If you are old, go by all means; but if you are young, stay away until you are older. The scenery of Alaska is so much grander than anything else of the kind in the world that, once beheld, all other scenery becomes flat and insipid. It is not well to dull one's capacity for such enjoyment by seeing the finest first.
—HENRY GANNETT

On my first day in the Interior Department, September 17, 1934, fire destroyed the greater part of Nome. This remote town had leaped into fame in Alaska's romantic gold rush days. A major "strike" in nearby creeks and the discovery of gold on the adjacent Bering Sea coast, within a year after the stampede to the Klondike, drew thousands of prospectors from the Yukon Territory on the Canadian side of the border to Alaska. Nome became a "boom town," but the boom was brief; by 1934 its population had dwindled from twenty thousand at the turn of the century to a scant fifteen hundred. It remained a tourist attraction for those hardy enough to make the trip, but then the fire destroyed even that claim to fame. Yet Nome still retained its importance as the principal trading and distributing area for a vast region, the headquarters of the Second Judicial Division and the seat of a number of branch agencies of the federal government whose principal offices were in the territorial capital, Juneau.

The fire wiped out virtually every business, most of the municipal and federal agencies and the greater part of the residential district. The city was in serious trouble, and it was the responsibility of the new Division of Territories and Island Possessions, six thousand miles away in Washington, to act as agent and coordinator of government relief. We promptly requested $50,000 from Harry Hopkins's Federal Emergency Relief Administration for food, clothing and temporary shelter. We secured a grant and loan from the Public Works Administration to rebuild the federal and municipal structures and to help the people of Nome plan for the city's reconstruction. The United States Coast Guard, rushed its cutters *Chelan* and *Northland* to the stricken city. The Red Cross responded to our first appeal. Meanwhile, Nome's people exhibited the energy and ingenuity typical of the frontier. Committees to grapple with every problem were immediately organized, and the dispossessed were given food and shelter.

Our problems were complicated by the need for speedy action. In 1934 the only transportation between Nome and the outside world was by ship, and within five or six weeks the Bering Sea would freeze. Boats would have to sail immediately from Seattle with whatever materials and supplies were needed through the long winter until the late spring "break-up." The dogsled was still the only overland means of transportation in and out of Nome once winter had set in; commercial air service between the territory and the States was still six years away.

Yet in less than a week after the fire, "Bob" Ellis, one of Alaska's best-known bush pilots, flew from Seattle to Nome in a pontoon plane carrying four passengers important to Nome's emergency, having made only two stops en route, one at Ketchikan, seven hundred miles north of Seattle, and one at Tanana, halfway across the main body of Alaska; reaching Nome through a dense fog. It was a great feat of daring and skill. Nome had no harbor; vessels had to lie half a mile offshore and their cargoes had to be transferred to lighters. To make matters even worse, the fall of 1934 was troubled by more severe storms than usual; the first snow fell on October 15, and a blizzard and howling gale followed a week later. But working against time and nature, we rushed relief supplies to Nome by ship from Seattle and evacuated several hundred survivors. A thousand or more chose to stay to begin the arduous task of rebuilding their lives. By November, when the weather finally closed in, reconstruction was well underway. One thought cheered the victims of the disaster. It might have happened two months later—after the last boat had sailed.

My first year and a half in the Division of Territories was largely devoted to Puerto Rico's pressing needs. Alaska's problems were handled in the division by Paul W. Gordon, a Quaker and devoted public servant, who had been superintendent of Indian Affairs in Alaska, and, of course,

by Anthony J. Dimond, Alaska's delegate to Congress. So I had delayed
going to Alaska, but in the winter of 1935–1936, president Charles Ernest Bunnell of the University of Alaska invited me to deliver the commencement address the following May and that seemed an excellent opportunity for a visit.

On May 9 the S.S. *Alaska* moved away from its Seattle dock. Its
passengers gave more than a clue to the land for which they were bound
—and its people. On board were no fancily dressed tourists. There were
grizzled miners bound for the creeks, operating personnel for the canneries, a few traveling salesmen, employees of the summer-activated outdoor government services, wives and young girls in slacks, children
warmly bundled up against the cool breezes of a sea voyage. Everyone
was friendly and informal.

We entered the "Inside Passage," a thousand miles of protected water-
way stretching north-northwest from Puget Sound to Skagway. The jag-
ged Olympic Mountains to port, and the Coast Range crests with Mount
Baker to starboard, ushered in a jouney unique in its intimacy of land and
sea. Only twice, beyond the northern tip of Vancouver Island, and again
past the Queen Charlotte Islands in Canadian waters, was there a brief exposure to the swells of the open ocean. Our course often followed narrow
channels, and wound between forested slopes rising more and more
steeply on both sides of the ship. Communities were few, habitations between them almost nonexistent. Occasionally a totem pole revealed a tiny
Indian settlement. Farther north in Alaskan waters the mountains rose
even higher; the timber line appeared; above it, meadows of a special brilliant green and bare rock crowned by snows. Great waterfalls generated
their misty spray and glistening glaciers discharged their crystal cargo of
blue-white icebergs into the sea.

Our first stop was Ketchikan, which appropriately had adopted the title
of "Alaska's first city." Against a pleasing backdrop of steep forested hills,
culminating in graceful Deer Mountain, the city extended along the east
shore of Tongass Narrows, a branch of the Inside Passage. The sheer terrain had forced its houses upward, tier on tier. Inland along a rushing
creek the slope was more gradual, but it was this creek, with its abundance of salmon, that had given birth to Ketchikan. Canneries established
by California enterprises processed more salmon there than in any other
place on earth. In the mid-1930s, the catch was reaching its all-time high.
The harbor was crowded with brightly colored fishing boats, moored to
each other for lack of dock space—a forest of masts matching the vertical patterns of the forested hillsides. Fisheries and forestry—they were
Ketchikan's present and future potentials. All houses were of wood; on
many, an outside flight of stairs led to a hillside perch with a spectacular
view. The streets were boardwalks of heavy planking.

My stay in Ketchikan, as in other stops on the *Alaska*'s run, was limited to her few hours in port. I was met by a delegation including the mayor, genial Jack Talbot, A. H. Ziegler and Harry McClain—leading attorneys—and Norman ("Doc") Walker, a territorial senator, who took me on a tour of the city. Luncheon was with the Rotary Club at its weekly meeting. I was scheduled to be the speaker and discuss the functions of the government subagency which I headed. In my opinion, its chief aim was to help the people of Alaska develop the territory as they thought best. Their views would be our principal consideration; we were not trying to run Alaska from Washington.

I had made up my mind that this first trip was to be a voyage of exploration and education. My information about Alaska had been secondhand: books, government reports, correspondence with Alaskans—official and otherwise—conversations with those who had lived in Alaska. I wanted to listen. But as a visiting VIP I was expected to speak with oracular authority. Instead I gave my impressions of the small part of Alaska I had seen and spoke of the desirability of adding tourism to the territory's other industries. My audience listened politely, but I suspected that their minds were set on fishing and mining.

Visiting the curio shops in my morning tour of Ketchikan to see what Indian and Eskimo arts and crafts were offered, I found that the miniature totem poles destined for the tourist trade were "made in Japan." They were usually bone rather than wood and it seemed odd that the residents would sell such a product instead of their own local handicrafts. I inquired whether the Bureau of Indian Affairs could not encourage a greater production of local handicrafts and thus diminish off-season unemployment—inevitable in a fishing economy—but I was told that there was little interest among the younger generation of Indians in pursuing ancestral crafts. Totem-pole carving and erection had ceased, and even the totem poles of an earlier day were neglected and falling into disrepair. I resolved to discuss Alaska's regrettable lack of concern both for one aspect of her historic past and her future potential for tourism when I returned to Washington.

Leaving Ketchikan, the *Alaska* moved northward between islands and shores dense with luxuriant growth of spruce, hemlock and cedar. They were virgin forests as yet untouched by the woodman's axe, but the number of dead treetops tapering starkly over the massed green aroused my curiosity. These, I was informed, were overripe trees crowded by their fellows and dying on the stump. Yet this was a national forest—The Tongass—and as such presumably dedicated to conservation and wise utilization, not disease, decay and death. Through the years, I was to learn—as one American-owned pulp and paper mill after the other established itself in neighboring British Columbia—that the politics of the

United States Forest Service had, at least as far as Alaska was concerned, become rigidified; its arbitrary attitudes and restrictions had for over thirty years prevented the proper use of Alaska's great timber resources. Not until midcentury, in response to the mounting critical clamor aroused by the wiser policies of neighboring Canada, was there a realistic reappraisal of Forest Service policy which permitted the careful utilization of Alaska's forest resources and finally ended nearly half a century of waste.

Wrangell, a fishing community on an island of the same name, and one of Alaska's oldest settlements, was our next stop. It had been an Indian village until Baron Wrangell, one of the later Russian governors, built a fort there, Redoubt Saint Dyonisius, to ward off the encroachments of the powerful and aggressive Hudson's Bay Company. After the Treaty of Cession in 1867, United States troops were stationed briefly at Fort Wrangell, and in the 1870s it was the starting place for the earliest gold-rushers. It had remained a mixed white and Indian community. The planked main street ran straight from the dock an eighth of a mile and then curved around the mud flats of the bay where fishing boats were moored in readiness for the season. I was taken on a quick tour of the village, but I would gladly have tarried over the marvelous collection of Tlingit headdresses, masks, shaman's rattles and other artifacts at both of Walter C. Waters's two curio stores. He infomed me with a smile that he believed in "working both sides of the street." Customers, he observed, had a habit of looking and then going to a competitor to compare prices. In Wrangell they went from one of Mr. Waters's stores to the other. If they bought at all, they bought from him.

There was just time to drive south some four miles along the shore, over Wrangell's only bit of highway, to Wrangell Institute, a boarding school for young "native" children conducted by the Office of Indian Affairs, one of three such institutions on Alaska. I visited the classes, inspected the children's woodcarvings, basketry, moccasins and other handicrafts and discussed the problems of the dual educational system with the principal, Mr. Charles W. Miller. In Alaska one set of schools was conducted for the children of aboriginal stock—Indians, Eskimos and Aleuts—by the Department of the Interior, supported by annual appropriations from the Congress, while another was conducted by the territory, for white children and children of mixed blood whose families led "a civilized life," a phrase which stemmed from Alaska's earliest days as an American possession when the indigenous inhabitants were largely primitives.

North of Wrangell, we saw ice cakes floating in the Inside Passage. They came from the LeConte Glacier, the southernmost and one of the most active of the tidal glaciers, winding down from the icecap which covers the coastal range in this region. Several other glaciers extending into tidewater were also visible beneath a granite shaft that reared some 1800 feet above the range's crest. It was called the Devil's Thumb and had hitherto, I was told, defied the most intrepid climbers. It was so steep that its seaward western face held no snow; it was a bare rock pillar, pinkish in the evening light.

The city of Juneau nestled in a small triangle sloping toward the water's edge below steep mountain parapets. It was an impressive setting for the territory's capital. Its snug site had been wrought by Gold Creek, a torrent rushing through a narrow canyon between the mountain walls and emptying into the Gastineau Channel. It was up this stream in 1880 that Joe Juneau and Richard Harris found gold, the first important strike in Alaska. While Mount Juneau on the northeast—a sheer three-thousand-foot rock wall—dominated the scene, the most impressive man-made structure clung to the vertical cliff south of town. It was the twelve-story mill of the Alaska-Juneau mine. At first glimpse it looked like a high luxury hotel, especially at night when its blazing lights were reflected in the channel. Another man-made structure, a handsome steel bridge recently completed with Public Works Administration funds, spanned the channel.

I was met by the governor of the territory, John Weir Troy, and other local dignitaries, and I sought their ideas about Juneau's as well as the territory's needs. As in virtually every Alaskan coastal community, a small-boat harbor or the improvement and enlargement of the existing harbor, a responsibility of the United States Army Engineers, came in for high priority. Airmail service, nonexistent at that time, also rated high, and I promised to work for both. Housing was likewise insufficient and hope was expressed that the newly established Federal Housing Authority would help speed construction.

In a stroll around town I observed some fine residences. But in the neighborhood of the mine and mine entrance, around the waterfront, and even through the central portion of the city, much of the housing was plainly slummy. One series of habitations under a single roof, called Robert's Row, were mere mansized kennels. I asked why these shacks were not condemned as health and fire hazards. Later I learned that some of the worst shanties were owned by the capital's leading citizens and were lucrative sources of income. Equally depressing were most of the dwellings in the Indian village on the flats just above the high-tide level. They were plainly visible from many of the surrounding and more loftily perched homes, including the porticoed Governor's Mansion.

Governor Troy planned to accompany me to the interior, and I was more than happy to have his company and the benefit of his experience. He was a genial man in his midsixties, who had come to Skagway in the Klondike days and was now the owner of Juneau's newspaper, the *Alaska Daily Empire*. It had been founded by another newspaperman, John F. A. Strong, who also came to Alaska during the gold rush. Appointed governor in 1915, he had leased the paper to Troy. But he was denied reappointment by President Wilson following the discovery that he was a Canadian by birth and although a resident for years in the territory had never been naturalized as an American citizen. His ineligibility had been exposed by his own newspaper's lessee, John Troy, who acquired possession of the paper when Strong left Alaska. Now, in 1936, Troy was governor and the paper was run by his son-in-law, Robert W. Bender, who had married his elder daughter, Helen. He, too, joined our party to the interior as did Ike Taylor, highway engineer and the executive head of the Alaska Road Commission. This agency, four years previously, had been transferred from the War Department to the Department of the Interior.

Hours after leaving Juneau, we passed through Icy Straight into the open Pacific. Shoreward the mighty Fairweather Range soared to its apex in 15,300-foot Mount Fairweather, a great natural Gothic cathedral of spires and crenelated crests glistening in the bright early evening light. The next day, at Yakutat, the sky was overcast and I had to forgo the sight of Mount Saint Elias, which I was told would be "right over there" if it were clear. Yakutat was an Indian village, the northernmost Tlingit community. Its tribal house, a community meeting place, was adorned with painted totemic designs. We visited the salmon cannery some three miles from the village, traveling over the narrow-gauge freight railway which enjoyed the name of "Yakutat & Southern R.R." Its officials, the manager informed me, were granted passes on any of the railroads in the United States.

Our next stop was Cordova, the name given by Spanish explorers to a small Indian settlement called Eyak on Orca Inlet in the eastern part of Prince William Sound. It was a fishing community that packed clams and crabs in addition to salmon. After the discovery of rich copper deposits in the Chitina Valley on the north slope of the Coast Range, and their purchase by a syndicate formed by J. P. Morgan and the Guggenheim Brothers, a railroad had been built from Kennecott to Cordova to bring out the ore. Like other Alaska coastal communities, the town was perched picturesquely on a steep slope, the houses rising from a waterfront crowded with fishing boats. Beyond these, on the outskirts of the town, a lovely little lake, Eyak, served as a landing field for float planes. Nearby a landing strip for planes on wheels was under construction, a Public Works Administration project.

I visited both the territorial school and the government school where students were taught to hammer copper into trays, bowls, paper cutters and other handicrafts. I was impressed by this use of the dominant resource of the region until I learned that the copper was imported from the States in sheets. In the local jewelry store, however, I saw attractive use made of the azurite, malachite and other copper ores derived from the nearby deposits.

From Cordova, the *Alaska* proceeded into Prince William Sound which was dotted with forested islands and deep fiords. At the head of one long fiord, the Valdez Arm, the town of Valdez was situated against a background of lofty peaks and descending glaciers. It was a point of entry to the interior by means of the only road of any length in Alaska, the so-called Richardson Highway, whose northern terminus was Fairbanks. This road, begun by the Alaska Road Commission in the century's first decade, followed the trail blazed by prospectors to reach the Klondike and later the placers in the Tanana Valley. It was, in 1936, still a rough road.

Our boat was met by Mayor C. J. Egan and a committee of citizens who told me immediately that the town had a grievance. With one voice they protested the tolls which the Department of the Interior had placed on trucks carrying freight to Fairbanks on the Richardson Highway. The object of their wrath was Colonel Otto F. Ohlson, the manager of the Alaska Railroad. This government-owned carrier, completed thirteen years earlier after long delays, extended from the port of Seward 470 miles north to Fairbanks. Owing to insufficient appropriations it had been built inadequately; much of the construction was temporary and repair and maintenance were costly. The feeder-wagon roads with which the Department of the Interior had been expected to develop the railway's traffic had not been built for want of appropriations. The railroad's operating losses aroused the ire of Congress and in 1920 a Senatorial committee was sent to investigate. The committee ordered an approximately fifty percent increase of the already high freight rates. Angry protests from the dwellers in the interior followed. They sought to solve their difficulty by intensifying the use of the Richardson Highway and making Valdez instead of Seward the point of entry for their supplies. But the Congress viewed the Richardson Highway with a jaundiced eye because of its high maintenance costs and its adverse effect on the railroad's revenues. The Alaska Road Commission was transferred from the War Department to the Interior Department and the Secretary was ordered to levy tolls on the highway at his discretion. A charge of $9 a ton on its freight had been imposed by Secretary Ickes, who also appointed Colonel Ohlson as manager of the Alaska Railroad with orders to "get it out of the red." The tolls were a blow to Valdez; they made it even more difficult to compete with the railroad. Seward had already become the chief gateway to the interior and Valdez was now fearful of becoming a ghost town. It was also threatened with the transfer of the Third Judicial Division Court to Anchorage.

I had heard about this controversy in Washington. Delegate Dimond had protested the tolls ever since they had been imposed, but Secretary Ickes remained adamant. I had accepted the departmental point of view that the commercial users of the highway should contribute to the cost of its maintenance, and by the same logic, that the cost of operating the railroad should be borne by the passengers and shippers, but I was impressed by the plight of Valdez, which was a pathetically rundown and decaying community. I argued the Interior Department's side of the case, and promised to present the Valdez point of view in Washington, but I was not hopeful of being able to bring about a change, and said so. It was the first of many vivid illustrations of how decisions of distant men controlled the lives and destinies of Alaskans, and how different things could look on the scene from the way they looked in Washington.

As the *Alaska* swung back through the Valdez Arm and reentered Prince William Sound, the great Columbia Glacier came into view. The ship stopped its engines a quarter of a mile from the face of the glacier, a vertical wall 250 feet high over most of its three-mile convex front. The steamer's whistle blew several sharp blasts—a performance for the benefit of the passengers to show that the vibrations would bring about the fall of ice. Several masses did fall; huge pinnacles toppled with a thunderous roar and set up a heavy swell which gave the ship considerable roll. Of the many tidal glaciers along the Alaskan coast, none was more impressive than this giant.

At the head of beautiful Resurrection Bay lay the city of Seward, our next stop, where we were greeted by Mayor Don Carlos Brownell. I spoke to the Chamber of Commerce at lunch, chatted with Ernest F. Jessen, editor of the tri-weekly Seward *Gateway* and visited the Jessie Lee Home, a Methodist mission for "native" children. Then we left for Anchorage on the Alaska Railroad in a special car provided by Colonel Ohlson. On the way north we saw Dall sheep grazing high up near the rocky summits of the Kenai Mountains, and on one occasion the train slowed down and blew its whistle to avoid striking a cow moose and calf on the tracks. The railway had obviously presented difficult engineering problems. The grades were steep and at one point a high wooden trestle curved and doubled back on itself to form a complete figure eight. The train took these trestles at a snail's pace.

We stopped briefly at Lawing on Kenai Lake to visit "Alaska Nellie." Nellie Neil, born in Missouri, the eldest of a family of twelve children, came to Seward when the construction of the railroad had begun, and her life and livelihood had been associated with it ever since. She had cooked for the advancing construction gang, then managed the railroad's round-house at Dead Horse Gulch. Hunting was her pastime, and she acquired the finest collection of big-game trophies in Alaska. With her husband, Will Lawing, she established a hunting and fishing lodge at the eastern end of Kenai Lake, a stone's throw from the railroad tracks. The train always stopped for fifteen minutes and "Alaska Nellie" displayed her trophies and gave a brief talk, profiting only by the sale of her book telling her life story. She was a slight woman, perhaps sixty-five years old, costumed in britches and boots. She had rigged fishing lines from a window in her log cabin to the lake. The lines were attached to a bell and whenever a rainbow trout hooked itself, the bell rang and the fish was retrieved.

Late arrival at Anchorage caused a scheduled luncheon to be changed to a dinner. The Anchorage Grill, a restaurant on Fourth Avenue, the town's principal thoroughfare, was filled to capacity and United States Commissioner Thomas C. Price acted as master of ceremonies. He voiced a complaint that I was to hear repeatedly against the arbitrary acts of a distant bureaucracy. Governor Troy also spoke and presented the view, widely held by Alaskans, that since the federal government owned over ninety-nine percent of the land in Alaska, and made it next to impossible to acquire any of it so that it was unavailable for revenue, it was proper that the federal government contribute substantially toward Alaska's development. If Uncle Sam would turn over the lands to Alaska, we could get along without such help, the Governor said. He also pointed out that more and more land was being withdrawn by various federal bureaus, making homesteading—already hopelessly snarled in red tape—exceedingly difficult.

The next morning we visited various federal offices, and I noted their cramped condition. The town needed a new federal building and a new post office and I promised to work for them. I also visited the plant of the Anchorage *Times* and met its editor and publisher, Robert B. Atwood. Anchorage, I discovered, was little more than a frontier village. Its streets were unpaved; its stores and houses were one-story, and vacant spaces in the heart of the business district far exceeded those occupied by buildings. But it was a town laid out for future growth. A vast plain extended ten or more miles behind it to the foothills of the Chugach, an area which could easily accommodate a million inhabitants. The plain was sheltered by high mountains from the rainbearing clouds of the Pacific; summer heat and winter cold were tempered by the embracing arms of the sea, and to the north, the great Susitna Plain with its myriad lakes stretched

150 miles to the monarch of the continent, Mount McKinley, visible from Anchorage on every clear day. It was an ideal site.

Saturday, May 16, was a special occasion, and Colonel Ohlson took me to nearby Palmer in his "dodgemobile" or "speeder," an auto fitted with flanged wheels for use on the railroad. It was the first anniversary of the settlers who had come to the Matanuska Valley under the sponsorship of the Department of the Interior, and the anniversary was denoted "Colony Day." A community hall in the three-story school building, erected the previous summer, was crowded. Addresses were made by Governor Troy, Colonel Ohlson, me, and by Ross Sheely, a valley farmer who had been appointed manager of the Alaska Rural Rehabilitation Corporation, the project's corporate name.

Luncheon was served out of doors and young and old alike entered a variety of contests—tug-of-war, sack races, husband-calling, horseshoe pitching, greased-pole climbing and pie-eating. I toured the valley looking at the new homes and barns. Most of the settlers were taking part in the celebration, but I found a few at home. I spoke to one whose tract was located on a ridge overlooking the entire valley, and commented on the beauty of the scene.

"If you could eat scenery," he replied, "this place would be paradise."

Considering the promises made to the settlers, many of their complaints were justified. Avoidable mistakes had been made, but I came away with the conviction that the experiment was a success.

I was due in Fairbanks the following Monday, which left no time to visit Mount McKinley Park en route, a journey that had to be made by rail. But flying northward in a small commercial float plane of the Star Air Service, a "bush"-grown operation, I saw Mount McKinley in all its shining glory. It was my first flight in Alaska, and I realized that the territory should be seen both from the air and from the ground. We landed on the Chena Slew, an arm, flowing through Fairbanks, of the Tanana River, and were met by Mayor Earnest B. Collins, who I learned had been a member of the first Territorial Legislature in 1913.

The men I met in Fairbanks were outspoken in their criticism of the Department of the Interior, which, I was beginning to realize, was the most disliked of all the federal departments in Alaska. Its opportunities for arousing and allaying discontent were, of course, far greater than those of any other federal agency. For in addition to having overall supervision of the territory, it also controlled the Office of Indian Affairs, the General Land Office, the National Park Service, the Bureau of Mines, the Geological Survey, the Alaska Road Commission, the Alaska Railroad; and would, in the near future, manage Alaska's wildlife and fisheries. The Forest Service of the Department of Agriculture, the Coast Guard of the

Treasury Department, and the Alaska Communications System, which was operated by the Signal Corps of the United States Army, performed important jobs in the territory, but it was, in essence, a fief of the Department of the Interior, and its secretary was the Lord of Alaska. As his representative, I often had difficulty defending departmental policies.

The University of Alaska lies a few miles west of Fairbanks. In 1936 it consisted of a few drab and unpretentious buildings on a hillock overlooking the Tanana Valley. Charles Ernest Bunnell had been its only president since it was founded as the Alaska Agricultural College and School of Mines, a land-grant college, which opened its doors in the fall of 1923 with six students. By inheritance, environment and experience, Charlie Bunnell was admirably suited for the task to which he was dedicating his life. His youth had been spent on a Pennsylvania farm and after high school and two years of a private academy, he had worked his way through Bucknell. He played on the football team, was one of the editors of the college paper, won a coveted prize for oratory, and was graduated in 1900 *summa cum laude*. He then applied for a teaching position in Alaska and found himself that fall in the government school on Wood Island adjacent to the larger Kodiak Island. His pupils were almost wholly Aleut, the Eskimoid aborigines who inhabited the Aleutian Islands and the Alaska Peninsula when the Russians invaded Alaska in the second half of the eighteenth century. Subsequently he taught in Kodiak and Valdez where he became school principal. Meanwhile he had earned a master's degree in economics and was now determined to study law. He read under a Valdez attorney, passed the territorial bar examination and was admitted to partnership in the office of the lawyer under whom he had studied. In 1912 he purchased his partner's interest in the firm, practiced law under his own name, and also engaged in business, securing a half interest in a lumber concern and a company manufacturing sheet metal.

In 1914 he received the Democratic nomination for Delegate to Congress but was defeated in the general election by James Wickersham who had served in the post since 1908. Later that year he was appointed Federal District Judge for the Fourth Division by President Wilson. He moved to Fairbanks, served the full four-year term and was reappointed to a second term. While on this bench he served not only in his own division but, owing to the illnesses of the judges in the Third and First Divisions, held court there also. In 1921 the regents of the agricultural college selected him as the first president.

Dr. Bunnell lived by himself in a modest cottage on one side of the hill and did his own housework. I spent most of the day with him and after he cooked a delicious steak dinner, we moved to the porch where he answered my questions for several hours. Due South across the broad Tanana Valley, one hundred miles away, three mountains which Dr. Bunnell identified as Deborah, Hess and Hayes lifted their snowy peaks above the Alaskan range. Far to the southwest, 150 miles away, Mount McKinley was turning pinkish. It was eleven-thirty and broad daylight. It was my first experience with the darkless nights in those far northern latitudes.

"This is wonderful," I said, "but what about the long dark nights in winter?"

"We don't have long dark nights up here," Dr. Bunnell said. "There is seldom an overcast in winter. The stars are so brilliant, and with the snow on the ground there isn't any real darkness. And on many nights, we have the aurora lighting up everything. Come up next winter and see for yourself."

I reserved a slight skepticism over what I suspected might be a bit of Chamber-of-Commerce talk, but I was to find that Dr. Bunnell had, if anything, understated the case. Over a decade later, when the Geophysical Institute of the university had been established, night-sky brightness was subjected to specific photometric measurement over extended periods to gauge the amount of light on nights that were auroraless, moonless and cloudless—that is, with starlight alone—and likewise to estimate the amount of illumination provided by the aurora. The first of these objectives was beset with difficulty because "it was discovered that almost every night displayed noticeable auroral activity." "It may be stated," concluded Dr. S. L. Seaton, director of the Institute, who conducted the observations, "that very few nights at College, Alaska, show absence of Aurora."

The gymnasium was the setting for the commencement exercises. The entire student body, numbering about one hundred and fifty, with a representative group of Fairbanks citizenry, constituted the attendance. The seniors, nineteen men and five women in caps and gowns, filed in. A majority of them had wholly or partly worked their way through college. Dr. Bunnell, I learned, devised work opportunities for them during the school year, and at times loaned them money from his personal funds to tide them over a difficult period. In addition, nearly all the students had jobs during the summer vacations in the mines, on the highways, on fishing boats and in offices. No country-club college this. These youngsters had to earn their education.

The subject of my commencement address was "A Challenge to Democracy." It seemed to me an appropriate topic at a time when Mussolini was riding high in Italy, Hitler had taken possession of Germany, Spain had been stifled by a fascist dictatorship and Russia was boasting of a "dictatorship of the proletariat" that made the tyranny of the czars seem benevolent by comparison. Our own system was far from perfect, but problems that had led to bloody revolutions in other countries were being solved in America without a departure from the democratic process. But "making democracy work" was and would continue to be an unending challenge. Democracy was not something we could expect to run smoothly without concern, effort and universal participation. Each generation would have to fight to preserve it.

Later in the day I was conducted over the most famous gold creeks in the Fairbanks area by Roy B. Earling, general manager of the Fairbanks Exploration Company which was the principal placer-mining enterprise in the territory and the dominant business in northern Alaska. It was a subsidiary of the powerful United States Smelting, Refining and Mining Company, whose headquarters were in Boston. Mr. Earling showed me the thawing, stripping, dredging and hydraulic operations, including the daily "clean-up" on the great dredge when the gold was separated from tons of muck and gravel. Discovery of gold in 1903 had created Fairbanks and gold mining continued to be the area's principal economic mainstay.

Our party left by train for Mount McKinley Park the next morning. At the ranger headquarters a few miles in, Harry Liek, the superintendent, showed us the park's kennels and the handsome huskies that were used to patrol the park in winter. Among them was a young female wolf that had been captured as a pup and would be bred to a husky. Three-quarters husky, one-quarter wolf produced the best type of sled-dog in the park rangers' view.

We drove into the park by bus, and stopped for lunch at the Savage River Camp where, during the summer season, tourists were lodged in tents and fed in a central dining hall. As we drove on we were treated to a display of the park's wildlife—moose, wolves, brown bear and grizzlies, Dall sheep grazing on the slopes not far above the road, and numerous ptarmigan. At mile sixty on the ninety-mile highway through the park, our advance was blocked by a wall of drifted snow. It was tantalizing to learn that just a few miles farther on the really magnificent views of Mount McKinley would begin, but the exhibition of wildlife more than rewarded our visit. I learned that adequate accommodations for tourists were the park's most pressing need. I promised to see what might be done when I returned to Washington.

We drove back to Fairbanks on the railroad auto-car late that evening, and toward midnight we began to see the sunrise and sunset at the same time. A tall tale? Not at all. In this latitude at that time of the year, the sun sets, not in the west, but just west of north. It then describes a short and shallow curve just below the horizon and rises within a couple of hours just east of north. While the light was waning in the northwestern sky, it was waxing in the northeastern sector. A conical mountain due north separated sunset and sunrise and made this phenomenon even more evident.

The next morning I flew to Nome. The first half of our trip lay over the Yukon River. For hundreds of miles in this western part of Alaska, it courses through a mammoth swamp of its own creation. So flat is the land that the river has engraved a fantastically serpentine course on the terrain. The numerous digressions from its present course—some old and almost obliterated by regrowth, some recent—were marked by winding swaths in the scrub timber, and by curved pools left stagnant in the abandoned grooves. Occasionally, when the banks of the river rose above the surrounding swamp, there was a small settlement. I expressed a desire to see one and we landed in Ruby which is on firm, high ground on the river's south bank. It was a mining community subsisting on placers lying some miles south. There was not much to see, but my visit gave me a chance to experience a typical Alaskan airfield. It was a small clearing on a hillock at the back of the village. The only sign that it was an airfield was a wind sock. Landing and taking off, we just missed the trees. There seemed to be no margin for error and no radio-range facilities. The pilots merely held up a moistened finger to the breeze and took off. What these early bush pilots lacked in equipment and aids to aviation they made up in skill. The village of Ruby itself consisted principally of a street of log cabins along the river, and a general store typical of these remote outposts of civilization. It included a little of everything in the way of canned foods, clothing and hardware—at prices that reflected the long and various hauls to that distant point.

From Ruby we flew on to Nome where I noted that reconstruction in the wake of the great fire was virtually complete. After only a brief stay we returned to Juneau and there, after discussing their problems with the heads of every federal and territorial agency, I was taken through the Alaska-Juneau mine by L. H. Metzger, its superintendent. This enterprise was the one survivor of various mining operations in the Gastineau Channel area since the discovery of gold fifty-six years before. Earlier operations had been run across the channel on Douglas Island, principally the Treadwell mine which in the 1890s was said to be the largest hard-rock goldmining operation in the world. When it caved in, in 1917, and was flooded by salt water, the mine was closed. The Alaska-Juneau, controlled by the Bradley family of San Francisco, had acquired the surrounding claims and was a highly skilled operation. It was a distinctly "low-grade" mine, extracting only about a dollar's worth of gold from a ton of rock. The mine tunnels into which I was taken did not merely go into the bowels of the earth, but extended laterally and vertically up into the mountain. The rock was brought to the top story of the mill and then carried by gravity through its successively lower levels. At each level, the ore was crushed into smaller fragments, washed with running water and then flowed over concentration tables on the lowest level where the heavier gold, separated first by gravity and then by amalgamation with mercury, was extracted. I was shown a gold "brick," the product of the last "clean-up," worth, I was told $33,000. It was half the thickness and about twice the length and width of a building brick. It weighed eighty pounds. The mine employed about a thousand men, most of them single. The A-J, as it was always referred to, was considered an indispensable community asset by the businessmen of Juneau. It had been exempted from all local taxation. In exchange, the mine's high-pressure water system was available to the city's fire department.

One of Juneau's scenic assets was, and is, the Mendenhall Glacier, a tongue of the 700-square-mile Juneau icecap. Governor Troy drove me to it on the Glacier Highway, and a loop from the main road brought us within several hundred yards of the mile-and-a-half-wide face of the glacier. A footpath led to the edge of the torrent which roared out from under the southern edge of the ice, forming a great cave of the deepest blue. I asked Governor Troy whether he thought the Mendelhall Glacier might not eventually prove to be a greater asset to Juneau than the Alaska-Juneau mine. I gathered from his smile that the question would be deemed something of a heresy around Juneau.

On Sunday a fishing party was arranged by James Simpson McKinnon, the Governor's naval aide. We took a cabin cruiser up the channel and beginner's luck was with me. I caught a twenty-five-pound king salmon, landing it after twenty minutes of expert coaching. We ate the salmon that evening at a party given by Dr. Walter W. Council, Health Commissioner of the Territory, a famous sportsman and a great spinner of hunting yarns. I also had time to visit the Territorial Museum, which was located in a large room the full width of the second floor of the Federal and Territorial Building. It had an excellent collection of the products of Alaskan Eskimo, Aleut and Indian cultures. Outstanding was the basketry, including the already rare white baskets of the Aleutians, even finer than the finest Panama weave, and elaborately designed brown Tlingit baskets made of spruce-root fibers. I was shown around by the curator, Father Andrew Kashevaroff, a priest of the Russian church.

A final swing around southeastern Alaska again took me north of Juneau. As the trip would include various Indian communities, I asked Charles Hawkesworth, assistant director for Alaska of the Office of Indian Affairs, to come along. Heading for Haines, we saw the Fairweather Range soaring into a cloudless sky and I asked our pilot to swing over Glacier Bay, a wonderland of tidal glaciers which had been set aside as a national monument ten years previously. We skirted the range and swung back over Lynn Canal, the terminal fiord of the Inside Passage, which cuts straight and deep for seventy miles into the continent. Passing over Davidson Glacier, we soon spied the gray symmetry of Chilkoot Barracks. There we were greeted by its commanding officer, Colonel Ralph Dusenbury, and his charming wife Eleanor. We inspected the infantry post built in the later Klondike gold-rush days to preserve order, and strolled to the adjacent village of Haines, a mixed white and Indian community where we visited the school and the Presbyterian Indian Mission.

We then drove twenty miles inland along the rushing Chilcat River to the Tlingit village of Klukwan. It consisted of one curving street along the stream with about twenty frame houses on each side. We were graciously admitted to several homes and saw a rare collection of house totems which, having been indoors, were well preserved, their red and blue coloring mellowed to a pastel-like softness. Some of them were decorated with human hair; others had been anointed with oil derived from the oulachan or candle fish. When I was told they were virtually the only remaining examples of house totems, I expressed fear that they might be destroyed by a fire that could easily consume a village in which there was no fire-fighting apparatus. The poles should, of course, have gone to a museum, but they were prized as the personal possession of each householder.

Returning to Haines, we flew twenty miles north to Skagway, a community whose glory was largely in the past. There, and at neighboring Dyea, the greater part of the gold-rushers to the Klondike started up the White and Chilkoot passes. The population was now a scant six hundred. Its chief economic prop was the Canadian-owned White Pass and Yukon Railroad, whose initials W.P. & Y.R., I was told, stood for "Wait patiently and you'll ride." The town's setting in a narrow valley between towering peaks seemed inviting to tourists, but the townspeople complained that the railroad authorities rushed passengers from boat to train and prevented their patronizing the local curio shops in favor of the shops at Whitehorse, the Canadian terminus of the railroad. The chief attraction in Skagway was a collection of gold-rush memorabilia at the local hotel, the Pullen House. Its owner, Harriet Pullen, a large, hearty and cheerful woman whose reddish hair was turning gray, had come to Alaska with five dollars in her purse, and had made a living for herself and her children by baking pies for the gold-rushers.

Our next stop was Petersburg, and at the dock we were welcomed by Earl Ohmer, the city's greeter and best-known character, owner of the local shrimp cannery and a one-man Chamber of Commerce. He was dressed in Western garb—leather waistcoat crossed by a heavy nugget chain, five-gallon hat and puttees; a brown Vandyke beard completed his get-up. According to him, Petersburg was the best town in America. It had been founded nearly forty years earlier by Peter Bushman, who had encouraged the immigration of Norwegians directly from the old country. They had come and grown prosperous, principally as halibut fishermen, but salmon and shrimp were also important in their economy. The harbor was crowded with white fishing boats.

From Petersburg we flew to Sitka, the ancient Russian capital, and the capital of Alaska until 1906. The town was beautifully situated along a winding shore with a circle of incisive peaks in the background. Despite their majesty, their restrained middle distance permitted a man-made edifice to dominate the scene. It was the Cathedral of Saint Michael the Archangel, rising from the heart of the town. This exquisite memorial of the vanished Russian era was an important symbol of Alaska's past. A wooden structure painted light gray, it was topped by a chastely ornamented octagonal belfry and a slender bulbed green dome.

Sitka's present was symbolized by another imposing structure which dominated the waterfront; it was the impressive three-wing Pioneers Home, a brown brick building with a red-tiled roof. In 1913, Alaska's first territorial legislature had established the first old-age pension ever enacted by any American legislative body; and in 1915 the second legislature provided for the construction of this home for aged prospectors. Thus the people of Alaska through their elected representatives recognized their obligation to the men who had undergone the hardships of early pioneering to "open up" the territory.

Visits to several southeastern villages completed my itinerary. They were Hoonah and Klawock, both Tlingit communities; Hydaburg, the only Alaskan community of Haida Indians; and finally, Metlakatla, founded by an Anglican missionary, "Father" Duncan, who brought his flock of Tsimshian Indians from British Columbia in the 1880s, and established a uniquely prosperous and self-contained community.

In my brief stay in Ketchikan prior to departure for Washington, I had an unforgettable experience. My arrival was unheralded and no one met me, so I wandered around town and presently dropped into a lunchroom for a snack. It was a small place, just a counter and some stools. I sat down and engaged the girl who waited on me in conversation. I told her of my trip and asked her about herself. She told me she had come from "down below" some months previously, and then began to give me her impressions of Alaska. When she had filled my order, she served herself, came out from behind the counter, sat down on the stool next to mine and we continued our conversation. The incident seemed to symbolize the mark of Alaska. It could not have happened anywhere else in America.

I had learned that the territory was not without serious problems, problems that I would have to work to solve in Washington. But I had also learned that Alaska's people were its greatest asset. Honest, straightforward, unaffected by caste or class, unafraid of hard work, they represented a kind of democracy that had long since vanished from many other parts of our country.

16

HAWAII AND A
PACIFIC ADVENTURE

*The loveliest fleet of islands that lies
anchored in any ocean.*
—MARK TWAIN

Hawaii did not suffer the neglect and colonial discrimination of our other territorial possessions—with one exception. It was not permitted to refine more than a small percentage of its own sugar; the balance was processed in mainland refineries. There was also some discrimination in favor of Florida and Louisiana cane-sugar growers and the beet-sugar growers of the western states, through quotas set by the administration in Washington and supported by the Congressional representatives of the benefiting states. Like Alaska, Hawaii was represented in the Congress only by a voteless delegate, and these refining restrictions and import quotas were a serious bone of contention. As Hawaii was included under my jurisdiction, it was up to me to come to its defense when a bill sponsored by the Department of Agriculture sought to continue these discriminatory practices. In March 1937, testifying before the House Agriculture Committee, I said:

> Our protest is embodied in the fact that this bill perpetuates a new geography. It creates two kinds of territory for America. It creates a continental and offshore America. We cannot recognize such a division. . . . Only one terminology should be used in this bill as far as all parts of America are concerned and that is the word "domestic."
> The question is one of principle. . . . We feel that Hawaii and

Puerto Rico are entitled to exactly the same kind of consideration that Florida and Louisiana will be entitled to. . . . If the total quota is to go up, Hawaii's and Puerto Rico's should go up too. If it is to go down, we are willing to be cut accordingly. But we wish to be treated as any other part of America or other Americans are treated.

The Washington *Herald* reported that "A fight broke out yesterday between the Agriculture and Interior Departments over the Administration's pending sugar bill. . . . Dr. Ernest Gruening, Interior Department official in charge of territories and islands, lodged an emphatic protest against the bill." The administration backed my stand and the discriminations against Hawaii were partially but not wholly rectified.

My point of view, apparently unprecedented in a federal agency, was appreciated in Hawaii. I got more than the usual friendly welcome when Dorothy, Huntington, Peter and I arrived in Honolulu that September. Governor Joseph Poindexter, a widower, invited us to stay at the official residence, "Washington Place," and arranged a comprehensive tour of the islands. There was not much that the happy, carefree Hawaiians wanted. I suggested a national monument or two where the scenery struck me as spectacular, especially the Waimea Canyon on Kauai, and asked various groups to forward their views, pro or con, to me in Washington. Some local irrigation and housing problems needed attention, but the Hawaiians' most immediate concern focused on the forthcoming arrival of a large joint Congressional delegation which would hold hearings on statehood.

The party included eight senators and fourteen representatives, amplified by wives, children, staff members and press representatives, and the Honolulu *Advertiser* irreverently headlined their arrival "Congressional Junket Party Totals 51." Nevertheless, it was the first serious hearing on Hawaii's future status on its own home ground. The delegation was, of course, royally entertained by civilian and military officials. The high spot in the welter of festivities was a luau given at her home by the Princess David Kawananakoa in honor of Senator and Mrs. Millard Tydings —he was chairman of the delegation—to which the Congressional visitors and prominent Hawaiians, over one hundred in all, were invited.

I was asked to sit in on the statehood hearings and occupied a seat next to Representative John E. Rankin of Mississippi. The case for statehood was presented by Delegate Samuel Wilder King. Other witnesses exemplified the ethnic diversity of Hawaiians of Polynesian, Japanese, Chinese, Korean and Filipino origin, as well as those of white and mixed descent. After several Japanese had testified, Rankin turned to me and said, "Mah Gawd, if we give them folks statehood we're lahkely to have a senator called Moto." That kind of prejudice would recur through the next twenty years of Hawaii's efforts to gain statehood. Actually, Hawaii's ethnic diversity and racial tolerance were, in my view, one of the most cogent reasons for its admission to the Union.

There were, of course, many well-placed Hawaiians who did not favor statehood, preferring the control they and their associates exercised in "the big five"—the large sugar and pineapple enterprises which dominated the islands' economy. But I felt from inquiries I had made that the majority of rank-and-file Hawaiians would welcome statehood, not so much because they needed it, but because they believed it to be just. My own view, formed then and never altered, was that Hawaii as a state would be an asset to our country and a valuable bridge between East and West. Rudyard Kipling notwithstanding, East and West had met in Hawaii and had mingled harmoniously.

The New England missionaries who sailed around Cape Horn in the early nineteenth century had with a rare acceptance of racial differences —rare among Anglo-Saxons at least—imparted standards of order, industry and social justice which fused beneficially with the islanders' hedonistic way of life, and created a society which could and would integrate later immigrants of every race. It has been said in derogation of the missionaries and their descendants that they "came to do good, and did well." The fact is that they did both.

My Pacific journey had a dual purpose. Besides studying Hawaii's needs, I wanted, if possible, to extend the reach of American aviation. Pan-American Airways was then the only United States airline operating in the Pacific. It had pioneered flights to the Asian mainland and now wanted to establish commercial service with the Antipodes. Its planes were "clippers," the big flying boats which required water-landings, and its commercial objectives had national military overtones. War in the Pacific was already foreseen as a possibility.

The range of Pan-Am's clippers precluded nonstop flights from Hawaii to New Zealand and Australia, and the two way-stations currently in use were unsatisfactory. The first, Kingman Reef, a thousand miles south of Honolulu, was a semicircular protrusion only a few feet above the ocean's surface at high tide; it was swept by great swells when the sea was rough, making it uncomfortable and even dangerous for the passengers when the plane put down for refueling from an anchored tender. The second stop, Pago-Pago on the island of Tutuila in American Samoa, was narrow, surrounded by steep hills and equally risky. Better landing sites were needed and if they could be found, they would fall under the Division's supervision. In May 1936 President Roosevelt had transferred jurisdiction over a number of small Pacific islands to the Department of the Interior to be the responsibility of the Division of Territories and Island Possessions.

Before leaving for Hawaii, I had visited Jay Pierrepont Moffat, a career

State Department officer in charge of the European desk. Several European nations as well as the United States had claims to uninhabited islands in the Pacific and the negotiations were his responsibility. He told me that under an informal agreement between Great Britain and the United States, a study was underway to determine the claims and rights of each. These claims were various and complex, but the study was proceeding in a leisurely fashion with the understanding that neither nation would take any overt steps to assert possession until the whole field had been surveyed and an agreement reached. Moffat was aware of Pan-Am's needs and put me in touch with S. Whittemore Boggs, the State Department's geographer, who briefed me on what islands were subject to the prospective negotiations. I had also been briefed by Pan-Am's president, Juan Trippe, about the specific needs of the airlines. Thus informed, and with the grudging consent of Secretary Ickes, I planned an island-hopping itinerary following my visit to Hawaii.

We left Honolulu aboard the Coast Guard cutter *Roger B. Taney* bound for the Line Islands, a group of tiny American-held islands strung out along the Equator south of Hawaii. On board were Richard Blackburn Black, a civil engineer, whom I had engaged to direct whatever island operations would develop, and twelve young Hawaiians, graduates of the Kamehameha School, four of whom would be settled on each of the Line Islands to make weather observations and build a coral rock lighthouse. We carried all the necessary equipment and supplies for a three-month sojourn, after which the boys would be relieved and replaced by others.

Our first objective was Kingman Reef, which we circumnavigated so that I could ascertain its shortcomings at firsthand; then, slightly to the southeast, Palmyra, politically a part of the city and county of Honolulu and owned by the Fullard Leo family. It was not one island but a number linked into one, surrounding several lagoons. It was a boy's dream of a tropical paradise, with tall coconut palms interspersed with equally towering Australian pine. Its white beaches were crowded with aquatic birds of all kinds, so unused to the intrusion of man that they remained undisturbed as we gingerly walked through them. The island abounded in a species of coconut crab, large crustaceans which had developed the practice of climbing the palm trees and snipping off the coconuts, then, after descent, opening and devouring their contents. The taste of coconut was, in fact, preserved in their delicious white flesh. In the crystal clear waters of the lagoons, we could look down ten or more fathoms to see schools of tropical fish of every brilliant hue darting among the no-less-brilliant coral formations. Palmyra entranced me as an ecological masterpiece—possibly unique—which should be preserved as a national monument, and I resolved to urge this on my return.

The purpose of our visit was to pick up coconut seedlings from Palmyra to plant on the Line Islands. There was an interesting interrelation on these and similar barren islands between vegetation and rainfall. When an island was devoid of vegetation, a low approaching rain cloud would be divided and driven past by the hot air rising from its sun-heated sands. If enough coconut palms could be planted and nursed to production, this cover of verdure would be receptive to the rain clouds, and the rain in turn would foster additional vegetative growth.

Christmas Island, our second stop, would have been an ideal location for a refueling station. It was some thirty miles long, mostly flat, and even large planes could have landed on the hard-packed surface of its coral sands. Its large lagoon could have accommodated seaplanes with equal ease, but there was one hitch. In the 1880s, maps had labeled the island "U.S.-Br.," indicating an approximately equal claim by both nations. But in the 1890s the British had moved in and granted a concession to a French priest from Tahiti, Father Rougier, to plant and harvest coconuts. Twenty-five Tahitians were currently working on the island under the direction of a Czech manager, while a British administrator was in charge. The United States had forfeited its half-claim.

Jarvis Island was an American claim and landing through a gentle surf, we spent the day unloading supplies, including drums of water. I was given the opportunity to drive the center stake for the lighthouse and to break the first coral slab for its foundation. Our next stop was Pago-Pago, the capital of American Samoa where we were welcomed by the governor, Captain McGillivray Milne, USN, and his staff. We spent two days among the Samoans—handsome men and women clad in the traditional *lava-lava* costume—living much as they always had. We visited their schools, were permitted to peep into their thatched-roof homes and were treated to a Kava ceremony, an ancient rite. I did not know whether the administration would transfer Samoa to the Interior Department as it had the Virgin Islands, but I thought that in case that were to be done, I should learn as much as possible about this southernmost of Uncle Sam's possessions.

We paid a courtesy call at Apia, the capital of Western or British Samoa, before we again headed north to investigate the Phoenix Islands. We arrived at Sydney, an island of that group, on November 14 and did not land but paused long enough to observe and photograph a sign nailed on a palm tree which read:

THIS ISLAND BELONGS TO HIS BRITANNIC MAJESTY KING GEORGE V. IT WAS VISITED BY H.M.S. LEITH JANUARY 1937.

L. C. P. TUDWAY
CAPTAIN, R.N.

Landing on Baker Island

On Phoenix, our next pause, there was a similar sign. The British had evidently decided to anticipate the outcome of the negotiations and to claim sovereignty of the islands in the Phoenix group, a violation of the agreement with the United States.

We found a similar sign on Enderbury Island which we explored briefly but found unsuitable for seaplane landings. Canton Island, just to the north, was another story. The island had achieved worldwide attention six months earlier when it was found to be the best observation point for a forthcoming total eclipse of the sun. A Harvard-Yale expedition had requested the State Department to secure permission from the British government to land, but was told that this was not necessary since neither nation acknowledged the other's sovereignty. The party left Honolulu on a seaplane-tender and anchored at the entrance to the island's lagoon. Twenty-four hours later, the Australian cruiser *Sydney* arrived with a contingent of British and Australian scientists. It signaled the American vessel to weigh anchor and move away, but its commander declined and replied that he would help the British locate a suitable anchorage. The two parties unloaded their equipment, made their observations and both left a concrete marker embedded with the enameled flag of their country. Subsequently, however, the British established a radio station on the island which again appeared to be a violation of the agreement between the two nations.

Canton was ideal for our purpose. It was an atoll, twenty-seven miles in circumference. Its land surfaces extended in every direction and would thus permit the construction of any number of airstrips in line with prevailing winds. The lagoon was large enough to accommodate all the seaplanes in the world. We explored the island thoroughly, arousing the curiosity of two British residents about the reasons for our visit which we did not feel it necessary to satisfy.

We made two more stops to land men and supplies on Baker and Howland islands, and then I returned, via Honolulu, to the United States and Washington. I reported the details of my trip to Secretary Ickes and then was summoned to the White House. I found Jay Pierrepont Moffat waiting in the anteroom to the Oval Room. When we were ushered in, President Roosevelt greeted us with "Are we in an acquisitive mood today?"

I told him we were. I outlined my exploration of possible island bases and recommended that we move in on Canton and Enderbury, the latter simply for the purpose of bargaining with the British. The President agreed, called in Marvin McIntyre and instructed him to inform Admiral

Line Islands expeditionary force on Howland Island

Russell Waesche, Coast Guard Commandant, that we would take possession of the islands on the next trip of the *Taney*. The move was to be
kept a top secret until the landings had taken place. Moffat was to inform
his chief, Secretary Hull. I did not realize it, but President Roosevelt, by
not directly notifying Secretaries Ickes and Morgenthau, would arouse
their opposition to the undertaking.

On the morning of February 19, 1938, the day the *Taney* was to sail, I
had just returned to my office after a conference with A. C. Park, Deputy Commissioner of the Bureau of Lighthouses, to confirm that all the
equipment necessary for a landing on Canton and Enderbury was on
board the *Taney*, when I was told that Admiral Waesche wanted to talk
to me immediately. I called and he reported that he had written instructions from Secretary Morgenthau that the *Taney* was not to sail without
written confirmation from the State Department that Canton and Enderbury were to be visited. It was difficult to get anything in writing in so
short a time, but through Moffat I got such a confirmation signed by
Judge Walton Moore, counselor of the State Department and under the
existing setup, its second ranking official. Morgenthau refused to accept it
and insisted that it had to be signed by Secretary Hull. Hull was furious
because the authorization by Moore was the prescribed formula. Meanwhile, Admiral Waesche had sent a telegram to the *Taney*'s captain de-
laying its departure, and Dick Black, who was responsible for all the arrangements in Hawaii, was frantically trying to get me on the line to find
out what was going on. To complicate matters, Morgenthau was
unreachable, at least by me or by Moffat. Marvin McIntyre located him
at last, and told him that the landing was on the President's order and
that he should stop his obstruction. Finally, Admiral Waesche sent another telegram countermanding his first, and I called Dick Black in Hawaii to reassure him that the *Taney* was to be allowed to sail according
to our original plans.

The mission was accomplished flawlessly. The *Taney* landed equipment and men on the islands, but as Black was about to raise the American flag on Canton, he was confronted by the British senior radio operator on the island who said, "I am instructed to inform you that this is
British territory and to protest against your raising the American flag."
Black, undaunted, replied, "And I am instructed to take possession on behalf of the United States and to raise the American flag. We are both
carrying out our orders."

When the occupation of the islands was revealed in a State Department
release, the British Foreign Office made emphatic protest. The State Department's reply sought to be as soothing as possible by pointing out that
the occupation was for air navigation purposes only, and that if the British wanted to make use of the planned facilities, they could enter into ne-

gotiations with Pan-American Airways. However, the British replied that the American occupation would prevent a plan to settle two hundred natives from the crowded Gilbert and Ellice Islands on Canton. As Canton was barren, the State Department's reply expressed a polite skepticism. In response the British Foreign Office quoted from a report by the Commissioner of the Gilbert and Ellice Islands. They really did have a plan, and it was an interesting revelation of British policy. The two hundred prospective settlers were to plant coconut trees on Canton, and in the seven years before they began to bear, they were expected to subsist on fish, shellfish, turtles' eggs and other land and marine life which would be supplemented by a daily ration of rice "strictly recoverable in coconuts." In other words, the British Empire would keep books on these poor natives through the years to see that each rice recipient ultimately repaid "the Crown" in coconuts. One could not help contrasting American policy. Our Hawaiian colonists on the Line Islands received all their subsistence and were paid $3 a day, which would enable them to save some $270 in their three months' stay on the islands.

When the State Department proved unresponsive to its protests, the British Foreign Office suggested admission of a British airline to Hawaii. That proposal was not accepted because it would have been impossible to refuse a similar permit to Japan and that was considered undesirable. Still the British persisted, and after several exchanges, President Roosevelt proposed that the United States and Great Britain establish a condominium over the islands for fifty years and leave the determination of ownership and use until that future time. The British accepted that solution.

Pan-American Airways requested and received a license to operate on Canton, and proceeded to build the necessary facilities. It was able to make Canton the only stop between Honolulu and Auckland or Sydney, eliminating the marginal landing at Pago-Pago. When I visited Canton two years later on the first flight of the New Zealand Clipper—to which I had been invited by Juan Trippe—I found a bustling community. The British had not sought to establish aviation facilities on the island, but as a matter of national pride decided to keep a representative there. We found him and his wife fishing—necessarily, they told me, for their subsistence. Their efforts were supplemented by a case of groceries supplied weekly with the compliments of Pan-American Airways.

The passage of time would finally dispose of the issue to which we had devoted so much energy. The ever-increasing range of aircraft, the replacement of "prop" by jet, made nonstop flights between Hawaii, Australia and New Zealand possible and eliminated the need for Canton except for emergency landings. So our adventure became a mere minor footnote to history.

17

ALASKA, 1938

*It is refreshing to hit a place where no-
body seems to be mad at anybody.*
—ROBERT C. RUARK

Secretary Ickes was to make his first visit to Alaska in the summer of
1938 and wanted me to be there. Although he and I knew that we were
not in accord on some departmental matters affecting the territories, particularly Alaska, I wanted to get his support for the projects my 1936 trip
to Alaska had convinced me were desirable. Moreover, he had recently
exhibited concern for one of the problems of our offshore possessions. He
had, in the early summer of 1937, unburdened himself to me on the subject of a major water diversion project in Colorado known as the "Big
Thompson." It was proposed to tunnel through the Rocky Mountains
and carry the water of the Big Thompson River from the west to the east
slope. Ickes denounced the project. "Its sole purpose," he said, "is to irri-
gate land to grow more sugar beets. The sugar-beet industry is a parasitic
industry. It employs child labor and low-cost Mexican labor. Instead of
growing more sugar beets, we should increase our sugar quotas in your
offshore territories, Hawaii and Puerto Rico. They want me to put up
$30 million dollars of my public-works funds for the Big Thompson. I'll
never do it."

I was impressed. Although this was the first I had heard of the Big
Thompson project, what Ickes said seemed to make sense. Our tropical
territorial possessions were suffering discrimination with regard to their
principal crop, sugar, because they were voteless in the Congress and
could not resist the powerful "beet-sugar block" supported by the senators and representatives from midwestern and western states. So I men-

tally applauded Ickes's determination to stand up for our less influential island possessions.

My interior applause was premature. When Ickes was appointed Secretary of the Interior by President Roosevelt, he had inherited as the first assistant secretary and the number-two man in the department, Theodore A. Walters, a former attorney general of Idaho, to whom the President —in response to pleas from western Democratic senators—had promised this post. Walters's presence irked Ickes. Whenever he left town, Walters automatically became acting secretary, and found out everything that was going on in the department, including matters that Ickes wanted to keep to himself. Walters died suddenly late in 1937, and Ickes began his campaign to promote Ebert K. Burlew, his "administrative assistant and budget officer." He was inviting trouble. In his fifteen years in the department under various secretaries, Burlew had antagonized several powerful western senators, including Thomas J. Walsh of Montana, George W. Norris of Nebraska and Key Pittman of Nevada. When Ickes sent Burlew's name to the Senate for confirmation, it was referred to the Committee on Public Lands and Surveys, whose chairman was Alva Adams of Colorado. The "Big Thompson" was Senator Adams's pet project. Before hearings on Burlew's appointment began, Ickes approved the "Big Thompson" project and committed the required $30 million in Public Works Administration funds to begin its construction.

The hearings which opened on January 11, 1938, attracted considerable attention since they presaged a lively scrap—always an attraction in Foggy Bottom—and were expected to expose much in the way of questionable practices in the Interior Department. Burlew, who was quietly referred to in the department as "the oversecretary" because of his apparent hold on Ickes, was both distrusted and disliked because he was deemed—rightly or wrongly—responsible for the wire-tapping, desk-searching and general snoopery that were part of the way Ickes ran his department. Burlew denied any connection with these alleged acts, and the departmental witnesses at the hearing, knowing what was good for them, gave the safely correct although not always the expected answers. The hearings lasted a month, the printed report, covering 616 pages, was favorable, and under Chairman Adams's benevolent guidance, the committee recommended Burlew's appointment, with only Senator Pittman dissenting in a long minority report.

Within minutes after the Senate confirmation of Burlew, I was summoned to Secretary Ickes's office.

"What's this I hear about your opposing my will to have Burlew confirmed?" Ickes said.

"What do you hear?" I asked.

Without answering Ickes continued, "And your wife's face registered distinct disappointment when Louis Glavis failed to testify as some people hoped he would."

I couldn't help laughing. "The only answer I can think of, Mr. Secretary, is 'so what!' "

When I reported this exchange to Dorothy that evening, she told me that during one session, Irene Moran,—the wife of Congressman Edward Carlton Moran of Maine—who had accompanied Dorothy to the hearings, said to her, "There is a man sitting on that window ledge who hasn't taken his eyes off you."

He must have been Harold Ickes's expression-watcher.

As often as we had clashed on various departmental matters, I did look forward to showing Ickes around Alaska so that he might see at firsthand some of the problems I had been working to solve ever since my visit in 1936. Among these were hotel accommodations for Mount McKinley National Park. The purpose of our great national parks was only partially fulfilled unless the National Park Service could furnish accommodations, either by its own action or through a concessionaire, so that people could enjoy the park's wonders. During my visit to Mount McKinley, I had seen that the tenting accommodations supplied by the concessionaire, Jim Gaylen, were inadequate, and when I returned to Washington, I went to work on the project.

The problem was that the only approach to the park was by railroad and its station was some sixty miles from where tourists could get the first satisfactory view of what they had all come to see—20,300-foot Mount McKinley, the highest mountain on the North American continent. Clearly it would be impractical to unload a trainful of visitors at the station and then transport them some sixty or more miles over a relatively poor road before lodging them for the night. The road, incidentally, was not a Park Service project. It had been built to open up a goldmining district, the Kantishna, which lay just north of the park's northern boundary, ninety miles west of the railroad. So the park's housing needs were twofold: a hotel near the railroad station at the entrance to the park, and another somewhere beyond the sixty-sixth mile of the ninety-mile road, where Mount McKinley could be viewed in all its magnificence. Naturally we had to begin at the entrance.

I had several conferences with Park Service personnel and we managed to persuade Secretary Ickes to give us a grant for a hotel at the entrance. The amount he gave, however—only $350,000—was insufficient for a hotel whose capacity should be at least two hundred guests—the average number of a trainload of passengers. As the plans neared completion, I was asked to approve them which, regretfully, I could not. I argued that the hotel would be too small. The plans were nevertheless approved and construction began in the early summer of 1937. If all went well, the hotel would be ready for occupancy in the late summer of 1938, or at the latest for the entire summer of 1939. Once completed it would be available the year round. Despite my misgivings about the design, I was pleased that we had made what seemed like a substantial start for the tourist business.

Another project that was underway was the construction of a federal building for Anchorage. I had spoken to a number of government officials, but the project seemed to depend upon convincing Postmaster General James A. Farley of the need for a new post office which the federal building would contain. Jim told me that a great many communities had priority over Anchorage. I argued that since all the places with priorities had two senators and voting representatives to fend for them, the executive officials of the government should take the territories under their wing and give them a "break." I told Jim about the discriminations against Alaska in the matter of road construction, agricultural and other appropriations, and a few weeks later he telephoned me: "We've got your Anchorage federal building on the list."

My return trip to Alaska would permit me to check up on the progress of these and other projects, and I knew I had a lot more to learn about the Territory, in particular about the fisheries which were its principal commercial pursuit and which affected the lives of more Alaskans than any other activity. In 1936 I had been there before the start of the fishing season. On this trip I was to precede Secretary Ickes and it seemed a good opportunity to look into the fishing industry. To get some pointers on whom and what to see, I consulted Frank T. Bell, commissioner of the Bureau of Fisheries of the Department of Commerce, who told me that the best way to proceed was to go with him aboard the Bureau of Fisheries vessel *Brant* which was sailing from Seattle on July 2. I had planned to take my son Peter, who was then fourteen, along and Commissioner Bell said he would be happy to have the boy aboard. The voyage proved to be an education and an adventure for both of us.

Perhaps the most memorable of the many stops we made was at the Pribilof Islands where we were able to observe the demonstration of a highly successful government enterprise in conservation. The two main islands, Saint Paul and Saint George, with their abundant fur-seal "fisheries" had, shortly after the purchase of Alaska, originally been leased to private companies headquartered in San Francisco. But by 1910, the herd—which had once numbered in the millions—had been reduced to 130,000. The Bureau of Fisheries then took over, and with careful management and conservation once again built up the herd. Some fifty thousand seals were harvested annually thereafter, grossing over a million dollars from the pelts and by-products. The islands were administered by the Bureau of Fisheries. Every male adult worked for the government, receiving in 1938, annual wages amounting to about $500 in cash, with food, housing, light, water and medical services free of charge. Old-timers were also taken care of. The seal industry supported everything.

Our voyage ended when the *Brant* dropped Peter and me at Seward where Colonel Ohlson, the manager of the Alaska Railroad, took us northward to Mount McKinley National Park. My objective there was to select a tentative site for the second hotel within the park. The hotel at the park's entrance was nearing completion, but I did not stop as I knew that in two weeks Secretary Ickes and Thomas C. Vint, the architect, would be here. Harry Liek, the park superintendent, drove us to mile 66 on the park road where Jim Gaylen had set up a tent camp at the proposed hotel site. Views of the mountain were better farther on, so a second site was proposed at the south end of Wonder Lake. However, this spot was low and mosquito-ridden, and I suggested that we climb the slope on the west side of the lake. Here, at three hundred feet above the lake

Jim Farley's party en route to Anchorage, 1936

level, we had a splendid view of the valley at our feet, and of the range. A still better site lay just outside of the park on Wickersham Dome with Wonder Lake in the foreground.

We returned to Anchorage and from there to Seward on the "No. 111," a fourteen-passenger auto-car, to meet Postmaster General Farley who was coming to Alaska to officiate at the ground-breaking ceremonies for Anchorage's new federal building and post office.

"Hello, Doc!" he called out from the upper deck as his ship approached the wharf. "What are you doing up here?"

"I'm here to show you a fine territory," I shouted back.

Farley's two daughters, Betty and Ann were with him, along with his secretary Ambrose O'Connell, Eddie Roddan, and Joe Knight, a member of the Illinois Democratic Committee. We all piled on the "111" and started right off in order to get ahead of the slower passenger train. About thirty miles from Anchorage we had a flat. It took the engineer one hour—with passenger help—to change it. Colonel Ohlson posted himself two hundred yards in back with a red flag to hold up the passenger train in case it overtook us. Three miles from Anchorage another tire blew out. As we were already late for a scheduled luncheon, the colonel decided to take a chance and proceed. We bumped along for about a mile, then the tire came off and the car slid off the rails, so there was nothing left but to walk the rest of the way to a spot where automobiles could meet us and take us to the luncheon. We trod along the tracks singing "I've Been Working on the Railroad," "In the Good Ole Summertime" and other ditties of the day. The weather was perfect but so warm that our collars wilted. Jim Farley comforted the chagrined colonel by saying the walk was a "great break" for him; he had been sitting for days and had been longing for some exercise. We all got it.

We finally made the luncheon, and talks by Farley and others were broadcast. Everyone's spirits were buoyed by Farley's good sportsmanship and friendly sallies. Later in the afternoon we all attended the ground-breaking ceremony with Farley wielding the spade. Then back to Seward on the repaired "111." Farley had come up just for the ceremony and on our way down I had a chance to fill him in on some of Alaska's problems. He was thereafter, as he would have put it, "in our corner."

An interesting project came to my attention while I was in Anchorage. In the absence of airfields, float planes were the prevailing type used in Alaska. The problem in Anchorage was the range of the tides—some thirty-six feet—the second highest in the world. At low tide vast mud flats were exposed in the adjacent waters of Cook Inlet and Turnagain Arm, stranding airplane passengers far off the mainland. Just outside Anchorage, however, there were two approximately circular lakes—

Hood and Spenard—a few hundred feet apart. The longest diameter of each, about five-eighths of a mile, was insufficient for many planes to take off safely, but Hugh Brewster, the chief inspector of the Bureau of Air Commerce, flew me over them and pointed out that a canal connecting the two would furnish a water runway of ample length. There was, however, no appropriation to build it. It occurred to me that we might be able to use Civilian Conservation Corps labor. The CCC was one of the imaginative New Deal projects created to lift the country out of the Depression and give young men opportunities for useful work and a modest livelihood. So I wired Robert Fechner, its director in Washington, who granted permission. Work began later that summer and the joined lakes eventually became the parking place for perhaps the largest aggregation of privately owned float planes anywhere in the world. Anchorage residents used them to reach their camps on other lakes to which there were then no roads.

Alaska's roadlessness was one of the territory's most serious problems. The persistent refusal of Congress to include Alaska under the Federal Aid Highway Act of 1916, coupled with the rejection, year after year, of individual projects proposed by the Alaska Road Commission, spurred my curiosity to see what little highway mileage there was. So Peter and I flew to Fairbanks to join Ike Taylor, the territorial highway engineer. As we started down the Richardson Highway, which extended from Fairbanks to Valdez on the coast, I discovered that the word "highway" was a misnomer. It was a low-grade gravel road, narrow and rough; but it was, in fact, one of the few, and one of the best, highways in Alaska. I could see that road construction would have to be a top-priority concern when I returned to Washington.

We drove south to Chitina, and at the end of the branch road known as the Edgerton Cut-off, we were met by F. A. Hansen, manager of the Copper River and Northwestern Railroad. He took us in an auto-car to Kennecott, the location of the famous copper mines, a distance of sixty-five miles. There we were met by W. A. Richelsen, manager of the mines, who took us to his home for the night. I wanted to see both the railroad and the mine because it had been announced that after thirty years of operation both were to be closed down that fall. The mine—once one of the world's richest—was no longer profitable, and the railroad, which had been built specifically to transport ore from the mine to the coastal town of Cordova, would no longer serve any useful function. It was, of course, a serious blow to the mine workers, railroad employees and everyone else up and down the line who depended on the operation of the mine.

Our visit to the mine was a memorable one. We were first carried in ore buckets lifted by an aerial tramway from the mine's ground level of

2500 feet to the 5500-foot-level of the Bonanza mine, one of the four composing the Kennecott operation. The horizontal distance was about three-and-a-half miles and took thirty-five minutes; at times the bucket swung dangerously close to the slope of the mountain, at other times we were suspended in mid-air. The longest span of 1665 feet carried us 520 dizzying feet over Bonanza Creek. A second aerial tram carried us still higher, and once at the top of the mine, we went down into various shafts and watched the extraction of the last consignments of ore. Our descent was even more nerve-racking than the ascent since the buckets were filled and each of us was perched in a separate bucket swinging on top of the ore. Peter said he enjoyed every minute. At the bottom once again, we went through the mill, the power plant, the hospital and a score of cottages and several bunk houses—the whole conglomeration to be abandoned. It was a saddening prospect.

No less sad was the realization, during our return journey on the railroad, that the most superlative of all the scenic trips in Alaska would soon be unavailable to the public. The railroad itself was an incredible engineering feat, passing over moving glaciers and bridging the turbulent Copper and Chitina rivers. Tourists had been permitted to make the trip, but now that business would also be lost. When we reached Cordova, I met with a group of townspeople to discuss what, if anything, might be done to lessen the devastating economic blow to their community. The decision to close the mine was final. Richelsen had told me that the owners had expended considerable sums prospecting for new ore deposits throughout the Chitina Valley and surrounding mountains, and had found none that would justify the continuing operation of either the mine or the railroad. But it was my hope that some way might be found to keep the railroad—the town's only link with the interior—going as a tourist attraction, and it occurred to me that the extensive Kennecott buildings could easily be adapted to hotel accommodations. Perhaps the solution lay in making the mine and surrounding scenery a national park or monument and I would offer that proposal to Secretary Ickes.

In Valdez, just west of Cordova, I found no diminution of the bitterness over the Richardson Highway tolls that I had encountered two years previously. Ike Taylor, Peter and I again set out on the Richardson Highway, this time driving north en route to Fairbanks, and during our trip I began to appreciate the difficulties of road maintenance in Alaska. A sudden rain could easily wash out the highway. Glaciers, sometimes advancing a hundred feet a day, were another threat, and glacier-fed torrents tossed boulders weighing tons on the highway as if they were pebbles. We had to cross raging rivers and extricate ourselves from beds of quicksand. We encountered herds of caribou and saw the destruction caused

Ernest on ascent to the Kennecott Mine, 1938

by recent forest fires. Approaching Fairbanks we had to proceed cautiously through water pouring over the road from the overflowing Tanana River. We traversed at least fifteen "lakes" from fifty to a hundred yards long, some of which covered our running board. But for the fact that Ike's car was high-slung, we would not have been able to make it through. It seemed incredible that the federal government levied a toll for that road.

In Fairbanks I ran into Robert Marshall, chief of the Division of Recreation and Lands of the Forest Service. The son of Louis Marshall, the distinguished New York lawyer, he was a "wilderness fan" whom we had known well in Washington. Finding a number of blank spaces on the map of Alaska, where insufficient federal appropriations had left regions unmapped, Marshall decided to spend a summer in one of them, located at the headquarters of the upper Koyukuk River, north of the Arctic Circle. He became so interested in the people and their way of life there that he decided to return the following year, and stayed fifteen months making his headquarters at Wiseman, one of two tiny communities in a region of some fifteen thousand square miles drained by the tributaries of the upper Koyukuk with a total population of seventy-seven whites, forty-four Eskimos and six Indians. A few of them lived in Bettles, a community of little more than a store and a dozen cabins on the Koyukuk some thirty miles above the Arctic Circle; a few were miners who worked the creeks in summer and holed up in nearby cabins in winter. Marshall's book, *Arctic Village*, published in 1933, was a fascinating social and economic study of Wiseman which he dedicated "To the People of the Koyukuk who have made for themselves the happiest civilization of which I have knowledge."

Marshall informed me that he was going to revisit Wiseman after an absence of seven years and asked whether I would like to go. Of course I would. It would be my first visit to the Arctic which, despite its sparse population, comprised one-fifth of the territory. We flew northwest from Fairbanks with Herman Lerdahl of Wien Airways, a bush operation

Ernest in Glacier Bay

started by the three Wien brothers, Sigurd, Noel and Fritz, which was gradually developing into an important air service in the north. We flew over country that was emptiness itself. Winding rivers had carved the level terrain with their abandoned courses; countless ponds and lakes dotted the region, many of them mere thawing of frozen ground. Our first stop was Allakaket on the south shore of the Koyukuk exactly on the Arctic Circle, an Indian Village of about twenty-five log cabins. Across the river was Alatna, which consisted of six houses inhabited by Eskimos. Two recent intermarriages between these ethnic groups had broken the long-established aversion to such matings. It was deemed progress by the schoolteacher, Miss King, and by Miss Kay, the nurse, both of the Episcopal mission of Saint John in the Wilderness located there. There was no Bureau of Indian Affairs school; the mission supplied both the teacher and the nurse.

Our plane landed on a gravel bar in the river and we were rowed to shore by an Indian boy named Simon. Most of the villagers, and all of the men except two traders, were engaged in salmon fishing. It was extremely hot this August 4, and a sunbath would have been in order but for the mosquitoes. The community's chief occupation was fur trapping which accounted for the two traders who exchanged the furs for clothes, canned goods and other articles, most of the transactions being in trade and not in currency.

As we took off, heading north for Wiseman, our next stop, the country became more rolling although no less vacant. On the northern horizon the Endicott Mountains of the Brooks Range began to appear. After an hour we entered the valley of the Middle Fork of the Koyukuk and landed on a level strip. All Wiseman came out to meet us. There was no question of its people's affection for Bob Marshall. The town's only auto, a battered model-T Ford which had been flown up in parts and assembled there, transported us to a roadhouse, the center of the community's social life. We shook hands with everyone, Eskimo men and women, a few white men, their Eskimo wives and their attractive and joyous children. The only white women in the village were Mrs. George Rayburn the newly wed wife of the territorial schoolteacher, and Mrs. Martin Slisco, the Yugoslav wife of the storekeeper who, after he had been in Alaska for thirty years, returned to the old country to bring back his young and beautiful bride.

The village consisted of some twenty well-built, log and sod-roofed cabins. The number of fair-sized trees, cottonwoods and spruce, was astounding at that latitude, 67.6. Equally astounding was the ease with which we had reached this remote and isolated spot and then returned to Fairbanks. It seemed to me not merely a modern miracle but evidence of the very special importance of aviation to Alaska.

Our next excursion took us northeast of Fairbanks by auto on the 165-mile road to Circle, the northernmost point in Alaska accessible by highway. A small collection of log cabins, a store and a schoolhouse, Circle was situated on the Yukon River and was mistakenly thought to be located on the Arctic Circle when the town was named. Actually it was sixty miles to the south. Circle Hot Springs, our next stop, proved to be a surprise. Approaching a central house and several cottages, we were amazed to see a garden with tomato plants six feet high, loaded with large tomatoes. There were also melons and nearly every type of vegetable, many thought to be ungrowable in Alaska. The explanation was quite simple; hot water from nearby thermal springs was piped through the ground under the garden, and with the more than twenty hours of sunlight in May, June and July, vegetables flourished. The water which left the springs at a temperature of 130° F. was also piped through the buildings of this establishment, supplying both their heat and hot water. And there was an open-air swimming pool into which the hot water flowed after running through the buildings. The establishment was advertised as "The Carlsbad of the North," but it was so far north that it attracted few customers. Nevertheless, here was the potential for a first-class thermal resort.

Back in Fairbanks again, we decided to indulge in bonehunting. The discovery of the remains of prehistoric animals in the area was a concomitant of the hydraulic process used to recover gold. In the late twenties when extensive goldmining operations on the creeks in interior Alaska began, powerful streams of water were turned on the frozen muck to uncover the gold-bearing gravel underneath. But the process also uncovered the bones of mammoth, mastodons and other long-vanished species, and they were uncovered intact while excavation by a steam shovel would surely have broken and destroyed many of them. When the bones of saber-toothed tiger, eohippus (a small prehistoric horse), camels and lions began to appear, it was realized that here was treasure—within a figurative stone's throw from the University of Alaska campus on Ester Creek —that would be more highly prized by scientists than the gold which was being mined. So the collection, identification and classification of these osseous finds was initiated under the joint auspices of the University of Alaska and the Museum of Natural History in New York. The paleontologist in charge was Otto Geist of the university.

We visited Dr. Geist's workshop where he was reconstructing the skull of a mammoth and preparing it for shipment, wrapped in rice paper and then encased in cement. I asked him whether the presence of lion and tiger bones meant that Alaska had once had a tropical climate, but he said that in the view of some zoologists the lion's mane was a survival of life in a colder climate, and that the lioness had lost her mane first. He also said that some human bones had been found but no one knew whether mastodon and man had been contemporaneous in Alaska.

Equipped with rubber boots, old clothes and a gunny sack, Peter and I went on a bone-hunt of our own with Dr. Geist. We descended a steep slope of frozen muck until we reached a place about seventy feet below the surface where the gravel was exposed. Dr. Geist directed us to pick up all bones. Later we would discard the useless fragments. It was so warm that we took off our shirts and worked bare from the waist up. We found a considerable number of bison vertebrae and shoulder blades, but the first good find was the maxilla of a young mammoth with teeth in place. Dr. Geist said he would have it polished and sent to us in Washington. Then Peter found the femur of a mammoth, half as high as he was and weighing twenty-five pounds. It was in almost perfect condition and Dr. Geist pronounced it the best find of the day.

The time was fast approaching for Secretary Ickes's arrival. To prepare for it, I spent another day at Mount McKinley National Park reevaluating the various sites for the new hotel. I also had a chance to reexamine the hotel which had just been completed at the park's entrance. It struck me as a complete fiasco; the dining room was too small, the rooms were not much larger than cubbyholes, and very few had baths. No one was happy with it and a hearing was planned to question all those concerned with its construction. I thought the hearing should be held by Secretary Ickes, who had the ultimate authority to decide what remedial measures should be taken.

The Secretary and his wife were to land in Seward and we traveled to meet them in the "B1," an old-fashioned private railroad car made of wood, with a double bedroom, kitchen and dining room. Colonel Ohlson proposed to turn it over to the Ickeses for their use. The Secretary had just been remarried to an attractive and intelligent woman forty years his junior, and their trip to Alaska was also something of a honeymoon. The B1 was very light and so shaky that eating supper on it was quite a feat. Soup remained in the plate with difficulty, as did coffee in the cup. However, for the Ickes party, Ohlson intended to add the observation car which was heavy and steady.

The Ickeses arrived on the S.S. *McKinley*, and after they were driven around Seward, we departed for Anchorage, stopping at Kenai Lake for lunch. Mrs. Ickes remarked it was the first time in her life that she had traveled in a private car and that a train had stopped while she lunched. Both the Secretary and Mrs. Ickes were very jolly. During the trip north, I had a chance to report to Ickes on my latest impressions of Alaska. I told him of the bitterness in Valdez over the highway tolls and urged their abolition. He said "No." I also urged him to visit Chitina and Kennecott, so that he could see this famous mine while it was still in operation and appreciate the consequences of its closing. I also wanted to enlist his support in keeping the Copper River and Northwestern Railroad in operation. I stressed the sensational beauty of the region and its potentialities as a national park. If he did not go, I said I would like to return and take some Park Service personnel with me. He agreed.

In Anchorage that evening, both Secretary and Mrs. Ickes spoke well in response to welcoming speeches. The Secretary was witty, caustic but tactful, and at all times meaty. He got a big laugh by saying that if Congress did not appropriate sufficient funds to rehabilitate the Alaska Railroad, he would get the appropriations committees to ride on the B1 and "shake it out of them."

When we arrived at Mount McKinley Park Station, Ickes, viewing the new hotel from the car, expressed strong disapproval. He said it looked like a factory and that he fully expected to hear the whistle blow. He, too, found the dining room wholly inadequate; an average arriving trainload of passengers would have required four sittings to get through a meal. The lobby was too small, there were too few rooms, beams in the ceilings were inferior—they had already split and would have to be replaced—the power house, which had cost $68,000, was unnecessary —a diesel engine in the basement would have sufficed—and its tall smokestack was a blot on the landscape. He concluded that he would hold a hearing the next morning and try to fix the responsibility for the blunders.

Harry Liek, the superintendent of the park, who was supposed to be in charge of the hotel project; Gutterson, the architect; Victor Rivers, the construction engineer, and Thomas C. Vint, the supervising architect of the National Park Service were summoned for the hearing. Colonel Ohlson and I were also present, and it was a ghastly revelation of administrative inefficiency. It soon became clear that Harry Liek, whatever his other merits, was wholly unqualified to superintend an assignment of this nature, but the fault was not his; he should never have been given such a task. Both the architect and the construction engineer were equally inexperienced and unqualified, but the unhappiest figure of all was Tom Vint, who, as the "supervising architect," was the one man fully responsible both for the design of the hotel and for the appointment of the other three. He had no explanation for the hotel's various deficiencies.

The Secretary found that at least $75,000 had been wasted. It would now be necessary to tear out the end of the dining room and extend it so that it could accommodate a trainload of guests at one sitting, and a wing would have to be added to bring the total number of accommodations to one hundred rooms. The additional funds would be supplied by the railroad; fortunately, Colonel Ohlson had accumulated a surplus of $125,000 during the preceding year. The Secretary gave all the principals a dressing-down, tempered with post-honeymoon kindliness. He relieved Harry Liek of his responsibility for the project, ordered Gutterson back to Washington, and told Rivers he could stay on as long as he was satisfactory to Vint. For his part, Vint was to be held responsible for such errors as could, on checking in Washington, be ascribed to him. In future he was to consult with Ohlson on all matters and, in the event of disagreement, Ickes was to be notified personally. The Secretary's conduct of the hearing and his decisions were correct, I felt; it was Ickes at his best, and I thought it fortunate that he had been on the scene when there was still time to rectify some of the more glaring errors.

I left the Secretary to meet Frank Heintzelman, the Regional Forester for Alaska; he had a conservation problem he wanted, with my support, to take up with Ickes. He felt that some new highway construction near the western boundary of the Chugach National Forest linking Seward with Turnagain Arm would make the Russian River—a famous trout stream—too easily accessible to fishermen and campers. Thirty-six-inch rainbow trout were being taken from it and they were abundant. The river should have been included in the national forest, but it was not. Its northward course was bisected longitudinally in several places by the 150th meridian which formed the western boundary of the Chugach National Forest. So arbitrary and artificial a boundary which ignored the contours and physical features of the land was clearly an error of earlier bureaucrats, committed when the Chugach was set aside as a national forest in the century's first decade. It was typical of the way decisions affecting Alaska were made in Washington.

There existed in Alaska no general provision for regulating sport fishing. Heintzelman proposed, therefore, that the Chugach Forest's boundary be moved westward a few rods where necessary to include the river's west bank, making it a part of the forest where fishing and camping could be regulated. The Forest Service had the training and legal authority for just such regulation. It seemed like a simple and sensible move to preserve a superlative fishing ground, and I told Heintzelman that I would be glad to recommend to Secretary Ickes that he relinquish the necessary land to the Forest Service.

There was some question, however, whether Ickes would agree to the proposal because of his animosity toward the Department of Agriculture. For several years he had been waging an unremitting battle to have the Forest Service transferred from it to the Department of the Interior. He had pulled every possible wire, and considered the opposition of any who did not favor the transfer as an unfriendly act, but so far his campaign had met with little success. He was, however, an ardent conservationist, and Heintzelman reminded me that at his suggestion the Forest Service was planning to relinquish a million acres from the Tongass National Forest to the Glacier Bay National Monument. Under the circumstances, he hoped that Ickes, as a *quid pro quo*, would yield the few acres necessary to save the Russian River in the interests of conservation.

I presented the arguments for Heintzelman's plan to Ickes and he said he would like to have Heintzelman accompany him to Glacier Bay to show him just what lands would be involved in the transfer. They set out together on the Coast Guard cutter *Spencer*, and meanwhile, since Ickes had decided not to go to Kennecott, I went, accompanied by Harry Liek, John D. Coffman, the Park Service's chief forester, and Peter, to begin an intensive three-day study of the Chitina Valley's potential as a National Park. The first leg of our journey took us by plane over the spectacular peaks, glaciers and canyons of the valley. We were on the look-out for locations from which most of this grandeur could be seen and made accessible to the public, and we explored one or two promising sites on foot. Finally we visited the Kennecott mine again and considered the possibilities of transforming the tram lines and ore buckets into facilities that tourists might use, and of converting mine buildings to provide the necessary accommodations. Everyone agreed that both the Chitina Valley and the mine were up to the very highest National Park standards, but there were two major drawbacks. We had no idea whether the Kennecott would be for sale or otherwise available, and clearly maintaining the Copper River and Northwestern Railroad through the valley to and from the mine would be prohibitively expensive. The most practical alternatives would be the construction of a highway that followed the railroad's right of way, or an extension of a cut-off from the Richardson Highway that already existed, neither of which would present difficult engineering problems. We were all enthusiastic about the project, but I knew that our enthusiasm would not be enough to bring it into being without Secretary Ickes's support and the necessary appropriations from the Department of the Interior.

We rejoined the Secretary's party in Juneau and Frank Heintzelman told me he had gotten along famously with Secretary Ickes during their trip to Glacier Bay. While not definitely committing himself to yielding enough land to save the Russian River, Ickes had said that he favored the plan and asked Heintzelman to put it in writing. Heintzelman was certain Ickes would approve. I was not so certain.

Another touchy subject in Alaska was drunkenness among the Indians, and again Ickes had jumped in with both feet. He had visited the Indian community of Hoonah and found most of the adults intoxicated. Such debauchery was all too common at the end of the fishing season when, for a brief period, cash was plentiful. Later in the year, when the money was gone, the consequences were destitution and misery, particularly among the children. Ickes had blasted, somewhat indiscriminately, the white people of Alaska for selling "rot-gut whiskey" to the Indians, and he had wired William Zimmerman, Jr., assistant commissioner of Indian Affairs, to come to Alaska at once and with Claude M. Hirst, the bureau superintendent for Alaska, to look into the matter. The most obvious solution, Ickes declared, would be to have the next territorial legislature pass laws prohibiting the sale of liquor to Indians with penalties for both seller and buyer. But I felt the problem was much more complex than that. First, there was some question whether the legislature had the power to enact such laws. The "natives" of Alaska had been granted full citizenship by Congress in 1924. I doubted whether such restrictive legislation could be applied only to them, even assuming that it was desirable. I thought the problem could be attacked in another, simpler way. Drunkenness seemed to be much worse in some villages than in others, a difference that could be ascribed to the presence or absence of liquor stores. Why not tighten up the licensing of these stores and regulate more carefully where, by whom and to whom liquor was sold?

I was unable to go with Zimmerman and Hirst on their tour of native villages, but I did decide to go to Hoonah to see for myself the conditions that had so shocked Ickes. There, Wendell Cordle, the Indian Bureau schoolteacher, and his wife, both of whom had served in Native communities all over Alaska, told a horrifying story of what liquor was doing to the Indians. Nearly the entire population of the village was drunk and would dissipate in about sixty days every cent earned during the fishing season. The rest of the year, there would be no alternative but to go on relief. Children, Cordle said, also started drinking at an early age, which increased their susceptibility to disease and their death rate.

There were two liquor dealers in Hoonah, and Cordle said there was no reason why they should have been granted licenses. Under territorial law, outside of incorporated towns, a license to sell intoxicating beverages could be obtained through a petition signed by a majority of the citizens over twenty-one years of age residing within two miles of the place where the liquor was to be sold. Granting the license was entrusted by law to Federal District Judge George F. Alexander of the First Judicial Division, who made it a practice to award a license whenever the above conditions were met, even though it was not mandatory, and he had repeatedly stated that liquor was ruining the Indians. However, the petitions were not always obtained legally. The applicant for a liquor license was often the village storekeeper who invariably extended credit to his customers and was thus in a position to exact their signatures on his petition. But in those villages where the necessary signatures had not been obtained, no liquor was sold and conditions were much better.

Cordle told me that the mayor of Hoonah was a good man, did not drink himself, and tried to prevent the general intoxication, but he was without influence because under the old Indian social order he was of low caste. The distinction between nobles—that is, chiefs—ordinary people and slaves still prevailed among the Tlingits, although slavery had disappeared half a century earlier largely due to the efforts of missionaries. Nevertheless, the descendants of former slaves were still looked down upon and considered inferior. Cordle shared my view that restricting the sale of liquor to Indians was the best way out of a difficult problem; they would still get bootleg liquor and make potent home-brew, but in much smaller quantities. Unless alcoholism was checked, he said, all the other efforts on behalf of the Indians would be in vain.

I went to see Judge Alexander and asked him why he granted liquor licenses in Indian villages. He said he felt he had no choice if the necessary signatures were on the petition. I pointed out that the law did not compel him to grant a license and that his refusal to do so would go a long way toward solving the problem. But he continued to assert that he had no right to refuse. Clearly the solution would rest in new and more restrictive licensing procedures, or in a new judge who would administer the present procedures with greater discrimination.

James Wickersham, for many years a federal judge in Alaska, agreed that liquor was destroying the Indians and that liquor licenses need not and should not be granted in Indian villages. I called on Wickersham, then in his eighty-first year, at his home on a hilltop overlooking Juneau. He had served not only on the bench but had been repeatedly elected as Alaska's Delegate to Congress. He was a man of many abilities. In addition to his distinguished service in the judicial and legislative branches, he had engaged in various mining and exploring ventures. His was the first attempt to climb Mount McKinley, which he had reached on foot from Fairbanks in 1903 through unexplored wilderness. On his way there and back, he made the first exploration of the Kantishna River and announced prophetically that within a year "the Kantishna would be an important goldmining district." The trail to it from the Nenana River, ninety miles to the east, would in time be the one road in Mount McKinley Park.

Wickersham had also compiled a bibliography of writings about Alaska which had been published in 1927 by the Alaska Agricultural College and School of Mines. In fact, it was through his efforts in Congress that the college, which later became the University of Alaska, had been established. In large part this bibliography of more than ten thousand items was a catalogue of his own library, the most complete collection of Alaskana in existence. He had also just published a book of Alaskan reminiscences entitled *Old Yukon*.

I had a long and interesting talk with Wickersham about Alaska's problems. He agreed that mining taxation was inadequate and should be increased. He also believed that land should be taxed to prevent mortmain holdings of those who left the territory and of others who made no use of the land but merely held it indefinitely waiting for some increase in value not due to their own efforts. I asked him why the Alaska Railroad— whose construction by the federal government had been undertaken, largely through his efforts, after various attempts by private enterprise had failed—had not been built from Chitina to the interior. He said he had not recommended the existing route; President Wilson had chosen it. At the time there was a good deal of feeling against J. P. Morgan and the Guggenheims in connection with the "looting of Alaska" and that had doubtless influenced Wilson. He said the present route, which traveled up the center of the Kenai Peninsula, was both impractical and uneconomical. Much more preferable would have been a route along either the eastern or western coasts of the peninsula. Even better would have been an extension of the railroad from Cordova to Chitina which had already been built by the Morgan-Guggenheim syndicate and which the government could have acquired.

"But didn't you lead the fight against the syndicate?" I asked.

"I did," he replied, "at least against some of their tactics, but I certainly would not have opposed the government's acquiring the railroad and extending it into the interior. Of course, for a time I hoped that the government would build not merely one but two railroads over different routes. The legislation I sponsored and Congress approved authorized two routes, but only one was built."

Wickersham also had a deep interest in preserving Alaska's historic past. He told me about the Lincoln totem at Tongass which he said he had been trying to save for many years. When Secretary of State William H. Seward visited Alaska in 1869, he stopped at Tongass and addressed the Indians on Abraham Lincoln, the Great Emancipator. He told them how Lincoln had brought freedom to the oppressed and assured them that his principles would guide government policies toward Alaskans and bring them many blessings. Thereafter at a council of chiefs, it was decided to make a totem to the "greatest of all chiefs." The next year the totem pole was carved from a large red cedar and erected with other totems in the village. Wickersham had a photograph which he thought was taken about 1880 that showed no fewer than twenty-eight totem poles standing, including the Lincoln pole. The likeness was unmistakable, right down to his tall, black hat. Another photograph taken about 1905 showed that one of the arms, which were akimbo, had broken off.

Wickersham had repeatedly requested that the pole be saved from destruction, but nothing had been done. I promised to see what I could do. I said I would try to get the Coast Guard cutter, *Haida*, on which I was returning to Seattle, to stop at Tongass so I could assess the present status and condition of the Lincoln totem and see what could be done to preserve it. Later I spoke to Heintzelman about preserving totems and suggested that we make application for the necessary funds from the WPA. He was keenly interested in the project.

Secretary Ickes had returned to Washington and my visit, too, was drawing to a close. There was just time for me to see Glacier Bay National Monument and inspect the million acres that the Forest Service intended to transfer to it. We flew to Glacier Bay in a Marine Airways plane, one of the southeastern bush operations which was expanding into a regular service, and there was no question about the unique beauty of the area. It had been established as a national monument twelve years earlier, but as yet there were no accommodations for visitors. It was Heintzelman's idea—and a very good one—to tackle the tourist problem by securing some discarded passenger vessel and anchoring it in the bay for use as a hotel. It could be left there through the winter, or towed back to Juneau at the end of each summer season.

We were favored with perfect weather during our visit, but when we sailed out of the bay to look over the wide, flat area that the Forest Service had offered to yield, I was forced to conclude that the enlargement proposed by Heintzelman to Secretary Ickes, and eagerly accepted by him, was not only unnecessary but positively objectionable. The additional area was without scenic value, and it could be administered, I felt, only with substantial additional expenditures. There were also a number of homesteaders, miners and Indian hunters and trappers, all of whom would be displaced by the transfer.

On my return to Juneau, I expressed my objections to Heintzelman. He said I was probably right but that he could not withdraw from the position he had taken vis-à-vis Ickes. He was still optimistic that Ickes would consent to adjusting the western boundary of the Chugach National Forest to save the Russian River's rainbow trout.

As it happened, the transfer of over one million acres to Glacier Bay National Monument went through, and there were immediate protests from the homesteaders who were dislodged. The Interior Department aggravated their grievance by reporting adversely on bills introduced by Delegate Dimond to secure adequate compensation for the losses they suffered. They were eventually obliged to settle for much lesser sums than they were entitled to for the loss of their homes and their years of effort to establish them.

Secretary Ickes, on the other hand, did not yield a square inch of his dominion over the western shore of the Russian River. The excessive fishing that Heintzelman feared and wanted to avert came to pass. By the time, three years later, that the Fish and Wildlife Service, now in the Interior Department, had secured the necessary authority to control sport fishing, the damage had been done. The thirty-six-inch rainbow trout of the Russian River were only a memory. Ickes's General Land Office still firmly held the line—the one hundred and fiftieth meridian.

One of the books I had picked up in Seattle on my way north was entitled: *Wildlife Restoration and Conservation*. It contained the proceedings of the North American Wildlife Conference, February 3–7, 1936 called by President Roosevelt and included an address by the Honorable Harold L. Ickes. In it he quoted a speech by himself made earlier:

> The real trouble with the conservation movement in this country is that it is divided into small cliques and factions. It is not a cohesive coherent movement. Forces that ought to be united and working disinterestedly for the common good are too busy struggling for their own selfish interests so that, due to the resulting confusion of counsel, the exploiters are still largely having their wanton way with the natural resources of America. It is high time for all of us who pay more than lip-service to conservation to unite in the common cause, realizing that conservation is a single objective and not a congeries of policies.

And Secretary Ickes continued:

> Since I have been Secretary of the Interior, I have never overlooked an opportunity to cooperate with any other divisions of the government interested in the preservation of wildlife or in conservation in any of its aspects.

I reread it several times when Frank Heintzelman told me sadly what hadn't happened on the Russian River.

Peter and I returned to Seattle on the seventeen-year-old Coast Guard cutter, *Haida*, which was going south for her annual overhaul and carried the families of its personnel as well as its normal complement of officers and men. The ship left her regular course to permit me to inspect the "Old Kasaan National Monument" on Prince of Wales Island. It was supposed to be the finest collection of totem poles in Alaska in their original setting, although closely rivaled by those at Tongass. They had been deemed of sufficient importance to be set aside by the Interior Department as a national monument in 1916. As we drew near, it was possible to see some thirty poles along the shore which at first glance looked like dead trees. We landed in a small boat and I saw that what had once been a great assemblage of poles had been so ruined by weather and neglect that scarcely four or five were capable of restoration. The carving on most of them had rotted away. In others, bushes and trees were growing from cracks, hastening their disintegration. The whole area was buried in a jungle growth of underbrush which made penetration difficult. In the midst of this tangle, we found what no doubt once had been a well-kept Indian grave. The top had come off and the bodies in the two coffins inside, of an adult male and a small baby, were exposed to the elements. What had been a fence around the grave had crumbled, and other graves were in similar condition. It was a monument to administrative inefficiency and neglect.

The devastation at Tongass was similar. Of eighteen poles still standing—others had fallen—all but two were so badly decayed that restoration was impossible. Fortunately, the Lincoln pole, although pretty far gone, was among the least damaged. Both arms were missing and the top hat was so fuzzy with vegetation that it was scarcely recognizable. The figures at the base were still visible but badly decayed. Practically all vestiges of paint had disappeared.

I radioed Heintzelman to urge him to hasten his request for funds from the WPA, and when I got back to Washington, I went to see Harry Hopkins immediately. It took a little doing to persuade him to agree to grant the application. The notion of restoring totem poles brought broad smiles to WPA officials. Wasn't this the boondoggliest of boondoggles, they wanted to know? But they finally agreed that the project was worthwhile. Heintzelman took over thereafter. With both WPA and CCC funds and labor, an energetic program of pole repair, restoration and—where the poles were too far gone—reproduction was undertaken just in the nick of time. Totem-pole carving had virtually ceased in Alaska. No new poles had been erected for a generation. Only a few of the skilled carvers—men of advanced years—were left. But they were now enlisted and put to work.

One hundred and fifteen poles were restored or duplicated. They were placed in the Indian villages of Saxman, Hydaburg, Klawok and New Kasaan, and in the part white, part Indian communities of Ketchikan, Wrangell and Juneau. The poles in the Sitka National Monument were also repaired and repainted. In addition, Heintzelman had exact reproductions of three native community houses with their inside totems erected at New Kasaan, on Shakes Island at Wrangell, and on the Tongass Highway, a few miles north of Ketchikan where they could be seen from passing steamers. The Lincoln likeness—some five feet high—was rescued and brought to Juneau where, after treatment with the proper preservatives, it was enclosed in a glass case and placed in the territorial museum. James Wickersham lived long enough to see the realization of the project he had worked so many years to achieve.

18

RANGING FAR AND WIDE

*We are always coming up with emphatic
facts of history in our private experience
and verifying them here. All history becomes subjective: in other words there is
properly no history only biography.*
—RALPH WALDO EMERSON

I might have wished that the area of my responsibility as Director of the
Division of Territories and Island Possessions could have been a little
more compact, but it was spread out to the north, south, east and west,
and I was stimulated by its diversity, which seemed to me to lend substance to Emerson's dictum. Back in Washington from my trip to Alaska,
I again turned my attention to Puerto Rico, and in particular to its university. Having created a fine physical plant for the university, it seemed
obvious to me that we should build up the quality of the educational
services it provided. I had long felt that a university was and should be
the soul of a state, the fountainhead of its spiritual and intellectual leadership, and a guide and consultant in solving its social and economic problems. That had not been in any sense the case in Puerto Rico. It was my
hope that we might now steer it in this direction.

The university had made a fair start in 1924 under the chancellorship
of Thomas Eliot Benner, an able and enlightened educator. However,
after only four years, he was forced out for purely—or, better said,
impurely—political reasons. His insistence on merit in faculty selections
had antagonized the legislative members who controlled the university's
board of trustees. Then followed a period of stagnation and lethargy
under the temporary administration of Dr. Gildo Masso. The university de-

clined in every respect, particularly in Hispanic studies. Dr. Carlos E. Chardon, his successor, was essentially an agronomist with no wider interest in university development. Political intervention, which he did not resist, increased. When he was succeeded by a well-meaning, but totally unqualified political appointee, Juan B. Soto, the university declined still further.

The university's many deficiencies resulted in its being denied a place on the approved list of regional associations of colleges following an investigation in 1937 by Frank H. Bookes, director of admissions of Columbia University. I had meanwhile asked for and received a report on the university from one qualified to make a knowledgeable estimate of its defects and requirements. He was Richard Pattee, for some years a teacher there of history and political science, and the coach of its debating team. Brought up in the Southwest, he was completely bilingual and bicultural. He added to his adverse report a largely unfavorable analysis of the qualifications of every faculty member.

It seemed to me that if we could get a commission of educators of high standing to go to Puerto Rico and report on the university's needs, we could make it not only a first-class insular institution of higher learning, but an inter-American university, a bridge between the Anglo-Saxon and Hispanic cultures of the western world. As such it would be of great benefit both to Puerto Rico and the United States in strengthening inter-American relations toward which the Roosevelt Administration had made such a hopeful start. I described my plan to Secretary Ickes and offered to approach American educators to see whether we might not create a commission for that purpose. He agreed.

My first choice was Isaiah Bowman, president of Johns Hopkins, eminent geographer and widely traveled scholar. He accepted and agreed to be chairman. Then we went over the list of the other names I proposed. I suggested we raise our sights following a dictum of Henry David Thoreau: "Men hit only what they aim at; so they had better aim high." Bowman agreed enthusiastically. "We can't get everyone we want," he said, "but we can try."

So we invited President Harold Willis Dodds of Princeton, President Livingston Farrand of Cornell, President Frank Parker Graham of North Carolina, and David Livingston Crawford, president of the University of Hawaii. Bowman vetoed President Robert Maynard Hutchins of Chicago on the grounds that he was eternally flippant, and Abraham Flexner, one of the three distinguished Flexner brothers, on the grounds that he was difficult to deal with. We also asked Alvin Johnson of the New School for Social Research, Victor Selden Clark because of his scholarly Brookings Institute study of Puerto Rico, and Senator Elbert Thomas of Utah, not so much because he was a senator—although that would be helpful if we needed some federal appropriations—but because he had been an enlightened professor of political science at the University of Utah before entering public life. Thomas Benner, then Dean of the School of Education at the University of Illinois, was included for his special qualifications. I felt we should also have a competent lawyer and teacher of law because of the university's law school needs, and at Felix Frankfurter's suggestion I invited Max Radin, a professor of law at the University of California. Richard Pattee was asked to be the commission's secretary. Because I was hopeful that we could promote a graduate school of tropical fisheries to add to the existing school of tropical medicine and to the graduate schools of tropical agriculture and tropical forestry we were trying to establish, we also included a fisheries expert, Reginald Fiedler. The commission finally consisted of Bowman, Benner, Clark, Crawford, Graham, Johnson, Radin and Thomas, and April 6, 1939, was fixed as its departure date for a ten-day investigation of the university.

The commission was enthusiastically received in Puerto Rico and its stay unmarred by any untoward incident. When its report was completed, it pointed to the unique geographic and cultural advantages which made the university a logical site for a hemispheric role. But it was clear that Puerto Rico's financial resources at the time were insufficient to achieve such an objective and that federal and private foundation aid would be required. Having proposed a number of structural changes in the university, the report dealt gently with the institution's defects, merely pointing out that it had "not developed as far as mainland state universities" and did "not offer a typically full university program." It was obviously the desire of the commission to give as little offense to Puerto Rican sensibilities as possible. But in subsequent conferences, its members made clear that a new chancellor was imperative as a first step.

Implementing the commission's recommendations and selecting a new chancellor would, of course, take time; but when, sometime later, Rexford Guy Tugwell was proposed as the new chancellor, I felt that the university would be in excellent hands. Tugwell had both an intimate knowledge of Puerto Rico's conditions and excellent academic credentials. Even the fact of his being a "continental" was no impediment, since his appointment was favored by the party in power which was headed by Luis Muñoz Marin, who had broken away from the Liberal Party, created the new Popular Democratic Party, and had won the election in 1940. The rug was pulled out from under my hopes for the university, however, when President Roosevelt appointed Tugwell governor of Puerto Rico early in 1941.

Tugwell accepted the appointment but also sought to hold the chancellorship as well. He requested Secretary Ickes to write President Roosevelt asking him to sign an executive order, a draft of which he enclosed, to permit him to occupy both positions. Ickes did so, but the move aroused —understandably—such a furor in Puerto Rico that Tugwell was obliged to give up the chancellorship.

There the matter lay until the leadership necessary to bring about the needed changes was found within the university itself. It came with the appointment of a young teacher of political science, Jaime Benitez, Puerto Rican born with degrees from Georgetown and Chicago universities. Surviving political changes for more than a third of a century thereafter, he gradually transformed the University of Puerto Rico into a steadily improving institution, adopting many of the Bowman commission's recommendations. While the role I had envisioned for the University as an inter-American institution was never sought and achieved as such, it continues as a possibility. The commission, however, furnished an impetus and Puerto Rico produced the needed individual.

Whatever my other concerns, Alaska could not be ignored for long. In the winter of 1937–1938 I had talked repeatedly with Delegate Dimond and Warren Magnuson, congressman from the First Washington District, about the possibility of building a highway from the States to Alaska. The idea was not new. An Alaska highway engineer, Donald MacDonald, had been advocating it for years. Various commissions, both American and Canadian, had looked into the matter, but so far nothing had happened. The idea never completely died, however, and during late 1938 and early 1939 we had several visits from T. Duff Patullo, the Premier of British Columbia, who was trying to stimulate enthusiasm in Washington for the project. The machinery began to move again slowly with the establishment of the Alaska International Highway Commission, consisting of five members, one of whom would be an Alaskan, to meet with a similar Canadian commission and recommend a route. The President appointed Magnuson as chairman, and Thomas L. Riggs, the United States-Canada boundary commissioner and former Governor of Alaska; James L. Carey, highway engineer for the State of Washington; Donald MacDonald the Alaskan highway engineer, and myself. After a preliminary organization meeting in Seattle, we met with the Canadian commissioners in Victoria.

The American commissioners—myself included—realized that while the choice of a route through Canada would probably follow Canadians' wishes, we would prefer a route as far west as practicable so that branch roads might connect the highway with the principal cities of southeastern Alaska—Ketchikan, Wrangell, Petersburg, Juneau and Skagway. A route along the rugged coast was obviously out of the question, but one just east of the coast range seemed most desirable from Alas-

ka's standpoint, and indeed had been declared feasible by the American
and Canadian commissioners who had studied it in the early 1930s. This
became known as the "A" route and like the "B" route, then favored by
the Canadians, would utilize the 650 miles of already constructed highway running north from the border to Prince George. It would then join
the three-hundred-mile road to Hazelton, the farthest north extension of
any road in western British Columbia, and from there extend to Atlin,
Whitehorse and Fairbanks. It would not, like the "B" route, pass through
Dawson and would have longer mileage in Alaska.

The Canadian commissioners suggested that it would be well if we
made an aerial reconnaissance—as they just had—of the two routes
and they recommended the airline that had taken them on their flight.
The four American commissioners present—Governor Riggs was unable to attend—agreed that, since we were already in British Columbia,
we should make the flight. Within minutes, two representatives of Canadian Airways Ltd. were on hand. We told them that we would like to fly
over the "A" route through Whitehorse to Dawson and return by way of
the "B" route. They told us they had just the plane, a new two-motored
De Haviland. The round-trip distance was about 2400 miles, and allowing
for overnight and other stops, would last three days each way, weather
permitting. They produced a contract for us to sign. The price stipulated
was $1800. We agreed without hesitation. After all we were guests of our
Canadian neighbors, but we gathered from the broad smiles of the airline
officials that they felt they had made a highly profitable arrangement.

They further urged that there was room for a photographer aboard,
and when we assented, Mr. Lucien Roy of Associated Screen News, Ltd.
came on with a hundred pounds of photographic equipment. When the
plane landed two hours later on Lake Williams, it was unable to take off
again. After a long exchange of profanity for our benefit between pilot
and co-pilot, we were told we would have to break up. Magnuson, the
pilot, the photographer and I would go on. MacDonald, Carey and the
co-pilot would follow in another plane. We objected. We said we
wanted the comments of the two engineers on the commission as we observed the terrain. But there was no alternative; the pilot insisted. So we
flew on and waited impatiently at a northern resort several hours further
along. On the third day the rest of the party finally arrived in a Junkers
freight plane in which only one of the two engineers, sitting in the co-pilot's seat, could look out; the other had to lie in darkness with the baggage. We protested emphatically again this breach of contract. Not only
had we been promised one plane for the four of us but we had also been
urged to take on another passenger, the photographer with one hundred
pounds of equipment. Then what was our amazement when the pilot

Peter Gruening on one of the high Wrangell Mountain peaks, 1938

asked us to sign a contract for the second plane for another $1800. We refused indignantly. The pilot said he couldn't move unless we did. "All right, take us back," we said.

"Not until you have signed," the pilot said. With some difficulty we managed to reach Premier Patullo by phone and he instructed the pilot to take us on. The four members of the commission were not again reunited. But when we met again at Vancouver, the airline company's men were at the float presenting the second bill. We refused to pay it. We had assented without argument to their original contract, but they had broken it. They continued to dun us, however, even after our return to Washington, and finally, to our amazement, Premier Patullo got into the act. "Oh hell why don't we pay it?" the chairman ventured. "Over my dead body," I said. "They seem to think Uncle Sam is made of money, as many Canadians appear to believe; there is a principle at stake." We did not pay it.

In spite of this dispute, the trip proved useful both in surveying the alternative routes and in sampling public opinion about the highway itself. We stopped for the night at Whitehorse, a town dominated by the White Pass and Yukon Railroad which opposed the construction of the highway. Its president, we learned, had expressed his opposition at a hearing held there a couple of weeks earlier by the Canadian commission. He had said that the scheme was "visionary and impractical," that it would "take many years to build a road that will be passable," that Yukon Territory was already "amply supplied with transportation facilities" and the proposed highway would serve "no useful purpose." However, we discovered that we had at least the tacit support of Mr. Horace E. Moore, the publisher of the *Whitehorse Star*, subtitled "Voice of the Yukon." He called on us at the Whitehorse Inn, took us to our room, and after seeing that the door was shut whispered, "I'm for the highway, but the paper can't say it."

Other Canadian and Alaskan communities were openly enthusiastic. In Dawson, the *Dawson News*, subtitled "British Empire's Farthest North Newspaper," stopped its presses to headline "American Commissioners

Representative Warren Magnusen and Ernest Gruening plotting the Alaska Highway route

Arrive." The town was but a shadow of its former Klondike gold-rush days and the highway would have been an obvious boon. In other smaller communities, everyone hoped the highway would "pass our way." But unfortunately, the time for building the highway was not yet ripe. Predictably enough, the Canadian commission recommended the "B" route, the American commission recommended the "A" route, and the project was confined to legislative limbo until both countries suddenly found themselves at war.

In 1939 Europe was already at war and Secretary Ickes began to promote a plan for a mass resettlement of European refugees in Alaska. It was launched by means of a brochure entitled "The Problems of Alaska Development." In my opinion, the brochure was completely misleading, and the Secretary and I once again found ourselves in opposite camps.

The brochure had been prepared by Felix Cohen, a member of the legal staff of the department's solicitor, Nathan Margold. Neither man had any firsthand acquaintance with Alaska, but their enthusiasm for the plan convinced them of Alaska's potential ability to absorb fifty thousand immigrants. Assistant Secretary Oscar L. Chapman, who had been asked to lend his name to the report, took the precaution of seeking the views of Interior officials familiar with Alaska. John D. Coffman's comment was typical of most of them. He wrote: ". . . altogether too optimistic. Only the roseate side is presented and the many difficulties which must be overcome are either omitted or minimized." President Isaiah Bowman of Johns Hopkins University, to whom the brochure was also submitted, declared it to be "the most slipshod and unworthy report of its kind that I have ever seen." Few persons were better qualified to judge. He had done extensive research in pioneer settlement. But no attention was paid to his criticism, and thereafter his advice and cooperation on the project were not sought.

In view of so much adverse criticism, Oscar Chapman declined to make the report his own. Undersecretary Harry Slattery was then asked to endorse it. Slattery had had a fine record as a courageous public servant before coming to the department, but like so many others after a few years of working under Ickes, he seemed to have lost his fighting spirit. Perhaps it was the result of Ickes's practice of tapping telephones, installing dictaphones and having the desks of his "underlings," as he referred to Interior Department personnel, searched to ascertain the extent of their loyalty to him.

The brochure became "The Slattery Report." In principle I was in sympathy with its dual proposal to help the persecuted victims of totalitarianism and to develop Alaska's resources. With about one inhabitant to every ten square miles, according to the 1930 census, Alaska could easily accommodate more people. And I pointed out to Secretary Ickes that there was probably less prejudice in Alaska against aliens than in any part of the Union. A large proportion of Alaskans had been foreign-born, and one heard various accents throughout the territory. But there were basic objections to the proposal, which I put in writing in a memorandum to the Secretary.

After quoting some of the adverse comments of Interior officials familiar with Alaska, I wrote:

> The legislation now being drafted and under consideration contains one provision against which I have registered my objections—namely the raising of the immigration quota for Alaska exclusively. I object to this because, first, it is wholly contrary to the principle which above all others has been established for the last five years in the Department—that the Territories are entitled to equal treatment with the States—and second, I consider it fundamentally un-American and undesirable to create a peculiar category of immigrants and prospective citizens denied the right of free movement and compelled to live in one region, virtually making Alaska a concentration camp. I question the constitutionality of such a project, doubt whether it would be adopted by Congress and question the possibility of its enforcement if adopted. A special enforcement agency watching over these prospective citizens in Alaska would be necessary to see that they did not slip out to the mainland. Also the provision would be universally resented in Alaska. If kept in the bill, it will prejudice a great many people against a desirable project.
>
> I question whether special legislation is necessary. Ample opportunities exist to test the feasibility of the whole undertaking with a very considerable number of refugees who have arrived in this country since the persecutions began in 1935. Tens of thousands are already here without economic opportunity or prospect—certainly a far larger number than can with any degree of practicability be settled in Alaska in the near future. . . .

But whatever the legality of the proposal, its most serious drawback was the provision that the refugees could settle only in Alaska, and would simply be dumped down to sink or swim, without any regard to their own preferences and abilities or to Alaska's particular needs. I suggested that a single project be developed on a test basis to determine the practicality of the resettlement scheme, and proposed that the mineral hot springs in Alaska be taken over and developed as thermal resorts. I listed six of them and particularly called attention to Circle Hot Springs, whose potentialities I had noted during my visit there. It had been taken over by creditors and could probably have been acquired easily. Among the refugees already in our country, it was certain there were doctors, masseurs, trained nurses, hotel managers, and no doubt some who had actual experience in the famous spas of Europe. With twenty-four-hour daylight during the summer months and built-in warmth during the winter, accessible by rail and highway, by riverboat and by air, Circle Hot Springs had obvious and unique attractions. But I found no enthusiasm in Secretary Ickes except for his plan, unchanged and undiminished.

The proposal came up at one of Secretary Ickes's staff conferences to which all the department's agency heads and subheads were summoned. These conferences were painful affairs—and a total waste of time. Presumably they were intended to exchange views with the Secretary, to acquaint the agency heads with each other's problems and to effect a departmental *esprit de corps*. But it was evident that the only individuals inclined to speak were those who offered some flattery to the Secretary; anyone who ventured an opinion contrary to the secretarial view was usually excoriated before his associates.

In one meeting in 1938, Arno Cammerer, Director of the National Park Service, arose to report that he had polled various members of the service concerning the proposal to transfer Admiralty Island to the Park Service as a national monument and bear refuge. The proposal was a part of Secretary Ickes's effort to take over the Forest Service, which, despite his unceasing efforts, the President refused to approve. If Ickes could not get it transferred as a whole, he would try the piecemeal approach. Heavily timbered Admiralty, largest island in the Alexander Archipelago, some two thousand square miles in extent, was the very heart of the Tongass National Forest. Cammerer, a friendly, mild-mannered individual, arose and said, "Mr. Secretary, perhaps you would like to have a report on the Park Service's views on the Admiralty Island proposal. The staff all agree that it does not have the scenic values to justify its being made a monument. Also the brown bear are multiplying far faster than they are being taken by hunters, and so there's really no conservation problem and no need———"

He got no further. "I'm the one who makes policy!" Ickes screamed. "If there are those who don't want to follow my policies, I'll accept their resignations at once. I'm growing sick and tired of this type of disloyalty!"

When the resettlement proposal came up at a staff conference, the Secretary spoke again about loyalty. It pained and angered him that certain members of the department were disloyal. He was currently encountering opposition to settling refugees in Alaska and he wanted it known that it was "departmental policy," that he had discussed it with the President and that the President had felt that five thousand refugees could be settled in Alaska every year for ten years. He said that he was now having experts from different bureaus go over the Slattery Report, which was to be reissued, and that he would welcome any suggestions or critical comments. But let it be clearly understood that this policy had been established and he would not tolerate opposition. We all knew that critical comment would, on this issue as on others, evoke the screaming denunciation we had witnessed many times before.

When the final draft of what was called "The Alaska Development Corporation Bill" was completed and ready for submission to the Bureau of the Budget and the Congress, I declined to "surname" it, the procedure by which a departmental policy was, and is, launched in the federal government. The draft of any proposal prepared for a cabinet member or department head is accompanied by numerous carbon copies, one of which is a different color so that it can be easily identified for secretarial scrutiny and later for filing. This copy has a small grid in the upper right-hand corner where the officials concerned "surname"—that is, sign—signifying merely that they have read and approved the proposal. When the proposal crossed my desk, I sent it along to the assistant secretary's office without my signature. Presently it came back with a note from Solicitor Margold saying that the secretary expected the signature of the Director of the Division of Territories and Island Possessions and that I would be well-advised to sign. Then Michael W. Straus, the department's director of information, who had been brought in from Chicago by Secretary Ickes, dropped by to tell me that I was out of step with the department and that it would be wise for me to sign. So I attached a note to the carbon copy which had been returned for my signature. It read:

I do NOT approve the appended draft and cannot therefore add my endorsement. My objection to the legislation as now drafted lies essentially in section 9 by its inclusion of non-quota immigrants, uniquely, for Alaska.

In a press release publicizing the proposal, Secretary Ickes declared that it had "received one of the most comprehensive endorsements of any major, far-reaching, national development ever proposed in the United States." Nevertheless, he had difficulty in securing Congressional sponsors for the bill, usually an easy matter for a cabinet officer.

I found myself wondering whether Secretary Ickes's refusal to face the realities did not mask another purpose—possibly a "play" to the diverse ethnic groups in this country with his eye on the 1940 Democratic presidential nomination. For it should have been plain to him that the peculiar and unprecedented immigration provision would never pass the Congress, even without the opposition of Delegate Dimond whose views and mine were identical. Why not, as I continued to urge in meetings and by memoranda, try one or two clearly feasible projects with some of the refugees already in America?

And so, while a few worthwhile enterprises might have been started, and the talents of a certain number of dislocated persons beneficially utilized to Alaska's, the nation's and their own advantage, nothing was accomplished. For after this legislation died in the committees of both Houses of Congress, the zeal of the sponsors of "Alaska development" vanished. No attempt whatever was made to carry out any part of it.

As far-flung as the territories and islands under my jurisdiction seemed to be, they were soon to be extended even farther. In mid-January of 1939, I received a call from Secretary Hull's office summoning me to the State Department. I did not know for what purpose, and when I inquired, I was given to understand that the matter could not be discussed over the phone. On the appointed day, I found a considerable gathering at the State Department, including Army, Navy and Coast Guard officers. Hugh Cumming, Jr., of the State Department presided and the purpose of the conference, he told us, was to establish United States sovereignty in Antarctica. In recent years the United States had been negligent of its territorial claims, and he cited the Pacific Islands as an example, "as Director Gruening well knows." But now we intended to assert our claims—which were substantial—on the Antarctic continent, starting with the discoveries along the coast of Antarctica by Captain Nathaniel Palmer in 1830, by Charles Wilkes of the United States Navy just a century ago, and the two more recent expeditions under Admiral Richard E. Byrd. Other nations were making claims and it was now considered necessary to assert ours. Cumming named Marie Byrd Land, Enderby Land, an island named Heard on the seventy-fifth meridian and about the fifty-fifth parallel, and some other areas which the United States could rightfully claim. These and others would be colonized to assure our sovereignty. Cumming assumed that the Division of Territories and Island Possessions would have charge of the colonization and said the President had suggested that I be called to the conference. Strict secrecy was enjoined on everybody. The next move was to secure definite authorization from the President to the various cabinet officers involved. That was not my problem, but finding colonists would be. Obviously, they could not be relieved at quarterly intervals as on our Equatorial Islands, but would have to stay a year. I wondered whether Alaskan Eskimos might not make the ideal recruits if they were willing to go.

Because of the secrecy of the plan, it was imperative to get funds without attracting attention. Under-Secretary Sumner Welles thought it might be possible to tap the State Department's special fund to start with and urged us to talk to George Messersmith, the department's budget officer. The State Department was also in touch with Admiral Byrd in Boston who, we all assumed, would play the principal part in the proposed expedition. We suspected that he had originated the idea of a government-sponsored and -financed undertaking and had sold the idea to President Roosevelt. Byrd's two previous explorations of Antarctica had been financed by private funds. Meanwhile, I was reading Byrd's *Little America*, his just published *Alone*, and everything else about the Antarctic that I could find.

I also conferred with a most interesting man about his Arctic experiences. He was Arthur Treadwell Walden, whom I first met in 1910, when I spent a few days of summer vacation in Wonolancet, New Hampshire, where Walden and his wife Catherine kept a modest, homelike inn. He had regaled his guests with tales of his experiences in the far north. He had gone to Alaska in quest of adventure in 1896 and became proficient at dog-team driving, then virtually the only mode of transportation. He had written of his experiences in 1928 in an interesting narrative, *A Dog-Puncher on the Yukon*. He was a dog-fancier and when I first knew him he was engaged in cross-breeding collies and Saint Bernards to produce a marvelous breed of canines which could be used by his winter guests as sled dogs to pull them around the the New Hampshire hills. His special knowledge came to Admiral Byrd's attention and he became his principal dog-musher in the 1928 Antarctic venture, bringing along some of his own dogs. He was then fifty-six years of age and the oldest man in the expedition. His firsthand information about the little-known continent was of great interest and value to me.

By mid-February I had seen the President, who told me he wanted Admiral Byrd to stand by and help organize the expedition. Byrd had assured him that if the Congress did not supply sufficient funds, he felt certain he could raise what was needed from private sources. Byrd had meanwhile come to Washington and we had several conferences. Richard Black, whom I had recalled from the Pacific, was entrusted with drawing up a memorandum of the expedition's needs. It was agreed that there would be at least two expeditions, one to the region of "Little America" and one to Enderby Land. Our conferences were joined by Paul Siple who had been a Boy Scout in Byrd's first expedition in 1928, was now teaching geography at Clark University and was eager to go.

We were still troubled by the injunction for secrecy, for we had to approach Congress. It was finally decided that Burlew and I should go to the House and talk confidentially with Representative Edward Taylor, chairman of the Appropriations Committee, and Clifton Woodrum, chairman of the Ways and Means Committee. They suggested that an appropriation allegedly for our Equatorial Islands might get by unnoticed, and they called a closed off-the-record meeting of the two committees which we found wholly sympathetic to our purpose.

But it was obvious that too many people were now "in" on the undertaking to keep it under wraps. The press was making inquiries and answers would have to be given. So it was decided that for the present the settlement idea and the assertion of United States sovereignty would be soft-pedaled; it would be merely another Antarctic exploratory expedition, but unlike the two previous ones, officially sponsored by the federal government.

Final decisions on Antarctica were made at a meeting in the Oval Room of the White House on July 7. Admiral Byrd presented the President with a large organizational chart of the expedition. The President looked at it and said with a smile, "This looks like a lot of organization for a very little money." We had received word that the Congress had appropriated $340,000. The President appointed Admiral Byrd to command the expedition, which was satisfactory to all of us, and he said he would also appoint an executive committee representing the Navy, Interior and Treasury (Coast Guard) departments. Hugh Cumming said he thought that the State Department should be included. The President shook his head and remarked teasingly, "All you do is write nasty notes to other nations; you don't have to be on the committee." But it was finally agreed that State should be included, since the expedition really involved international matters. I would represent the Interior Department and was named chairman of the committee; Admiral Russell Waesche represented the Coast Guard; Captain C. C. Hartigan the Navy; and Hugh Cumming, Jr., the State Department. The committee was named "The United States Antarctic Service" (USAS)—one of several titles I had suggested to the President—and placed in the Division of Territories and Island Possessions.

It was decided to establish three bases in Antarctica spreading over the 180 degrees of the Western Hemisphere, the point being that we could probably use the Monroe Doctrine to justify that claim. This, it was further decided, did not preclude going over to the other areas in the Eastern Hemisphere to assert claims there, but because of the lateness of the season, that would probably have to wait until the following year.

At our first executive committee meeting, we confirmed the use of three ships: Admiral Byrd's old ship, the *Bear of Oakland*, now reconditioned, the Coast Guard's icebreaker, *Northland*, both to sail from Boston, and the Bureau of Indian Affairs' *North Star*, which would sail from Seattle. They all got off in October, and landed their personnel and equipment without mishap. It looked like the beginning of a great historic episode: the peaceful conquest of the last of the world's continents.

In recognition of the services rendered by the USAS, the expedition christened several landmarks in its honor—the "Richard Black Coast," the "Gruening Glacier" and the "Executive Committee Range"— Antarctica being the only place where a landmark could be named for persons still living. Much valuable mapping and research were accomplished, but the occupation of Antarctica lasted only two years and its overall aims would not be achieved. The imminence of World War II took priority, and the men, ships and equipment were recalled. For several years thereafter there was no continuing United States presence in Antarctica, although there were two expeditions under United States Navy auspices in 1947 and 1948. Interest was renewed in the International Geophysical Year, 1957–1958, and the value of scientific research in Antarctica reappreciated. It was resumed under various government agencies, and in 1965 when I visited Antarctica in the company of Dick Black and Senator Frank E. Moss of Utah, it was being carried out under the auspices of the National Science Foundation and the Office of Naval Research, the Navy supplying the logistics and housekeeping. The Treaty of 1959, providing that for thirty years Antarctica would be preserved for peaceful purposes, was enacted in my first year in the United States Senate. It was subsequently ratified by the twelve nations having interests in Antarctica. The United States, however, reserved its territorial rights as a safeguard against all eventualities at the expiration of the treaty.

The USAS was only one of many casualties of the Second World War. The plan for what the Park Service had already prospectively named the "Kennecott National Monument," after it had been recommended by various departmental echelons, was forgotten in the greater concern for national defense. It was perhaps just as well; the shortage of funds would have certainly precluded the necessary development of public recreational facilities and accommodations, as it had the hotel within Mount McKinley Park which, even today, has not been built. Even if the Kennecott area had become a national monument, it would have remained inaccessible to the public.

But Palmyra, the uninhabited Pacific island paradise, was a permanent casualty and an irremediable loss. The Navy felt it needed that island for defense purposes, although it could have used Canton and Enderbury instead. It uprooted the trees, in the process destroying a natural bird sanctuary; blasted the lagoons, opening them to sharks; and irretrievably ruined that unique ecological masterpiece.

The proposal to use a ship as a hotel for the Glacier Bay National Monument was lost for a different reason. We had taken the idea to Ickes, who accepted it enthusiastically and told us to go ahead and find a ship. The United States Maritime Commission was helpful in our efforts. I spoke to Admiral Emory S. Land, its chairman, to my friend Carl Moran, former Maine Congressman and now a member of the commission, and to Commissioners Thomas Woodward and Admiral Wiley. They told us what ships were available. With National Park Service officials and two men from the commission's staff, we drove from Washington to where the Patuxent River empties into Chesapeake Bay. There, moored together, were four big liners taken from the Germans during the war. Two of them, the former *Kaiser Wilhelm II*, rechristened the *Monticello*, and the *Kronprincessin Cecilie*, renamed the *Mount Vernon*, had been used as transports during the war and would have required extensive renovation. The other two, the *America* and the *George Washington*, which had been most recently used by a commercial shipping line, were in better condition and we went through the latter carefully. She would have made an ideal hotel but was really much too large for use in Glacier Bay. We could have got her and had her towed to Glacier Bay for nothing, but reconditioning would have cost at least $150,000, and if we spent that much, people might well ask why not build a hotel? Besides we were doubtful about getting the $150,000.

Then the Maritime Commission offered us the Munson Line's *American Legion*. She was being taken out of service and would be given to us fully equipped. Our Park Service group and I traveled to Brooklyn where she was in dry dock and I saw she had been greatly improved since my trip on her to Montevideo in 1933. We concluded that we could not have found a better ship, and the Maritime Commission secured the President's approval to operate the ship itself.

However, when Burlew, Ohlson, Vint and I went jubilantly to report our good luck to Secretary Ickes, he said, "Well, I've changed my mind. Since the Alaska legislature won't do what's right, I'm not going to do anything for Alaska." He referred to the 1939 legislature's refusal to enact an eight percent gross gold tax which he had requested. I argued that there was no reason why we should not do what *we* thought was right and Ickes finally agreed to take the matter up with the President, although he said he would do it without enthusiasm. We told him that the President had already assured the Maritime Commission that it could let the Park Service have the boat.

I soon discovered, however, that we were not the only ones interested in the ship. A man named Ralph Dellevie wanted to secure a cruise ship to take to both Alaska and Hawaii, and he had his eye on the *American*

Legion. I told him I was sorry but we had already secured her for Glacier Bay, though perhaps we could combine a Glacier Bay and a Hawaiian cruise. We went to Commissioner Moran and only then found out that Burlew had notified the commission that the Park Service did not want the *American Legion* and orders had been given to dismantle her. I'll confess that I was boiling mad. It was yet another instance when Ickes said he would do one thing and then turned around and did the exact opposite.

Notwithstanding such frustrations, life in Washington during the late 1930s was a kind of golden interlude. Our country, thanks to Roosevelt's leadership and a generally enlightened Congress, was recovering from the great Depression. There was a feeling of accomplishment among those who had participated in this democratically wrought revolution, and apart from the stalwarts of the New Deal, the national capital was thronged with interesting people many of whom Dorothy and I entertained in our N Street home in Georgetown.

One of the memorable events of that time was the aftermath of the refusal of the Daughters of the American Revolution to allow Marian Anderson, the Negro contralto, to sing in Constitution Hall. The DAR denied the hall's use to any Negro performers or organization, and I joined an *ad hoc* committee to find another auditorium where she might be heard. But this was 1939 and Washington was still rigidly "Jim Crowed." After countless refusals, Oscar Chapman, Assistant Secretary of the Interior, the leading member of our committee, asked Secretary Ickes to let her have the auditorium of the new Department of the Interior Building. It seemed to be our last hope, but Ickes brusquely said no. Two days later Chapman came back to Ickes with another proposal. "How about the steps of Lincoln Memorial?" It was an inspired idea; the building was a responsibility of the National Park Service.

"I told you I didn't want anything to do with it," said Ickes and appeared to close the discussion.

"Wait a minute, Mr. Secretary," Chapman persisted, "there will certainly be a crowd of a hundred thousand people and a nationwide hook-up."

"I'll preside," said Ickes.

On the night of the concert, a crowd variously estimated at between seventy-five thousand and a hundred thousand jammed around the Lincoln Memorial and stretched halfway down the Mall to the Washington Monument. On the platform with our committee were Justice and Mrs. Hugo Black, and Senators Wagner, Capper, Minton, Austin and Guffey. Oscar Chapman and Mrs. Caroline O'Day, a representative from New York, came down the steps from inside the monument with Marian Anderson between them. Secretary Ickes introduced her in a speech worthy of the occasion. Her mellow, vibrant voice rang out well beyond the reaches of that vast and sympathetic audience. It was a memorable event due largely to Chapman's ingenuity and persistence. Later he was also able, overcoming strenuous objections, to desegregate the National Park Service public facilities in Washington—the golf courses, tennis courts and swimming pools.

The year 1939 also saw the appointment of Robert Morss Lovett as the government secretary of the Virgin Islands. I recommended him for the post and he served with distinction for several years, but then ran afoul of a war-engendered witch-hunt in the Congress which led to withholding his salary and forcing his resignation. His offense consisted of membership in a variety of organizations devoted to peace and other liberal or left-wing causes. However, his character and ability could not be so easily impugned. After his forced resignation he was promptly invited by Rexford Guy Tugwell, then the governor of Puerto Rico, and Jaime Benitez, the chancellor, to teach at the University of Puerto Rico.

Even into the late 1930s, Puerto Rico continued to suffer from Washington's political whims. On May 12, 1939, I learned that Blanton Winship had resigned as governor and that Admiral William D. Leahy had been appointed in his place. It was a startling piece of news, since I had met with Winship only a week before when he was returning to Puerto Rico full of plans for the future. The President had apparently consulted no one about the change. Later that day Secretary Ickes said he had known about the Leahy appointment and that in his judgment it was a very good one, but he refused to answer whether he had recommended Leahy. I thought it was a very poor appointment in spite of Leahy's distinguished career as a naval officer. He knew nothing about Puerto Rico, spoke not a word of Spanish and had no familiarity with economic or social questions. But Roosevelt had a soft spot for admirals, and the general assumption was that he had become "fed up" with the incessant stream of complaints from Puerto Rico. As it was the first gubernatorial appointment since Puerto Rico's removal from the jurisdiction of the War Department, I thought that a civilian would have been more appropriate. I also thought that we should have sounded out the Puerto Rican legislature before the appointment was made to see if it would be acceptable. If a military man was in order, Colonel Wright would certainly have been welcomed by the Puerto Ricans; even more welcome would have been the appointment of a Puerto Rican.

Teofilo Maldonado of San Juan's *El Mundo* reported that the reaction to Leahy's appointment was very adverse. I asked him whether this feeling came from a particular political faction and he said, "No, from everyone." In his opinion, Puerto Rico was being treated like a little Gibraltar, as if defense were the only issue, and he added that there was a great deal of sympathy for Winship and indignation at his abrupt dismissal. He said a great many people liked Winship; he was popular, on the whole, and those who did not like him merely felt that he was not the proper man for the post. No one questioned his sincerity, his honesty or his devotion, and when it became known that he would soon be leaving, there were spontaneous expressions of appreciation and applause and cheers when he appeared on the streets. On the other hand, Leahy's name was jestingly pronounced "Lija," the Spanish word for sandpaper.

Actually Leahy's incumbency was brief and untroubled. President Roosevelt soon appointed him ambassador to France and he was succeeded by Guy Swope, a professional accountant and former congressman from Pennsylvania, who after his defeat for reelection was appointed auditor of Puerto Rico. When Leahy left, Swope was moved up into the governorship and served only six months before he was succeeded by Rexford Guy Tugwell, who had been an economic consultant in Puerto Rico for Secretary Ickes. Tugwell served a four-year term, and then, at long last, a Puerto Rican, Jesus T. Piñero, was appointed governor in 1946 by President Truman.

Muñoz Marin continued to play an important part in Puerto Rican affairs, even though in 1938 the Liberal Party repudiated both its independence stand and his leadership. He organized a new party, the Popular Democratic Party, and by effective campaigning under the slogan "Land, Bread and Liberty" achieved a plurality in a three-way split election. Four years later his party was reelected, this time by a substantial majority. Meanwhile, harboring increasing doubts about independence, he began to work in Washington for a new status for the island. In 1950 the Congress went one step beyond appointing a Puerto Rican as governor; the governorship was made elective, and Muñoz Marin was elected. We had long since composed our past differences and Dorothy and I were present at his inauguration, where he was obviously the idol of the Puerto Rican people. The new status he persuaded the Congress to grant in 1952—called "Commonwealth" in English, and "Estado Libre Asociado" in Spanish—gave Puerto Rico complete self-government under a constitution drawn up and ratified by Puerto Ricans. Most significant for Puerto Rico's welfare was the continuation of the practice, which dated from the beginning of United States rule, providing for no federal taxes and retention by Puerto Rico of all customs revenues. Muñoz Marin had indeed achieved his dream of having his cake and eating it too.

Under his leadership, Operation Bootstrap introduced sweeping social and economic improvements to the island. By allowing industrial enterprises to pay no federal taxes and a ten-year exemption from Puerto

Rican taxes, Operation Bootstrap was able to attract a great number of mainland industries. Despite some failures the program became increasingly successful, due in large measure to the ingenuity and ability of two Puerto Ricans, Teodoro Moscoso and Rafael Pico.

When I visited the island in 1968, I found it flourishing and full of optimism and bounce; and I was gratified to learn that much credit for the start of Puerto Rico's economic revival was given to PRRA efforts in the 1930s. The cement plant had been producing uninterruptedly and profitably for thirty years; the hydroelectric development had brought electricity islandwide at low costs; the multiple agricultural activities, now relegated to second place in the island economy by the new industrialization, were giving Puerto Rico a balanced and diversified economy.

In the fall of 1968 Muñoz Marin's Popular Democratic Party suffered its first defeat in the twenty-eight years of its existence. Four years before, he had declined to be a candidate for the governorship after three terms in office, and Roberto Sanchez Vilella, one of his able young associates, was elected. Differences arose between them and Sanchez Vilella was denied renomination by the party in 1968. It named a less charismatic candidate, and the Partido Puertoriqueno Progresista, formed from the old Republican Party, elected Luis Ferré, an enlightened industrialist, as governor, capturing the House and falling one seat short of winning the Senate.

Muñoz Marin took the defeat hard and not long after resigned his Senate seat and announced his retirement from public life. But his accomplishment stood and a prosperous and autonomous Puerto Rico, socially, economically and spiritually reborn, would have a free choice in the future to retain its commonwealth status or seek either independence or statehood. The latter was favored by Governor Ferré, but was not an issue in the 1968 campaign and would not be pressed in the immediate future. But perhaps even more important, the 1968 election demonstrated that the Puerto Ricans were firmly committed to the principles of democratic government and peaceful political transition, principles which few Latin-American republics, or indeed their mother-countries, Spain and Portugal, have been able to achieve. The United States can point with pride to Puerto Rico, no longer "hopeless" as President Roosevelt characterized it a third of a century earlier. We can now point with equal pride to Alaska and Hawaii which have achieved statehood, and to the elective governorships of the Virgin Islands and Guam, where the basic principle of government by consent of the governed has been combined with economic progress. So the thought I expressed to FDR in 1934, that a democracy should not have colonies, has pretty well materialized.

19

TERRITORIAL GOVERNOR

Any influence, from whatever source,
that tends to decrease the citizen's sense of
personal responsibility for the integrity of
his government is a source of danger to the
democratic state.

— JOHN LORD O'BRIAN

Early in August of 1939, I received a call to come to Secretary Ickes's office. He greeted me with "How would you like to be governor of Alaska?"

"What about Governor Troy?" I asked.

"He'll resign with the understanding that he won't be prosecuted," said Ickes.

"Is it that serious?" I asked. "Are there really valid grounds for prosecution?"

Apparently there were. Whenever a high government official signs a contract involving the expenditure of public funds, he has to sign an "oath of disinterestedness" by which he swears that he has no personal interest in the transaction and in no way stands to profit by it. Troy had signed such an oath for printing done for the government by the Alaska *Daily Empire*, which he owned. It was a criminal offense. Everyone knew that he owned the paper and that it had received government printing contracts for years. I assumed that he had been merely careless; perhaps someone had laid the printed oath on his desk with some other papers and he had unwittingly signed it. Further, he had been in failing health for some time and was increasingly unable to carry on the duties of his office, which were being largely performed by his secretary, Harry G. Watson.

Under those circumstances it seemed to me a ruthless and indecent way of forcing him out of office. While his views on Alaskan affairs differed radically from Secretary Ickes's, his appointment had been viewed with favor in Alaska and he had been appointed and reappointed with Ickes's approval.

"Well, I'm offering you the governorship," said Ickes.

"I think an Alaskan should be appointed," I replied.

"That's just what we don't want," snapped Ickes. "We want someone to go from here."

"I want to think it over," I said, "but I incline to the view that I should not take the post."

"I want your answer right now."

"If I have to give it right now, my answer will have to be 'no.' But I can see no reason why I shouldn't have time to consider so important a step. I'm going on vacation shortly and I want to wait until I return before deciding."

"I want your decision before you go."

Although the offer was a complete surprise to me, I knew that it was President Roosevelt's idea, and not Ickes's. He, I was convinced, would never have offered it to me of his own accord. I felt I should discuss it with the President before deciding. I dictated a letter to Ickes in which I repeated that if my answer had to be immediate and before my departure it was "no." And then I left for a month's vacation.

Following my departure a peremptory call to return to the Secretary's office came to mine. My secretary, Estella Draper, informed the Secretary's office that I had already left. She was given a grilling as to my whereabouts, but she informed the Secretary that I was traveling by automobile.

It was a splendid vacation after five years of intense activity. Dorothy, Peter and I visited Dorothy's parents at North Scituate and other friends around Boston, returned to our Maine haunts for days of tennis, swimming and camping, and then back to our summer home and friends at Rockport. That summer the European situation was becoming graver every day, and the radio in our car was always turned on to catch the reports of Hitler's latest moves. While driving around Rockport on September 2, we heard the following news flash:

> Washington: President Roosevelt today appointed Ernest Gruening, Director of the Division of Territories and Island Possessions, as Governor of Alaska. . .

That is how it was done. A few days later I saw the President. I thanked him for his confidence in me, but informed him that I had told

Secretary Ickes that I felt I ought not to accept the appointment. "I think an Alaskan should be appointed, Mr. President," I said.

"Such as who?" he asked.

"Tony Dimond, for one; that would be the best and most popular appointment you could make," I said. "Charlie Bunnell, the president of the University of Alaska, would be another wonderful choice. You couldn't go wrong with either of them. And there are others. I'll be glad to submit some more names. It definitely should be an Alaskan."

"Ernest," said the President, "Alaska has lost touch with the federal government. There's a lot of the New Deal that hasn't come to Alaska. You know your way around here. You know what we're trying to do. You know how to get it done. You can be of great help to Alaska. I think you ought to go."

"All right, Mr. President," I said.

"It's a wonderful opportunity, the most interesting assignment I know of in the government," said the President. "And come in to see me whenever you're in town. I want to keep in touch with you."

"Thank you, Mr. President," I said. "You know that Secretary Ickes doesn't like anyone to make an appointment with you without his permission."

"You come in whenever you want to," said the President with a smile. "Good luck, Ernest."

My departure for Alaska was, however, to be delayed for several months. President Roosevelt had decided to send up no names whatsoever for confirmation at the special session of Congress he had called. He wanted the Congress to concentrate on the neutrality legislation and nothing else. That meant that I would have to wait until the session was over and then receive another recess appointment, or wait until the regular session of Congress convened in January.

After conferring with Tony Dimond, I hoped it would be the latter. He had shown me a telegram indicating opposition to my appointment from the Democratic Committee of Southeastern Alaska on the grounds that I was a nonresident. Tony told me that he would have to present this and similar protests when my name came up for a hearing in the Senate. He also said that he, too, had written the President opposing my appointment because he thought an Alaskan should be named. I told him I agreed and related my conversation with the President. I also told him that I thought Governor Troy had been getting shabby treatment. I said that if the President had written him a letter suggesting that he resign on account of his health—a legitimate request—I was sure Troy would have acceded; but forcing him out as an alternative to prosecution was contemptible. Tony was going to Alaska and I urged him to see Troy and suggest to him that he withdraw his resignation and ask to be retired on the grounds of his health. Tony agreed. Shortly thereafter he saw Troy at Bell Island Hot Springs near Ketchikan. Since my assumption of the governorship had been postponed beyond the date of Governor Troy's resignation, September 15, he had already been requested by the President to continue to serve, first until October 15, and then until his successor was installed. Troy considered this something of a vindication and made it clear that he felt his health was really too poor to justify any further attempt to prolong his tenure. When he finally did resign, it was ascribed to his wish to retire because of ill health.

The President sent over my commission—a recess appointment—on November 15. Secretary Ickes called me to his office and suggested that I issue a statement saying I would probably not be in Alaska long. I asked him what the purpose of such a statement would be. He replied that there would be opposition to my appointment and the President might not want to send my name up again when Congress convened. "In that case," he continued, "we wouldn't send your name up until the end of the session, or perhaps not send it up at all. But you would have had six or seven months anyhow, and then we would find something else for you."

I told the secretary that I would issue no such statement and that I was not interested in having "something else" found for me. It was evident to me that his purpose was to have my appointment unconfirmed by the Senate as long as possible to make sure I carried out all his orders, and if I did not satisfy him, to try and persuade the President that he had made a mistake in appointing me. Fortunately, I had been forewarned, even if I had not been able to see through his clumsy and disingenuous maneuver, for I had learned that a few days previously he had expressed great indignation at my refusal to support his proposal to resettle European refugees in Alaska. "If Gruening doesn't carry out policy," he had said, "I'm going to ask the President for his resignation."

I became convinced that the only opposition to my confirmation would come from Ickes himself—exerted under cover. Tony Dimond had made it clear to me that his opposition was based solely on the issue of appointing a non-Alaskan, and that if the President had made up his mind to appoint a non-Alaskan, he would prefer me to anyone else.

On the eve of my departure for Alaska, I received a reassuring letter from Senator Lewis B. Schwellenbach of Washington. Ever since his election in 1934, he had gone out of his way to assist Delegate Dimond and me on Alaska matters. A few weeks previously, we three had seen the President, as a last resort, about the still-unsettled need for a vessel to carry freight and passengers to and from the Alaska Peninsula and the eastern Aleutians, and the President had suggested that we seek a special post-office appropriation—which we later did. Schwellenbach had just returned from Alaska and wrote:

> There is really no deep-seated opposition to your appointment. Of course, the Alaskans always want to make a showing on the appointment of anybody outside the Territory and they have made that showing in the form of their protest. Having done so, they are perfectly satisfied. As a matter of fact, I think that they probably realize that they will be better off with an outsider than they would dealing with somebody selected up there on a political basis. So I would suggest that you act on the assumption that you are really welcome and not be timid with them about discussing your point of view on any problem. I am not flattering you when I say that you did make a very good impression on your two visits to Alaska. You will go into the job with as friendly a reception as any non-Alaskan could possibly have.
>
> The Secretary is very unpopular in Alaska. They lay all of their troubles of every nature upon him. Therefore I would suggest, if I may, that you, if you consistently can, present yourself on your own and not as a representative of the Secretary. I think it would be fatal for you, either in speeches or conversations to give the impression that you are there as the Secretary's emissary. I don't know how many people said to me, 'Well Gruening's all right, but he has been working for the Secretary for a number of years and that's the chief thing we don't like about his appointment. . . .'
>
> When I got back I dropped a note to the President telling him not to worry about opposition to your appointment. Apparently he was not very much worried about it.

Dorothy and I journeyed across the country by train, spent several days in Seattle, and sailed for Alaska on the S.S. *Yukon*. We reached Ketchikan early on December 4. It was pitch-dark, but seventy people assembled at 7:30 A.M. for a breakfast at the Blue Fox restaurant. It was a warm and friendly welcome and there were no less warm greetings during the short stops at Wrangell and Petersburg.

At Juneau we were given the key to the city and the swearing-in ceremony took place that evening in the governor's office in the Federal-Territorial building. A number of persons whom I would have expected to be present were not, such as former Governor George Parks. I learned later that the ceremony, which was broadcast over the local radio station, was deliberately arranged to make it a wholly Democratic Party affair, although, ironically, it had been the leading Democrats who had actively opposed my appointment. "Jack" Hellenthal, Democratic National Committeeman for Alaska, presided, and introduced "Mike" Monagle, notary public and secretary of the First Division Democratic Committee, who administered the oath of office. Hellenthal then introduced me as "the Democratic governor of Alaska." I did not want to start a controversy at the very beginning of my term; otherwise I might have said something to the effect that I was not a "Democratic governor" but governor of Alaska.

When the party broke up, I asked "Bob" Bartlett to stay. His full name was Edward Lewis Bartlett and I had first met him several years earlier when he was secretary to Delegate Dimond. He had been appointed by the President as secretary of Alaska less than a year previously, an office that had few duties. They consisted principally of being "Keeper of the Territorial Seal" and acting as governor in the governor's absence from the territory. Harry Watson, the secretary to the two previous governors, had consistently kept the secretary of the Territory from the work of the governor's office. I liked Bob Bartlett exceedingly, and I proposed to him that he assume a considerable share of the work of the governor's office. He agreed.

I had let Harry Watson know two months earlier that I expected him to resign. He had plenty of time to look for another job, but he had not done so. I now told him that I had other plans for his position. He had been under fire from the Comptroller-General's office for the misuse of a government truck, and for the conflict-of-interest investigation that also involved Governor Troy. He said that he had been in no way responsible for either incident. I told him it was not for me to judge, but that if he felt an injustice had been done him, he should make every effort to clear the record with the Comptroller-General. Apparently he was able to do so, for he was soon employed by the Civil Aeronautics Administration and held his position there until his death years later.

In his place I appointed Estella Draper, who had been my secretary in and out of government for eleven years. I had instructed her, as I would other secretaries and staff members, that they should never hesitate to express disagreement with any of my actions. If they thought that a letter I had dictated should be modified, or not sent at all, they should say so. On occasions secretarial criticism saved me from sending a letter which on second thought seemed inadvisable. I always welcomed such challenges from my staff and it enhanced our collaboration.

The duties of the governor's office had been expanded through the years by successive territorial legislatures which had gradually created a system of government by boards—with the governor serving as chairman of most of them. I found myself chairman of the Board of Administration, the Board of Examiners, the Board of Budget, the Banking Board, the Board of Road Commissioners, the Board of Trustees for the Alaska Pioneers Home, the Board of Public Welfare, the Territorial Historical Library and Museum Commission, and the Canvassing Board.

These boards were of two types: those whose members were appointed by the governor subject to confirmation by the legislature, and those whose members were elected territorial officials. Thus they furnished a kind of insulation against too much executive power. Board members were independent of the governor and not subject to his wishes, a system that had been devised as protection against the governors appointed by Washington. The governor of Alaska, I soon discovered, had merely the power to persuade.

The staff of the governor's office was small—a secretary, an assistant secretary who combined the duties of stenographer-typist and filing clerk, and an accounting clerk—and a substantial part of our time was taken up in governmental housekeeping. In addition, many Alaskans passing through Juneau on either the north or southbound boat wanted to see the governor just to say hello. Most callers brought some useful item of information, some "lead" to a condition somewhere that needed investigating. But it was never customary to ask for an appointment or to inquire whether a call would be convenient. Alaskans merely dropped in and expected to see the governor without delay. If I was tied up in a board meeting or some other conference, I made it a practice to leave it briefly, greet the caller personally and ask him to wait. Similarly Tony Dimond had explained to me that he could not stay at the Governor's House when he came to Juneau, which I always invited him to do, because he had to stay at a hotel where any old-timer would feel free to come to his room for a chat. The same thing happened to me when I began to travel around Alaska; callers seldom bothered even to announce themselves or to knock before they entered my room, and it might be any time of the night or day. It was all part of the natural democracy of the time and place.

One matter, that I deemed important soon occupied me. The Navy had begun work on two bases, at Sitka and Kodiak, and a third was to be located at Dutch Harbor. The program represented the first stirrings of national defense for Alaska, and a three-part contract for the employment of labor on this new naval construction had been entered into between the Navy, a State of Washington contracting firm and a score of AFL building trades unions in Seattle. The arrangement was discriminatory against Alaskan labor virtually to the point of its exclusion. It provided that the first man in each union would be hired in Seattle. This meant that each craft—carpenters, masons, boilermakers, plumbers—supplied not only the first man, but as many men thereafter as the union could produce. The contract also provided that these men would have their transportation paid to and from the work sites, and in case of injury or illness, in addition to compensation, they would receive transportation back to their homes in the States.

Alaskan workers were excluded from these provisions. There were many unemployed in Alaska. I had had several conferences with them immediately after my arrival in Juneau and they called my attention to their inability to secure work on the new naval bases. An Alaskan worker, skilled or unskilled, seeking work on these Navy projects, had to pay his way from the Alaskan mainland to Baranof or Kodiak Island and apply there for employment. If denied it, as all who tried had been, he was totally out of pocket for his transportation there and back.

I questioned a representative of the contractors about this matter, and he gave me some reassuring figures about the proportion of men "locally hired." But on checking with Alaskans who had vainly sought employment on the bases, I found that these purported Alaskans appeared to be nonresidents who after their arrival from Seattle had gone through some local inscription process. I therefore wired local officials in Sitka and Kodiak, asking them to send me the facts about all of the men employed on the bases to ascertain how many were bona fide Alaska residents and how many were outsiders. I also asked to have details of any subterfuges that may have been practiced to make non-Alaskans appear as residents.

I felt this issue was fundamental from several standpoints, and I was prepared to fight it to the limit. Apart from the matter of common fairness, if the federal government sponsored or participated in such discrimination against Alaskans, it would scarcely be possible to argue effectively against the practice when indulged in by private employers. Fishermen and cannery workers were also imported by the salmon industry, while native Alaskans went without work, and I was ready to do battle on that issue, too.

A telegram from Mayor Tom Tilson of Sitka informed me that he could not get the information I wanted, and the story was the same in Kodiak. I decided to go to Sitka in person, accompanied by Walter Sharpe, the director of the Unemployment Compensation Commission, and Joseph T. Flakne who directed the Employment Service. We sailed for Sitka and went directly to Japonski Island where the base was being constructed. The officer in charge was a Lieutenant-Commander Cronin. After he heard what I wanted, he told me that the records were in charge of a Lieutenant Stribling whom he would try to locate. There was an unexpected delay in finding Stribling, perhaps because the employment officer of the contracting company had been on board the ship with us and knew why we were coming. Obviously the Navy was stalling, and after waiting two hours, we went back to Sitka and found Stribling ourselves. I told him I wanted to look at the payroll to see where the workers originated. He replied that he had just received a message from Seattle prohibiting him from giving that information to any unauthorized person. I said that I considered the governor of Alaska an authorized person. He finally agreed, reluctantly.

As Sitka had other problems I wanted to look into, I left Sharpe and Flakne to go back with him to Japonski to see the records. There Stribling stalled again, going into huddles with various people and finally producing an extract from an alleged message from his supervisor in Seattle which said that information about employment was not to be given to any non-Navy person. He had not thought of that when he talked to me. At Sharpe's and Flakne's request he then agreed to wire Seattle to secure modification of the alleged order, but by ten o'clock the next morning when our boat was about to leave, no reply had been received. I told Lieutenant-Commander Cronin I would report his behavior to those higher up. I had already made up my mind to go to Seattle and, if unsuccessful there, to Washington.

Meanwhile, feeling that discrimination could best be met by exposure, on my return to Juneau I gave an interview to the *Daily Empire* and the weekly *Press*, and spoke about it over KINY, the radio station. The Associated Press carried the story. The reaction among Alaskans was naturally favorable, but it drew a blast from the contractors, who charged me with interfering with the defense effort. A week later in Seattle I met with the contractors, the AFL leaders and the officer in charge of the Sitka and Kodiak construction contracts, Commander R. E. Thomas. While it was too late even to secure equality of opportunity for Alaskans, since work on both bases was underway, I wanted to prevent further discrimination; there would be some vacancies at Sitka and Kodiak, and there would be another project at Dutch Harbor. So I asked the contractors either to establish employment offices in Juneau and Anchorage or to have an employment official visit the principal Alaskan coastal towns at regular and announced intervals to interview Alaskan applicants. I also asked that their transportation be paid to and from the job. The union leaders were agreeable; they had already secured employment for virtually all their members who wanted it. The contractors, however, were opposed and Commander Thomas supported them. There must be no interference with their efficient conduct of the job. After much battling, it was agreed that any Alaskans hired would have their transportation paid for from their residences to the base. But there was no agreement that would improve the likelihood of their employment.

I took my case to Washington and went to see Admiral Ben Moreell, chief of the Bureau of Yards and Docks, a big, tough former Navy football player. He, too, gave me a runaround. He said he would have to get the facts. I told him that the facts were all available, and that he could check them by telephone to Seattle. When I returned the next day, he informed me that the original arrangement with the contractors would have to stand unmodified, and he even withdrew the payment of transportation for Alaskans.

My next hope—but not my last—was the secretary of the Navy, Charles Edison, son of Thomas Alva Edison, the inventor. If I failed there, I would take it to the President. Edison called in Admiral Moreell who firmly resisted all change. After an hour's animated debate, Secretary Edison brought the discussion to a close with words that were music to my ears: "Admiral, I am compelled to agree with the governor. I want you to carry out his proposal to have the contractors' employment manager visit Alaskan centers every six weeks. And they should make the same arrangements for transporting the Alaskans as for other workers."

It was a gratifying victory, even if a belated one. But there was still time to forestall similar discrimination on Army construction which was to begin in a few weeks on the Air Corps testing station near Fairbanks, Ladd Field. I sent Flakne there, and Major George of the Corps of Engineers promised that all available Alaskan labor would be put to work. And he was as good as his word. But we had won only one skirmish in what would prove to be a continuing struggle. The battle for priority of employment for Alaskans would have to be fought over and over again.

In Sitka, faced with the impending prosperity brought by the new naval air station, I found an almost incredible municipal helplessness. As we walked around town, the Mayor, Tom Tilson, a Scandinavian whose name was originally Tollekson, and Leslie Yaw, the principal of the Sheldon Jackson School and a member of the City Council, presented this dilemma. New houses were being built on muskeg ground and there was need for streets and sewers. The city's income from assessments of real and personal property was only $9,000 and its total revenue during the year just ending, including licenses and fees, had been only $17,000. I told the mayor he should immediately hire a competent man to reassess all property adequately. Actually new sewers and streets had been installed the previous year at municipal expense but with no charges levied on the abutters. The city light and water services were a monopoly of one W. P. Mills, an aged widower, who also owned the cold-storage plant and much else, including, as it turned out, a majority of the city fathers. The best information I could get was that he had been given a franchise for fifty years at some earlier date which no one knew about, and the document

—which I asked to see but which could not be found—did not even give the city a free or reduced rate for its own electricity.

On top of all this, the existing plant was not able to supply the town's expanding power needs. The new houses would have to do without electricity. Furthermore, the power company was not even taxed. "Why not?" I asked. And why not, on pain of taxation, compel the owner to enlarge his generating capacity to supply the city's requirements, which surely the unfindable franchise agreement must have provided. The plant could not be taxed, the mayor said, because it was outside the city limits. "Why not tax the distribution system?" I said. That apparently had not occurred to the mayor and the Council. But better yet, I suggested, why not have the city buy the plant and make the necessary enlargements of its generating capacity to supply the needed power and establish equitable rates? I gave them the name of a responsible stateside firm which had experience in installing municipal light and water plants and could determine how much Mills's property was worth. Actually, that firm, Burns and McDonnell of Kansas City, had not long before shown what it could do in Alaska. It had superintended Ketchikan's purchase of the utilities run there by the Foshay Company of Minneapolis, and had converted them into a municipal service, a transaction brought about by the wise leadership of Ketchikan's lawyer-mayor, Harry McCain. Under the subsequent management of W. T. Stuart, Ketchikan provided lower rates for its combined telephone, light, power and water services than any place in the United States, and the highest per family consumption, five thousand kilowatt-hours a year. With all that, the Ketchikan utilities were showing a substantial profit and when the bonds were retired would be able to return $50,000 to $75,000 a year to the municipality. Since Sitka had no funds and no borrowing capacity, I said I would try to get the necessary funds from the Public Works Administration.

The mayor asked me to sit in on a meeting of the City Council and present my ideas. I recommended that it send a telegram to Burns and McDonnell to come up and appraise Mills's utilities. The council agreed until Mills said that he would not accept any appraiser but his own. Only two members of the Council stood firm. Mills let it be known that his price for his power and water company was $150,000. I told the Council that I would have difficulty in getting PWA or other funds unless an honest and objective appraisal were made.

Thus matters appeared deadlocked. In Washington, a few weeks later, I discussed the problem with Delegate Dimond, who proposed introducing legislation to permit Sitka to issue bonds in excess of its statutory limit for $200,000 to purchase the utilities. I feared Congress might not act. But defense was a powerful lever. A supporting letter from Lewis Compton, acting secretary of the Navy, brought a unanimous committee vote and the bill was passed on July 29, 1944. It required approval of fifty-five percent of Sitka's voters, which was easily obtained.

I had secured the services of a hydroelectric engineer, R. V. L. Wright of the Bureau of Reclamation, to come to Alaska to assist Sitka and Kodiak with their power problems. The legislation had provided that the price for the acquisition of Mills's company could not exceed $120,000. Wright, after looking them over, said they were barely worth half that amount and that the money could better be spent on a wholly new system. But a majority of the Council felt it had an obligation to deal with Mr. Mills.

Sitka's problem appeared to be nearing solution, but then it was complicated by the arrival of a Ketchikan banker, William A. Bates, who was opening a branch bank there and had sold Mayor Tilson the idea that he could handle the whole transaction. Bates sought to persuade the Council that a Seattle stock-brokerage firm that he would retain would "do all the underwriting, paperwork, provide the engineering services and so forth." I argued that the fees and costs which his plan involved would eat up what little was left from the Congressional authorization for rehabilitation after Mills had been paid off. Mills had finally agreed that his property was worth $115,000 and would take no less. Sitka's attorney, R. E. Robertson, had informed the Council that Mills was entitled to an additional sum for "goodwill." I blew up at that and said that Mills had been overcharging the town for years owing to the innocence of the city fathers, and that instead of being additionally compensated for "goodwill," there should be a deduction for something that might be called "illwill." I felt that Sitka's attorneys seemed to be representing Mills rather than Sitka.

Mr. Mills fared well. In addition to collecting a high price for his company, the Council, with some dissenting votes, gave him a power rate of one cent per kilowatt-hour for his cold-storage plant. In consequence I was much put out with Leslie Yaw, who was obviously a high-minded person, but who had nevertheless consistently favored Mills's interests at the city's expense. I spoke to him as I never had to a public official before and would not again, for it was improper for me to do so. I said to him, "Leslie Yaw, you have been a faithless public servant." He replied that he was just trying to keep matters on a friendly basis.

However, my visit had paid off, I felt, in sharply increased assessments and the immediately urgent problem was solved. But I came away with the conviction that Sitka—and doubtless other Alaskan communities —needed a city manager. That conviction was reaffirmed a year later when Sitka's new mayor, Jack Conway, told me that the combination of Bates, Robertson, and their Seattle associates had cost Sitka some $60,000 in appraisers' fees, underwriting costs, commissions and other charges.

During my first year as governor, I visited a number of other communities to ascertain their needs. At Haines the problem was to find a use for Chilkoot Barracks—soon to be declared surplus—as a tuberculosis sanitarium, an arts and crafts center or a tourist facility. In Skagway, seventy-five citizens, at a dinner arranged by "Ma" Pullen, wanted an airport, of course, but even more, a bit of road. They could not drive outside the town limits—the town had several taxis but no place to go—and they hoped for a road to Dyea in the neighboring Taija Valley, where the gold-rushers had started up the Chilkoot Trail to the Klondike. The valley would be accessible if about seven miles of road were constructed along the shore. That struck me as reasonable and I assured the people that I would get it for them. However, when I proposed it in Juneau to the two other members of the Board of Road Commissioners, Ike Taylor and Oscar Olson, they looked at me as if they thought I had gone mildly insane.

"Why," said Taylor, "that would be a recreational road."

"We've never done that," said Olson.

"Well, let's establish a new precedent," I said.

"I'm against it," Taylor said.

"A year and a half ago," I recalled to him, "you took me on a 125-mile road that led only to a mine at Nabesna. Tourism is the best economic prospect for Skagway. Why aren't its people entitled to it?"

I persisted and did get a survey, and when that was completed, the start of construction. But for each of the next six years, I had to keep wheedling for the meager funds necessary to push the road just one mile farther. It was a far more difficult undertaking than I had imagined. The road had to be quarried out of the face of granite cliffs. But it was done with determination by a fine old Swedish-born Skagwayan, Ludwig Frolander, who with little equipment and few helpers blasted his way foot by foot through solid rock. Several years later, I would dedicate the steel bridge across the Dyea River at the road's terminus. Throughout its length it provided superb views down Lynn Canal. It should have been named the "Frolander Highway."

One WPA project which I secured with much effort was a municipal swimming pool in the "Bowl," a beautifully situated recreational area at the base of Mount Juneau. Mayor Lucas and the City Council wanted to drop the project because of a $2,400 sponsor contribution the city would be obligated to make. Knowing how much greater the demand for WPA projects was than the supply, and how relatively fortunate the successful applicants were, I insisted that Juneau's chance of future projects would be greatly diminished if it did not carry out its commitment. They saw the point.

And why, I asked the mayor and the city engineer, should there not be some kind of a city plan which would take into consideration the water-front areas? All the mud then being excavated to make the Juneau small-boat harbor was being barged down the channel and dumped into deep water, whereas it could have been used as fill on the waterfront tidal flats.

Mayor Levi Kilburn of nearby Douglas wanted a gymnasium for the Douglas school and also raised the question of a small-boat harbor for Douglas, as soon as Juneau had one. So it seemed logical to arrange for a meeting of the two mayors and the members of the Alaska Planning Council to discuss regional planning for both towns and the adjacent areas. It struck me as odd that Juneau and Douglas had not united and pooled their resources but were duplicating their municipal and educational functions. But when I broached the subject, I ran head on into a major obstacle—sentiment. Douglas, a shrinking community with no economic mainstay of its own, except two restaurants which furnished some "nightlife" after Juneau's bars and restaurants closed, had, until a quarter of a century earlier, been larger than Juneau. When its great Treadwell mine had caved in and flooded in 1917, never to reopen, Douglas dwindled into a mere straggling residential suburb of Juneau. But its people's pride was strong and resisted amalgamation. However, both mayors agreed to appoint committees to confer with each other to formulate a program. I got the gymnasium for the Douglas school as a WPA project, but lost out on an indoor swimming pool.

With war clouds rising ominously across the Atlantic and Pacific, Alaska, except for the beginnings of the two naval air stations, was defenseless. Ladd Field, near Fairbanks, whose construction had also just begun, was to be merely a cold-weather aeronautical testing station designed to train flyers in Arctic conditions.

Except for Billy Mitchell, for six years Delegate Dimond had been a lone voice on behalf of defense for Alaska. As early as March 1934, after he had been in Congress just a year, he had pleaded for military bases in Alaska. His pleas went unheeded. In November 1937, he tried again and wrote Chief of Staff General Malin Craig, asking his support for an Army Air Corps base. Craig refused "for the reason that the mainland of Alaska is so remote from the strategic areas of the Pacific that it is difficult to conceive of circumstances in which air operations therefrom would contribute materially to the national defense."

But now in 1940 there was greater wisdom in the high command and Dimond's proposal, programmed to cost $12,104,000, was approved by General George Catlett Marshall, the Deputy Chief of Staff of the Army. He had asked my opinion about the location of the base and I had recommended establishing it on the railroad just north of Anchorage. Both Delegate Dimond and I had testified for it before the House subcommittee on appropriations for the War Department, and while we had received no recognizable reaction, we assumed that since the base had War Department sanction, the subcommittee would go along. We were wrong.

The military appropriation bill for the coming fiscal year was just under a billion dollars—the last time it would be so low—and Tony Dimond informed me that the Alaska base had been eliminated from the budget. I immediately telephoned General Marshall. "If there's one item out of the 65 million dollars they've cut which we must get back, it's the Alaska base," he said. "I've asked for a special meeting of the subcommittee to reconsider it."

General Marshall, Major-General H. H. Arnold, Chief of the Army Air Corps, Delegate Dimond and I appeared before the subcommittee. They were unmoved. "We're not going to waste any money on Alaska" was the consensus. But the fortunes of war were with us. Before the subcommittee had concluded its hearings on May 17, Goering's Luftwaffe had bombed Rotterdam, Hitler's armies had seized the Netherlands, swept through Belgium and begun the invasion of France. The atmosphere had been altered. The Senate restored the base; the House concurred. Thus Fort Richardson and adjacent Elmendorf Air Base came to be, and other bases would follow. Another important link between Alaska and the States was forged in mid-June of that same year when regular commercial flight and airmail services were established, with the inauguration by Pan-American Airways of twice-a-week clipper flights between Seattle, Ketchikan and Juneau.

Other transportation problems, however, were a long way from a solution. Freight rates on the steamers plying between the States and Alaska had long rankled Alaskans. The price of transporting an article was often greater than its cost. The 1939 territorial legislature had asked for an investigation. While still director of Territories, I had presented Alaska's grievance to the United States Maritime Commission which was reluctant to act, but which finally agreed to a hearing, after investigating the situation. Their investigator, Irwin Heine, came to Alaska during the summer of 1940 and reported that he was meeting considerable resistance in getting information. He had talked with John Bishop, the manager of Behrends—Juneau's closest approximation to a department store— who had given him verbally many good leads—that, for instance, light bulky objects were charged by volume, and small heavy objects by weight. But when Heine returned to get specific figures, Bishop had regretfully informed him that he had been ordered by Jack Mullen, the store's owner, not to supply the information. Heine met similar resistance elsewhere. Some of the merchants, although not all, were unconcerned by high freight rates, for they passed the charges on to their customers, augmenting their own profits by adding a bit extra to the freight rates and blaming it all on transportation costs. It had become a current wheeze, when haircuts were raised to two dollars and a half, for the barber to reply to any protests, "It's the freight."

The Maritime Commission hearings began in Juneau with a good attendance. I asked Mildred Hermann, a lawyer and a public-spirited woman active in club affairs, to attend and report them by radio every evening. It was desirable, we thought, that the people be informed what their freight costs were. A number of the smaller merchants were willing to testify candidly, but the bigger, more influential companies put on a well-rehearsed show. The Alaska Steamship Company presented several witnesses including William Pullen, manager of the local Alaska Light and Power Company, owned by a San Francisco family. He read the answers to questions asked by the company's attorney, Herbert L. Faulkner, which had evidently been prepared in advance. The burden of his replies was that freight rates—which had been increased again right after the hearings were authorized—were just, equitable and perfectly proper in view of the higher cost of labor. Upon cross-examination, David Scoll, a young attorney for the Maritime Commission, asked him whether his labor costs had gone up and he replied, "Twenty percent in all classes of labor." But when Scoll asked him whether this included salaried and clerical employees, he said, "Oh no." Scoll then asked him whether he had increased his rates on light and power and passed the costs on to the public, or absorbed them, to which Pullen replied proudly, "Our light and power rates have not changed up or down in seventeen years." He was apparently unaware that probably no other power company in the country had failed to reduce its rates during that period. Asked by Scoll what percentage of dividends his company was paying, he said, "Do I have to answer that question?" Faulkner shook his head, and Pullen replied, "I decline to answer that question on advice of counsel."

Other witnesses put on by the Alaska Steamship Company represented the Columbia Lumber Company and the Juneau Lumber Company. They thought the freight rates were just fine. Scoll revealed, however, that R. E. Robertson, one of the attorneys for the steamship company, was president of the Columbia Lumber Company and that Faulkner was a director and counsel for the Juneau Lumber Company. The Juneau Chamber of Commerce was conspicuously absent throughout these hearings. Predictably, both Faulkner and Robertson were among its officers, past or present.

As we were to learn, the Maritime Commission seemed to be for all intents and purposes in cahoots with the carriers. The Roosevelt Ad ministration had sought to remedy this situation in 1936 by abolishing the United States Shipping Board; but its substitute, the United States Maritime Commission, proved no different, as its successor some years later, the Federal Maritime Board, would likewise continue to disregard the public interest. The Maritime Commission's 1940 investigation clearly revealed that freight rates to Alaska were needlessly high and the latest increase unjustified, but as usual the Commission took no action. The lobbyist who for many years successfully kept the Alaska Steamship Company's freight rates where it wanted them was Alaska-born Henry Wadsworth Clark, known as "Eskie," a sobriquet acquired during his Harvard days on the fancied assumption that every Alaskan must be an Eskimo. Actually Clark was part Tlingit Indian.

There was, incidentally, no tax on the steamship companies, another example of the general disregard for the territory's needs by its successive legislatures, which were dominated by absentee interests through their resident lawyer-lobbyists. In Juneau, Herbert L. Faulkner and R. E. Robertson headed the capital's two leading law firms, and between them represented mining, shipping, canning and banking interests. There were likewise no taxes on lighterage companies, airlines, construction companies, building contractors, light and power companies, cold-storage plants, motion-picture theaters, radio stations, garages and filling stations, newspapers and banks. Their financial obligation to the territory was limited to a nominal license fee. There was no tax on gasoline. Residents outside of incorporated towns paid no municipal taxes although they freely used the town's facilities—schools, roads, fire and police protection. The owner of one of the three dairies on the highway running north of Juneau, none of which paid any taxes, had successfully led a protest against paying to have his daughter transported to school in Juneau. As a result, the dwellers along the twenty-nine-mile highway, who paid no other taxes, also paid nothing to have their children transported at the expense of the territory.

Knowing that while the executive proposes, the legislative disposes, I felt it essential to propose an adequate although modest revenue system for the territory, and consulting with the members of the next legislature, I found a majority of them favorably inclined. In arriving at these proposals, I had had the benefit of several tax studies previously made, and the advice of a United States Treasury expert, Frederick G. Lusk, who had been loaned to us by Secretary Morgenthau. Our program included a general property tax to apply to real estate and improvements thereon, but not on personal effects or intangibles; a corporation income tax which would enable the territory to tax the profits on mining operations, canneries, cold-storage plants, utilities, transportation companies and motion-picture houses, while at the same time the various license taxes which brought in virtually no revenue would be repealed; and a personal income tax which would augment the income tax on corporations, and levy taxes on outsiders who came to Alaska for a few months, made substantial incomes and then left.

Believing that drafting the proposal required expertise that might not be found in Alaska, I secured the services of Alfred Harsch, Professor of Taxation Law at the University of Washington Law School, who had drafted tax measures for the Washington legislature. The cost of his services was defrayed by the Public Administration Clearing House of Chicago, whose executives, Louis Brownlow and Herbert Emmerich, generously made funds available as a public service. Harsch would come to Juneau in December and stay through the session in order to be able to explain the tax provisions to the legislators.

Predominantly favorable expressions of support from the legislators made me reasonably optimistic, although I should have been warned by the realism of President Bunnell. While asserting that a general tax program was indispensable, he pointed out that the territory had gone for over a quarter of a century without one and had gotten the habit. He added that some of the legislators were, in essence, employees of the big mining companies, including Senator O. D. Cochran of Nome, and could not be counted on to support any additional taxes or to favor expenditures, no matter how necessary.

An even more adverse view was voiced by a House member from Juneau, John L. McCormick, and his wife Betty, who was active in civic affairs. John called my attention to the fact, which I had not realized, that the previous legislature had increased the gold tax exemption from $10,000 to $20,000. The bill which achieved this had been sponsored by Senator Cochran, had received all eight Senate votes and had passed the House by a vote of thirteen to three. McCormick was one of those voting against it. As most of those legislators would return for the new session, this did not make the outlook too promising.

Also, as I began to weigh the prospects, I recalled that some years earlier, before I knew I would have any interest in Alaska, I had at a cocktail party in New York heard a man named James Fozzard tell with relish how with a few cases of liquor he would, every other year during sessions of the biennial legislatures, keep the Kennecott mines from being taxed. He had rooms in the Gastineau Hotel and would dispense whiskey freely to the legislators; it was as easy as that to secure their grateful compliance. In Juneau in 1940 I was able to verify from B. D. Stewart, Commissioner of Mines, and other old-timers, the validity of "Big Jim" Fozzard's boasts.

In mid-August I had word that two Congressmen from the War Department Appropriations Subcommittee were en route to Alaska on the clipper and were going to Anchorage on the Coast Guard cutter, *Haida*, to inspect the new defense construction. They were L. Buell Snyder of Pennsylvania and a new member, George Mahon of Texas, whom I knew fairly well. It was late afternoon when they arrived, and I invited them to come to the house for dinner and to spend the night, but they wanted to leave immediately and asked me to accompany them. On board the *Haida*, I met their escort officer, Lieutenant Colonel Stephen Sherrill, who mentioned that he was the General Staff's expert on Alaska. Interested in finding out what the General Staff's latest views on Alaskan defenses were, I asked him when he had been in Alaska before. He replied, somewhat uncomfortably, that this was his first visit. I offered to be of service to him in any way I could, but when the *Haida* emerged from the protected waters of the Inside Passage, started across the gulf and began to roll heavily, Lieutenant Colonel Sherrill retired to his bunk and was seen no more on the voyage.

When we reached Seward forty-eight hours later, we were met by General Buckner and Colonel Ohlson, and rode to Anchorage in his private railroad car. There we met two other Congressmen, Joseph Starnes of Alabama and David Terry of Arkansas, who had flown in from Fairbanks. The next morning we were driven out to the base where the land had been cleared and construction was in full swing. The four Congressmen were photographed driving a nail and immediately departed for the States in an Army bomber. I regretted that the General Staff's expert on Alaska had missed an opportunity to become more expert.

I spent much time and care on my first message to the fifteenth Territorial Assembly, and delivered it on its opening day, January 29, 1941. It was, I thought, a practical speech, listing those territorial needs that could be met with a minimum of controversy. I quickly learned, however, that the legislators had minds of their own.

After my address, the House convened separately and adopted a memorial sponsored by Representatives James V. Davis and Harvey Smith, asking the enactment by Congress of a bill—previously introduced by Delegate Dimond but which he had decided not to press—forbidding the appointment of a nonresident to the governorship. As my appointment had long since been made, it was merely a gesture of hostility which the two sponsors continued to show. Davis had only one eye and reminded me of Long John Silver. A popular legislator, he was the principal stockholder in a local airline, owner of a local transportation vessel, a fish-trap licensee and otherwise a successful entrepreneur. Smith and his wife operated a "sporting house" in Anchorage. His biography in the

House journal listed him as a "property owner." Apparently, neither man had much use for me.

The lobbyists were present in force and I soon discovered the extent of their influence. In addition to Faulkner and R. E. Robertson, whom I had already met, they included W. C. Arnold, a lawyer for the canned-salmon industry and a former United States Commissioner in the little border community of Hyder, and Jack Clawson, an employee of Captain Austin E. Lathrop of Fairbanks, the Republican National Committeeman from Alaska, and owner of the Fairbanks *News Miner*, the city's lone daily, radio stations in Fairbanks and Anchorage, a motion-picture theater in both cities and a coal mine—indeed Alaska's principal resident tycoon. He had loaned Clawson to the salmon interests as a lobbyist.

Then there was Archibald William Shiels, president of Pacific-American Fisheries, one of the largest of the absentee salmon-packing concerns. He arrived at the beginning of the session and stayed until four days before adjournment, then sailed for home in Bellingham, Washington, remarking to a friend that there was no use staying any longer since everything was "in the bag." He was sufficiently interested, however, to telephone from Bellingham on the last night of the session about the fate of a measure which, had the legislature been able to achieve it, would have frozen the ownership of fish traps in the possession of their present licensees, a bill obviously desirable from the standpoint of those who had traps. These large structures, located near the mouths of salmon streams, were tremendous fish-catchers and were bitterly opposed by fishermen. They had been abolished in neighboring British Columbia and in the salmon-producing states of Washington and Oregon; but in Alaska, they were granted on a yearly basis by a federal regulatory agency and it was no secret that a previous federal commissioner had left office a rich man. Of the more than four hundred fish traps in Alaska, over ninety percent were owned by absentees, and Pacific-American Fisheries alone had sixty. Obviously, enactment of the bill was worth a fortune to existing licensees. Yet it had been disguised as a revenue measure, since it raised the annual license fee from $200 to $300, and was so presented in the news-columns of the *Daily Empire* which had long been the mouthpiece of the absentee interests. The price increase was mere bait, as an all-important paragraph toward the end of the bill provided that if two or more applicants for a fish-trap license sent in their applications and payments to the treasurer of the territory, he should retain only the one sent in by the existing trap owner and return the others.

I was unaware of this joker, and it was obvious that some of the legislators, who included quite a few who sympathized with the fishermen and were opposed to fish traps, were likewise unaware, for it passed the

House by a vote of fifteen to one and on the last day of the session by a vote of five to three in the Senate. It would have become law either with my signature or without it, but for a fortunate happenstance.

It was the last night of the session. The lobbyists had won. On the Senate floor there was much revelry; bottles were passing from hand to hand and the floor attendance was no longer confined to legislators. I was surprised to see Herbert Faulkner among the crowd. His dignity and urbanity were in contrast to the prevailing riotousness and I heard someone ask him, "Why are you here, Bert?"

"I just wanted to make sure that House Bill 112 got through," he replied.

I did not recall what that bill was but felt that a measure of such special concern to Bert Faulkner required investigation. It was unusual for lobbyists to want any legislation enacted; their business was to block bills. So I returned to my office, read the bill carefully, and after discovering its real purpose, decided to give it a pocket veto. I did not announce my decision. Two days later, Norman Banfield, a junior member of Faulkner's firm, came to get a copy of the act and gasped when he found the bill had not become law. Two days later Tony Dimond sent me a telegram from Washington urging me to veto the bill. I wired back that I already had. He wrote me that he was greatly relieved; he had just heard of the measure and was afraid it was too late to stop it. It would have been if I had not overheard Bert Faulkner's expression of interest.

It was, however, the only defeat the lobbyists suffered. Operating on the principle that Alaska should spend as little as possible on its own needs, they were influential in killing sorely needed social and educational legislation, and successfully fought every tax reform measure that would have affected their absentee employers. Their victory was so overwhelming and their performance so crude and shameless that I resolved to take the matter to the public and issued a "Message to the People of Alaska" to give them my view of what had happened. Lathrop's *News Miner* suppressed it, but Frank Gordon of Fairbanks, one of the uncontrolled legislators from the Fourth Division, read it aloud at a Fairbanks Chamber of Commerce luncheon, and I was swamped with so many requests that I had to order a second printing.

I was, of course, disheartened by my setbacks with the legislature, but that same year, 1941, I had better luck with the Washington bureaucracy. Earlier in my term, concerned that no action had yet been taken on the highway to Alaska, I raised the matter with President Roosevelt during a trip to Washington in December, 1940. I had seen him only once since my departure for Alaska a year before.

He greeted me with his usual cheerful smile, then looking grave asked,

"Have you found out who is responsible for the illegitimate bears in Alaska?"

I sensed a joke coming.

"You know," he said, "that you have bears under the jurisdiction of the Department of the Interior and bears under the jurisdiction of the Department of Agriculture. Now if a bear belonging to Interior meets and mates with a bear belonging to Agriculture, to whom does the offspring belong?"

The President answered his own question. "We can't have another fight between Harold Ickes and Henry Wallace over them. The answer is that the offspring belongs to Congress."

The bears disposed of, I said, "Mr. President, I've come to ask whether there isn't going to be some action on our highway to Alaska."

"It's a grand project, Ernest, a grand project. We ought to build it."

"Well, why don't we?" I asked.

"You go over and tell Cordell Hull that I want him to start negotiations with the Canadians."

"It would be much more effective if you'd tell him," I said.

The President laughed and pressed a button on his desk. In came his military aide, General Edmund ("Pop") Watson.

"Call Secretary Hull and tell him that I'd like him to start negotiating with the Canadians about that highway to Alaska, and to talk with Governor Gruening about it."

I spoke with Hull the next day. "The Canadians don't really want us to build that highway," he said, "but we'll talk to them and see what can be done."

I told him that I felt that the Canadians would get at least as much benefit as we would, that Premier Duff Patullo had shown his great interest in several conferences with Delegate Dimond and me, and that I suspected that any apparent Canadian reluctance might well be for bargaining purposes to get the United States committed to paying the greater portion of the costs.

I recalled to the secretary a conversation I had had a year earlier with Bruce Hutchinson, correspondent of the *Vancouver Sun*, who had called on me in Washington to inform me that considerable work would have to be done in Canada before the highway became a reality, and reported that the attitude of most Canadians was "If Uncle Sam wants this highway, let him pay for it." I told him that I believed the highway would be mutually advantageous, and while the United States might help finance the Canadian portion, I could see no reason why we should pay anything substantial toward its costs. If the Canadians felt otherwise, there just would not be any highway. I suggested to Secretary Hull that there was a bit of poker involved here, and that if we played our cards right, we could win the hand.

"We'll try it," Hull said, "and do the best we can."

Negotiations were reopened, and several months later when I was in Washington again, I had a phone call from Assistant-Secretary Adolf Berle who had been conducting the negotiations. He was one of the ablest men in our foreign service. "The Canadians really don't want us to build that highway," he said, "but if we can assure them it has military value, they'll let us go ahead."

"Well, it's obvious that it has military value."

"You may think so, and I may think so," Berle said, "but the Canadians will not accept that unless we can get the Army to say so. Can you get the Army to say so?"

"Of course I can," I said confidently.

I reported this conversation to Warren Magnuson and together we drafted a letter to the secretary of war, Henry L. Stimson. It gave a detailed description of both the "A" and "B" routes with the arguments for each, stating our preference for the former, and asked that the War Department express an opinion as to which of the routes would be preferable from the Army's standpoint. Two weeks later on April 26, 1941, the reply came:

> The War Department considers that the construction of such a highway cannot be justified on the basis of military necessity. Because of this view, it is believed that it would be inappropriate to comment upon the relative merits of the two suggested routes.

The letter was signed "Henry L. Stimson, Secretary of War."

We were momentarily stunned. Our letter had stated that construction of the highway had "the entire support of the commanding officer in Alaska," but perhaps we should go directly to the top of the military hierarchy. We promptly drafted a one-page memorandum to General Marshall, who was now chief of staff. We said what seemed to us uncontrovertible, that in the event of war sealanes might be cut by submarines, and the highway would then be indispensable as a route to Alaska. We followed this the next day with a call on General Marshall.

He said that our memorandum had been referred to the General Staff for study. "Would you mind telling us," I said, "who on the General Staff has that Alaska highway study?"

The answer came back, "Lieutenant Colonel Sherrill."

"Oh, I know Colonel Sherrill," said I happily, pleased at the prospect of not being obliged to talk to a complete stranger.

We were in Sherrill's office the next morning. We greeted each other warmly, recalling the stormy passage across the Gulf of Alaska the previous summer.

"Now about the Alaska Highway," I began.

"Hold everything," he interrupted. "I am no longer the General Staff's expert on Alaska. As of today, I'm the expert on Atlantic bases from Newfoundland to French Guiana." He was, I suspected, even less informed on those than he had been on Alaska. He told us he had never visited any of these prospective sites.

We had another surprise in store for us when I showed him Secretary Stimson's letter.

"I drafted that letter," he said.

"How did you conclude that the highway was not a military necessity?" I asked.

Sherrill paused. "Do you want me to take my hair down?"

We said we would appreciate his frankness. "The truth is," he said, after further reflection, "and I might as well level with you because it's now going to be up to someone else, that if I'd said 'yes, it's a good project,' I would have had to come up with answers I didn't have. How much will it cost? How long will it take? What equipment will be needed? Which is the better route? So I thought I'd say 'no.' I didn't think much of the project anyhow."

We chatted on, and gradually the whole process that had led to the adverse decision became clear. It demonstrated once again that in a government bureaucracy, civil as well as military, the person who drafts the initial letter often determines the final decision. Sherrill had drafted the letter, and the carbon copy surnamed by him had gone to his immediate superior, a colonel. He, too, knew nothing about the merits of the highway and wanted more information before passing it on to his superior. He went back to Sherrill, who naturally defended his position. The colonel agreed, surnamed the letter and passed it on. Their superior, a brigadier-general, equally uninformed, checked back again, heard the same story, and then added his signature. With three names, the letter began to acquire momentum. The major-general next in line would no longer question it; his superior, a lieutenant-general would follow suit and the letter finally found its way to the secretary of war's desk. So it became departmental policy.

It was hard to believe that one so little informed about Alaska would be entrusted with appraising the merits of the highway. But there it was. We would see much more of the same kind of military ignorance. We went back to General Marshall and asked for reconsideration. He said the highway would be given further study. I reported our experience to the

President. He said, "Don't worry; we'll get it built." But nothing happened until our nation was at war.

Even then, however, it was difficult to get the necessary machinery moving. In January 1942 I called on Frank Knox, secretary of the Navy, whom I had known well as a newspaper publisher in New Hampshire. "Frank, I suppose you've got all the ships you want," I said banteringly.

"What the hell are you talking about? You know we haven't got anything."

"You must have," I said, "or else you would be doing something about building the highway to Alaska."

Knox grabbed the phone. "Get me Secretary Ickes." When he reached the secretary of the Interior, he said, "Your governor of Alaska is here in my office wondering why *you* haven't done anything about building the Alaska highway."

Ickes's reply, which I could not hear, must have been colorful. I had violated one of his rules; namely that no one in his department could make an appointment to see another cabinet officer without his permission. But I had made up my mind that as a presidential appointee, confirmed by the Senate, I was not his subordinate and not bound by his orders, if I saw no good reason to be so. Nevertheless, as a result of this encounter, the Alaskan highway was brought up at the next cabinet meeting and the President appointed a committee of three—the secretaries of War, Navy and Interior—with instructions to proceed at once with the construction of the highway.

Much to our regret, the recommendations of the American and Canadian commissions that had studied the project were disregarded. The highway would follow neither the "A" nor the "B" route, but an entirely different route farther east, over terrain that had never been surveyed. The agency that made the determination was the United States-Canadian Joint Defense Board, justifying its decision on the grounds that the new route linked three airports built by the Canadians the previous summer at Fort Saint John, Fort Nelson and Watson Lake. The United States Commission drafted a long report of protest, reiterating the arguments for the "A" route. Warren Magnuson, its chairman, denounced the new route as a 100-million-dollar blunder. I deplored it because it eliminated the possibility of sideroad connections with southeastern Alaskan communities. We felt that the "A" route was shorter, more direct, less costly, and could be built more quickly. And no one of us was impressed by the financial arrangement under which the United States agreed to pay the entire cost of construction and the cost of maintenance for the duration of the war and for six months thereafter. Nevertheless, we concluded that any highway was better than none. It was completed in an amazingly short time by the

United States Army Engineers and opened with appropriate ceremonies at Jacquot's camp on Lake Kluane on November 20, 1942.

There was one comforting aftermath. I was able to persuade Brigadier General James A. O'Connor of the Corps of Engineers and head of the Northwest Service Command with headquarters at Whitehorse to construct a branch road to extend the road running north from Haines to the Canadian boundary until it joined the Alaskan highway about ninety-five miles west of Whitehorse at a point designated as Haines Junction. This hundred-mile addition had not been included in the "C" plan. My plans were aided by the pile-up of freight on the docks at Skagway which overtaxed the facilities of the White Pass railroad. The "Haines Cut-off," as this extension came to be known, furnished a new land route from Alaska's panhandle to the interior of Alaska and to the great outside.

20

AT WAR

*War is a terribly destructive force, even
beyond the limits of the battle front and the
war zone. Its influence involves the whole
community. It warps men's judgment, dis-
torts the true standards of patriotism, breeds
distrust and suspicion among neighbors, in-
flames passions, encourages violence, devel-
ops abuse of power, tyrannizes over men
and women even in the purely social relations of life and terrifies whole communities
into the most abject surrender of every right
which is the heritage of free government.*
—ROBERT M. LAFOLLETTE

The *McKinley*, which was to take me to Seattle on my way to Washington on December 6, 1941, was rescheduled to leave the next day. But
early that Sunday morning, the seventh, a phone call informed me that
there was a further delay and she would not leave for another twenty-
four hours. It was pitch-dark and snowing heavily. I welcomed the postponement called out cheerily to Dorothy, "I won't be leaving till tomorrow," and went back to bed.

At ten o'clock the phone rang again and a man who identified himself
as "Tom Gardiner living out on the highway" said he had been listening
to a broadcast from Seattle's KIRO. He heard that the Japanese had attacked Honolulu and Manila by air, that many civilians had been killed
and much damage done to our fleet at Pearl Harbor. It seemed hard to
believe. I called our local station KINY which had heard nothing. So I
called the station manager at his home and suggested that he get to his of-

fice immediately and start giving us the news. Then I called the Signal Corps and found they were getting confirmatory reports from Station WLW in Cincinnati. The surprise Japanese attack was all too true.

It was imperative to notify as many men in positions of responsibility as possible. I called Frank Metcalf, Director of Civilian Defense, told him to organize a meeting of the local civilian defense committee which I had organized on a territory-wide basis some months earlier, and make all preparations for the emergency. I phoned Mayor Lucas and Captain Walther of the Juneau National Guard Company and Bob Bartlett, all of whom were incredulous. By noon KINY was broadcasting more details, confirming that the army and navy in Hawaii had been caught napping. It was evident that the attack had been planned for weeks and that the Japanese ambassadors who had come to Washington to propose negotiations had been a blind designed to lull the American people and our military into a false sense of security. The civilian defense committee met that evening in the City Hall and arranged for a blackout the following night. Meanwhile I had sent messages to all directors of civilian defense in the territory and had talked to General Simon Bolivar Buckner, head of the Alaska Command. My trip to Washington was, of course, postponed.

It was reported or rumored that the Japanese had also planned air attacks on various Alaskan coastal cities, but foul weather all along the coast had made such raids impossible. Had these raids been made, they would have found us as unprepared as Hawaii—indeed far more so. If alerted, Hawaii had the planes and coastal defense guns to repel the attack; Alaska did not. When some days later Admiral Kimmel and General Walter C. Short were relieved of their commands in Hawaii, General Buckner remarked, "There, but for the grace of fog, go I."

Monday morning we listened to the President's "Day of Infamy" speech asking for a declaration of war. Alaska was woefully unprepared. It was clear to all of us that, as Japan's conquests in the Pacific expanded, Alaska would come next. Our four National Guard companies, which I had organized only a year before, had been federalized, becoming the 297th Infantry. That was hardly enough and I felt it desirable to organize a Territorial Guard in which every able-bodied male not subject to the draft or engaged in essential war work would be enrolled. We visualized the possibility of Japanese landings in Alaska and were determined that they would meet guerrilla resistance every step of the way. The need for such a force was more than ever brought home to me by a talk I had in February 1942 with Admiral Ernest King, chief of naval operations, who said that it was doubtful whether we could hold Alaska in view of more pressing commitments. When I told the President how few planes the army and navy had in Alaska, he said, "How many planes do you think I have to defend New York?"

General Buckner liked the Territorial Guard plan and the first week in January he specified a formidable list of points that he wanted it to guard, including Signal Corps communications stations, weather stations, bridges, railroad tunnels and terminals, coal mines, power plants, water-supply stations, telephone exchanges, oil tanks, docks and a variety of civilian airports. Many of these points, it seemed to me, should have been the responsibility of the military, but General Buckner insisted that he could not dispose his troops for guard duty; they had to be held for use en masse for defensive and offensive operations. I said we would do our best and asked him to assign two officers to me to help me organize the Territorial Guard. He sent me two men who had served in World War I, Major Marvin R. Marston and Captain Carl Scheibner, and I decided to assign each to one-half of the territory, Marston to the west, Scheibner the east.

We had no time to lose. Marston, who had had some contact with the Eskimos on Saint Lawrence Island, and I started off immediately in a small float plane to organize the villages in the Kuskokwim. Many of the army officers stationed in Alaska had a depreciatory attitude toward the "native" people—Indians, Eskimos and Aleuts. Not Marston. I was very favorably impressed by his performance, and after our trip, I wanted to report on what we had accomplished to the officer whom General Buckner had assigned as a liaison with my office, Lieutenant Colonel Hobart Murphy. I discovered that he was the one who had picked Marston and Scheibner. We had dinner and after a few cocktails, he waxed confidential. "Governor, you don't want Marston," he said.

"Why don't I?" I asked.

"Because he's no damn good."

"Why did you assign him to me then?" I asked.

Murphy looked embarrassed.

"So you wanted to get rid of him, is that it?" I asked.

Murphy admitted it.

"Well, it may interest you to know that I do want him. He's first-class in every way."

I had already sensed that Marston's offense was that he wanted action; he was no apple polisher, and in cutting corners to achieve what he considered desirable objectives, he had found it necessary to step on a few toes. He had, I knew, overcome considerable resistance to build an enlisted men's club on the base. Aware of his unpopularity with the brass, I made a special point of thanking General Buckner for assigning him to me. "He's a very good man," I said.

"Of course he is," said Buckner. "You don't suppose I would have assigned him to you, if I hadn't thought so."

I was pleased to have restored Marston in the command's good graces, or so I thought. But six months later my request for his promotion was turned down by General Buckner. When I was on Adak where General Buckner was headquartered, I asked him why.

"Because he's no damn good," said Buckner.

"Let me tell you, General," I said, "there's no other man in Alaska who could have done what he has." And I described how he had driven a dog-team long distances through the Arctic wilderness in subzero temperatures to deliver rifles and ammunition when the army supply system had failed. Marston ultimately got his lieutenant colonelcy.

Because of the importance of the Territorial Guard, I felt it essential to go to each village in person. We would call a meeting, usually at the Bureau of Indian Affairs school, and I would explain that now that our country was at war and Alaska likely to be invaded, I wanted every able-bodied man ready to defend his home. The government would supply rifles and ammunition.

Up until then, I had had very little contact with the Eskimos. I was aware that in some cases they had been badly treated by the whites, and I did not know what resentment might lurk behind their smiling faces. I encountered none, only the greatest willingness to serve their country. This was made vivid to me at Cape Prince of Wales on the westernmost tip of the Seward Peninsula. The King Islanders were also there, having come to trade their fox-skins and ivory carvings. After pointing across the sea, the direction from which the enemy would come, I asked, "Now, who is qualified to serve? Out here a boy of sixteen is a man. If he can handle a rifle, he can enlist."

Sitting at my feet was a handsome, well-built youngster who looked about eighteen.

"How old are you, son?" I asked.

"I'm four . . ." he started to say and then corrected himself. "I'm sixteen."

"Well," I said, "I'm proud of you. Even if you're only fourteen, if your father says you can join, I'll enroll you." He was enrolled. Later I encountered a five-foot-eleven youngster strolling across the tundra near Haycock. Four ptarmigan were hanging from a rifle slung across his shoulders. He had brought them down with the rifle, not a shotgun. He was twelve years old. He was enrolled.

The Japanese did attack Alaska, bombing Dutch Harbor on June 3, 1942, and occupying the Aleutian islands of Attu and Kiska. Now there was even greater urgency to organize and equip the Territorial Guard. In a few of the white communities, men asked how much they would be paid. No Eskimo ever asked that question.

A further illustration of their patriotism came on Saint Lawrence Island, where stormy weather held us for several days. The local guard unit was organized on the first day. The next day was spent with the same group discussing village problems. The following day I said to them, "The planes that you see patrolling overhead, the rifles and ammunition which our government is giving you, cost money. In addition to fighting the war is the problem of paying for it. You have in your village treasury some funds from the sale of your fox-skins and ivory. Over on the mainland we buy war bonds which help Uncle Sam pay for the war."

The village leaders went into a huddle. Then an elder spoke up. "We have fifteen thousand dollars in the village treasury. We buy fifteen-thousand-dollarsworth of bonds."

"Hold on a minute," I said. "I'm proud of you. But you mustn't do that. You may need some of this money. Over on the mainland people give maybe one-tenth of what they have. Besides there will be more bond issues later."

After another huddle, the spokesman said, "We hear what you say, Governor, but Uncle Sam has been very good to us. So we buy fifteen thousand."

I finally persuaded them to invest only part of that.

These Eskimos proved to be the eyes and ears of the army in Alaska, and their services were invaluable. At the war's end I wanted them included in the regular military establishment, but I encountered some resistance in the National Guard Bureau because of the Eskimos' nomadic hunting habits. I could not guarantee a full attendance on a given night, fifty-two weeks in the year, nor the size of the units. This difficulty was overcome by enrolling them in scout battalions, a new designation.

After the war, a National Guard encampment was established at Fort Richardson which included an Eskimo scout battalion. A special ceremony was held in the auditorium on the base and all the top "brass" from the Army, Navy and Air Force was there. In front of us in their seats were three hundred Eskimo scouts. Captain Frank Clayton proceeded to call their names and as each came to the platform I conferred his award: "Marksman, Sharpshooter, Expert." As the roll call continued I was increasingly surprised at the large number of recipients. When all the awards had been made, I said, "I want to congratulate you men of the Second Battalion. It's a wonderful showing. As for those few who did not get an award, I'm sure you will next time."

At this point Captain Clayton interrupted me. "Every one of these men got an award, Governor."

I turned to Major General Julian Cunningham, the Alaska Army Commander, and asked, "Isn't this an unusual showing?"

"Unusual," he said. "It's unprecedented. I've never known of a unit with a hundred-percent-marksmanship record."

Those were the Alaskans who had served, and continued to serve, their country cheerfully, patriotically, efficiently, modestly. The full story of their service written by Marvin R. ("Muktuk") Marston under the title, *Men of the Tundra, Eskimos at War*, was published in 1969 with an introduction by me and an epilogue by Major General C. F. Necrason, Adjutant General of the Alaska National Guard.

Along with bravery and devotion to duty, war inevitably brings its fair share of absurdities. This became painfully evident when Alaskans began to find large excisions in the magazines to which they subscribed. The asininity of this procedure was revealed when the same magazines arrived at newsstands or other distributing agencies untouched.

I telephoned General John L. DeWitt, head of the Western Defense Command in San Francisco and followed that up with a written protest. General DeWitt informed me that he considered that kind of censorship totally unnecessary, but that the policy did not originate in his command but in the civilian Office of War Censorship in Washington. However, the military in Alaska had established a censorship policy of its own. The high command at Elmendorf ordered that no material relating to Alaska's rivers, mountains or shorelines could be taken out of the territory. To enforce that policy, the baggage of persons going "outside" was searched. Whenever a copy of Robert Service's, *The Spell of the Yukon* was found, it was confiscated. The Yukon was a river! When Robert Atwood, the editor and publisher of the Anchorage *Times*, wrote a kidding editorial about this idiocy, the Fort Richardson censor forbad its publication. That censor, after a promotion to a lieutenant colonelcy, was subsequently deposed after he had shown signs of mental disturbance.

To make matters even worse, some four hundred clerks in Seattle, wives of men stationed in Alaska and others, were opening all mail coming to and from the territory. Excerpts were placed in sheets of foolscap size at the top of which were printed the abbreviated initials of some thirty government agencies, including the British, to which these excerpts might be sent. Letters from husbands to wives, from parents to children, business communications—all were subject to this scrutiny and distribution. I could see no reason why such snoopery should be imposed exclusively on Americans living in a territory. I decided to take my protest to Washington where I found Delegate Dimond in accord with my view. Together we called on Byron Price, a former Associated Press editor, who was now in charge of the Office of War Censorship. I registered my protest.

"We get a lot of valuable information that way," Price said.

"You'd get a lot more if you tapped every telephone wire and put someone under everybody's bed," I told him. "Moreover, you have no legal authority for doing this."

"I think I have," said Price.

He did not tell me that a bill granting that authority in the territories and outlying possessions, which he, in fact, did not yet have, had just passed the House and was awaiting action in the Senate. But he said that he would give my complaint consideration and suggested that I return next week. It was a Thursday. On Saturday I read in the morning paper that the legislation had been passed by the Senate unanimously the previous day.

In those days, a procedure subsequently adopted by the Senate to call for reconsideration of a bill immediately after its passage and then moving to "lay that vote on the table" was not always practiced. I knew that without it, a bill could be recalled within twenty-four hours on the next calendar day. *The Congressional Record* showed that no action for reconsideration had been taken. I immediately called on Senator George Norris of Nebraska, who shared my indignation. He told me to see Senator John Danaher of Connecticut, Chairman of the Judiciary Subcommittee in charge of the legislation. Danaher, still a first-term senator with the face of a cherub, was also incensed, and when the Senate session opened on Monday, he moved for reconsideration and recalled the bill. The New York *Herald Tribune* reported the action.

The Senate took the unusual course of recalling a bill it had unanimously adopted on Friday authorizing censorship of communications between the United States and its territorial possessions, after sharp protest by Ernest Gruening of Alaska who charged abuse of existing censorship.

The Senate Judiciary Committee thereupon granted my request for a hearing and called a meeting of the full committee for the next morning.

I picked my evidence carefully—a collection of intercepts that had been sent to the Department of the Interior. Among them were parts of letters from Interior Department employees written to their wives in the States, voicing criticisms of some departmental policies and personnel in Alaska. They were obviously not intended by the writers for Interior Department inspection. Other excerpts were from letters written by residents of various states, living in Alaska, to their senators, which made the members of the Senate Judiciary Committee even angrier.

The committee called Byron Price to a closed session and criticized him sharply. Chairman Frederick Van Nuys informed the press that he had asked Price why, if he was convinced—as he had alleged—that authority already existed for censoring mail between the United States and its territories, he had requested legislation granting such powers.

Price's reply was that he wanted it in case a damage suit came up. "In other words," said Van Nuys, "he thinks it all right for him to do so as long as he does not get into trouble about it. And now he wants us to protect him."

The Senate Judiciary Committee concluded that there was no more right to censor a letter between the United States and Alaska than between any two states. It was a victory for the principle of equal treatment of territorial residents. The opening of letters and the clipping of magazines was stopped; the Seattle branch of the Office of War Censorship was closed.

There would be, however, other wartime absurdities in Alaska which I was powerless to stop, chiefly perpetrated by the military. Shortly after war was declared, President Roosevelt had by executive order created an Alaska War Council to be composed of the senior representatives, in Alaska, of various federal agencies. I was named chairman of the council and our function was to establish a working liaison with the military. We were therefore interested to learn that the military planned to build a base at Excursion Inlet some seventy miles northwest of Juneau, where materiel, supplies and troops would be assembled and then proceed under convoy to the end of the Aleutians to expel the Japanese from Kiska and Attu.

I asked Bob Bartlett to come with me to the site. There was nothing in the inlet except a small cannery. A great amount of building material would have to be transported there; docks would have to be built, power and water supplies installed. We already had these facilities in Juneau, and Bartlett and I both felt that much time and cost would be saved by locating the base there. Knowing how long it would take to complete the project at Excursion Inlet, I was convinced that building the base there would delay action which the military now considered urgent.

As phone communications of classified material were interdicted, I flew to San Francisco to see General DeWitt. I made it plain that I was not approaching the subject from a Chamber of Commerce standpoint, but I told him that we already had both the facilities and the manpower in Juneau—some eight hundred soldiers were stationed there—and that building the base there would be a great saving of time, to say nothing of money.

"I've already signed the order for Excursion Inlet," the General said.

"Well, unsign it," I said. "Not a stick of lumber has been laid down at Excursion Inlet. Merely change your order to read Gastineau Channel, or Juneau. We have all kinds of room there, or at Auke Bay or on Douglas Island."

"I never reverse my decisions."

Construction of the base began shortly, but long before it was completed the Japanese had been driven off Attu and had evacuated Kiska. The $25 million spent on the base at Excursion Inlet had been wholly wasted. Yet the construction continued. I asked the commanding officer there, Colonel Norris, why it was being completed. He thought for a while and said, "The next war."

"Against whom?" I asked.

"Maybe Russia" was his reply.

But after the base was completed, prisoners of war were brought in, all the facilities were dismantled and the salvaged materials shipped elsewhere.

Excursion Inlet was not an exception. Virtually every base in Alaska was built either wrongly or in the wrong place. At Sitka the Navy built an air station on Japonski, a diamond-shaped island about a mile long and half a mile wide. When it was nearly completed, it was discovered that no provision had been made, and no room left, for the army, which was expected to defend a naval base in the event of a hostile invasion. What to do? The army could not be put on the mainland of Baranof Island because it would then be separated from the airbase by a hundred yards of water. So it was decided to move out into Sitka Bay, flatten half-a-dozen dome-shaped granite islands and use the rock to build a causeway between the airbase and these newly created flat islands where the army would be located. It raised the cost of the base from the allotted $2,900,000 to $50,000,000. And if the war had come to Sitka, one bomb dropped on the causeway would have separated the army on its insular retreats from the navy on Japonski.

Commander Jack Tate explained to me that Auke Bay near Juneau would have been a much better site for the airbase, but Japonski had been selected because the navy still had title to a coaling station there which dated back to the early days after the cession from Russia. Experience had proved to the navy that it was easier to persuade Congress to add millions of dollars to any existing structure, even an outhouse, than to begin somewhere else from scratch.

At the Kodiak Naval Air Station, the first inspection came when the base was nearly completed. The inspector found the buildings much too close to each other. One or two bombs would destroy everything. "Disperse!" was the order. It was carried out. The navy dispersed all over Kodiak Island. But at the second inspection to survey the finished result, it was found that the base had been over-dispersed; its various vital structures were impractically far apart. So the base was rebuilt a third time to strike a happy mean between the first two attempts.

At Dutch Harbor, the third of the Naval Air Stations, the airstrip had

to be cut out of a cliff at right angles to the prevailing winds. It was op-
erationally unsafe. On the eve of hostilities, General Buckner wired the
War Department for authorization to build another field that would satisfy navy requirements. Permission was granted. The nearest level ground
was on Umnak Island fifty miles away. The field was built there, with
some difficulty in landing the equipment, for Umnak had no harbor.
Dutch Harbor had a fine harbor but no field. The combination was likened to a blind man carrying a lame man on his back.

When the United States began to supply planes to the Russians, they
insisted that our flyers could not deliver them in Siberia, but that their
flyers would pick them up on American soil. So it was deemed advisable
to construct an airfield between Ladd Field at Fairbanks and the field at
Nome where the Russians would take off for home. The distance between Fairbanks and Nome was considered too great for safety. For the
intermediate field, a site was selected about halfway at the village of Galena alongside the Yukon River.

When the first grading began, the old-timers were horrified. "You can't
build a field there," they said. "It will be flooded in the spring breakup.
Build it on one of the benches on the nearby hills."

"Don't tell us," said the army engineers.

At the next spring breakup, the field, nearing completion, was flooded.

"See what we told you," said the old-timers.

"Nothing to it," said the engineers. "We'll just raise the level of the
field six feet. That'll do it. It will only cost $9 million."

"Oh no," said the old-timers. "Last spring's flood was a very small one.
Every third or fourth year there's a really big flood. It will cover and cut
away even your raised runway."

And so it proved.

Nothing daunted, the engineers said, "We'll dispose of this problem.
We'll build a dike and divert the waters of the Yukon around the field."
(Cost figures, classified.) The dike diverted the waters; it diverted them
through the village of Galena which has been subject to flooding ever
since.

When the Fort Richardson-Elmendorf complex was built, everyone
was naturally in a hurry. Bulldozers cleared away the forest. The barracks were erected on a World War I model in neat rows, equally spaced
apart, their copper roofs glinting in the sun. Suddenly, someone woke up:
"What about camouflage?" The trees were gone. "Let's send for the
army's top camouflage expert." He came, a brigadier general.

General Buckner told me the story with great relish. He and the visiting expert cruised aloft, slowly, in a helicopter. "What'll we do?" asked
Buckner after the base and surrounding terrain had been surveyed.

"Do *nothing*," said the army's camouflage expert. "The Japs will never believe we built a base like that. Put some structures four or five miles away in the woods that look as if you were trying to conceal them. If they ever get this far, that's what they'll try to hit."

One is left to wonder, when Uncle Sam is building bases all over the world, not subject to the observation of fellow-Americans, how many of our overseas installations have been so misbuilt or badly placed.

Even the war could not overshadow Alaska's internal problems, and as the 1943 biennial session of the legislature neared, I had to make up my mind what kind of message I would deliver. With one exception, the 1941 session had rejected all my proposals, but even more serious was its failure to take advantage of the great war-engendered construction boom by allowing its vast profits to go totally untaxed. Yet the composition of the 1943 legislature offered no ground for encouragement. O. D. Cochran of Nome, attorney and lobbyist for the absentee mining interests, was slated to be president of the Senate; James V. Davis, the most ruthless and predacious of the House members, to be Speaker. Joseph W. Kehoe, a newly elected member from Seward, who was sympathetic to my tax program, advised me not to attempt to bring it up again. "If you do, they'll even do less for you; they're in full control." So I decided to make a few recommendations and leave it at that. Sooner or later the prevailing "take it all out and leave nothing" policy would have disastrous consequences.

These consequences were already apparent to those legislators, still relatively few, who were concerned with the territory's welfare and the permanency of residence. There was a continual exodus of small businessmen who had done well in Alaska and then sold out and moved "down below." I made it my business to interview them and ask why they were leaving. I was so entranced with the beauty, the freedom and the potentials of Alaska that I could not see why anyone would want to leave. But Alaska could not furnish the advantages they would find in the States, they said. Their teen-age daughter could have dancing and art lessons; their boy would have a good gym and an indoor swimming pool in his high school and a greater variety of sports; in Alaska there was only basketball. They would have better medical attention and more cultural advantages, whereas everything in Alaska was second-rate. Even the motion-picture theaters showed only Grade B five-year-old movies. In many cases the departing Alaskans had "made it" in Alaska and were looking for better surroundings. And one could foretell that those to whom they sold their businesses would follow suit in a few years, when they too had "cleaned up."

The solution to this problem seemed simple to me. We should "put

more butter in the cake." But how to do that with legislatures controlled
by those dedicated to the opposite? Perhaps these legislators represented
their constituents' real sentiments. There seemed to be a widespread inferiority complex among many Alaskans, which was in contrast to their
supposed "pioneer spirit." If that was the case, perhaps we should try to
change that point of view. Alaskans had every reason to be proud of themselves and of their land, but why should its people's needs be neglected?

We were at war, and winning it was a primary consideration, but that
did not preclude the normal legislative functions. So my message to the
legislators stressed that even during a war against totalitarianism we had a
chance to demonstrate by our actions how much better results a free society could obtain. I knew my tax-reform proposals were a lost cause, so
instead I presented a list of possible economies to stay within the territory's meager budget, which we were required by law to do. Among these
economies was the elimination of the bounties on eagles, wolves, hair
seals, coyotes and trout—all of which were part of an expensive and
short-sighted territorial delusion. A quarter of a million dollars had been
spent on bounties in the last two years. I had urged their aboliton in 1941;
and I again called attention to them, particularly to the bounty on eagles.
A dollar was being paid for each pair of claws of this noble bird under
the misconception that it was a predator on salmon. I was unable to secure repeal of the bounty legislation, but I exercised my power of item
veto and eliminated the appropriation from the budget. Actually, the
1943 legislature did as little that was constructive as the 1941 session, although it amended existing legislation I had urged to make possible the
hiring of city managers. I reminded them again of the revenues they were
forfeiting and pointed out that much profitable construction was still untaxed. But it fell on deaf ears.

There was, however, one new and important problem in the territory,
and the foundation for its solution was laid in the 1943 legislature. I had
found that the pure democracy and egalitarianism of Alaskans which had
so impressed me was subject to one basic exception. It did not apply to
the native people—the Indians, Eskimos and Aleuts. They were excluded from many establishments and segregated in motion-picture theaters. A sign in the Anchorage Grill, "We Do Not Cater to Native and
Filipino Trade," which I had seen on my first visit to Alaska, haunted me.

In 1940 I had paid a visit to the grill and took a seat on one of the
stools at the counter over which that sign hung. "Who's the boss around
here?" I asked the waitress. She replied, "George." "I want to see
George," I said.

She went to the back of the restaurant and from the kitchen came a big
man in a white chef's cap and uniform. He was George Grames, a naturalized citizen, born in Greece.

"What's the idea of that sign, George?"

"Oh, we have to have that sign to keep the customers," he said.

"Here's one customer you won't keep," I said pointing to myself, "if that sign stays up."

"How's that?" asked George, evidently surprised.

"Well, how would you like to go into another eating place down the street and see a sign: 'We Do Not Cater to Greeks.'"

I then gave George a pep talk about the meaning of America. He went over and removed the sign. "It will never be up again," he said.

I dropped into the Anchorage Grill on various occasions thereafter, and the sign had not reappeared. And I saw native families eating along with other patrons. No one seemed troubled by it. But I was not equally successful elsewhere.

Across the Gastineau Channel from Juneau on Douglas Island, there were two restaurants that catered to the "nightlife" of Juneau. One of them, the Douglas Inn, had painted over its entrance: "No Natives Allowed." The owner, John Marin, was an Italian by birth, and I was informed he had changed his name from Marini.

"You have a sign over your establishment that is very offensive to the native people here," I said to him. "Won't you please paint it out and stop the practice that it indicates you follow?"

"I can't have a lot of dirty, drunken natives in my place," he replied.

"You can't have, and needn't have, *any* people who are dirty or drunk," I told him. "But why call them 'natives'? I've seen people stagger out of your place, and they weren't natives. If any person, native or white, is drunk, disorderly, or otherwise objectionable, you can exclude him—but as a person, not as a member of a race."

We discussed the matter for a while and he said he would think it over. But nothing happened. Then after we entered the war, I sent for Marin again. "John," I said, "we're at war now. Native boys are being drafted like white boys. Some of them will be killed. We're fighting a government which propagates the idea that one 'master race' is superior to all others. The United States is opposed to that idea and all that goes with it. So I urge you to paint out that sign."

This time Marin promised that he would, but he did not keep his promise. No doubt he took counsel with others who said, "Tell that Cheechako governor to go jump in the channel." The sign remained.

Then I made up my mind that I would try to have legislation introduced at the next session of the legislature to provide equal treatment in public places and make violations a misdemeanor. I first went to Speaker Jim Davis. We were far apart on revenue measures, but I thought I might appeal to him on an issue that did not mean more taxes. He said he would introduce a bill eliminating all discrimination based on race, but only "by request." That clause, signifying that the bill's sponsor was not really for it, led me to tell him that I was glad to have him go ahead with the bill, but I would try to get a Senate sponsor who really favored the move.

Davis's bill included not merely prohibition of discrimination in public places but also opened the local schools to "native" children, thus going beyond what I felt was practically attainable at the time, since the Bureau of Indian Affairs—known locally as the "Alaska Native Service"—had an established system of separate schools. I did not like the separate school system but doubted that we could achieve all these changes at once, especially as they involved federal policy which the legislature was powerless to alter. My apprehension materialized when, in a hearing on Davis's bill before the whole House, it was opposed by R. E. Robertson, president of the Juneau School Board, on the grounds that it would place an unwarranted burden on the Juneau school system. The bill was defeated, nine to seven.

Meanwhile Senator Norman R. Walker of Ketchikan had agreed to sponsor a bill which would only ban discrimination in public places. When I told Senator Walker I would urge its passage strongly in my message, he said, "Don't do it, Governor. The legislators don't like to have the governor tell them what to do; it's likely to lose votes." So I refrained, and it passed the Senate seven to one. The House killed it, eight to eight. But the story did not end there.

While greatly disappointed by this defeat, I felt that the closeness of the vote made prospects of a future reversal favorable, and I laid plans to enlist hitherto unutilized support—that of the native people themselves.

Discrimination against native Alaskans was not confined to restaurants and movie houses; its most blatant expression came with the war. During a visit to Ketchikan, I was called upon by a delegation of native young women who reported that native girls were being excluded from the USOs, the recreation centers provided for members of the armed services. The absurdity, as well as the cruelty, of this practice lay in the fact that while native young men in uniform were admitted freely to the USOs, their sisters were not. And this discriminatory practice was carried so far that if a native GI and a white GI were walking or talking together on a street corner, and a native girl—perhaps the sister of the native soldier—joined them, an MP would come along and order them to "break it up."

The policy originated from the headquarters of the Alaska Defense Command in Anchorage, which exercised overall military authority in Alaska. So I flew to Anchorage and took up the matter with General Buckner. His position was that the policy was designed to protect the virtue of the native girls. I was unable to shake him. Although a product of the border state of Kentucky, Buckner had the color prejudice of the deep South and held it strongly. On another occasion he told me how he had sought to dissuade Benjamin O. Davis, a black who later rose to the highest rank in the armed services of any of his race, from pursuing his military career. I decided to go over Buckner's head, so I flew to Washington and took up the matter with President Roosevelt who promised to have the Alaska Defense Command overruled and the practice of excluding native girls from the USOs stopped. It soon was, on order from the secretary of war.

A few weeks later I received a telegram from Nome which read:

I am a girl, seventeen years old, half-white, half-Eskimo. My father was a soldier in World War I. I have two brothers in the Army in this war. Last night I went to the theater with a friend of mine, a sergeant in the Army. He paid for the tickets. When we sat down the usher came and ordered me to move to the other side of the aisle. When I refused, he called the police and had me ejected. When I struggled, I was arrested and spent the night in jail.

The custom in Nome's one motion-picture house was to seat Eskimos on one side of the central aisle, and the whites on the other. I promptly sent a telegram to this young girl, expressing my regret and telling her it should never have happened in America, and would not have happened if the equal treatment bill had passed in the last legislature. Another telegram was sent to the Mayor of Nome, Swedish-born Edward Anderson, denouncing the incident and asking for an explanation. He wired back that he considered it most regrettable and that it would not happen again.

Using what influence I had, I could fight selected incidents of discrimination, but I knew the final outcome of the battle rested with the native people themselves. In pursuance of that objective, I presented my views to the Thirtieth Annual Convention of the Alaska Native Brotherhood which met at Hoonah. I said that the native people—comprising at that time three-sevenths of the territory's population—were entitled to a larger share in the territory's political and economic life. There were no natives in the legislature. I urged them to take advantage of a newly enacted bill I had asked Delegate Dimond to sponsor, which doubled the size of the Senate and provided proportionate representation in the House, raising the First Division's (Southeastern Alaska) delegation from four to eight members. With six thousand natives out of a population of 24,000, they were entitled to two representatives, who, if elected, could help end discrimination.

They followed my advice and in the 1944 primaries nominated two outstanding members of the Indian race, Frank Peratrovich, a merchant from Klawok, and Andrew Hope, a boat-builder from Sitka. In the Democratic primaries they ran respectively first and third among fifteen candidates for eight places. In the general election they ran second and third out of a field of sixteen, gratifying evidence that racial prejudice was not considerable and that the majority of Alaskans were willing to judge and elect their representatives on the basis of merit.

In the Second Division (Northwestern Alaska), whose population was eighty percent Eskimo, no Eskimo had ever been elected to the legislature. This was chiefly due to the denial of polling places to a majority of its communities. Extension of the franchise was opposed by a group of whites in Nome who, by limiting the number of voters, had been able to control the selection of the legislative delegation. Overcoming considerable resistance in the Clerk of Court's office in Nome, I was able to establish polling places in a number of remote communities whose people had never had the opportunity to vote.

Casting about for a worthy candidate, I found him in Percy Ipalook of Wales, a Presbyterian minister and a full-blooded Eskimo. He was hesitant about running and felt that he should obtain the consent of his superior, the Reverend Earl Jackman. I went to see Reverend Jackman in New York on my next trip east and got it. Percy Ipalook ran and was elected first to the House of Representatives and later to the Senate.

I considered the principle of representation for a large segment of our population by a member of their own race so important that I deliberately refrained from suggesting to Percy Ipalook on which party ticket he should run. It would clearly have been to the advantage of the Democratic Party for him to run under its banner, but I felt that this basic issue should not be tinged with partisanship. Consequently, Percy Ipalook made his own choice; he filed, ran, was elected and reelected on the Republican ticket. Since then Eskimos and Indians have served in every Alaska legislature. Following a term in the House, Frank Peratrovich was elected to the Senate, and was succeeded in the House by another Tlingit Indian, Frank L. Johnson of Kake. An Eskimo, William E. Beltz of Nome, was elected to the House in 1948, was later elected to the Territorial Senate and became president of the Senate in the first legislature after statehood. When he died, he was succeeded in the presidency of the Senate by Frank Peratrovich. The performances of the legislatures were improved by the participation of Alaskan natives.

In spite of its internal problems, Alaska's chief concern was in helping win the war. I spent considerable time in the Aleutians during our military's westward course to expel the Japanese. I wanted to see what was happening, to assist in removing obstacles where I could, and to encourage our troops. The campaign was dogged by the foulness of the fog-shrouded, gusty Aleutian weather, by unfamiliarity with the terrain and by interservice rivalries. From the first, General Buckner and Rear Admiral Robert A. Theobald, the navy commander, clashed and neither one got along with Air Corps Brigadier General William D. Butler. They were not reticent in letting me hear about their differences. When Buckner wanted Theobald to move his ships to Tanaga and Theobold refused on the grounds that the anchorages were unsafe, Buckner said to me, "He's as tender of his bottoms as a sixteen-year-old girl." Theobald lost out, and was transferred and replaced by Rear Admiral Thomas C. Kinkaid.

The Japanese-occupied island of Attu was the main target of their combined operations. An invasion was mounted and I reached Attu while the battle was in progress. Many mistakes had been made. The footgear issued our men was wholly unsuitable. More men were disabled by frostbite and trench foot than by enemy action, and amputations were frequent. Instead of using—in part at least—the acclimated forces stationed in intermediate Alaskan posts—Cold Bay, Umnak, Adak—the contingents for Attu, trained for service in North Africa in California's hot dry Mojave Desert, were sent to our coldest, wettest terrain. Generals DeWitt's and Buckner's protests were overruled by the War Department.

The campaign started off badly; its commanding officer, Major General Albert E. Brown, with no Alaskan experience, was soon relieved and Major General Eugene M. Landrum, who had directed the occupation of Adak, replaced him. I divided my time during the battle between General Landrum's tent in Massacre Valley, from which we could see action, and the seaplane tender *Casco* under the command of Commander William Everett Cleaves, who gave all his orders with the courtesy usual in civilian life, but exceptional in the armed services, especially in wartime.

The brightest event in the Aleutian campaign was the defeat in March 1943 by a naval task force, under the command of Rear Admiral Charles Horatio McMorris, of a Japanese force twice its size and firepower. But the long-planned recapture of Kiska ended somewhat ingloriously. The island had been shelled continuously by a reenforced fleet and bombed from the air for three weeks. A tremendous invasion-force had been assembled under command of Vice Admiral Kinkaid—over thirty thousand combat troops including a regiment of Royal Canadian infantry. When they landed, they found that the Japanese were no longer there; they had been evacuated two weeks earlier by submarines. Nevertheless, some of our men panicked in the fog and believing that Japanese were still there, shot each other. Twenty-four died at the hands of their comrades and fifty were wounded.

The war came very close to me in other ways. On August 5, 1944, I received a telegram which read: "The War Department regrets to inform you that your son Huntington is missing in action." He had volunteered early in the war, had been trained in California, achieved a second, then a first lieutenancy, and was attached to the Eighth Air Force in England. I did not dare tell Dorothy and kept this terrible news to myself for a week. Then came the joyful tidings that Huntington was "interned in a neutral country."

He had had two engines shot out of his B-24 by flak in a raid on Kiel. It was his eleventh mission over Germany. He knew that he could not make it back to his base in England, so he had turned his plane north-ward and landed in Sweden. He was made an air-inspection officer. After some months there he was flown back to his base in England by Colonel Bernt Balchen, who was conducting this secret route of return. Under the rules of war, Huntington was not allowed to resume active combat duty.

Our younger son Peter also had a passion for flying. He made his first solo flight in Washington on his sixteenth birthday, July 28, 1939—the first permissible date. He volunteered for service, became a fighter pilot and was commissioned a second lieutenant, but to his great regret the war ended before he got overseas.

The war aggravated the problem of absentee control in Alaska, not only in industry and government, but also in labor. I urged Frank Marshall, the local organizer of the American Federation of Labor, to start an Alaska Territorial Federation of Labor. Up to that time decisions affecting Alaska's organized labor had been made in union headquarters in Seattle, San Francisco, Indianapolis, and these decisions invariably favored non-Alaskan workers. Seattle-based unions dominated employment in the canneries and in the fishing grounds, and the industry favored them. Longshoring in Alaska, which should have provided wholly local employment, was in part performed by the seamen who manned the commercial vessels, thus adding to their seamen's pay and taking wages that should have been earned in every Alaskan port by resident dock workers. Then in 1943 a convention was called in Juneau of delegates from all local unions and central labor councils, and the Alaska Territorial Federation of Labor was born. It was an important first step.

We were winning a corresponding battle with absentee government. Navy headquarters had been moved from Seattle to Kodiak, and the army's from the Presidio in San Francisco to Elmendorf. But during the war, the Coast Guard's headquarters in Ketchikan was moved to Seattle. I fought for its return. A board headed by Admiral Richmond made a study and recommended it be returned to Juneau. I abstained from any effort to determine where in Alaska the district headquarters should be; my concern was merely to get it back to Alaska.

LEFT: *Lieutenant Huntington Gruening*

ABOVE: *Second Lieutenant Peter Gruening*

Delegate Dimond had been offered and had accepted the judgeship in Alaska's Third Judicial District. But who was to succeed him in his important post as the territory's only representative in Congress? He had to carry a burden that in a state would be shouldered by never fewer than three men—two senators and a representative, all with votes. Three well-known Alaskans announced their intention of running: Henry Roden, a former senator and now attorney general; A. H. Ziegler, former mayor of Ketchikan and a leading attorney there, both of whom would run as Democrats; and L. V. Ray, also a former senator and a prominent Seward attorney, as a Republican.

I thought that Bob Bartlett, who was just forty, would make an excellent delegate and urged him to run. But he felt that all his opponents were too well-known and that he lacked the political know-how, and the necessary funds. I told him he could be elected and that I would raise the money. He continued to be reluctant, but he decided to run. I swung around the territory and sang Bob's praises everywhere. I raised $3500 which in those days was enough. Informed opinion did not concede much chance for Bob; but he carried the primary, and with the Democratic tide running high, won the general election, starting a long career of effective public service to Alaska. As his successor as secretary of the Territory, I proposed Lew Williams, the editor and owner of the Wrangell *Sentinel* and he was appointed.

I thought that the people of Alaska would want to make some gift to Tony Dimond in appreciation for his long service, and the response to my initiative was more than generous. I was able to purchase four paintings by Sydney Laurence, two watercolors by Joseph Kehoe and a beautiful silver tray from my friend, William Spratling, master craftsman, who had revived the silvercraft industry in his shop in Taxco, Mexico. I also opened the proceedings of the House Committee on Territories in the Capitol, which honored Tony Dimond. The many words of praise he received from his colleagues were both sincere and well-deserved. He had been a great delegate and would acquit himself no less well as a judge.

The war, which had touched Alaska's shores, was by this time retreating to the far reaches of the Pacific. But that did not lessen the military's absurdly restrictive policies. A small hospital in Petersburg was in danger of closing because it could not get a trained nurse. The nurse who had worked there, the wife of a Coast Guard officer who was stationed in the town, had been sent out of Alaska when war was declared two years earlier, in conformity with the Alaska Defense Command's order that wives of service personnel should be evacuated. There was now no good reason why she should not return. The commandant of the Coast Guard was willing, but the decision rested with the Alaska Defense Command. So I wired General Buckner, asking that the nurse be readmitted. A telegraphic reply signed "Gault, Adjutant," curtly said "Request denied."

I was puzzled by this answer, and so was Tony Dimond. Together we drafted a letter to General Buckner, stating in detail the reasons for our request, which were simply matters of common sense. In reply I received a telegram referring to the previous denial and the original evacuation order. This one was signed "Shick, Adjutant."

My relations with the military had been most friendly. I had considered it my obvious duty to cooperate with them in every way and had never failed to do so. My relations with General Buckner in particular, had been cordial. But now I was forced to conclude that cooperation with the military was no longer a two-way street. Shortly thereafter, the Alaska Defense Command requested my approval for the withdrawal of Fire Island "for the defense of Anchorage." Fire Island lay just off Anchorage at the head of Cook Inlet where it was joined by the Turnagain and Knik arms. The war was nowhere near Anchorage, and it was ludicrous to consider it necessary for defense purposes. I wired back:

"Only reason for the withdrawal of Fire Island is to supply duck-hunting ground for the brass. Request denied."

Then I received a letter from a Mrs. Frye in Kodiak. She was the wife of a soldier stationed there; her presence which had escaped the vigilance of the military had now been discovered, and she had been ordered evacuated. She had just given birth to twins and she wrote that she had no close relatives or friends in the States and that her evacuation with her infant sons would constitute a great hardship. She pleaded with me to intercede with General Buckner.

Thinking that this time, perhaps, I would have better luck, I wrote General Buckner giving all the obvious reasons why an exception to the evacuation order should be made for Mrs. Frye. A reply came back, not from an adjutant, but from General Buckner himself: "I shall decide this matter as I see fit." The evacuation order was not lifted. I could see no justification for such a needlessly haughty attitude, and I wired Warren Taylor, a Kodiak attorney, to get out an injunction against General Buckner's action. I also requested George Folta, who had been assigned to me as counsel for the Interior Department, to appear in my behalf as "a friend of the court." I admit I was incensed and I wrote to Warren Taylor that I hoped he would make those twins as famous as Romulus and Remus.

Legal action proved unnecessary. Shortly thereafter General Buckner was transferred to the Pacific and Major General Charles H. ("Pete") Corlett, the friendly commanding officer at Kodiak, canceled Mrs. Frye's evacuation order. General Buckner was killed in action on Okinawa on the eve of our victory there, and I have always regretted that we were not able to patch up our differences. But I still feel very strongly that military encroachments upon the civil rights of any citizen must be implacably resisted, even if they are imposed in the press of a wartime emergency. The long-established practice of subordinating our military establishment to civilian control, a practice that is fundamental to a democracy, must be vigilantly guarded by every citizen, and by the officials they have chosen to represent them.

21

POSTWAR "PROGRESS"

*There is nothing more arduous than the
apprenticeship of liberty.*
— ALEXIS DE TOCQUEVILLE

The war put Alaska on the map. Its new highways and airfields would be the tools of postwar progress, and many GIs who had served there would stay, infusing new life, ideas and energy into the territory. My message to the enlarged legislature in January 1945 was directed at the need for taking care of our returning veterans, not merely by legislation especially designed for them, but by transforming Alaska into a land of opportunity that would benefit all its citizens. And I was hopeful that, at last, the necessary social and economic reforms would not fall on deaf ears in the legislature.

One reason for my optimism lay in the fact that the powerful canned-salmon industry was enjoying unprecedented prosperity and profits and might therefore modify its opposition to revenue reforms. The federal government, itself a large purchaser, had guaranteed salmon prices at approximately one hundred percent above what they had been in prewar years. Costs had risen only a fractional degree, and these were more than offset by the industry's relief from brokerage charges, advertising and other selling expenses. Perhaps now the industry would be willing to stop biting the hand that fed it. Another reason for my optimism was that gold mining had been suspended during the war as inessential, and because of the reduced revenues from gold, other tax legislation would be required. The gold lobby as an ally of the canned-salmon lobby would be eliminated.

I urged the legislature to enact veterans' benefits, to create a development board as every state in the Union and our sister territory Hawaii had long since done, a Department of Health with a full-time health commissioner, and concomitant appropriations to combat our shocking incidence of tuberculosis, a Department of Agriculture, a Department of Taxation to ensure that the few taxes that were levied would be collected—they had been largely evaded, especially the $5 so-called school tax, the only contribution nonresident fishermen, placer miners and construction workers were asked to pay—a teachers' retirement act, a housing agency, a recompilation of our laws, a referendum on statehood, some improvement of our labor legislation, increased salaries for our territorial employees, and, of course, revenue reforms. Those proposed in 1941 but not enacted, had been revised, and among them was a new measure which would both produce revenue and achieve a needed social and economic reform—a progressive fish-trap tax.

As it turned out, I was too optimistic; lobbyists still exerted a powerful influence over the members of the Senate, although their influence in the House was on the wane. A case in point was the fate of Representative Stanley McCutcheon's bill "to provide benefits for returning veterans." It passed the House, sixteen to eight, but in the Senate it was referred to the Committee on Finance and Corporations—composed of Allen Shattuck, chairman, Frank Whaley, Ed Coffey and Leo Rogge—which reported a unanimous "do *not* pass" and kept the bill buried in the committee throughout the session.

Fortunately, an antidiscrimination bill fared better. I put as much feeling as I knew how into an appeal for this legislation, and I was cheered by the presence in the joint assemblage of the newly elected "native" legislators, Frank Peratrovich and Andrew Hope. The antidiscrimination bill was introduced by Edward Anderson, the former mayor of Nome, who had promised me that he would not allow the theater segregation incident there to recur. It passed the House with little debate by a vote of nineteen to five, but when it came up in the Senate, it was violently opposed by Allen Shattuck. "Far from being brought closer together, which will result from this bill," he said, "the races should be kept further apart. Who are these people, barely out of savagery, who want to associate with us whites with five thousand years of recorded civilization behind us?" Frank Whaley also opposed the bill, saying that he did not want to sit next to Eskimos in a theater; they smelled.

According to established legislative custom during the debate on the bill, an opportunity was offered to anyone present to voice his views. A young woman, Mrs. Roy Peratrovich, rose in the gallery and said she would like to be heard. She came to the floor, crossed it and sat next to the president on his raised platform. The packed gallery was tense with expectation; clearly passage of this bill would spell profound social change in Alaska.

"I would not have expected," Elizabeth Peratrovich said in a quiet, steady voice, "that I, who am barely out of savagery, would have to remind gentlemen with five thousand years of recorded civilization behind them of our Bill of Rights. When my husband and I came to Juneau and sought a home in a nice neighborhood where our children could play happily with our neighbors' children, we found such a house and had arranged to lease it. When the owners learned that we were Indians, they said 'no.' Would we be compelled to live in the slums?" Mrs. Peratrovich went on to give other instances of the discrimination she had encountered. She was a beautiful woman; her intelligence was obvious, her composure faultless, and her plea could not have been more effective. When she finished, there was a wild burst of applause in the gallery. The Senate passed the bill, eleven to five. A new era in Alaska's racial relations had begun.

The fight to regulate fish traps also provided its dramatic moments, but in this case the outcome was not so successful. Opposition to fish traps was widespread not only because of the fishermen's antagonism, but because they represented a crude and highly lucrative vested interest enjoyed by a very few, almost wholly nonresidents. Because of Alaska's Organic Act, enacted by the Congress in 1912 under pressure from the California and Washington State salmon interests operating in Alaska, the regulation of Alaska's fisheries was retained in the federal government and there was no territorial fishing agency. The legislation under consideration, House Bill 35, proposed a territorial fisheries commission which would, hopefully, regulate fish traps in a way that would favor individuals and residents rather than the large absentee corporate interests. I knew that fish traps could not be abolished completely; it would have been impossible at that time since the federal Fish and Wildlife Service of the Interior Department, under the directorship of Ira Gabrielson, was not troubled by the monopolistic and absenteeist aspects of the present setup, but favored fish traps and would have prevented their abolition. House Bill 35 proposed a system of progressive taxation on fish traps; to the existing $200 tax, $100 would be added for each trap under the same ownership, reaching a maximum of $1600 for chain ownership of any traps above fifty. In addition there would be a tax of $2 per thousand for all fish caught over a hundred thousand. It was estimated that these taxes would produce $1,200,000 for the biennium, as well as diminish the evils of monopoly and absentee ownership.

The House enacted the bill, nineteen to five. In the Senate the bill was referred to the Committee on Taxation and Revenue which reported it favorably with two dissents. It was then referred to the Committee on Finance and Corporations which brought in a unanimous "do *not* pass" report. Thereupon a motion was carried on the floor that the Senate resolve itself into a Committee of the Whole to consider the bill, and that Mr. W. C. Arnold, representing the canned-salmon industry, be heard. Arnold made an able presentation, saying that the tax provisions were confiscatory and discriminatory. He felt that singling out absentees for discrimination was unfair; they were all good Americans interested in Alaska, and he identified and gave personal tribute to the individuals who headed the absentee corporations.

Senator Frank Gordon then requested that Representative Warren Taylor be heard in favor of the bill. At the request of Senator Joseph Green, Frank Marshall, president of the Territorial Federation of Labor, was also heard in its favor. Mr. Arnold was then heard again, as were Taylor and representative Peratrovich. Then at the request of Senator Frank Gordon, I was asked to appear. I was called from my office, went to the floor and reiterated the arguments I had used in my message. When I had finished, Senator Walker spoke up and said, "Governor, I used to think after World War I there would never be another war. I was wrong. So I've decided to vote against this bill." It was a perfect *non sequitur*. But it was the first intimation that Walker would vote against the bill. He had assured me he was for it, but he had also assured me that he supported my tax proposals—and had been instrumental in defeating them.

The suspense was prolonged by having action on House Bill 35 postponed until the following day. From the moment the doors opened the galleries were packed. The House recessed and its members filed in and stood at the rear of the chamber. I had decided to listen and sat in the gallery. So did Arnold.

Eight votes were cast in favor of the bill and eight against. It was a tie and the bill was defeated. The canned-salmon lobby had won a tremendous victory against public sentiment. Further, it appeared that the Senate had no desire to ascertain just what the public sentiment was when it defeated a bill sponsored by Peratrovich in the House to provide a referendum on whether fish traps should be abolished.

Now only six days were left in the session. Much good legislation had been enacted by the House and was awaiting action in the Senate. There were over twenty of these bills, some of which were noncontroversial, such as a bill to provide for the much-needed compilation, annotation and publication of the statutes of the territory. It had been requested by all four district judges and by every bar association in the territory, but it would be an expensive project.

Some desirable measures that I had recommended were enacted. Bounties on eagles were abolished, but there was still the obligation to pay for the claws turned in during the previous four years. My veto of the necessary appropriation in 1941 and 1943 did not relieve the territory of its responsibility to pay. 128,273 eagles had been killed while the legislation was in effect. Fortunately, they had not been exterminated, and multiplied rapidly so that I later felt justified in offering some to any state with a similar habitat that wanted them, provided the Alaska legislature agreed.

The referendum on statehood had passed unanimously in the House and in the Senate, fifteen to one. So had the antidiscrimination bill and measures providing for a full-time Commissioner of Health with a modest appropriation to combat tuberculosis, an Alaska Development Board, a Department of Agriculture and a Housing Authority. A teachers' retirement bill had also passed, and a measure to increase their salaries and those of all other territorial employees by fifteen percent. Old age assistance was increased from $45 to $60 a month; and unemployment compensation, rejected in both previous legislatures, was enacted.

The problem was that, except for a one-cent-a-gallon tax on motor fuel and a slight increase in liquor taxes, no new revenue measures had been enacted. Before the session, the Territorial Board of Budget had estimated a deficit for the biennium of $1,655,576. And now there were all these additional commitments. How were these obligations to be met? After the cannery interests had defeated the income- and property-tax bills, it became known that they had, as their spokesmen in the Senate put it, "come to the rescue" of the territory in the previous sixteenth assembly by paying an additional nickel-a-case tax; and although the tax was good for two years only and not a permanent levy, they were again planning to assume their role as territorial savior by a similar offer. However, their offer, which was embodied in Senate Bill 53 and sent to the House, was not quite as "generous" as the one offered in the preceding session. The cannery interests would pay four cents a case on "pinks" and eight cents a case on "reds," but for one year only. The measure would have added a paltry $250,000 to territorial revenues, about one-tenth of what was needed for each of the coming two years.

It was the fiftieth day of the session, the last day on which bills could be received from either house without a two-thirds vote. With several vital tax measures passed by the House still pending in the Senate, the House waited until the next day to see what the Senate would do. Noting no action there, the House then amended the Senate four- and eight-cent bill by adding a zero to each of these figures and making them apply for both 1945 and 1946. This, in the absence of all other revenue measures, would have provided approximately $2,250,000, just about what the territory needed for the biennium. The Senate rejected it and conference committees could not reach agreement. The House modified its stand and reduced its figures, but the Senate conferees refused to alter the original bill and finally voted to postpone it indefinitely.

I reviewed the performance of the legislature in another "Message to the People of Alaska," discussing the important measures that had been enacted and defeated and naming those who had been for and against. In describing the deadlock over the canneries' offer, I wrote:

In my view, it was improper and undignified for the Territory to put itself in the position of "accepting" as a gift a crumb which the canned salmon industry graciously offers the people of Alaska from its sumptuous banquet table. What this proceeding amounts to is that the chief lobbyist for the canning industry comes to Alaska, surveys the situation and tells the legislators how much, or rather how little, they may spend, and graciously offers to make up the modest deficit provided only it is modest enough. He is to be the judge; and his pliant and compliant emissaries in the Legislature accede to his estimates. This is a wholly unworthy and humiliating position for a great Territory which aspires to be a sovereign state. The correct attitude for the Territorial representatives in both houses, if they represent the people of Alaska, is to determine what expenditures they shall make and then to *impose* the necessary taxes. If the Territory wishes to assume the degrading position in which it would have found itself had it accepted the miscroscopic 4 and 8 cents one-year tax, it would be selling its birthright for less than a mess of pottage.

My message bestowed high praise on the House, which it fully deserved, and pointed out that the Senate "had petered out in a shabby fiasco." It had not even gone through the customary final ceremony of adjournment, notifying the House and the Governor that it had concluded its business. This disorganization brought about one fortuitous occurrence at the very last minute: it raised *all* territorial employees' salaries. I had urged this course of action, pointing out that their salaries were substantially below the federal scale, but it met opposition from the Senate Finance Committee. It was returned to the House but came out of a groggy conference with a fifteen percent raise tacked onto every salary based on the April 1, 1943, stipends regardless of any previous raises. As the final draft applied the increase to "all other territorial employees" and repealed "all acts in conflict with this act," it included all schoolteachers and the university faculty, which was more than I had hoped for.

After the session adjourned, I finally woke up to the unpleasant truth that Senator "Doc" Walker had been double-dealing with me. He had volunteered early in my term as governor to assist me in every way; I had accepted his offer in good faith, and considering him an experienced legislator, I had asked his advice and discussed my ideas with him. He had expressed unqualified support for my tax program; yet it was he who had moved to postpone the income-tax bill indefinitely after it had passed the House. Needless to say he would have been under no obligation to support my efforts, but when he vouchsafed full accord with them and offered to support them, I assumed he was a man of his word. I was now informed that the canned-salmon industry had financed his campaigns for election in 1932 and 1936, and had assisted him financially when his drugstore was in difficulties during the Depression. Had it "planted" him on me to find out what my plans were? That would scarcely have been necessary since in my addresses around Alaska, to Chambers of Commerce and service clubs, I made no secret of my hopes and purposes. I said nothing to "Doc" Walker, but he was obviously aware that I was now "on to him" and he began a campaign of definite hostility. He became a sort of Dr. Jekyll and Mr. Hyde, charming and gracious one moment and vicious beyond reason the next.

The canned-salmon industry's methods to influence other senators became clear after the 1945 legislative session. Ed Coffey, who had come to the House as a fisherman's candidate in 1937, was reelected in 1939, and then elected to the Senate thereafter, had been set up in the insurance business with the canned-salmon industry's multiple policies as his reward for services which he thereafter rendered faithfully. Grenold Collins, a young impecunious aviator, blossomed out after the 1945 session as Libby, McNeil and Libby's western representative, with an office on Anchorage's main thoroughfare and a brand-new twin-engine plane. Bob Hoopes, who had been a mucker working on the creeks near Fairbanks, was now the owner of a new filling station. Leo Rogge had also been rewarded. Dropping into the office of the Wrangell *Sentinel*, while her ship stopped on its way north, Mrs. Rogge had burbled, "Leo and I have just had the most wonderful trip to Seattle, courtesy of Mr. Arnold." Stanley McCutcheon told me, and it was confirmed by Warren Taylor, that they had been offered $25,000 between them if they would oppose the progressive fish-trap tax legislation. The offer was made through a fellow legislator.

I had secured a kind of respite from any organized hostility from the canned-salmon industry and its minions by my relative passivity during the 1943 legislative session. I had not followed that session up with a "Message to the People of Alaska." But now that I had, after the 1945 session, openly attacked the canned-salmon industry's methods, it would make every effort to discredit me. My renomination and confirmation for the governorship in 1944 had taken place without opposition, but that would not happen again. The campaign against me would have the support of most of Alaska's newspapers: "Cap" Lathrop's *Fairbanks News Miner*, and his *Anchorage News*, the *Ketchikan Fishing News*, edited by

Sid Charles, and the Alaska *Daily Empire*, whose editor, Helen Troy
Monsen, had reversed her earlier friendly attitude. She was, of course,
under the influence of her attorney, Herbert L. Faulkner, partisan and
attorney for absentee interests, and her hostility was no doubt intensified by my accidental discovery that the royalties for the *Alaska Guide*
by Merle Colby, a WPA project, had been deposited to former Governor
John Troy's account while he was living and to his estate after his death.
The discovery came when a letter to my office was found to contain a
check for several hundred dollars made out to Troy from the Macmillan
Company, the book's publishers. In Alaska, as in the States, the governor
was the official sponsor of the project, but the royalties were due to the
United States Treasury. When I discovered this, I had to bring it to the
attention of federal authorities, which thereupon sought reimbursement
from the Troy estate. It required action by the United States Attorney,
Patrick Gilmore, to bring this about.

The year 1945 was both a happy and a tragic one. It brought the victorious conclusion of the most destructive war the world had ever known,
but even before that victory, it also brought the death of one of the
world's great statesmen, Franklin Delano Roosevelt. The President had
made a special trip to see me in Alaska the year before. "Sim" McKinnon,
who had been my naval aide in the first months of my governorship and
had become chief of staff to the Alaska Naval Command, called on me in
August 1944 to ask whether I could be in Juneau on a certain day. I told
him I was planning to be in Anchorage. He said that an important visitor
was coming to see me, but when I asked who it was, he said he was not
at liberty to tell. It was not difficult to guess, and I agreed to stay. On the
appointed day, Captain Gordon MacLane of the Coast Guard and I went
to Auke Bay where the cruiser *Baltimore* was anchored: Admiral Leahy
and General Watson greeted me cheerfully as we climbed up a rope lad-
der, and there, with cheerful greetings of his own, was the President. At
lunch he said, "Ernest, do you remember what they would call this
weather off the coast of Maine? The down-easters would say it was an
'open and shet day.' "

After lunch we went fishing in one of the ship's launches. The President caught a halibut and a flounder, and I, two salmon. "We'll have
them for dinner tonight," Roosevelt said. It was a jolly occasion, and at
5:00 P.M., the *Baltimore* weighed anchor and departed.

That visit had an intriguing background which dated from my fight
against Byron Price's attempt to single out Alaska for wartime censorship.
After the third hearing by the Senate Judiciary Committee at which
Price was again sharply criticized, I had heard from Secretary Ickes. He
told me that Steve Early had come from the White House to tell him to tell

me that the President wanted me to lay off Byron Price. Knowing of the close relationship between Price and Early, I conjectured that Price had gone to Early with a complaint against me, and then Early had sold the President the idea of sending him to tell Ickes that I was to stop attacking Price. Actually I had stopped after the first hearing.

I had a few days left before my return to Alaska and I went to see the President. But for the first time I was not permitted an appointment, and I could tell from General Watson's attitude that I was not to speak to him under any circumstances. This was a blow because I felt that had the President known all the facts he would have seen me, and that my actions had been misrepresented to him. I had the unhappy feeling that I had lost my entree to the White House.

So when I learned that the President was coming to Juneau, I thought it was part of a planned itinerary. But both Admiral Leahy and General Watson each made a point of taking me aside to tell me that the President had put into Auke Bay for only one purpose—to see me. And the President, while not saying so in so many words, had nothing of particular moment to discuss that would have justified the visit. It was out of the *Baltimore's* course. Except for a brief nap after lunch, the President spent all the ship's six hours in port with me. Perhaps he knew that my feelings had been wounded and sought to lay that hurt to rest.

I had no difficulty in seeing the President when I called at the White House the following December. The "Battle of the Bulge," the last desperate German counteroffensive of the war, was on. The President was deeply worried about our casualties and was not receiving visitors. I was the only official caller that day. It was the first time I had ever seen him other than his usual debonair and buoyant self. He looked depressed and thin.

The news of his death the following April came as an unexpected shock. Dorothy and I loved that man. The next generation may need to be reminded that he surmounted crippling polio and labored through our country's longest and most burdensome presidential years in a wheelchair, able to stand only with the discomfort of steel braces on his legs and with the support of someone else's arm. Yet he was always blithesome. Serious conferences were brightened by his gaiety and enlivened by his mirthful quips. "If I've accomplished nothing else," he said to me once, while discussing caste and class in America, "I've shifted the seat of power from the Metropolitan to the Cosmos Club." He shifted much more—indeed, the course of history. He lifted our country out of its worst Depression with no violation of democratic procedures, and carried the nation to victory in World War II. Historians will, I am convinced, rank him with Washington, Jefferson and Lincoln.

At home, his innovations were denounced as "socialistic": unemployment compensation ("Imagine paying people for not working!"), Social Security, bank-deposit insurance, the minimum wage, public power—but they have all endured. A patrician, he and his wife were idolized by the plain people. I had this feeling brought home to me as early as the fall of 1936 when I dropped into the Saint Botolph Club in Boston and was hailed by some of the club regulars with friendly derisiveness: "You and Charlie Warren (the historian of the United States Supreme Court) are the only members who are really for Roosevelt." But when I signed for my room the British-born clerk, who had heard this remark, said, "Yes, the members seem to be hostile to Mr. Roosevelt, but I shall vote for him and so will all the boys who work here."

Because of the variety of problems I encountered as director of the Division of Territories and Island Possessions, I was able to see Roosevelt often. I was always impressed by his knowledge of the situations on which I had come to brief him, and by his receptiveness to new ideas. He seldom rejected them out of hand. When something novel was proposed, his reaction often was "Let's try it."

When President Harry S. Truman took office, he issued a general invitation to the governors to come and see him when they were in Washington. But hearing that he would be in the State of Washington in June, I thought that would provide a good opportunity to see him, so I wired Matt Connelly, his secretary, asking for an appointment. He replied that the President would be in Olympia as Governor Mon Wallgren's guest and I would have to make my arrangements through him. So I telephoned Mon who invited me to come down.

President Truman was most agreeable. We had lunch on the lawn of the governor's mansion; the only other guests were Senator Magnuson and Nick Bez, a Seattle cannery man. I told the President about the impending referendum on statehood and asked him if he could see his way clear in his first State of the Union Message to Congress next January to give statehood a "plug." Without hesitation he said he would.

After the rejection of measures to aid Alaska's veterans by the 1945 legislature, I made up my mind to call a special session with the announced purpose of enacting them, which I figured would make legislative opposition more difficult. Opponents to veteran's legislation in 1945 had advanced the lame excuse that the war was not yet over, and that we should wait until it was, although several hundred veterans had already returned. The unexpectedly rapid collapse of our enemies and the war's end with V.E. Day and V.J. Day coming in rapid succession nullified that argument. So I called a special session of the legislature in 1945 to convene in March 1946 when most of the GIs would have returned and would be

Felix Frankfurter   *Charles W. Ervin*

breathing down the legislators' necks. Some additional proposals were also to be pressed at the special session. Our incidence of tuberculosis—nine times greater than in the States—imperatively required action. The 1945 legislature had appropriated only a paltry $30,000 a year for it.

Veterans' legislation fared well in the special session. The Alaska World War II Veterans Act set up a commission of five members with a paid executive, a commissioner of Veterans' Affairs, to administer the act. It provided loans to veterans up to $2,500 for educational, domestic and other purposes, and up to $10,000 to acquire homes, farms, fishing boats and gear, or mining equipment. It fixed the interest rate at four percent, one-half that currently required by banks. The bill also provided a bonus of $10 for each month of military service. If veterans who had elected to take the bonus wished also to have a loan, they could have it by repaying the bonus. After one loan had been repaid, the veteran could borrow again. The only serious argument about the bill was over the method of financing it. I urged a bond issue, for which I knew we would get Congressional approval, but I lost that part of my plea. The bill provided a tax of one percent on the revenue from all retail sales and services, and one-half of one percent from the revenue of wholesale sales and exports, until the sum of $3,500,000 had been collected, which would then become a revolving fund, replenished by the repayment of the loans. The veterans' bill passed the Senate, twelve to four, and the House, twenty to three.

Frank Gordon   *Hubert Clinton Herring*

The legislature also appropriated $250,000 for combating tuberculosis, authorized the acquisition of small medical hospitals which would be declared surplus by the army as well as medical supplies and equipment, acquisition of a motor-vessel that would be used as a floating clinic along Alaska's coast, and several other health measures. This legislative action was stimulated by the effective presentations of the newly appointed Commissioner of Health, Dr. C. Earl Albrecht, who had come to Alaska as a Moravian medical missionary, settled in the Matanuska Valley and had served as the senior surgeon at Fort Richardson. A dedicated public servant, he also went to Washington and secured the authorization and the necessary appropriation for a native hospital in Anchorage where tuberculosis for the first time received adequate treatment, a step which marked the beginning of the effort to compensate for a long-standing neglect which had cost many Alaskans' lives.

In addition, the special session approved a land-registration act which required real property owners to register their holdings with a small fee, which if unpaid for a time incurred foreclosure; it was a means of recovering the property of owners who had abandoned it, left the territory and could not be located, thus representing an attempt to solve an increasingly prevalent mortmain problem. The legislature also raised teachers' salaries and established minimum wage-levels, and at long last enacted adequate workmen's compensation and a retirement system for all territorial employees. The session also legislated much needed revenue measures. It imposed an additional pack tax of ten cents a case on king salmon and four cents on other species, and adopted, in modified degree, the progressive fish-trap tax which it had rejected in 1945. A corporation operating more than three traps would pay an additional $200 per trap for all over ten, and $4 per thousand for all fish above one hundred thousand caught in any one trap.

It was with great pleasure, therefore, that I was able to say in my "Third Message to the People of Alaska:"

> Considering that the Extraordinary Session lasted only 30 days, its achievement will in my judgment rank as high as that of any legislature in Alaskan history. For this accomplishment the members of the Legislature and the people of Alaska are to be warmly congratulated.

After the message appeared, Senator Frank Gordon, who had consistently supported my efforts, said to me, "Governor, you were altogether too kind. The lobbyists succeeded again in avoiding any basic taxation, and in fastening a sales tax on the people. Considering the fortunes the fish-trap operators have been making, these little increases are peanuts. The canned-salmon lobby is unreconstructed, and they will continue to fight you when our needs are going to be crucial."

"I hope you're wrong, Frank," I said. "It was a relief to be able to praise the legislative performance for the first time."

Frank Gordon who, to my regret, had decided not to run again for the Senate, was right; he was wiser than I was, as I would learn. Actually there was evidence of trouble in that very session. Senate Memorial No. 1, introduced by Senator Norman R. Walker, asked "the Honorable Harry S. Truman, President of the United States, the Congress of the United States, and the Honorable Julius Krug, Secretary of the Interior, to remove the present governor from office with all possible dispatch." It passed by a vote of nine to six. But minutes later, the House adopted House Memorial No. 2, introduced by Representative Stanley McCutcheon: "That the House of Representatives commend Governor Ernest Gruening for his efforts in behalf of the people of the Territory of Alaska . . . and that a copy be dispatched to the President of the United States." It passed by a vote of sixteen to seven.

This hassle had its amusing aspects. Invited by Senator Gordon to appear—if I wished—to answer the charges against me while the Walker Memorial was being debated, I accepted, and told the Senate that "it is a privilege to be invited to one's own execution." The charges were that I had used my office for political purposes. Senator Walker also produced a troller who had given an affidavit published in the *Empire* that I had called him to my office and talked politics with him whereas he wanted to discuss fish prices. The story was wholly manufactured, and when I consulted the United States Attorney about possible action, I discovered that the man had a long criminal record under three aliases and had served time for forgery. The Associated Press reported on the hearing as follows:

> After a big build-up, the Senate's hearing on charges brought against Governor Gruening proved a flop. The chief executive was able to show that most of the sallies launched at him were based on opinion or trivialities.

In spite of my difficulties with the Senate, the veterans' bill would in time prove to be the most valuable piece of legislation enacted thus far —and possibly thereafter—in my terms as governor. It not only benefited thousands of veterans whose economic stability it established, but gave Alaska's economy a tremendous and continuing lift. Without it, the thousands of homes and business activities, as well as the educational opportunities it made possible, would never have come into being. It was variously amended and amplified through the years, but the capital it furnished at low interest rates, totaling $53,795,605 by the end of 1972, gave Alaska's population the beginnings of a permanence which it had lacked.

Other important changes were in the wind for Alaska. Earlier that year I went to Washington after the Christmas holidays and was happily on the House floor in January 1946 when President Truman, in his first State of the Union Message, magnificently fulfilled the promise he had made to me the previous June in Olympia. If the people of Alaska in the forthcoming referendum on statehood voted for it, he hoped that the Congress would enact legislation granting it. He urged similar action for Hawaii. He was the first President to endorse statehood for Alaska.

Then in February, Secretary Ickes, who had made no secret of his differences with the Truman Administration, submitted his resignation to the President, saying, however, that there were matters that still needed his attention and that he wanted to make his resignation effective some weeks hence. The President considered this stipulation a bluff and accepted his resignation as of the next day. Oscar Chapman became acting secretary and virtually everyone in the department hoped and expected he would become Secretary. He had served as a member of the so-called junior cabinet for fourteen years, longer than anyone in American history, and was respected and liked. It had apparently been President Truman's intention to offer him the post, but he was visited by Bernard Baruch and John Snyder, Secretary of the Treasury, who persuaded him to appoint

Ernest Gruening thanking President Truman for his statehood support

Julius A. (Cap) Krug, a utility executive with a reputation as a good administrator. Oscar Chapman was made Undersecretary.

I welcomed Ickes's retirement. His relations with the Division of Territories and Island Possessions had been marred by arbitrary actions and arrogant interference. Unfortunately, Ickes's good qualities—battling effectively for a worthy cause, which he had done on various occasions —were more than offset by his shortcomings. Chapman informed me that Ickes's last act before leaving office was to take five cases of Virgin Island rum with him. It had been a matter of amusement in the department that, in his occasional entertaining, this government-manufactured product, which he appropriated free of charge, would be the sole alcoholic beverage served. Other actions similarly belied his sobriquet of "Honest Harold." The chickens and eggs from his farm at Olney, Maryland, which he sold, would be delivered in a government car, fueled by gas paid for by the government, and driven by a chauffeur on the federal payroll, prerogatives which he would never have tolerated in a subordinate. When he was invited to speak, as he often was, he would exact a handsome fee and travel expenses, then assign himself to an official errand in the region and also collect transportation costs from the government.

John F. Kennedy, Lyndon B. Johnson and Ernest Gruening at the 1960 Democratic Convention at Los Angeles

Two of his chief executives, Nathan Straus, director of Housing, and Far-rington Carpenter, director of Grazing, told me of specific instances when Ickes had done this.

After he left office, an elaborate recording apparatus was found—and removed—from the lower righthand drawer of his desk; he had used it to record conversations with visitors without their knowledge. Senator Clinton P. Anderson of New Mexico told me that he was once the victim of that kind of snoopery. Ickes excerpted what he wanted from Anderson's recorded conversation and sent it to an individual about whom the Sena-tor had been led to make statements that could be interpreted as disparag-ing. In a speech on the floor of the Senate several years later, Senator An-derson referred to those one thousand pounds of recording equipment and another eight-hundred-pound apparatus removed from the Secretary's private dining room.* Yet Ickes posed as a great libertarian. Earlier in my newspaper days, I had learned to be wary of men who wanted to be known as "Honest Dan" or "Honest John." "Honest Harold" was the great myth of the New Deal.

* *Congressional Record*, page 9682, June 21, 1956.

Secretary Krug started off well. He made an excellent impression in Alaska in the course of a ten-day visit which included seldom-seen Barrow, and, having listened to every Alaskan who wanted to be heard, he devoted himself on his return to Alaska's accumulation of problems.

Alaska's inadequate transportation by sea, air and land, and the effort to improve all three, would be a major concern during the next several years. Alaska needed an overland route from the Atlantic Coast along the Great Circle, a route that would also be the shortest passage to the Orient. The Anchorage Chamber of Commerce conceived the idea of sending a group on a chartered plane over the proposed route and enlisting support in the key cities along the way. I joined the party. In Washington we were welcomed by Secretary Krug and received by President Truman. The only discordant note came from Senator Hugh Mitchell of Washington who said he would seek a Congressional investigation of my participation. "I intend to ask why the governor of Alaska," Mitchell told the press, "can spend so much time in Minnesota, Illinois, Indiana and Washington in the interest of a private commercial airline which wishes to by-pass the traditional transportation lines through Seattle which have served Alaska in the past and must serve the territory in the future."

Mitchell was mistaken in saying that we favored any one airline; we were interested only in the route. But his insistence that Alaska must be served through Seattle echoed the narrow, selfish, colonialist outlook of his predecessor, Senator Wesley Jones, who had fastened the strangulating Jones Act on Alaska. Mitchell's attitude, however, was not shared by Congressman Henry M. Jackson, later senator, who with his colleague, Warren Magnuson, never allowed the presumed interests of Seattle to work to the detriment of Alaska.

Shipping to Alaska was also in a state of chaos. In addition to the excessive maritime freight rates, Alaska was subjected to a series of shipping tie-ups in which it was held as a hostage. The situation again pointed to the need to develop alternate supply routes to what in terms of transportation were virtually two islands—southeastern Alaska and western Alaska. Some relief, before the shipping situation became desperate, was furnished by army supply vessels. This and a battery of other problems would confront the next session of the territorial legislature, but instead of moving to solve them, my adversaries in the Senate spent most of their time trying to get rid of me.

The Eighteenth Territorial Legislature, convening in January 1947, began explosively. Senator Walker had announced his candidacy for the Senate presidency. He was nominated by Senator Ed Coffey and seconded by Senator Joe Green. Gunnard Engebreth, a newly elected Republican senator from Anchorage, nominated Andrew Nerland, and the nomination was seconded by Earnest B. Collins of Fairbanks, Republican, also newly elected. He, as well as another newly elected Republican senator, Charles D. Jones of Nome, had served in the House in the First Territorial Legislature in 1913. When the roll was called, Senator Victor Rivers, Democrat, newly elected, and Frank Peratrovich, who had come to the Senate from the House, abstained from voting, thereby permitting Nerland to win. The Senate was still Democratic by a margin of nine to seven, but the House, for the first time in more than a decade, had swung to a thirteen to eleven Republican majority, and elected Oscar Gill, Republican of Anchorage, as Speaker. Up to this time Alaska's legislatures had been overwhelmingly Democratic since the Roosevelt landslide in 1932.

The abstention of two fellow Democrats which lost Walker the presidency of the Senate triggered an incredible speech. Walker rose and in a voice trembling with anger said, "This day, like Pearl Harbor, will live forever in infamy. Christ said, 'One of you will betray me,' but two"— and here he held up two fingers—"have betrayed me. They will wear the badge of infamy, the curse of Judas Iscariot, and the brand of Cain unto their dying day. I've been a Democrat since I was old enough to vote, but I am filled with shame to have such men representing the party here. These men are Benedict Arnolds. They are bereft of all decent concepts."

There was dead silence in the packed galleries following this outburst. Rivers and Peratrovich rose to assert calmly that they were good Democrats and considered their abstention in the public interest. They resented Walker's performance in the 1946 special session and his subsequent vigorous campaigning in the 1946 election for legislative candidates who would support the "Walker bloc" in both houses. He had been only partly successful. Frank Whaley had been defeated for reelection. His opposition to the antidiscrimination bill and the revelation of his olfactory sensitivity to Eskimos had lost him their votes, and veterans resented his indifference to their needs and that, although an able-bodied aviator, he had not served in the armed forces. Alaska Linck and Curtis Shattuck, candidates for the Senate, had also been defeated on the basis of their House records, as had Harvey Smith for the House. But Walker had been successful in defeating for reelection to the House Jess Lander and Warren Taylor from the Fourth Division, Stanley McCutcheon from the Third, and Joe Krause and Chris Hennings from the First. He had also tried—unsuccessfully—to unseat Steve McCutcheon who had been elected to his father's Senate seat after the senior McCutcheon's death. It had become known that in order to achieve his objectives Walker had offered Republican candidates his support. So Democrats outside the "Walker bloc" were not critical of Rivers's and Peratrovich's abstention. Andrew Nerland was a widely respected figure. He was president of the Board of Regents of the University of Alaska and was known for his scrupulous fairness.

In my message to the legislature, I again reviewed the territory's needs. The influx of population rendered school expansion and enlarged university accommodations essential. Federal funds for airport and highway construction were available on a uniquely favorable three-to-one matching basis, but to take advantage of them required revenues. In the eight months since the establishment of the Office of Veterans' Affairs, the revenue from the Veterans' Fund sales taxes had proved insufficient to take care of the applications. We had advanced 896 Alaskan veterans $1,539,000 in loans and paid $236,000 in bonuses. But 353 loan applications were waiting unfulfilled, and more would shortly come. It was clear that the avoidance of adequate revenue legislation during the past four sessions, coupled with new and greater demands on the territory's treasury, required immediate action. I again outlined a number of possible revenue measures, but a few legislators had other business on their minds.

Senator Green promptly introduced Senate Bill No. 1 and Representative Oscar Gill introduced House Bill No. 1. These were, in the parlance of the Juneau *Empire*, designed "to strip the Governor" of all the powers conferred upon him by the legislature. The two versions differed slightly. The House bill was "laid on the table" thirteen to eleven; the Senate version passed the Senate, twelve to four, but was defeated in the House, seventeen to six. However, other attempts to curtail my function followed in quick succession. A bill by Senator Walker to remove the governor from the Board of Administration and replace him with the attorney general was amended in the House on motion of Representative McCutcheon and seconded by Edward Anderson to restore the original language. After lengthy conferences there was no agreement and the bill died.

Then Senators Coffey and Green introduced a bill to abolish the Development Board. This was also intended as a slap at the governor. Coffey, in his public attacks on me, had stated that as long as I was governor no new business would come to the territory. This was part of the theme that my efforts to secure tax measures would "affright capital." He attributed the Republican gains in the 1946 election to my actions, but actually those October elections foreshadowed a nationwide trend which, in the States in the November 1946 elections, resulted in the Republican Eightieth Congress. Alaska had again proved a reliable political barometer.

The Coffey-Green effort to abolish the Development Board did not meet with popular favor. The Board was rightfully credited with saving the people of Alaska vast sums by successfully opposing the maritime freight increases. It was also at that time trying to secure a pulp mill in Ketchikan, working to overcome the obstacles which had long prevented such an industry from coming to Alaska, an effort that would shortly succeed. The bill passed the Senate by a vote of nine to seven. In the House it was defeated by a tie vote twelve-twelve. But that was not the end of the campaign. The next incident in the comedy was a memorial introduced by Representative Hoopes "that the Office of the Governor of Alaska be declared vacant and that Senator Walker be appointed to fill the vacancy so created." It was obvious that Walker, and not Hoopes, had written the memorial, since it was full of high praise for Walker. The memorial was treated with much levity by the galleries and was defeated, thirteen to eleven.

And so it went. As the session was drawing to a close, it was depressingly evident that not only would it follow the bad example of the 1941 and 1943 sessions but would do even worse. One good revenue bill after another, if it survived a House vote, would be unceremoniously killed in the Senate. One of the evidences that the 1947 legislature was hitting a new low was the disgraceful way it treated President Bunnell. This able and dedicated educator, through whose almost unaided efforts the University of Alaska had been kept alive during the twenty-five years of his presidency, was heckled and sneered at when he presented the needs of the territory's one institution of higher learning. As a result of the attitude of legislators who argued that "it would be much cheaper to do away with the university and let students go 'outside,' the university was a shabby, rundown, inadequate plant staffed by a wretchedly underpaid faculty. President Bunnell presented only four humble construction needs and a request for operating expenses that totaled $1,321,530. He also hoped for a southern branch of the university in southeastern Alaska. In response, a House bill by Anita Garnick of Juneau and Frank L. Johnson of Kake for $250,000 for the university was passed by the House, thirteen to eleven. The five members of the Fourth Division who were from Fairbanks to which the university was adjacent—A. F. (Joe) Coble, Robert Hoopes, Maurice Johnson, L. F. Joy and Lawrence Meath—all voted against it. The Senate declined to receive it.

In another "Message to the People of Alaska" I again reviewed the irresponsible performance of their legislators. I pointed out how they had failed the veterans, how they had forfeited federal three-to-one matching funds for airfields and highway construction, and how—incredibly— they had incurred obligations approximating three and three-quarter million dollars more than anticipated revenues, all of which, in my view, came pretty close to being a collapse of responsible government. Finally, it was necessary to call the Board of Administration to freeze all expenditures while we tried to decide just how the territory's meager revenues should be spent.

The university was left high and dry, and to prevent its closing I took it upon myself to borrow money against the assumption that the next legislature would be responsible for the debt—a risky assumption in view of past legislative performances. Fortunately, James Wooten, president of Alaska Airlines, offered on behalf of the company to lend $25,000 to the territory without interest. Other corporations felt obliged to follow suit, but Alaska during the next two years went through a difficult crisis.

The delinquent legislators began to hear from their disgruntled constituents, and several of the worst offenders, including Doc Walker, asked me to call a special session to meet the crisis. I refused and added, "I'm hopeful that by waiting we'll get a legislature that will do what you now promise to do. I haven't forgotten all the promises you've broken in the past." But I confess I was discouraged. I began wondering whether I had not wasted six years.

22

ALASKA TURNS THE CORNER

*The mode in which the inevitable comes
to pass is through effort.*
—JUSTICE OLIVER WENDELL HOLMES

My preoccupation with Alaskan affairs could not preclude interest and participation in the affairs of the nation as a whole. In fact, I think I may have had something to do with a change in the course of American history. If I did, it came about in this way.

As a territorial governor, I attended the fortieth annual Governors' Conference at Portsmouth, New Hampshire, in mid-June, 1948. The proceedings followed this established routine. Four subjects were selected for general discussion at round tables attended by approximately one-fourth of the governors, and these subjects were given a preliminary discussion and ideas were exchanged at a breakfast attended by the governors assigned to each round table. Almost at the start of the breakfast I was attending, Governor Thomas E. Dewey of New York led off by saying: "The most important thing this Governors' Conference can do is to expose the teachers' lobby. They come into every state when a legislature is in session and work for higher salaries. The fact is they're overpaid. They work only five days a week and only forty weeks in the year. They're the biggest liars since Adolf Hitler."

The outburst took the ten breakfasting governors by surprise. Its intemperance astounded us. We knew that Dewey would, before the end of the month, be nominated as the Republican Party's candidate for the Presidency and would in all likelihood be elected. So there was dead silence for several minutes. Then Governor James H. Duff of Pennsylvania asked, "Are you going to bring this up at the general meeting?"

"Yes, I am," said Dewey, "but I'm going to move to make it a closed session and exclude the press and the public." At this there was even greater astonishment. Such a move would be without precedent; these general discussions had always been open to the press and the public.

"What do you propose to have the Governors' Conference do?" asked Duff.

"I want the Conference to hire two of the best public-relations men in the country, and if necessary, pay them $50,000 apiece to show up that lobby."

The governors were again dumbfounded but few wanted to tackle the next President of the United States. Dewey was asked several questions about his experiences with the teachers and his answers made clear that he and they had been at swords' points.

When we gathered for the general meeting, the galleries were jammed. After the address of welcome by Governor Charles M. Dale of New Hampshire, the embarrassing task of requesting the visitors in the galleries to leave fell to Governor Horace Hildreth of Maine, the conference's chairman. Governor Dewey then reenunciated his proposal to start a publicity campaign to show up the teachers' lobby.

Again there was a stunned silence among the assembled governors. Then Governor Earl Warren of California, who two weeks later would be nominated as Dewey's running mate, said, "Tom, out on the coast we wouldn't know what you are talking about. In my state many of our teachers are paid less than the school janitors."

Dewey was not to be crossed. "Ever since you raised the minimum to $2400 in your state of California," he said, "our teachers have been crying for more. Your action forced me to agree to a minimum of $2000. Our teachers are mighty well paid, what with promotions, retirement, only five-days-a-week work and three months off in the summer. I'm going to fight that lobby with everything I've got. We get only about $30 worth of education for every $100 we pay. If the Governors' Conference will stage a counter campaign, I'll double my state's contribution to the conference."

Only one other governor, Thomas I. Mabry of New Mexico, arose in opposition. "In my state," he said, "we are short about six hundred teachers. Common labor gets a dollar an hour. I see no reason why the governors should take action against the teachers such as you propose." The other governors remained silent. It was clear from their total lack of support for the proposal that none of them shared Dewey's views, but it was no less evident that few wanted to tangle with the probable next President of the United States. In the end, the conference quietly ignored Dewey's proposal.

I was outraged to think that someone with these views could be our next President. They ran counter to ideas which I held deeply and had expounded time and time again in my messages to the Alaska legislatures, urging increases in teachers' salaries. In fact, only a year before, at the Governors' Conference in Salt Lake City, I had expressed the view that teachers are the most important element in our society, the people to whom we entrust the teaching of our future citizenry. I also rebelled at Governor Dewey's effort to clap press censorship on ideas and intentions which he had freely expressed to over forty governors. I felt the public had the right to know. Perhaps my journalistic background motivated me; it was a "good story" and there had been no injunction of secrecy placed on the governors. So that night I telephoned Drew Pearson and, finding him interested, sent him a written account of what had happened. He released the story a week later in his widely syndicated column, "The Washington Merry-go-round," but not before he had checked by telephone with some of the governors who had also been at that breakfast —whose names I gave him—and so had heard Dewey level his blast at the teachers twice.

After the story appeared and had attracted the attention of teachers, members of parent-teachers associations and others, a denial was issued by Jim Hagerty, Dewey's press man. This led the Democratic National Committee to check with several of the governors who had been at the conference. Some of the Republican governors were reluctant to be interviewed but Democratic governors confirmed the truth of Pearson's column.

Dewey was nominated for President at the Republican National Convention a few days later, but his attitude toward teachers was not forgotten. It was discussed at great length at the eighty-sixth annual meeting of the National Education Association in Cleveland the second week in July. Telegrams were sent to the four presidential candidates asking for their views. Replies were received from Harry Truman, Henry Wallace and Norman Thomas and were printed in the record of the proceedings. But no reply came from Thomas E. Dewey.

It should be recalled that throughout the 1948 presidential campaign, the pollsters, political commentators and editorialists were unanimous in forecasting Dewey's election. Truman's victory was the greatest surprise upset in the history of presidential elections. The electoral college vote was Truman 303, Dewey 189, a difference of 114 votes. But Truman's majorities in a number of states were so small that I have often wondered if Dewey's violent attack on teachers which I helped expose, and which mobilized the members of the profession and their friends and relatives as well as parent-teachers groups to vote against him, may not have been the reason for his unexpected defeat.

Even before Truman's surprise reelection that November, the voters of

Alaska, who went to the polls in October, came up with a surprise of their own. At long last Alaskans realized how an effectively organized minority in the legislatures had betrayed their interests and had left the territory in a deplorable state. The performance of the 1947 legislature had finally revealed in all its crudity the complicity of absentee influence and seducible legislators. At their next opportunity, the people of Alaska acted in conformity with a recurring American tradition. They "threw the rascals out," and the 1948 elections marked a turning point in Alaska's history.

The territory's financial crises had become so acute—with unpaid bills, unpaid teachers, and other overdue obligations such as veterans' loans and bonuses exceeding $3,000,000—that I decided to call a special session of the legislature two weeks before the regular session to start clearing up the staggering mess. The legislators wasted no time. House Bill No. 1, levying a net income tax, was introduced on the second day, followed in minutes by House Bill No. 2, levying a property tax.

The Alaska income tax was based on a new approach, wholly different from the drafts which had been rejected by the preceding three legislatures. As I had come to see, to the pain incident to paying an income tax was also added the headache of making it out. The average taxpayer was confronted with the dilemma of either not recording his income and deductions adequately and risking penalties, or of overpaying and thus defrauding himself. In states having income taxes, as most states had by then, this annual anguish had to be undergone twice a year, once for the state tax and once for the federal tax. Why not eliminate one of these calculations?

So I had proposed that our territorial income tax be geared to the federal income tax which would save the taxpayers at least one headache. It would also simplify checking and collection since territorial authorities would have access to the individual's federal income tax and could rely on the vigilance of the Federal Bureau of Internal Revenue. The 1949 Alaska income tax was based on ten percent of the federal, which subsequent legislators might raise or lower; but apparently this was a new concept, and I was amazed that more states had not adopted this obvious formula.

The regular session moved to enact additional revenue reforms including a uniform business-license tax, a tobacco tax, an augmented fish-trap-license tax, raw-fish taxes, and increased fishermen's-license taxes. These measures provided revenue from sources which had previously yielded little or none.

They did not go unchallenged, however. During the third week of the session, Winton C. Arnold came to call.

"Sit down, Judge," I said to him cheerfully. Arnold had been a United States Commissioner at Hyder, a magistracy below the federal judiciary, but he enjoyed being given the title of judge.

"No, I'll stand," he replied. "What I've got to say won't take long. I've come to serve notice on you that we're not going to pay those taxes. They're outrageous, they're confiscatory; we're going to take all of them to court and meanwhile we'll tie you up with injunctions so you won't be able to meet your payrolls."

"That's very interesting, Judge," I said. "But why tell it to me? Why not go down to the second floor and tell it to the legislators who are passing these tax bills?"

"Because this is your legislature," said Arnold.

"Do you mean the others have all been yours?" I asked.

Arnold did not answer. If he had, it would have had to be in the affirmative. He had been an effective lobbyist. The canned-salmon industry did take all these tax measures to court. But with the exception of one minor aspect of the fish-trap bill relating to the tax on trap-caught fish, every one of the measures was sustained.

In my view, education had to be one of Alaska's top priorities, both at the school and university levels. These new revenues would provide the funds necessary to meet the territory's educational needs by building adequate school facilities and by paying teachers the salaries they so richly deserved. But the legislature did not stop there in its attempt to right past wrongs. The veterans' sales tax fund, terminated by the 1947 legislature, had ceased to operate. I asked for and got its restoration. Failing in its efforts to abolish the Development Board, the 1947 legislature had not voted it funds. Even so the board had managed to survive on a much reduced and inadequate basis. I asked for and received restoration of its funds. I likewise requested and secured funds for housing which had reached a critical shortage, for a retirement fund for territorial employees, for improvement of labor legislation, for the reestablishment of the National Guard, and for a fisheries commission which would prepare the way under statehood for control and conservation of Alaska's greatest natural resource. I also asked that a Statehood Commission be set up that would help speed the day of the full self-government that statehood would bring, and that request, too, was granted. And among many other sorely needed reforms was an act barring billboards on Alaska's highways so that visitors would not have to peer at the splendor of Mount McKinley between signs proclaiming the relative virtues of "Old Crow and Old Grand-Dad."

Working with enthusiasm and indifference to long hours, the legislature truly merited this enduring tribute: "The Nineteenth Legislative

Assembly did what eighteen previous legislatures were unable to do."
These words were uttered on the closing night of the session, March 24,
1949, by Senator Andrew Nerland, born in Norway, veteran of twelve
legislative sessions, and the man with the longest and most distinguished
record of legislation in Alaska's history. Admittedly Alaska's elder statesman, he added that this had been "the best legislature in the territory's history."

My subsequent "Message to the People of Alaska" summarizing the
performance of the nineteenth legislature was full of unqualified praise.
Thinking of the territory's history, I wrote:

> In Alaska few, if any, fur seekers, gold rushers, seasonal migrants
> to the canneries and fishing grounds, and finally the traders and re-
> tailers, came with any thought of permanent residence. Theirs was
> not the traditional purpose that has animated Americans from the
> landing of the Pilgrims and that carried their descendants across the
> Alleghanies, the prairies and the Rockies. There was no vision of
> hewing a home out of the wilderness for their children. With "get it
> and get out" a widely accepted practice, with little invested in civic
> improvement, health and welfare, in roads, in community facilities,
> Alaska offered scant prospect of realizing the American dream. The
> 19th legislature, however, turned a new page in Alaskan history. On
> that page, the elected representatives, responding to an awakening
> consciousness throughout the Northland, wrote the decision to make
> Alaska henceforth a creditable example of the American way of life.
> Their legislation spelled out the desire of an ever-increasing number
> of Americans to consider Alaska their home.

I knew now that my years in Alaska had not been wasted, but as my
second term as governor drew to a close, rumors flew, both pro and con,
about my reappointment. It was opposed by Alaska's absentee mining,
steamship and salmon-canning interests, and their retainers in the territory
who included some of the legislators who had served those interests. One
daily newspaper in each of Alaska's four principal cities was violently opposed to my reappointment. A rumor that had circulated widely for years
was that State of Washington politicians subservient to Seattle-based
canned-salmon and steamship interests could influence Truman, to whom
they were close, and that Nick Bez, the Seattle canneryman whom I had
met in Olympia in 1945 when I had lunched with President Truman and
Washington's Governor Wallgren, had his foot in the White House door.
This report proved unfounded. When Interior Secretary Krug presented
his recommendation for my reappointment, the President told him that he

had never had any intention of not renominating me, and he sent my name to the Senate that same day, March 12, 1947.

However, it would not be acted upon for over a year. The Republican Eightieth Congress, following the counsel of Senator Hugh Butler of Nebraska, chairman of the Committee of Interior and Insular Affairs, decided they would wait rather than attempt to defeat my reappointment, which did not seem a promising prospect. They expected a Republican president to be elected the following November who could be counted on to nominate a Republican for governor, allowing my unconfirmed nomination to die on the vine.

Their expectations were in vain. Truman was reelected. With the Democrats again in control of the Eighty-first Congress, I hoped that my renomination would be confirmed, as it had been on two previous occasions, without a hearing. But after Senator Joseph O'Mahoney, the new chairman of the Committee on Interior and Insular Affairs, decided to hold one, the opposition press in Alaska not only hailed this as a great victory but assumed that it would result in my rejection. By the time of the hearing on April 1, 1949, there had been such a build-up of publicity that the large caucus room in the Old Senate Office Building was filled to overflowing. Eleven of the thirteen committee members were present seated at a long table, bathed in klieg lights facing the press.

"Cap" Lathrop had chartered a plane to bring five witnesses to oppose my confirmation. This delegation included an attorney, A. H. Ziegler of Ketchikan, who would act as ringmaster. When their mission became known, Stanley McCutcheon, legislator and Anchorage attorney, and others chartered a plane whose cost was shared by those who came to support my renomination. As the hearing opened Austin E. Lathrop, his secretary, Miriam Dickey, Ziegler and the witnesses who opposed my reappointment were gathered at the committee's right. There were, however, forty-five witnesses facing the committee ready to testify on my behalf. They included a wide diversity of professional, business and working men and women, as well as Indians, Eskimos and Aleuts. They had filled the plane and many who wanted to come had to be left behind.

The first of Lathrop's witnesses, Frank Angerman of Fairbanks, a machinist and a Representative in the previous session of the House, testified that I had pressured him in favor of reestablishing the National Guard which he, representing a labor viewpoint, had opposed. The next witness, George Miscovich, a placer gold operator who had also served for the first time in the last session of the House, charged that I was trying to repeat in Alaska my Puerto Rican efforts at a "planned economy." He testified that I was "encouraging radical elements," that I had opposed absentee ownership without which "the territory would be no place," that I

Fifty-five Alaskans en route to testify for Governor Gruening's confirmation

for a third term, 1949

was building "the most powerful political machine ever seen in Alaska," that I had "broken up the Republican Party" and would do the same to the Democratic. He was, however, unable to cite specific facts, and his prepared statement had a literary quality which was not in accord with his educational endowments. The explanation for that came out in the testimony of the next witness, Charles D. Jones of Nome, a senator in the last two legislatures.

"When all else fails," he said, "Gruening plies the legislators with cocktails and cultured conversation in the governor's mansion amid surroundings more luxurious than most of these unpretentious Alaskans from mining and fishing communities and Eskimo villages have ever seen before." Then suddenly Jones put down his prepared statement and said, "Oh, I don't talk like this."

"Do you mean that you did not write this?" asked Senator O'Mahoney.

"Of course not," he replied.

"Who did then?" Senator O'Mahoney inquired.

"Cap Lathrop's secretary."

There was a reaction among the large audience in the hearing room.

"How would you have said it, in your own words?" asked Senator Anderson, with a twinkle.

"Well," said Jones, "he gives them plenty of booze and lots of conversation."

There was widespread laughter. The audience was attending a good show.

"May I suggest, Mr. Jones," said Senator Anderson, "that the Committee would greatly prefer to have every bit of it just as you have given it in your own language."

Jones complied. "Let me tell you, brother," he said, "the way he is throwing it out, you know, we have an expression, that what he peddles makes the grass grow green on the Kougarok. He's got it. Dairy farmers know what it is."

Other witnesses came forward, but the revelation that their statements had been ghost-written clearly damaged their testimony. Cap Lathrop, complaining that I had consistently sought larger appropriations for the Alaska Development Board, charged that I opposed the entry of capital to Alaska and that while awaiting the committee's decision on my renomination he had "stopped plans on building." He tempered his criticisms gracefully by saying, "Governor Gruening . . . is in my view a fine man. I like him in many respects; I like him because I get ideas from him."

Marcus Jensen, a Douglas merchant, in addition to repeating that I had dominated the previous legislature, charged laxity in the Territorial Veterans' Administration, which was true, but had been corrected by the discharge of the responsible official. Attorney Ziegler apparently felt that the hearing was not getting the desired results. He testified that he "sincerely believed, as do thousands of other Alaskans, that the welfare of the people of Alaska demands the rejection of confirmation," but because it was impossible to get people to testify to the damaging facts, he suggested that the committee send an investigator throughout Alaska who would "tell the people that their answers to him will be kept strictly confidential." Only in that way, he claimed, would the committee get to know the true picture. Senator Eugene Milliken opposed such "a ridiculous suggestion." "Mr. Chairman," he said, "I think it is perfectly obvious that we cannot approve or condemn a man in confidence. If we visited Alaska and merely had . . . people whispering in our ears, but refusing to get on the stand and testify, where would we be? . . . . We cannot condemn or approve a man on that kind of stuff."

With that the committee recessed and announced it would hear the proconfirmation witnesses in the afternoon. But when it reconvened, Ziegler announced that he had one more witness, Representative Robert Hoopes. Hoopes entered breathlessly, saying that he had just come off a plane and had not even had time to shave. Ziegler stated that Hoopes, who had earlier presented a written statement, had an important supplemental statement that he wanted to wait until Monday to file. Chairman O'Mahoney agreed.

Stanley McCutcheon came forward on my behalf, stating that there were forty-five witnesses that were "about the best cross-section of the people of Alaska you will ever see." After his testimony, Chairman O'Mahoney limited further testimony to seven additional witnesses but asked McCutcheon to introduce and identify the others. None of those who testified was cross-examined by the committee. In fact, Senator O'Mahoney told me after the hearing, "It wasn't really necessary to hear any of them after we had heard the opposition."

I was then asked to present my case and, if I desired, to refute charges of unduly pressuring the Alaska legislatures. I said that there was a good deal of talk about how I dominated the legislature, but while it was somewhat flattering to my powers, it was simply not true. I pointed out that the governor of Alaska has less power than the governors of most states, or even the governor of Hawaii. All of the important officials in Alaska are elected, not appointed; they are wholly independent of the governor and are responsible to no one but the people. As for the question of lobbying in the legislature, I did not deny using what powers of persuasion I had to influence the passage of those measures I thought essential to the territory. I felt it was my duty, as well as my right as a free citizen, to tell people what I think, just as it was the province and the duty of the legislature to modify, adopt or reject my views. And, I added, anyone who knows Alaskans would know that nobody can tell them what to do.

The hearing concluded at 6:40, an unusually late hour. The following Monday, Representative Hoopes brought his unfinished testimony to the committee rooms. He had flown to Texas and picked up copies of the document published seventeen years previously in the Hearst papers about my mission to England at the behest of the Mexican government to stir up the British miners to strike in the interest of world revolution. Senator Anderson then secured a copy of the Senate hearings which had shown that this and all the other documents in that Hearst exposé were forgeries. Calling this to Hoopes's attention he said, "You can present this if you wish, but you are liable to be charged with contempt of the Senate." Hoopes decided not to present it.

The Committee recommended my reappointment by unanimous vote and the Senate confirmed it by a voice vote.

The chief concern of my next, and as it happened my last, gubernatorial term would be statehood for Alaska. The majority of Alaskans had voted for statehood in an October 1946 referendum, but that mandate was a long way from realization. First it would be necessary to create a large body of favorable public opinion to which Congress would respond, and to overcome some obvious objections: the smallness of our population, which the 1940 census gave as 72,225, and the unprecedented obstacle of our noncontiguity with the other states of the Union. Also there was the prevalent myth, dating from the "Seward's Folly" stigma, that Alaska was a "land of snow and ice" unfit for human habitation—at least by white men. That obstacle, too, had to be overcome, so I accepted as many invitations as my gubernatorial duties would permit to present the case for statehood. My campaign and Alaska's cause were aided by a *Time* cover, which pictured me with the forty-ninth star, and a friendly feature article. And also in our favor was Alaska's strategic importance in the postwar antagonism between the United States and Soviet Russia.

The impact of the so-called Cold War hit hard in the State of Washington. In August 1949, the people of the Puget Sound area awoke to a horrible reality. The Air Force had decided to move the Boeing plant to Wichita, Kansas. Boeing was Seattle's largest industry, employing 25,000; the pending move would dislocate between fifty and seventy-five thousand people. Boeing employees would have to choose between losing their jobs or selling their homes and moving halfway across the United States to start life anew in unfamiliar surroundings. Either alternative would be a disaster both for the community and for the families affected. The Seattle Chamber of Commerce called a meeting of all concerned to see what, if anything, might be done. Its President, Nat Rogers, asked me to attend. My relations with the Chamber of Commerce had not been particularly friendly, but I was glad to accept.

When the meeting assembled, present in the large ballroom of Seattle's Olympic Hotel were the state's leaders in politics, finance, business and labor. And at one side of the head of the table was the state's congressional delegation. They all looked glum. Stuart Symington, secretary of the Air Force, began by explaining to the concerned citizenry the reasons for this fateful decision. Tall, handsome and personable, Symington said that while it was regrettable, it was a military decision dictated by necessity. It had been made by Lieutenant General Kenneth B. Wolfe, Deputy Chief of the Air Force for Materiel, who sat beside him in the light blue uniform of the Air Force, but he, Symington, had approved it. Why? Because the Air Force knew that the Russians had great numbers of planes that could fly the 2400 miles from eastern Siberia to the Puget Sound area, drop their bombs on the Boeing aircraft factory and then return to their base; Wichita was 3600 miles away from the Russian bases and therefore out of range.

The members of the Washington delegation voiced a plaintive protest. Everyone agreed it was a terrible thing, but how could they argue against a policy based on consideration of high strategy? Besides, the removal procedure was already underway. I felt no such inhibitions. I had seen at close range the stupidities committed by our military planners in Alaska. Another costly asininity was about to be perpetrated. I was feeling particularly rambunctious when called upon to give my views.

"We, in Alaska," I said, "do not believe in hoisting the white flag to halt the advance of the red flag. What is proposed is a twentieth-century retreat from Moscow, and it will be as disastrous as was Napoleon's in the nineteenth. If the range of Russian bombers today is twice 2400 miles, how long do you suppose it will be before it is increased to twice 3600? The installation in Wichita will hardly be completed before that will have happened. Suppose you do move Boeing. What about the other installations you can't move? You can't move the Grand Coulee and Bonneville dams. Their demolition from the air would be more disastrous than the loss of Boeing. What about the atomic energy plant at Hanford? Are you planning to move that?

"I am shocked that it is the Air Force, supposedly the striking arm of our military establishment, that is initiating this 'turn tail and run behind the Rockies' policy. I am amazed that the flying branch of our armed services, instead of emulating the eagle, the American symbol of air power, should follow the example of lesser birds and pursue a policy that is both ostrich-headed and chicken-hearted."

I could see Symington's face crimsoning. "In my family," I continued, "we've been very partial to the Air Force. Both my sons were Air Corps pilots in the war. But I'm thinking of shifting my allegiance to the Navy whose slogan is still 'Don't give up the ship' and has no plans that I am aware of to move the Bremerton Navy Yard up the Mississippi River. I have never appreciated as much as I do today, the wisdom of Clemenceau's dictum that 'war is too important a matter to leave to the generals!'"

There was a large map of North America hanging next to the Congressional delegation, placed there to illustrate the Boeing problem. I went to it and swung a pointer around the northern and western coasts of Alaska. "If there were a radar screen all along this coast to warn of the approach of Russian planes," I said, "and if we had plenty of interceptor planes in Alaska, the Russians would never be able to fly across Alaska, heading this way. Their planes would be shot down. They would have to fly southwest around the Aleutians and then southeast again, and Puget Sound would then be just as far away as Wichita."

There was a loud burst of applause when I finished. People came up to thank me. Stephen Fowler Chadwick, past national commander of the American Legion, said, "Governor, that was the finest fightingest speech I've ever listened to." Charles Lindeman, publisher of the *Seattle Post Intelligencer* said, "That helluva speech you've made might just save us."

Incredible as it may seem, my suggestion for a radar screen was apparently a new idea to the military planners. A week later, the Air Force rescinded the plan to move Boeing. Three months later it announced that it had transferred $50 million to begin construction along Alaska's Artic and Bering Sea coasts of the Distant Early Warning (DEW) System. It had done so without going to Congress which was not then in session. The DEW line was also extended across Canada's northern border.

A few days after the Air Force reversal was announced, Dorothy received a dozen American beauty roses from President Rogers and I a warm letter of appreciation: "You've saved Boeing. I can't tell you how grateful we all are. Is there anything we can do for you?" I replied that I was delighted with the outcome and there was nothing that I wanted done for me. Alaskans would always be glad to help out their nearest neighbor. But on second thought, since he had asked, there *was* something that the Seattle Chamber of Commerce could do. It had never endorsed statehood for Alaska as other West Coast Chambers of Commerce had done. Mr. Rogers wired back that it would be done immediately. A week later I received a letter from him. He regretted to inform me that all Alaskan matters were referred to and passed upon by the Alaska Committee of the Chamber, and that the committee had decided that it could not adopt a resolution endorsing statehood for Alaska, because that would be political.

I replied, "The so-called Alaska Committee of the Seattle Chamber of Commerce is dominated by men who view Alaska as King George the Third and his ministers viewed the Thirteen Colonies, an area to be ruled and exploited by distant men through their representatives in the colony, but never to be treated on a basis of equality. Two years ago, the Seattle Chamber endorsed statehood for Hawaii. That wasn't political, was it?"

Mr. Rogers then telephoned to ask me to come to Seattle and sit down with members of the Alaska Committee. I said, "No, thank you. I'll come down to thank them after they have done for Alaska what they did for Hawaii." They never did. As the battle for Alaskan statehood progressed during the next decade, one West Coast Chamber of Commerce after another adopted a resolution endorsing statehood, but never Seattle, not even when Alaska statehood, eight years later, was imminent.

An interesting footnote to this episode occurred after I had succeeded in getting the Civil Aeronautics Board to make Portland a co-terminus with Seattle on flights to and from Alaska, the only plus in my otherwise unsuccessful efforts to stimulate Portland to compete with Seattle for the Alaska trade. For this I was taken severely to task by Ross Cunningham, political editor and columnist for the Seattle *Times*. So I dropped Ross a note: "If you'll pause in your booing, you might recall Boeing."

The Defense Department's plan to build a radar screen around Alaska's northern and western coasts proceeded rapidly, but the essential corollary of that warning system, supplying the territory with a sufficient number of fighter planes and other defenses, was completely ignored. In fact, after VJ Day the defenses still under construction in Alaska had been abandoned and no new installations were being built. Our military commanders, a succession of excellent officers, Howard (Pinky) Craig, Nathan Twining, William Kepner, Frank Armstrong, shared my concern. The Russians were within naked-eye view of the coast of Alaska. They were actively developing the region just across the Bering Sea, extending the limits of agriculture farther east and north, bringing in industry and harnessing their rivers. That much was known. What accompanying military development there had been or would be was shrouded behind the Iron Curtain. But certain it was that if the Cold War became hot, Alaska would be the first victim.

With that conviction, I began to campaign as vigorously for Alaskan defense as I was campaigning for statehood. In telegrams to the chairmen and members of the Armed Services Committees of the Senate and House, I said that if Alaska was going to be another Pearl Harbor, let them not say they had not been warned. As a result U.S. *News and World Report* interviewed me, and a five-page interview entitled "Alaska—Another Pearl Harbor?" appeared in their November 18, 1949, issue. In it I expressed my view that Alaska could be taken by a minor-scale airborne invasion. There were only about seven thousand troups in Alaska, and the reason we had no more was that there was no housing for them. And, of course, I emphasized that not only would statehood indicate United States determination to hold Alaska, but that two senators and a representative with votes could do much more to get adequate defenses than a voteless delegate could.

Favorable editorial comment followed and, goaded by it, the Senate Armed Services Committee sent up three of its members, Lester Callaway Hunt of Wyoming, Democrat, Leverett Saltonstall of Massachusetts, and Wayne Morse of Oregon, Republicans, to survey the situation. A slight improvement in Alaska's defenses followed but defense expenditures were far greater on our Atlantic Coast which, in my view, was far less vulnerable. It seemed clear that our only recourse, both for achieving adequate defenses and statehood, lay in mobilizing public opinion.

Ever since Alaskans voted in favor of statehood in 1946, I had been trying to win the support of the governors of the forty-eight states. My first attempt came with the 1947 Governors' Conference at Salt Lake City. The conference had adopted a rule that all resolutions had to be passed by unanimous vote. I appeared before the Resolutions Committee to ask for a pro-statehood resolution and there was some amusement and some opposition. I was told that if a resolution were to be considered for Alaska, there would have to be a similar one for Hawaii. I wholly favored it. I considered Hawaii, with its large population, economic stability and fiscal responsibility, better qualified at that time for statehood than Alaska, which had not yet put its house in order. But the governor of Hawaii, Ingram M. Stainback, was not enthusiastic about statehood and so it fell to me to present the case for both territories. However, he gave statehood lip service, and so two resolutions, one for Alaska and one for Hawaii which I drafted, were approved.

It was a victory, but only the beginning of a long battle. Next year at the Governors' Conference in Portsmouth, New Hampshire, I presented the same resolution and expected that this time it would pass easily. But I got a message from a friendly governor, Roy Turner of Oklahoma, who had just left the Resolutions Committee and said, "You better get down to that meeting. Stainback has been there and told them that communism is rampant in Hawaii, and while he did not say he was against statehood, he left the definite impression that this was not the time to grant it to Hawaii—and if Hawaii is dropped, Alaska might well be too." So I found myself again defending the cause of Hawaiian statehood. Having worked closely with Samuel Wilder King, Hawaii's delegate to Congress and later its governor, and with his successor, Joseph Rider Farrington, editor and publisher of the *Honolulu Star-Bulletin*, I knew that the tales of communism in Hawaii were grossly exaggerated. They were being propagated by opponents of statehood, of whom Stainback was really one, as his later advocacy of "commonwealth" status for Hawaii would demonstrate. Fortunately, I was able to sway the committee, and statehood resolutions for both territories were adopted for a second time.

There was no difficulty at the next Governors' Conference at Colorado Springs in 1949. For Oren Long, a strong advocate of statehood, had become Hawaii's governor, and later would be one of its first two senators. Thus our two Pacific territories presented a united front at both this and the next Governors' Conference at White Sulphur Springs. But the following year in Gatlinburg, Tennessee, an unanticipated obstacle appeared. Governor Frank Luasche of Ohio was presiding and as he went down the list of resolutions, they were unanimously approved by a chorus of "ayes." Then, last, came the statehood resolution for Alaska and Hawaii. There was a hearty chorus of "ayes," but when he called for those opposed, there was one loud "no." It came from Governor Herman Talmadge of Georgia. "The motion is defeated," said Governor Lausche.

There was a breathless pause at this unexpected development. Finally, Governor Alfred Driscoll of New Jersey spoke up. "This resolution has passed four previous Governors' Conferences. Would the distinguished governor of Georgia tell us why he opposes it?"

"I don't mind at all," said Governor Talmadge. "The people I represent are opposed to the admission of any states whose senators are not likely to take our position on cloture." He referred, of course, to the fondness of southern senators for unlimited debate, that is, for the "filibuster" which they were using to block civil-rights legislation.

I rose and began to speak, and after I had talked for about fifteen minutes, I could see that most of the governors were getting fidgety. This was the last item on the agenda and all were anxious to get away. As I continued, Governor Frederick Payne of Maine, who was friendly to our cause and whom I had come to know well when I was a newspaper editor in Portland, went over to Talmadge and whispered in his ear. I continued to speak. Another governor, Sidney McMath of Arkansas, went up to Talmadge. What they were saying, they told me later, was "Please lay off, Herman. This guy is going to keep us here all afternoon." They were right. I was determined there would be no cloture on my remarks.

Finally, Governor Talmadge rose and asked me to yield. He said, "I shall withdraw my vote in opposition to statehood. I want the record to show that I am not voting, but that if I did vote, it would be against statehood." I thanked Governor Talmadge for his gallantry and have never forgotten it.

At the next Governors' Conference in Houston in 1952, it happened again. There, governors James Byrnes of South Carolina and John S. Battle of Virginia, both opposed to statehood for the same reason Governor Talmadge had been, joined him in announcing their opposition to the resolution but abstained from voting so that the resolution would not be defeated. That was the last time, however, that a resolution for statehood for Alaska and Hawaii was sought and adopted at a Governors' Conference. President Eisenhower's appointee, B. Frank Heintzelman, who succeeded me as governor, was opposed to statehood, and the last territorial governor, Mike Stepovich, was not an enthusiast. I was fearful that the failure of my successors to seek a statehood resolution in the ensuing six years before it was finally achieved would be used as an argument against it. But public opinion for statehood was rising and the support of other governors was no longer as necessary as it had been, as long as they did not reverse their previous endorsements.

Even more important than the support of the governors was action in the Congress. The first House hearings on statehood had been conducted in April 1947 on a bill (H.R. 206) introduced by Delegate Bartlett. They were led by Representative Fred L. Crawford of Michigan, chairman of the Subcommittee on Territorial and Insular Possessions of the Committee on Public Lands. Crawford had acquired considerable knowledge of our dependent areas and was sympathetic to their problems and needs. The hearings lasted seven days and heard thirty-one witnesses; only three had opposed statehood. My testimony came last and consumed two and a half hours. We had made a good start.

In my first six years as governor I had taken no vacations; I had never felt the need for one. The assignment was stimulating; the trips around the territory and to Washington provided a variety of excitement. But now I welcomed every opportunity to use my accumulated leave to sell statehood. In the decade following the 1946 favorable referendum vote, I delivered over two hundred addresses all over the United States. I talked to service clubs—Rotary, Kiwanis, Lions, Civitans—to women's clubs, American Legion and VFW posts, to conventions, to university and church groups. In some instances I illustrated my lectures with Kodachromes I had taken. With or without slides the appeal was the same. I spoke of Alaska as a land of unsurpassed beauty with its juxtaposition of mountains and sea, its virgin forests, its bountiful variety of wildlife, its riotous flora, its friendly people. But Alaska had its problems, too, and I told of the neglect and discrimination Alaskans had suffered, and of their desire for the equality of statehood. A question period followed each talk, and when the question was asked, "What can we do to help you get statehood?" the answer was quite simple. They could help by writing just three letters, one to each of their two senators and one to their congressman. I also called on the newspaper editors in each city I visited to try to enlist their support for the cause. As a former editor my reception was always pleasant, and in addition to statehood for Alaska we would discuss journalistic problems.

It further occurred to me that a national committee of distinguished Americans supporting Alaskan statehood would be very influential, and I began a campaign of letter-writing and personal appeal to secure a committee of one hundred. When I visited Tokyo, I asked General Douglas MacArthur to join the committee and he replied, "I'll be glad, like Abu Ben Adhem, to lead the rest." By 1949 it was quite a star-studded group.* After their acceptance I wrote each one requesting that he write to his senators and representatives. Many did and their influence was tremendous. Some of them spoke publicly in support of statehood. Eleanor Roosevelt wrote about it in her syndicated newspaper column. The support of William Green and Phillip Murray—respectively the heads of the AFL and the CIO, brought the rank and file of organized labor to our

* The committee consisted of Ellis Arnall, General H. H. Arnold, Rex Beach, Dave Beck, Adolf A. Berle, Jr., Francis Biddle, Sarah Gibson Blanding, Harold Boeschenstein, Governor John W. Bonner, Joe E. Brown, Belmore Browne, Mrs. J. L. Blair Buck, Pearl Buck, Rear Admiral Richard E. Byrd, James Cagney, Arthur Capper, William S. Carlson, Hodding Carter, Stuart Chase, Morris Llewellyn Cooke, Bartley Crum, Homer Cummings, Jonathan Daniels, Jay N. Darling, Clarence P. Decker, John Dewey, Major General William J. Donovan, Michael Francis Doyle, Governor Alfred E. Driscoll, Cyrus Eaton, Jr., Major George Fielding Eliot, James A. Farley, Marshall Field III, Dorothy Canfield Fisher, Douglas Southall Freeman, Ira N. Gabrielson, John Nance Garner, William Green, Joseph C. Grew, John Gunther, Vice Admiral Harry Hamlet, Mrs. J. Borden Harriman, Oveta Culp Hobby, Hamilton Holt, Palmer Hoyt, Rupert Hughes, Croil Hunter, Mrs. Ellsworth Huntington, Eric Johnston, Al Jolson, Jesse Holman Jones, Bishop Gerald K. Kennedy, Robert M. LaFollette, Jr., James M. Landis, Wilbur La Roe, Jr., Herbert H. Lehman, Governor Thomas J. Mabry, General Douglas MacArthur, Archibald MacLeish, E. B. MacNaughton, Governor Sidney S. McMath, Malcolm Muir, Philip Murray, Jeannette Paddock Nichols, Admiral Chester W. Nimitz, Howard W. Odum, Robert P. Patterson, Governor Val Peterson, Cornelia Bryce Pinchot, Daniel A. Poling, Henry Varnum Poor, Grantland Rice, Eddie Rickenbacker, Kenneth Roberts, Eleanor Roosevelt, James Roosevelt, Arthur Schlesinger, Jr., Robert E. Sherwood, Kenneth C. M. Sills, James G. Stahlman, Vilhjalmur Stefansson, Governor Adlai E. Stevenson, John W. Studebaker, Herbert Bayard Swope, Governor Roy T. Turner, Governor Earl Warren, Bradford Washburn, Wallace H. White, Jr., Governor G. Mennen Williams, Joseph R. Wilson, Henry M. Wriston, Wilson W. Wyatt, Alvin C. York and Darryl F. Zanuck.

side. The five-star generals, MacArthur and Arnold, and five-star Admirals Nimitz, "Wild Bill" Donovan, wartime head of the OSS, Secretary of War Robert Patterson, and George Fielding Eliot, writer on military affairs, all gave their assurance that Alaskan statehood would not weaken, but strengthen America's defense.

Partly as a result of these efforts, plus those of the Alaska Statehood Committees whose moving spirits were Robert and Evangeline Atwood, and William L. Baker, Ketchikan editor, the House enacted Delegate Bartlett's statehood bill, H.R. 206, in March of 1950. The Senate hearing the following month would be our next hurdle.

Seeking for a way to get it off to a good start, I telephoned Earl Warren, governor of California, and asked him whether he could attend as one of the witnesses. Without a moment's hesitation, Warren asked, "When do you want me?" I told him the hearing was scheduled for the following Monday at 10:00 A.M. "I'll be there," he said.

I met him at the Washington airport that morning. Given the time difference, he must have arisen at a very early hour. He followed Oscar Chapman, secretary of the Interior, the first witness, who had succeeded Julius Krug in that post. Warren spoke extemporaneously and eloquently, urging "prompt and favorable action . . . on the Alaska statehood bill." In response to a question from Senator Anderson as to how he felt on statehood for Hawaii, he gave Hawaii's cause no less support than Alaska's.

Unfortunately, the Senate took no further action, but clearly I owed Governor Warren a debt of gratitude. When I asked him how much we owed him for his transportation, pointing out that the Alaska Statehood Committee had funds for such a purpose, he declined to accept anything. He returned to California immediately, having come for just that purpose. It was, therefore, a great satisfaction to me the following year to have the Board of Regents of the University of Alaska agree to invite Earl Warren to give the commencement address and allow me to bestow upon him an honorary degree.

With the support of distinguished men like Earl Warren, I knew it would only be a matter of time before Alaska achieved statehood. But if our campaign seemed to proceed by inches, one of the reasons was the Department of Interior's continuing attempts to treat the territory as its own personal fief. This attitude was particularly evident in its handling of Alaska's native population and its efforts to establish native reservations —a policy wholly unrelated to the question of aboriginal or possessory rights. The natives would have no title or rights on these reservations; they would merely become permanent wards of the Bureau of Indian Affairs. Secretary Ickes had begun the policy over my strenuous objections, and it was revived by his successor, Secretary Krug, when he issued orders to set aside a 750-square-mile reservation for Barrow, 2300 square miles in the Kobuk Valley for Shungnak, and one hundred thousand acres for Hydaburg. The residents of each of these areas had not been consulted and when hearings were held subsequent to the order, they all expressed their opposition. But the Interior Department was determined to achieve its purpose. Elections were scheduled, and when the voters in each area rejected the reservation, they were told another election would be held. Meanwhile BIA officials were making every effort to convert them.

Since no one in Alaska—either natives or whites—wanted the reservations, I requested Senator O'Mahoney, chairman of the Committee on Interior and Insular Affairs, to hold a hearing. At it, on February 2, 1950, both Delegate Bartlett and I testified emphatically against the reservations. At about the same time, however, Secretary Krug's resignation had been requested by President Truman for wholly unrelated reasons. Krug had started off well as secretary of the Interior; he had made an excellent impression in Alaska. But he had been neglecting his duties and had become involved in personal affairs inconsistent with his high office. But the reservation program had been, and was being, promoted by Assistant Secretary William Warne and BIA personnel for the sole purpose of keeping the natives as wards and perpetuating themselves as warders. Criticism was so intense, however, that the program was dropped by Krug's successor, Oscar Chapman, who also disapproved of it.

But other factors were working beneficial changes in native affairs. One interesting corollary to the establishment of the DEW line across Northern Alaska was the training of natives to man the stations. RCA, which operated the stations for the Air Force, was at first opposed, but in time was persuaded that hiring and training natives would obviate the costly turnover of white technicians from "down below" who would predictably soon become bored in their isolated Arctic posts and would also have problems of acclimatization. So I urged the BIA to seek an appropriation to pay RCA to train natives in industrial and communications electronics. The BIA cooperated handsomely and allocated $600,000 to train 125 natives. In August of 1962, the first group of ten Alaskan Eskimos and Indians, having completed eighteen-month training courses at the RCA Institute in New York, came to Washington and were received at the White House where I introduced them to President Kennedy. Twelve other Alaskan natives were enrolled in the RCA Institute in Los Angeles and others were being recruited. Thus Alaskan natives were not only provided with useful and well-paid employment, but prepared for careers in electronics.

Another hurdle to Alaskan statehood lay in the difficulty of attracting industry to the territory. Unquestionably, Alaska was rich in natural resources, but at times, they were considered too remote and inaccessible for profitable development. There was no lack of absentee exploitation of those resources that were accessible, and exportable, but Alaska needed industries that would develop, not deplete its resources and would contribute to the growth of the territory. For that reason, I was delighted in 1948 when I received a letter from Richard Mellon introducing J. P. Growden, chief hydraulic engineer of the Aluminum Company of America, headquartered in Pittsburgh. Growden was in Alaska on the lookout for a source of low-cost hydroelectric power, the essential factor in reducing bauxite to alumina, the preterminal product in the manufacture of aluminum. The bauxite would be transported from Surinam. I accompanied Growden on some of his exploratory flights, and he came to the conclusion that one of the finest power potentialities in North America, indeed anywhere, lay at the upper end of Lynn Canal in the Skagway-Dyea area where the waters of the Yukon could be made to drop to tidewater some 2500 feet below. Four years later in August 1952, Alcoa made a sensational announcement; it would invest $400 million in establishing a gigantic plant in the Taija Valley. The current would be supplied by damming Miles Canyon on the upper Yukon and bringing down the water in a tunnel forty feet in diameter through the mountains to tidewater. The plant would process one hundred thousand tons of aluminum annually. It would require the establishment of a community of twenty thousand people. Alcoa's spokesman, Leon Hickman, vice president and general counsel of the company, visualized it as a modern town, a community of families with up-to-date facilities. It was a magnificent project. It would deplete no Alaskan natural resources, use an imported raw material, utilize only the gravity of perpetually falling water, supply a product needed in our economy and give employment to thousands on a permanent year-round basis.

Everyone in Alaska was enthusiastic. The problem of getting the necessary land over and beyond the existing 160-acre limitation on public domain acquisitions could be easily disposed of. I had talked to Secretary Chapman and he had set the wheels in motion. Construction was to start the next spring and we did not want to lose any time. A bill drafted in the Interior Department for prompt introduction at the next session of Congress provided not only for the sale to Alcoa of public domain land at the nominal price of $2.50 an acre, but permitted Alcoa to acquire privately owned land by right of eminent domain. No one questioned the reality of this unexpected bonanza. It was no fly-by-night promoter's venture. It had been announced by the responsible heads of the leading industry in its field and was backed by the prestige of the Mellon family. As might be expected, there was a lot of hasty buying and selling of lots in Skagway. Those who bought were sure of a good thing; those who sold were pleased at their profits but wondered whether they would not have been wiser to hang on for higher prices.

Unfortunately, everyone was in for a great disappointment. By the following January, the sad news filtered out of Canada that the Dominion and British Columbia authorities would not approve the project. They had other plans for their Yukon water, and through the Aluminium Company of Canada would utilize it at a place called Kittimat on the coast of British Columbia. Alcoa authorities appeared stunned; they stated that they had been assured of Canadian cooperation. But the assurances were all verbal; they had nothing in writing. There had been an unfavorable public reaction in Canada to giving away its waters. Hugh Keenleyside, deputy minister of resources in Canada during that period, later told me that there had never been a valid commitment to Alcoa. The mystery remains how so responsible a corporation as Alcoa could even contemplate a $400-million project without a written agreement.

Alaskans would be in for further disappointments in their slow march toward self-sufficiency and statehood. But as early as 1949, Dorothy and I had designed a fifty-star flag which we hung from the governor's mansion, while the official forty-eight-star flag flew from the flagpole in front. We both were confident that two new stars would eventually be added to Old Glory.

23

TRANSITION

It is useless to maintain that social progress takes place by itself, bit by bit, in virtue of the spiritual condition of the society at a certain period in its history. It is really a leap forward which is taken when the society has made up its mind to try an experiment; this means that the society must have allowed itself to be convinced, or at any rate allowed itself to be shaken; and the shake is always given by somebody.

—HENRI BERGSON

Throughout my terms as governor, I made many good and loyal friends in Alaska, and I also made some enemies. Such, I knew, was the nature of any political office, but on occasion even a political enmity can be carried too far. For over a decade I had been vilified by the Alaska *Daily Empire.* Baseless charges were made, and corrections in the form of letters to the editor were denied publication. Press releases from the governor's office were omitted or altered; news stories were not merely slanted but the facts distorted; the editorials were poisonous. Then in the late 1940s, the *Empire* launched a campaign to picture me as procommunist. It was nourished by a report of a California legislative committee, a replica of the House of Representatives Un-American Activities Committee, which "exposed" the so-called Garland Fund. This fund had been established from an inheritance of $900,000 left to a young man, Charles Garland, of a prominent Massachusetts family. Garland had adopted a Tolstoyan philosophy and was both a pacifist and a vegetarian. Believing that inherited wealth should not be accepted, he had decided to decline his legacy, but was persuaded by Roger Baldwin, director of the American Civil Liberties Union, to make it available for liberal causes. And so the "American Fund for Public Service" was born.

A news dispatch from Sacramento reported that I was a director and officer of this fund which, in the prevailing hysteria of the McCarthy era when liberalism and communism were considered to be synonymous, was tantamount to an indictment. It was grist for the *Empire*'s mill; the dispatch was reprinted prominently. As I had never been either an officer or director of the fund, I issued a statement to that effect; the *Empire* printed it with the word "denies" in quotation marks. I had known of the fund through Lewis Gannett, one of my associates on the *Nation* in the early 1920s who was a director, and Roger Baldwin had once asked my endorsement of one of the fund's projects. But there my knowledge ended, and Bob Bartlett, checking with the House Un-American Activities Committee, found that my name did not appear in its records of the Garland Fund and wrote the *Empire* to that effect. I would have been glad, had I been asked, to participate in the rewarding task of giving away these funds to causes that I considered deserving. But I had not been asked, and so I simply stated that the dispatch from California was false.

There the matter lay until three years later when the *Empire* dug up the report on which the dispatch had been based, and on the front page under an eight-column headline, "Red 'Garland Fund' Exposed!" printed photostatic reproductions of three pages of the document. It was the "Fourth Report of the Senate Fact-Finding Committee on Un-American Activities" of the California legislature, and the passages alleging my association with the fund were specifically marked by the *Empire*. This time I wrote Lieutenant Governor Goodwin J. Knight, who had been president of the California Senate when the report was issued, asking him to check on how the misinformation about me had been obtained. Receiving no answer, I wrote again, and Knight wrote back expressing regret that the members of the committee were now scattered and that he had been unable to get a reply from Senator Jack B. Tenney, its chairman. It was obvious, of course, that the *Empire*'s elaborate front-page display of this three-year-old California report was an attempt to tar me with guilt by association, even if that association was nonexistent.

Another issue which attracted far more attention, and was inflated, misrepresented and exploited for weeks, was referred to by the *Empire* as the "Palmer airport scandal." That was its presentation of a legitimate effort by the territory's Aeronautics and Communications Commission to secure the maximum federal matching funds under the existing laws for the construction of an airport in the Matanuska Valley. I was chairman of the commission, ex-Navy pilot George S. ("Tony") Schwamm was its executive officer, and its other members were Sheldon Simmons, Neil K. Foster, Jack Carr and Frank Barr—all well-known Alaskan pilots. In this attempted smear of all concerned, which included Stanley McCutcheon, the counsel for the commission, the *Empire* had the assistance of Nebraska Senator Hugh Butler who was seeking ways to discredit Alaska's statehood efforts. Butler, who had received his information from Alaskans hostile to the administration in Juneau, particularly Marcus Jensen of Douglas, a territorial legislator, denounced the Palmer airport procedure in the Senate and called for an investigation by the Committee on Expenditures in the Executive Departments of which Senator John McClellan of Arkansas was chairman. The subcommittee chairman was Senator Clyde Hoey of North Carolina. Hearings were held in Washington in January 1951, and testimony was taken from civil Aeronautics Administration and territorial officials. It revealed only that the Alaskans had worked closely with and had been guided by the Civil Aeronautics Administration (CAA) in its attempts to secure matching federal funds. But the chief counsel for the subcommittee, Francis D. Flanagan, and its investigator, Carmine S. Bellino, had apparently received their cue from Senator Butler and were eager to secure an adverse verdict which the subcommittee rendered. In consequence, Comptroller General Lindsay Warren issued a ruling that the requested federal funds for the Palmer airport not be granted. The ruling was hailed in the Senate by Hugh Butler and echoed gleefully by the *Empire*.

However, the Department of Commerce, within which the CAA was located, disagreed. It made an investigation of its own and then requested the Comptroller General to reconsider his decision. An investigation by the FBI, which we requested, likewise found that the performance of both CAA and territorial officials had been wholly legal and proper. The federal funds were released and the Palmer airport was built. In fact, Alaska's Aeronautics and Communications Commission, spurred by the energy and determination of "Tony" Schwamm, went on to construct some forty airports and seaplane facilities which withstood the ravages of time, weather and misrepresentation.

The *Empire* finally overplayed its hand and dug its own grave. On September 25, 1952, it splashed the news of the so-called Chilkoot Scandal across its front page. According to the *Empire*, Treasurer Henry Roden, Highway Engineer Frank Metcalf and I had diverted territorial money into a private account in a Juneau bank. The truth was, not surprisingly, a far cry from the *Empire*'s version of the story.

For more than a year a small privately owned and operated steamboat, the *Chilkoot*, had conveyed passengers between Juneau and Haines. It was not a profitable operation and was due to be suspended, but the service was important, for it linked southeastern Alaska with the interior by way of the Haines Cut-off. The Board of Road Commissioners, which consisted of the governor, the treasurer and the highway engineer, decided to acquire and operate the ferry, which it had the authority to do. After several weeks of operation, the crew complained of delay in the payment of their wages. Formerly they had been paid at the end of each round trip, but under government operation, their pay went through the red tape of the auditor's office and payment was held up for weeks. They threatened to quit. Exploring a way to meet this problem, the Board consulted the Attorney General, J. Gerald Williams, who approved a plan whereby the fares collected on each journey were deposited in a special bank account from which the purser of the *Chilkoot* could pay the crew's wages. This simple expedient had been suggested by Treasurer Henry Roden who was a former attorney general of the territory.

The implications of the *Empire*'s news story, however, were clearly that the governor, the treasurer and the highway engineer had diverted government funds for themselves. The story, the headlines and the accompanying editorial were patently libelous. The casual reader, uninformed about the background of the story, could only conclude that all three of us were embezzlers. So Roden, Metcalf and I entered a suit for libel against the *Empire*. We each asked for $100,000.

The case would normally have been tried in the federal district court in Juneau. But then in a syndicated column in the *Empire* titled "Criswell Predicts" there appeared the prediction that "Three self-respecting men will not prevail against a poor lone widow." The "poor lone widow" was, of course, Helen Troy Monsen, owner and editor of the *Empire*, and as this blurb was obviously a local insertion designed to influence public opinion, our attorneys, Buell Nesbitt and Wendell Kay, asked for a change of venue which Judge Walter Hodge granted.

The trial took place in Ketchikan. Herbert L. Faulkner represented the *Empire*, and ironically, the most damaging testimony against the newspaper was given by one of its own employees, Jack McFarland, the managing editor. He said that "the main purpose of the paper seemed to be to find something which would either cripple or embarrass the Gruening administration. . . ." We won the case, and the jury awarded each of the plaintiffs $5,001 damages, of which one dollar was compensatory and five thousand dollars punitive. Judge Hodge rejected a motion for a new trial and Faulkner appealed the verdict to the United States Circuit Court in San Francisco. But concluding that "the record contains a mass of evidence disclosing malice," the circuit court affirmed the verdict of the district court.

Three years elapsed between the two trials, and interest on the awards was added to the final payment. Nesbitt and Kay, who had handled the case most skillfully, averred that Ketchikan was a "low award town" and that if the case had been tried in Anchorage, the award would have been substantially larger. However, Roden, Metcalf and I were not interested in the amount, but in vindication and in checking the kind of defamatory and irresponsible journalism of which the *Empire* had been guilty for a decade. The paper was sold shortly after the publication of the libelous story, partly to pay for the cost of the trial and the awards, and because the other stockholder, Dorothy Troy Lingo, Helen Troy Monsen's sister, realized that the *Empire* could not prosper under her sister's management.

In addition to my battle with the *Empire*, my last term as governor was marked by yet another collision with the Alaska legislature. The 1953 lawmakers swept in by the Eisenhower landslide, were overwhelmingly Republican, and they did not wait long to turn the clock back. The first House bill, to repeal the property tax, was passed by a straight party vote, twenty to four. I vetoed it, and in my veto message pointed out that if the bill passed, Alaska would be the only area under the flag that had no property tax. Furthermore, the tax was the lightest in the Union and its repeal would discriminate against those enterprises inside incorporated towns, since they would continue to pay the tax while those just outside would not. However, the legislators had made up their minds and the Senate overrode my veto by the just sufficient two-thirds, eleven to five. Another veto that was overridden was of Charlie Jones's Senate Bill No. 1 which placed a bounty on wolverines. It appeared that a wolverine had raided Charlie's food cache. Wolverines had not been included in the various bounties still in effect and it shocked me that we were now going to exterminate an animal that was virtually extinct except in Alaska. Five thousand dollars was to be appropriated for that purpose with a $15 bounty per wolverine. The fact that wolverines had long been a source of income to fur trappers, and that they could be sold live to stateside zoological gardens for $30 to $100 each had no effect on the legislators, and the bounty was enacted over my veto.

Two related bills to change the composition of the unemployment compensation commission were also vetoed and the vetoes overridden. The first was to abolish the existing commission in order to get rid of an incumbent, the public's representative, Ralph Rivers, who had been Alaska's attorney general, but suffered, in the legislature's view, by being a Democrat. The existing commission consisted of three members, one representing industry, one labor and one the public. The new bill eliminated the public's representative and created a commission of four, two representing industry and two labor. In my veto message I pointed out that this arrangement would invite deadlocks and later events would prove that it did. The other bill created a commission composed of legislators to investigate Alaska's executive departments and stipulated a *per diem* of $35 for its members. It was a clear violation of the Organic Act that provided that "no member of the Legislature shall hold or be appointed to any office which had been created, or the salary or emoluments of which had been increased, while he was a member . . ." Again my veto was overridden along straight party lines.

Some bills reached me on the last day of the session so that my vetoes could not be returned to the legislature. One such bill lowered the tax on raw fish. In my veto message I pointed out that the legislature had already reduced the territory's biennial income by $1,750,000 and that in consequence some vital services, which I listed, would have to be curtailed. Another bill amended the existing law for the creation of utility districts by taking away the power which had been vested in the people to create such a district by popular vote and giving it instead to the District Judge. In my view, a right which the people enjoyed should not be taken away by a legislature but only by the people themselves in a referendum.

Perhaps my keenest disappointment, however, was the defeat of House Bill No. 7, "An Act providing for the calling of a Constitutional Convention, the ratification of a Constitution, the election of State officers and for other purposes." Conceived by Wendell Kay, it was sponsored by the four Democratic House members and then referred to the Special Committee on Statehood which was predominantly Republican.

Even though I felt the 1953 legislature had undone some of the things for which I had worked and which I had hoped would be enduring, as the end of my governorship—April 10, 1953—neared, I could not but reflect how kind the political fates had been. They had vouchsafed me the longest term not only of any Alaskan governor, but also, I believe, one of the longest of any state or territorial governor since the founding of our republic—thirteen years, four months and five days. It was this occupational longevity which alone made possible the fulfillment of a program of self-reliance for Alaska and Alaskans, or at least laying a solid foundation for it. Clearly, had I had but one or even two of the prescribed four-year terms, my administration would have ended after the disastrous 1947 legislature, with a bankrupt territory, political dissension, and a record of having been unable to do anything about it in two terms. It was not until late in March, 1949, after I had been in office several months over eight years, that the vindicating 1949 session marked an historic turn and threw open the portals of progress.

My third term in office should normally have ended on December 5, 1951, and, ironically, I owed the extension of my term to the Republican

ABOVE: *Ernest Gruening testifying for statehood before the Senate Interior Committee, 1950*

RIGHT: *Alaska's first lady, 1939–1953*

OPPOSITE ABOVE: *"St. Louis Post-Dispatch" cartoonist's view of the plight of unrecognized "Tennessee Plan" Alaskan congressional delegation*

OPPOSITE BELOW: *The Governor's Mansion in Juneau*

"SENATOR" GRUENING

"SENATOR" EGAN

CONGRESSMAN RIVERS

ALASKA, WE ARE HERE!

Eightieth Congress which declined to confirm my nomination on the assumption that a Republican President would be elected in 1948 and would replace me. After Eisenhower's election in 1952, the opposition press in Alaska suggested that I resign promptly and allow the President to fill my place without delay. But I felt I should show my appreciation of the Eightieth Congress's inaction by my completing the term it had unintentionally granted me. Besides, April was a much better time than December to move into the cabin Dorothy and I had at Eagle River Landing.

I had many other causes for gratitude, particularly for the wonderful help that had been given me. Dorothy had made the governor's mansion a paragon of hospitality. We had welcomed there and enjoyed the company of countless Alaskans and visitors from afar. We would not have been able to do it without the assistance of Marguerite Doucette, who had been born in Luxembourg, and had worked for us before we came to Alaska. Officially she was our cook, but in reality she was a female chef, a master of culinary craftsmanship. She would be unflustered if Dorothy said to her at perhaps four in the afternoon, "Marguerite, a plane has just landed with thirty people on board. We're planning to have them for dinner." And a perfect dinner would always be ready.

Dorothy was able to rise to every occasion and her activities ranged far beyond the social. She had a kindergarten on the top floor of the governor's mansion when that form of early childhood education was not available in the Juneau school system. She initiated the Alaska Music Trail, an excellent program which brought many talented musicians to our still-remote territory. She had also founded a Juneau branch of the League of Women Voters and had served as a nurse's aid during the war. I could not have done without her love, encouragement and support.

I had been most fortunate in my collaborators, particularly in a succession of efficient naval aids. J. Simpson ("Sim") McKinnon, a lifelong resident of Juneau, first introduced me to its society. He was followed by warmhearted Bob Schoettler, also a Navy alumnus, and then by Warren Caro. A lawyer in civil life, Caro, a wartime enlistee in the Coast Guard, became the officer of the port in Petersburg and was then transferred to the Governor's Commission of the Arts. He did not look forward to reverting to legal practice; his interest was in the theater. My own experience made me sympathetic to one who wished to change his profession. So I wrote my old friend Theresa Helburn in New York. We had first met as children on shipboard, and years later we had won the mixed doubles tennis championship at Rockport. She had been instrumental in founding the Theater Guild, and on my recommendation Caro secured a position as its executive. My last aide was Lieutenant Commander Ed

Chester of the Coast Guard, who combined meticulous attention to detail with good judgment on matters of policy. He and his wife Isabel were of great help and fitted admirably into our official family.

In my office Juneau-born Katie Torkelsen was a spring of good humor and a devoted secretary who had started as an assistant to Estella Draper. She was ably seconded by Jean Marsh who later married Dr. Roderick MacKenzie. Invaluable as assistants were George Sundborg and Burke Riley who climaxed his Alaska service as secretary of the territory. All of these associates had the characteristics of intelligence, independence of thought and dedication for which I will always be grateful.

My departure from office was cheered by the very generous gift of an automobile from friends who remained anonymous, and an equally generous full-length editorial in the Anchorage *Times* entitled "Alaska's Greatest Governor." I left the governor's mansion with only one regret. After an apparently promising start in the early 1950s, our campaign for statehood had gone into a decline. Senator Hugh Butler, all powerful in the counsels of the Eisenhower Administration, continued to oppose it and was unscrupulous in his efforts to block it. President Eisenhower himself seemed to have lost his earlier enthusiasm for it, and his Secretary of the Interior, Douglas McKay, who, as Governor of Oregon, had repeatedly supported statehood resolutions in the Governors' Conferences, was now meekly following the adverse trend. Frank Heintzelman who succeeded me as governor was openly opposed to statehood for Alaska.

*Dorothy's
painting
of our
Eagle River
cabin*

Unforeseen developments would change this picture, but for a while the outlook seemed bleak. It occurred to me that Alaska's case and the record of its long neglect and discrimination should be set forth objectively and authoritatively in a book. Such a book would be helpful to our statehood cause and various publishers had expressed an interest. So I signed a contract with Random House, and Dorothy and I moved to our cabin, where I started pounding my typewriter to produce, a year later, *The State of Alaska.*

Although I was no longer governor, my thirteen years in Alaska qualified me, I felt, to continue to act as its spokesman. In fact, both Dorothy and I now considered Alaska our home and the campaign for statehood remained one of my chief preoccupations. In addition to my book, I was able to secure publication of articles advocating statehood in the *Atlantic, Harper's, Current History* and other magazines, and as I talked to various audiences, I felt that public sentiment for Alaska was growing, as indeed the Gallup polls showed. I admit I experienced an occasional lapse into gloom, but I did not share the pessimism of some of my fellow-workers in the cause. At last things did begin to look up, and the first new ray of hope came from Alaska itself. The poor performance of the 1953 legislature resulted in a political reversal—almost numerically exact—of the composition of its successor. The 1955 Senate consisted of twelve Democrats and four Republicans, the House of twenty-one Democrats and three Republicans, and its most important action was the passage of House Bill No. 1 which called for a convention to prepare a constitution for the State of Alaska. It was a vindication of Wendell Kay and his fellow Democrats who had sponsored a similar bill in the 1953 legislature only to have it rejected by the Republican majority. It would prove a major step toward achieving statehood. Sentiment for statehood was growing in Alaska, and it increased when President Eisenhower reneged on his support for statehood, even though he still favored it for Hawaii. He had been persuaded by Senator Butler that Hawaii would elect two Republican senators who could bolster the party's slender senate majority, while Alaska would, in all probability, elect Democrats. Butler had once been no less violently against Hawaiian statehood, and had issued a statement opposing it on the grounds of communist infiltration. But before the 1952 convention, Senator Robert Taft, then seeking the Republican presidential nomination, had, with Delegate Joseph Farrington's promise of the support of Hawaiian delegates to the convention, agreed to "take care of" Butler. Butler was supporting Taft's candidacy and so he changed his mind about Hawaii. Political considerations outweighed principle.

Alaskans were also outraged by the provisions of the McCarran Act which compelled us to stand in line on entering the "lower 48" and identify ourselves as Americans. Quite apart from experiencing annoying delays as we passed through "immigration" in Seattle, we felt that being an Alaskan was the same thing as being an American. Another factor in the rising tide of statehood sentiment was the active support of the Fairbanks *News-Miner*, which after owner Cap Lathrop's death, was sold to C. W. Snedden, who reversed that paper's policy of opposition to statehood. Although he was a Republican and supported Republican candidates with a biased news and editorial slant, Snedden nevertheless criticized President Eisenhower editorially for his lack of information about Alaska which he revealed in press conferences when he was trying to justify his lack of support for Alaskan statehood.

The bill for a constitutional convention called for the election of delegates to take place on September 13, 1955. Fifty-five delegates were chosen and when they assembled on the campus of the University of Alaska on November 9, I delivered the keynote address. The similarities between the discrimination suffered by our colonial forefathers and that experienced by Alaskans gave me the theme—a new approach—and I developed it under the title *Let us End American Colonialism*. It was issued in pamphlet form and became a useful statehood campaign document. The convention was an unqualified success. In addition to drafting what political scientists declared to be "one of the best state constitutions ever written," the convention took a step of far-reaching consequence which the delegates had not anticipated. It arose from an inspired recommendation of a public-spirited New Orleans businessman, George H. Lehleitner.

In researching American history, Lehleitner discovered that a number of territories had departed from the conventional procedures for seeking admission to the Union as states. The first of these was by an area west of the Carolinas. Its people, envious that the area immediately to the north —Kentucky—had achieved statehood in 1792, and displeased that the first three Congresses had not done likewise for them, called a constitutional convention, drafted a state constitution, elected two senators and sent them to the national capital. Four months later they brought back statehood for Tennessee. A similar procedure had been followed by Michigan, California, Minnesota, Oregon and Kansas.

Lehleitner had served in the navy during World War II in Hawaii and was sympathetic with its statehood aspirations. He proposed this Tennessee procedure to Joseph Farrington, Hawaii's Delegate in Congress, but he and his predecessor Samuel Wilder King, shortly to become governor, both leaders in the statehood fight, felt this approach unnecessary. They were convinced that President Eisenhower and Speaker Joseph W. Martin would put Hawaii through. But nothing happened. Lehleitner then transferred his interest to Alaska, and suggested that we follow Tennessee's example. It sounded like a fine idea. I urged various of our delegates to give Lehleitner's proposal a hearing; they did so on January 23, and after his very convincing presentation, adopted it by unanimous vote. They placed it on the ballot at the next primary election in which the people would also vote to accept or reject the constitution. They voted for both.

Democratic and Republican conventions met and nominated their candidates. I was nominated for the six-year Senate term; William Egan, legislator since 1941 and president of the constitutional convention, for the four-year Senate term; and Ralph Rivers, former legislator and attorney general was chosen for the House of Representatives. My Republican opponent was John Butrovich, a Fairbanks insurance man, a senator and an able and personable legislator. Unwisely he chose to run for both the United States Senate and for reelection to the Alaska Senate, and that enabled me to win by the narrow margin of 14,109 votes to Butrovich's 13,301. It is my opinion that had Butrovich filed only for the United States Senate he would have won.

The following June I was a member of the Alaska delegation to the Democratic convention in Chicago. I had headed the delegation four years earlier when I was governor and that year we had given our votes to Estes Kefauver for whom I made a seconding speech. But when Adlai Stevenson won the nomination on the third ballot, we all supported him enthusiastically, and now that he seemed likely to try again in 1956, we were still behind him. Stevenson had come to Alaska in 1954 and Dorothy and I had entertained him at our cabin. His wit, his charm, captivated everyone, and he delivered a major address in Anchorage advocating statehood. The impression he created was in marked contrast to that of Secretary of the Interior McKay. He had visited Anchorage a week earlier and when pressed for his views on statehood, lost his temper and asked his questioners why they could not "act like ladies and gentlemen."

However, my ardor for Stevenson had been somewhat dampened by a meeting which Bob Bartlett and I had with him in April prior to the convention. We found him evasive on what he would do for statehood if elected, but now at the convention, the hour of decision was at hand. Bartlett and I had seen Kefauver, who might again be the nominee, and he gave us his unqualified assurance that he would use the full powers of the presidency to get statehood for Alaska. Then we went to Stevenson for a similar assurance.

"How does the South feel about it?" he asked.

"The South, with a few exceptions, is against it," I said.

"Then I can't be for it."

"Adlai," we both chorused. "Where are your principles? This is the issue of government by consent of the governed."

"You've been on record for it repeatedly," I reminded him.

"The most important thing is to hold the South in the Democratic Party," Stevenson said.

"The South isn't going to run out of the party on the issue of Alaska statehood," I told him.

Although we argued for half an hour, we could not shake him. He repeated that while he personally favored statehood for Alaska, he was not going to fight for it if it meant antagonizing the South. Bartlett and I walked away, disappointed and disillusioned. We would support Stevenson, but with much less enthusiasm than before, and we recorded our feelings in a long letter which we both signed. We were forced to conclude that with all his charm and brilliance, Stevenson would be a weak President. We contrasted his Hamlet-like attitude with that of Kefauver and we were glad when he became Stevenson's running mate.

The next great "break" for the cause of Alaska's statehood was the replacement of Douglas McKay by Frederick A. Seaton as Secretary of the Interior. Seaton, a newspaper publisher and radio station owner in Nebraska, had been appointed to the Senate in 1951 by Governor Val Peterson to fill the vacancy caused by the death of Senator Kenneth Wherry. I had promptly called on Seaton with a view to "selling" him on statehood. He said he was totally uninformed but would be glad to hear what I had to say. I was in his office for two hours. On parting he said, "I want to talk to Joe Farrington about Hawaii. Come back in a few days and I'll give you my answer." I was not optimistic. The most inveterate opponent of statehood at that time was Seaton's senior colleague from Nebraska, Hugh Butler. I assumed that Seaton would consult with him and reflect his views. So I was more than pleasantly surprised when I entered his office a week later to hear him boom out, "I've made up my mind. I'm for statehood now—for both Alaska and Hawaii."

I had during the previous years done intensive research on the struggle of each territory to secure statehood. I had read the records of every debate in both Houses of Congress beginning with Vermont, the fourteenth state, and I had learned many fascinating and little-known facts that would stand us in good stead in our struggle. One of the most interesting was the story of Nebraska whose admission to statehood, coincidentally, took place in 1867, the same year as the purchase of Alaska. Amazingly, Nebraska had not fulfilled the requirements for admission to statehood; Senate hearings uncovered instances of flagrant fraud in counting the votes presumably cast for statehood, and when a recount resulted in less than a majority, President Andrew Johnson vetoed statehood for Nebraska. However, Johnson was at the height of his unpopularity in the Congress; he had escaped impeachment a few weeks earlier by the narrow margin of one vote. And so with mighty whoops the two Houses overrode his veto and Nebraska came into the Union.

In my testimony before the Senate Interior and Insular Affairs Committee on April 29, 1950, I had told this story as an illustration of a state coming into the Union with far less justification than Alaska had, and I enjoyed being able to tell it when Butler was present. When two years later I told the same story to another Nebraska senator, Fred Seaton, who had never heard of it, he was fascinated, and asked me to write it out in detail. I also wrote a speech that Seaton delivered in the Senate unchanged. Of course it was a strong pitch for statehood for both Alaska and Hawaii, and it was the only speech that Seaton delivered during his nearly thirteen months in the Senate, for he decided not to run for election, and left the Senate at the expiration of his term in January of 1953. Now three years later he was back in Washington and at the hearing on his confirmation as Secretary of the Interior, Senator James Murray placed Seaton's Senate speech into the hearing record and asked him if he still felt the same way. He said he did, and would do everything he could to persuade President Eisenhower that Alaska should have statehood immediately.

It was an important victory, but there was yet another cloud on the horizon. I told Seaton there were reports that the statehood bill which the administration would require for its approval might contain a provision for partition whereby a large part of northern and western Alaska would be kept in territorial status for defense purposes and statehood would be given only to the more populated areas. I was vehemently against any such partition and told him that if necessary it could be better achieved by land withdrawals. Further, I said that Alaskan sentiment was unanimous against partition and that partition would raise new problems, including the need to establish some form of a government for the part of Alaska left as a territory. Seaton said he saw the force of these arguments, but he could not say just what the White House would require. But he reaffirmed his support for statehood even if the terms were somewhat unfavorable. Otherwise it might be postponed indefinitely.

We discussed the governorship. Although it was not yet publicly known, Seaton had already quietly fired Heintzelman and the governor's office was now occupied by Waino Hendrickson, the secretary of Alaska, who was serving as acting governor. Seaton said he had not yet selected a successor to recommend to the President. I strongly recommended Robert Atwood, giving my view that he and his wife, Evangeline, would make a wonderful team, and urged Seaton under no circumstances to let the "Fifth

Division" name the governor. He asked me what the Fifth Division was, and I explained that it was a term we used to describe the Seattle interests that had always exploited Alaska and opposed any increase in self-government. Seaton then asked me to name a few who would be considered Fifth Division nominees. I named Paul Robison, John Manders, Henry W. Clark and Norman Banfield. Seaton said that Clark and Banfield had already been recommended to him for the governorship, but he was planning to go to Alaska shortly to survey the possible appointees.

After leaving Seaton's office, I went to Bob Bartlett and suggested we call on Nathan Twining and see how he stood on partition. As Air Force Chief of Staff he was certain to be consulted about Alaskan defenses, and we should do our best to convince him that partition would be folly and wholly unnecessary. He said he had never been asked about it but could see no necessity for it. He would so testify subsequently.

The next step in our campaign took us to Tennessee. Dorothy and I flew to Nashville with Estes and Nancy Kefauver to publicize the origin of the "Alaska-Tennessee" plan. Governor Frank Clement rolled out the red carpet for us, and our mission received favorable attention on radio, television and in the two dailies, the *Tennessean* and the *Banner*. Back in Washington we made the rounds of senators and congressmen. They fell pretty generally into three categories: those favoring statehood; those opposed, mostly from the South; and the largest category, those who listened without committing themselves. I kept a daily diary which recorded our encounters with the ninety-six senators and 435 representatives.

We rented office space not far from the Capitol. One of my tasks was to mail out copies of my keynote address to the constitutional convention along with personal letters to every member of Congress, to newspaper editors, commentators, political scientists, to the members of the Nationwide Committee of One Hundred, to members of my Harvard College class, to anyone, in fact, who might be helpful. I also sent out copies of my book, *The State of Alaska*.

We were formally welcomed in the Senate on January 14, 1957, not to the floor but to the Diplomatic Gallery. The proceedings were opened by Senator Spessard Holland of Florida, an early supporter of statehood for both Alaska and Hawaii. After wishing us success in our mission, Senator Holland asked us to rise and we were greeted—as the *Congressional Record* reported—with "prolonged applause." He then called on Senator Murray of Montana, chairman of the Committee on Interior and Insular Affairs, which would be in charge of the statehood bill; and Senators O'Mahoney of Wyoming, Kefauver of Tennessee, Kuchel of California, Neuberger of Oregon, Humphrey of Minnesota, Capehart of Indiana, Payne of Maine, Thye of Minnesota, Wiley of Wisconsin and Morse of

Oregon who spoke in support of statehood. We were early informed, however, that if we got statehood, we would have to run again. As all three of the men Alaska sent to Washington were Democrats, the Republicans understandably took that position, although that had not been required of earlier "Tennessee-plan" states. But as insistence on maintaining our status would have lost us Republican support and jeopardized our objective, we agreed that the statehood legislation would so provide.

We had our answers ready to the familiar objections to Alaskan statehood: the smallness of our population and noncontiguity. Why should such a small handful of people have two senators when even the great state of New York had only two? Our response was that if this view had prevailed in the early days of the republic, we would still have only thirteen states. Furthermore, we needed statehood in order to grow. As for noncontiguity, jet planes brought Alaska closer to the capital in travel time than was any other state at the time of its admission. We had figures to show just how long it had taken the senators and representatives of each new state, on its admission, to reach the national capital.

There were other less tangible objections, however, and we learned to our regret that the two most powerful, and indeed key figures in Congress—Lyndon B. Johnson, Senate Majority Leader, and Sam Rayburn, Speaker of the House—were not favorably inclined toward statehood. Rayburn told me so frankly, but said he was less opposed to Alaska than to Hawaii—a view held by almost all Southerners and many Northerners. I asked Rayburn why the difference in his feeling. "Hawaii has too many Japs," he said, and "Alaska is on the continent." Nevertheless, he said he would not try to prevent the statehood bill from being brought up, but as added insurance I asked former President Truman to call Rayburn. He said he would, and did, reporting to me: "Don't worry, keep on plugging; Sam will be all right."

In late July we got both bad and good news about Rayburn. Bob Bartlett reported that Rayburn had told him there would be no action on statehood until the next session. So our Tennessee-plan delegation called on him. We asked whether he would make a public statement to that effect, which would allay the anxiety and disappointment in Alaska that would inevitably follow the news of the bill's postponement. "You may say that I will support the bill," he said, "and will try to bring it up in January if we can get a rule."

"If we can get a rule?" I asked in surprise. "Is there any doubt about it, with your support?"

"There is always doubt about it," he replied. So we were left with this contradiction. Rayburn *had* made a definite commitment that the bill would get on the floor in the next session. But we were in doubt whether we were not getting another run-around.

Meanwhile, Mike Stepovich, Fairbanks attorney and territorial senator, had been appointed governor of Alaska. Interior Secretary Fred Seaton was a guest at a dinner party at our home and I asked about the new incumbent. "I couldn't appoint Bob Atwood," Seaton said. "There was too much opposition within the party in Alaska." It was evident that Bob was considered too "liberal" by some of the Republican stalwarts, but I was disappointed that, if Seaton considered him a good choice, he had not managed to overcome their objections.

Our delegation went home in the interval between the two sessions of the Eighty-fifth Congress, and that fall another subject of controversy arose in Alaska. Oil deposits were discovered in the Kenai Peninsula, a large part of which, nearly two million acres, had been set aside in 1940 by presidential executive order as the Kenai National Moose Range. This had been done on the recommendation of Ira Gabrielson and carried out without a hearing by Secretary Ickes. I welcomed the discovery. The territory's economy was in bad shape; gold mining was no longer profitable and the salmon industry was suffering from overfishing and federal mismanagement. Revenue from petroleum resources was sorely needed. But exploration and drilling for oil were savagely fought against by all but one of the major conservation societies, as well as by the Fish and Wildlife Service, on the grounds that oil development would destroy the moose's habitat. Hearings were held in Washington and I testified as a conservationist solicitous for the moose but no less concerned for the two-legged species whose habitat required an economy to subsist. The Isaac Walton League's executive, Burton Atwood, testified to his conviction that moose and oil could co-exist without detriment to either, and Secretary Seaton compromised by opening up one-half of the moose range for oil development. So Alaska was not only saved from bankruptcy, but the foundation was laid for a new and expanding economy. For the oil strike in the Kenai led to further exploration and discovery of other vast oil deposits, of great fields of natural gas, and to the birth of a petrochemical industry. Concomitantly the moose multiplied and spread all over Alaska.

In my continuing campaign for statehood, I went to New York just before the second session of the Eighty-fifth Congress to try to strengthen our newspaper support. I visited every editorial sanctum and got encouragement in each. At the *Herald-Tribune*, Irita Van Doren, editor of the weekly book supplement, gave me the galley proofs of Edna Ferber's forthcoming book on Alaska which was to be out on March 27, and asked me to review it. My friendship with Edna Ferber had begun years earlier when she used a passage from my book, *Mexico and Its Heritage*, as the title of a short story and of a book of her short stories, *They Brought Their Women*. Having been an admirer of her fiction, I suggested that she write a novel about Alaska and told her of our problems and our desire for statehood. She became interested, and made several trips to Alaska for background. The novel, *Ice Palace*, made a strong case for statehood. While some literary critics felt that it was not up to her best work, one of them, Clifton Fadiman, referred to it correctly as "the Uncle Tom's Cabin for Alaska," and that useful label gained currency. Thousands who might not have been interested in nonfiction accounts about Alaska did read her novel, and in the spring of 1958 the book stimulated many pro-statehood letters to members of Congress. They came at just the right time.

When the Congress reconvened, a new obstacle to our efforts appeared when minority leader William Knowland announced that when the Alaska statehood bill came up he would move to tie the Hawaii statehood bill to it. That would defeat both. Hawaii's cause had much less support in the Congress than Alaska's; the only way to secure favorable action on both bills was to try to enact the Alaska bill in this Congress and to postpone action on Hawaii until the next.

Earle Clements, who had been defeated for reelection as senator from Kentucky in 1956, was helping us in the Senate and urged me to try to get seventeen Republican senators to agree to vote against Knowland's proposal. His count showed that thirty-three Democrats would oppose it, and if I could line up the necessary Republicans, we could defeat it. Egan and Rivers agreed that I should undertake the effort and I was assisted by Senator Thomas Kuchel, Knowland's junior colleague from California, who agreed to oppose Knowland's move and to line up other Republicans. While a number of Republicans refused to commit themselves, I was able to get promises from Aiken, Flanders, Barrett, Payne, Allott, Javits, Langer, Morton, Hoblitzel, Cooper, Beall, Dworshak, Bricker, Young and Dirksen. Dirksen told me that tying the bills together had been prearranged at a conference of Republican leaders at the White House. Knowland was soon apprised that he did not have the necessary votes and so dropped his move to unite the two bills.

Then began the slow process of lining up legislators' support for Alaskan statehood. By April we had a pretty good count. Allowing for unexpected changes of mind, we felt we had a substantial majority in the Senate and a less certain one in the House. My efforts were now directed at bringing new influences to bear on those whom we listed as opposed or doubtful. We had the support of a variety of national organizations on which we could call. The most active were the Veterans of Foreign Wars, the Jaycees, the Kiwanis International and the General Federation of Women's Clubs. Leslie Wright of this organization was most effective; she would contact the president of each state federation and turn her loose on the doubtful congressmen. In the farm states we had the support of the National Grange, and some of the governors whom I had gotten to know were most helpful, particularly Governor Alfred E. Driscoll of New Jersey.

Members of my college class also rendered valuable assistance. Kenneth B. Keating, Republican, then representing the Thirty-eighth New York district which included Rochester, told me that he would never vote to admit Alaska. He had, he said, three times as many people in his district as Alaska had in the entire territory. I consulted my classmate Harper Sibley, one of Rochester's leading citizens and a former president of the United States Chamber of Commerce. He invited me to come to Rochester as his guest and address the local Chamber of Commerce. He converted Kenneth Keating, whom I would get to know well after we were both elected to the Senate in 1958. Similarly my classmate Ward Murphey Canaday, chairman of the Board of the Willys-Overland Company in Toledo, was instrumental in winning over Senator John Bricker. To find the "man behind the man" was an ever-intriguing pursuit. Often there was none, but in some states, in the South particularly, there would be a tycoon, banker, utility or oil magnate who could pretty much tell a senator or congressman how he would like him to vote. I had had a curt turn-down from big, blustering Robert Kerr of Oklahoma, himself a millionaire oil-man. Clark Clifford, counsel for the Phillips Petroleum Company, told me that Kerr would do anything that Kenneth Stanley Adams, chairman of the Board of Phillips Petroleum, asked him to do. I telephoned Irene Ryan, the only woman mining engineer in Alaska, whose bill in the 1957 territorial legislature had facilitated petroleum development, and asked her to get Philip O'Rourke, the resident Phillips representative in Alaska, to telephone Kenneth Adams to let Kerr know that he favored statehood. Two days later I heard from Bob Kerr. He asked me to repeat the arguments I had given him for statehood, to which he had scarcely listened before. He now indicated that he was favorably inclined and subsequently voted aye. By getting Kerr we also got Allen Frear of Delaware. Albert Gore of Tennessee was converted by a call from James G. Stahlman, the president and publisher of the Nashville *Banner*.

By mid-May it became clear that our battle for statehood would be fought chiefly on the House floor. We were not going to get a "rule." Howard Smith, the crusty old Virginian who was chairman of the Rules Committee, ably seconded by the no-less-conservative William Colmer of Mississippi, the No. 2 Democrat, was stalling and made no secret of it. But this implied a challenge to Speaker Sam Rayburn and that was good news. The opening gun was fired on May 21, when Wayne Aspinall of Colorado, the ranking Democrat on the House Interior Committee, moved that the House resolve itself into the Committee of the Whole to consider H.R.7999. Noah Mason of Illinois, Republican and a schoolteacher by profession—whom I had vainly sought to convert by citing a New York congressman's opposition to the admission of Illinois in 1818—objected. Points of order were raised by Howard Smith of Virginia and Clarence Cannon of Missouri who was an authority on procedure and whose principal point was that the bill contained matter not pertinent to statehood, as well as appropriations which were not proper in a legislative bill. Aspinall replied at length, and Smith then took over the battle with another point of order, citing many precedents. Finally Speaker Rayburn was ready to rule:

> The Chair was not notified by anyone that a point of order would be made against consideration of the bill, but anticipating that such a point of order would be made, the Chair, in company with the parliamentarian of the House, has made a research of decisions of Speakers heretofore.

Of course Rayburn knew what was going to happen. He too cited precedents, then ruled against the point of order.

We had won the first test. The second was on Aspinall's motion to bring up the bill. As the roll-call proceeded, it was difficult to tell who was ahead; we were not permitted to keep score in the gallery, which struck me as a strange infringement on personal liberty, but which was a provision in both Houses. Some members who had faithfully promised to support the bill ran out on us, but the motion prevailed 217 to 172. The Southerners—all Democrats—were almost solidly against it. All the Republican leaders, Martin, Halleck, Arends, Brown, Allen, Wigglesworth and Taber, voted "no"; but many of the younger Republicans did not follow their leaders. It was an encouraging showing, but we were told that we must not count that vote as a final victory; quite a few who had voted to bring the bill up would switch on the bill itself.

It had been agreed that the time for debate would be divided equally between Leo O'Brien of New York and A. L. ("Doc") Miller of Nebraska, ranking Republican on the Interior Committee, who would represent the opposition. O'Brien led off by pointing out that his name, rather than Delegate Bartlett's, was on the bill so that it could be sponsored by a representative from the most populous state of the Union, an implicit refutation of the much-used argument that it was unfair to states with large populations to give Alaska two senators. The colloquy was chiefly with John R. Pillion, New York Republican, who repeated his earlier assertions that Alaska was being used as a shoehorn to get Hawaii admitted, that its two senators and representative would be "selected by communist agents," and that once Alaska was admitted, Harry Bridges would send one hundred agents to take over the new state. His performance was the all-time low in the whole Alaska-Hawaii statehood battle.

On Tuesday, May 27, we were anticipating amendments to strike the enacting clause which would kill the bill, and another equally fatal one to recommit the bill. Both were offered by Walter Rogers of Texas. There was a primary in Kentucky that day and by agreement there would be no roll-call; any action subject to a roll-call would be taken the next day. Consequently many of our supporters were absent, while the Dixiecrats were there in force. So, on a teller vote, the enacting clause was stricken by 116 to 106. Psychologically this was damaging. It looked as if the opposition had gained control.

We had to get busy. We met in Leo O'Brien's office with Wayne Aspinall and Representative Gracie Pfost of Idaho, and went over the list of those missing. We were on the phone most of the night. The following day was our zero hour. The first vote was on the motion to recommit. The yeas and nays seemed about even, but when the roll-call was about two-thirds finished, Bob Bartlett waved a cheery signal from the floor. The vote was 199 to 174 in our favor, a twenty-five-vote margin. So far so good. The opposition did not weaken. The next motion to strike out the enacting clause was defeated by a voice vote, our majority of twenty-five shouting louder than the rest. Our long night's work had paid off. On final passage the vote was 208 yeas to 166 nays, with fifty-three not voting.

We now transferred our activities to the Senate and called again on the doubtful or opposed, marshaling all our powers of persuasion. Then on June 23, Mike Mansfield, acting majority leader in the absence of Lyndon Johnson, asked that the Senate proceed to the consideration of H.R.7999. Opposition to statehood was presented by Senators Willis Robertson of Virginia, James Eastland of Mississippi and Strom Thurmond of South Carolina; pro-statehood speeches were made by Senators Estes Kefauver, Hubert Humphrey, Spessard Holland and Frank Church who missed no opportunity to interject some excellent comments and raise the already high level of the debate. The debate continued day after day. Senator Mike Monroney introduced his "commonwealth" bill as a substitute for statehood; Senator George Smathers endorsed that proposal, which also had Fulbright's blessing. John Marshall Butler, Republican of Maryland, made a long speech against statehood, so did Prescott Bush of Connecticut. Francis Case of South Dakota and Ralph Yarborough of Texas both spoke in favor.

On June 30 we sensed victory. Of the various amendments designed to kill the bill, the most crucial was the one giving the President the right to withdraw the northern half of Alaska either in whole or in part for military purposes. The statehood opponents declared that it was unconstitutional. We had long known that the whole proposal was phony and had been put in as a face-saving device for the President. However, the Southern bloc, using this as a pretext, argued that this section was vital to national security, and that when it was thrown out by the courts—as it surely would be—it would leave Alaska defenseless. It was obvious that the opposition was picking up some strength for a motion to recommit the bill to the Armed Services Committee "for clarification." As the voting proceeded, it was also clear the opposition had made a dent. But not enough. The move was defeated, fifty-five to thirty-one. That was the high tide of the Confederacy. That was Gettysburg. When Strom Thurmond brought up his amendment to exclude the proposed withdrawn areas from the state, he could muster only sixteen votes. Thereupon Eastland, who was putting forth an amendment to recommit the bill to the Judiciary Committee, threw in the sponge. He merely offered his remarks for the record without delivering them, and said that in view of the previous votes it would be useless.

The presiding officer, Senator Richard Neuberger, then asked whether

Dorothy Gruening showing Anchorage Times headline to Bill and Neva Egan

President Eisenhower signing Alaska's statehood bill, 1958

there were any more amendments. There were none and Senator Knowland asked for the yeas and nays on final passage. They were ordered, but
there was a further delay. Senator Thurmond wanted to make a speech
and did at length. Senator Leverett Saltonstall asked unanimous consent
to insert a statement giving his reasons for voting against the bill. Senator
Henry Jackson wound up with a tribute to those who had helped statehood. He was interrupted by senatorial cries of "Vote! Vote!" So
Presiding Officer Neuberger uttered the usual formula: "The question is
on the passage of the bill. The yeas and nays have been ordered, and
the clerk will call the roll."

There were sixty-four yeas and twenty nays. We had won a twelve-
year battle. When six months later, on January 3, 1959, President Eisenhower signed the proclamation admitting Alaska as the forty-ninth state
the forty-nine-star flag was unfurled. Its design had been a closely
guarded secret. Several hundred variations had been submitted. The significant change was that the stars—seven rows of seven—were, for
the first time, staggered. We all thought it excellent.

24

IN THE UNITED STATES
SENATE

*The Senate is the most honorable and
independent station in our government, one
where you can peculiarly raise yourself in
the public estimation.*

—THOMAS JEFFERSON

During my terms as Alaska's governor and the hectic years that followed
fighting for statehood, our sons Huntington and Peter had grown to man-
hood. Hunt, safely back from the war in Europe, fulfilled our hopes that
he would stay in Alaska by becoming a pilot for Alaska Coastal Airlines,
one of the two amphibian commercial companies that served southeastern
Alaska and had its headquarters in Juneau. He had graduated from Harvard in 1938 and, in 1940 in San Francisco, married Elizabeth Ingalls
whom he had met in Cambridge. Betty and Hunt came to Juneau after
the war with their young son, Clark, who had been born in 1943, and
several years later their happiness and ours was increased by the birth of
twin boys, Winthrop and Bradford.

Peter had decided that he wanted to go to a West Coast university, and
while I would have preferred Harvard, we had all begun to think of ourselves as westerners. He enrolled at the University of California in Berke-
ley in the fall of 1941 but left at the end of his freshman year to enlist in
the Army Air Corps. He was graduated in the class of 44J at Williams
Field, Chandler, Arizona, where I delivered the graduating address and
had the thrill of pinning on his wings. The war over, Peter expressed a
desire to write, and his letters home showed that he had talent. He

thought he would like to get a job on a newspaper. I encouraged him, but told him I would not give him letters of introduction to my newspaper executive friends. If I did, he would never know whether or not he was "making good" on his own.

He did just that. At the San Francisco *Chronicle*, its dynamic editor, Paul Smith, offered him a job as a copy boy, assuring him that that was the way everyone started on the *Chronicle*. But after applying at several other dailies, he called at the office of the United Press to get some advice from Frank Bartholomew, its vice president. "Well, I got more than I hoped for; I got a job," Peter wrote us, and "it made me feel better that I was actually offered the job by someone other than a friend of Dad's." He spent five months in Sacramento covering the California legislature and then got word he would be sent to Hawaii. "Of course I am elated," he wrote from Honolulu. "Hawaii is and has been my Shangri-La." But within a few weeks, he wrote of his disappointment. Hawaii was in the throes of a prolonged dock strike and the islands were torn by civil strife. The strike was finally settled that fall and the tensions and hard feelings it created gradually died away.

Later that same fall Dorothy and I had an opportunity to visit Hawaii. Secretary of the Treasury John Wesley Snyder had started on a Pacific tour by way of Alaska; his trip on a Coast Guard plane would include three days in Japan, two in the Philippines, one in Guam and a stop in Hawaii. He invited me to come with him, and if I was being treated to a free ride to Hawaii, I was determined that Dorothy should come too— at our expense, of course—so that we could both see Peter.

Peter arranged to have his vacation coincide with our visit and Dorothy and I have always remembered it as an episode of supreme happiness. We found that Peter was already widely loved in Hawaii and his gift for friendship reciprocated. He was a stimulating companion; his analysis of contemporary events and his estimates of the individuals who shaped them were extremely perceptive. His verve was contagious and his company highlighted every gathering. I enjoyed reliving through him my own early newspaper experiences.

After our return to Alaska, Peter wrote that he had been made UP night bureau manager in Honolulu, and in April of 1950 he was sent to Midway to report on the abandonment of the net tender *Elder* which had exploded and caught fire en route to the Eniwetok atomic tests. He also covered President Truman's historic meeting with General MacArthur on Wake Island. Then came the unexpected news that he would be married. The letter reached us in Juneau the day before the event. The girl he was marrying, Nadine Unger Roosevelt, had been born in Honolulu of parents of German descent, and had been previously married to George

Emlen Roosevelt, Jr. Peter had known her since the previous August, but we had not met her during our visit to Hawaii. We wired our love and expressed the hope for an early visit to us in Alaska.

They did come that summer and we found Deedee as lovely as Peter had described her. We also learned more of her history. She had been married and divorced once before her marriage to Roosevelt and a baby by her first marriage had drowned. She had not had a very happy family life at home, but in the weeks she and Peter spent with us, largely at our Eagle River cabin, which Hunt and a carpenter-neighbor had built, they both seemed radiant and we welcomed her warmly into our family.

Shortly after returning to Honolulu, Peter wrote us that he had been offered the position of business representative for the UP in San Francisco. It was a great honor, his supervisors told him. So Peter moved to San Francisco. But we were shocked beyond measure to learn that his marriage with Deedee was ending by mutual consent. She did not want to leave Hawaii. We were deeply saddened and expressed our hope that the breach could be closed, but it was not, although the separation and divorce took place without bitterness or recrimination.

Peter did well in his business apprenticeship in San Francisco and early in 1951 was transferred to Portland, Oregon, where he would be, as he wrote, "on my own in a new country which will be an interesting challenge." When the war broke out in Korea, he asked to be assigned there as a war correspondent. He went late in 1951 and stayed a year. The UP then sent him to Singapore as "Manager for Southeast Asia," an important promotion. He arrived there on May 10, 1952. His territory included Malaya, Burma, Indochina, Indonesia and the Philippines, and he succeeded in renewing canceled UP contracts and extending the news service in several areas. In Saigon he found "the stickiest and most intriguing situation of any so far in my news and business experience with all the elements of an Oppenheim thriller." The French colonial forces in Vietnam were engaged in a bloody battle with the communist Vietminh, a battle that they would soon lose, and although Peter was chiefly concerned with the business aspect of the UP in that war-torn country, he wrote several dispatches that had a prophetic ring in the light of the tragic events that have since occurred in Southeast Asia.

Early in 1954 Peter was offered and accepted the general management of the UP in Australia and New Zealand, but before he reported there, he went to the Indonesian Republic. Two months later, after four weeks in Java and Sumatra, he wrote from Jacarta:

I am still in Indonesia with scarcely any idea when I shall leave and little inclination to do so. This trip has been extremely pleasant and informative and I am most reluctant to return to the orderly but sterile surroundings of Her Majesty's crown colony. Singapore, an antiseptic and hermetically sealed anomaly in the Asian scene, is a comfortable and efficient headquarters but colorless in comparison to the stimulating areas adjacent.

Indonesia is my favorite country in Southeast Asia. It is a terribly alive and precocious young nation of 80 million people emerging from its 300-year-old cocoon of servitude under the Dutch. Rich in culture and valuable resources, Indonesia is a fiercely proud and independent youngster doing its best to toddle a middle path between the armed camps of the cold war. Anxious to be left alone to shape its own destiny, it is at the same time friendly and suspicious of its fellow nations which preach that neutrality is next to enmity. Indonesia's leaders and intellectuals remember with painful vividness their years in Dutch jails for the crime of wanting their country free, and find it difficult to believe that the "Free World" of today is what it claims to be. Colonialism as practiced by the Dutch, English, French, and yes, Americans, still strikes a far more strident note than communism. Except for the short period in her fight for independence, communist leaders in Indonesia were fighting against the Dutch right along with the patriots. When communist leaders attempted to take over the government by coups in '46 and '48, the country quickly nipped the rebellions and executed the culpable, showing a realistic attitude toward the threat of communism when it became a danger of a "clear and present" nature. Indonesia's views toward the fight against the French in Indochina by the Vietminh are consequently not too hard to understand. . . .

One could spend years here and only scratch the surface of the aesthetic possibilities. In short, I find Indonesia a highly stimulating place. Adding to the enjoyment has been the friendliness of the American Ambassador, Hugh Cumming, an old friend of both Dad and Hunt. When I first arrived I heard from the Embassy that the Ambassador was most anxious to see me. Shortly afterward I had lunch with him and he recalled the trip to Montevideo with Dad in 1933.

"Ernest and I viewed each other with great suspicion. He thought I was an impossible reactionary and I confess I thought of him as a dangerous wild-eyed liberal. It was amazing after 21 days aboard the ship—striking an occasional 'blow for freedom' together—we found there wasn't such a wide divergence in our thoughts after all." He also told me of taking Hunt out of internment in Sweden and getting him a job at the American Embassy, before Hunt was smuggled back to England through Bernt Balchen's "underground" airway. Cumming is a very likable person and is certainly an improvement over his predecessor, H. Merle Cochran, who single-handedly caused the fall of one of the Indonesian cabinets and also had me tossed out of his office. (I don't know which was the greater crime!) Cumming asked me to extend an invitation to you folks to come out to Indonesia and stay with them.

Peter arrived in Australia in June and two weeks later reported he had been "whirling in a maelstrom of appointments, introductions, trips to Melbourne and other areas . . . settling into the new routine, house hunting, and rounds of farewell and welcoming cocktail parties, luncheons and dinners . . ." For the next several months, according to all reports, he did a first-rate job for the UP, and then early in January of 1955, he wrote us that he was about to be married again. His bride was Nancy Monkton, the daughter of a prosperous sheep-ranching family. Several years older than Peter, she was the mother of two children by an earlier marriage, a nine-year-old girl and a four-year-old boy. Dorothy and I were apprehensive. Recalling the circumstances of Peter's previous marriage, our message of love was accompanied by a plea for fuller consideration and less haste. But Peter went ahead. We were unable to go to Australia to attend the wedding.

The marriage lasted seventy-eight days. One night his wife simply walked out on him.

We should probably have gone to Australia to be with Peter, but our finances were at low ebb. I had left the governorship two and a half years previously with only a small retirement income, and was earning my living by writing and lecturing. Moreover, Peter seemed to be recovering from his initial shock. To one friend he wrote that it had put him "in a real tailspin for a month or so, but I'm leveling out again." But then a few months later on October 24, I received a call in Washington from the UP Office in New York informing me that Peter was missing and had been for several days. I at once called Hunt in Juneau and he flew to Australia immediately. When he arrived there, he was given the shattering news that Peter's body had been found in his car on a little-traveled road some miles from Sydney. He had taped a tube to the car's exhaust and had taken his life.

Our anguish was deepened by the incredibility of it all. His many Australian friends had no explanation. His marriage had clearly been a mistake, but he seemed to have recovered from that. Nor could any remotely compelling reason be found in his business life; he had had one or two setbacks which could only be considered minor in view of his successes.

Everyone who wrote to Hunt and to Dorothy and me said there had been no hint of the impending tragedy. Friends, business associates and even his competitors spoke of his charm, intelligence and business acumen—and of his zest for life. There were many such letters; he had made many friends and not only in Australia. He left a trail of affection all over the Pacific, and years later I met people who spoke of him with genuine feeling.

Hunt bore the ordeal of arranging for Peter's funeral bravely. His inquiries led only to the baffling conclusion, which persists, that Peter had everything to live for. Perhaps the nearest approach to an explanation came in a letter to Dorothy from a good friend of Peter's, Aviva Nathan. She was a young woman from Tel Aviv—a former member of the intelligence department of the Israeli Independence Army—whom Peter had known in Singapore. She had come to Sydney just prior to Peter's death and wrote:

> When I met him in Sydney for dinner, he again told me of his work, which he loved and that his marriage had been a mistake. But he seemed to have recovered from any heartache he had about it. . . . As you know, he suffered from moods of depression, and when in that mood talked of suicide, but, of course, I did not believe it. . . . Peter was overworked too. I phoned him two days before his death. Peter was very much depressed and sounded most unhappy. . . . He said he was a failure and couldn't make anyone happy. I would have gone to him, but Sydney is so big and I had only just arrived. I did not know my way about. . . . I told him he sounded terribly unhappy and he said "It's just one of those days; I'll get over it."

It does not really explain why Peter took his own life, but it suggests that in one of his moods of deepest depression, he acted impulsively.

The battle for Alaska statehood in the second half of the 1950s was a blessing to me personally; it helped to take my mind off Peter's tragedy. Dorothy, too, was hard hit by the loss of the second of our three sons, but she was unflagging in her dedication to our common cause.

Agreement had been reached about the candidates for the new statewide offices. For the governorship the Republicans nominated John Butrovich, the Democrats William Egan. For Secretary of State, Hugh Wade, Democrat; Brad Phillips, Republican. For the Senate races Bob Bartlett would be opposed by R. E. Robertson, and Mike Stepovich would be my opponent. For the House, Ralph Rivers would be opposed by Henry Benson who had been the territory's commissioner of Labor.

Expecting mine, the Democratic candidates were expected to be push-overs. But the Stepovich-Gruening race was a different matter.

The difference arose largely from the determination of Interior Secretary Seaton to elect at least one Republican senatorial candidate. Bob Bartlett was considered unbeatable, and so the Republicans concentrated on Mike Stepovich. Their campaign was assisted by the *Fairbanks News Miner*, whose publisher, C. W. Snedden, had originally proposed Stepovich to Seaton. Mike was a most attractive and popular young man with a truly lovely wife and a photogenic family of eight children. The *News-Miner* put out a calendar with a colored photograph of the Stepovich family which was sent to every Alaskan household. Each one must have cost at least a dollar, but as it contained the *News-Miner*'s imprint, it could be deducted as an advertising expense. I saw these calendars in homes even in remote Eskimo villages. They were a potent reminder to cast a vote for the head of a fine family.

The Republican campaign tried to picture Stepovich as an early and ardent supporter of Alaskan statehood. He was photographed in Washington with Senator Knowland and Secretary Seaton, and Seaton was able to secure favorable spreads in the Luce publications. An article in *Life* described Stepovich as the dynamic symbol of a newly reborn Alaska and *Time* planned a "cover" story which would make him appear as the real catalyst of statehood. Unfortunately, his legislative record showed that he had opposed statehood on every possible occasion. In the 1951 legislature, a memorial requesting immediate statehood sponsored by seven Democratic members of the House was referred to a "Special Committee on Statehood" of which Stepovich was chairman, and from which it never emerged. In the same session, a memorial for an elective governor, a device to kill off prostatehood action, was sponsored by Stepovich. In the same session, he had voted to table a bill to appropriate $35,000 for the work of the Alaska Statehood Committee, a bill sponsored by Gunnard Engebreth, a Republican. His record in the 1953 and 1955 sessions on the statehood issue was similar. The Democratic Third Divisional Committee published these facts in a flyer headed "When and Why Mike Stepovich Shifted to Statehood." The exposé made Seaton's efforts to identify his candidate with the statehood cause pretty ridiculous.

Stepovich's record was also vulnerable on other issues. He had voted against salary increases for teachers and for a reduction in teachers' retirement, against new buildings for the University of Alaska and against establishing community colleges. He had voted twice against abolishing fish traps and against the creation of the Alaska Department of Fish and Game. He had voted against the improvement of the Workmen's Compensation Act, against a bill for the care of sick and disabled fishermen,

against construction of National Guard armories, against fiscal reorganization, and against the Alaskan Visitors Association designed to develop the
tourist industry. Our newspaper ads urged people to "Reelect Ernest
Gruening who is FOR the things Stepovich is AGAINST."

I challenged Stepovich to debate; he declined and the Anchorage *News*
supported his decision. In a leading editorial it said: "Why should Mike
waste his time in debate with a man who is perhaps the best qualified
public speaker in Alaska? Would the Golden Gloves champion accept a
match with the world heavyweight?" Our reply to that was obvious.
George Sundborg, who was in charge of the campaign publicity, designed an ad which asked: "Would it be bad for Alaska to have that kind
of a man speaking up for the New State in the United States Senate?"

My publicity made an appeal to the nineteen- to twenty-year-olds who
were now, under Alaska's constitution, able to vote for the first time. I
called their attention to a bill I had sponsored in the 1945 legislature—
Senate Bill No. 1—to give the vote to Alaskans who were eighteen
years of age. It had passed both houses and was signed by me on February 6, the first bill approved by that legislature. But under the restrictive
Organic Act of 1912, it had to be approved by the Congress and Congress declined to do so. Under statehood, I pointed out we could enact
such legislation.

I continued to have an underdog complex because of Stepovich's larger
vote in the primary. For the last two years, I had spent most of my time
in Washington while Stepovich was campaigning in Alaska. There were a
lot of recent comers to Alaska who might not know me, so I felt it desirable to walk up and down Anchorage's main thoroughfare to solicit
votes. I would stop a passerby, hold out my hand and say, "My name is
Gruening. I'm a candidate for the United States Senate and I'd appreciate
your vote."

One heavy-set individual whom I stopped drew his hand away and
said, "You're Gruening? I'd sooner vote for the devil."

I was taken aback, but fortunately I remembered the good advice given
me by experienced campaigners never to lose one's temper. "You know,"
I said, "he'd be a tough guy to beat. But if he decides not to run, do you
suppose you could switch to me?"

The man looked at me steadily for a moment and then said, "Why you
son of a bitch, I might vote for you yet."

Secretary Seaton came to Alaska to campaign for Stepovich and we
were quick to remind the voters that now that we were a state "we could
get the dead hand of the Interior Department off our throat." Seaton's
campaign was, however, counter-productive. Many resented the secretary's injecting himself into a political race. Vice President Richard

Nixon also came to Alaska to speak for Stepovich and the other Republican candidates, and that was enough to enable us to bring up Senator Frank Church of Idaho and Senator John Kennedy of Massachusetts to speak for the Democrats.

We had a cocktail party for Kennedy at my son Hunt's house in Juneau and that evening he spoke at both the Twentieth Century Theater and at a public dinner at the Baranof Hotel. The Lacey Street Theater was packed when he spoke in Fairbanks, and in Anchorage I introduced him to a thousand in the Anchorage High School auditorium. During the question period that followed his speech, Bob Kederick, a pro-Stepovich columnist for the Anchorage *Times*, asked whether it would not be better to have one Democratic and one Republican senator. Kennedy replied that in the next Senate there would be thirty-four Republicans and sixty-two Democrats. Why send a man who would serve on the bottom rung on the minority side of the least important committees when you can send two senators and a representative who are already widely known and respected? "Reelect the team that brought statehood!" The applause was thunderous. Frank Church's eloquence and youthful appearance also captivated his audiences. Kennedy and Church more than offset Nixon and Seaton.

On election night, Dorothy and I, surrounded by well-wishers, listened to the returns at the home of Irene and Pat Ryan. Irene's brother, Pat Irvine, had been an effective campaign manager. I won the election. My majority was not great, only 2581 votes, but it represented a shift of 4302 votes since the primary. Egan, Wade, Bartlett and Rivers were also elected. And the Democrats made a clean sweep in the legislature: eighteen to two in the Senate; and in the House, Democrats numbered thirty-three, Republicans five, Independents two. Apparently the Republicans had really expected to elect at least one senator from Alaska; Secretary Seaton had assured them that they would. Sam Shaffer, *Newsweek*'s knowledgeable Washington correspondent, told me later that the Alaska's Democratic sweep had killed off Fred Seaton politically.

The Eighty-sixth Congress convened on January 7, 1959. Bob Bartlett had previously expressed his desire to be "the senior senator," which I offered to concede, but he insisted that we toss and he won. I was henceforth "the junior senator" from Alaska. The swearing-in ceremony was most impressive. Our so-called Class of '58, the result of a rising Democratic tide, had an unusually large number of new Democratic senators, fourteen in all. They marched down the aisle in groups of four in alphabetical order accompanied by their senior colleagues, the exception being Stephen Young of Ohio who refused to be accompanied by Frank Lausche, a nominal Democrat, because Lausche had supported John

Bricker against Young in the campaign. Bob Bartlett and I came last and were given the special distinction of being accompanied down the aisle respectively by majority leader Lyndon B. Johnson and majority whip Mike Mansfield. Standing beside Vice President Nixon who administered the oath of office to us, we then drew slips from a box held by Felton Johnston, Secretary of the Senate, to determine the length of our terms —two, four, or six years. Bartlett drew the two-year term, I the four-year; the most desirable six-year term remained perversely in the box.

The first three days of the new session were consumed by a recurring fight to curb the filibuster by amending Senate Rule XXII. A group of liberals, headed by Paul Douglas and Clinton P. Anderson, wanted the rule amended to impose cloture by a majority vote. Lyndon Johnson's compromise amendment provided the imposition of cloture by two-thirds of "those present and voting"—a very minor modification. While I felt strongly that the Southerners' filibustering to block civil-rights legislation was intolerable, there were countervailing arguments in favor of extended debate to prevent hasty decisions in moments of national hysteria and to give time to allow public sentiment to mobilize. The need of a state with a small delegation—such as Alaska's with only one congressman—to protect itself against majority action detrimental to its interests predisposed me to the very moderate—indeed insignificant—change proposed by Johnson. We in Alaska had endured shameful discriminations by the Congress which a filibuster could perhaps have prevented. After hours of debate, Senator Douglas's amendment for a straight majority to achieve cloture was defeated sixty-seven to twenty-eight. An amendment by Senator Thruston Morton of Kentucky to achieve cloture by a three-fifths vote lost fifty-eight to thirty-six. I voted against both proposals.

As I listened to the well-reasoned presentations pro and con, I found myself mentally vacillating. I was not wholly happy at the thought of a minority imposing its will to prevent action. Still there were valid, constitutionally established practices for a two-thirds vote, such as for the ratification of treaties and the overriding of a presidential veto. But my determination to support the Johnson amendment was finally secured when William Langer reasserted his long-established opposition to any limitation of debate in the Senate, "the one place left in the world for free and untrammeled discussion," and quoted the elder Robert LaFollette and Charles McNary that "a good bill has never been killed by a filibuster, but many a bad bill has been prevented from becoming a law by a few fighting liberals." And still remembered was President Truman's request for legislation to draft striking railroad workers into the army which was rushed through the House in only two hours, but died after six days of Senate debate. So both Bartlett and I voted for Johnson's amendment which was adopted by seventy-two to twenty-two and terminated that Congress's debate on a hardy biennial. Ten Senate years later I would become convinced that we had been right and that "extended debate"—a euphemism for the filibuster—was truly a guardian of our liberties.

On my second day I was happy to cosponsor bills for Hawaiian statehood, for improvements of the Federal Airport Act, for the stimulation of the production and conservation of coal, and for federal support of schools. I asked for membership on the Committee on Interior and Insular Affairs and the Committee on Public Works which were granted me. Bobby Baker, "Secretary to the Majority," asked whether I would not like another minor committee appointment—Government Operations—and I accepted.

Also on that second day the Senate membership went to the House of Representatives at the other end of the Capitol to hear President Eisenhower's State of the Union Message. Among Democrats, it was considered uninspiring, a platitudinous rehearsal of the need for economy and a balanced budget that did not correspond with the realities of the current recession, the 12.9-billion-dollar deficit for that fiscal year and the President's expressed hope for a tax reduction, which was an illusion, we felt, especially in view of the 47-billion-dollar defense program he said was essential. His budget message dealt largely with defense, mutual security and foreign aid—all of which he urged be increased substantially, at the same time warning that "we must examine new programs and proposals with a critical eye." This, we soon learned, meant "no new starts." And as we examined the proposed appropriations for matters that seemed to us essential to the nation's well-being and progress—education, health, housing, airports, highways—they struck us as inadequate. The coming session might well develop into a contest between the Congressional majority to secure what it deemed essential in these vital domestic fields, and the presidential veto or threat of veto to curtail Congressional efforts. This is exactly what happened, and this struggle was particularly pertinent to the Alaska delegation; we all keenly felt the need of catching up with the rest of America to compensate for the near century of flagrant neglect.

Actually, Alaska had at that time a larger proportion of unemployment—fourteen percent—than any other state. I addressed the Senate on this issue in support of an amendment by Senator Pat McNamara of Michigan, I cosponsored, to extend the duration of unemployment compensation. Alaskans' unemployment had been aggravated by a treaty with Japan negotiated several years earlier, without consultation of Alaskan authorities and in woeful ignorance of the pelagic habits of the Pacific salmon. The treaty fixed the meridian up to which high-seas salmon-fishing was permitted too far east. In consequence the Japanese were taking such quantities of Alaska-spawned salmon that Alaska's important Bristol Bay area was closed to salmon-fishing. The amended unemployment compensation bill passed by a narrow margin of forty-nine to forty-six along almost straight party lines; a few Southerners joined the Republicans, a foreshadowing of what could be the line-up in the Congress.

The differences between the President and the Democratic majority in the Congress were highlighted by the administration's desire to wreck the rural electrification program established a quarter of a century earlier by the Roosevelt Administration and still bitterly opposed by the privately owned utilities. The issue involved transferring the authority to make loans to REA cooperatives from the agency's administrator to the Secretary of Agriculture, and increasing the existing two percent interest rate on these REA loans. Maintaining the existing set-up was of particular importance to Alaska where electric cooperatives were being formed, a program I had worked for as governor; in fact, the first Alaskan REA loan had just been made to a cooperative in the Bristol Bay area. I took an active part in the debate and the President's veto was overridden sixty-four to twenty.

For me, this was a time-honored battle, believing as I did that low-cost electric current was a commodity essential to modern living which should be made available to the public without private profit and at a price sufficient only to meet the costs of investment and operation. For that reason, I actively sought the development of Alaska's vast hydroelectric potential which, as yet, had hardly been touched. The only federal hydroelectric project at that time was a dam at the outfall of Eklutna Lake north of Anchorage. But there were other desirable sites all over Alaska—at Bradley Lake in the Kenai Peninsula, at Long and Crater lakes near Snettisham some thirty miles south of Juneau—a study of which I recommended—and most important, at the Rampart Canyon on the Yukon. Here a dam could create an installed capacity of nearly five million kilowatts, twice the capacity of Grand Coulee Dam, at that time the largest hydroelectric project under the American flag. Further, the power could be produced and transmitted to all parts of Alaska at an extremely low cost. So I requested and secured a resolution of the Public Works Committee for a preliminary investigation of the Rampart Canyon site by the Corps of Engineers. A modest $100,000 was granted.

I think I expressed the feeling of most of my Democratic colleagues when on May 19, after discussing the hydroelectric program, I called attention to the Senate passage of an excellent housing bill, an area redevelopment bill and an airport construction bill—all of which were awaiting action in the House. I said that both houses were operating "under the dark shadow of a veto threat and felt themselves shackled by the unimaginative, regressive and wholly deficient administration policy of no new starts." The President did veto the airport, housing and area redevelopment bills and also a bill sponsored by the Alaska delegation to increase the acreage for oil leasing in Alaska, a measure designed—in compensating partly for the high cost of operation in Alaska—to attract the major petroleum producers. After the veto, however, we were able to reenact it in a modified form. We had less luck with the airport bill veto. I called attention to the statements made by Secretary Seaton while he was campaigning in Alaska the previous fall, asserting the administration's approval of funds to extend the Anchorage and Fairbanks airport runways. But the President's budget contained no provision for either, and after his veto we had to content ourselves with a bill that did not include them.

The veto of the bill providing for housing and urban renewal seemed particularly ill-advised since the draft originally introduced in the Senate had been drastically whittled down to meet what were believed to be the President's standards. In the course of my protest I said: "It makes no economic sense to label housing programs in the United States as 'extravagant' while threatening to call the Congress into special session if additional funds for foreign aid—including housing programs in foreign lands—are not voted by this Congress." Herblock, the *Washington Post*'s cartoonist, depicted President Eisenhower looking at four framed pictures of his various domiciles—the farm at Gettysburg, Camp David in Maryland, the house built for him off the golf course in Augusta, Georgia, and the White House—and saying: "I see no housing shortage."

While funds for our domestic needs were subject to repeated scrutiny and control, the vast funds destined for foreign aid—the administration sought $3.8 billion in 1959—were not. For both expenditures and appropriations—except the foreign-aid program—the procedure required authorization first by the appropriate subcommittee, then by the full committee and finally passage by the whole body, a process duplicated in both the House and the Senate. In contrast, the agency which administered foreign aid—at that time called the International Cooperation Administration (ICA)—merely presented what it called an "illustrative budget" to the Foreign Relations Committee of the Senate and the Foreign Affairs Committee of the House which approved it with little real probing. Foreign-aid appropriations received the same uncritical assent in both Senate and House Appropriations Committees.

In effect, foreign aid was virtually a secret program—secret to a degree even from the senators and representatives who passed judgment on it. Senate and House members were permitted to see the volumes of graphs, charts and tables prepared by the ICA, but as these were "classified"—that is, marked "secret"—we were not allowed even in discussion on the floor to reveal the projects and the amounts allocated to each. Moreover, even this restricted preview was meaningless since the ICA was free to depart from it. But the administration contended that this procedure gave the program the flexibility it required. For fifteen years the Congress had accepted this formula, and while I favored the purposes of the program, I felt that a "double standard" between foreign aid and domestic expenditures should no longer apply. It amounted to giving the executive branch a blank check in this vast field; it was an abdication by the Congress of its constitutionally prescribed function, and a violation—in spirit at least—of the Constitution's provision that "no money shall be drawn from the Treasury, but in consequence of appropriations by law."

Senator Fulbright, chairman of the Foreign Relations Committee, had invited suggestions to amend the procedure, and I presented a proposal that would require the ICA to present its projects and the amount to be spent on them in detail before the committee, and to be bound by its commitments as would be any federal agency; in other words, to apply to the foreign-aid program the procedure used for all other federal projects and expenditures. The proposal came up for debate, and in the final debate on July 7, I pointed to the action of an ICA representative in Laos who had recently increased the annual pay of its army—the total cost of which was borne by the United States—by a million dollars, in compliance with a request by the Laotian government, but which the State Department had specifically ordered him to reject. The Congress had not been informed of this episode. "It would appear," I said after presenting these facts to the Senate, "that the control of the program no longer resides in Washington but is scattered throughout the world. Not only has the Congress lost control over the spending under the foreign-aid program, but officials of the Departments of Defense and State and of the International Cooperation Agency have delegated authority to approve expenditures of sizable sums of money to mission heads wherever they may be. When the head of a mission in face of contrary instructions from his superiors can commit the United States Government to the expenditure of a million dollars annually, it is my opinion that the time has come to pull in the reins and subject the expenditure of funds under this program to the same controls as are exercised over funds expended for domestic programs."

Senator Fulbright, however, opposed the amendment. He said it "would completely disrupt the administration of the program." I replied that under the provisions of the bill the President could use ten percent of the total foreign-aid appropriation as he saw fit; this provision was not affected by my amendment, and ten percent of $3.8 billion, or of whatever amount was finally voted, certainly provided ample flexibility. But the opposition of a committee chairman is difficult to overcome, especially by a freshman senator. The vote was fifty-three nays to thirty-eight yeas. But given the number and names of those who supported the amendment, I considered it a moral victory and merely the first skirmish in what I hoped would be a continuing battle against an unsoundly administered and costly program.

The battle would be renewed, and shortly. Two weeks later, on July 21, Senator Mansfield introduced into the *Congressional Record* the first two of a series of articles by Albert M. Colegrove, published in the Scripps-Howard newspapers. They revealed that American taxpayers had already spent roughly two billion dollars to help the new, anticommunist nation of South Vietnam, described the waste and corruption, and the efforts of United States officials to conceal it. It was further proof of my point and addressing my colleagues, I said, "The question I would now raise is this: Has the time not come for Congress to reassume its control over the power of the purse with respect to foreign-aid spending? How many more scandals in how many more countries must be ferreted out before the Congress will hold the foreign-aid program to strict budget and accounting controls?"

One happy event—no longer controversial—was the admission of Hawaii to statehood. On March 11, the Senate voted favorably by seventy-six to fifteen, and the following day the House passed it by 322 to eighty-nine. The speed with which this action was taken—early in the session with relatively little debate—was in part the result of Alaska's long struggle for statehood.

On August 24, we welcomed our Hawaiian colleagues, Oren Long and Hiram Fong, to the Senate. I had known Long as superintendent of Public Instruction in Hawaii, then as secretary and as governor of the territory. Hiram Fong's story would have put Horatio Alger's heroes to shame. Son of an indentured Chinese laborer, he had graduated with honors from the University of Hawaii, worked his way through Harvard Law School, and become a successful businessman and a director of many corporations. He had also served in the Hawaiian legislature and was now the first of his race to be elected to the United States Senate.

Hawaii sent Dan Inouye to the House of Representatives. Inouye, the son of a naturalized Japanese, was the principal in a unique and historic incident. When asked to raise his right hand to take the oath of office, he could not do it. He had lost his right arm in battle, in Italy, fighting for his country in World War II. He raised his left hand, and two years later he would do so again in the Senate. Viewing the ceremony, I recalled the oft-asked question by opponents of Hawaiian statehood: "How would you like to have a senator called Moto?" The answer was that we liked it and him very much. Inouye rapidly endeared himself to all his colleagues and became one of the Senate's leaders. Meanwhile two more "Motos" were elected to the House, Spark Matsunaga, and Patsy Mink, both excellent.

I found I had another struggle on my hands when I tried to secure subsoil rights for homesteaders on the Kenai Peninsula. Shortly before the big oil strike there in 1957, the Geological Survey had declared all lands in the Kenai Peninsula prospectively valuable for oil and gas, where previously they had been declared agricultural only. The Interior Department's Bureau of Land Management thereupon had required the homesteaders to submit waivers of their subsoil rights within thirty days, or forfeit the right to patent—that is, ownership. These homesteaders had completed all the requirements for patent (clearing and cultivating land, constructing access roads, building homes, etc.) before the Geological Survey's declaration, and had expended a great deal of hard work and money in the process. In many cases patents should have been issued them before the new declaration, but were not because of delays in the Bureau of Land Management whose efficiency left much to be desired. This high-handed action struck me as wholly unjust and unwarranted and I determined to introduce remedial legislation. But first I had to move fast to get the thirty-day and then ninety-day ultimatums extended. My bill, S.1670, introduced on April 12, not only gave these homesteaders their subsoil rights, but quit-claimed the United States in the cases of those homesteaders who had been stampeded into giving the waivers.

There was, however, an unconscionable delay in getting the Interior Department's report on the bill despite my repeated requests while the extended time limits were expiring; it was a deliberate bureaucratic move to prevent enactment. And when the report finally came, it was adverse. Opposition of a department to a bill affecting it is almost invariably fatal; but there was evidence that in the preceding fall, when Secretary Seaton was campaigning in Alaska, he had met with Kenai homesteaders and promised them that he would favor legislation preventing forfeiture of their rights. Yet now his department had rendered a report opposing this very legislation.

Fortunately, a tape-recording of Secretary Seaton's remarks had been made. I quoted them in my correspondence with Seaton and presented them at the hearings of the Senate Subcommittee on Public Lands, which I chaired at the request of the chairman, Senator O'Mahoney. So the bill was reported to the full committee and to the Senate, and with an amendment in the House which limited its effect only to the Kenai Peninsula (my draft had included other areas where similar conditions existed) was enacted by both Houses toward the end of the Eighty-sixth Congress's second session and became Public Law 86-789. Some two hundred homesteaders were benefitted; and knowing what an arduous, back-breaking task homesteading in Alaska is, and how beset with man-made difficulties, I rejoiced for them. Secretary Seaton had the grace not to recommend a veto.

The session's single most gratifying action from Alaska's standpoint was the enactment of an "Alaska Omnibus Act," the legislation needed to adjust the transition from territory to statehood. It involved no small amount of painstaking research and lengthy hearings. The legislation followed a precedent set with the admission of Oklahoma, New Mexico and Arizona. If authorized—there would be transition grants totaling $28.5 million over a five-year period, in part as compensation for the continuing discrimination against Alaska in highway funds, although the report on the bill made clear that these grants were by no means the equivalent of the sums of which Alaska had been deprived through the years. The act provided for the state's take-over of the federal airports and the establishment of a federal judicial system. The excellence of the act was largely due to the solicitude of Harold Seidman of the Bureau of the Budget. I reported the bill to the Senate on June 3 and it was passed by a voice vote, having previously passed the House whose slightly differing version was accepted by the Senate.

In the closing days of the first session, the President vetoed the public works bill. He had vetoed this bill once before, and the House sustained that veto by a margin of two votes. The bill was then reenacted with a two-and-one-half percent reduction on each item. In his second veto message, the President said the bill contained sixty-seven unbudgeted items —that is to say, new starts. It included appropriations for the Tennessee Valley Authority as well as a variety of other projects all over the country. Funds to study hydroelectric development in Rampart Canyon had been reduced from $100,000 to $50,000 in the previous public works bill, and now to $47,500 in this one. It also contained appropriations for small-boat harbors in Dillingham, Juneau and Seldovia. The charge that these were "pork barrel" items was made by opponents and in the press, but in my view they were nothing of the kind. Small-boat harbors were needed by Alaskan fishermen, and the ramps and floats were provided by local funds. This time, fortunately, the House overrode the veto by 280 to 121, and the Senate by the ample margin of seventy-two to twenty-three.

In June, Senator Moss of Utah and I joined Senator Paul Douglas on the south shore of Lake Michigan to have a look at some five thousand acres of the Indiana Dunes which Douglas wanted set aside as a national monument. The preservation of this ecological masterpiece was a special concern of his. Originally it had stretched the full twenty-five-mile length of Lake Michigan's southernmost shore which lies within the State of Indiana. Behind white sandy beaches, these dunes actually extended more than a mile inland and contained unusual and exotic plants and animal life. But this unique natural heritage had been invaded from the west to make way for the industrial cities of Gary and Hammond. As we entered what was left of the area, the acrid fumes of industry assailed our nostrils and throats, and the waters of the lake were red and yellow with rusted, cast-off machinery and chemical effluent. At the time of our visit, some five miles beyond Hammond had escaped the destruction and pollution of air, beach and water, and at the eastern end some three miles had been preserved as a state park. There was imminent danger that the rest might go. Two steel companies—National, headed by George M. Humphrey, former Secretary of the Treasury, and Bethlehem—were each planning to erect a mill and develop a harbor in front of them. Moss and I urged speedy action on the Interior Committee and we joined in sponsoring a bill introduced on July 29 by Senator James Murray to set aside not only this area but a number of others as national seashores and national lakeshores. Under it in the following years, I was privileged, with some of my colleagues on the Interior Committee, to see set aside for posterity not only what was left of Indiana Dunes, but the Cape Cod, Padre Island, Point Reyes, Assateague and Fire Island national seashores. In retrospect I know of no more valuable actions taken by the Congress in the 1960s.

Hearings before the Senate committees on Interior and Insular Affairs and Public Works had established that, while the United States was still ahead of Russia in water-resources development, Russia's progress was "a stern warning that this Nation must not adopt a complacent attitude that would allow us to drift into an assumption of unassailable superiority." With that conclusion as a preamble, the previous Congress had resolved that the two Senate committees continue their "joint findings and recommendations of ways and means to accelerate the development and utilization of the natural resources of the United States." To my pleasant surprise this was interpreted in the Eighty-sixth Congress as a study trip to Russia to see what it was doing to develop its hydroelectric power. Three freshmen, Frank Moss, Edmund Muskie and I were appointed to make the study.

We left Washington in mid-September, accompanied by a staff of experts, and spent a month in Russia, visiting eleven dams on eight rivers. They included the Kuybyshev and Stalingrad dams on the Volga, the former completed, the latter in operation, and the Bratsk dam two-thirds of the way across Siberia near Irkutsk which harnesses the Angara River, the outflow of Lake Baikal, the largest body of fresh water in the world. Each of these dams exceeded in installed and generating capacity anything in the United States. Still bigger dams were on the drawing boards. Our experts concluded that the Russians could overtake the United States in power production in a little more than a decade. They were already superior to us in long-distance transmission of electric energy.

Throughout our journey we had knowledgeable guides who were eager to display their hydroelectric accomplishments, but who also left us free to wander. Official hospitality could not have been exceeded with its sumptuous luncheons and dinners, the opera and the ballet. And we had many opportunities to meet with Russian professionals and workers. Without exception we found only friendliness. The mass of the people, we noted, were living in poverty but were confident of improvement. Their standard of living, their true income, was diminished by the high cost of goods, which were pretty shoddy, sold in government stores where they were obliged to buy in the absence of competitive private enterprise. Women had a greater occupational equality with men than in the United States, including both menial jobs and professional employment. If one conclusion was impressed on me, making due allowances for the relative brevity of our visit, it was that the people of our two countries really had nothing to quarrel about, and, if left to their own devices, would be friends. It was, and is, I am convinced, little groups of men called "governments" who foster suspicion, distrust, antagonism and fear —and the responsibility is shared equally by both the Russian and American governments. My colleagues came to the same conclusion.

When we returned, our subcommittee of three issued a 206-page report with individual contributions by the experts who had accompanied us. It pointed out, in a passage which I neither wrote nor inspired, that "The greatest undeveloped hydropower potential on the North American Continent is concentrated in Alaska." At least we had begun our studies of the hydroelectric potentials of our mightiest river, the Yukon, and I was determined to press for greater development of Alaska's power resources.

A major theme of President Eisenhower's State of the Union Message to the second session of the Eighty-sixth Congress was the need to fight inflation "as we would a fire that imperils our home." Yet only three days later, on January 10, 1960, the Federal Maritime Board granted an increase of ten percent in freight rates to the Alaska Steamship Company. A request by the Alaska congressional delegation for a hearing before such action was taken had been denied, and this increase followed hard on the heels of another fifteen percent increase in 1958, which made a total of twenty-six and one-half percent in the last two years.

I took to the Senate floor, reviewing our long-standing battle with the

steamship company, now Alaska's only maritime carrier, and the so-called
regulatory agencies that controlled it, denouncing their latest performance as "seaway robbery." But in spite of that, and a telegram of protest
to President Eisenhower from our delegation, asking, at the very least, the
120-day grace period provided by law, the rate increase was not suspended. The hearing was granted, but its possible benefits were nullified
by the misleading provision, which Alaska had experienced before, that
the increases would be held in escrow and refunded to the shippers if
they were found unwarranted. The spuriousness of this proposal was
self-evident. The freight increases had already been passed on to the customers of every merchant. How could they be refunded to the
consumers—the real victims? The increase remained, and the inflation-
ary spiral begun by governmental action before the echoes of President
Eisenhower's urgent plea had died away continued.

But there was more—and worse—to come. A week after the Federal Maritime Board's action, our delegation learned through the newspapers that the Alaska Railroad was also raising its rates ten percent. I again
took the floor of the Senate to point out that this increase was by a
wholly owned government enterprise, and to criticize "the striking disparity between the pronoucements and the actions of this administration."
And I followed a telegraphic protest to Secretary Seaton with a letter
which cited the protests of two prominent Alaskans who were also Republicans. Nevertheless, the railway increase remained in effect and its in-
flationary consequences were immediately felt.

The President's budget message was again strikingly deficient in proposed items for domestic needs, but lavish with foreign-aid expenditures,
which led me to voice another protest. This time I was joined by the two
West Virginia senators, Robert C. Byrd and Jennings Randolph, who deplored the President's veto of a modest bill aimed at finding new uses for
coal, in order to aid the sorely depressed areas of that and other coalmining states, while at the same time aid to coalmining was being given in
some thirty foreign countries. Alluding to Alaska's principal industry, fisheries, Senator Byrd asked me whether I was aware of the aid program's
expenditures to "rehabilitate the fishing industries of other countries some
of which were engaged in fishing before Leif Ericson or Columbus came
to America, "while Alaska's ailing fisheries were completely ignored. I replied that it was only one of several such flagrant contradictions in the
administration's policies.

The difference in the administration's—indeed the two political
parties'—attitude on domestic versus foreign appropriations was shortly
made crystal clear in the debate early in February on the federal aid to
education bill. An amendment by Senator Joseph Clark of Pennsylvania

to include aid for teachers' salaries in addition to school contruction resulted in a tie vote. On reconsideration, Vice President Nixon broke the tie so that the inclusion of teachers' salaries was defeated. Reintroduced in a diminished form, the bill was still opposed predominantly by Repbulicans and a few Southern Democrats, but it passed fifty-four to thirty-five. In a colloquy with Everett Dirksen, the Republican minority leader, I said, "The Senator from Illinois has said he is opposed to aid to American schoolteachers. Will he be opposed to the aid for foreign schoolteachers included in the foreign-aid program, which the President will send us?" Senator Dirksen evaded the issue with a funny story.

I then started to read, and, after a sampling, placed in the *Congressional Record* the projects for education in the foreign-aid bills submitted to the Congress in the five previous years of the Eisenhower Administration. These projects went to fifty-nine countries at a cost of $128,334,501, and many specifically included teachers' aid. In none was it excluded. The exhibit required nine pages of the *Congressional Record* in small type.

In mid-February the Senate began a long battle for civil rights. To head off such legislation, eighteen senators from nine southern states resolved to filibuster. They were determined to keep the Senate in continuous session for five, and at times, six days a week. So with some exceptions—for there would be considerable absenteeism—we, who favored civil rights, were expected not to leave the Capitol except on Sundays or for very special reasons. And those of us who took the challenge seriously slept in our clothes on cots adjacent to the Senate chamber, in our offices, or in the Senate "gym." These naps were often interrupted by "live" quorum calls at 2:00, 3:00, or 4:00 A.M. and by a total of forty-three yea and nay votes. Of these I missed only one—on a motion by Lyndon Johnson to recess until noon the next day, a welcome break in our rather gruelling self-enforced routine. The debate lasted nearly eight weeks, concluding at sixteen minutes before 9:00 P.M. on Saturday, April 8, the Senate having adjourned the night before at 12:21 A.M.

At the start of debate, civil-rights legislation presumably had bipartisan support—all the Democrats except the eighteen Dixiecrats and all the Republicans. But the latter soon began to slip away. The administration was lukewarm about the whole civil rights issue and minority leader Everett Dirksen led the defectors. It was he who moved successfully to table amendments by Senators Douglas, Hart, Javits, Keating, Hennings and Carroll for desegregation of public schools, open housing, fair employment practices and other measures. It became evident after a few weeks that protection of voting rights would alone survive and that was the administration's wish. Majority leader Lyndon Johnson, although a sincere civil-rights advocate, also seemed to feel that this was about all we could achieve under the circumstances. The voting rights provisions, the use of federal registrars and referees and other related provisions would, it became clear, depend for their success on the zeal with which the Department of Justice implemented their enforcement.

I spoke at length on the debate's last day, voicing my criticism of the legislation and my disappointment at its many omissions. But I decided that what little was left in the bill was worth voting for, a conclusion likewise reached by the other truly committed civil-rights advocates, for on final passage by a vote of seventy-one to eighteen, only the die-hard Southern opponents voted against it. They had been beaten in their efforts to defeat all of the legislation, but kept on trying until the last minute.

Even though Alaska was now a state, conflicts with the Secretary of the Interior continued. In April, Bob Bartlett and I objected to Secretary Seaton's withdrawal of 607,800 acres of public domain near Fairbanks as a missile-testing range, which he thereupon issued under a license to the Defense Department. This action was in violation of the so-called Engle Act which forbade the withdrawal for military purposes of any area in excess of five thousand acres without the consent of Congress. Although the land was expropriated by the secretary of the Interior instead of by the Defense Department, it was clearly against the law. Had the law been followed, a defense-minded Congress would doubtless have approved the withdrawal, but the hearings preceding such assent would have served to protect affected citizens and spelled out the terms on which the military would operate. It was just another of the arbitrary decisions imposed on Alaskans by the Interior Department bureaucracy.

Another followed shortly when Seaton moved into the field of Alaska fisheries which, under the Statehood Act, had been transferred from the Interior Department's Fish and Wildlife Service to the state. Seaton set aside a large fishing area in southeastern Alaska for exclusive Indian use and ordered the installation of eleven fish traps for three villages. Alaska's state constitution had barred fish traps; moreover, the villagers did not want them and had gone on record to that effect in a resolution of the Alaska Native Brotherhood. But operating under the paternalistic attitude traditional with secretaries of the Interior, Seaton decided they must have them. The State of Alaska took the matter to court and ultimately the Supreme Court. Justice Felix Frankfurter rendered the majority opinion and overruled the secretary, but the state had been put to needless effort and expense.

The totally unexpected and distressing news of the death of Oregon's Senator Richard Neuberger came on March 9. It was a great personal loss to both Dorothy and me, and indeed a deep sorrow to the Senate and to our Alaska delegation in particular. A promising career of exceptional dedication and versatility had been cut short. He had served as a captain in the Corps of Engineers that built the highway to Alaska, had given his time and talent generously to promote Alaska's interests, including statehood, and had continued to serve the state in the Senate.

I wired William Beltz, president of the Alaska Senate, and Warren Taylor, Speaker of the House, suggesting a memorial and urging that one of Alaska's many unnamed mountains be named for Dick Neuberger. A 6749-foot peak, recommended by Representative Robert Sheldon of Fairbanks, the highest summit of a range fifteen miles southeast of Tok junction and visible from the Alaska highway, was submitted to the Board of Geographic Names which approved the choice of Mount Neuberger.

Neuberger had announced his candidacy for reelection. When he died, only forty-eight hours remained before the closing date for filing. I telephoned his wife, Maurine, and urged her strongly to file—a decision

Dick and Maurine Neuberger

difficult for her to make at such short notice under the circumstances. Dick and Maurine had for several years served together in the Oregon legislature, she in the House, he in the Senate, a unique husband and wife legislative team. I felt that no one could better continue Dick's work. She agreed and was elected in 1960. She served well for the next six years, distinguishing herself particularly as a consumers' advocate. Her book, *Smoke Screen:Tobacco and the Public Welfare*, sounded one of the earliest warnings against the danger of cigarette smoking. She chose not to run for a second term.

I was gratified when the Department of Agriculture, under Ezra Taft Benson, presented to the Congress a program for forestry research, conservation and utilization that would cost six million dollars for the next fiscal year. I was less pleased when the Bureau of the Budget slashed it to $1,780,400, I criticized the action on the Senate floor and listed—as I had with educational grants abroad—the foreign forestry-aid programs which had been approved by the Eisenhower Administration in the preceding five years. They included grants to China (Taiwan), Vietnam, India, Iran, Jordan, Lebanon, Liberia, Pakistan, Turkey, Spain, Yugoslavia, Haiti, Paraguay, Cambodia, Korea, Laos, Libya, Somalia and British Guiana. In this small British colony alone we spent in one year—1958 —the sum of $2,150,000, or one-fourth more than the Eisenhower Administration was willing to spend for forestry in the whole of the United States, including Alaska and Hawaii.

"Truly shocking" was what I called the President's veto of the pollution-control bill, which provided federal matching grants for municipalities and states to enable them to build sewage-disposal and treatment plants. The reason given was that pollution control was primarily the responsibility of state and local governments. I pointed out that, on the contrary, some two thousand rivers were interstate, that such rivers as the Missouri, the Mississipi and their tributaries drew their pollution from more that a score of states, and that such interstate pollution was surely, in part at least, a federal responsibility.

Again I contrasted domestic spending with what was being done in foreign countries. Arkansas, for example, wholly bordered on the east by the Mississippi and crossed by several mighty tributaries, would have received $3,587,570 under the bill and would have been obligated to put up twice that amount. Yet in 1957 the Karachi water and sewage-disposal plant in Pakistan had received $3,795,000 in American dollars with no matching requirements. I cited other such contrasts: Rangoon, Burma's capital, had received $2,045,000 to construct a water supply and sewage system; Panama, $2 million. However, the House failed to override the veto. A start made then would have forestalled far worse pollution in future years.

The battle against the disparity between generosity abroad and penu-
riousness at home had its lighter moments. I sponsored a bill to appropriate $20 million a year for the next fifteen years for Alaska highways.
When it was suggested by one of the members of the Public Works
Committee that Eisenhower would probably veto it, Thurman D. Sherard, Alaska's chief highway engineer who was testifying before the committee, said with some feeling that a staff member of the International Cooperation Administration had stopped in his office in Juneau on his way
to the Far East to superintend the contruction of a highway—from
Rangoon to Mandalay.

"With whose money?" asked Chairman Jennings Randolph.

"The United States will finance it," said Sherard.

"Maybe," said Senator Oren Long, a member of the committee,
"Alaska and Hawaii should secede and as foreign governments get the
help from Uncle Sam we can't get now."

I was inspired to start writing on a pad before me, and after a few minutes said, "Members of the committee, I've just composed a poem which
may be appropriate to the occasion. It is entitled 'On the Road to Mandalay' with apologies to Kipling. May I read it?"

"Perhaps you should sing it," suggested Oren Long.

But I read it.

> By the old Moulmein Pagoda
> Looking eastward to the sea,
> There's a Burma project settin'
> And I doubt it works for me.
> But the White House says we've got to,
> And the foreign echoes say
> Come you back you Yankee dollar
> Come you back to Mandalay.
>
> On the road to Mandalay
> Where the ICAers play,
> Can't you hear bulldozers chunkin'
> From Rangoon to Mandalay?
> Just another give-away
> When the dough comes up like thunder
> From the good old USA

I would try again to eliminate this "double standard" in foreign and
domestic expenditures. I proposed an amendment to the foreign-aid bill
which would require that all nonmilitary projects abroad for flood con-

trol, reclamation or other utilization of land and water resources be studied by competent engineers and the cost-benefit ratio be determined as they were (and are) for such projects in the United States, and that no project be undertaken unless the benefits exceeded the costs. Senator Fulbright opposed the measure. He said there was no justification for requiring the same standards abroad as at home; there was a large element of political necessity in these projects overseas. He was joined by minority leader Everett Dirksen—a tough combination. Nevertheless, the amendment was defeated by only five votes.

My next amendment provided that projects for flood control, hydroelectric development, and harbor, housing, hospital, highway or airport construction, if they were estimated to cost more than a million dollars apiece, be presented separately for the approval of Congress. I pointed out that scores of projects in this country costing far less than a million dollars were subjected to scrutiny, and approval or rejection by the appropriate committees of both Houses of Congress, and I asked why large foreign-aid projects and programs should not require specific justification and approval by Congress. Fulbright and Dirksen again said no, that this would wreck the program. Senator Allen Ellender, who had made it a practice to travel abroad extensively at his own expense, called attention to the many large projects which the United States had undertaken in foreign countries, and which had then been abandoned. Senator Russell Long of Louisiana ventured the guess that the chairman of the Foreign Relations Committee could not tell the Senate how many construction projects costing more than a million dollars were included in the pending bill. Fulbright did not respond. But the closeness of the previous vote had alarmed the foreign-aid advocates and the debate went on at some length, Lyndon Johnson granting an additional hour to each side. My amendment was defeated fifty-two to twenty-three.

I was humbled. My next amendment merely required that the Congress be informed in advance what military assistance would be requested for each country. Fulbright said he would not oppose that and it was approved by a voice vote. The foreign-aid bill, authorizing expenditures of $4 billion—which did not include an additional loan program generally repayable in soft currencies—was finally passed by a vote of sixty to twenty-six. I voted against it, convinced that the program was wasteful and ineffective and that unless some serious effort was made to improve its procedures and administration, it did not merit support. My opposing vote was also a protest against the "double standard."

The continuing disparity between the administration's words and deeds prompted me on June 14 to make a speech on the Middle East. I had been disenchanted with the Eisenhower-Nixon-Dulles foreign policy ever since it had turned against Britain, France and Israel, and had voted with the Soviet Union in the United Nations to impose sanctions upon them for moving to recapture the Suez Canal after Nasser had seized it in violation of all treaties. Saved from defeat by the United States, Nasser, Egypt's dictator, was now denying passage through the Suez to ships of all nations carrying supplies to and from Israel. The Arab nations had never ceased to wage war on Israel and were continuing their efforts to strangle this tiny young republic. In response to protests against American policies that were giving comfort to the Arab design, Vice President Nixon had written a letter to Label Katz, president of B'nai B'rth, saying: "With regard to the matter of the Suez Canal the United States has unequivocally affirmed its support of the principle that there should be freedom of transit through the canal for all nations. This policy has been enunciated publicly and repeatedly."

Fine words, but they were negated by a loan of $50 million from the International Bank for Reconstruction and Development to Nasser to widen and deepen the canal. While allegedly an international agency, there was no question that had the United States wished to exercise its influence it could have prevented this action. The president, the three vice presidents and the treasurer of the bank were all Americans, and while decisions were made by a majority of the eighteen directors representing a variety of countries, all the Americans on the board had voted for the loan. Certainly the loan should have carried a commitment to allow freedom of transit as had originally been provided in the treaty which Nasser had violated. This at least would have furnished evidence that the United States meant what its Vice President affirmed so emphatically.

Moreover, when the Senate attempted to insert a moderate amendment to this effect in the mutual security bill, we were informed that the administration was adamantly opposed to it. The amendment was sponsored by Senator Paul Douglas in Illinois with twenty-eight cosponsors of whom I was one. It stated quite succinctly that "the purposes of this Act are negated and the peace of the world is endangered when nations which receive assistance under this Act wage economic warfare against other nations assisted under this Act, including such procedures as boycotts, blockades, and the restriction of the use of international waterways." Further, it stated that "assistance under this Act . . . shall be administered to give effect to these principles, and, in all negotiations between the United States and any foreign state arising as a result of funds appropriated . . . these principles shall be applied as the President may determine and he shall report on measures taken by the administration to insure their application." I spoke for the amendment, saying that I believed it "highly desirable that the United States stop appeasing dicta-

424   *Many Battles*

tors, especially when they are in definite violation of their own agreements." The amendment was opposed by Fulbright and Dirksen but supported by Johnson and Mansfield and passed forty-five to twenty-five.

In my speech on the Middle East, I called attention to the plight of
Israel, surrounded by militantly hostile nations with populations fifty
times as numerous and an area a thousand times as great. Yet it remains an
oasis of democracy in a desert of backwardness ruled by dictators; Israel,
alone among the nations in the Middle East, embodied the principles of
self-government and freedom that our nation professes. Its dedication and
determination were converting their arid sliver of earth into a civilized
homeland blooming with agriculture and flourishing with small industries.
It had established new standards of education, health and welfare in this
long-stagnant backwater, and served a unique role among nations as a refuge for the persecuted Jews from other countries. Why did not the Arab
leaders, instead of wasting their substance in fighting, emulate Israel and
attempt to improve the lot of their own distressed people?

What I did not know, and would learn only gradually, was that the
concluding lines of that amendment, generally assumed to be necessary to
secure adoption, really denatured it. The phrase "as the President may determine" meant, of course, that he might interpret the act as he wished,
not as the Senate indicated its purpose to be. And so aid to Nasser would
continue and the administration's pious protestations would again be nullified by its actions. This steady encroachment of executive power upon
the legislative, or rather the steady abdication by Congress of its powers
to oversee the executive was of deepening concern to me.

When a bill came up to extend for four years the provisions of the
Sugar Act, I was interested because of the long-standing efforts by the
continental growers—beet and cane—to diminish the quotas of our
offshore areas. The bill sponsored by Senator Wallace Bennett of Utah, a
beet-sugar-producing state, gave the President the power to set the quotas
for one year at a time. Senator Bennett justified this because Fidel Castro
had taken over the government of Cuba and it might be desirable to cut
the Cuban quota when Congress was not in session. I argued that this
provision would diminish the present powers of Congress, which had always set the quotas. Senator Bennett said, "Yes, but we must remember
the President has the ultimate responsibility for conducting our foreign
relations." I replied that "we all appreciated the very grave situation
which had arisen in Cuba. Certainly it required attention, not merely by
the executive, but also by the legislative branch. Nevertheless, I hope the
Congress will consider very carefully any proposal for a further diminution of its powers and relinquishment of them to the executive. I think we
have traveled a long way in that direction, far too far indeed, and I think
we should scrutinize the bill very carefully from that standpoint." There

was no further scrutiny of that provision, however. It remained in the bill and became law.

On the last day of June, President Eisenhower vetoed a federal pay bill that increased salaries and wages of government employees by an average of 8.35 percent. He denounced it as an example of legislative irresponsibility. But the Congress was in a rambunctious mood. The House overrode the veto by a whopping 345 to sixty-nine. I think I expressed the Senate's feeling—or at least that of a large majority—when I urged an overriding of the veto saying:

> For 7 years we have been told by the White House what legislating we could do and what we could not do. During the 86th Congress . . . we have been told by the President of the United States what we could not do in regard to legislation for airports, highways, aid to schools, classroom construction, teachers' salaries, housing, small business, area redevelopment, anti-pollution control, public works and for resource and conservation development. The needs of the American people in these vital fields have been slighted and impaired by veto or threat of veto. We are now being told what we cannot pay our federal employees. I think it is time for the Congress to resume its legislative function.

The Senate overrode the veto seventy-four to twenty-four.

There was an interesting illustration in the Eighty-sixth Congress of how conservationists could disagree. Secretary Seaton wanted legislation to create the Arctic Wildlife Range, an area of nine million acres in the northeast corner of Alaska. It was introduced by request in the House by Representative Herbert Bonner of North Carolina and in the Senate also by request by Senator Warren Magnuson, chairman of the Committee on Interstate and Foreign Commerce. Magnuson appointed Bob Bartlett as chairman of a subcommittee to study and report on the project. Bartlett held hearings in Washington and in Ketchikan, Juneau, Anchorage, Seward, Valdez, Cordova and Fairbanks. The bill had the support of conservation organizations and their officials, members of Alaska sportsmen's organizations, game guides and some others. But it was opposed by a larger number of Alaskans, including Governor Egan and the state legislators, who adopted a joint memorial of protest. Their opposition was based on the bill's provision that the area would be administered by the secretary of the Interior, that there were already sufficient game refuges and ranges, and that under federal highway legislation, this withdrawal could increase Alaska's annual contribution to the cost of road construction by $275,000.

It was evident at the first hearing that those testifying for the bill had little or no knowledge of the area to be withdrawn. Ross Leffler, assistant secretary of the Department for Fish and Wildlife, admitted as much. This was true also of the top conservation organization officials. Their testimony was confused, because the objectives of the bill were confused. It was to be a range, not a refuge; hunting and trapping were to be permitted; it was "to preserve . . . a wilderness area," but mining was to be allowed which would require road construction and structures. It was touted as a tourist attraction, but the area would be virtually inaccessible to tourists, and without accommodations. Dr. John Buckley, a naturalist and the only administration witness who had firsthand knowledge of the area, testified that it was "not a great game area in regard to total number of animals, nor perhaps total number of species of animals." Its one justification, he felt, was that it contained a unique combination of both Arctic and sub-Arctic conditions.

I opposed the bill because it seemed to me unthinkable that after the Interior Department's failure in the management and conservation of Alaska's fishery and wildlife resources, the new state, which had set up its own far-more-qualified fish and wildlife organization and had offered to make this range a state-managed project, should be asked to turn it back to that discredited federal control. Moreover, if an additional range area —on top of the more than twelve million acres already set aside for federal refuges and parks—were to be withdrawn, why not set aside one with more abundant wildlife, grander scenery and greater accessibility to the public, such as the Chitina Valley in the Wrangell Mountains area, and set it up under state control?

Bob Bartlett shared my view. His subcommittee did not report the Senate bill and it died. But in his last week in office, as the Eisenhower Administration expired, Secretary Seaton signed an executive order creating the Arctic Wildlife Range. Governor Egan urged that the state take control of the range, and both Bob Bartlett and I would have accepted that solution. But Secretary Seaton would not agree. It was yet another example of the executive branch deliberately flouting the will of Congress, and of a Secretary of the Interior's arbitrary action in violation of the express wishes of Alaska's authorized spokesmen.

25

ACTIVITIES AT HOME AND ABROAD

In the end I came to realize that you may gain almost as much ground by making and losing a good fight for a good cause as if you had won it.

—GIFFORD PINCHOT

In June of 1960 the Senate had unanimously approved a resolution authorizing the Committee on Interior and Insular Affairs to conduct an investigation of conditions in American Samoa. Volunteers for this assignment were sought, and Oren Long and I accepted. There was a certain appropriateness in our selection. Both of us were "Pacific" senators; both had been appointed territorial governors. Oren Long's public service in Hawaii had made him particularly interested in the Polynesian race; my directorship of Territories and Island Possessions had made me keenly aware of the problems of our outlying possessions. Samoa had been outside my jurisdiction, but I knew that it, too, had its share of problems.

The motivation for the Senate's action was not wholly fortuitous. Pago Pago, capital of American Samoa, was slated as the site for the fifth conference of the South Pacific Commission in July 1962. This commission, which met every three years, was an advisory and consultative body set up in 1948 by the six governments responsible for the administration of island territories in the South Pacific: Australia, France, the Netherlands, New Zealand, the United Kingdom, and the United States. Curtis Cutter, Dependent Areas Officer of the State Department, voiced a concern which we shared. At this time world attention was focused on the problems of colonial areas, and because this conference would meet in the only American-held territory in the South Pacific, it would assume unusual importance. Further, in addition to the member nations, indigenous representatives from sixteen Pacific territories, observers from the United Nations agencies and reporters for the press, radio and television would also attend. It was desirable that they go away correctly impressed. But it was clear to us shortly after our arrival in early December of 1960 that facilities for a three-week conference were totally inadequate. So Oren Long and I sent a telegram to the Bureau of Budget with copies to President-elect Kennedy, explaining the problem and requesting that $415,000 be added to the budget to supply an assembly hall and dormitories. Compliance was one of the first actions taken by the incoming Kennedy Administration.

American Samoa, under Navy rule since 1900, was in 1951 transferred by executive order of President Truman to the Department of the Interior, a change expected to promote the islanders' welfare. But nothing further was done in the first four Eisenhower years. In 1956 Secretary Seaton had issued a good statement of administration policy and objectives, but again no appreciable action was taken to implement them, although the department drafted a constitution for Samoa which was adopted in 1960. The economy and the physical conditions of the islands were in wretched shape and it was obvious that of all our outlying areas, Samoa had been the victim of the most flagrant neglect.

Yet the people were fervent in their loyalty to the United States. They did not desire to join Western Samoa which after a decade and a half as a New Zealand mandate wanted and would shortly achieve independence. We found no consensus of opinion among Samoans about their political status. There was little enthusiasm for an elective governor, some demand for a nonvoting delegate in Congress, and some for a change of their status as "nationals" to American citizenship, although many were apprehensive that it could change their way of life. Their concern—and ours—was for economic improvement.

With the help of an excellent staff of consultants, our committee submitted a 184-page report on the most urgent needs of the islands. Chiefly, we recommended the inclusion of Samoa in eleven federal programs made available to our other insular possessions but denied to Samoa, and called on Congress to face up to its responsibilities.

I am happy to say we got some results. On the recommendation of Secretary Stewart Udall, President Kennedy appointed Rex Lee as governor. As a former assistant director of the Division of Territories and Island Possessions and former Deputy Commissioner of the Bureau of Indian Affairs, he was the right man for the job. He knew his way around the bureaucratic labyrinth and had established good relations with key committee members in Congress—of supreme importance since Samoa's neglected needs required appropriations. Lee began with determination and enthusiasm to try to satisfy those needs, using our report as a blueprint to which he could refer on his frequent returns to Washington in quest of funds. Perhaps his most brilliant single achievement was to introduce educational television, then in its infancy, to Samoa. He had first to secure a $40,000 grant from Congress to explore the idea and to make it applicable and available to the islands.

Just after we submitted our report, the *Readers' Digest* sent a staff correspondent to Samoa and in July 1961 printed a devastating article titled "Samoa: America's Shame in the South Pacific." But only four years later the same writer, Clarence W. Hall, wrote another article for the *Digest:* "Samoa, America's Showplace in the South Seas," with the subtitle "From a Pacific slum to a Polynesian paradise in four years; the dramatic story of a man who helped an island people help themselves." Both accounts were accurate. Rex Lee's achievement exemplified what I have long come to believe; in this complex modern world in the grip of vast impersonal forces, the individual still counts, supremely. Lee's determination, administrative ability and know-how accomplished amazing results. The success of his programs was facilitated by a friendly and enlightened administration; both the White House and the Congress were cooperative.

The Senate included in our authorization to visit Samoa a trip to Guam and the Pacific Trust Territories for which the United Nations and the United States were sharing responsibility. With the limited time at our disposal, we were able to visit Truk, Ponape, Saipan, Tinian, Kwajalein and Majuro, and were impressed with the problems that would confront the ultimate governmental authority over these widely scattered islands —ninety-six of the 2100 inhabited—with their diverse populations, ethnic and linguistic differences, physiographic variations and the special requirements of each insular microcosm. It was still too early to hazard a guess as to where the eventual sovereignty would reside, but it was both Oren Long's and my hope that the Micronesians would desire some form of association with the United States and that our policies would be conducive to such a choice. In Guam we found the Guamanians prospering and pleased at having their first native governor, Joseph Flores. Senator Long and I introduced bills early in the next session of Congress to provide a voteless deputy from both Guam and Samoa in the House of Representatives on the same pattern as Puerto Rico's Resident Commissioner, but we were unable to persuade a majority of the Interior Committee to approve.

We rejoiced at the election of John F. Kennedy and of Lyndon B.

Johnson. In my two years in the Senate both had been friendly to me, and the. latter particularly helpful in ways a majority leader can be. The new young President's charm filled us with an anticipatory glow. He combined both princely courtesy and easy informality. Bob Bartlett and I called on him at his Georgetown home after his election. As fellow-senators we had addressed each other by our first names. When we greeted him as "Mr. President," he came back with "Why not 'Jack'?" We both murmured something about his altered status, but he said engagingly, "Nothing is changed. You're Bob and Ernest to me and I hope I'll continue to be Jack to you."

The new administration brought with it some long-needed changes, although not in every instance. At Stewart Udall's confirmation hearing as secretary of the Interior, I reminded him of the arbitrary actions in Alaska taken by his predecessors, and cited as a striking example Secretary Seaton's move to set aside the nine-million-acre Arctic Wildlife Range, after the Congress—following extensive hearings—had rejected the proposal. I asked Udall to review this last-minute action of a lame-duck secretary and accede to Alaska's request that it be made a state-managed range. Udall agreed that Seaton's performance was improper, but never took the requested remedial action.

On the other hand, at a press conference Udall summarized the new administration's hydroelectric power policies thus: "The Eisenhower Administration regarded public power as a necessary evil; we regard it as a necessary good." And so, as early as June 26, I introduced a bill for the construction of the Crater-Long Lakes power project thirty miles south of Juneau, with the assurance of administration support. I had conducted a hearing on this project in Juneau the previous September as a member of the Irrigation and Reclamation Subcommittee of the Interior Committee, and had ascertained its desirability.

Other bills, vetoed or emasculated under the threat of veto, were reintroduced with White House favor. Area and public works redevelopment, an increased minimum wage, highway and airport construction —measures so sorely needed in Alaska—were now welcomed by the Kennedy Administration. And this time the forestry research laboratory to study the unassessed timber resources of interior Alaska —which had been slashed in a previous bill by administrative budget cuts—was in the President's budget with a $300,000 appropriation. It was approved and located on the campus of the University of Alaska.

On February 6, in company with eleven other senators and twelve House members and their wives, I went to Guadalajara, Mexico, to attend the first United States-Mexican Interparliamentary Conference. Meetings of Congressional and Canadian Parliament members had been authorized by the Eighty-fifth Congress and the first conference held. It seemed to me and others that we could do no less than enter into a similar arrangement with our southern neighbor, and I was happy to be a cosponsor of the enacting legislation as well as of a bill to present a statue to Mexico to celebrate the hundred-and-fiftieth anniversary of its independence. Mexico asked for a statue of Abraham Lincoln.

Our relations with Mexico, long turbulent, had greatly improved through the years, but unlike Canada with its common bonds of language and ideology, Mexico was not yet taken for granted as a friendly neighbor. Mexican-American relations were still somewhat strained, and as the conference got underway, I noted considerable caution on both sides. The experience was new; there was mutual apprehension of offending sensibilities. This would eventually change, and several conferences later there was as much freedom from restraint as among gatherings of our own nationals—a gratifying development which coincided with a steady removal of the causes of friction between the two governments. But at that first conference, it was the generous and exquisite Mexican hospitality that soon broke down all psychological barriers. For me it was an opportunity to renew old friendships and visit many of the places I remembered so well from earlier trips. Mexico had effected dramatic social, economic and political changes in those intervening years, but one thing that had not changed was the courtesy, graciousness and kindness of the Mexicans themselves.

President Kennedy had appropriately labeled his administration the "New Frontier," and it was my primary concern, during the first year of his term in office, to see that Alaska was included as part of that frontier. With a galaxy of cosponsors, I introduced a bill to assist Alaskan fisheries which were depleted by overfishing and suffering from federal mismanagement as well as from foreign competition stimulated by the largesse of our foreign-aid program. It was enacted.

One incident revealed President Kennedy's accessibility and cooperativeness. An order originating in the Treasury Department would have lifted a ten-year ban on the importation of Russian crabmeat, even as the Alaska king-crab industry was in its infancy and still struggling to find a market. I phoned the secretaries of State, Commerce and the Treasury in protest, and was informed at 10:45 A.M. on Saturday, March 11, that the announcement lifting the ban was scheduled for noon that same day. I then telephoned President Kennedy. He was in conference. When I explained the urgency of my call, he left the conference, talked to me, grasped the situation immediately and within minutes ordered suspension of the order. Then he called me back to tell me what he had done.

The Federal Water Pollution Control Act of 1961, introduced by Senator Dennis Chavez, chairman of the Public Works Committee, provided for a research and field laboratory in each of the six regions into which the country was divided: Northeast, Middle Atlantic, Southeast, Middle West, Southwest and Pacific Northwest. This last region included Montana, Idaho, Wyoming, Washington, Oregon and Alaska. When it came up in the committee, it was clear to me that Alaska would not get that laboratory. It would go to one of the states with a larger delegation. I offered an amendment to add a seventh region, Alaska. I argued that the different climatic and physical conditions in Alaska's sub-Arctic and Arctic regions required a laboratory of their own. I argued further that the problem of water pollution in Alaska was different from that in the "lower 48," that in Alaska the problem would be to prevent pollution whereas in the older states it would be to undo already existing pollution. The committee accepted my amendment and it was included in the bill the Senate passed.

The House, however, had a similar bill sponsored by John Blatnik of Minnesota which did not include this amendment. The bill itself had some difficulty, but a motion to recommit was defeated on a straight party vote, and went to conference. Fortunately, the Senate conferees stood firm for a separate Alaska region, and a pollution research laboratory, a $2½ million structure, was established on the campus of the University of Alaska. It subsequently demonstrated that Alaska was making the same mistakes as every other state, but it also presented comprehensive programs to correct existing water pollution and prevent it in the future.

Alaska's different conditions required constant readjustment to the legislation drafted for other states. An excellent bill to provide federal assistance to education, restoring what had been lost in the previous Congress by Vice President Nixon's tie-breaking vote, nevertheless had a formula for the allocation of funds which would have been very unfair to Alaska. It did not take into account the much higher construction costs there. A more realistic formula was worked out by Alaska's economist George W. Rogers and accepted by the Senate Committee on Labor and Public Welfare. But we really had to prove our case. A similar situation was presented in the Housing Act of 1961, which provided a maximum cost of $2500 per room. I was able to persuade the Senate that $3000 would be a more realistic figure and the amendment was accepted.

A man-made explosion with minor national and international repercussions took place when agents of the Fish and Wildlife Service, stationed in Alaska, arrested Eskimos throughout the vast northland, charging them with violating the migratory bird treaties with Canada and Mexico by shooting ducks allegedly out of season, and confiscated their guns. For a people dependent on hunting for food this was a serious issue. Protests poured in to the Department of the Interior and to the Alaska delegation. They came from all over Alaska, from whites as well as natives, including one from Governor Egan. But Secretary Udall stood pat. "The law is the law," he said and backed up his agents.

After a bit of hurried research, I took to the Senate floor and demonstrated that no such action by responsible enforcement agents had taken place since the ratification of the treaties forty-six years earlier. Further, there was provision for Eskimos taking ducks for food and no conservation interest had been violated. It was clear that the Fish and Wildlife agents, with little to do since the State of Alaska had taken over their functions, had shown an excess of misplaced bureaucratic zeal. Finally Secretary Udall modified his position, and while the Eskimos lost the confiscated ducks, they got back their guns.

President Kennedy proposed that the nations of the western hemisphere join in an "Alliance for Progress." Its basic motivation, only delicately referred to by an allusion to the "alien forces which once again seek to impose the despotisms of the Old World on the people of the new," was fear of communist subversion aroused by Fidel Castro's regime in Cuba. Nine days later the President sent Congress a comprehensive reorganization plan for the foreign-aid program. It recognized that existing concepts were unsatisfactory and had "begun to undermine confidence in our effort both here and abroad." The new approach included "development loans" through various lending agencies, some repayable in dollars, some in local currencies and some at low or no rates of interest. Since economic programs could not "succeed without peace and order," military assistance was also necessary; but this would be separated from the agency, which administered other grants, and turned over to the Department of Defense. For the military, President Kennedy requested $1.6 billion, while the cost of economic programs (exclusive of loans) would remain at what it had been, $4 billion. An innovation was that there would be a five-year commitment instead of, as hitherto, yearly appropriations.

I was very sympathetic with the high purpose of the "Alliance for Progress," although, having some familiarity with Latin America, I was also conscious of its difficulties. And I was most impressed with President Kennedy's awareness of the shortcomings of previous foreign-aid programs and his expressed determination to rectify them. In addition to my general interest in foreign relations, I now had a special mandate. The committee on Government Operations had been divided into subcommittees, and I was chairman of one of them, Foreign Aid Expenditures.

When the foreign-aid bill came to the Senate, I voted against Senator Byrd's amendment to eliminate the five-year commitment. I had some doubts as to the constitutionality of loaning public funds without interest to foreign countries, but felt that that objection, if valid, would probably be raised by my senior colleagues who considered themselves constitutional experts. However, I did try to prevent what I foresaw as an abuse by proposing that American loans not be *reloaned* at a rate more than five percent higher than the rate our loans carried. The justification for this was that in Latin America interest rates varied and were in some instances as high as thirty-six percent a year. It seemed to me objectionable that the beneficiaries of low-interest or interest-free loans should make unconscionable profits at the expense of those for whom the loans were intended.

Chairman Fulbright declared his opposition to my amendment as he had to a similar amendment—introduced by Senator John Williams of Delaware—fixing the reloaning rate at a maximum of eight percent. Fulbright reported that the State Department considered both amendments unduly restrictive. It wanted a compromise, worded: "Funds . . . shall not be . . . reloaned at an interest rate considered excessive by the Development Loan Committee . . . but in any event not higher than the legal rate of interest of the country in which the loan is made." The joker in this wording, however, was that the legal interest rates were twelve percent in Brazil and Paraguay, thirteen percent in Peru and fifteen percent in Chile.

There was a good deal of support for both amendments, but Fulbright's prevailed, forty-eight to forty. I had not actually called up my amendment, and convinced of its desirability and encouraged by the closeness of the vote on Fulbright's alternative, I decided to wait, believing that I might make some converts. In this objective I was greatly aided by the report of a meeting on August 16 at Punta del Este, Uruguay, of the nations of the western hemisphere which had agreed to a program committing the United States to make fifty-year loans at low or no interest rates. The report, published in the Washington *Post* of August 17, revealed that Secretary of the Treasury Douglas Dillon had committed the United States not only to making fifty-year, no-interest loans, but that there would also be no repayment of principal for ten years.

It was an opportune moment to call up my amendment. However, it was objected to by John Sparkman, ranking Democrat on the Foreign Relations Committee, speaking for Chairman Fulbright, who was absent. He reminded the Senate that it had already adopted the Fulbright compromise. Nevertheless, I offered my amendment again. Sparkman offered an alternative amendment proposing the same language that Fulbright had offered. Although it had been accepted two days earlier, it was now defeated, fifty-three to thirty-eight. My amendment to limit reloaning interest rates to not more than five percent was then adopted, seventy-four to sixteen. Senator Joseph Clark, a strong supporter of the foreign-aid programs, voted with me on both these roll-calls, and congratulated me on "beating the machine." I felt I had done the program a service.

I voted for the Foreign Assistance Act of 1961 on final passage, hopeful that the reforms President Kennedy had proposed would materialize, although I felt a kind of fraud was being perpetrated on the American people when fifty-year loans with no interest, no repayment for ten years and no likelihood of repayment ever, were called "loans." They should have, in all honesty, been called grants which I was sure they would prove to be.

I had further striking evidence of the need for tightening the financial controls on foreign aid when, after the end of the first session of the Eighty-seventh Congress in November 1961, serving as one of two on a sub-committee of the Public Works Committee, I looked into the Inter-American Highway. It had originated in the Roosevelt Administration as a part of the Good Neighbor Policy and provided for the construction of a highway extending from the United States through Mexico and the six Central American countries. There was also the vague intention of extending it someday through South America. The United States had agreed to pay two-thirds of the construction costs, while the other countries paid one-third of their part of the project. Mexico, however, had declined American financial aid and decided to pay the entire cost of its part of the highway.

The project was being carried out by the Bureau of Public Roads of the Department of Commerce, with Congressional supervision lodged in the Public Works Committees of both Houses. Each year one of its sub-committees would inspect and report. It was the Senate's turn to report and I again got an education in inefficiency.

We were not able to drive over all of the Inter-American Highway. Construction schedules had not been met and our ride would be interrupted by an unfinished and impassable portion over which we had to fly. On our return to Washington, we reminded the Bureau of Public Roads that when it appeared before the committee in 1955, it had requested an additional $25,730,000 to complete the highway. Commissioner of Public Roads C. D. Curtis and Francis C. Turner, deputy commissioner and chief engineer, assured the committee that the figures arrived at by Mr. Turner were accurate. Turner confirmed it. However, in 1957 the Bureau had requested an additional $10 million and that was voted on the assurance that it would really and truly be enough. Now in 1962 we were told that $32 million more were needed to complete the highway. Thus the Bureau's estimate turned out to be incorrect by $42 million, an error close to two hundred percent. Our report expressed our censure and said that

Congress might not have agreed to go ahead with the highway had it known that it would take $67,730,000 instead of $25,730,000. Turner was not long after promoted to the post of United States Highway Commissioner, the federal bureaucracy's way of rewarding incompetence.

We made one other interesting discovery. The one-third contribution which each country was pledged to provide was, with the exception of El Salvador, paid out of foreign-aid funds. In Guatemala, Honduras, Costa Rica, Nicaragua and Panama, Uncle Sam was paying the whole bill for the highway. This had never been revealed by the ICA or its predecessors. We had to find it out for ourselves—an example of the shoddy lack of responsibility of that agency's officials. Nor would that agency's complaisance and indifference to its obligations serve to promote the self-help which it was supposed to encourage in Latin-American recipients of American aid.

In talking to Bureau of Roads officials as we traveled on the Inter-American Highway, I gathered that they were planning—after its completion—to maintain it, using the same two-thirds, one-third formula. This shocked me. If the United States was going to maintain highways all over the world after we had built them, not only would this become a bottomless financial pit, it would also defeat one of the alleged purposes of our foreign-aid programs—namely to help the recipient countries become more self-reliant. Moreover, the law under which we had agreed to construct the highway specifically provided that each Central-American country would thereafter maintain it. Obviously, that provision was being circumvented when foreign-aid funds were used in maintenance as well as construction. So I offered an amendment to the Foreign Assistance Act of 1962 prohibiting the use of United States funds to maintain a highway which had been built with our money. It seemed to me proper, but its opponents argued that unless the United States was willing to maintain such roads, they would go to pot and our original investment would be wasted. My amendment was defeated, forty-two to thirty-nine.

A problem arose in Alaska that required a Congressional airing which would also prove beneficial to home-buyers in several other states. About a hundred families in the Anchorage and Eagle River area had purchased prefabricated homes—from a concern with headquarters in Indiana—that proved so defective as to be almost uninhabitable when winter's cold arrived. These homes had been acquired by means of Federal Housing Administration loans and were promoted and designated as "FHA-insured." This merely meant that the company which sold these houses was insured against default, but it had been assumed that the houses also conformed to FHA specifications. The Anchorage representative of "Modern

Homes, Inc." had disclaimed responsibility for the defects and the local representative of the FHA washed his hands of the problem by telling the indignant purchasers that it was a matter of negotiation between them and the company. They had felt compelled to hire an attorney.

Clearly the designation "FHA-insured" could reasonably be interpreted by the buyer as an assurance of satisfactory workmanship. I felt that the good faith of our government should not be impugned or jeopardized, and that *caveat emptor* had no justification when people were dealing with a federal agency. Alaskans had had all too many unpleasant experiences when they relied on the information given them by a federal-agency official, only to find out that they had been misled and had no recourse.

I aired these views and the facts about the defective housing on the Senate floor, reading into the *Congressional Record* some of the detailed complaints I had received. At the same time I sponsored a bill to amend the National Housing Act to hold the FHA responsible for defects in "FHA-insured" homes. But speedy action was required—it was too late for the legislation to be enacted in the Eighty-seventh Congress—and I called on Robert Weaver, the administrator of the Housing and Home Finance Administration—a highly responsible and responsive public servant—for prompt remedial action. He at once sent a team of inspectors to Alaska and served notice on the company that unless the defects were rectified it could no longer receive the FHA-insured mortgage arrangement. The repairs were made.

One gratifying result of this victory was extension of the reform throughout the United States. My Eagle River constituents, except for some worry and temporary distress, had won their battle, but I was hopeful that the victory would not end there and that the words "FHA-insured" would not continue to mislead other Americans. With Secretary Weaver's support, an amendment was incorporated in the Housing Act of 1964, giving all who had bought homes with FHA-insured loans the same protection we had extended to Alaskans. The bill was enacted and became Public Law 88-500. Robert Weaver was subsequently appointed by President Kennedy to head the Department of Housing and Urban Development and was the first black to become a member of the Cabinet.

A debate over an appropriation for Alaska illustrated a difference in Republican and Democratic ideology—and also the value of having one's party in the majority. At issue was the restoration of $375,000 to the Department of the Interior's appropriations bill, to enable the Bureau of Indian Affairs to recondition a vessel to serve ninety-eight Indian and Eskimo communities along Alaska's long coast. Such service had been in effect since 1922, but the boat previously used was no longer big enough because of population increases in these native communities. The item had been in the House bill, but was deleted in the Senate Appropriations Committee on a motion by Senator Karl Mundt. The BIA had assumed that the item would be approved automatically. When the bill reached the Senate floor, Senator Mundt opposed the restoration of this item; he referred to it no fewer than eight times as a socialistic enterprise. I explained that commercial vessels, those of the Alaska Steamship Company, would not serve these small communities and that only by a government-owned vessel could they be supplied. The item was restored by a vote of forty-eight to forty-three. Every one of the yea votes was cast by a Democrat.

The supply of gold in the United States was steadily dwindling, and while this was a national problem related to balance of payments and therefore involving certain larger aspects of our economy, it was also the special concern of those in Congress representing the goldmining states, particularly California, South Dakota, Alaska and the western states generally. Gold has a dual role in our economy; it is important both as a monetary symbol and medium of exchange, and for its many commercial and industrial uses. Yet despite its importance, gold mining was being subjected to impediments suffered by no other industry. It had been suspended by presidential order during World War II, although this had not been done by other gold-producing countries—Canada, Australia and South Africa—and the abandoned goldmining machinery had deteriorated or been converted to other uses. And in the twenty-eight years since President Roosevelt had in 1934 increased the price of gold from $20.70 to $35 an ounce, other costs had risen so rapidly that gold mining was no longer profitable. The industry could not raise its prices because it was compelled by government decree to sell only at that price and only to the federal government—a unique discrimination in our presumed free-enterprise economy. Thus the decline in domestic production had accelerated the diminution in the United States Treasury's gold supply stored at Fort Knox. However, lifting the government-imposed ceiling and raising the price of gold was strongly resisted by the Treasury Department, which on this issue spoke for the administration.

As a member of the Interior Committee's Subcommittee on Minerals, Materials and Fuels, I wanted to explore all the possibilities. John Albert Carroll of Colorado, chairman of the subcommittee, agreed to hold hearings on a resolution sponsored by Senator Clair Engle of California to subsidize gold mining by offering incentive payments not to exceed $35 an ounce. I testified at length for the measure and cited in detail the subsidization of all kinds of mining in other countries under our foreign-aid program. Not unexpectedly, the reports from the Treasury, State and Interior Departments were adverse. Their reasoning was derived from the Treasury, for all used virtually the same language: "The enactment of a measure providing for such payments would be definitely harmful by encouraging uncertainty and speculation with regard to future gold prices."

It made no sense to those of us in favor of the subsidy. Nothing in the resolution hinted at any change in the value of gold; it merely offered a subsidy of so much per ounce, the equivalent of offering to increase a goldminer's wages. We finally had a meeting of the full Interior Committee and called Robert V. Roosa, Undersecretary of the Treasury for Monetary Affairs, whom we knew to be the author of these adverse pronouncements.

Mr. Roosa told us that even talk of a subsidy was creating alarm and apprehension in financial circles. I suggested that he reminded me of the quaking aspen tree whose leaves tremble even when there is no breeze. He replied that anything that raised a question concerning gold would make him quake. It was pointed out that Canada had for years subsidized gold mining and had greatly increased its production. He stuck to his story; Canada was different.

The committee, with Clinton P. Anderson presiding, was composed of men of experience and intelligence, successful in private and public life. Mr. Roosa's objections were incomprehensible to them. They reemphasized that the resolution said nothing about changing the price of gold, and they asked him whether a public statement by the President pledging that there would be no change in the price of gold would not offset the psychological fears he worried about. He said it would make no difference. Suppose the Congress enacted the resolution, he was asked. He would, he said, recommend a veto. Did he have any alternative solutions? None, he said.

Our committee members felt variously puzzled, angry and frustrated. We realized we were up against a mystique that would smother any effort to increase the domestic supply of gold. But Roosa's position and power were such that he was responsible for letting our goldmining industry fade away and become a memory, while it flourished elsewhere.

The Senate went through an unusual experience when it debated a communications satellite bill to establish a government-owned and -controlled authority. It had been introduced as early as February 26, 1962, by Senator Estes Kefauver with Senators Burdick, Gore, Morse, Neuberger and myself as cosponsors. President Kennedy had a different idea and sent us a bill providing for a private corporation organized for profit and subject to appropriate government regulation. It was this bill, H.R.11040, that came up in the House on May 2. Opposition was voiced by Representative Emmanuel Celler who declared, "We are creating a private monopoly . . . the bill does not contain sufficient safeguards to protect the public interest." Representative William Fitts Ryan stressed its monopolistic aspects, and pointing out that the government had already spent $471 million in the development of a satellite system and $25 billion in the space program, urged government ownership. However, the bill was enacted in the House by a vote of 354 to nine.

The administration's position had come as a surprise to some of us in the Senate, and not wholly a pleasant one, for it proposed to create "a communications satellite corporation for profit which will not be an agency or establishment of the United States Government." We thought of TVA and pictured what Roosevelt would have done. To place the emphasis in this great new adventure into space on private profit was disturbing, especially since vast sums of public money had already been spent. It seemed to us that the bill had been insufficiently studied. A few of us Democrats, at least, would be critical and—if our apprehensions appeared justified—in opposition.

Senator Russell Long, Democrat of Louisiana, opened the debate by saying that he was not necessarily for public ownership, but why give this cosmic field to a specific corporation before we even knew the complexity or dimensions of the undertaking. Bob Bartlett, who had filed an adverse minority report from the Commerce Committee on the bill, said we must not rush in with so little real knowledge of what was involved. It was already clear that the American Telegraph and Telephone Company would be the chosen instrument. Bartlett further enlivened the debate with a devastating attack on an AT&T vice president whose record of malfeasance he exposed in great detail and with a passion unusual in my generally mild-mannered colleague. It occupied five pages in the *Congressional Record*.

I was disturbed by the secondary role given to the State Department. The bill provided that negotiations with foreign entities would be carried on by the corporation, which was obligated merely to keep the State Department informed. Why should not the State Department do the negotiating? This was among the defects I criticized in my first speech. Senator Kefauver added his weight to the opposition, saying the bill would create a private monopoly and carve out an exception from the anti-trust laws. As the debate proceeded the evidence of what he called "the most extraordinary giveaway of a great asset I have ever known in the history of our country" began to pile up. But it was clear that only a small group of perhaps sixteen were recorded in opposition: Senators Bartlett, Burdick, Carroll, Church, Clark, Douglas, Gore, Kefauver, Long of Hawaii, Long of Louisiana, McNamara, Morse, Neuberger, Yarborough, Young of Ohio, and myself.

We got some unexpected outside support, however, when the AFL-CIO, which had favored the bill, now stated its opposition. And former President Truman, visiting in Washington in mid-August, was also unequivocally against private ownership. We were beginning to feel cautiously hopeful. If we could only keep the debate going, public sentiment might come to our rescue. Both Senators Morse and Kefauver tried to bring up other bills, but their motions were tabled. An amendment by Senator Gore to take the negotiating power from the corporation and restore it to the State Department was also defeated. Then on August 11, Mike Mansfield filed a cloture petition. Cloture had not been successfully invoked since 1927. We expected to defeat it. We were mistaken. It was adopted, sixty-two to twenty-seven. An analysis of the roll-call was interesting. All the Republicans except Goldwater and Tower voted for cloture, but Goldwater had reportedly assured Dirksen of his vote if it was needed. Two Southerners who had always denounced cloture voted for it. Four others, Byrd, Fulbright, Jordan and Robertson, absented themselves.

From then on every amendment was ruthlessly tabled by Rhode Island Senator John Pastore, the bill's floor manager. Many of them were not even discussed. I introduced an amendment which provided that inventions furnished to the corporation by the United States would not become the exclusive prerogative of the corporation; rather it would pay a reasonable royalty for them, and any results of the inventions supplied by the United States would be available to others on the same basis. The amendment was designed to prevent a further giveaway, and I asked that it be brought to a vote. It was tabled sixty-eight to twenty. And so the steam roller made possible by cloture rolled on and the bill finally passed on August 16, with our little minority voting nay. We had been beaten on every count; not even obviously desirable amendments had been accepted. But we had no regrets.

After the adjournment of the Eighty-seventh Congress in October 1962, I went to the Middle East to study our foreign-aid program in ten countries. It would be the first serious on-the-spot investigation of these programs, and why the Senate Foreign Relations Committee had never undertaken such studies before was hard to understand. Both Senator Hubert Humphrey and I had suggested it to Chairman Fulbright, but he said that this was not the function of his committee, and that it was not equipped to do it. Had he felt otherwise, it would have saved the federal government billions of dollars; but more important, it would have made far more effective the programs which Senator Fulbright by and large supported when they were presented to Congress by the successive federal executive agencies which—under changing names (ICA, Mutual Security, AID)—administered foreign aid.

I selected the countries to be studied: Turkey, Iran, Syria, Lebanon, Jordan, Israel, Greece, Tunisia, Libya and Egypt. The investigation took sixty-one days of intensive work and resulted in a 472-page printed report, analyzing how, why, when and to what extent these programs had succeeded or erred, along with twelve pages of "findings and recommendations" on how to correct these errors. Had these recommendations been followed, our foreign-aid programs would have been vastly improved and the growing disillusion with the programs at home and abroad largely averted. That so little improvement resulted was in great measure due to the virtually unquestioning acceptance of the programs presented by the executive branch, by the two committees charged with responsibility for them, the Senate Committee on Foreign Relations and the House Committee on Foreign Affairs. For the concept persisted that the conduct of foreign policy was the responsibility and prerogative of the executive branch, as indeed it had been and should be, except for the constitutional provision to "advise and consent" to treaties by the Senate and its confirmation of nominations of foreign-service officers. But now for the first time in our history vast sums of money were being used as an instrument of foreign policy, and this new element should, under Congress's constitutional "power of the purse," have made it an equal partner with the executive. I had urged that course repeatedly, but the Congress had never really assumed its responsibility.

The report listed twenty-three other spigots, apart from the annual foreign-aid appropriations, through which American dollars were funneled to foreign countries. I discovered that most of my colleagues were unaware of their multiplicity. The report also noted the tendency of AID administrators to proceed on the assumption that any nation in the so-called Free World not only should, but was entitled to receive American aid, regardless of its internal situation, its political stability or the sincerity of its desire to raise living standards. Our study made crystal clear that all nations were not equally ready or equally entitled to receive economic assistance. I raised this point with Averell Harriman, one of our most experienced diplomats, and one of vast influence in high circles when the Democrats were in power. "Why don't we," I urged, "select in each region three or four countries whose officials are reasonably honest, public-spirited and enlightened, capable of administering our aid and willing to cooperate, and make these countries showcases, using their example to tell others that if they do likewise, they too will get our foreign aid?"

Harriman rejected the idea. "There isn't time. We can't discriminate. We've got to give to all."

I disagreed and was often criticized for it. Foreign aid had unqualified and unquestioning "liberal" support, and efforts to improve foreign-aid programs were usually viewed askance by most of my friends and by liberals in general. I was not against foreign aid, by any means, but I was against the way it was being applied.

What we learned on our trip to the Middle East confirmed my opinion. I was impressed by the Shah of Iran, who was, in effect, leading a social and economic revolution in his country "from the top," and by the young King Hussein of Jordan, whose nonviable principality was sustained largely by American funds in the belief that it would serve as a buffer state between Arab extremists and Israel. The task of counseling the harried monarch was being admirably carried out by William Macomber, the chief of mission. He was hopeful that given a period of peace our AID program would put Jordan on its feet. But the shadow of Egypt's ruler, Gamal Abdel Nasser, was cast over the whole Middle East. We were made aware of it in every country. In Beirut, Charles Habib Malik, internationally known Lebanese philosopher and educator, and his country's ambassador to the United States from 1945 to 1953, felt that the United States was making a fatal mistake in continuing to support Nasser. Malik said Nasser was using American funds to stir up revolt in Lebanon, Syria, Jordan and elsewhere, and that our idea of Nasser's indispensability was nonsense.

In Jerusalem, Abba Eban, then Israel's Minister of Education and truly a statesman, confessed that his forecast thirteen years earlier that time would soften and diminish Arab hostility was wrong. In consequence Israel had to spend a large part of its revenues for defense, to the detriment of other worthwhile activities. Further, there was no defense agreement between Israel and the United States; in fact, Israel was one of the few countries in the free world not included in some mutual defense pact. Israel was trying to provide for its own defense, but American aid to Nasser was adding to Israel's defense burden, and our recent recognition of the revolutionary regime in Yemen, which Egypt had been supporting with its armed forces, was a great boost for Nasser.

We had terminated aid to Israel. However, Levi Eshkol, the finance minister, indicated that Israel would welcome its resumption. Israel publicly acknowledged its debt to its American benefactors; no other country we visited exhibited a similar expression of appreciation. In my view, of all the recipients of our foreign aid, Israel was the best qualified to receive it and had made the best use of it.

Tunisia, smallest of the Arab countries except for a few sheikdoms on the Arabian Peninsula, and less endowed with natural resources than the others, was fortunate in having a government that was both cooperative and honest. It was the only Arab country that had accepted the Peace Corps; the others had rejected it because of its racial composition. Tunisia leaned more to the West than its neighbors, but occasionally had to rectify this by making pro-Arab noises. I found President Habibi Bourguiba an expansive and dynamic extrovert. He expressed the belief and hope that with the completion of a ten-year American-aid plan, Tunisia could get along without further help. He emphasized his purpose to live and let live, to forget past grudges and indulge in no hates. I congratulated him on his emancipation of Tunisian women; the traditional veil had been abolished. Referring to recent troubles with Algeria, he said there might be danger of aggression stimulated by Nasser. But military aid was limited to eight percent of the Tunisian budget, which Colonel William Knowlton, our military advisor, felt was enough. It was a welcome change from some of the high allotments in other countries. Our aid was spent chiefly to effect agricultural improvements, support small industries utilizing local products and stimulate tourism.

Libya, by contrast, presented an example of foreign aid misspent. Independent since 1951, a federation of three provinces, Tripolitania, Cyrenaica and Fezzen, the country was ruled by seventy-four-year-old King Idris, who insisted on maintaining three capitals, Benghazi, Tripoli and Baida, and incurred the costs of moving the government back and forth between them as well as building palaces in each for members of the royal family. The United States mission likewise had to move its personnel and arrange for quarters, to keep up with the government. In 1954 the United States had entered into an agreement with Libya to establish an airbase —Wheelus—near Tripoli. The United States agreed to make an initial payment of $7 million for the ground rent, with an annual payment of $4 million for five years, followed by $1 million annually until 1970. Our military-aid program was also started at that time. The base itself employed Libyans whose yearly payroll amounted in 1962 to $1,676,800 and whose maintenance and other costs contributed another $1,000,000 annually into the economy. But that did not prevent the government from exacting—under threat of expropriation—double the rentals agreed upon, to which the United States acceded. Later, in 1968, Libya expropriated the base completely.

Our aid program, which began in 1952, had poured millions more into Libya to support a number of conceivably desirable projects, but without exception both the funds and the projects were handled with conspicuous inefficiency. Libya had also received $9,400,000 from the United Nations Technical Assistance Program and the United Nations Special Fund. These funds, too, were mishandled. A World Bank mission leveled severe criticism at the poor coordination, duplication, and lack of fiscal responsibility exhibited by Libyan officials, all of which it attributed to our incredibly lavish foreign grants and loans.

Libya was, of course, a backward country even by Middle East standards. Power was concentrated in the king and his court clique, made up of tribal chiefs, wealthy merchants and aristocratic families. Uninterested in making reforms, the regime resorted to repression in order to maintain power. No opposition was tolerated, political parties were banned, strikes prohibited. Corruption and favoritism, we were told, were universal. In contrast with Tunisia, Libyan women were maintained in their inferior status. But compared to Tunisia, Libya was a rich country. The great oil strikes by foreign petroleum companies with concessions in Libya were responsible for the government's soaring revenues. In view of those, I could recommend that United States economic assistance to Libya cease. The government could well afford to support its own economic development, and I felt that whatever money it wasted should be its own.

Our tour of Egypt revealed a mine of conflict and contradictions in American foreign policy. Our Ambassador, John S. Badeau, said he was strongly pro-Nasser and considered his regime the most stable in the Middle East. Again we were pouring millions into the Egyptian economy, and although these funds were labeled "loans," they were, in reality, little more than grants made at the expense of the American taxpayer. I asked Badeau how he could justify these expenditures; he replied that it was useful to have a United States "presence" in Egypt. Feeling that I was perhaps not attuned to this "Alice in Wonderland" atmosphere, I sought a chance to discuss our foreign-aid program with Dr. Edward Sagendorph Mason, professor of economics at Harvard and a member of a commission—headed by General Lucius Clay—appointed by President Kennedy to appraise the American-aid program. He had been in Egypt before. He said his commission's report would be very critical; in his view, we were "attempting to do too much for too many"—a conclusion that corroborated my own. He said all ambassadors wanted an AID mission in every country to which they were accredited; they were then strongly tempted to influence AID to make its terms as favorable as possible and thereby ingratiate themselves with that country's government.

In Ambassador Badeau's opinion, United States relations with Nasser had vastly improved and the Israel issue was "on ice"; while there had been no real change in the hostility between the two nations, there was no present danger of its erupting into greater violence. However, it appeared to me that there was another "presence" in Egypt. Nasser's intervention in Yemen was being supported by Russian arms and military assistance, and it was clear that Nasser was playing one benefactor off against the other to get exactly what he wanted.

I had an opportunity to meet and speak with Nasser. He struck me as a shrewd man and a pragmatic politician. When I asked about his armed intervention in Yemen, he said that the war there was a revolution against one of the most barbarous and reactionary regimes in the world—tenth century, he called it. King Feisal of Saudi Arabia, fearing the movement might be contagious, had rushed arms and gold to the Iman, whereupon the revolutionists had appealed to Nasser for help. He had given it, as he would whenever any Arab country was the victim of external aggression. This story, however, did not coincide with the information given me by our military mission that Russian planes had carried troops from Cairo to Yemen the day after the revolution broke out.

When I brought up the question of Israel, I got what I came to know as the conventional reply. Nasser said that Israel had wantonly attacked Egypt in 1956, making common cause with Britain and France. Further, a million Palestinians had been driven out of Israel and wanted to go back. I asked whether some peaceful solution to the hostility between the Arab states and Israel were not possible. Nasser said no, not until the Palestinians could return to their homeland and Israel ceased to be a religious state and offered equal treatment to all races. He said that there was no discrimination against Jews in Egypt and that his opposition was to political Zionism—the standard Arab position. Then I asked about birth control and Nasser said he favored it, but that it would be difficult to persuade the *fellaheen* who put their children to work at the age of seven. Education was the answer, he felt. When I asked him what he considered his chief problem, he said raising the standard of living of the people, which he admitted the population increase made difficult.

The whole interview was pitched in a very moderate tone. Nasser never showed any deep passion and expressed himself in a matter-of-fact way. He conveyed an image of sincerity and objectivity, but that did not quite square with his intemperate blasts over the Cairo radio and his ability to stretch the truth to suit his own political purposes. Ambassador Badeau admitted that Egypt was a police state, although not a ruthless one; but he also said that Nasser, with Russian aid, was building up a sophisticated war machine for aggressive purposes. Nevertheless, Badeau was firm in his enthusiasm for Egypt's ruler. I was less enthusiastic. Our report to the Senate recommended that the continuance of the American financial-aid program to Egypt be conditional upon "Egypt's prompt compliance with the terms of the United Nations' settlement of the Yemen dispute, and Egypt's reversal of policy so as to cease production of missiles, warplanes, submarines and other implements of war clearly designed for aggressive purposes."

In Israel and Lebanon, foreign-aid programs had been effectively carried out, largely due to the character of the support given by their people. The programs had ended, however, and our report did not recommend their resumption. It did recommend continuation and possible increases of the programs in Tunisia and Jordan. For Syria, in view of its political instability and consequent lack of a climate in which economic development could take place, we recommended that except for commitments already made, American economic assistance should stop. And for Turkey and Iran we recommended continuation of the programs provided certain reforms were made.

We could not ignore the still unsolved problem of the Palestinian refugees. We visited several of their camps, seeking as many views from the refugees, and others, as possible, and devoting a long section of our report to the problem. We came to the sorrowful conclusion that the Arab leaders did not desire a solution beneficial to the refugees, but rather preferred to keep the fires of resentment burning and the refugees as pawns in their campaign against Israel. But we also concluded that the United States, which was paying the largest share of maintaining the refugees, should promote, and if necessary pay for, their resettlement in various underpopulated Arab regions and insure their permanent rehabilitation and integration there.

I came back from my tour of the Middle East to face a reelection campaign in Alaska. The Democrats and the Republicans were at each other as usual, but that fall Alaska was deeply rent by an issue that had been bitterly controversial for many years. My first inkling of it had come in the fall of 1959, when Senator Moss and I returned from our study of power development in Russia via the polar route to Anchorage. At the airport we were met by representatives of the press and radio. "What do you think of the capital move idea?" one of the reporters inquired.

"What's that?" I asked.

"Bob Atwood has started a campaign to move the capital from Juneau to western Alaska."

It was news to me, but I said I thought it was a very bad idea; it would be needless, costly, wasteful and arouse sectional bitterness.

The proposal, I discovered, had been launched a day or two before in the editorial columns of the Anchorage *Times* but had not as yet elicited any repercussions. I was perhaps the first to denounce it, and so became the target for an editorial attack in the *Times*, and, as I continued to fight the move vigorously, a sort of central figure in a battle that would last several years.

An editorial in the *Times* following my declared opposition charged that I had always been partial to Juneau, because my home was there, and that I was responsible for moving the Coast Guard headquarters from Ketchikan to Juneau. I replied by letter, pointing our that during World

War II, when the Coast Guard headquarters was moved to Seattle, my efforts were directed at bringing it back to Alaska—the location there was immaterial and had been decided by the Coast Guard. And I countered by reminding the *Times* that I had recommended that the first Army Air Force base be located near Anchorage, which it was. After some delay my letter was printed, with a few essential passages deleted. But I had taken the precaution of sending a copy to Norman Brown, editor of the Anchorage *News* who gleefully reprinted the whole letter with the deleted passages in large red type. The most significant deletion challenged Bob Atwood's charge that I was opposed to the capital move because I had a home in Juneau. I simply said that if owning a home in Juneau explained my partiality, perhaps his extensive vested interests in and around Anchorage explained his.

Groups differing on this issue began to mobilize; in Anchorage a "Capital Building Committee" favored the move, and in Juneau-Douglas, "Alaskans United" were opposed. Those in favor of the move proposed to do it by means of the initiative permitted by Alaska's constitution if a petition was signed by ten percent of the number voting in the preceding general election and resident in two-thirds of the election districts. Both Governor Egan and Senator Bartlett opposed moving the capital, and the issue became largely sectional; the Anchorage area supported it, southeastern Alaska opposed it, and other areas were slightly opposed. At the primary election on August 9, the move was defeated by 23,972 to 18,865.

Those of us who opposed the move assumed that the adverse vote had settled the issue, but we were mistaken. The closeness of the vote encouraged the capital movers. We were disturbed at the continuing uncertainty and resulting ferment, and decided to go to court. We contended that since the Alaska constitution provided in Section Twenty of Article XV that "the capital of the State of Alaska shall be at Juneau," the capital could not be moved by means of a referendum secured by an initiative, but required approval by a constitutional convention. The capital movers contended that Article XV which included Section Twenty was labeled "Schedule of Transitional Measures," and that by implication, naming Juneau the capital was a transitional measure. To test this contention, twenty-three residents of twenty-five cities filed a suit in the Superior Court in Juneau to enjoin the secretary of state from placing the initiative on the ballot. Judge James Von Der Heydt issued the injunction. But the capital movers then appealed the decision and the Supreme Court overruled it by a two-to-one vote, finding that the capital could be moved by initiative. This, of course, intensified the activity on both sides.

The first initiative had read that the capital should be moved to "within the Cook Inlet-Railbelt Area," which would have assured its location in or adjacent to Anchorage. The second initiative provided that the capital site be not within thirty miles of Anchorage, and the location would be selected by a committee of senior senators from each senatorial district. It was a clever move designed to increase the appetite of those areas that felt a new capital would be an economic bonanza.

I campaigned actively against the initiative, making four successive television appearances in Anchorage. Those in favor of the move claimed that Juneau was inaccessible by highway and its airport frequently shut down by weather and that it was far from the centers of population. I contended that few airports, including Anchorage's, were immune to the weather, that the cost of building a new capital, presumably to house ten thousand people, was a total waste of the state's funds, and that in a majority of states the capital was not necessarily near the center of population. I also pointed to the needless destruction of values in Juneau, and the sectional bitterness that would be engendered.

Throughout the campaign, the Anchorage *Times* was highly biased in favor of the move, both editorially and in news treatment, presenting supporting articles on the front page and burying opposing articles. Letters from readers that disagreed with the paper's stand were not published, and Alaskans United was forced to present its side of the story as paid political advertisements. On the last day of the campaign, the *Times* published a poster about three feet long and six inches wide with the legend "Ernie, Go Home." I had it framed and hung in my office.

The vote on November 6, 1962, resulted in a victory for the retention of Juneau by 32,325 to 26,542. On the same day, Governor Egan was re-elected and so was I, defeating my opponent, Theodore Stevens, by some eight thousand votes. Stevens was an able young lawyer from Anchorage who had served as United States attorney in Fairbanks during the Eisenhower Administration and had been a special assistant to Secretary Seaton. The chief issues in that campaign were the relative merits of Democratic and Republican policies, and Alaska voted in favor of the Democrats.

26

KEFAUVER, KENNEDY

America is never going to find security in suppression. America is never going to find any security in beating down ideas. America is going to find strength only in free men who have the right to speak and think as they wish. . . . However distasteful some of the persons who have strange ideas or are crackpots or what not may be . . . in a free government a great deal of good may come from letting them pop off whenever they want to as long as they do not advocate the use of force and violence in an effort to destroy the government.

—ESTES KEFAUVER

Whatever may come before me as President—on birth control, divorce, censorship, gambling, or any other subject—I will make my decisions in accordance with . . . whatever my conscience tells me to do in the national interest and without regard to outside pressures or dictates.

—JOHN F. KENNEDY

During the Eighty-eighth Congress, which convened in January of 1963, I found myself embroiled in many of the same issues that had come before the Senate in previous sessions. While our little group of sixteen senators had lost the battle to make our country's first venture into space with communications satellites a nonprofit operation, we had not given up. Some of the doubts we had expressed—but, because of cloture, had been unable to develop fully—appeared to us justified by later events. And now in the authorization bill for the National Aeronautics and Space Agency (NASA), there was an item for $45,175,000 to be given for research to the American Telephone and Telegraph Company, which under the Communications Satellite Act of 1962 (now Public Law 87–624) had become the agency for the program. Our group objected strenuously. In a long statement on August 8, 1963, which Senator Wayne Morse, who was absent on official business, had asked me to read, he said that in his nineteen years in the Senate he had seen many special-interest and pressure groups attempt to take advantage of the American people. But never had he seen a more gross attempt to pick the taxpayers' pockets. "We cannot have it both ways. If the corporation was going to earn profits, it must also bear the expenses." To require the taxpayers to pay for the corporation's profits was, he believed, immoral.

Senator Kefauver joined the battle once again and reemphazied that the newly created Communications Satellite Corporation was a private monopoly which, according to the sponsors of the act, had been "created for the special purpose of relieving the taxpayers of research expenditures." He noted that in addition to the specific grant proposed for the Communications Satellite Corporation, $4.6 million of the $539,185,000 destined for "administrative operations" would also go to the satellite program, making the corporation the beneficiary of some $50 million dollars. He proposed an amendment providing for reimbursement to the United States of any such authorization used by the corporation. It seemed reasonable and it had fourteen of us as cosponsors.

Majority Leader Mansfield proposed a unanimous-consent agreement under which there would be a two-hour debate the next day, half the time to be controlled by the senator offering the amendment and half by Senator Clinton Anderson, chairman of the Aeronautical and Space Science Committee. There were several reservations of the right to object to what seemed to some of us too short a time, but the unanimous consent request was agreed to.

The debate began the next day and Senator Anderson, opposing the Kefauver amendment, said that it "would place an inequitable burden on the corporation." As the debate continued, Senator Kefauver told me he was not feeling well and was going over to the Senate gymnasium to lie down. The next morning I learned that he had gone to the Bethesda Naval Hospital and would undergo surgery for an aortic aneurism, a major operation, but usually successful.

In his absence Senator Anderson requested that I control the time on behalf of the Kefauver amendment. It gave me pleasure to quote the explicit assurances of various senators—expressed in the committee hearings and the floor debate of the previous year—that the costs of satellite communications research would be borne by private enterprise. The senators included Humphrey, Goldwater, Keating, Javits and Pastore. I ventured to hope that they would therefore support the Kefauver amendment.

Senator Anderson, one of the Senate's ablest parliamentary strategists, offered an amendment "in the nature of a substitute," to the Kefauver amendment; but in effect it relieved the corporation of any compulsion to reimburse the federal government. Our group voted against it. Since it was a substitute for the Kefauver amendment, we could not also vote on that. It would not have mattered; the result would have been the same. We had been defeated again, but we felt we had made the record clear. It *was* a giveaway. It was so-called private enterprise supported by the American taxpayers.

A call to the hospital brought word that Kefauver was resting comfortably and that the operation would take place the next day. It came therefore as a devastating shock to learn that he had died. The aneurism had burst before the operation. It should have been performed immediately, and not postponed till the next day.

I felt that the nation had suffered an irretrievable loss. It is often said that no man is indispensable. But Estes Kefauver represented to me a combination of qualities not found to the same degree in any of his contemporaries. He was indeed a battle casualty, for he was engaged in a struggle for what he considered the public interest, a fight against monopoly, intrenched privilege and the covert alliance of big business and its representatives in government.

A man of indomitable courage and inflexible adherence to principle, Kefauver combined tenacity with gentleness, modesty and a patient tolerance for opposing views, rare in one so earnestly devoted to a variety of difficult causes. I never knew him to lose his temper or to become angry —at least visibly—in debate. Unlike most senators he was not a good speaker. His public utterances lacked passion and oratorical flourishes; they were delivered in a low monotone. This in itself helped conceal the quiet determination with which he pursued his objectives on behalf of the largely unrepresented groups in our society. In him, as his colleague, Albert Gore, stated simply, the people lost a champion and a true friend.

He waged a heroic and almost lone battle against abuses in the drug industry, a task that required highly specialized and technical knowledge. His concern was not merely for the people's health but for their pocketbooks. In the middle of his fight he got an unexpected and needed break through the efforts of a dedicated researcher in the Food and Drug Administration, Dr. Frances Kelsey, who had uncovered the deforming effects on the unborn of a drug, thalidomide, and was trying to convince a sluggish medical bureaucracy to have it barred from use. Kefauver asked me to appear on television with him and Dr. Kelsey in support of his bill to regulate the drug industry. My being a doctor as well as a senator would, he felt, be useful, and together we discussed the abuses that the bill would attempt to correct. It was finally passed as the Drug Industry Act, but Kefauver had to battle the industry lobbyists and its supporters in both Houses. It was signed after adjournment of the Eighty-seventh Congress by President Kennedy on October 13, 1962. He had helped the cause several weeks earlier by giving the "President's Distinguished Service Award," the highest award available to a federal employee, to Dr. Kelsey.

Perhaps the outstanding example of Estes Kefauver's courage came during the hey-day of McCarthyism when the charge that anyone was "soft on communism" was deemed to be politically lethal. To demonstrate their freedom from such an imputation and undoubtedly in many cases because they considered "the communist conspiracy" a real menace to our democratic institutions, representatives and senators sponsored legislation to outlaw the Communist Party. There was a bandwagon rush to support it. In the debate Kefauver questioned whether this had ever been done before to a political party, whether such a precedent might not be unwise, and whether any recourse or appeal was possible once the action had been taken. Receiving no satisfactory answers, he resolved to vote against it. His staff pleaded with him not to do it, warning that it would be political suicide. But Kefauver refused to be stampeded and said that our American institutions were not so fragile as to be impaired by a few communists in our midst. The bill was passed eighty-one to one—the one being Estes Kefauver.

In his crusade against organized crime, he exposed its connection with some of the big-city political machines and thereby earned their enmity, but this did not faze him in the least. He was unswervable from what he considered the path of rectitude. Although he was a Southerner, he was totally free from racial prejudice and refused to sign the Southern Manifesto calling for massive resistance to desegregation and civil rights. He suffered many defeats. He tried repeatedly and vainly to establish a Department of Consumer Affairs. Twice he hoped to be the Democratic nominee for the Presidency, but he took his setbacks without bitterness or rancor. In my view he was equaled or surpassed in greatness in this century by just one other senator, George W. Norris.

Of the many problems faced by the Eighty-eighth Congress, unemployment was among the most serious. In the spring of 1963, it had reached 6.1 percent; nearly five million Americans were out of work. I had long considered this our nation's number one economic and social problem. A year earlier, the Senate Public Works Committee had reported an Accelerated Public Works bill with an authorization of $600 million. The amount struck me as wholly inadequate and I sponsored an amendment to raise it to one-half the amount authorized for that year's foreign-aid program, which would have approximately quadrupled the authorization. The committee did not accept the amendment, but the amount appropriated was raised fifty percent to $900 million. This, I felt, was still inadequate, and the intervening year demonstrated it. The program ran out of funds while unemployment was mounting and worthwhile projects totaling over a billion dollars, ready to go, could not be financed. So at this session I introduced a bill with eight cosponsors to raise the authorization to $2,645 million although even that amount did not bring this domestic appropriation to parity with foreign-aid expenditures.

To demonstrate the bill's necessity, I wired the governors of all the states asking them to submit a detailed list of desirable public works projects on their agendas, with the costs of each and the number of man-hours each would employ. In less than three weeks, replies had come from twelve governors whose projects totaled $1,566,220,905. It was clear that my request for $2,645 million was far from sufficient, and in presenting the bill on the floor, I said:

> We shall either spend this $2,645 million on constructive investments in the future economic strength of the United States—in schools, hospitals, roads, sewer and water works, dams, airports and the like—or we shall spend that and much more in the next 27 months and in the years to come in unemployment compensation and in welfare payments, and suffer the loss of tax revenue which fuller employment will generate.

After several setbacks, I finally won passage of the bill, but not until the next Congress. The new bill, "The Public Works and Development Act of 1965," carried an authorization of $3.25 billion which I had proposed as the equivalent of that year's Foreign Assistance Act. It was passed by the Senate on June 1, 1965, 71–12, and six weeks later by the House 246–138. President Johnson signed it on August 27. Earlier I had also worked to secure the passage of the Alaska Public Works Act.

But employment was not Alaska's only nagging problem. In the early

1960s, the coastal waters of Alaska were penetrated by Russian and Japanese fishing vessels. In addition to catching salmon and killing whales, Russian poachers tore up Alaskans' crab traps. Although occasionally a Russian or a Japanese vessel would be apprehended and its captain arraigned and fined, the penalties—with the State Department invariably interceding for the lightest possible sentence—were insufficient to deter other violations, as were the State Department's diplomatic protests after each incident. Further, the Coast Guard in Alaska, with the longest coast line of any district to protect, was inadequately equipped with planes and vessels. The Russian ships, once spotted, were faster and got away.

Alaska's largely littoral population was embittered by these repeated violations. I wired President Kennedy, asking him to station destroyers in our waters, and I added that I found it hard to see how we could sign a treaty with Russia which implied friendlier relations, when the Russians were continually violating international law and other treaties respecting our waters. I was referring to the nuclear test-ban treaty, but because it was then under negotiation, the Executive wished to avoid confrontations, and nothing was done to discourage poaching. It then occurred to me that one way to obtain larger enforcement capabilities was to extend our fishery limits from three to twelve miles. I spoke to that objective repeatedly, stressing that the three-mile limit was obsolete, established when three miles was about the maximum range of a shore-based cannon firing a round iron ball. Other nations had extended their limits. Peru and Ecuador were claiming a two-hundred-mile limit and arresting our tuna fishermen at that and even greater distances from their coasts. And to do it, they were using armed vessels given to them—presumably for national defense—under our foreign-aid program. Both State and Navy departments were opposed to extending our limits; even so, I introduced a bill for a twelve-mile fishing limit. It was not enacted in that Congress, but I felt it was bound to come.

In 1963 I became chairman of the Subcommittee on Minerals, Materials and Fuels of the Committee on Interior and Insular Affairs. Unsuccessful in my efforts to resuscitate the moribund goldmining industry, I struck gold—figuratively—with a bill to permit mining operations to receive the same tax treatment that was allowed for research expenditures in other industries—namely to permit them to deduct the costs of exploration, and to remove existing limits on the amount of exploration. I presented this reform as an amendment to the internal revenue bill in which it was incorporated. Despite an adverse report from the Treasury Department, that I refuted with a letter to every member of the committee, I was able to convince the Senate Committee on Finance that the immediate loss in revenue would be many times made up by the resulting discoveries and development of new ore deposits, and that the deductions were recoverable. Passage in the House was assumed by the support of Representative Al Ullman of Oregon, a member of the Ways and Means Committee, and it became law.

Another long battle appeared to be ending in victory when the National Park Service budgeted $1,111,800 for the contruction of tourist facilities in Glacier Bay National Monument. My criticism of existing policy was that in national parks and monuments a concessionaire was expected both to build and operate these facilities. It had worked well in national parks such as Yosemite or Yellowstone, which were near centers of population or easily accessible to large numbers of visitors who patronized them on a year-round basis. But given the shortness of the Alaska season—three to four months—it would be financially impossible for any concessionaire both to build and operate, and I felt the National Park Service had an obligation to make these natural wonders available to the public. Glacier Bay had been set aside in 1926; for forty years, only wealthy yachtsmen or government officials traveling on government vessels had been able to enjoy it. My reasoning finally prevailed, although it took more than one Congress to secure the necessary authorization and appropriations. A few years later I dedicated the well-planned and tasteful accommodations at Glacier Bay's Bartlett Cove. They soon attracted a host of visitors, and their enlargement was called for.

I also persuaded the Park Service to build a twenty-mile jeep trail in Katmai National Monument, so that visitors could ride to and then walk in the famous "Valley of Ten Thousand Smokes." At the urging of the National Geographic Society, which had organized an exploratory expedition after the great Katmai eruption of 1912, the valley was made a national monument. But until the trail was built, it had been inaccessible to pedestrians.

As a member of the subcommittee on government operations, I had the pleasure of meeting Rachel Carson who came as a witness to a hearing on environmental hazards and the control of pesticides and other chemical poisons. Her charm and sincerity were impressive and I was able to tell the hearing that every once in a while a book appears that alters the course of history. Such was her *Silent Spring*, which for the first time alerted the nation to the perils of DDT and other pesticides. Already famed as a marine biologist and the author of *The Sea Around Us*, Miss Carson was also an ardent and persuasive ecologist. Her untimely death from cancer a few weeks later ended a career that would have been increasingly useful.

The annual foreign-aid controversy again reared in the Eighty-eighth Congress. My Middle East report had been given substantial circulation in Congress, as had the report by General Clay, both highly critical of our foreign-aid programs. The debate on the Foreign Assistance Act of 1963 lasted three weeks and ran late into the nights. The problem was still the same; Congress was expected to give the administration *carte blanche*. I offered several amendments. One provided that no aid could be furnished to any country which the President determined was engaging in or preparing to engage in aggression against any other recipient of our aid. "The United States is buying both butter and guns for aggressor nations," I said in my presentation, "and we must stop it now." Senator Fulbright proposed a weaker substitute—which was defeated—and my amendment was approved 65–12. The debate made clear that it applied to Egypt's Nasser and to Indonesia's Sukarno, who was then waging war against the new nation of Malaysia.

Nevertheless, despite the clearly manifested purpose of the Congress, the amendment was ignored by the State Department, and aid to Nasser continued. After my return from the Middle East, but before the report appeared in print, I had written President Kennedy of "my firm conviction that United States foreign policy in the Middle East is set on a disaster course as surely as it was when we thought we would appease Hitler." And with an implied reference to the President's book, *While England Slept*, I added, "I fervently hope that no future historian will be able to write a book concerning this period of United States activity in the Middle East, entitled *While America Slept*." I followed it with a supplementary letter two days later. The President asked Assistant Secretary of State Federick G. Dutton to reply. It was a long, carefully worded evasion of all the realities. It underscored what I had learned through the years, namely that the State Department is virtually a law unto itself and changes little under different administrations. It had been and continued to be pro-Arab.

I was equally unsuccessful with an amendment to raise the interest rate on development loans from the prevailing three-quarters of one percent —over $1.3 billion had been loaned on those terms—to the rate charged by the United States on its securities. It was opposed by Senator Fulbright and defeated, 44–30. I then offered a substitute raising the interest rate to two percent, which was likewise opposed by Fulbright who supported a committee amendment which retained the three-quarters-of-one-percent interest for five years, whereupon it would rise to two percent. My amendment was defeated, 47–41.

Another amendment to stop all military aid to Latin America was inspired by events in the Dominican Republic. After thirty years of savage tyranny, General Rafael Leonidas Trujillo was assassinated and there followed the first honest election in that small country's history. Juan Bosch, a civilian, was elected president, but within days he was deposed in a military coup by *Trujillistas,* and the legislature elected with him, abolished. A similar coup followed in Honduras. A year earlier in a speech entitled "Military Aid to Latin America is Defeating the *Alianza Para Progresso,*" I had described the coup in Peru in which military men trained in the United States, using Sherman tanks supplied as part of our military-aid program, had overturned the democratically elected government of President Manuel Prado. Similar coups had taken place in Brazil and Argentina.

In presenting the amendment, I pointed out that none of the goals of our military-aid programs in Latin America had been achieved—not hemispheric defense, not standardization, not modernization, not a reduction in forces, not even that much-to-be-desired by-product, an understanding by the Latin-American military of their role in a modern democracy. I placed in the *Congressional Record* the amounts already spent on military aid to Latin American: $714 million to twenty-one countries. For the current bill, $74.1 million was requested.

Subject to a minor modification, Fulbright said he would not oppose the amendment. It was adopted by voice vote and survived in conference with the House. Of course there was nothing to prevent a Latin-American country from buying arms either from the United States or from another country—a practice some would engage in despite their pressing economic and social needs—but at least it would no longer be a part of our foreign-aid program.

I offered another amendment to stop aid to colonies. We had been giving aid to French and British Guiana and British Honduras. I could see no reason why that was not the responsibility of the "mother-country." But on Senator Fulbright's assurance that such aid would be discontinued, I withdrew the amendment.

Going through the recipients of our foreign aid one by one, I sought to show where substantial savings could be made. We were still giving military assistance to thirteen now-prospering European countries, totaling $900 million. Japan likewise was prospering, yet still received $67 million in military aid. Argentina and Brazil were chaotic with military upheavals; their promise to reform in terms of the commitments made at inter-American conferences in Bogota and Punta del Este were not being carried out and our AID administrators were not pressing the issue. Algeria and Morocco were following Nasser's policies and arming to join in the war against Israel. Libya was now oil rich. I estimated that by cutting our military aid to these and other countries, we could save $1,868 million. I also called attention to our numerous AID officials in the newly emerging African nations, who were offering economic assistance, plans and programs even before the new government had taken office or had a chance to stabilize itself, as we had done so unwisely in British Guiana. I felt that their former colonial masters should take on that responsibility. I was still not satisfied with the bill in its final form; however, I felt that our foreign-aid programs had been somewhat improved by the amendments, and I voted for the Foreign Assistance Act of 1963.

The upheavals in Latin America made me increasingly concerned about the Alliance for Progress. Perhaps its premises were too idealistic; it was probably too much to expect the oligarchies that dominated the Latin-American countries to give up their entrenched privileges, to permit the breakup of their vast landholdings, and to agree to an equitable tax system. But it was also the function of our AID administrators to shape programs in accord with these premises and insist upon adequate performance. They did not do it. They vacillated, and the recipient governments soon felt that their compliance was not essential.

I voiced my fears as early as July 17, 1962, and repeatedly thereafter, often in colloquies with Wayne Morse who, as chairman of the subcommittee on Inter-American Affairs, knew more about Latin America than anyone in the Congress. We wanted the Alliance for Progress to succeed, but saw it steadily heading for failure.

This was, in part, responsible for the growing disappointment I began to feel with President Kennedy's Administration, a disappointment which was shared by other old New Dealers who had cheered his summons to seek new frontiers. We were charmed by his verve, his style and his accessibility. Obviously, things were better than under the Eisenhower Administration. But we had expected things to be very much better and markedly different under President Kennedy, and they were not. Like his predecessor, he seemed more concerned with defense and foreign aid than with the needs of folks at home. His domestic initiatives were faltering; the promised civil-rights and tax legislation were not enacted in the Eighty-eighth Congress's first session.

Perhaps a clue to my disappointment can be found in a statement made by President Kennedy on a nationwide television broadcast in December of 1962: "There is no sense in raising hell and not being successful. There is no sense in putting the Presidency on the line on an issue and then being defeated." But I believed that the greatest battles are often fought by men who are defeated time and again, and keep on fighting. Should not a worthy cause be fought for regardless of ultimate victory or defeat? Many of us got the feeling that President Kennedy had a lack of real conviction. What he did always seemed more conservative than what he said. Senator Albert Gore remarked to me in early September of 1963, "Jack has gone conservative," and he forecast the loss of many seats in Congress in 1964, adding, "When Democrats go conservative, voters go Republican." It had never occurred to me that President Kennedy had "gone" conservative. He was just more conservative than we had anticipated. There was not, I think, much intensity in our disappointment; it was tentative and qualified by the hope that the Kennedy we had pictured would emerge.

On October 21, 1963, I spent almost an hour with him at the White House—a generous slice of Presidential time. He came out to escort me into the Oval Room. He first mentioned a nice letter he had received from Dorothy. She had written praising his United Nations speech and he had acknowledged it. I began our discussion by telling him that I wanted to carry Alaska for him in 1964; I was mortified that we had failed to do it in 1960. Then I listed some of the matters that required attention: electrification, better understanding of Alaska's special needs by the federal regulatory agencies, unemployment, the decline of the fishing industry, the Russian poaching problem, my hopes for a twelve-mile fishing limit and some means to revive the goldmining industry. Finally, I aired my views on foreign aid and particularly the Alliance for Progress, at which he interjected, "I've been following the Senate debate." He was a good listener and a sympathetic commentator. I left with a feeling of deepened affection and the hope that he would shortly be getting into his stride.

But his life was cut short by the catastrophe in Dallas on November 22. I was in my office being interviewed by a reporter from the New York *News* when one of my staff rushed in to tell me the President had been shot. I went at once to the Senate floor where prayers were being offered. Whatever history's assessment of John F. Kennedy's public service, one enduring achievement was his establishing that a man's religion is no bar to the nation's highest office, and he will be loved and remembered for the princely gallantry he lent that office during his tragically short sojourn there.

27

A GREAT VICTORY AT HOME:
DISASTER OVERSEAS

I have a dream . . . I have a dream that my
four little children will one day live in a
nation where they will not be judged by
the color of their skin but by the content
of their character.
—MARTIN LUTHER KING, JR.

The currency of speech has been debased
over many years by the lies and distortions
of American military and political leaders
in Vietnam. They still talk about victory
when the simplest citizen can see it for the
bloody mistake it was.
—ANTHONY LEWIS

The Vietnam malaise is rotting out the
shining heraldry worn by American fight-
ers for two centuries.
—CHRISTOPHER WREN

Nineteen hundred and sixty-four was a memorable year. It brought one of
the worst natural disasters visited on any part of the Union, an epoch-
making civil-rights bill, and a plunge into the longest war in our nation's
history.

Early in the second session of the Eighty-eighth Congress, a House-passed civil-rights bill faced expected resistance by eighteen Southern senators. But although we sat late, the round-the-clock filibuster of 1960 was not repeated. After eleven weeks of debate, beginning in February, during which all crippling amendments were defeated and strengthening amendments approved, the opposition had had more than ample opportunity to present its arguments, and a cloture petition was filed on June 6. The bill passed four days later, 71–20. In voting for it, I took pains to reiterate my support of cloture by the existing two-thirds majority of those present and voting, a rule which had just demonstrated its workability.

The Civil Rights Act of 1964 strengthened the enforcement procedures of school desegregation and of the voting rights provisions enacted in 1960. It also provided for equal employment opportunity and for equal access to public accommodations. While it was obvious that resistance to these reforms would continue in the South, and their validity depend on the commitment of the enforcing officials, the bill represented substantial progress. "Colored" and "White" signs would shortly disappear from airport, bus and railway stations and from lodgings. The achievement was in no small measure due to Hubert Humphrey, the majority whip and the bill's floor manager, who combined unswerving persistence with good nature in steering the measure through the Senate, and to the manifest support of President Lyndon Johnson whose stand on equality and justice for the Negro was also unswerving.

Late in the evening of Good Friday, March 27, the radio brought news of a tremendous earthquake in Alaska. In seconds, it seemed, an area of about fifteen hundred miles from east to west and two hundred miles from north to south had been damaged; the intensity of the quake reached the record high of 8.6 on the Richter scale. It was accompanied by tsunamis, popularly known as tidal waves, which added to the destruction of the coastal cities, Seward, Kodiak, Cordova and Valdez, and the native villages on Kodiak Island and in Prince William Sound. Anchorage was hard hit but escaped wave-damage, fortunate in that its thirty-six-foot tide was at dead low, and that the quake struck at 5:37 P.M. when stores and office buildings were empty, their daytime occupants on their way home and thus escaping the collapsing structures. Under these circumstances the death toll of 115 was amazingly light. But there were great personal tragedies—two children of one family swallowed up as the earth opened, whole families wiped out as the Valdez pier dropped out of sight, a score of children drowned as a great wave swept over the island village of Chenega.

President Johnson acted swiftly. Within hours Edward McDermott, Director of Emergency Planning, other officals, Bob Bartlett and I were on our way to Anchorage in the presidential jet. The control tower at the airport had been destroyed and the runway severely damaged, but we managed to land. We spent two days in Alaska inspecting the destruction in the five stricken cities and other areas in between. It was hard to believe the evidence of our own eyes. Great buildings had collapsed. Private houses had been demolished or were badly askew. In Anchorage's fashionable residential section of Turnagain-by-the-Sea, not only had a score of houses on the bluff been swept out to sea in fragments, but the ground on which they had stood had been washed out with them. In Seward the horror had been intensified when great oil-storage tanks ignited, and burning oil swept through the town on the tidal wave's crest. In some communities the level of land had been raised by many feet, in others lowered. Massive reconstruction was called for. The total cost of rehabilitation was estimated at $750 million.

On our return President Johnson proposed the formation of a President's Commission for Emergency Planning and suggested to us that Senator Clinton Anderson be appointed as its chairman. Some $20 million in emergency disaster funds were made immediately available and Congress was asked to appropriate $40 million more, which it did promptly. Various federal agencies were mobilized and went to work. Repair of the public sector—highways, the Alaska Railroad, airports, harbor installations, telephone lines, federal buildings and schools— quickly got underway. But the hard-hit individual was not, in my judgment, getting adequate relief. I took this problem to Eugene Foley, head of the Small Business Administration which handled "disaster loans." The legislation setting up that service provided that disaster loans "should not exceed three percent." I ascertained that its administrator could, at his discretion, make loans at a lower rate—indeed, at zero percent. So I urged Foley to give Alaskans the same treatment accorded foreign borrowers under our foreign-aid legislation, namely three-fourths-of-one percent. Foley declined, saying that those loans were made only to foreign governments. I corrected his misapprehension and gave him long lists of such loans to private businesses abroad. It was embarrassing for me to press this point. Senator Anderson, who was devoting much time and effort to the Alaska disaster, quite apart from his senatorial duties, was opposed to it. Yet I felt it my duty to raise the issue and to mobilize as much public sentiment for it as possible. I could see no reason why Alaskans should not be afforded the same interest rate as foreign borrowers. I entered the following comments in the *Congressional Record:*

For a man who has lost his business, the building which housed it, and the inventory and still has a loan on either or both at the bank, the difference between 3 per cent and three-fourths of one per cent may well be the difference between recovery and failure.

There is one further justification for making the foreign rate available to our own American disaster victims. The rehabilitated businessman soon begins to pay taxes to municipality, state and Nation. No such benefit results from the foreign loan.

The Small Business Administration was adamant, however, in arguing that the requirements of foreign policy accounted for the difference. But I persisted and began to get some popular support. Both the Anchorage *News* and the Seattle *Post-Intelligencer* supported my stand editorially. They were joined by the AFL-CIO Executive Council and the National Executive Committee of the American Legion. Similar endorsements of the lower interest rate came from the National Congress of Parents and Teachers and from the International Longshoremen and Warehousemen's Union. I put them all in the *Congressional Record* with appropriate comments.

The issue came to a head on June 3, when the Senate Interior Committee heard testimony on behalf of the amendments to the Alaska Omnibus Act. These amendments called for the lower interest rate on disaster loans, and a proposal that the contributions from the Housing and Home Finance Agency to disaster-damaged urban renewal projects be made on a 90–10 matching basis instead of 75–25. I had offered both these amendments, but the latter alone was approved, and only partially. It would apply only to cities of under six thousand population, which would exclude Anchorage. I protested, but Senator Anderson's view that Anchorage could afford the higher matching ratio prevailed.

When the bill came before the Senate on June 30, I introduced my amendments once again, although it was unlikely that the Senate would overrule the Interior Committee. Senator Anderson asked that they be considered *en bloc* and expressed the hope that they would be rejected. They were, on a voice vote. Then on July 23 we met to consider the House bill, which was more generous than the Senate bill, credit for which belonged to Representative Ralph Rivers and to the sympathetic attitude of Interior Committee Chairman Wayne Aspinall. The Senate bill had fixed the interest rate at three-and-five-eighths percent; the House bill at two. I rose and once again called attention to the fact that more than $1 billion was being loaned to foreign countries at three-fourths of one percent. I also expressed my hope that the Senate would accept the House amendment which provided 90–10 matching funds for urban renewal, which would include Anchorage. That was accepted, and the other differences were referred to conference in which the Senate version was slightly improved. But I lost the battle for lower interest rates.

Federal assistance to the victims of the Alaskan quake totaled $393,246,000 of which Alaskans would repay $66,228,000. We had reason to be grateful to President Johnson, and despite our differences, to Senator Anderson, to Edward McDermott and a host of others who had worked tirelessly and effectively to help Alaska. The final bill for earthquake relief was more generous than the original drafts and I felt my efforts had been justified. Bob Bartlett and I did not agree on my stand for the lower interest rate. Nevertheless, I shall forever maintain that it was just and proper.

A tragedy of even greater proportion slowly began to engulf the entire nation during the 1960s. There was not much talk of Vietnam on the floor of the Senate in my first two Congresses—the Eighty-sixth and the Eighty-seventh. I knew little more than what I had read in the newspapers, and found most of my colleagues no better informed. The United States presence in Vietnam, by force of circumstances a commanding one, had attracted little public attention. It had been wrought and was maintained wholly by executive action, Congress voting the appropriations with scant questioning. So I did a little studying and what I found was intriguing.

Our intervention in Vietnam began in the Eisenhower Administration, when the French, who were fighting to retain control of their Indochinese colonies, requested American aid. Foreseeing defeat, the French sought desperately to have American troops sent to save them. Vice President Nixon and Admiral Arthur Radford, Chairman of the Joint Chiefs of Staff, urged it, but General Matthew Ridgway, army chief of staff, was opposed. He felt it would be disastrous, sharing General Douglas MacArthur's publicly expressed view that "anyone who counsels our getting into a ground war on the continent of Asia should have his head examined." President Eisenhower explored it, but finding he could not get Congressional support nor Britain's—Winston Churchill was opposed to any joint venture—he rejected it. But he did give the French massive financial aid—$1.8 billion, four times France's own contribution—in the sixteen months before the fall of Dien Bien Phu, and sent a military mission to help train a Vietnamese army to fight for the French.

The French were beaten and a nine-nation conference met in Geneva in 1954 to draw up the accords which provided for the independence of Cambodia, Laos and Vietnam. For purposes of demobilization, Vietnam was to be temporarily divided at the seventeenth parallel into two regions, but within two years north and south were to be reunited and nationwide elections held. Meanwhile, the United States helped install as South Vietnam's premier Ngo Dinh Diem—a Vietnamese who had been living in monastic seclusion in the United States—and not long after, backed him for the presidency in a rigged election which deposed the ruling Emperor Bao Dai. To Diem, who looked promising at first, President Eisenhower offered economic aid subject to good performance and reforms that would promote freedom and economic well-being. These reforms did not materialize but substantial aid went to Diem nonetheless, and strengthened his hold on his office. Diem, a Catholic, turned out to be a ruthless tyrant, imprisoning hundreds without trial, suppressing freedom of assembly and press, and persecuting the Buddhists who were numerically a majority. His oppressive rule precipitated a civil war.

A further cause for civil war came when Diem reneged on the agreement in the Geneva accords to hold elections—a reversal the United States supported, although it had pledged itself to the elections through the official declaration of Undersecretary Walter Bedell Smith on July 21, 1954. The reason for the United States reversal was the near certainty that Ho Chi Minh, the North Vietnamese leader—regarded as the nation's liberator—would be elected, and he was a communist. That ruled him out, regardless of any prior American commitments, although Ho had fought side by side with the Americans in the expulsion of the Japanese and had expressed his hopes for the future of Vietnam in the vocabulary of America's revolutionary patriots. A Moscow-trained communist, he shared his people's millenial aversion to the Chinese and would have been a firm bulwark against a Chinese invasion of Southeast Asia. He was, above all, an ardent nationalist and incarnated his people's desire for independence and opposition to all foreign domination—Chinese, French, Japanese and American. But the American leadership's policy was based on the unwarranted assumption that communism—which had been born in Russia after World War I with the fall of Czarism—had become a homogeneous monolithic force plotting to conquer the world, and therefore, supported John Foster Dulles's "domino theory" that if Vietnam "fell," as China had in 1949, all Southeast Asia would fall; then the Philippines, Australia, New Zealand, and we'd be fighting them on the beaches of California! So it is interesting to speculate what might have happened if we had adhered to our commitments. Had Ho been elected, it would have resulted in a situation analogous to that in Yugoslavia, where the United States supported Tito—to the tune of over $1 billion—although he was a communist. Ho, like Tito, was not a part of the "Communist Conspiracy" and therefore independent of Moscow, as he would have been of Peking. In all probability, a unified Vietnam under Ho would have maintained a neutral stance in the Cold War. However, United States policy in rejecting the unifying election created a *de facto* state of South Vietnam, without legal justification, made civil war an enduring reality and entrapped us into supporting the new state.

In my opinion, a unified nation, even under communist rule, could not have been worse than the strife-torn, dictator-ridden and corrupt regimes which the United States continued to keep in office in South Vietnam while the whole country was laid waste by war.

President Kennedy inherited the problem of Vietnam, and by the middle of his term he had become disillusioned with Diem and discouraged with the Vietnamese prospect. His administration, represented in Saigon by Ambassador Henry Cabot Lodge, was not unsympathetic when a military coup removed Diem and his brother Ngo Dinh Nhu from power, but prior to that time President Kennedy had changed existing policy of no military intervention by the United States, by sending in so-called advisors to help Diem stay in office, a deception which I criticized on the Senate floor in my first discussion of Vietnam, on October 7, 1963:

> We have been and are heavily engaged in Vietnam to the extent of 12,000 "advisors." They are supposedly "technicians," but of course they are troops, and it is sheer hypocrisy to pretend they are anything else. It is only costing us a million dollars a day, but far more serious, it has cost us the lives of 100 American young men.

Moreover, Kennedy's action was in violation of the 1954 Geneva accords which prohibited "the introduction into Vietnam of any troop reinforcements and additional military personnel." That was why the personnel President Kennedy sent were called "advisors," and it was the beginning of the "credibility gap" between the administration's words and its actions, although it would not be called that until President Johnson took over the conduct of the war. That gap was widened by administration propaganda to the effect that we were fighting "communist aggression from the north." But in fact it was a civil war being fought by both South and North Vietnamese against the oppressive regimes of Diem and the military dictators who succeeded him and their perpetuation of a separate South Vietnam. The rebel ranks included noncommunists as well as communists, and their goal was the reunification and independence of their divided country.

President Johnson in his first three months in office made no significant statements concerning Vietnam. I hoped he would get us out of this needless entanglement and said so in a speech in the Senate on March 10, 1964, entitled "The United States Should Get Out of Vietnam." I said that no vital American interest was at stake in Southeast Asia, and that despite our massive military and economic aid, the situation there was deteriorating. Pointing out that we had already spent over $2.5 billion in Vietnam, I said, "I consider the life of one American boy worth more than this putrid mess. I consider every additional life that is sacrificed in this forlorn venture a tragedy. Someday . . . if this sacrificing is continued it will be denounced as a crime."

Since President Johnson had inherited a mess that was not of his making, he was free, I pointed out, to reverse our policy in Vietnam, and I urged him to disengage immediately, to relieve all our military of combat assignments and bring them home at once. It would have been easy at that time. Only two hundred of our boys had died in combat. Had Johnson taken this advice, he would have saved some 45,000 American lives and the maiming of thousands of other young men; he would have kept America's good name; he would not have laid waste a small country we were there presumably to help; he would not have killed thousands of Vietnamese noncombatants and made refugees of millions more. And he would have gone down in history as one of our greatest presidents, for his leadership in effecting desirable domestic programs was unexcelled. Unfortunately, the war nullified these great gains at home and eventually forced his retirement.

No report of my Senate speech appeared in the New York *Times*, or in any of the three Washington dailies. It seemed to me that the first clear-cut demand to get out of the war by anyone in public office was news. The wire services had carried summaries of it and I concluded that my views ran counter to the editorial policies of these papers which had censored them. I called Turner Catledge, then the New York *Times* managing editor, and speaking to him as an old newspaperman, asked "How come?" He said that it had been a mistake of judgment and that later in the week the *Times* would publish a summary of conflicting views on the war, which it did, inevitably minimizing my position.* Nevertheless, as a result of the wire-service coverage, I received a flock of letters running, in the first batch, one hundred to one in support of my stand. The writers included university deans and professors, business leaders, clergymen of var-

* *The Columbia Journalism Review* in its winter 1970–1971 issue entitled "Vietnam, What Lessons?" published an analysis by seven responsible journalists of press, radio and television coverage of the war. Its "lead" article by Jules Witcover, Washington correspondent of the *Los Angeles Times*, discussed the failure of the metropolitan dailies to report what he termed my "historic speech" of March 10, 1964. That failure, in the view of Don Stillman of the West Virginia School of Journalism, "was part of the general breakdown of the media's responsibility to check on the actions of the Government." In further proof of that point, failure to check on the official account of the Tonkin Gulf incident was almost total; the Charleston, *West Virginia Gazette* and I. F. Stone's *Weekly* being the only organs that appraised the deception correctly.

ious denominations and retired military men. They encouraged me to keep on. My view was also supported in a syndicated column entitled "Vietnam: It Isn't Worth the Cost" by John S. Knight, newspaper owner and publisher and a past president of the American Society of Newspaper Editors. His was one of the very few dissenting journalistic voices at that time.

The killing of six more Americans in Vietnam led me to repeat my plea for withdrawal on March 16. On March 20 I joined in a colloquy with Senator Wayne Morse, who denounced Secretary of State Dean Rusk for characterizing those who opposed the war as "quitters" and "lending aid and comfort to our enemies." Since the latter was the Constitution's definition of treason, and as Wayne Morse and I were then the only outspoken Congressional opponents of the war, we were quite properly resentful. And on April 15 I pointed out that our casualties in Vietnam were more than doubling and criticized Secretary Rusk's statement at a Manila meeting of representatives of the Southeast Asia Treaty Organization that the United States might extend the war into North Vietnam. I repeated my conviction that it was "a war we cannot win. . . . It is a war which bears only the remotest relation, if any, to our national security."

On May 7, speaking on "The Tenth Anniversary of the Surrender at Dien Bien Phu, France's Disaster in Southeast Asia: A Lesson for the United States," I drew what seemed to me the increasingly obvious conclusion, repeating as I would again and again that all Vietnam was not worth the life of a single American boy. My words went unheeded; on the contrary, a message to the Congress from President Johnson on May 18 indicated that the war in Vietnam would be escalated. He asked Congress to add $125 million for Vietnam on top of the $3.4 billion already provided for foreign assistance. Both Senator Morse and I registered our opposition. On May 22 I proposed to bring the war in South Vietnam to the conference table, a plea strongly supported by Senator Morse. I repeated that plea on May 27, and on June 3, proposed a United Nations cease-fire in South Vietnam. This was the first time a United Nations-sponsored cease-fire in Southeast Asia had been proposed in the Senate, or as far as I could tell, anywhere. It was ignored by the press; neither the New York *Times* nor the Washington *Post* mentioned it, although again it was carried by the wire services. But both these major newspapers responded editorially that to negotiate successfully the United States had first to increase its military strength. I replied, "In other words we have got to kill more American boys as well as Vietnamese and spend more millions of dollars before we do what we know we will have to do ultimately. What utter folly!" And I added that we should stop the killing not merely of American boys, but of South Vietnamese, cease bombing villages with napalm and burning innocent men, women and children who had no part in the conflict except as its victims. But the need "to negotiate from strength" would be stressed again and again by our policy makers and their journalistic supporters and lead us ever deeper into the Southeast Asian morass.

Then on the night of August 4, President Johnson reported to a nationwide television audience that on August 2, there had been an unprovoked attack by North Vietnamese vessels on an American destroyer on routine patrol in international waters in the Gulf of Tonkin; that he had ordered a second destroyer to accompany the first; and that on August 4 the attack on both vessels had been repeated, constituting clear acts of aggression, which required a response by the United States; and that he had ordered an air raid in reprisal on North Vietnamese ports and installations and would ask Congress for a resolution, which would show its support of his purpose to repel such acts of aggression in the future.

The joint resolution, drafted in the White House, was received in both houses of Congress the following day. After "whereasing" that "naval units of the Communist regime in Vietnam" had "deliberately and repeatedly attacked United States naval vessels lawfully present in international waters . . . part of a deliberate and systematic campaign of aggression against its neighbors and the nations joined with them in the collective defense of their freedom," the resolution asked the Congress to approve of and support the President's taking all necessary measures to repel armed attack and prevent further aggression. It authorized the President to use U.S. armed forces anywhere he saw fit in Southeast Asia.

In the Senate, the resolution was referred to the Foreign Relations and Armed Services committees, which after listening to Secretary of Defense Robert McNamara, Secretary of State Dean Rusk, and Chairman of the Joint Chiefs of Staff, Earle Wheeler, voted to report the resolution, Wayne Morse dissenting. In the House, it was referred to and reported favorably by the Committee on Foreign Affairs, and its chairman, Thomas E. Morgan—on August 7—urged immediate passage. After an hour's "debate" consisting of expressions of approval—with the sole exception of George Brown of California—it was adopted by a vote of 416 to zero.

Senator Morse had been vociferous in his objections to the resolution when it was in committee, and he repeated his objections when it came to the floor of the Senate. But Senator Fulbright, the floor manager of the resolution, recommended its "prompt and overwhelming indorsement." There was some questioning of the consequences of its enactment by Senator George McGovern and by Senator Gaylord Nelson, who feared that it portended a "complete change in the mission we have had in South

Vietnam for the past ten years." Fulbright replied that the resolution was consistent with what the United States had been doing. Nevertheless, Senator Nelson was not convinced, and on the third and last day of the debate, after pointing to the widely divergent opinions of the senators as to what the resolution really meant, he offered an amendment which would have limited our role in Southeast Asia to training assistance and military advice—our avowed policy. Senator Fulbright refused to accept it.

I detailed my objections to the resolution on the second day of the debate, and again on the third. But the resolution was adopted by eighty-eight yeas to two nays, that of Senator Morse and mine. The ten absent members were all recorded as supporting the resolution.

What none of the senators and representatives knew, however, was that they had been misled about the Tonkin Gulf incident. The facts would not be fully revealed until four years later when, on February 20, 1968, the Senate Foreign Relations Committee reopened an investigation into what actually had or had not happened in the Tonkin Gulf.

But even before these subsequent disclosures, Senator Fulbright publicly and repeatedly expressed regret for his sponsorship and support of the Tonkin Gulf Resolution. He said he had been deceived. The Congress had been bamboozled into giving the President the unlimited power he sought to wage war in Southeast Asia. Had the Congress not been misinformed by the executive branch, the resolution would never have been adopted.

A summary of the true facts revealed that the destroyer *Maddox* had not been, as alleged, on a routine patrol in international waters. She was a spy ship, outfitted with elaborate electronic equipment; she had penetrated the territorial waters of North Vietnam and was engaged in hostile operations against a country with which we were not at war. Furthermore, her penetration of North Vietnamese waters took place at the very time when South Vietnamese vessels supplied by the United States Navy, with crews trained by it, were raiding North Vietnamese ports, and shelling their installations. It would not have been surprising had the North Vietnamese been unable to distinguish these acts of aggression from the presence of United States destroyers. Moreover the *Maddox* had fired the first shots. The United States destroyers involved in the encounter on August 2 were not hit, except for one bullet hole, reportedly in the *Maddox*, nor were they hit on August 4. Neither vessels nor crew suffered any damage. Indeed, it was not clear that an attack on the *Maddox* and *C. Turner Joy* on August 4 ever took place. It was also revealed that nearly nine hours before President Johnson's television address and his order to attack North Vietnamese installations, the following message was received

at the Pentagon from Captain Herrick of the *Maddox*, who had been promoted to commodore when his command included a second destroyer,
the *C. Turner Joy*, on August 4. Obviously he was the one man who knew
what had and what had not happened on August 2 and 4:

> Review of action makes many recorded contacts and torpedoes
> .fired appear doubtful. Freak weather effects and overeager sonarmen
> may have accounted for many reports. No actual visual sightings by
> Maddox. Suggest complete evaluation before any further action.

Yet this message, known early on the afternoon of August 4 by secretary of Defense Robert McNamara and President Johnson, was concealed
from the Senate and House leaders meeting later that day at the White
House to be briefed by President Johnson with his version of what had
happened in the Tonkin Gulf, which he would also give the American
people over television later that night. And it was further concealed from
senators and representatives during the committee hearings of Senate and
House, and during the debate in each house on the following days. Surely,
had they known of it, they never would have voted for the Tonkin Gulf
Resolution.

The truth about the Tonkin Gulf incident, whose administration version plunged our country into the longest and costliest war in our history, became available to the American people only four years later. It
became known because Senator Fulbright, aware that he had been misled
by the administration, reopened the hearings on the Tonkin Gulf incident
before the Foreign Relations Committee and called in all the principals in
the affair. Their testimony made clear the official misrepresentation that
had surrounded the incident four years earlier.

The administration denied any duplicity, of course. In concluding his
testimony at the 1968 hearing on Tonkin, Secretary McNamara declared:
"the suggestion that in some way the United States induced the incident
on August 4, with the intent of providing an excuse to take the retaliatory action which we in fact took, I can only characterize such insinua-
tions as monstrous." But at a closed session of the Foreign Relations
Committee three years before, William P. Bundy, assistant secretary of
state for Far Eastern Affairs, admitted under Fulbright's questioning that
he had prepared drafts of a resolution to achieve the result of the Tonkin
Gulf Resolution several months before the August 1964 incidents occurred.

In sum, while the Johnson administration was charging that its action
was to repel and prevent aggression, it was itself the aggressor, a paradox
applicable not only to the Tonkin Gulf incident but to the whole war in
Southeast Asia.

Many people asked me right after the Senate vote, and later at various times, why I had voted against the resolution. I had no other alternative. I was convinced of the folly of our military involvement in Southeast Asia, and having declared my opposition to it nearly five months earlier and having reiterated it subsequently, I could only view the Tonkin Gulf Resolution as a blank check to the President to escalate and widen that involvement. Moreover, the text of the resolution, apart from its misrepresentation of what happened in the Tonkin Gulf, embodied three falsities which aggravated the whole deception. The action authorized was *not*, as the resolution declared, consonant with the Constitution of the United States and the Charter of the United Nations, nor was it in accordance with our obligations under the Southeast Asia Collective Treaty. Article 1, Section Eight, of the Constitution does not permit the President to wage war at his own discretion. The Charter of the United Nations specifically forbids the action authorized by the resolution and proposes wholly different alternatives. And so does the Southeast Asia Collective Treaty.

Of course when I voted "nay" I did not suspect, any more than did my colleagues, that the Tonkin Gulf incident was largely spurious. But during the ensuing months as I watched the presidential credibility gap widen, I began to wonder whether the incident had not been another "Reichstag Fire." I once asked Senator Fulbright, after he had changed his view about it, but before the full facts were uncovered in 1968, whether he did not think it might have been such. "I've suspected it," he said, "but I haven't any evidence." Certainly the incident may not have been planned, but the Johnson Administration had provoked and welcomed it, had misrepresented it, and had it not occurred, would have found another pretext to plunge us more deeply into the war. The draft prepared three months before the incident by Assistant Secretary Bundy demonstrated that conclusively.

Since the members of Congress were unknowingly voting on and approving a wholly false presentation of what had happened when the true version would have become available had they been informed of Captain Herrick's telegram, it is not incorrect to say that the United States was lied into the war.

That fall Lyndon Johnson ran for the Presidency against Barry Goldwater. Goldwater preached a belligerent policy which called for whatever it took to "win" the war in Vietnam, whereas President Johnson's campaign utterances conveyed to millions of Americans that he hoped for and would achieve peaceful solutions to inherited foreign entanglements, particularly in Southeast Asia. Johnson said repeatedly that he would not send American boys to fight a ground war in Asia, and on the strength of these promises, he was swept into office overwhelmingly. Goldwater carried only six states. Meanwhile plans were maturing in the Pentagon to do exactly what Johnson had promised not to do. He had deceived the Congress in August and he was now deceiving the American people during his campaign.

In his State of the Union Message on January 4, 1965, the President deepened that deception when he said of Vietnam:

> Why are we there? We are there, first, because a friendly nation has asked us for help against Communist aggression. Ten years ago the President pledged our help. Three Presidents have supported that Pledge. And we will not break it.

These statements were untrue. The record is bare of any such request. Eisenhower gave Vietnam no military help, although the military mission he had sent to train the Vietnamese to fight for the French remained after the French defeat. Kennedy sent several thousand "advisors." But these Presidents acted on their own initiative and not in response "to a request for help," and when Johnson refers to *three* presidents, he includes himself. Johnson went further in an address at John Hopkins University on April 7, when he said:

> We are there because we have a promise to keep. Since 1954 every American President has offered support to the people of South Vietnam . . . . Thus, over many years, we have made a national pledge to help South Vietnam retain its independence. I intend to keep that promise. To dishonor that pledge . . . would be an unforgivable wrong.

Thus a myth was invented and perpetuated—that the United States had a commitment to send military aid to Vietnam. History will verify that the only firm commitments made by a President were those made to the American people by Lyndon Johnson in his 1964 election campaign, when he said that he would not send American boys to fight a ground war in Asia.

After the adjournment of Congress in the fall of 1964, the Government Operations Committee authorized a continuation of my on-the-spot studies of our foreign-aid program, this time in Latin America. My study included Colombia, Venezuela, Ecuador, Peru and Chile, and I learned from several of our ambassadors that they had been given explicit instructions by Secretary Rusk to request the president of the country to which they were accredited to support United States intervention in Vietnam. President Johnson, they were told to inform the Latin-American Chiefs of State, wanted to show their flags alongside ours in Southeast Asia. Two ambassadors confided that they were embarrassed, knowing that the request would not be well received, but since these countries received United States aid, their leaders found it difficult to refuse. But in no country was there a meaningful acquiescence. Uruguay offered to send an ambulance. Brazil agreed to send coffee of which it had an unsold surplus.

Early in 1965, President Johnson's tragic escalation of the war began when, in a so-called tit for tat retaliation for a Vietcong raid on the American outpost at Pleiku, planes were dispatched to bomb North Vietnam. The administration blamed Hanoi for the raid, but in fact, as newspaper correspondents later revealed, the Vietcong had used mortars of American make or left-over French arms, captured from or given them by South Vietnamese troops. Up until that point, the administration claim that it was fighting "aggression from the North" had been a myth. Now infiltration from the North began, and Russia and China supported North Vietnam with arms. The retaliatory bombing raids, which thenceforth became fixed United States military policy, did not stop this infiltration; they caused it.

I discussed the Pleiku attack and subsequent bombings in the Senate and my comments appeared in the *Congressional Record* under a standard heading, "The Mess in Vietnam," although these were not my only criticisms as the political chaos in South Vietnam grew and our involvement deepened. I began to receive invitations to speak and give my views, and in April of 1965 I debated the Vietnam issue with Assistant Secretary of State William P. Bundy in an upper West Side Manhattan high school on invitation from that district's Congressman, William Fitts Ryan. Whenever I was invited to speak, I requested that the opposing view be presented. After several such encounters the State Department declined to furnish speakers. The matter came to a head when I was scheduled to speak at Ohio State University. I asked that the State Department be requested to send someone to present its case. It declined. Finally the office of the university president telephoned Secretary Rusk's office and was told that the department could spare no one for that purpose.

The reasons for the State Department's withdrawal were clear. It was beginning to get unfavorable audience reactions and press reportage, both at home and abroad. My stand was still far from popular, however, and needless to say I did not escape unscathed. I was attacked by syndicated columnists James J. Kilpatrick, Fulton Lewis, Jr., and others, and addressing the Anchorage Republican Club, Theodore Stevens—then a member of the Alaska legislature—declared that "No man, unless it is Senator Wayne Morse, has done more to harm American security at home and our prestige abroad then our junior senator." But on the whole I did not incur many unfavorable criticisms. The press generally ignored my

statements, as it did Senator Morse's, while giving plenty of coverage to
the administration's pronouncements and to those of the war's supporters
in Congress and elsewhere. Nevertheless "The Mess in Vietnam" was becoming so patent that more and more questions were being asked, largely
about our conduct of the war, rather than the legality of or justification
for our intervention. I questioned both, but I also expressed the view that
if we could not solve the problem by negotiation, we should confess our
error and get out.

Full-page advertisements in the New York *Times* sponsored by clergymen, lawyers, university faculties, and other groups were demonstrating
growing opposition to our Southeast Asia adventure. I inserted them in
the *Congressional Record*. And I found an increasing number of my Senate
colleagues unhappy about the war, but without being able to offer any
solution. A new attitude was springing up among them and many others;
in fact, for a time it was a widely expressed cliché. It admitted that the
United States had made a mistake in going into Southeast Asia, but we
were *there* now, and so we had to keep at it. I could not see why we had to

*Wayne Morse and Ernest Gruening—the two "nos" in the Tonkin Gulf
Resolution, 1964*

Ernest Gruening addressing an anti-war rally in Washington, 1965

compound our errors, keep on killing more of our boys and squandering more billions. Not only was this a war we could not win, but I had become convinced it was a war we should not *want* to win. I had also come to the conclusion, and said so, that far from stopping communism we were helping it. Bombing Vietnamese villages, north and south, burning homes with napalm, making thousands of homeless refugees and driving our tanks over the South Vietnamese rice paddies could hardly succeed in "winning the hearts and minds of the people."

Finally, I was convinced—and declared—that if the Chinese and Russian rulers, who, in the official view, were our real enemies in this war, had wanted to devise a policy that would bring us down, they could not have conceived a better one than we were pursuing, bogged down in a hopeless Asian land war, sacrificing thousands of our young men, wasting billions of dollars, creating dissension at home, and forfeiting the respect and sympathy of the rest of mankind. I said, and would repeat, that no good whatever could come out of our involvement in an undeclared, utterly unjustifiable, needless and illegal war. I voiced those views whenever I spoke, and I was gratified by the increasing number of antiwar rallies and "teach-ins," including one at the outdoor Sylvan Theater in Washington on April 17, which twelve thousand attended.

In a message to Congress on May 4, 1965, requesting a supplemental appropriation of $700 million, President Johnson frankly stated that no funds were needed to supply our armed forces in Vietnam which had sufficient funds for the time being, but that the request was a means of securing approval of his conduct of the war. I attacked his proposal at length on May 6 and voted against the appropriation. I was joined by Wayne Morse and Gaylord Nelson. In the House, seven voted against it: George Brown, Philip Burton, Don Edwards, Edith Green, John Conyers, John Dow, and William Fitts Ryan. We were rewarded with a cartoon in the York, Pennsylvania, *Gazette* headed "Profiles in Courage." Thereafter I decided to vote against every military appropriation and Senator Morse and I did so, joined occasionally by Stephen Young of Ohio, a former combat veteran who had visited Vietnam several times and disapproved of our presence there. For I had concluded that merely speaking against the war was ineffective. The only way to put an end to it was to exercise our constitutional power over the purse. Indeed, President Johnson had once taunted the Congress, saying: "I don't care what speeches you make against the war as long as you vote my appropriations."

Of course this action evoked criticism. "Don't you want to back our boys?" I was asked. "I sure do" was my answer. "I want them *back* home!" Actually, had the Congress voted down a military appropriation bill, it would not have deprived the men at the front of a single rifle, bullet, or plane. The materiel authorized by the appropriations did not reach the front for a year or more; there was always plenty in the pipeline. But a "no" from the Congress on military appropriations would have brought the war to an early halt.

On August 19, 1965, I had a chance to express my views to President Johnson. He had telephoned to thank me for some remarks I made on the floor in praise of his domestic program. I told him that while I had done that gladly, I differed wholly from him on his Southeast Asia policy and would like to tell him why.

When we met, I reviewed my criticisms of the war, challenging its legality as well as its conduct. I said that in my view his expressed determination to "win" the war was a mistake. It could not be won; rather I suggested that our only hope was to revert to the Geneva agreements and make a firm commitment for a cease-fire, withdrawal of all American troops and a Vietnam-wide election supervised by the United Nations.

Giving my views on the war to President Johnson, August 19, 1965

He said he would consider my recommendations and discuss them with his advisors. I then told him I was planning that afternoon to offer an amendment to the draft legislation to provide that no draftees be sent to Southeast Asia without their consent and without approval of Congress.

"Don't do that; please don't do that," the President said.

I gave the President my reasons, and he then said, "If we're not out of there by next January, you can do anything you please. We won't be sending any draftees down there before that."

In response to his request and his assurances, I said that I would not introduce the amendment, but I would immediately send him a draft of the amendment and a copy of the speech I had intended to make supporting it, and I did so.

He telephoned me the next day, August 20, repeating what seemed to me a somewhat modified statement, that no draftees would be sent to Southeast Asia before January 1966, and the following day I received a two-page letter from him, the first paragraph of which read:

I deeply appreciate your forbearance in not introducing your amendment to the Defense Appropriations Bill which would have prohibited the sending of draftees without their consent to Southeast Asia. I confirm what I told you during our telephone conversation yesterday—no persons drafted into the military service during the remainder of this year will be assigned to Southeast Asia before January 1966.

We were not "out of there" by January. On the contrary our participation had been greatly and rapidly escalated. So on January 26, 1966, I announced that I would offer the amendment—cosponsored by Senator Morse—to one of three bills, whichever came up first. I related my conversation with the President of August 19 and introduced into the *Congressional Record* the letter I had sent him immediately thereafter. I did not think it proper to insert the letter he had sent me. I gave my reasons for the amendment; there had been no declaration of war, and it was unlikely there would be one. Therefore I felt the Congress should decide whether or not draftees were to be sent to Southeast Asia. I asked whether it was fair to send draftees with little or no training while the Armed Forces Reserves, on whose training three-quarters of a billion dollars had been spent annually, were not being utilized in Vietnam. Theoretically our country was at peace. If these young men, the draftees, were to be sent into battle, should not Congress which had enacted the peacetime conscription law make the determination and accept the responsibility for sending them into combat? However one might feel about the war, there was a difference in the obligation to serve, between men drafted involuntarily and those already in the armed services who had voluntarily enlisted, knowing they would have to go where they were sent.

My announcement brought me hundreds of approving letters, some of which I read into the *Congressional Record*. They were a striking exhibit of the growing gap between the people and their government, for they described the many hardships suffered by draftees and their families and protested our involvement in an unjust and immoral war. There were now two hundred thousand American soldiers in Vietnam, and thirty-three thousand of them were draftees.

Debate on the Supplementary Military and Procurement Bill began on February 24, and I introduced my amendment on March 1. Senator Richard Russell, chairman of the Armed Services Committee who was in charge of the bill, objected. "I merely wish to say that this innocent-sounding time-bomb would absolutely destroy our Armed Forces. It would require that every unit from the squad level up be called, to determine who would be eligible to go to Vietnam." If the amendment were adopted the thirty-three thousand draftees already in Vietnam, he said further, would remain without relief, and if they were pulled out, the units would have to be re-formed. Senator Mansfield moved to table the amendment and the vote was 94–2, only Wayne Morse and I in opposition. I would introduce the amendment again the next year, but with no more success.

The debate on the procurement bill continued for several days. Wayne Morse had alerted the Senate that it foreshadowed a major change of policy. It provided for an escalation of half a million men and allowed the secretary of Defense to establish installations which he determined "to be vital to the security of the United States." Morse declared that this would mean enduring occupation of Vietnam by the United States. He was further outraged at giving the secretary of Defense that blank check. Why should not the Congress determine what installations were to be established? And that phrase "vital to the security of the United States." How could they be, in Vietnam?

Morse said he would move to amend the bill and if the amendment failed, he would vote against it. His amendment was to repeal the Tonkin Gulf Resolution. It was a challenge to those senators who had in the last year and a half protested that they had not dreamed that the Tonkin Gulf Resolution would bring bigger escalation. Senator Mansfield moved to table the Morse amendment. It was tabled 92–5, the five being Fulbright, McCarthy, Young of Ohio, Morse and myself. On final passage of the bill only Morse and I voted "nay." It passed the House 393–4 with only

Brown and Burton of California, Conyers of Michigan and Ryan of New York voting "nay."

The United States had now irrevocably escalated into a major war. I continued my opposition to the war all through the spring of 1966. At hearings conducted by Senator Edward Kennedy with a view to improving draft procedures and eliminating some of their inequities, I testified to my conviction that the draft could *not* be reformed. What difference did it make *how* you were selected to become cannon fodder in an unjustifiable war? The draft ought to be abolished, certainly at least for service in Southeast Asia. The horrors of the war had become apparent to an increasing number of our young men. They faced being compelled to serve in a war that they considered unjust and immoral, to kill people against whom they felt no grievance, possibly to be maimed or killed in the process, or if they refused, to go to jail for five years of hard labor. This, I declared, was an infamous dilemma, to which no American, no member of a society which vaunted itself as "free," should be subjected. My views of the draft did not prevail, however, and many young men followed their consciences and either went to jail or left the country. They were not, I said, "slackers," to use the World War I epithet. Had this been a war for the defense of our country, they would have gone almost to a man.

They would tell me so with deep conviction on the campuses where I spoke. I was invariably asked by those nearing draft time what I thought they should do. I felt obliged to tell them that I could not advise them; I could not counsel them to go into a war which they—like I—considered unjust and immoral; neither could I counsel them to refuse to go, and incur not only imprisonment, but the possible ruin of their future careers when they returned to civilian life. It was a decision each had to make for himself, but I felt remiss that I could not be more helpful.

It was the widespread unhappiness and revulsion among our youth, engendered by that dilemma, that George Wald, professor of biochemistry at Harvard, in a notable address in Boston, diagnosed as the cause of their alienation and of campus unrest; young men were questioning whether they had a future. He also made the amendatory suggestion that to the "military-industrial complex," which President Eisenhower had warned against in his farewell address, "Labor" should be added. I hailed this as a realistic appraisal, having become painfully aware that the labor movement had lost the idealism and wider range of concern that had once characterized it—and its leaders and members alike, content with their employment in the factories which produced napalm, bombs and the other implements of war, had become part of the military establishment. But a fourth component, I suggested, should also be added; it should be labeled the "military-industrial-labor-congressional complex." For Congress had consistently supported the war and was a full partner in the complex; it had always had the power to end the slaughter and had failed to do so.

Attempting to arouse the Congressional conscience, I continued to criticize the war from the floor of the Senate. It was to no avail. When I spoke on June 21, 1966, on "Why Not Face the Truth About Vietnam?" our troop strength had reached three hundred thousand in Vietnam, forty thousand in Thailand and seventy thousand aboard the fleet off-shore. The number of Americans killed had passed four thousand and the wounded twenty thousand. We had been bombing North Vietnam for sixteen months, and the administration was planning to send more troops and continue the bombing. I repeated my proposals for an effort at peaceful solution. Stop the bombing. Lay the issue before the United Nations. Agree to negotiate with the National Liberation Front. Ask for a cease-fire. Promise to hold Vietnam-wide elections supervised by the United Nations. Agree to abide by the results and pledge a phased withdrawal as soon as peace is established. It might not work. But why not try it?

Yet despite my protests, and the mounting dissension of the American people as a whole, the Congress refused to act in any way to contain what had come to be known as "Johnson's War." And President Johnson continued to wave the Tonkin Gulf Resolution in the face of Congress and the public in support of his escalation and his determination to achieve military victory. "Nail that coonskin to the wall" was his injunction to the soldiery on his visit to Vietnam in 1967. And his gestures at negotiations were irrelevant, unrealistic and continually undercut by his insistence on conditions our "adversaries" could not possibly accept. Finally, the rising tide of public opinion—which President Johnson thought he could ignore—pulled him down. Senator Eugene McCarthy's stand on Vietnam and his showing in the New Hampshire primary early in 1968 foreshadowed President Johnson's defeat, and he chose not to run for reelection. But the damage had already been done—and has yet to be undone. Had Lyndon Johnson acted upon the advice I gave him on March 10, 1964, instead of listening to the counsels of Dean Rusk, the brothers Bundy, Walt Rostow, the joint chiefs of staff and Robert S. McNamara, he would have spared the nation, Vietnam and himself a terrible tragedy.

There is little satisfaction, however, in being able to say "I told you so," even to a President of the United States. But it was gratifying to both Senator Morse and me that ours were no longer the lone voices raised in opposition to the war. My criticisms of the President's policies continued unabated throughout 1967 in speeches from the Senate floor, in public addresses and television appearances, and in newspaper and magazine articles. And in 1968 in collaboration with Herbert Beaser, who did the writing, we published a 664-page volume entitled *Vietnam Folly*, which detailed the historical background of the steady American descent into the Southeast Asian quagmire. President Johnson was, of course, resentful of the critics of the war, denouncing them as "Nervous Nellies." But he exhibited no personal displeasure in my case and without exception treated me with consideration. And on his pause in Alaska in 1966 to assist Governor Egan's campaign for reelection, he gave me a photograph of himself with the inscription "To Ernest Gruening, a fighter always for what he believes right, from his friend, Lyndon Baines Johnson."

This struck me as such a generous action that I decided to record it gratefully here. But I was disillusioned when a man of national repute and unimpeachable veracity, whom I had known well for many years, related to me verbatim that the President, after denouncing the Senatorial critics of his war policy, said, "I'm smarter than they are. I'm going to get Wayne Morse. I'm going to offer him an assignment which he won't refuse. It will ruin him." He then outlined the words of encomium and flattery he would use to get Senator Morse's agreement to serve. The assignment was to act as mediator in a strike of the machinists' union against the airlines in 1966. Morse did agree, feeling it was his duty to accept an assignment for which he was exceptionally well qualified. Yet, although he was a proven friend of organized labor, he could not support all its demands. And in his 1968 campaign for reelection, the machinists' union, a substantial segment of organized labor in Oregon, came out against him and provided the slender margin of his defeat.

President Johnson had achieved his objective.

Not knowing this and assuming that he would be grateful to Morse for the special service he had rendered, I suggested to President Johnson after Morse's defeat, that he nominate him for the Supreme Court vacancy created by Earl Warren's resignation. The President had already nominated Abe Fortas, but the nomination had run into a Senate filibuster which would prevent confirmation in the expiring Ninetieth Congress. Morse, a former professor of law and dean of the University of Oregon Law School, as well as an outstanding constitutional scholar, was not only supremely qualified but would have been confirmed by the Senate.

28

CONTRACEPTION:
THE BREAKTHROUGH

Whatever your cause it's a lost cause unless you control population.
—PHYLLIS T. PIOTROW

"Birth control," the term originated by Margaret Sanger, was still widely taboo in the early 1960s. Despite her half-century of crusading and the efforts of "Planned Parenthood" groups, no relaxation or repeal of the laws forbidding physicians to impart contraceptive methods had taken place. Organized opposition by the Roman Catholic hierarchy, assisted by lay organizations such as the Knights of Columbus, had sufficed to prevent any action by state legislatures. Even discussion of the subject with a view to remedial action was assumed to be, and indeed was apt to be, politically lethal. Newspapers, too, were still subjected to the same pressures I had encountered in Boston in the century's second decade. The subject had never been discussed in Congress.

Perhaps the first sign of recognition in government circles of the importance of birth control came in 1959 with a report by General William H. Draper, Jr., who had been appointed by President Eisenhower to head a committee to study the foreign-aid military-assistance program. General Draper's report stated that foreign aid, especially in Latin America, could not succeed as long as the excessive population growth continued; and it recommended that a portion of our aid be devoted to bringing about a better understanding in the developing countries of the problems that accompany population growth. Credit for the first serious presentation of this subject in Congress, however, belongs to Senator Joseph S.

Clark of Pennsylvania, who gave a major address on August 15, 1963, entitled, "The Time Has Come To Speak Out on the Problem of Population Control." Clark also introduced a concurrent resolution, which I cosponsored, urging the President to encourage research on population control within the National Institutes of Health, and to create a Presidential Commission on Population to inform the government and the people of the nature of the problem and to make appropriate recommendations. The resolution was referred to the Senate Committee on Labor and Public Welfare. No hearings were held, and President Kennedy's death precluded any action by him, although he had at a press conference expressed sympathy for further studies.

I felt the government had to go beyond "study." I visualized legislation that would make a start on limiting or slowing down population growth, and communicated with a variety of interested people to get their ideas of what might be done. Meanwhile, I thought it advisable to build up as much Congressional support as possible—for the subject was still considered politically perilous—by publicizing it. These efforts were given further impetus by President Johnson's declaration in his State of the Union Message that he would "seek new ways to use our knowledge to help deal with the explosion in world population and the growing scarcity in world resources." It was the first forthright declaration on this issue by a President of the United States.

My ideas about the necessary legislation began to crystallize. I decided to make it moderate—an entering wedge. The bill I conceived merely provided two new positions in the federal government with the rank and title of Assistant Secretary for Population Planning, one in the State Department, and one in the Department of Health, Education and Welfare. Their functions would be to publicize the population problem and to provide the pertinent materials—on request—the former to foreign governments and institutions, the latter to states, communities, institutions and individuals at home. The emphasis was wholly on voluntary participation; no one was obliged to ask for the material, to accept it, or to use it, if accepted. The legislation also authorized a White House Conference on Population in 1967. The bill had six co-sponsors, Senators Bartlett, Bass, Douglas, Moss, Tydings and Yarborough—a disappointingly small number—but six more joined us after hearings were underway. Companion bills were introduced in the House by Morris Udall of Arizona and Paul Todd of Michigan.

Early in 1965 I had been made chairman of a new subcommittee on Foreign Aid Expenditures of the Committee on Government Operations. My population-control bill, S.1676, was referred to it. When hearings opened on June 22, 1965, they received a welcome assist from Dwight D.

Eisenhower, who as President had opposed federal action in this field. General Draper told me that Eisenhower had changed his mind, so I wrote asking whether he would be willing to testify, or if not, to submit a statement. His letter from Gettysburg, dated June 18, was the first hearing's "*pièce de résistance;*" it was an unqualified endorsement of our purpose. He wrote in part:

> I am delighted that your committee is concerning itself with the subject, one that I consider constitutes one of the most, if not the most, important of the critical problems facing mankind to-day. . . .
>
> I realize that in important segments of our people and of other nations this question is regarded as a moral one and therefore scarcely a fit subject for federal legislation. With these feelings I can and do sympathize. But I cannot help believe that the prevention of human degradation and starvation is likewise a moral—as well as a material —obligation resting upon every enlightened government. If we now ignore the plight of those unborn generations which, because of our unreadiness to take corrective action in controlling population growth, will be denied any expectations beyond abject poverty and suffering, then history will rightly condemn us.

There was further encouragement. Two weeks earlier, on June 7, the United States Supreme Court ruled 7–2 that the 1879 Connecticut birth-control law was invalid and an "invasion of the right to privacy." Richard Cardinal Cushing of Boston had expressed his opinion concerning a similar Massachusetts law, declaring that Catholics did not need the support of civil law to be faithful to their religious convictions, and did not seek to impose by law their moral views on other members of society. And the New York *Times* had just reported that eighty-one Nobel Prize Laureates had petitioned the Pope to reconsider his stand on birth control. I cited Cardinal Cushing in the statement that opened the first hearing, and it seemed to me that we were off to a good start.

Our progress was slow, however. In the next three years, we held thirty-two hearings and heard from Presidents of the United States, senators, representatives, federal and state executives, heads of state in foreign countries, demographers, sociologists, penologists, geneticists, clergymen of various denominations, lawyers, physicians representing varieties of medical practice, social workers, representatives of labor and industry and anyone else who was concerned. I made every effort to present all sides of this isssue, and solicited the views of those opposed, but the amount of adverse testimony, by a few Catholic laymen, was slight; not a few, including priests, testified favorably. I invited Archbishop (later Cardinal)

O'Boyle to testify, but he declined. He had had the unprecedented experience of having his congregation at Saint Matthew's Cathedral in Washington walk out when he was counseling them to adhere to the papal pronouncements on this issue.

Dr. John Rock, Emeritus Professor of Gynecology at the Harvard Medical School, told our subcommittee that the purpose in writing his book, *The Time Has Come: A Catholic Doctor's Proposal to End the Battle over Birth Control*, was to present to his church not only the dangers of uncontrolled population growth, but also to propose a theologically acceptable birth-control measure. The church had not accepted it. I asked him whether he expected any change in the position of the church. Having been a Catholic for seventy-five years, he had, he said, complete confidence in his church's eventual action, but the speed with which it would act left much to be desired. He added, however, that the pressure now being brought to bear on the church would bring much faster action than in the cases of Galileo, usury, and autopsies.

"It took a little while for the church to come around to the position taken by Galileo, did it not?" I asked.

"About three hundred years" was Dr. Rock's reply.

Ernest Gruening with his office staff, Washington, 1965

One of the Senate subcommittee birth-control hearings

Dr. Donald Barrett, professor of sociology at Notre Dame, author of two volumes on *Problems of Population*, and a member of the Papal Commission on Population and Birth Control, felt family planning was essential, but that "rhythm" was the only method acceptable to the church. However, a professor of chemistry at Boston College, Dr. André de Bethune, and his wife appeared on their own volition to tell of their experience with the rhythm method. They expressed their firm belief in the principles and precepts of their church, and desirous of spacing their offspring, they had tried both the calendar and basic body temperature rhythm methods with the conscientiousness of their faith and the meticulousness of their scientific training. They had nine children in eleven and a half years. The de Bethunes were people of intelligence and education, with a firm determination to make the rhythm method work. Did they think that, with people of less education and less restraint, the probabilities of failure would be even greater? Dr. de Bethune answered affirmatively. Other witnesses testified to the difficulty of getting birth-control information, and testimony was also offered on intra-uterine devices and on the effectiveness of the "loop" which our ambassador to India, Chester Bowles, said was being distributed gratis in that country with success.

Our cause received another boost when President Johnson, speaking at

San Francisco in June of 1965 on the Twentieth Anniversary of the United Nations, said:

> Let us in all our lands—including this land—face forthrightly the multiplying problems of our multiplying population and seek the answers to the most profound challenge to the future of the world. Let us act on the fact that less than $5 invested in population control is worth $100 invested in economic aid.

This second emphatic Presidential plea for action on the population issue was followed by others. So when David Bell, administrator of AID, appeared before our subcommittee's next round of hearings the following April, I asked him what his agency was doing overseas to implement President Johnson's exhortations. Bell replied that this was "a sensitive and complex area . . . in which policy making . . . should be done by the governments concerned, not by the United States." He was opposed to earmarking funds for action in this field.

When I went through a list of countries receiving foreign aid in alphabetical order, asking him what was being done in each on population matters, he had very little information. Yet he felt no additional legislation was needed. He proposed "to stand by the key elements of the agency's policy in the population field." AID would consider requests for assistance in this field—as in others—only if they were made or approved by the appropriate authorities of the requesting government. AID's view was heavily influenced by its belief that public and private leaders in the developing countries were fully conscious of the urgent need for action. Results, he said, could not be expected quickly.

Thomas C. Mann, Undersecretary of State for Economic Affairs, also testified and said the State Department had been "active in the formulation and expression of international policies and programs on population matters. . . ." "However," the department had "also been keenly aware of the many complexities involved" and "would not advocate any specific policy that another country might follow." The department had all the authority it wanted and was doing all that needed to be done. It did not require a new assistant secretary; it already had a "Special Assistant on Population Matters." The subcommittee and I felt this was a disappointing and negative approach. But we realized that the State Department was slow in accepting new ideas and translating needs into action. Senator Clark, at an earlier hearing, had testified that he had found "something less than enthusiasm on the part of foreign-service officers" for getting into so controversial a field. However, he hoped for a more positive response on the home front.

The new secretary of Health, Education and Welfare, John W. Gardner, had a reputation for being a man of both vision and action. He had held important posts in both public and private life, and had been president of the Carnegie Foundation before becoming a member of President Johnson's Cabinet. His appointment was widely acclaimed, an enthusiasm I shared. When he testified before our subcommittee, however, I found his attitude both negative and evasive. He read a memorandum that he had issued to his department on taking office, which stated that he had assigned to the assistant secretary for Health and Scientific Affairs, responsibility for population problems, and he saw no need for additional legislation or for a White House Conference. It was clear to me from his subsequent testimony that his department, far from tackling the population problem head on, intended to do little or nothing in this field.

Then I asked Secretary Gardner how much was to be spent on family planning. He referred me to Dr. Philip Lee, the assistant secretary for Health and Scientific Affairs. Lee could not say; it would depend on the rate at which local and state programs were developed. I asked him what specific instructions had been issued by the department and regional offices with respect to family planning. He referred me to Surgeon-General William H. Stewart who, we discovered, had merely transmitted the Secretary's memorandum to all the bureaus of the Public Health Service.

With this additional confirmation of his department's do-nothing attitude, I told Secretary Gardner, "There is absolutely no evidence from your words or actions that you are really concerned about population problems. It is almost without precedent for the President of the United States, since his election, to make twenty statements in favor of any one issue. And yet your department, which has—and should have—major responsibility for this program does not even list it among its activities. I would have hoped that there would be an assistant secretary for Population Problems exclusively, instead of which you do not even add population problems to the multiple duties of the assistant secretary for Health and Scientific Affairs. I consider this an evasion of the issue. The difficulty with this whole problem is that people have been afraid of it— and your department is afraid of it, too."

There was more discussion, but little clarification. Senator Metcalf, a member of the subcommittee, joined in the criticism of HEW's performance, and finally I suggested to Secretary Gardner that I hoped he would reconsider his department's responsibility to deal with population control and come up with a more constructive program.

Secretary Gardner did not testify again before the subcommittee, although he was invited to reappear at his convenience. But impressive confirmation of his department's failure in the population field came a short time later in a report by the Ford Foundation written by Oscar Harkavy. Senator Tydings cited extracts from this report at a subsequent hearing to bombard Dr. Philip Lee. "It is clear," Tydings quoted from the report's opening paragraph, "that none of the Department of Health, Education and Welfare's regional offices or operating agencies presently places high priority on family planning, or is certain what precise functions it is expected to carry out in this field. . . . A clear signal from the Secretary that vigorous support is an integral part of DHEW business seems necessary." The report then detailed sixteen ways in which the department needed to reform in order to deal effectively with population matters. "The President of the United States speaks, but the Secretary does nothing. I think it is tragic," said Tydings. "History is going to show that Secretary Gardner missed a golden opportunity to do something about the war on poverty in his years as Secretary, letting the bureaucracy of the department control the situation and do nothing when he could easily have been doing something."

The "clear signal" the Harkavy report deemed necessary did not come during the remainder of John Gardner's secretaryship, although he did establish, some months later, the post of deputy assistant for Family Planning and Population and appointed the highly qualified Katherine Ottinger to the post. But why, after all this time, Senator Tydings wanted to know, only a *deputy* assistant secretary?

It was difficult for any of the subcommittee members to understand why the President's repeated urgings for action—there were to be forty before the end of his term—met with so little response from the federal agencies. I wrote the President to raise this question, and I said that if the proposals in S.1676 were unsatisfactory the subcommittee would gladly accept and sponsor any legislation that the President felt would achieve his repeatedly declared objectives. The answer came back that the hearings had aroused so much favorable sentiment that improved action by the agencies was inevitable and no specific legislation was needed.

I had, myself, come to the conclusion that the real value of our hearings was educational; the newspaper and radio coverage had been excellent. Further, I realized that the bill itself was becoming obsolete and inadequate; it asked for no appropriations, but rather left requests for funds to the concerned departments. In view of their demonstrated lack of interest and effectiveness, that approach clearly would not produce the desired results. The attitude in HEW improved markedly when Assistant Secretary Wilbur Cohen succeeded John Gardner. But the hearings—week after week for three years—made federal action on birth control not only acceptable, but imperative.* This was demonstrated when the next Congress, the Ninety-first, enacted Senator Tydings's "Family Planning Service and Population Research Act of 1970" by a unanimous Senate vote and with only a handful of opponents in the House. The Act, Public Law 91-572, authorized a $382 million appropriation for birth-control information on request. It created an Office of Population Affairs in the Department of Health, Education and Welfare with full authority to do what was needed. It underwrote research into new and better methods of contraception. Meanwhile the Foreign Assistance Act of 1970 provided $175 million for the promotion of birth-control programs abroad.

At a luncheon on Capitol Hill on January 28, 1971, organized by the Population Crisis Committee to celebrate this final breakthrough, I recalled witnessing the arrest of Margaret Sanger fifty years earlier, in Town Hall, New York City, for attempting to speak on "Birth Control: Is It Moral?" We had come a long way! The problems of overpopulation at home and abroad were overwhelming, but at long last we had made a start in trying to solve them. Much would depend on the dedication and effectiveness with which the federal bureaucracy carried out the intent of Congress. But concerned organizations, "Planned Parenthood" and the Population Crisis Committee—to which I had been invited to be a consultant and director—and a public opinion increasingly aware of the relation of population growth to environmental deterioration and economic regression would, hopefully, exercise the needed vigilance, and promote the new concept and objective of zero population growth.

Margaret Sanger died in 1966, aged eighty-two, having lived to see the beginnings of the breakthrough in the cause she originated and for which she had battled so indomitably. "The issue is to raise the question of birth control out of the gutter of obscenity into the light of intelligence and human understanding." Thus, early, Margaret Sanger defined her purpose and her mission.

"When she started her crusade in 1914," wrote Emily Taft Douglas in her excellent biography, *Margaret Sanger, Pioneer of the Future*, "federal, state and local laws were all arraigned against her. She was jailed eight times. The medical profession denounced her, the churches excoriated

---

* The hearings, complete with numerous graphs, charts, tables and reprints of letters, statements and articles, ran over six million words and filled eighteen volumes when issued by the Government Printing Office. Their completeness was in no small measure due to the dedication of Laura M. Olson of my staff. A one-volume condensation was published with the title *Population Crisis*, and an excellent account of the hearings appears in *World Population Crisis: The United States Response*, by Phyllis Tilson Piotrow, published by Praeger Publishers.

her, the press condemned her and even liberal reformers shunned her. She entered the fight alone, a frail young woman without much education, with no social or financial backing, with nothing but conviction." Yet she persisted, and achieved a society-wide conversion productive of more human happiness, of more social and economic value, and of more far-reaching significance than any single reform in history.

Closely allied to my efforts to stimulate federal action on the problem of population control was my belief that the government must be responsive not only to the material needs of the American people but to their spiritual needs as well. In the early fall of 1964 I read a report by a Commission on the Humanities created by three respected bodies in American letters—The American Council of Learned Societies, the Council of Graduate Schools, and the United Chapter of Phi Beta Kappa. One sentence struck me forcibly:

> If the interdependence of science and the humanities were more generally understood, men would be more likely to become masters of their technology and not its unthinking servants.

Our rampant technology could, obviously, effect great achievements—largely because of massive government support. But its dominance needed to be balanced by a greater emphasis on the humanities, which had never evoked remotely comparable federal concern.

I pondered the problem, and after some research and consultation, I drafted a bill to establish a National Humanities Foundation as a federal agency. I was gratified to find twenty-nine of my colleagues enthusiastic about the idea, and I planned to introduce the legislation on January 6, 1965, the first day of the new session on which bills could be received.

I did not know that President Johnson in his State of the Union Message two days before would say, "To help promote and honor creative achievements, I will propose a National Foundation of the Arts." As I listened, I hoped he would elaborate on that proposal, but he did not. However, my bill, while including the arts, went far beyond the President's proposal.

Under the terms of my bill, the foundation would develop and encourage a national policy for the promotion of scholarship, education, research, creative work and performance in the humanities and the arts. These were defined to include the study of languages (ancient and modern), literature, history and philosophy; the history, criticism and theory of art and music; the history of religion, science and law; the creative and performing arts, including the theater and the dance: and those aspects of the social sciences with humanistic content. The bill now had thirty-six co-sponsors and was referred to the Senate Committee on Labor and Public Welfare, which promptly began hearings before a subcommittee, chaired by Senator Claiborne Pell of Rhode Island. He also subsequently sponsored a bill, which I likewise co-sponsored, differing in some respects from mine, and companion bills were introduced in the House. The legislation was enacted in record time by unanimous vote in the Senate and in the House without a roll-call. It was signed by President Johnson on September 29, 1965, and became Public Law 89-209.

The newly created National Foundation for the Arts and the Humanities had two separate but closely cooperating entities, the National Endowment for the Arts and the National Endowment for the Humanities. After Henry Allen Moe, former president of the Guggenheim Foundation, served briefly as temporary chairman, the President appointed Barnaby C. Keeney, who had been president of Brown University, as the foundation's chairman, an excellent choice. The President also appointed twenty-six citizens outstanding in their fields to comprise the National Council on the Humanities which would act in an advisory capacity. Chairman Keeney's first report described the beginning of what he termed "an enterprise unique in the history of the United States, and an agency unique in the Federal Government."

Congress was generous in its funding. The first year's appropriation was $10,727,000. The next year, 1967, it was $13,985,000. By 1970 it had risen to $17,910,000, and for fiscal year 1971 to some $33,000,000. Even so, the demands for scholarships, stipends and grants for research far exceeded the available funds, although these were augmented by provisions for matching grants from private foundations, instituions, and philanthropic individuals.

The foundation made use of television, books and pamphlets. It infused the humanistic approach into other widely divergent fields. And it wisely concentrated on matters of current national relevance, while not eschewing studies of the past, particularly—as is often the case—when what had gone before was closely related to contemporary problems. An example was a study of the relations of the United States government and the American Indian before 1900, designed to approach and appraise intelligently the contemporary problems relating to the descendants of America's aboriginal inhabitants, which the foundation rightly deemed "of immediate national concern."

The foundation contributed further to understanding in this field by creating a documentary film, *The Cherokee: The Trail of Tears*, a dramatization of the forcible removal of the Cherokee Indian nation from Georgia and the Carolinas to "Indian Territory" (later Oklahoma) in the 1830s. The picture, which lasted nearly an hour and a half, was shown on

134 television stations and reached an audience estimated at between eight and ten million, informing this generation about an almost-forgotten episode in American history. Critics praised the production for its historical accuracy as well as for its artistry.

In the very few years of its existence, the National Endowment has provided substantial assistance in the humanities and the arts, and has won enthusiastic recognition from institutions, groups and individuals. It has helped demonstrate that in the midst of doubt, dissent, and many unsolved problems, ours is not—as is so often alleged—a purely materialistic society. The foundation, under dedicated and intelligent leadership, has driven a small but penetrating, wedge into that concept. That appreciation for its work is growing was demonstrated by the appropriation for fiscal year 1972 of $39,000,000. While even more generous appropriations are needed and desirable, seldom have so many worthwhile cultural projects been stimulated and initiated in so short a time.

I considered my part in bringing the foundation into being a most important victory. But on another project of an entirely different character —although possibly of comparable importance—I met total defeat: The Rampart Canyon Dam on the Yukon. This canyon, at almost the exact geographical center of Alaska, and about halfway along the Yukon's flow through the state, had long been considered a great potential power site, perhaps the greatest in North America. But nothing had been done about it, even though Alaska—with only one-fourth of one percent of its hydroelectric potential developed, and otherwise dependent on sub-soil fuels with high transportation costs—needed low-cost electricity not only for the individual consumer, but also to restore an economy already gravely impaired by the cessation of gold mining and the depletion of fisheries—both consequences of federal action beyond Alaska's control.

I was an outspoken advocate for the Rampart Canyon project from the moment I was elected to the Senate. In May 1959 I got the Senate Public Works Committee to adopt a resolution requesting the Corps of Engineers of the United States Army to undertake a detailed investigation of the Rampart site, and the study, funded from year to year, indicated the feasibility of a concrete gravity dam with an installed capacity of five million kilowatts, which would cost $1.3 billion. It would be the largest hydroelectric dam in the western world, generating two and a half times as much power as Grand Coulee, our largest hydroelectric project.

The reservoir behind the dam would cover an area of some ten thousand square miles, ten percent larger than Lake Erie, and would require some eighteen years to fill. The submerged area—the Yukon flats—is a vast swamp and uninhabited except for seven small Indian villages on the river. The flooding would, to all intents and purposes, destroy no property values. To study the marketability of the power generated by the project, the Corps of Engineers had retained the Resources and Development Corporation, a New York firm headed by David Lilienthal and Gordon Clapp, who had initiated hydroelectric development in the Tennessee Valley. Their report indicated not only that a market would exist for all of Rampart's power, but that further up-river development would be needed to meet the eventual demand.

In the summer of 1963, in company with others, I visited the seven Yukon villages that would be submerged. The inhabitants lived miserably; their houses lacked running water or inside toilets. In winter they had to get water by melting snow or chopping through the ice covering the Yukon. These people eked out a meager subsistence from hunting, trapping and fishing, supplemented by welfare payments. They would, if the dam were built, be required to move to a new village which would be constructed according to their choice, on the shore of the man-made lake or on the river below the dam. Resettlement presented no alarming problem; a number of villagers had already moved voluntarily from the aboriginal sites to secure a better location.

In addition to vastly improved living conditions, the project would also assure the natives a variety of new employment. There would be jobs during the construction of the dam and of the new community which the construction would bring into being; timber would have to be cleared in the area behind the dam; sawmills would be established and the local residents trained in a variety of new skills. It was all part of the program. Further, a freshwater fishery to be developed on the lake would also attract tourism. And the ever-present danger of floods after the spring break-up would be eliminated. In talking to the villagers, we found— with the exception of one old-timer in Rampart village—no one who did not welcome the project.

In short, the project looked favorable from every standpoint. But opposition shortly arose. The opening salvo was fired at a Detroit wildlife conference by Ira Gabrielson, director of the Wildlife Management Institute, in these fighting words:

> There is a new proposal now for a project that dwarfs all previous projects in the unprecedented magnitude of fish and wildlife resources and habitat that would be destroyed. It is the proposed Rampart Dam. . . .
>
> The 500-foot dam would block sizable upstream migration of salmon in the Yukon. . . .

The impoundment would cover the Yukon flats that produce on the average of 1-½ million ducks and geese a year. . . .

Moose and fur-bearers also would suffer . . .

Rampart Dam is synonymous with resource destruction.

There was a special irony in Ira Gabrielson's sounding the tocsin. As one of the nation's leading conservationists, he had been welcomed by Alaskans as director of the Fish and Wildlife Service where he was in charge of Alaska's greatest natural resource, its salmon fisheries. But his incumbency spelled the gravest conservation disaster since game and fishery management had come to be recognized procedures. Under Gabrielson's directorship and that of his assistant and successor, Albert M. Day, the salmon pack—over the unceasing protests and ignored remedial proposals of Alaskans—dropped from nearly 7,000,000 cases to 1,600,000 the lowest point in sixty years. The industry was saved from extinction only by the coming of statehood and the establishment of a knowledgeable state regulatory agency.

It was also Gabrielson who, as the head of the Wildlife Management Institute, fought Alaskans' efforts to develop a new economic resource after the discovery of oil on the Kenai Peninsula. It was he who prophesied that this new resource would, if developed, destroy the moose and its habitat. But in spite of his prophecy, the moose multiplied and oil revenues saved the territory from bankruptcy. Finally, without impugning Gabrielson's devotion to the abstraction which he was unable to materialize in practice, it was not generally known that the Wildlife Management Institute was financed in large measure by gunmakers and ammunition manufacturers, and its officials' testimony could scarcely be considered disinterested. To cite—as Gabrielson did in opposition to Rampart—the millions of man-days of recreation in duck shooting that would be lost, was revealing. Was preserving the ducks in Alaska so they could be blasted from the skies in the States, really a praiseworthy demonstration of conservation?

Nevertheless, conservation societies took up the cry against Rampart, and they were abetted by officials of the Interior Department's Fish and Wildlife Service who campaigned openly against the project. Its office in Sacramento broadcast the warning that "if Rampart is built, there will be one less duck in every California sportsman's bag!" The Department of the Interior was, by law, charged with the responsibility of making a study of the effects of the dam on fish and wildlife, and if it proved adverse, to propose palliative or remedial measures.

But even before this study was undertaken, these officials were active in their publicly expressed opposition. It became so flagrant that I called it to Secretary Stewart Udall's attention in writing, citing specific examples and indicating that this was not part of their prescribed function. But the Secretary did nothing about it, and his officials' unrestrained campaign of opposition foreshadowed his own, which would suffice to kill the project. He voiced his opposition just as the Corps of Engineers, having completed its studies, was about to recommend the project. "We cannot afford to antagonize the sportsmen" was Udall's justification to me. Yet President Kennedy had warmly endorsed Rampart, and when Udall himself had come up for confirmation as Secretary of the Interior in January 1961, he had stated that "our objective as a nation should be the maximum development of power resources," and promised that this would be his policy.

A somewhat amusing example of the extreme opposition we met appeared in the May 1965 issue of the *Atlantic* in the form of a piece by Paul Brooks entitled "The Plot to Drown Alaska." An announcement of the article in the previous issue featured a photograph of a moose swimming—a sight familiar to Alaskans but which implied to the uninformed that the poor animal was drowning. Mr. Brooks had unsurpassed credentials. A naturalist by avocation, he had been to Alaska and had published in the *Atlantic* two years previously an article entitled "Alaska: Last Frontier." It was an effective plea for conserving Alaksa's natural assets and concluded that Alaska offered what history seldom afforded—a second chance. With this I found myself in complete accord and inserted the article in the *Congressional Record*. But in his later article he concluded that Rampart was "an ill-conceived project that would destroy that chance forever," as editor, Edward Weeks summarized Brooks's purpose in an introductory note. That is where Paul Brooks and I disagreed.

There—of course—had been no "plot." The legislative process we had followed for six years had been regular and above board. And to claim that a man-made lake occupying two percent of Alaska's area would "drown" the state was a manifest hyperbole. So I wrote Weeks asking for the opportunity to reply. The *Atlantic* granted it but gave me less than half the space accorded Brooks. I entitled my piece "The Plot to Strangle Alaska," which was justified, I felt, by the concerted effort—some of it clandestine—to kill a project designed to speed Alaska's development. I presented all the arguments in favor of the project, and to my surprise the *Atlantic* gave Brooks a chance for further reply in a piece which followed my article. But his reply, in my view, so largely misinterpreted my presentation that I requested a chance for a rebuttal. This was not granted, but in essence I believed then, and still believe, that with imaginative and creative management, Alaska's environment and the habitat of its wildlife would be enhanced, not destroyed, by the Rampart Dam.

This exchange occurred almost a decade ago, but the issue—

conservation versus development—is more acutely relevant today than ever. Indeed I consider it among the paramount issues confronting the American people. Unfortunately, the issue is fraught with emotionalism on both sides. In general, I am on the side of the concerned environmentalist and consider myself not only a conservationist but a fervent one. But where I disagree with some of my fellow conservationists, whom I class as extremists, is that their concern omits the essential part of the problem —the human element. They are interested in preserving the habitat of a variety of feathered, furred, and scaled creatures. That's good. But man requires a habitat too, and without a viable economy does he have one?

Conservation and development can and must be reconciled: we need both. They can and must co-exist, and this requires a dispassionate appraisal in every situation of the pros and cons of the values that may be lost and those that may be gained. I welcome and applaud the conservationists' efforts and goals. They are campaigning against the human greed and stupidity which have so tragically destroyed much of our environment and may threaten man's very survival on our small planet. But sometimes these friends of nature are, in their laudable zeal, misguided, too.

The Sierra Club, for example, bitterly fought the Colorado's Glen Canyon Dam. Its officers still deplore that lost battle. But where there was once a parched, uninhabited desert, there is now beautiful Lake Powell, with its clear and sparkling waters and facilities for fishing, swimming, and boating.

While some of the canyon is now under water, its scenic values are nevertheless enchanced because its towering walls are mirrored in the lake's waters. An attractive Interior Department brochure describes the site as "the Jewel of the Colorado." Who shall say that man's imagination and labor did not, in this instance, enhance unspoiled nature? By the same token, the Sierra Club sought to prevent the harvesting of overripe timber in the northern part of Alaska's Tongass National Forest. Yet scientific logging designed for perpetual yield is the essence of conservation.

In a land of infinite beauty, with towering peaks rising from the ocean, tidal glaciers, high waterfalls and many other sights to lift the spirit of man, the Yukon flats are, in my opinion, anything but beautiful. A great body of clear water over them could be an enhancement and supply a habitat for new varieties of wildlife. But even more important, the people of Alaska are entitled to low-cost electricity; it has become an essential of modern life. Equally essential are hydroelectric reserves to avert the power shortages in our country that have been long foreseen and are now upon us. The Rampart project could supply some of these needs.

Alternatives to Rampart? Alaska's other hydroelectric sites—which may also need development—could not equal Rampart's low-cost power output. Fossil fuels pollute the atmosphere and are exhaustible. Nuclear power and the disposal of its wastes are still a source of peril. Perhaps one day man's ingenuity will find other alternatives, but as of now hydroelectric power is still the cleanest, safest, most enduring source of energy. Once harnessed, nature's force of gravity is at the service of man indefinitely. I am still in favor of Rampart, even though in 1971 the Corps of Engineers shelved the project, reporting that rising costs had made the cost-benefit ratio unfavorable "at this time." Had the dam been started in the mid-sixties when the Corps was ready to proceed, it would soon be completed. One of these days, I believe it will be built.

Another regrettable failure—not of intention, but of implementation —was President Kennedy's Alliance for Progress. I had long been concerned about our foreign-aid program, and my effort to instill the principles of both economy and common sense into this huge governmental expenditure had been rewarded with some degree of success. I had a unique opportunity to combine my interests in both the foreign-aid program and in Latin America, when Senator McClellan, chairman of the Committee on Government Operations, thought that a study of the program in Latin-American countries similar to the one I had made in 1962 in ten Middle-Eastern countries would be useful. So in the fall of 1965 I went to Colombia, Venezuela, Peru, Ecuador and Chile, and after a preliminary survey it seemed desirable to select only one of them for exclusive study. I chose Chile, because of these five countries it appeared to be the most promising for a demonstration of what foreign aid could accomplish. First, the United States and Chile had already cooperated on a relatively large scale in a program to help Chile recover from the 1960 earthquake, for which the Congress had authorized $100 million. Second, our aid to Chile had been the highest per capita in Latin America; our contribution could not be faulted for insufficiency. Third, Chile seemed one of the most hopeful prospects for an effective aid program; it was stable, homogeneous, literate and it had a long history of free elections, honestly conducted. It had not suffered the frequent military coups that had afflicted its sister republics. Nor did it have—like Peru, Bolivia, Ecuador, Honduras, and others—a large unabsorbed indigenous population that spoke its own language and lived out of the mainstream of the country's economy. Fourth, Chile had a promising resource base and a democratic government, under President Eduardo Frei Montalvo of the Christian Democratic Party, ostensibly committed to Alliance for Progress goals.

It was recognized, of course, that not all the findings of my study would be applicable to every AID program in Latin America. Nevertheless, this approach would prove useful, it was hoped, in revealing both the positive and negative aspects of the program, and in spelling out the guidelines necessary to achieve success. The report was titled "United States Foreign Aid in Action: A Case Study," and it was a *factual* report. Every foreign-aid project in Chile was described in detail and the facts spoke for themselves. The report, compiled with the assistance of Mrs. Rieck Bennet Hannifin of the Legislative Reference Service of the Library of Congress, totaled 229 pages and, unfortunately, largely described a succession of failures. There was goodwill on both sides, but inadequate planning, lack of competence, inability to interrelate ends and means, and basic cultural differences accounted for the gravely disappointing results.

Subsequently, the Senate Foreign Relations Committee for the first time adopted a similar procedure to examine in depth our foreign-aid programs in each individual country, and in 1969 it published a case study of Colombia. Both Chile and Colombia were considered by AID administrators to be potential "showcases" for American aid. Yet this later report, like the case study of Chile, revealed a disappointing succession of failures. And if we have failed in these two countries, then the Alliance for Progress has failed.

I take no pride in having predicted that failure as early as 1962. But it seemed to me, then as now, that the collapse of our well-intentioned programs can be traced to a pervasive fear of a communist take-over in Latin America. To prevent that, we have poured millions of dollars into the pockets of the oligarchies of these countries, and have supported in power the most repressive of right-wing dictatorships, both of which have prevented land reform, equitable taxation and all the other social and economic reforms that would truly benefit the people. We have, in a very real sense, aggravated and prolonged the grievances of the people, and may well have increased, rather than diminished the threat of left-wing extremism.

Yet, while the prospects for Latin America and for aiding its people effectively do not seem very promising, they are not hopeless. In January 1970 the *Atlantic* published an article by Arthur Schlesinger, Jr., "The Lowering Hemisphere," which analyzed the failure of past policies and rightly ascribed the blame to both Latin Americans and North Americans. But he offered no solution, and I submitted some remedial proposals which the *Atlantic* published in its June issue. In summary, I suggested that the previous troublesome giver-recipient relationship be avoided by entrusting the choice of programs and projects to the Latin Americans themselves. I also proposed increasing their deficient technical knowledge by scholarships in appropriate American institutions, and by the loan of our technicians. I further proposed joint ownership of foreign-financed corporate enterprises, as successfully practiced in Mexico; abolition of military aid; alterations in the provisions of our foreign-assistance legislation designed solely to promote the sale of American goods; and an all-out educational assistance program to encourage family limitation. While I have long had reservations about multilateral financing, largely because I believe that it removes the control from the Congress where it belongs, that control has been so poorly exercised that I would be willing to try alternative methods. Hopefully, the lessons of the last ten years will be taken into account in any future programs, but unless we are adamant in refusing economic and military support to totalitarian regimes, these programs, too, will be doomed to failure.

It is gratifying to me that our foreign-aid program as a whole has finally come in for the kind of careful scrutiny that I tried to encourage throughout my years in the Senate. In a foreword to a highly critical report by the General Accounting Office,* Senator Fulbright, the chairman of the Senate Committee on Foreign Relations, wrote on March 29, 1971:

> In recent years, the Committee on Foreign Relations has become increasingly skeptical of the manner and methods used to implement this country's foreign aid program. . . . The future of foreign aid is bleak indeed until a new program can be developed which will command greater respect and rapport both with the public and the Congress than the current program commands.

The findings of his committee and the GAO report taken together, Fulbright added, "tell a tale of bureaucratic woe, mismanagement and insufficiency—feebly attempting to promote a sort of updated version of "dollar diplomacy". . . . [It] tells a tale of disregard for Congressional intent and of the use of foreign-aid funds as a kind of diplomatic pork barrel. . . . If we are to build a successful foreign-aid program we simply cannot afford to repeat the mistakes of the past; the gravity of our economic situation does not permit us that luxury."

It is interesting to contemplate just how luxurious our foreign-aid programs have been. From 1946, when they began, to 1971, 136 foreign countries have received $131,530,600,000. With the interest paid on what the United States borrowed to make loans to these countries $67,858,-067,000, the grand total of Uncle Sam's largesse has been $199,388,667,000. It is depressing, however, to reflect how much of this money was

---

* "United States Economic and Military Foreign Assistance Programs: Compilation of General Accounting Office Reports, Findings and Recommendations to the Committee on Foreign Relations, United States Senate, Ninety-second Congress, First Session."

wasted and misspent; how much good one-half of that astronomical sum, wisely spent, would have helped emerging peoples help themselves— and how much good the other $100 billion could have accomplished for our own neglected needs in slum clearances, education, health, depollution, and in creating employment opportunities through public works, raising living standards generally, and improving the quality of life at home.

Excessive spending by the military was also a concern of mine during my Senate service, and on that issue I can record one success and one failure. When the Military Assistance and Sales Act came up in July 1966, I introduced an amendment designed to have our allies in the North Atlantic Treaty Organization share some of the costs of the new construction in Belgium that was necessary when De Gaulle ousted NATO from France. I had inspected these facilities which were now to be abandoned and discovered that the United States had been paying costs running into millions of dollars. The Senate adopted my amendment in an attempt to check the profligate way our military planners were disposing of American funds.

I also urged a reduction in the three hundred thousand troops the United States had maintained in Europe since the end of World War II over twenty years before. In a major speech entitled "Our Obsolete Concepts About NATO—1949 Solutions for 1966 Facts," I documented the great changes that had taken place in Europe and how our massive and costly presence there was no longer necessary. It was warmly commended by Senator Mike Mansfield, who had earlier striven for the same goal and would do so again. But both the Johnson and Nixon administrations have persisted in this needless expenditure.

Another domestic issue of particular interest to me revolved around the whole question of native claims to land in Alaska. The problem originated with the Organic Act of 1884 which provided:

> That the Indians or other persons shall not be disturbed in the possession of any lands actually in their use or now claimed by them, but the terms under which such persons may acquire title to such lands is reserved for future legislation by Congress.

By the terms of this same act, the Department of the Interior was charged with the responsibility for investigating native claims and advising the Congress on the necessary legislation; yet for more than three-quarters of a century the department had ignored its responsibility, in spite of the rising discontent of Alaska's native citizens. The problem was particularly acute in the Alaskan "Panhandle," where the Tlingit and Haida Indians had been deprived of all their lands when virtually the entire area was taken over by the federal government to create the Tongass National Forest—during President Theodore Roosevelt's Administration.

This question was finally settled by the United States Court of Claims, effective August 19, 1965, with an award of $7.5 million to be divided among all persons of Tlingit or Haida blood residing in the United States or Canada. But for the rest of Alaska's natives, it was clearly incumbent upon the secretary of the Interior to carry out the mandate of the Organic Act of 1884, unmodified subsequently, particularly in view of Alaska's affirmation of the validity of native land-claims in the Statehood Act. So I urged Secretary Udall, soon after his appointment, to send up a draft of a legislative proposal. It was important that this legislation originate in the Interior Department because it would require the department's endorsement. But there were also several new urgencies. The Statehood Act granted Alaska the right to select 103 million acres from the public domain for its own development, which it intended to do as rapidly as possible; and the rush of new people to Alaska during and after World War II was troubling the natives who, for the first time, were beginning to encounter newcomers in areas where they had traditionally been the sole residents.

Spurred by the approaching Tlingit-Haida award, native associations began to form throughout western Alaska to urge settlement of their long overdue claims, and to assert claims to areas which would soon include virtually all of Alaska and even parts of Canada. Some of these claims overlapped and some were clearly exaggerated, but a settlement was nevertheless imperative. Still Udall did not act, despite repeated proddings from the Alaska delegation. Further, in view of the natives' claims, he declined to process the state's land selections, a function necessary for their validation. In May 1966, at a meeting of the subcommittee on Indian Affairs of the Senate Interior and Insular Affairs Committee, I noted that Udall had failed to act on thirteen state selections totaling 15,668,168 acres. We soon found that this was part of a deliberate policy which would become a "freeze" of all land selections and withdrawals, including the patenting of homesteads by homesteaders who had fulfilled all the necessary requirements. Obviously, the paralysis had to be ended and the whole issue resolved by Congress.

Native claims in western Alaska were not as clear-cut as those of the Tlingit and Haida in southeastern Alaska where the Tongass National Forest had taken all their land. In western Alaska, lands had been withdrawn for three great national parks and monuments—Mount McKinley, Katmai and Glacier Bay—the Chugach National Forest, various wildlife refuges, military installations and lands for the support of the

University of Alaska. But these were ostensibly for the general good, and much more land was still left in public domain. So there was some question as to what extent the natives had been "disturbed in the possession of any lands actually in their use or occupation." However, a majority of Alaskan sentiment inclined to the view that the depressed economic and social condition of the natives required some remedy and that settlement of their land-claims would provide that remedy.

When Udall finally sent up a draft of some remedial legislation, it provided that the land awarded the natives would be held in trust by the Department of the Interior, a provision wholly objectionable to the natives, and to me, since we felt it essential that they get out from under the department's century-old control, which had spelled stagnation while other ethnic minorities had progressed. Meanwhile, other legislative drafts were submitted which I introduced "by request." They contained all the provisions that the native groups I conferred with favored and whose views I shared. But not until 1968 was the first hearing held. Chairman Henry M. Jackson of the Senate Interior Committee, who presided, asked me to make the arrangements; and so that none of the more-than-a-hundred witnesses desiring to be heard should be denied, the three days of hearings in Anchorage started at 6:00 A.M., an hour unprecedented in Senate history.

It was too late for enactment in the Ninetieth Congress—many more hearings would be required—and while the Senate enacted a good bill in the Ninety-first Congress, the House failed to act. What might and should have been disposed of in the 1960s dragged on into the 1970s. Not until the last month of the first session of the Ninety-second Congress—on December 18, 1971—did the legislation emerge. But the delay resulted in a more generous settlement. "The most generous settlement that has ever been made to a native group in our history," said Senator Jackson, who managed the Senate version of the bill. It provided $962,500,000, of which $462,500,000 came from the federal treasury and the remainder by collecting two percent of the receipts for mineral leases from the state. Forty million acres of land—of which approximately one-half included both surface and subsurface rights—were given to the natives. An estimated 55,000 Eskimos, Aleuts and Indians were benefited, the eligible being those who could demonstrate that they had twenty-five percent native blood. Some 220 villages were included in the settlement and provisions were made to have former Alaskan natives, now resident outside of Alaska, participate in the settlement. The bill was highly complex; its effectiveness cannot be determined until after the passage of some years and will, of course, depend in large part on the integrity and intelligence of native leadership. But it provided an opportunity that Alaska's native population had too long been denied.

Another matter vital to Alaska, which had deeply concerned me, appeared at long last to be approaching at least a partial solution. It was Alaska's roadlessness, due to its total exclusion for forty years from the Federal Aid Highway Act. This important legislation, enacted in 1916 just as the automobile was becoming a practical means of locomotion, provided federal matching funds for the states, with the understanding that the highways would be built to certain standards set by the federal government. The eastern states were granted fifty-fifty matching funds, but for the western states with large areas of public domain which could not be taxed by the state, there was a compensatory formula based on the state's total area, the proportion of public domain to the total area, the state's population and the existing post-road mileage. Contemplating Alaska's vast area and the proportion of public domain—virtually total—Congress shuddered and refused to include the territory. Other outlying areas, such as Hawaii and Puerto Rico, were subsequently included, but not Alaska.

In 1956, further discrimination took place. Under President Eisenhower's program for a vastly improved highway system, financed on a pay-as-you-go basis by additional taxes on tires, trucks, trailers and gasoline, Alaskans were obliged to pay these taxes but were excluded from the program. Aroused by this forty-year injustice—now aggravated—Senator Neuberger sought to include Alaska by proposing that one-half the public-domain-formula applied to the states be applied to Alaska. But even this was deemed too generous, and only one-third of the formula was permitted in the two years before statehood.

With statehood, Alaska was finally included in the Federal Aid Highway Act, but catching up required something more than the annual allocations. In Alaska, nearly all our communities were unconnected by either a highway or a railway, a situation that would be unthinkable in the older forty-eight states. Federal executive support was needed to remedy this situation, and as early as 1961 I had secured the promise of it from Undersecretary of Commerce Clarence Martin, the highest federal official in charge of transportation. However, he insisted that before legislation to secure additional funds was introduced, there must be a highway study of Alaska to determine the exact nature of its needs. That study seemed to me wholly unnecessary, but I had to yield reluctantly as the price of departmental support. The Eighty-seventh Congress approved $400,000 for the study.

The report was due on May 15, 1964, but it soon became evident that there was small prospect of its completion by the statutory deadline. The date for the completion of the report was moved ahead to May 15, 1965. That date came and went, and still no report. For the next year I sought by phone call, letter, telegram and personal interview to urge the Department of Commerce to produce its promised executive branch recommendations for Alaska highway legislation. The report was lost in the maze of bureaucracy, shuttling between the Bureau of Public Roads, the Department of Commerce and the Bureau of the Budget. As the date of hearings on the Federal Aid Highway Act of 1966 approached, my efforts were redoubled. The report was finally extricated from the bureaucratic morass at 5:45 P.M. on May 10, 1966, the day before I was scheduled to testify before the Senate Public Works Committee.

The report was very disappointing; its recommendations were negligible. I was on my own, but my lone campaign to publicize Alaska's roadlessness had begun to impress my colleagues. I had told them again and again that Alaska had been deprived of $575 million through the years. I pointed out how the young State of Alaska had financed and was maintaining—without a cent of federal aid—a "marine highway"—a ferry system operating between Seattle and Alaska's southeastern ports. Now I sought, as an amendment to the highway act, an authorization for an additional $14 million a year for each of the next five years, a sum which would be used for both road construction and maintenance in Alaska. The subcommittee on public roads, with ten of its thirteen members present, voted unanimously for my amendment, and the Senate passed it.

But the House bill did not contain the Alaska provisions, and its conferees resisted adamantly the provisions in the Senate bill to take the additional appropriations from the highway trust fund. I was a conferee, and it was finally agreed that $70 million for the next five years would be authorized by direct appropriation from the Treasury. The conference report was accepted by both Senate and House, and I felt very happy about it. We were making a substantial start at catching up.

I was happy too soon. In the next year's Presidential budget, the necessary $14 million was not included, which presented an almost unsurmountable obstacle to getting it appropriated. I was pretty disgusted. However, through personal interviews with members of the appropriations committees of both houses, I was able to get the Senate committee to include $8 million and the House $4 million. In conference a compromise was reached at $5 million. It was a drastic cut, but at least it would be a start.

Again I was too optimistic. President Johnson withheld the appropriation from the 1968 Highway Act. The action of a President in withholding sums voted by Congress is, in my opinion, a usurpation of Congressional power; but it had been done before and has been done since. In that instance, however, the authorization remained valid for the next five years, and it would fall to others to see to it that these funds were appropriated.

Nineteen hundred and sixty-seven was Alaska's centennial year, and a joyful round of festivities was inaugurated in Juneau when I dedicated the $10-million, nine-story federal building which my membership on the Senate Public Works Committee helped secure. This was followed at Ketchikan, Sitka, Anchorage and Fairbanks by other dedications of centennial buildings and projects, including a monument to William H. Seward in Anchorage, amid enthusiastic crowds. In Fairbanks the members of the Constitutional Convention of a decade earlier assembled around the dedication of a memorial tablet. I addressed all these happy gatherings. An *Alaskan Reader* which I had compiled, with contributions by Washington Irving, Rudyard Kipling, William H. Seward, Jack London, John Muir and others no less famous, was published as part of the centennial.

Finally, in 1968, I was gratified to initiate the first Olympic-size swimming pool in Alaska—in a junior high school in Sitka. Its construction was largely due to the dedication of Mayor John O'Connell, who had done much to lift that community to high levels of urbanism after a century of man-made doldrums. It was just another example of what one individual can accomplish and how leadership in city, state or nation makes the difference between stagnation and progress. Swimming pools in Alaska's schools seemed essential to me, not only for the health and recreation of young boys and girls, but because Alaska's largely littoral population derived its livelihood from the sea, and every year an average of sixty persons drowned, in many cases simply because they had not been taught to swim. Other communities followed Sitka's lead; Juneau, in particular, where twenty-nine years previously I had started what, for a while, was an uphill battle, on my discovery that there was not an indoor pool in a single Alaska school. Then, local authorities felt that they could not afford it, and their attitude was abetted by the legislatures of that day. Now it will be a rare Alaska community that can afford *not* to have one.

After World War II, my son "Hunt" continued in aviation, flying for Alaska airlines, of which he has also been vice president. His happy marriage to Oline Sather of Petersburg has brought us three beautiful grandchildren, Kimberly, six; Peter Sather, four; and Tiffany, two.

My grandson, Clark, is a lawyer, associated with one we have long highly esteemed in the firm of McCutcheon & Gruening.

My grandson, Bradford, volunteered for infantry service in Southeast Asia and was in combat in Vietnam.

My grandson, Winthrop, graduated from the Airforce Academy and is a pilot. He married lovely Anne Fox of Juneau. They are stationed in Tacoma.

In the 1968 Senatorial race I had a primary opponent: thirty-eight-year-old Mike Gravel, born in Springfield, Massachusetts, of French-Canadian parentage, who had come to Alaska in 1956 and engaged in real-estate development. He was elected to the State House of Representatives from Anchorage in 1962 and was elected its speaker in 1964. On the Republican side, in 1968, there was a contest between Ted Stevens and Elmer Rasmuson, owner of a statewide banking chain.

The primary campaign was fought without issues. I presented my record, and my seniority. It was known that Mike Gravel was depending on a documentary motion picture which would be shown late in the campaign. Polls taken at intervals, early in the campaign, showed me winning by a margin of two to one or better.

Mike's film was shown on every television station in Alaska, twice a day, ten days before the election. Planes carried the film and a projector to every village. It was a professional production. It pictured Mike and his family undergoing the deprivation of the great Depression—although Mike, born in 1930, must have had little recollection of it. It showed him working his way through Columbia College as a taxi driver, and then in the United States Army in World War II, working with the French underground. To make sure the viewers understood this part of his career, he was shown with the Eiffel Tower in the background when he was on a furlough from his service with the French underground. Since he was only eleven years of age when the United States entered the war in 1941, and fifteen when it ended, he must have been the youngest young man enlisted in the Allied cause. (He did not mention his war service in *Who's Who* or in his *Congressional Directory* biography. But there it was in the film!)

Coming to Alaska without funds—according to the documentary—he started at the bottom and worked his way up in the real-estate business. The film had a great impact on and demonstrated the effectiveness of a new campaigning technique which had never been used before in Alaska. Polls taken three days before the election—after the picture had been shown for a week—indicated that Mike had caught up and that we were running neck and neck.

Mike won by 1694 votes. The unexpected defeat was hard to take, especially when disappointed Gruening adherents began to tell me how unfortunate they deemed the voters' verdict. They related that Mike had achieved the Speakership of the House by promising more committee chairmanships than there were. The president of a local airline told me that Mike had requested a $10,000 contribution to his campaign; he had refused, telling Gravel he was for Gruening, and if Gruening lost in the primary he was for Rasmuson, at which point Gravel had said to him:

"Get wise. Think what a United States Senator can do *to* an airline."

"Did you throw him out of your office?" I asked.

"No," was the reply. "I'll have to confess I weakened. I let him blackmail me."

I began to understand how Bob LaFollette felt when he lost to Joe McCarthy.

29

POSTSCRIPT

"Ruled by shady men, a nation itself becomes shady."

— HENRY L. MENCKEN

"Our mission in the cause of liberty is to be accomplished through a steadfast devotion to the cause of our inner life, and not by going abroad as missionaries, as conquerors, or as marauders among weaker peoples."

— JOSIAH ROYCE

"A great sickness grips our society. People have lost faith in our basic institutions. They have lost faith in the processes of government itself."

— ARTHUR BURNS

My last action as a senator was to represent the Committee on Interior and Insular Affairs at the inauguration of Luis Ferré as governor of Puerto Rico. A wealthy public-spirited industrialist, he had given the city of Ponce an art museum, a $3 million edifice—of which Edward Durell Stone was the architect—whose abundance of old masters, which Ferré had been collecting for years, would have constituted an outstanding collection in any one of our nation's largest cities. Dorothy and I would have liked to spend days rather than hours there. It illustrated

Ferré's desire to establish something really first-class in his native island, whose people had finally emerged from the inferiority complex derived from their earlier long-time colonialism.

My next four years were enhanced by the kindness of my fellow-Alaskans (and of others) who in various ways sought to make me feel that leaving public office had not ended my usefulness. In Juneau, a group including the Chamber of Commerce, adopted a resolution couched in generous terms, requesting that the unnamed 6,500-foot peak rising above Eagle River thirty miles north of Juneau be named for me, and providing a helicopter trip to its high slopes to signalize their action. This magnificent mountain with its hanging glacier, whose numerous wild goat we had often observed with field glasses from our cabin, had been several times painted by Dorothy.

At its fiftieth anniversary in 1972 the University of Alaska dedicated a splendid social sciences building in my name. Sheldon Jackson Junior College at Sitka awarded me a citation. Other numerous tokens of friendship were characteristic of Alaskans.

After leaving the Senate, my first activity was to testify on behalf of the confirmation of Governor Walter Hickel of Alaska to be Secretary of the Interior.

There was plenty of opposition. "Wally" had said that he did not believe in "conservation for conservation's sake." I knew what he meant; it referred to the long disuse of Alaska's timber resources in the Tongass National Forest while the trees became overripe and needed harvesting. But the conservationists mobilized their forces, and representatives of the Sierra Club and others testified against his confirmation. Wally was portrayed as a ruthless exploiter of natural resources and one who would favor private interests. Newspaper editorials and columnists gave this view currency.

There was much to refute these charges. Wally had resisted pressure from "sportsmen" who wanted to hunt musk-ox, and when the Alaska legislature enacted a bill permitting it, he vetoed it. This interesting Arctic mammal which had been almost exterminated by the mid-nineteenth century, was being restored under the direction of John J. Teal on Nunivak Island and a herd had been brought to the University of Alaska where they were being domesticated with a view to establishing an industry that could utilize their very fine wool and give the natives a new occupation in weaving it. Hunting musk-ox is as sportsmanlike as shooting a cow. Wally was instrumental in eliminating the bounties on wolverines, coyotes and hairseals. I knew that the allegations against him were unfounded and gave my view that he would make an excellent Secretary of the Interior.

The hearings lasted five days. Wally was thoroughly cross-examined and impressed the committee with his candor as well as with his willingness to learn. There were three negative votes and the Senate then approved him, seventy-seven to sixteen.

During the 1968 presidential campaign I naturally supported Hubert Humphrey. I was not only very fond of him personally, but admired his record as a liberal. One exception was his all-out support of the war. However much I disagreed with it, I understood his dilemma as Johnson's vice president. Yet I felt it unnecessary for him to out-Johnson Johnson. I had heard Hubert, at American Legion and VFW conventions, make speeches so jingoistic that they made me squirm; he had accepted all the officially propagated myths about the war. I likewise heard him address a gathering of Methodist bishops in an entirely different vein—one would never have thought it was the same Hubert. I felt that unless he disassociated himself from Johnson's war policies he would lose the election, but if he did disassociate himself, he could win. I urged him to resign the vice-presidency—but if he felt he could not do that, at least to declare a reversal of his pro-war stand on the basis of the obvious nullity of the United States' declared purpose to bring freedom and self-determination to Southeast Asia, and announce that, if elected, he would end the war and bring our boys back home. He could not bring himself to do it, and a very minor modification of his position in a Salt Lake City speech was insufficient—although it incurred the censure of LBJ who was giving HHH no help and was obviously not unhappy at the prospect of a Nixon victory.

Nixon's campaign pledge to end the war undoubtedly provided the slender margin of his victory. While with Nixon's past record of hawkishness, this was entitled to some skepticism, it was not unnatural to hope for the best. His initial declarations as President were soothing and unifying; they gave hope that there was possibly a "new Nixon." His appointment of Wally Hickel gave us Alaskans a cause for gratitude. During the ten previous years of statehood under two Democratic Presidents, Alaska had not received recognition with as much as a minor federal appointment, although we had sought an assistant secretaryship in the Department of the Interior, which in view of the importance of that Department to Alaska and of Alaska to it, was a reasonable aspiration. Now Nixon had gone far beyond expectations and precedent, and had not merely appointed an Alaskan to a cabinet post but to that very cabinet post.

In view of the war's impact on American lives, it was natural to expect that President Nixon would disclose his plan to end the war at the earliest opportunity—his inaugural, or his State-of-the-Union message; but they passed. Between Nixon's election in November 1968 and his assumption of office the following January 1,452 Americans were killed in combat and 9,501 wounded,

While I no longer had the forum and facilities of a United States Senator, and soon found that interest in my views had sharply diminished, I felt it imperative to speak out for a cessation of the slaughter, and did so whenever asked, particularly as the casualties continued month after month with no indication of a change of policy from the White House.

At a meeting which honored Wayne Morse and me and was sponsored by various church groups in the Capitol Hill United Methodist Church, I proposed two ways to get out of Vietnam, one by Presidential, the other by Congressional action.

President Nixon had been critical of campus violence in some of the student protests against the war. While I regretted the violence, it led me to say:

Violence—sanctioned and sanctified abroad—breeds lawless violence at home. If we want to diminish violence at home the administration must stop making violence compulsory overseas.

Actually while President Nixon appeared on campuses urging students to eschew violence and use reason—a very proper counsel—his actions belied his words, for he honored—by inviting them to the White House—a group of "hard hats" who had attacked and beaten up students demonstrating peaceably against the war.

The American people had to wait thirteen months after his election for President Nixon's plan, which he unveiled on December 3, 1969. Over eleven thousand more Americans died in Vietnam while he delayed. And what was the long-awaited plan? It was not a plan to end the war but a plan to continue it, as I declared publicly as soon as I had heard and read it.

On Moratorium Day I spoke at a high school in Bethesda at 9:00 A.M.; at Georgetown Law School at 11:00; in Farragut Square at 1:00; on the Johns Hopkins Campus at 3:00 and thereafter to a crowd ten thousand strong, massed around Baltimore's city hall. I spoke on campuses as widely separated as the University of California at Davis, and New York State University at Albany. I testified before the Massachusetts Legislature in favor of legislation originated by an enlightened clergyman—the Reverend John M. Wells, pastor of the Unitarian Church of Lexington—which provided that no citizen of Massachusetts would be compelled against his will to serve in an undeclared war. The legislation was enacted by both Houses, and signed by the governor.* Its ultimate validity would depend on the United States Supreme Court, but it was an important and historic action by the elected representatives of the State which enshrined Lexington, Concord and Bunker Hill.

I joined the "Stop the Draft" organization and spoke at public meetings it organized. I had expressed my view that the draft constituted involuntary servitude and was thus in violation of the Thirteenth Amendment to the Constitution, in a long letter to *The New York Times* which it published on July 21, 1969. The Selective Service Act—extended several times since its enactment in 1948, the first peacetime conscription in American history—was due to expire in June 1971, unless renewed by the affirmative vote of both Houses of Congress.

I was saddened when on March 31 only sixty-two members of the House, and on June 4 only twenty-three members of the Senate voted to let it expire. All honor to these minorities! It was hard to understand at a time when President Nixon was ostensibly "winding down the war"— to use the current phrase—and periodically announcing the withdrawal of troops, why 330 congressmen and sixty-seven senators would vote to send more draftees back there. Then, by narrow margins, both Houses rejected a one-year draft extension in favor of a two-year extension. This action, which sentenced more youngsters to be cannon-fodder in an obscene war and on behalf of an utterly discredited cause, was shrouded in the reasoning that such an action was a necessity before a determination of the practicality of an all-volunteer army could be made. I disagreed, and vainly lobbied against it.

When a young seaman, Roger Lee Priest, stationed at the Anacostia Naval Station in Washington, D. C., was court-martialed for circulating a paper in which he protested against the illegality of the war, I was asked by his lawyer to appear in his defense and I did. I was asked by the prosecutor whether I did not think Priest's statement was "subversive," and replied that I thought it the highest form of patriotism. Priest might have been given up to thirty years. He received a bad-conduct discharge.

I also appeared in defense of Norman Jacques, a former member of the Rhode Island Legislature, a conscientious objector who had refused induction. The United States District Judge in Providence, Edward Day, exhibited flagrantly unjudicial bias; I was convinced that the two-year sentence he imposed would be reversed, and on appeal the First Circuit Court in Boston declared it a mistrial. The administration, however, was determined to secure a conviction and again brought Jacques's case to trial in

---

* An account of this matter is found in *The People versus Presidential Power* written by Mr. Wells and published by Dunellan, New York.

the same United States District Court in Providence. But this time it was heard by a different judge, Raymond Pettine, whose fair conduct resulted in an acquittal. I was glad to appear on behalf of Jacques, as I would in similar cases when asked, because I considered that—contrary to pre-vailing public opinion—those who, following their conscience, refused to fight in an utterly unjustified war and incurred imprisonment or exile in consequence, were the unsung heroes of the war. It took courage to do what they did. And it took no less courage for those who *did* go, and af-ter seeing at firsthand the slaughter of civilians, the burning of women and children with napalm, the throwing of captives from helicopters and much else, refused to participate any longer, and deserted. So I would disagree with President Nixon's later pronouncements against amnesty.

I continued my anti-war activities on every possible occasion. I was gratified by the growing opposition to the war. Would it be sufficient to galvanize the Congress into effective action, to influence the vote against appropriations to carry on the conflict? For it was becoming increasingly clear that despite its hitherto almost total support of the war, whatever hope there was lay in the Congress. There was none in the executive branch as long as Nixon remained President. There was none in the judi-cial branch. The Supreme Court had avoided taking up the Massachusetts case which would have tested the issue of the constitutionality of the war, and provided an interesting measure of the "strict constructionism" pre-sumed of President Nixon's appointees. It voted eight to one, with only Justice William O. Douglas dissenting, ruling—in an opinion drafted by Justice Thurgood Marshall—that there could not be conscientious objection to a particular war. While this may have been technically in ac-cord with the provisions of the Selective Service Act, it was—in a larger sense—an absurdity that conscientious objection to all wars, even wars of defense of one's country, or a war to repel an invasion, was valid, but objection to a war as unjustified as the war in Indochina was not. Jus-tice Douglas's dissenting opinion had charted the right course.

On November 17, 1966, I had asked Secretary Udall to request the Na-tional Park Service to study the establishment of a "National Parkway" starting at Cordova and continuing up the Copper River Valley through the Wood and Abercrombie canyons and into and around the Chitina Valley. This was the superlative scenery which had entranced me back in 1938, and I had gotten two National Park Service men, Harry Liek and J. D. Coffman, to return there with me. We then had recommended it for National Park status, but, as I related earlier, World War II suspended all such undertakings.

Now, reassessing the project nearly thirty years later, it seemed to me that the area was almost too vast for a National Park—some ten thousand square miles—and I faced the objections that it would end and prevent hunting and mining. Copper ore had unexpectedly been uncovered as the Kennecott Glacier receded, and was being extracted without much effort or damage to the environment. Another likely objection was that the Park Service could probably not be able to provide accommodations. (For half a century we had been unable to get accommodations within Mount McKinley National Park. They are still lacking in 1973.)

Since the suspension of the Copper River and Northwestern Railway, coincidental with the closing of the Kennecott mine a generation earlier, the region was no longer accessible. A National Parkway would make it so and would withdraw permanently only the area actually needed, rendering the region's natural wonders available to the public, and perhaps stimulating construction by private enterprise of a lodge or two to accommodate visitors.

In order to revive the project I felt I should go there to reappraise my estimate. I asked Fred Machetanz—one of our great landscape painters, resident in the Matanuska Valley—to come along. I wanted to interest him in painting the Valley, recording some of its great peaks on canvas, just as Sydney Laurence had painted and glorified Mount McKinley.** I visualized a future Interior Department brochure in which some of Machetanz's paintings would reveal the region's scenic superlativeness. The Interior Department's Geological Survey was engaged in mineral studies of the Valley and obligingly put one of its helicopters at my disposal. This was the ideal way to explore and inspect the region. We flew low and slowly over it, landed on its peaks and tramped around from these easily attained elevations. Fred made sketches and also recorded by Kodachromes views that he wanted to paint. It was in late August of 1967 and the spectacular fall crimson ground-cover was before us in all its splendor.

With the change of administration wrought by the 1968 election, I took up the idea with the new secretary of the Interior, Walter Hickel. He was enthusiastic and agreed that we should hold hearings. Because of the opposition to setting aside so large an area as a National Park or Monument with their limitations on use, I suggested we devise a new category and a new designation for it, and proposed "Chitina Valley National Sce-

---

** Alaska is fortunate in its abundance of other excellent landscapists: "Rusty" Heurlein, Gil Smith, Harvey Goodale and his wife, whose brush name is Henne, "Scotty" McDaniel, Curt Wagner, Jr., Jennie Werner, and others, worthy successors of Sydney Laurence, who made Alaskans art conscious.

nic Area." Wally approved, but felt that since the area would include far more than the Valley, it should be called the "Wrangell Mountains National Scenic Area." We tentatively proposed that it be under the jurisdiction of the Bureau of Land Management, that hunting be permitted as well as mining—the latter under strict supervision to preclude ravaging the landscape—and that there should be no logging, since the virgin tree-cover of many species—spruce, birch, cottonwood, willow, aspen —was an essential element in the region's natural beauty. A substantial portion was to be preserved as wilderness. With these proposed guidelines we held hearings at Anchorage and Fairbanks, which Wally asked me to conduct, and there were further hearings at Cordova and Glennallen. Representatives of the Alaska Conservation Society approved; those of the mining industry expressed some fears as to the restrictions that might be imposed, and some voiced the Alaskans' apprehension of more large withdrawals. But the net reaction was favorable. Secretary Hickel ordered the area withdrawn from entry—always a necessary temporary measure to prevent speculative filing when the government plans an area's development—and the BLM was instructed to initiate the needed surveys.

I joined its party in August 1969, with Fred Machetanz again and George Sundborg, now the number two official in Interior's Bureau of Outdoor Recreation. After surveying it, with the advice of highway officials, we came to the conclusion that extending the Parkway through the Skolai Pass at the eastern end of the Chitina Valley to connect with the Alaska Highway in Canada—the plan which had been under consideration—was physically impracticable, but that aspect of the project was not important. George tested the fishery resources of one of the Valley's numerous lakes, Tebay, and found its rainbow trout abundant.

It looked as if the most beautiful and bountiful recreational area under the American flag would before long be made available to the public; and with a certain pride of discovery I could think of few undertakings of mine that I considered more worthwhile and more rewarding. Under the Alaska Native Claims Settlement Act of 1971, eighty million acres were set aside for purposes which the Secretary of the Interior would determine. They included the Wrangell Mountains and other outstanding scenic areas. Conservationist societies in the lower 48 states were lobbying to have all of it reserved for national parks, wildlife refuges and wilderness. Testifying on May 30, 1973 before the joint Federal-State Land Planning Commission, I urged adoption of the National Scenic Area designations and multiple use, except for timber harvesting, with perhaps ten percent set aside as combined wilderness and wildlife refuges, reiterating my view that conservation and development were not incompatible, that we needed and could have both. Hopefully both will be served by Secretary Rogers Morton's decision.

One objective which had long concerned me—availability of birth control for those who wanted it—was at long last recognized on the political front as urgent and essential, not merely for the individual, but for society. Two dedicated organizations, "Planned Parenthood" and "Population Crisis Committee" had been conducting effective educational campaigns—the latter under the dynamic leadership of General William H. Draper, Jr.—and after leaving the Senate, I was invited to become a director there.

The great change was signalized by Congressional action: allocation of funds under the Social Security amendments of 1967 for those in low-income brackets, and then by enactment of "The Family Planning Services and Population Act of 1970." While retaining the euphemism of "family planning" in its title, it created the "Office of Population Affairs" in the Department of Health, Education and Welfare, and through it—along with other prescribed activities—made $20 million a year available to supply American women, who needed the know-how and the wherewithal to forestall pregnancy, with both. And under the Foreign Aid program, the appropriations for the same purposes reached $125 million in 1972. That was a battle finally won.†

But although the United States birthrate had fallen gratifyingly to a record low, the desirable goal of zero population growth was still to be attained, and the burgeoning population of Asia, Africa and South America, with its disastrous consequences, invited appropriate missionary efforts as well as inclusion in the affluent nations' foreign-aid programs.

I had long held a deep-seated conviction that the judiciary was, or should be, the Palladium of the liberties of a free society, and that the qualifications of judges—integrity, ability, judicial temperament— should be held sacrosanct.

My first opportunity to translate that conviction into action came with Statehood when I felt obliged to forestall the appointment of Raymond John Kelly as Alaska District Judge. Kelly, who had been active in Michigan politics, was appointed by President Eisenhower to be chairman of the Railroad Retirement Board. The other two members, likewise Presidential appointees, were presumed to represent railroad management and railroad labor respectively. The chairman's role was to be a neutral, im-

† An excellent account thereof is *World Population Crisis: The United States Response*, by Phyllis T. Piotrow, published by Praeger, 1973.

partial balance-wheel between the two special-interest appointees. Kelly's performance was such that Eisenhower's secretary of Labor, James P. Mitchell, brought about his removal. Since he had previously been the National Commander of the American Legion, he was presumed to possess considerable political clout, and, needing employment, sought and was appointed by Eisenhower judge of Alaska's first judicial district, thus exemplifying Jeannette Paddock Nichols's aphorism that Alaska had long since become "a political preserve for the payment of small debts owed by big politicians to little ones." ††

With Statehood, Kelly sought the Alaska federal district judgeship, and his unjudicial declaration in a public address that he planned to be active in the new State's politics, added to his record on the bench, made it necessary for me to serve notice that I would oppose his confirmation; and he was not nominated.

In the three subsequent nominations of Alaskan federal judges, my support was solicited by various candidates, all—of course—Alaskans. I knew them all, and some were my friends. But invariably I replied that I would indicate no choice and depend on an investigation of all the candidates' qualifications by the Department of Justice, relying on its findings as to who was best qualified. I knew that this was not always the way in which judgeships were secured. Often—perhaps even generally, when a Federal District or Circuit Court vacancy occurred—a senator from that state or area would recommend a friend and do his best to get him nominated and confirmed; and such senatorial support, in the absence of a definitely adverse report from the Department of Justice, would be decisive. I had taken a hands-off position in the case of Walter Hodge, the first federal nominee after Statehood, then of Ray Plummer when Hodge retired—although convinced they were well qualified—and again when Alaska had been given a second federal judge. In that instance the Department came up with two names of men it considered well qualified, as did I. Both happened to be my friends, and I was delighted that they were recommended. Bob Bartlett, the other Senator, had a decided preference, and so we agreed on James Von der Heydt. (The other nominee, Robert Boochever, was subsequently appointed to the State Supreme Court). I have never in recent years heard our Alaska federal judges spoken of other than favorably. They have been what judges should be.

So, holding these views, I experienced a keen sense of frustration after President Nixon had nominated Clement Haynsworth of South Carolina, Chief Judge of the Fourth Circuit Court, to the Supreme Court, and his

†† Nichols, Jeannette P., *Alaska, A History*, 1963 (Arthur H. Clark Co., 1924).

qualifications were uncovered in hearings before the Senate Judiciary Committee. My frustration, on this and other occasions, was due to the recurrent realization that I could no longer register my vote in the United States Senate. Haynsworth's nomination was part of Nixon's "Southern Strategy," which was obviously racist. Haynsworth had consistently taken a reactionary stand on civil rights. But what defeated him was an insensitivity in matters of conflict of interest. He passed on cases involving securities which he owned. I telephoned a number of my former colleagues. I found those I talked with receptive, although few would commit themselves. But the result was gratifying. Haynsworth was rejected fifty-five to forty-five and the "no" votes included seventeen Republicans.

President Nixon then nominated G. Harrold Carswell whom he had previously appointed to the Fifth Circuit Court, promoting him from Chief Judge of the District Court of Northern Florida. This nomination was infinitely worse than Haynsworth's.

In 1948, while campaigning for a seat in the Georgia legislature, Carswell had said in an address to the American Legion:

> I am a southerner by ancestry, birth, training, inclination, belief and practice. I believe that segregation of the races is proper and the only practical and correct way of life in our states. I have always so believed, and I shall always so act. I shall be the last to submit to any attempt on the part of anyone to break down and to weaken this firmly established policy of our people . . . I yield to no man as a fellow candidate, or as a fellow-citizen, in the firm vigorous belief in the principles of white supremacy and I shall always be so governed.

Carswell was twenty-eight years old when he made this speech— scarcely a stripling—and its categorical character indicated a firmly held unchangeable credo. But after this damaging disclosure, Carswell went on television and declared that he now rejected these words and that they were "abhorrent" to his personal philosophy.

The hearings would reveal conclusively by Carswell's subsequent acts that he had not changed his philosophy and that he was lying when he said he had.

I found it difficult to believe that after this revelation, President Nixon would not withdraw the nomination, but instead he reiterated his support of Carswell and asserted his right to appoint judges, indicating that the Senate should forego its duty prescribed by the Constitution, to advise and consent to "Judges of the Supreme Court" (and others).

In addition to Carswell's blatant racism his performance on the bench had been distinctly inferior; an exceptionally large proportion of his judgments had been reversed by higher courts. He also had shown a grave lack of judicial temperament in his rude treatment of civil-defense lawyers. His was probably the worst nomination ever submitted for our highest court.

If I had been distressed by Haynsworth's nomination, I was nauseated by Carswell's and vowed to do all I could to get the Senate to repeat its rejection. But to my surprise I found the prospects unpromising.

When I spoke to Sam Shaffer, *Newsweek*'s experienced Washington correspondent, he replied:

> Not a chance. Unless the nominee has committed murder a week before the vote on confirmation, the Senate will approve him. They're not going to turn down the President's choice a second time.

I found a similar defeatist attitude among several senators I called on the phone. But to me Carswell on the Supreme Court was unthinkable. It would have degraded our entire judicial system and aggravated the already acute racial tensions.

Fortunately there would be a delay of several weeks before Carswell's nomination came before the Senate. Majority leader Mansfield had scheduled the Voting Rights bill's extension to precede the debate on Carswell. That delay permitted the enormity of Carswell's unfitness to become widely known, it permitted the mobilization of concerned members of the bar, and provided time for the needed editorial comment. Meanwhile I was telephoning as many of my former colleagues as I thought my views might influence. They included both Republicans and Democrats. While a number rejected my plea—some of whom surprised and disappointed me—I felt I had been helpful in persuading others.

The debate lasted three weeks. A low spot in Senate history was attained in the declaration of Nebraska's Roman L. Hruska, the ranking Republican on the Judiciary Committee:

> Even if he were mediocre, there are a lot of mediocre judges and people and lawyers. They are entitled to a little representation, aren't they, and a little chance? We can't have all Brandeises, and Frankfurters and Cardozos and stuff like that.

(Hruska was according Carswell more than his due. Mediocrity suggests a position halfway between good and bad!)

On the night before the vote I made several more telephone calls to my former colleagues. One was to Margaret Chase Smith with whom I had had friendly relations since my Maine days forty years earlier, and whose independence and integrity I had always admired. I talked with her for some twenty minutes, summarizing the case against Carswell. She told me she had not made up her mind—her usual custom not to reveal her vote in advance—but that she had taken home the arguments, pro and con, and would consider them carefully. I was convinced she would vote "no," and she did. I had a similar conviction about two other Republicans with whom I had talked, and I was also hopeful that I had been able to persuade Bill Fulbright, who through the years had taken the Dixiecrat position and had voted for Haynsworth. His "no" vote the next day went far to redeem that past.

I was on the Senate floor on April 8. The galleries were packed. The atmosphere was tense as the clerk called the roll. The first five votes were for confirmation; then Birch Bayh cast the first "no" vote. He had taken the leadership in the fight against Carswell, as he had against Haynsworth. The break came a few names later, when Marlow Cook, the newly elected Republican from Kentucky, voted "no." The final fifty-one to forty-five vote was gratifyingly larger than expected. At its announcement the visitors broke into applause and cheers despite Vice President Agnew's gaveling and threat to clear the galleries. The Senate had saved the country from a catastrophe. The vote revealed some oddities. Seven senators—six of them Republican—who had voted against Haynsworth, voted for Carswell, testimony to the tremendous pressure exerted by the Nixon administration.

On the morning of the second day thereafter, after ample time for reflection, President Nixon called the press and delivered an attack unequaled in vituperativeness and intemperance by any previous Presidential utterance directed at the Senate. He charged that as then constituted the Senate would not confirm a Southerner who was a strict constructionist, —an obviously untrue allegation. It would have confirmed by unanimity a Southern judge it deemed to have the necessary qualifications, as it did some months later when it confirmed Lewis F. Powell of Virginia.

Three beneficial results followed the Senate's action. Nixon's next nominee, Harry Andrew Blackmun of Minnesota, judge on the Eighth Circuit Court, was deemed well qualified and was confirmed unanimously. Carswell was persuaded to run for the United States Senate in the Florida 1970 primary, taking himself off the Fifth Circuit Court and out of the judiciary, and was defeated by eight-term Congressman William C. Cramer, an extreme conservative whom President Nixon had urged to run. The resulting split in the State's Republican ranks led to the election of

Democrat Lawton Chiles, who would obviously be a better senator than Cramer or Carswell.

Nixon is a lawyer, a profession which carries with it definite implications of performance and standards of conduct. His nomination of Carswell, his all-out efforts to secure confirmation after Carswell's unfitness had become manifest, his assertion that there would be judges like Carswell on the Supreme Court, dispelled any thoughts I might have harbored that there was "a new Nixon." The continuing disparity between his words and his actions on virtually every issue strengthened my view that he was still the same "tricky Dick" who, decades earlier, had defeated Jerry Voorhis and Helen Gahagan Douglas in contests for Congress by the shadiest of shady smear tactics, while his performance in the 1962 California gubernatorial campaign, managed by H. R. Haldeman, foreshadowed the Watergate shenannigans. Nixon was running against incumbent Edmund G. (Pat) Brown. A "Committee for the Preservation of the Democratic Party" sent a communication to every registered Democrat in the State deploring the extreme leftist views of Governor Brown's supporters. The scheme was concocted in Nixon's campaign headquarters, and it was Nixon himself who edited and strengthened the spurious communication—as it was found to be by Judge Byron Arnold of the California Superior Court on October 30, 1964—in upholding an injunction brought two years earlier by the Democratic State Central Committee.†††

His campaigning in 1970 with the avowed purpose of capturing control of the Congress, and his approval of the vicious divisiveness of his chosen Vice President merely brought those unworthy performances of yesteryear up-to-date. Both he and Spiro Agnew, hatcher of hate and vendor of venom, had the effrontery to charge the Democratic candidates with being inciters of, and responsible for, the violence that had been spreading in the land, a base and baseless charge that was effectively rebuffed on election's eve by Senator Edmund Muskie.

Nixon revealed himself further by his abrupt dismissal of Secretary Hickel, followed by a totalitarian-style purge in the Interior Department of those Hickel had brought there. Hickel had proved an excellent Secretary of the Interior. He had won over the previously suspicious and hostile conservationists. He had moved to stop the slaughter of the whale and the alligator. He had prevented the ruin of the Everglades by opposing and forestalling the construction of the international airport there. He

††† The episode is recorded by Joseph C. Goulden in the May 28, 1973 issue of *The Nation*, and Judge Arnold's comprehensive finding, documenting every detail of the conspiracy, was inserted in the May 7, 1973 *Congressional Record*, pp. 8377–8383 by Senator Floyd R. Haskell of Colorado.

had cracked down on the oil companies which had polluted the Pacific Ocean off Santa Barbara and had wrought similar damage in the Gulf of Mexico. That was part of his undoing in an administration to which the big oil companies were heavy financial contributors. He had also urged President Nixon to talk to the young people—good advice which Nixon later adopted, but it implied a criticism which the President resented. Finally, Hickel had voiced his disagreement with Agnew's performance in the campaign, suggesting that you could not "tear the country together."

Hickel's contribution was reconciling development and conservation, demonstrating that they need not be incompatible, and that both are essential: a view I fully shared. After two years, his was the only outstanding performance in the Nixon cabinet. So out he went!

The grounds for the pessimism I expressed two years earlier in the foreword about our country's future, persist. Killing has become an increasing monstrosity overseas and at home. Ours has needlessly become a militaristic nation, squandering its substance in excessive weaponry, which in the name of security has diminished security and the confidence in it which as a far less panoplied country we enjoyed for the first four-fifths of our national existence. And while this wanton extravagance proceeds through official deception and false alarms, the basic needs of our society are neglected.

Concomitantly, the first steps have been and are being taken to transform our nation into a police state. Spying is practiced not only by the FBI (whose function should be confined to tracking down criminals), and also by the Army (a new role for it) on individuals suspected of dissenting from administration policies, with compiling of dossiers on them which they are not permitted to see, but which may be used to their disadvantage without their knowledge when they seek employment or endorsement. On April 25 1971, newspapers published Attorney-General John Mitchell's statement that wire-tapping without a court order was in the interest of "security," a view reiterated by his successor, Attorney-General Richard Kleindienst. Coincidentally, Secretary of Commerce Maurice Stans, visiting in Greece congratulated its totalitarian regime's colonels on the "security" their rule conferred. In similar vein our Vice President brought our country's congratulations to the twenty-fifth anniversary of Francisco Franco's fascist rule in Spain. And Spiro Agnew's attacks on the media recall the intimidation of the press by Europe's dictators of yesteryear before they abolished its freedom entirely. Indeed, President Nixon has exhibited a special affinity for dictators. In the 1971 border-conflict between India and Pakistan, the White House made a point of proclaiming its neutrality in its public statements, but columnist Jack

Anderson revealed that President Nixon's instructions to his representatives on the scene were to "tilt" toward Pakistan. India is the closest approach to a democracy in Asia: Pakistan was ruled by a ruthless dictator. Anderson was awarded a Pulitzer prize for this exposé. In reprisal, federal authorities arrested Les Whitten, a reporter for Jack Anderson, charging him with possession of stolen property. He was accompanying the Indians who, in their raid on the Interior Department's Bureau of Indian Affairs, had taken its files and were now returning them. The charges were dropped, the incident merely illustrating the Nixon administration's vindictiveness toward its critics.

The Nixon administration's frantic attempts to prevent publication of the Pentagon papers—the first attempt in our nation's history by the federal government to impose "prior restraint," that is, to prevent publication by a newspaper—were further indicative of its purpose to limit freedom of the press. Fortunately, it had not yet succeeded in packing the bench in its image, which it has now virtually achieved. Suppression of the Pentagon papers was rejected by the United States District and Circuit Courts in Washington, New York and Boston, and on appeal to the United States Supreme Court the effort was quashed by a 6–3 decision with a ringing opinion by Justice Hugo Black. It declared that the drafters of the First Amendment intended precisely what publication of the Pentagon papers would achieve: that the press should be the vigilant guardian of our liberties, should protect the governed from the abuses of the governing such as the Pentagon papers had exposed, and that if the finding of the Court's minority upholding prior restraint of publication of news in a newspaper ever prevailed, it would make a shambles of the first amendment. The minority group referred to included the two Nixon appointees—the only ones at that time—Burger and Blackmun.

The administration's prosecution of Daniel Ellsberg (and Anthony Russo) for bringing the Pentagon papers to the press, was a sequel to its efforts to suppress them, and a further indication of its vindictiveness. In the course of their interesting "inside" history of the war in Southeast Asia, they exposed the duplicity of some officials high in our government. I was happy to testify in refutation of the charge that their publication was harmful to the national defense. Far from being prosecuted, Ellsberg should have been given an award for public service.

Judge W. Matthew Byrne Jr.'s declaring a mistrial and dismissing all the charges against Ellsberg and Anthony Russo with prejudice, ruling that they could not be tried again, brought another revelation of the Nixon administration's police-state methods, which included not only tapping Ellsberg's phone but breaking into his psychiatrist's office in search of information that might reflect on Ellsberg's mental balance. A further attempted tampering with justice was Nixon's invitation to Judge Byrne, during the trial, to visit him at San Clemente when he was offered the directorship of the FBI.

For the first time in our nation's history, following a Supreme Court decision, newspapermen were jailed for refusing to reveal to grand juries the sources of their reportage. This freedom of journalists to keep their informants' identity confidential, never before challenged, has enabled newspapers to bring to the people information of public interest which without such protection would never see daylight. All four Nixon appointees—with one other, Byron White, least qualified of the pre-Nixon incumbents—affirmed what the dissenting four justices considered a violation of the First Amendment's guarantee of freedom of the press. That freedom has thereby been seriously impaired.

Another method by which the Nixon administration is eroding the guarantees of the First Amendment is through the Internal Revenue Service, by threatening to deprive churches and religious associations of their tax-exempt status if they promote causes such as peace, interracial justice and other moral issues which conflict with administration policies. By threatening such deprivation, by harassment through protracted examination of the church's books and use of the subpoena, the government is making war on such institutions as the United Churches of Christ, the National Council of Churches, and the Unitarian Universalist Association. The IRS warned the Trinity Episcopal Church of Melrose, Massachusetts that giving space to a student peace group would endanger its tax-exempt status. A group of college and high-school students desiring to protest against the continuation of the war in Southeast Asia had sought and secured a room in the church for the meeting. But despite the Internal Revenue Service's threat, the church's minister, the Reverend Warren Radtke, assured me he would not yield to this intimidation, having meanwhile consulted his attorney and notified the American Civil Liberties Union. Similar warnings against allowing meetings of other groups under its roof have gone to other churches.

In a protest to President Nixon the National Council of Churches and the Synagogue Council of America declared

> We find intolerable the Government's overbroad and unparticularized use of subpoena powers in a general search of all this Church's financial records for a substantial period of time. We believe it can only have a chilling effect on the free exercise of a religion as well as upon the other great freedoms guaranteed by the first amendment . . . We reject the contention that the government is dealing not with this church's religious activities but with its 'politi-

cal' activities. There is no political issue that does not have a potential moral dimension, and no moral issue that does not have a potential political dimension. Neither our faith nor the Constitution will
permit our religious institutions to yield to any government agency
the power to determine the definition or the limits of religious activity . . .***

In this assault on the First Amendment, the administration target is not
only the press but the three other freedoms—"an establishment of religion" and "the free exercise thereof," "freedom of speech," and "the right
of the people peaceably to assemble."

President Nixon has repeatedly declared that his Supreme Court appointees will be "strict constructionists," meaning that he wants and ex-
pects them to construe the Constitution strictly. Yet no President has so
violated the Constitution in practice both in letter and spirit.

Article I, Section 8 of the Constitution vests the power to declare war
in the Congress. Both Johnson and Nixon have violated this by waging
war (in Nixon's case against three countries: Laos, Cambodia, Vietnam)
without a declaration by Congress.

The extent of Nixon's violation of that constitutional provision could
not have been more grotesquely illustrated than by his six months' saturation bombing of Cambodia in 1973, following a similar performance in
Laos for several years and in late 1972 in North Vietnam.**** There, he
could allege that he was trying to bring the North Vietnamese to the
conference table, an allegation of dubious validity which subsequently
demonstrated the uselessness of that barbarity in achieving the "peace
with honor" that he had vaunted. The Cambodian bombings, the Nixon
administration admitted, were for the sole purpose of compelling the
Cambodians to accept as their President one Lon Nol, an unpopular and
corrupt politician and a dimwit guided by soothsayers. The cost of each
sortie was $30,000. An average of 125 sorties a day was flown—a total
of over $100 million a month. During a Senate debate, May 30,
George McGovern—a World War II bomber pilot—adverting to the
domestic gasolene shortage, pointed out that each B52 sortie from Guam

*** *Censorship by Taxation: New Muzzle for Churchmen* by Joseph A.
Ruskay, in October 2, 1972 issue of *The Nation* gives a detailed account of
the administration's efforts to silence the ministry.

**** The bombing of Laos, concealed from the American people, was exposed in an "op-ed" article by Anthony Lewis in The *New York Times*, July
9, 1973. He reported that, in all, two million tons of bombs had been dropped
on that peasant country—two-thirds of a ton for every man woman and
child.

consumed 50,000 gallons of fuel. The moral costs to the American people are incalculable.

The cost to the Cambodian people—innocent victims of United States aggression—in killed and maimed is yet to be disclosed. The Congress tried for six months to stop this massacre. The Nixon administration would circumvent one measure after another, and it was not until the last week in June that House and Senate finally found and agreed upon a formula that appeared inviolable.

Briefly, on June 27 that is the way it looked. But before the day was over Nixon had vetoed the bill—an appropriation bill to which the prohibition of future bombing had been attached—declaring that continued bombing was essential to secure a negotiated peace and alleging the presence of North Vietnamese forces in Cambodia, a previously unpresented reason for United States bombing there. The House voted 241–173 to override, lacking thirty-five votes of the necessary two-thirds majority. The Senate promptly added the Cambodian rider to another appropriation bill, and Senate majority leader Mike Mansfield declared that he would attach it to other bills "again and again until the will of the people prevails." Senate sentiment had been consistently and overwhelmingly in favor of stopping the bombing. The outcome would depend on whether the House could muster the two-thirds majority to override future Nixon vetoes. It was a confrontation without precedent or parallel in United States history.

But faced with this threat and the impending and unprecedented constitutional crisis, President Nixon offered a compromise: he would bomb Cambodia six weeks more; thereafter after August 15, United States military action (amended in Congress to include all Southeast Asia) would require Congress's consent.

The Congress divided into two camps, debating the alternatives at great length and with deep feeling on June 29. There was the revulsion expressed by Senator Mansfield that acceptance of Nixon's proposal was "a capitulation and an abdication of the constitutional powers of the Senate," by Senator Kennedy that the compromise was an "infamy;" and by others urging the Congress to stand firm and continue to add amendments to appropriations bills calling for immediate cut-off of the bombing.

But there was the view of Senator Fulbright and the 15–2 Foreign Relations Committee vote that here at long last was the opportunity to end United States military action in Southeast Asia, that the two-thirds majority needed to override Nixon's veto was lacking in the House and that Nixon could otherwise continue to bomb indefinitely. The Senate approved the compromise 64–26, and the House, 236–160.

But if the evidence to condemn this senseless and despicable slaughter were not sufficient, the bombing was also in violation of the peace agreement drafted by Henry Kissinger and signed by the United States to end the war in Southeast Asia.

> Chapter VII entitled "Regarding Cambodia and Laos, Article 29 (B) Foreign Countries shall put an end to all military activities in Cambodia and Laos, totally withdraw troops, military advisers, and military personnel, armaments, munitions and war materials."
>
> Article 20 (C) The internal affairs of Cambodia and Laos shall be settled by the people of their countries without foreign interference.

Not only has Nixon ignored the Congress's constitutional authority to declare war, but he has also attempted to deprive it of the "power of the purse" vested in Congress by the Constitution, and has, in several instances, succeeded in doing it. His refusal to spend funds authorized and appropriated by Congress *after* his veto of the legislation has been overridden, is an illegal act and in violation of the Constitutional provision in Article II, Section 3, that the President "Shall take care that the laws are faithfully executed."

Not only has Nixon ignored the Congress but he has diminished the role of the executive branch. The Secretary of State has been downgraded and his truly essential functions transferred to a personal Presidential appointee, whose appointment is not subject to confirmation by the Senate, and who cannot be interrogated by it unless the President agrees. A staff of personal assistants who also do not require confirmation surround the President, make important executive decisions under a cloak of anonymity, and often make it difficult for cabinet members to see the President. The framers of the Constitution conceived of three branches of the federal government, the executive, the legislative and the judicial, independent and yet interdependent. President Nixon has steadily eroded that concept and increasingly arrogated to himself dictatorial powers.

It would seem incontrovertible that something has gone wrong and that the American people confront a challenge to identify what has happened and why and to seek remedies.

Why is it that the wealthiest nation on earth with an unsurpassed technological know-how has not been able to solve basic problems of living, has not stemmed the steady deterioration of our cities, the pollution of our land, air and waters—unspoiled and virginal at the beginning of our national life—has failed to diminish the mounting incidence of crime, to avert the alienation of much of our youth, and to lift substantial segments of our population from poverty, indeed even from hunger, which stunts its children mentally and physically and will later aggravate our social and economic problems.

With the greatest heritage of natural resources granted to any people and the peerless legacy of wisdom bequeathed us by the founding fathers, the great promises have been betrayed and remain unfulfilled.

What has happened to us? How has it come about? And what can we do about it?

At the risk of oversimplification I ascribe a large share of our nation's trouble to its leadership. I have made clear, I hope, through specific examples in this narrative, my belief, borne out by experience, that the democratic process does not function automatically. When there is a George Washington or an Abraham Lincoln, or to come closer to our time, when there is a Franklin Delano Roosevelt or a Winston Churchill, nations overcome obstacles however great. Contrast these two with their immediate predecessors, Herbert Hoover and Neville Chamberlain, who failed to meet the crises they confronted, and note the difference in their countries' courses under the sequent leaderships. Roosevelt lifted our country from the worst depression in its history without deviating from the democratic process. Churchill reversed Chamberlain's policy of appeasement and saved Britain from conquest.

The converse—bad leadership, of a Hitler or a Mussolini—is equally true. I have seen the success or failure of both kinds of leadership exemplified in nation, state and city.

Our rapid deterioration began with President Johnson's lying our nation into the war in Southeast Asia. Though his Tonkin Gulf Resolution was rescinded by the Congress in 1970, the war went on. It went on with consequences yet to be appraised, but all of them bad, because President Nixon likewise deceived the American people by his promise to end the war—and that did not mean to them four years or more later.

Where could there be a clearer illustration that two individuals, vested with a brief authority, used it to bring our great nation to such a pass? For in no war in our history has the responsibility been so assignable to two individuals as in the protracted conflict in Indochina. Johnson not only bamboozled the Congress into giving him the authorization he sought to wage all-out war in Southeast Asia, but deceived the American people into electing him by his repeated campaign pledges that he would not send American boys to fight a ground war on the Asian continent. The blood of the forty-five thousand American dead—all of whom have died in vain—and of the three hundred thousand American wounded, to say nothing of the millions of slaughtered or wounded Indochinese civilians, is on his head. In addition to propelling the country into the war, he, as no other President before him, personally directed the selection of targets to be bombed.

For their deceptions and for their authorizations—violating the Constitution—of genocide, both Johnson and Nixon deserved impeachment.

So, feeling deeply that a change in our national leadership was essential, and in order to play my small part in trying to implement that objective, I campaigned for the election of George McGovern. In my view he personified the needed values more than any other Democratic candidate, all of whom I knew well and liked personally. During the primary contests I campaigned in sixteen States. I attended the Southeastern Alaska convention at Sitka in May and was elected a delegate to the State convention at Fairbanks which endorsed McGovern. I was elected a delegate to the National Convention in Miami and shared the joy of all his supporters when, confuting all the polls, he was nominated on the first ballot.

My reasons for supporting McGovern, besides those previously indicated in my analysis of some aspects of Nixon's record, were Nixon's vetoes which were directed against what seemed to me our nation's great-

Ernest Gruening campaigning for George McGovern, 1972

est needs—education, health, unemployment, pollution abatement, correction of economic inequalities, etc.

There were also the evidences—still unconfirmed—of blatant corruption: the breaking and entering and burglarizing by men who shortly before had been or still were administration employees; the ITT scandal; the wheat deals by which big grain-operators were tipped off to forthcoming sales to Russia so they could make big profits denied the little farmers; and other evidences of improper administration favoritism for the rich and powerful. More disturbing was the lack of adverse public reaction. A decade and a half previously, a presidential assistant to President Eisenhower, Sherman Adams, had been forced out of office by public opinion for the impropriety of accepting a vicuña coat in return for a favor rendered. Was the lessened sensitivity of the American people to greater scandals fifteen years later a confirmation of Henry Mencken's aphorism: "Ruled by shady men, a nation itself becomes shady"?

Then there was Nixon's violation of all his campaign promises. He did not diminish inflation, unemployment or crime. All increased during his four-year term. But most flagrant in my view was his failure to end United States participation in the war. The responsibility for the other failures could be shared by subordinates and other administration officials. But prolonging the war—indeed widening it by extension to two other countries, Laos and Cambodia, and intensifying it in Vietnam—was exclusively the President's decision. There was no reason whatever why Nixon could not have ended our part in the war in the first weeks of his term, early in 1969.

Nixon's continuation thereof, while assuaging public opinion by the gradual withdrawal of our ground troops will have cost the American people twenty thousand more dead, over one hundred thousand wounded, some crippled for life, and not less than sixty-five billion dollars, with a resulting prospective increased tax burden or continued slighting of our long overdue, neglected domestic needs.

The cost to the Southeast Asians will—when told—disclose a horror story unrivaled in history. The dead, mostly noncombatants, will run into millions, for the saturation bombing, decreed by Nixon in early 1972, leveled schools, hospitals and hamlets with no military significance. When Olaf Palme, Sweden's premier, voicing revulsion at the 1972 Christmastime bombing of North Vietnam, shared by the leadership of other free nations, likened it to some of Hitler's performances, Sweden—and the United States—were penalized by the Nixon administration's request to Sweden that it not send us its ambassador. Was Palme wrong? In those bombings, hospitals and schools were hit—the invariable allegation that the air-raids were directed at strategic targets is tragically farcical—high-level B-52 bombings cannot pinpoint targets. The administration denied the North Vietnamese charge that the Bach Mai hospital at Hanoi had been bombed; then modified the denial by saying that it had suffered only minor damage as a result of pilot error. I wrote Telford Taylor, who, I heard, had been there. (Taylor, professor of law at Columbia University, was commissioned as a major in the military intelligence in World War II, rose through the grades to a brigadier-generalcy, was chief of counsel and United States representative in the prosecution of German war-criminals.) He was in Hanoi on December 22, the day of the bombing, and wrote me that the hospital had been "virtually destroyed." The patients had been removed to shelter earlier after an air-raid warning, but twenty-one of the hospital staff, including fourteen nurses and a doctor were killed.

At the third session of the International Commission of Enquiry into United States Crimes in Indochina, at Copenhagen in October 1972 (the previous two sessions were held in Oslo and Stockholm), a succession of horrors resulting from United States bombing was unfolded. I saw and heard a twenty-four-year-old teacher testify that her school was hit by a bomb. Its fragments tore her right arm so that it had to be amputated. (It was missing when she testified.) Six children were killed outright; ten others wounded, some of them permanently crippled.

So going back to 1972, there were ample reasons for voting for George McGovern. His basic issues: end the war now (he had been urging it for nine years), eliminate tax loopholes, reduce our bloated military budgets and take care of our domestic needs—antitheses of Nixonian policies—were surely desirable. But he lost, and lost overwhelmingly, and we got four more years of President Nixon.

Well, the people have spoken, and it is axiomatic among us Americans to abide by the result, consider that the popular verdict is not to be questioned but acknowledged as the final word and accepted more or less philosophically. I've always lived by that; but some questioning and reservations are nevertheless in order. The people can and sometimes do go wrong. They have in the past. Who will contend that the majority who in 1920 elected Warren G. Harding were right? Nor were his successors, likewise brought to high office by popular vote, successes. It took the people twelve years to wake up and give themselves a "New Deal," having suffered severely in the meantime. It can, must and will happen again if our great legacy is not to go down the drain.

After the November 1972 landslide, hope was expressed in various editorial comments in newspapers that had opposed Nixon's re-election, that with no more electoral battles to wage, with the opportunity to rectify some of his past questionable acts, he would move to diminish discord, to bring our people together, to end his public career nobly, and now write a shining page in history. Most Americans shared that hope and wished President Nixon well for such a prospect.

But that hope was soon shattered. President Nixon's first move after victory was to demand the resignation of Father Theodore Martin Hesburgh as chairman of the Commission of Civil Rights to which he had been appointed by President Eisenhower fifteen years earlier when the Commission was created. This distinguished educator, for twenty years president of the University of Notre Dame and a director of the Chase Manhattan Bank, had been unswerving in his stand for equal treatment and fair play, regardless of race or color. Firing Father Hesburgh, following Nixon's mistaken support of Harrold Carswell, could but lead to the depressing conclusion that the American people had placed a racist in the Presidency.

Nixon's bombing of Cambodia and Laos, extending through half of 1973, further nullified his claims of "peace with honor" and that his policies would secure "a peace that lasts." The obvious question the American people have every right to ask and to which Congress should have addressed itself, is "What business have we to try to impose our choice of rulers on three supposedly free and independent Indochinese nations?" There will never be peace there as long as the Nixonian policy continues. There will never be peace in Vietnam until its people *by themselves* determine their future. The United States' arbitrary action in the mid-nineteen fifties in creating, in violation of the Geneva accords, a separate South Vietnam, built civil war permanently into that country, and our costly military intervention merely intensified the conflict and postponed peace. Peace will not come to Southeast Asia until the Vietnamese themselves end their civil war, unpressured either militarily or financially by the United States. The Paris peace agreement—if it is to be taken seriously—makes peace even more unlikely by its recurring double-talk.

Chapter I, Article I declares:

The United States and other countries respect the independence, sovereignty, unity, and territorial integrity of Vietnam as recognized by the Geneva agreements on Vietnam.

Nothing could be clearer and more categorical. It should determine Vietnam's future insofar as such an agreement can. But Chapter IV, Article IX nullifies it, saying:

(a) The South Vietnamese people's right to self-determination is sacred, inalienable and shall be respected by all countries.

(b) The South Vietnamese people shall decide themselves the political future of South Vietnam through genuinely free and democratic general elections under international supervision.

The double-talk is repeated by Chapter V which prescribes the steps for the reunification of North and South Vietnam, but Article XIV of Chapter IV says:

South Vietnam will pursue a foreign policy of peace and independence. It will be prepared to establish relations with all countries irrespective of their political and social systems on the basis of mutual respect for independence and sovereignty and accept economic and technical aid from any country with no political strings attached. The acceptance of military aid in the future shall come under the authority of the government set up after the general elections in South Vietnam provided for in Article IX.

Another joker is found in Article XI in which "the two South Vietnamese parties . . . agree immediately to insure the democratic liberties of the people, personal freedom of speech, freedom of the press, freedom of organization, freedom of belief, freedom of movement. . . ."

The "two South Vietnamese parties" are the Viet Cong and the Thieu government. The former have been fighting for independence of *all* Vietnam for a quarter of a century, and for unification since United States' violation of the Geneva Accords. The Thieu government has taken the opposite stand. Moreover, it is unrealistic to expect Thieu to abandon the terrorism and oppression he has practiced since taking office. His rule has made a mockery of due process; legal procedures have ceased to exist; he has imposed the death penalty by decree, and opposition has been crushed by arrest, imprisonment, assassination and torture. Between 1969 and 1972, 40,000 civilians were executed without trial.

Finally, Article IV states:

The United States will not continue its military involvement or intervene in the internal affairs of South Vietnam.

But when Thieu arrived in Washington early in 1973 and was royally welcomed by the Nixon administration, he announced that he would expect a $700 million annual subsidy from the United States until 1980. Although there was no public response by the Nixon administration, one may assume that its policy of all-out support for Thieu will continue, despite the Article IV prohibition.

The same prohibition against interference in the affairs of Laos and

Cambodia in the same peace agreement, which I mentioned earlier, has already been violated by the Nixon administration which—on the record already established—cannot be trusted to keep its promises and commitments.

United States policy for two decades has been to prevent a communist regime from taking over in Indochina, on the assumption that such a regime would be totalitarian and oppressive. But the regimes the United States has supported have been totalitarian and flagrantly oppressive. Since Nixon has established an *entente* with Communist China and Russia, and will obviously make no attempt to overthrow their governments, what sense is there in trying to impose our design on the smaller nations in Southeast Asia immediately adjacent? It will not work, in any event. Our army of over half a million men supported by Navy and Air Force against a small nation which had neither, was unable to achieve our purpose in two decades.

So we come back to the question: Why don't we mind our own business, let the Southeast Asians settle their problems without our interference, and take care of our long slighted needs at home?

After President Nixon's reelection, his determination to ignore the Constitution's provisions which clearly define the functions of each of the three branches of government became increasingly evident, and each of his violations of the Constitution was a violation of his oath of office.

In our nation's greatest previous crisis, the nation was saved by the leadership of a great man, who as President Lincoln—after taking the steps necessary for a "nation conceived and dedicated" as ours had been, to endure—pointed up as the fruits of impending victory, that "government of the people, by the people, and for the people" would "not perish from the earth."

President Nixon, by contrast, has sought to make ours a government of the President, by the President and for the President's friends and supporters.

As Henry Steele Commager, probably the foremost living American historian, has summarized it:

> He has usurped or aggrandized authority in every field. Even in wartime there was no such broad-gaged and wide-frontal assault on the integrity of the constitutional system as we now have.

Nixon's effort to deprive Congress of its constitutional role as the appropriator and designator of where public funds should be spent—by impoundment—by refusing to spend them even after his veto had been overridden, awaits court action. His defense—that Congress would spend extravagantly and bring higher taxes—was invalid; Congress early agreed to his $260 billion ceiling, but insisted that Congress, not Nixon, determine how the funds should be spent.

Far more serious has been Nixon's assault on the freedoms guaranteed by the first amendment. Radio and television did not exist when our founding fathers wrote it. But as purveyors of news and other information, they are obviously entitled to the same freedom from abridgement as the press. They are, however, more vulnerable to such abridgement than the newspapers, because they are licensed by a federal agency, the Federal Communications Commission. It can revoke their licenses or not renew them if the bureaucrat in charge finds their presentations not to his liking. Such a bureaucrat, named Clay T. Whitehead, holding the position of "Director of the White House Office of Telecommunications," made a widely publicized attack on the media in 1972, charging them with broadcasting "ideological plugola" and "elitist gossip." No one seemed to know what he meant, except that he was obviously hostile. Two nationally known and respected commentators, John Chancellor of ABC and Walter Cronkite of CBS saw it as an escalation of administration attacks on the media, begun in 1968 by Vice President Agnew. But Whitehead left little doubt that he wanted the media to be subservient to the administration's interest. Charging them with bias, he warned that "station managers and network officials who fail to correct imbalance or consistent bias in the network—or who acquiesce by silence—can only be considered willing participants, to be fully accountable at licenses' renewal time." Meanwhile, the television and radio services were left in a state of uncertainty and apprehension. This was clearly another attempt at intimidation and censorship.

"Never in my twenty-one years in Washington and thirty-three in the news business have I seen such a blatant attack on the first amendment as we are witnessing and . . . if the press is in trouble, the people are in trouble," declared Warren Rogers, the outgoing president of the National Press Club in 1972.

But complete revelation of the Nixon administration's purpose is found in legislation it submitted in 1973 to Congress, which, if enacted, would further transform our once free society into totalitarianism. The bill was the subject of the leading editorial in the April 10, 1973, issue of the *New York Times* entitled "The U. S. vs. the People." Because it is so revelatory of the peril which our heritage of freedom faces, as well as the source of that peril, I quote essential parts of it:

The Nixon Administration has submitted to Congress the equivalent of an Official Secrets Act that could bring down an impenetrable curtain over virtually all governmental activities related to defense and foreign affairs. . . . The proposed legislation would give the executive branch and its huge army of officials ironclad protection from public scrutiny.

The proposal is a nightmare threat to freedom of the press, to the people's right to know, and to the very concept of government with the consent of the governed. It is all the more insidious because its provisions are buried in 336 pages of a Justice Department bill for revision of the federal criminal code, a complicated and in the main highly technical and legalistic document.

There is nothing complicated or legalistic, however, about the intent and the consequences of the code's section dealing with government secrecy. It would make it a felony punishable by fine up to $50,000 and seven years' imprisonment to disclose or communicate any governmental information concerning 'the conduct of foreign relations affecting the national defense.' Penalties would be applicable to government employees, reporters and officials of newspapers and broadcasting companies who, if in possession of any such information, did not return it to the government.

A further gag rule, applicable to present and former government employees would cover classified documents no matter how improperly they might be labeled, thereby seeking to give some 20,000 functionaries the absolute power of censorship that has never in the nation's history been deemed wise or essential even in time of war.

The proposed new powers would give the government virtually unlimited license to shape foreign and defense policies in insulation from either Congress or the people. The effect could be to make all fiscal arrangements of the military-industrial complex immune to public scrutiny. The proposal would make investigative reporting all but impossible, while making a criminal of the conscientious public servant who refused to conceal deceptive or wasteful practice as in the recent Fitzgerald or Rule cases. . . .

These proposals represent not so much a revision of the criminal code as an effort to rewrite the first amendment and subject the American people to a kind of guaranteed ignorance about the workings of their government. . . . Instead of protecting the nation's security, it would destroy access to information on which rests the foundations of popular government.

Nixon's design—furthered by secrecy unprecedented in our history—to flout the Constitution and transform our democracy into a police-state under his rule was making headway. The Congress was supine. The people, while increasingly apprehensive as their problems mounted, were apathetic. Then came the stunning revelations of Watergate with its un-believable orgy of criminality at the pinnacle of our government: burg-glary, forgery, character assassination, bribery, perjury, destruction of evidence, deception, violation of any law that stood in the way of pro-moting the continuation in power of Richard Nixon, the deliberate sabo-tage and subversion of the electoral as well as of the judicial process.

And so, at long last, the Congress began to stir. It still needs more re-solve to restore its constitutional role.

Then after months of Presidential resistance to a meaningful investiga-tion and disclosure, came the denials by President Nixon, alleging that he had been unaware of what had been going on in his official family for nearly a year, an attempted exculpation which strained credulity to the limit, and even if true, would convict him of gross negligence and incom-petence. But as the noose of accumulating evidence tightened, there came another explanation and attempted justification: "Security."

Security! It seemed like a substitute for Samuel Johnson's aphorism about patriotism.

What security? Whose security? Seldom, if ever, have the American people had more reason to feel *in*secure.

If a government official, federal, state or local, elected or appointed, a journalist and/or media man, a teacher, a minister, a civic leader, a social worker, or one of independent ideas, he could well suspect that his phone was tapped, his movements spied upon, his neighbors questioned about him, and experience an unprecedented personal insecurity.

Any of these and countless others would note the ever-rising tide of living costs, dread the approaching time when they would exceed the steadily devaluating family income, and experience an unprecedented economic insecurity.

A city dweller would feel the mounting peril of its streets and fear the moment when he or one of his family would be mugged, robbed and injured, experiencing an unprecedented physical insecurity.

This is the security, so diminished in the last few years, that should concern us and our government.

The "security" which President Nixon invokes is a fiction. It is a con-venient cover for malfeasance, and it can also be profitable.

A *New York Times* news dispatch of May 26, 1973 reported that $39,525 had been spent by the federal government to improve Nixon's San Clemente home. "Security" was the quick White House alibi when the news broke. But, like the Watergate disclosures, this item was only a beginning. A month later, a signed article by *New York Times* editor and columnist James Reston, entitled "Nixon's Fringe Benefits," disclosed that the General Services Administration had spent $703,307 on the San Clemente home and $599,907 on Nixon's Key Biscayne residence. It can scarcely be claimed, as of Watergate, that Nixon was unaware of it. A Congressional inquiry should determine how much of these substantial sums can legitimately be charged to "security," what federal officials are responsible for the use of government funds to improve a private home and to legislate—if a suggestion proves insufficient—that Richard Nixon reimburse the federal treasury for the balance.

As this volume goes to press on July sixteenth, President Nixon has announced that under no circumstances will he appear before Senator Ervin's committee for questioning, or turn over to it any of his own files that would permit it to ascertain the truth—as Nixon saw it—of the charges made, or to be made against him by some of his former associates. So the American people and their representatives in Congress would necessarily draw their conclusions from the testimony of others. While regrettable, President Nixon's response was only transitorily important, except as it reflected his attitude toward full and frank disclosure.

Whatever his part in Watergate, Nixon's undeniable guilt has been his attempted and partly successful subversion of our free society into a police state, abrogating our basic concept of "a government of laws and not of men," (even less, of one man)—a course which encompassed Watergate's multiple crimes, his various unconstitutional actions, his perversions of the electoral and judicial processes, his assaults on the first amendment's guarantees—all evidences, manifestations and consequences of his purpose. This, he deliberately originated and materialized. His is the sole responsibility for it, and his subordinates—mostly long-time associates—merely carried out his design in ways they felt would be acceptable to him.

The great experiment begun so daringly and so hopefully two centuries ago, that great legacy bequeathed to us by the patriots of that day, and whose bicentennial we are to celebrate three years hence, is too precious and priceless to be destroyed. I intend to devote my remaining years, however few they may be, to exposing this sinister subversion, to alerting my fellow-countrymen, and to trying to help restore the America that has been and has served us so well. I fired the opening gun of what I would consider the most important battle of my life in an address at Boston University on April 24 of this year. It was an appropriate place: the capital of the Commonwealth in which at Lexington and Concord were struck the first blows for freedom, and whose descendants of this day, not content to rest on past glories, had the wisdom—uniquely among the States—to reject Richard Nixon in the 1972 election. It was gratifying

that after I had recited the record—the record *before* the Watergate revelations—the audience rose to its feet and cheered when I gave my view
that Richard Nixon deserved impeachment and should be impeached.

That every phone conversation with President Nixon was taped without the other party's knowledge; his refusal to make available those tapes
that would enable the nation to ascertain the truth about the Watergate
crimes; the concealment by falsification of the records of the 3600 Nixon-
ordered B-52s March '69 to May '70 bombing sorties over Cambodia, contrasted with Nixon's April 30, 1970 assurance to the American people that
no raids had occurred—all these reveal a versatile depravity that staggers
the imagination and almost beggars characterization. At the very least, they
embody a repudiation of what America has meant to its people and has
stood for throughout our national life.

The rest of the nation needs to follow the example and recapture the
courage of those—past and present—who inculcated and preserved
the spirit of free men which has guided and galvanized America until yesterday. Along with our basic freedoms to speak, to write, to think as we
please, must also be freedom from fear. Men are not really free if they
have to wonder whether they are. Thus believing, and acting accordingly, we shall win this battle and make the America we love happen
again.

INDEX

INDEX

Y

Yarborough, Ralph, 393
Yaw, Leslie, 290, 292
Young, Stephen, 405, 406

Z

Zevada, Manuel J., 178
Ziegler, A. H., 213, 325, 355, 359
Zimmerman, William, Jr., 254